THE BITTERSWEET BOND

⚜ THE LOCHLAINN SEABROOK COLLECTION ⚜

AMERICAN CIVIL WAR
Abraham Lincoln Was a Liberal, Jefferson Davis Was a Conservative: The Missing Key to Understanding the American Civil War
Confederacy 101: Amazing Facts You Never Knew About America's Oldest Political Tradition
Confederate Blood and Treasure: An Interview With Lochlainn Seabrook
Everything You Were Taught About African-Americans and the Civil War is Wrong, Ask a Southerner!
Everything You Were Taught About the Civil War is Wrong, Ask a Southerner!
Give This Book to a Yankee! A Southern Guide to the Civil War For Northerners
Heroes of the Southern Confederacy: The Illustrated Book of Confederate Officials, Soldiers, and Civilians
Lincoln's War: The Real Cause, the Real Winner, the Real Loser
The Great Yankee Coverup: What the North Doesn't Want You to Know About Lincoln's War!
The Ultimate Civil War Quiz Book: How Much Do You Really Know About America's Most Misunderstood Conflict?
Women in Gray: A Tribute to the Ladies Who Supported the Southern Confederacy

CONFEDERATE MONUMENTS
Confederate Monuments: Why Every American Should Honor Confederate Soldiers and Their Memorials

CONFEDERATE FLAG
Confederate Flag Facts: What Every American Should Know About Dixie's Southern Cross
What the Confederate Flag Means to Me: Americans Speak Out in Defense of Southern Honor, Heritage, and History

SECESSION
All We Ask Is To Be Let Alone: The Southern Secession Fact Book

SLAVERY
Everything You Were Taught About American Slavery is Wrong, Ask a Southerner!
Slavery 101: Amazing Facts You Never Knew About America's "Peculiar Institution"
The Bittersweet Bond: Race Relations in the Old South as Described by White and Black Southerners

CHILDREN
Honest Jeff and Dishonest Abe: A Southern Children's Guide to the Civil War
Saddle, Sword, and Gun: A Biography of Nathan Bedford Forrest For Teens

NATHAN BEDFORD FORREST
A Rebel Born: A Defense of Nathan Bedford Forrest - Confederate General, American Legend (winner of the 2011 Jefferson Davis Historical Gold Medal)
A Rebel Born: The Screenplay (film about N. B. Forrest)
Forrest! 99 Reasons to Love Nathan Bedford Forrest
Give 'Em Hell Boys! The Complete Military Correspondence of Nathan Bedford Forrest
I Rode With Forrest! Confederate Soldiers Who Served With the World's Greatest Cavalry Leader
Nathan Bedford Forrest and African-Americans: Yankee Myth, Confederate Fact
Nathan Bedford Forrest and the Battle of Fort Pillow: Yankee Myth, Confederate Fact
Nathan Bedford Forrest and the Ku Klux Klan: Yankee Myth, Confederate Fact
Nathan Bedford Forrest: Southern Hero, American Patriot - Honoring a Confederate Icon and the Old South
Saddle, Sword, and Gun: A Biography of Nathan Bedford Forrest For Teens
The God of War: Nathan Bedford Forrest As He Was Seen By His Contemporaries
The Quotable Nathan Bedford Forrest: Selections From the Writings and Speeches of the Confederacy's Most Brilliant Cavalryman

QUOTABLE SERIES
The Alexander H. Stephens Reader: Excerpts From the Works of a Confederate Founding Father
The Quotable Alexander H. Stephens: Selections From the Writings and Speeches of the Confederacy's First Vice President
The Quotable Jefferson Davis: Selections From the Writings and Speeches of the Confederacy's First President
The Quotable Nathan Bedford Forrest: Selections From the Writings and Speeches of the Confederacy's Most Brilliant Cavalryman
The Quotable Robert E. Lee: Selections From the Writings and Speeches of the South's Most Beloved Civil War General
The Quotable Stonewall Jackson: Selections From the Writings and Speeches of the South's Most Famous General
The Unquotable Abraham Lincoln: The President's Quotes They Don't Want You To Know!

CIVIL WAR BATTLES
Encyclopedia of the Battle of Franklin - A Comprehensive Guide to the Conflict that Changed the Civil War
Nathan Bedford Forrest and the Battle of Fort Pillow: Yankee Myth, Confederate Fact
The Battle of Franklin: Recollections of Confederate and Union Soldiers
The Battle of Nashville: Recollections of Confederate and Union Soldiers
The Battle of Spring Hill: Recollections of Confederate and Union Soldiers

CONSTITUTIONAL HISTORY
America's Three Constitutions: Complete Texts of the Articles of Confederation, Constitution of the United States of America, and Constitution of the Confederate States of America
The Articles of Confederation Explained: A Clause-by-Clause Study of America's First Constitution
The Constitution of the Confederate States of America Explained: A Clause-by-Clause Study of the South's Magna Carta

VICTORIAN CONFEDERATE LITERATURE
Rise Up and Call Them Blessed: Victorian Tributes to the Confederate Soldier, 1861-1901
Support Your Local Confederate: Wit and Humor in the Southern Confederacy
The Bittersweet Bond: Race Relations in the Old South as Described by White and Black Southerners
The God of War: Nathan Bedford Forrest As He Was Seen By His Contemporaries
The Old Rebel: Robert E. Lee As He Was Seen By His Contemporaries
Victorian Confederate Poetry: The Southern Cause in Verse, 1861-1901

ABRAHAM LINCOLN
Abraham Lincoln: The Southern View - Demythologizing America's Sixteenth President
Lincolnology: The Real Abraham Lincoln Revealed in His Own Words - A Study of Lincoln's Suppressed, Misinterpreted, and Forgotten Writings and Speeches
Lincoln's War: The Real Cause, the Real Winner, the Real Loser
The Great Impersonator! 99 Reasons to Dislike Abraham Lincoln
The Unholy Crusade: Lincoln's Legacy of Destruction in the American South
The Unquotable Abraham Lincoln: The President's Quotes They Don't Want You To Know!

NATURAL HISTORY
North America's Amazing Mammals: An Encyclopedia for the Whole Family
The Concise Book of Owls: A Guide to Nature's Most Mysterious Birds
The Concise Book of Tigers: A Guide to Nature's Most Remarkable Cats

PARANORMAL
Carnton Plantation Ghost Stories: True Tales of the Unexplained from Tennessee's Most Haunted Civil War House!
UFOs and Aliens: The Complete Guidebook

FAMILY HISTORIES
The Blakeneys: An Etymological, Ethnological, and Genealogical Study - Uncovering the Mysterious Origins of the Blakeney Family and Name
The Caudills: An Etymological, Ethnological, and Genealogical Study - Exploring the Name and National Origins of a European-American Family
The McGavocks of Carnton Plantation: A Southern History - Celebrating One of Dixie's Most Noble Confederate Families and Their Tennessee Home

MIND, BODY, SPIRIT
Autobiography of a Non-Yogi: A Scientist's Journey From Hinduism to Christianity (Dr. Amitava Dasgupta, with Lochlainn Seabrook)
Britannia Rules: Goddess-Worship in Ancient Anglo-Celtic Society - An Academic Look at the United Kingdom's Matricentric Spiritual Past
Christ Is All and In All: Rediscovering Your Divine Nature and the Kingdom Within
Christmas Before Christianity: How the Birthday of the "Sun" Became the Birthday of the "Son"
Jesus and the Gospel of Q: Christ's Pre-Christian Teachings As Recorded in the New Testament
Jesus and the Law of Attraction: The Bible-Based Guide to Creating Perfect Health, Wealth, and Happiness Following Christ's Simple Formula
Seabrook's Bible Dictionary of Traditional and Mystical Christian Doctrines
Sea Raven Press Blank Page Journal: For Reflections, Notes, and Sketches
The Bible and the Law of Attraction: 99 Teachings of Jesus, the Apostles, and the Prophets
The Book of Kelle: An Introduction to Goddess-Worship and the Great Celtic Mother-Goddess Kelle, Original Blessed Lady of Ireland
The Goddess Dictionary of Words and Phrases: Introducing a New Core Vocabulary for the Women's Spirituality Movement
The Martian Anomalies: A Photographic Search for Intelligent Life on Mars
Victorian Hernia Cures: Non-surgical Self Treatment of Inguinal Hernia
Vintage Southern Cookbook: 2,000 Delicious Dishes From Dixie

WOMEN
Aphrodite's Trade: The Hidden History of Prostitution Unveiled
Princess Diana: Modern Day Moon-Goddess - A Psychoanalytical and Mythological Look at Diana Spencer's Life, Marriage, and Death (with Dr. Jane Goldberg)
Women in Gray: A Tribute to the Ladies Who Supported the Southern Confederacy

REPRINTS
A Short History of the Confederate States of America (author Jefferson Davis; editor Lochlainn Seabrook)
Prison Life of Jefferson Davis (author John J. Craven; editor Lochlainn Seabrook)
Life of Beethoven (author Ludwig Nohl; editor Lochlainn Seabrook)
The New Revelation (author Arthur Conan Doyle; editor Lochlainn Seabrook)

Lochlainn Seabrook does not author books for fame and fortune, but for the love of writing and sharing his knowledge.

SeaRavenPress.com

The BITTERSWEET BOND

Race Relations in the Old South
As Described by White & Black Southerners

This Highly Educational Compendium of Articles, Essays, Stories, Speeches, Letters, Poems, & Obituaries was
CONCEIVED, COLLECTED, EDITED, & ARRANGED, WITH AN INTRODUCTION BY THE AUTHOR,
"THE VOICE OF THE TRADITIONAL SOUTH," COLONEL

LOCHLAINN SEABROOK
JEFFERSON DAVIS HISTORICAL GOLD MEDAL WINNER

Diligently Researched and Generously Illustrated
by the Author-Editor for the Elucidation of the Reader

2022

Sea Raven Press, Nashville, Tennessee, USA

THE BITTERSWEET BOND

Published by
Sea Raven Press, Cassidy Ravensdale, President
Nashville, Tennessee, USA
SeaRavenPress.com • searavenpress@gmail.com

Copyright © text and illustrations Lochlainn Seabrook 2022
in accordance with U.S. and international copyright laws and regulations, as stated and protected under the Berne Union for the Protection of Literary and Artistic Property (Berne Convention), and the Universal Copyright Convention (the UCC). All rights reserved under the Pan-American and International Copyright Conventions.

PRINTING HISTORY
1st SRP paperback edition, 1st printing, July 2022 • ISBN: 978-1-955351-18-8
1st SRP hardcover edition, 1st printing, July 2022 • ISBN: 978-1-955351-19-5

ISBN: 978-1-955351-18-8 (paperback)
Library of Congress Control Number: 2022941386

This work is the copyrighted intellectual property of Lochlainn Seabrook and has been registered with the Copyright Office at the Library of Congress in Washington, D.C., USA. No part of this work (including text, covers, drawings, photos, illustrations, maps, images, diagrams, etc.), in whole or in part, may be used, reproduced, stored in a retrieval system, or transmitted, in any form or by any means now known or hereafter invented, without written permission from the publisher. The sale, duplication, hire, lending, copying, digitalization, or reproduction of this material, in any manner or form whatsoever, is also prohibited, and is a violation of federal, civil, and digital copyright law, which provides severe civil and criminal penalties for any violations.

The Bittersweet Bond: Race Relations in the Old South as Described by White and Black Southerners, by Lochlainn Seabrook. Includes an introduction, illustrations, index, endnotes, appendices, and bibliography.

ARTWORK
Front and back cover design and art, book design, layout, font selection, and interior art by Lochlainn Seabrook.
All images, image captions, graphic design, and graphic art copyright © Lochlainn Seabrook.
All images selected, placed, manipulated, cleaned, colored, tinted, and/or created by Lochlainn Seabrook.
Cover image: White baby Ada Peters Brown with black governess, 1860s, Library of Congress, © Lochlainn Seabrook.

All persons who approve of the authority and principles of Colonel Lochlainn Seabrook's literary work, and realize its benefits as a means of reeducating the world about facts left out of mainstream books, are hereby requested to avidly recommend his titles to others and to vigorously cooperate in extending their reach, scope, and influence around the globe.

The historical views expressed in this book are those of the publisher.

WRITTEN, DESIGNED, PUBLISHED   IN THE UNITED STATES OF AMERICA

DEDICATION

To my venerable Appalachian ancestors from Kentucky, West Virginia, Tennessee, North Carolina, & Virginia

FARMERS, COAL MINERS, RAILROAD MEN, CONFEDERATE SOLDIERS

"Noble souls,
through dust and heat,
rise from disaster and defeat,
the stronger."

EPIGRAPH

"The negro race in the South has advanced farther than any similar number of negroes anywhere on the globe, because it has had the privilege of coming into contact with the white people of the South. To the Southern white people we owe our language and our religion, all that we have learned and all that we have advanced in civilization."

Dr. Robert Russa Moton
PRINCIPAL TUSKEGEE INSTITUTE

Dr. Robert Russa Moton. Original 1916 caption: "The new principal of Tuskegee Institute, a full-blooded Negro, descendant of an African war chief, whose abilities as an administrator and as a leader of his race well fit him to carry on the work of the late Booker T. Washington."

CONTENTS

Notes to the Reader - Page 11
Introduction, by Lochlainn Seabrook - Page 17

CHAPTER ONE
1893-1896: Page 37

CHAPTER TWO
1897-1900: Page 85

CHAPTER THREE
1901-1904: Page 131

CHAPTER FOUR
1905-1908: Page 187

CHAPTER FIVE
1909-1912: Page 239

CHAPTER SIX
1913-1916: Page 321

Appendix A: Forrest's Independent Order of Pole Bearers' Speech - Page 375
Appendix B: Abraham Lincoln's Real Views on Race & Slavery - Page 377
Notes - Page 379
Food for Thought: Fruitful Quotes from Confederate Veteran - Page 392
Bibliography - Page 393
Index - Page 401
Meet the Author - Page 412
Learn More - Page 413

NOTES TO THE READER

"NOTHING IN THE PAST IS DEAD TO THE MAN WHO WOULD
LEARN HOW THE PRESENT CAME TO BE WHAT IT IS."

WILLIAM STUBBS, VICTORIAN ENGLISH HISTORIAN

THE TWO MAIN POLITICAL PARTIES IN 1860
☛ In any study of America's antebellum, bellum, and postbellum periods, it is vitally important to understand that in 1860 the two major political parties—the Democrats and the newly formed Republicans—were the opposite of what they are today. In other words, the Democrats of the mid 19th Century (formed by what we now call "right-wingers" or "traditionalists")[1] were Conservatives, akin to the Republican Party of today, while the Republicans of the mid 19th Century (formed by what we now call "left-wingers" or "progressives")[2] were Liberals, akin to the Democratic Party of today.[3]

Thus the Confederacy's Democratic president, Jefferson Davis, was a Conservative (with libertarian leanings); the Union's Republican president, Abraham Lincoln, was a Liberal (with socialistic leanings).[4] This is why, in the mid 1800s, the conservative wing of the Democratic Party was known as "the States' Rights Party."[5]

Hence, the Democrats of the Civil War period referred to themselves as "conservatives," "confederates," "anti-centralists," or "constitutionalists" (the latter because they favored strict adherence to the original Constitution—which tacitly guaranteed states' rights—as created by the Founding Fathers), while the Civil War Republicans called themselves "liberals," "nationalists," "centralists," or "consolidationists" (the latter three because they wanted to nationalize the central government and consolidate political power in Washington, D.C.).[6]

The author's cousin, Confederate Vice President and Democrat Alexander H. Stephens: a Southern Conservative.

In 1889 President Davis, who referred to the 1860 Democrats as "the conservative power of the country,"[7] himself explained the political situation at the time this way:

> . . . the names adopted by political parties in the United States have not always been strictly significant of their principles. In general terms it may be said that the old Federal party [Liberal] inclined to nationalism [then a term for big government], or consolidation [that is, consolidation of power in the Federal government], and that the Whig party [liberalistic], which succeeded it, although not identical

with it, was favorable, in the main, to a strong Central Government [liberalism and socialism]. On the other hand, its opponent, the Republican [Conservative], afterward known as the Democratic party [until the election of 1896, when the two parties reversed, becoming the parties we know today], was dominated by the idea of the sovereignty of the States and the federal or confederate character of the Union [Americanism or conservatism]. Although other elements have entered into its organization at different periods, this has been its vital, cardinal, and abiding principle.⁸

Since this idea is new to most of my readers, let us further demystify it by viewing it from the perspective of the American Revolutionary War. If Davis and his conservative Southern constituents (the Democrats of 1861) had been alive in 1775, they would have sided with George Washington and the American colonists, who sought to secede from the tyrannical government of Great Britain; if Lincoln and his Liberal Northern constituents (the Republicans of 1861) had been alive at that time, they would have sided with King George III and the English monarchy, who sought to maintain the American colonies as possessions of the British Empire. It is due to this very comparison that we Southerners often refer to our secession from the U.S. as the Second Declaration of Independence and the "Civil War" as the Second American Revolutionary War.

Without a basic understanding of these facts, the American "Civil War" will forever remain incomprehensible. For a full discussion of this topic see my book, *Abraham Lincoln Was a Liberal, Jefferson Davis Was a Conservative: The Missing Key to Understanding the American Civil War.*

THE TERM "CIVIL WAR"
☞ As I heartily dislike the phrase "Civil War," its use throughout this book (as well as in my other works) is worthy of explanation.

Our entire modern literary system refers to the conflict of 1861 using the Northern term the "Civil War," whether we in the South like it or not. Of course, this is purposeful, for America's book industry, which determines everything from how books are categorized and designed to how they are marketed and sold, is almost solely controlled by Liberals, socialists, globalists, collectivists, and communists, individuals

The American "Civil War" was not a true civil war as Webster defines it: "A conflict between opposing groups of citizens of the *same* country." It was a fight between two individual countries; or to be more specific, two separate and constitutionally formed confederacies: the U.S.A. and the C.S.A.

who will do anything to prevent the truth about Lincoln's War from coming out. An important aspect of this wholesale revisionism of American history is the use of the phrase "Civil War," which Yankee Liberals thrust into the public forum even as big government Left-winger Lincoln was diabolically tricking the Conservative South into firing the first shot at the Battle of Fort Sumter in April 1861.

The progressives' blatant American "Civil War" coverup continues to this day, one of the more overt results which pertains to how books are coded, indexed, and identified.[9] Thus, as all book searches by readers, libraries, and retail outlets are now performed online, and as all bookstores categorize works from or about this period under the heading "Civil War," honest book publishers and authors who deal with this particular topic have little choice but to use this deceptive term. If I were to refuse to use it, as some of my Southern colleagues have suggested, few people would ever find or read my books.

Confederate General Nathan Bedford Forrest, just one of many Southern officials who referred to the conflict of 1861 as the "Civil War."

Add to this the fact that scarcely any non-Southerners have ever heard of the names we in the South use for the conflict, such as the "War for Southern Independence"—or my personal preference, "Lincoln's War." It only makes sense then to use the term "Civil War" in most commercial situations, historically inaccurate though it is.

We should also bear in mind that while today educated persons, particularly educated Southerners, all share an abhorrence for the phrase "Civil War," it was not always so. Confederates who lived through and even fought in the conflict regularly used the term throughout the 1860s, and even long after—as this book attests. Among them were Confederate generals such as Nathan Bedford Forrest, Richard Taylor, and Joseph E. Johnston, not to mention the Confederacy's vice president, Alexander H. Stephens.

In 1895 Confederate General James Longstreet wrote about his military experiences in a work subtitled, *Memoirs of the Civil War in America*, while in 1903 Confederate General John Brown Gordon, the first commander-in-chief of the United Confederate Veterans, entitled his autobiography, *Reminiscences of the Civil War*. Even the Confederacy's highest leader, President Jefferson Davis, used the term "Civil War,"[10] and in one case at least, as late as 1881—the year he wrote his brilliant exposition, *The Rise and Fall of the Confederate Government*.[11] Authors writing for *Confederate Veteran* magazine sometimes used the phrase well into the early 1900s,[12] and in 1898, at the Eighth Annual Meeting and

Reunion of the United Confederate Veterans (the forerunner of today's Sons of Confederate Veterans), the following resolution was proposed: that from then on the Great War of 1861 was to be designated "the Civil War Between the States."[13]

A WORD ON EARLY AMERICAN MATERIAL

☞ In order to preserve the authentic historicity of the antebellum, bellum, and postbellum periods, I have retained the original spellings, formatting, and punctuation of the early Americans I quote. These include such items as British-English spellings, long-running paragraphs, obsolete words, and various literary devices peculiar to the time. However, I have corrected misspelled names to prevent confusion, and also *where possible*, inaccurate dates and locations (the inevitable result of old faulty memories). Bracketed words are my additions and clarifications (added mainly for my foreign readers), while italicized words are (where indicated) my emphasis.

INCLUDED MATERIAL DOES NOT EQUAL MY ENDORSEMENT

☞ The appearance of a view, idea, sentiment, or declaration in this book does not necessarily mean I accept, support, or condone it, or agree with it. This is a history book; that is, it is a work based on the historical record. The material in it is presented, not necessarily to promote all of the views contained herein, but for its educational value and to preserve authentic history for future generations.

A WORD ON RACE

☞ This is a work about what the Left regards as the "controversial" issues of race and race relations.[14] Due to the potentially inflammatory nature of ethnic studies, let me clearly state my views here.

I do not agree with or believe in the theory that one race is superior to any other. I do not even believe in or accept the concept of race; particularly the wholly unscientific version fabricated by Liberals, socialists, and communists.[15]

To the contrary, I promote, and have always promoted, the ideas of racial oneness, racial unity, and racial harmony as these concepts are laid out in the New Testament: "And God hath made of one blood all nations of men for to dwell on all the face of the earth."[16]

PRESENTISM

☞ As a historian I view *presentism* (judging the past according to present day mores and customs) as the enemy of authentic history. And this is precisely why the Left employs it in its ongoing war against traditional American, conservative, and Christian values. By looking at history through the lens of modern day beliefs—and, just as heinous, fabricating

Judging our ancestors by our own standards is dishonest, unfair, unjust, misleading, and unethical.

obviously fake history based on emotion, opinion, and political ideology—they are able to distort, revise, and reshape the past into a false narrative that fits their ideological agenda: the liberalization and Northernization of America, the enlargement and further centralization of the national government, and total control of American political, economic, and social power, the same agenda that Lincoln championed.[17]

This book rejects presentism and replaces it with what I call *historicalism*: judging our ancestors based on the values of their own time. To get the most from this work the reader is invited to reject presentism as well. In this way—along with casting aside preconceived notions and the fake history churned out by our left-wing education system—the truth in this work will be most readily ascertained and absorbed; truth that has been rigorously researched and forensically uncovered by myself using the scientific method. As Confederate Colonel Bennett H. Young noted in 1901:

> History is valuable only as it is true. Opinions concerning acts are not history; acts themselves alone are historic.[18]

CONTINUE YOUR SOUTHERN HISTORY EDUCATION

☛ Neither race relations in the Old South or Lincoln's War on the Constitution and the American people can ever be fully understood without a thorough knowledge of the South's perspective. As this book is only meant to be a brief introductory guide to these topics, one cannot hope to learn the complete story here. For those who are interested in additional material from Dixie's viewpoint, please see my comprehensive histories listed on pages 2 and 3.

Keep Your Body, Mind, & Spirit Vibrating at Their Highest Level!

YOU CAN DO SO BY READING THE BOOKS OF

SEA RAVEN PRESS

There is nothing that will so perfectly keep your body, mind, and spirit in a healthy condition as to think wisely and positively. Hence you should not only read this book, but also the other books that we offer. They will quicken your physical, mental, and spiritual vibrations, enabling you to maintain a position in society as a healthy erudite person.

KEEP YOURSELF WELL-INFORMED!

The well-informed person is always at the head of the procession, while the ignorant, the lazy, and the unthoughtful hang onto the rear. If you are a Spiritual man or woman, do yourself a great favor: read Sea Raven Press books and stay well posted on the Truth. It is almost criminal for one to remain in ignorance while the opportunity to gain knowledge is open to all at a nominal price.

We invite you to visit our Webstore for a wide selection of wholesome, family-friendly, well-researched, educational books for all ages. You will be glad you did!

Unique Books & Gifts for the Whole Family!

SeaRavenPress.com

LochlainnSeabrook.com
TheBestCivilWarBookEver.com
NathanBedfordForrestBooks.com

INTRODUCTION

"I believe that the best friend that a Southern negro can have is the Southern white man."
U.S. PRESIDENT WILLIAM H. TAFT

HISTORY TWISTING: FAVORITE PASTIME OF THE LEFT

WHEN IT COMES TO AMERICAN history, no subject has been as aggressively edited, garbled, falsified, distorted, and intentionally manipulated as that of race relations in the Old South. Little wonder. Our highly prejudicial enemies have had over 150 years to freely depict us, the white people of Dixie, in any manner they please. Typical descriptions of us have ranged from "a rabid, fighting people, slave drivers by instinct, traitors by nature, and secessionists by choice," to "a proud, aristocratic section who sought to perpetuate human slavery by plunging the country into war." But as Southern writer Annie Gwinn Masey states, "this prejudice will disappear gradually when historians study closely the South."[19]

George Limerick Cowan, Confederate Lieut., Gen. N. B. Forrest's Escort.

WHY I WROTE THIS BOOK

And that is one of the primary purposes of this book: to help erase the error-based, and thus needless, ignorance and bigotry still possessed by many people around the world concerning America's Old South. The intended methodology behind my book is simple: To provide a straight-forward presentation of unembellished facts and unbiased knowledge as gathered from eyewitness testimony.

In 1915, Fannie E. Selph, historian for a U.D.C. chapter in Nashville, Tennessee, wrote:

> It has been well said that "there are three things necessary to the greatness and glory of a State or nation: To make history, to write history, to teach history." Our Confederate heroes of the sixties have made history grand and noble. It is the responsible duty of the living South of to-day to see that this history is correctly written and taught and not only recorded in printed page, but inscribed in the hearts and minds of our children and then preserved as monuments standing out grandly through the coming years as a vindication of the truth and the right.[20]

While American abolition took place 157 years ago, truly, neither Southern blacks or whites will ever be completely emancipated until every Left-wing Yankee myth is debunked and the genuine history of the Old South is publicly and widely known. It is my sincere hope that *The Bittersweet Bond* will play a role in fulfilling that goal.

FACTS TO REMEMBER

Long time readers of my works will be surprised by very little in the following pages. They are now well aware, for example, that literally *nothing* in any mainstream history book can be completely trusted, that few if any of the statements and claims made in such volumes hold up to objective academic scrutiny, and that most are penned by radical Left-wing, America-hating, opinionated socialists and communists; many who conveniently avoid using footnotes and bibliographies, and nearly all who seem far more interested in propagandizing and indoctrinating than educating and enlightening.

As for my loyal readers, they already know that:

• American slavery, and particularly the Southern variety, was nothing even remotely similar to how it is portrayed in conventional history books.

• As many as 1 million Southern blacks willingly worked for, served in, or fought in the Confederate army and navy; five times more, in fact, than served in the Union army and navy.

• According to Victorian military authorities, like Union General August Valentine Kautz, a "soldier" is legally defined as anyone who serves in any capacity in the military and receives pay. This would include common laborers, servants, wagoneers, cooks, gunsmiths, wheelwrights, launderers, sutlers, teamsters, hostlers, musicians, etc., whatever their color or race.

• Technically speaking, authentic slavery was never practiced in the South, and the institution was regarded by all thinking people at the time as "indentured servitude," a mild form of temporary vassalage in which a servant can purchase his or her freedom at any time.

Popular fictional Southern character "Uncle Remus."

• Besides white slave owners, there were also thousands of black slave owners. Fact: twenty-five percent of all antebellum slave owners in the South were of African descent, many who owned both black and white slaves.

• The South was not responsible for American slavery. Both the American slave trade and American slavery got their start in the Northeast (Massachusetts to be specific), and our country's largest and one and only true slave empire, was New York City, a bonafide slavocracy that indulged in and perpetuated the institution for over two centuries. Indeed, "in the seventeenth century slaves were sold in most all [of] the New England States. Massachusetts, Rhode Island and Connecticut contained not less than 15,000 in 1761."[21]

• Abraham Lincoln was a lifelong member of the American Colonization Society, a white supremacist organization whose primary mission was to deport and resettle (that is, colonize) *all* African Americans in and on foreign lands—such as Liberia.

• Lincoln did not "free the slaves." His Emancipation Proclamation was unconstitutional, and thus null and void. Slavery did not legally end until eight months after his death with the ratification of the Thirteenth Amendment—which was created by a Southerner.

• Slavery is not a "peculiar institution," as the ill-informed enjoy referring to it. It has been an integral part of the founding and development of every known civilization, on every continent, from time immemorial.

Miss Aline Mobley, Rockhill, S.C., Chief Confederate Maid of Honor for the South Carolina Division, U.C.V.

• We are all, no matter our skin color, race, ethnicity, or nationality, the descendants of both slaves and slave owners—making the idea of reparations specifically for African American slaves unjustifiable.

• Millennia before the arrival of Arab, European, and Yankee slavers on Africa's shores, black Africans had already long been enslaving their own people, using some of the most horrific and inhumane forms of bondage ever recorded.[22]

• In fact, without Africa's prehistoric domestic slave system, as well as her enthusiastic participation and encouragement, the Atlantic Slave Trade would never have been possible.[23]

• Slavery continues unabated to this day in nearly every country (including the U.S.), with an estimated 40 million enslaved people around the world: 25 percent of them children, 71 percent girls and women.[24]

"RADICAL" & "ABOLITIONIST": LEFT-WING CODE WORDS

In the previous section, "Notes To My Readers," I touch on the subject of the great party reversal in the mid 1800s, at which time the

Democrats were politically conservative and the Republicans were politically liberal—positions that would not change until the presidential election of 1896, when the platforms of the two main parties reversed, becoming those that we are familiar with today: Conservative Republicans and Liberal Democrats.[25]

A related topic that is vital to any accurate comprehension of American slavery, the War Between the States, and more particularly white and black relationships in the Old South, is the duplicitous terminology used by the Victorian Left. I am speaking specifically here about the two words "radical" and "abolitionist" as they were coined, defined, and used by 19th-Century progressives.

So-called Yankee "radicals" and Yankee "abolitionists" were anything but the charitable egalitarians and zealous black civil rights activists guilefully depicted in Western textbooks. They were, in fact, socialists and communists, whose true aim was the destruction of traditional democratic society, which had originally been built upon slavery (of all races) dating back to earliest recorded history, including ancient Rome, Greece, Arabia, Egypt, and Mesopotamia—*all Caucasian civilizations*. Despite this historical foundation, under the autocratic dictates of the extreme Yankee Left, by the early 1800s abolition had become one of the tools it intended to use to accomplish its goal; not out of compassion for the slave, but out of hatred for white people, the South, capitalism, and the Constitution (which protected slavery countrywide at the time).

Lincolnite Salmon P. Chase of New Hampshire, infamous for his dislike of blacks, his apathy toward abolition, and his loathing of Southerners.

Nowhere is this fact better illustrated than by a series of comments uttered by Lincoln's future Chief Justice of the United States, Yankee Salmon Portland Chase (then governor of Ohio), to William D. Chadwick of Huntsville, Alabama. This conversation took place four years before the start of the War for Southern Independence. Looking back in 1891, Chadwick writes:

> Near the close of the winter of 1857, I visited Ohio at the instance of S. D. Cabiness, Esq., and Samuel C. Townsend, for the purpose of selecting a home for a number of slaves belonging to the estate of [Southerner] Samuel Townsend, deceased, and who, according to his last will were to be liberated and settled in some free State. Having letters to several distinguished gentlemen in Cincinnati, mainly of the clergy and the bar, and having made their acquaintance, I obtained from them letters to other intelligent and influential citizens in different portions of the State.

Among many others, I had letters to his Excellency Governor S. P. Chase. I called on him among the first men, after my arrival in Columbus, believing, from what I had learned of him from others, who knew him well, that he would take a deep interest in the matter of my mission, and that, owing to his thorough acquaintance with the physical and moral developments of the State generally, he would be found an efficient friend of those I represented. I was received by the Governor with apparent cordiality, and received from him much information in regard to the various negro schools, colonies, etc., in the State. But, to my utter astonishment, Governor Chase closed his conversation on the subject by remarking, with emphasis, that "for his part, he would rather never see another free negro set his foot upon Ohio soil." I asked his reason. "Because," said he, "their moral influence is degrading." I then remarked that it appeared to me a glaring inconsistency, in him and others in Ohio, to love our Southern slaves so much as to desire their freedom and clamor for their emancipation, and yet hate them so much as to be unwilling to allow them a home in their own State; especially so since, by the existing laws in the slave States the negro cannot be liberated and remain where he is." He replied: "I do not wish the slave emancipated because I love him, but because I hate his master...."[26]

Union General Carl Schurz, one of the many foreign socialists who served in Lincoln's military, campaigned for Liberal "Honest Abe" during the 1860 presidential election.

As will be ascertained in the following pages, in making these statements, Governor Chase was speaking not only for countless Ohioans, but for thousands if not millions of Yankees from other Northern states as well.

How do we know that the words "radical" and "abolitionist" were Left-wing euphemisms for "socialist" and "communist"? Because they themselves said so, as did their critics. After a communist insurrection (against the conservative French government) erupted in Paris in 1871, radical Left-wing "abolitionist" Wendell Phillips declared sympathetically: "There is no hope for France but in the Reds" (that is, the communists).[27] Another "abolitionist," Theodore Tilton, was even more forthright and transparent, stating:

The same logic and sympathy—the same conviction and ardor—which made us an Abolitionist twenty years ago, make us a Communist now. Half a dozen cabinets in Europe send each a representative to Congress of consultation; and these satraps, sitting like a committee of slaveholders, rule the workingmen of Europe. This may not be slavery; but it is tyranny. Hence, the International; in other words, Emancipation. Having been an Emancipationist, why should we not be an Internationalist?[28]

The source of many of the South's troubles, then and now: white racist German revolutionary Karl Marx, the founder of modern communism. A staunch admirer of Lincoln (to whom he once wrote an impassioned personal letter), as well as the President's pro-Labor and anti-states' rights views, many of Marx's friends served in the Lincoln administration and in Lincoln's armies.

Internationalism, defined as "a policy of cooperation among nations," is an important ideological aspect of both socialism and communism, which is why it was heartily sponsored by such individuals as Karl Marx (the founder of modern extreme radical communism), Mikhail Bakunin (noted revolutionary anarchist leader), and Leon Trotsky (a Bolshevik-Leninist and founder of the communist political concept known as Trotskyism).

That "radicals" and "abolitionists" were nothing but socialists and communists in sheep's clothing was patently clear to educated Southerners long prior to Lincoln's War. One of them, Virginia Senator Robert Mercer Taliaferro Hunter, spoke the following words before the U.S. Senate in 1858:

> Mr. President, if we recognize no law as obligatory, and no government as legitimate, which authorizes involuntary servitude, we shall be forced to consign the world to anarchy; for no government has yet existed, which did not recognize and enforce involuntary servitude for other causes than crime. To destroy that, we must destroy all inequality in property; for as long as these differences exist, there will be an involuntary servitude of man to man. Your socialist is the true abolitionist, and he only fully understands his mission.[29]

Conservative Yankee statesmen were also aware of the linguistic trickery being practiced by the Victorian Left. In 1860, "in a letter addressed to a public meeting," Massachusetts Congressman Caleb Cushing wrote:

The current suggestion that slave property exists but by local law is no more true of this than it is of all other property. In fact, the European Socialists, who, in wild radicalism . . . are the correspondents of the American abolitionists, maintain the same doctrine as to all property, that the abolitionists, do as to slave property. He who has property, they argue, is the robber of him who has not. *"La propriete, c'est le vol"* ["property is robbery"], is the famous theme of the [French] Socialist, [Pierre-Joseph] Proudhon. And the same precise theories of attack at the North on the slave property of the South would, if carried out to their legitimate and necessary logical consequences, and will, if successful in this, their first state of action, superinduce attacks on all property, North and South.[30]

German philosopher, nihilist, and anti-Christian Friedrich Nietzsche, who at one time had plans to establish a commune in Europe, linked abolition with socialism, saying:

The French Revolution is the continuation of Christianity. [French philosopher Jean-Jacques] Rousseau is the seducer: he again unfetters woman who is henceforth represented in an ever more interesting manner—as suffering. Then the slaves and [Yankee novelist] Mrs. [Harriet] Beecher-Stowe. Then the poor and the workers. Then the vice addicts and the sick. . . .[31]

Friedrich Nietzsche.

Virginia lawyer, writer, and intellectual George Fitzhugh easily saw through the euphemistic word games played by 19th-Century Liberals, and even confronted abolitionist-socialists with his view. In an 1856 letter to Boston "abolitionist" William Lloyd Garrison, one of early America's leading socialists, Fitzhugh writes:

Dear Sir: I am about to publish a work, entitled *Cannibals All! or, Slaves Without Masters*. I shall, in effect, say, in the course of my argument, that every theoretical abolitionist at the North is a Socialist or Communist, and proposes or approves radical changes in the organization of society. I shall cite Mr. [Horace] Greeley, Mr. [William] Goodell, S. P. [Stephen Pearl] Andrews, Gerrit Smith, yourself, and other distinguished and leading abolitionists, of both sexes, as proof of my assertion.[32]

Knowing the true meaning behind the word "abolitionist," naturally Fitzhugh also understood the "real object" of the Liberal Northern "abolition" movement. In the 1857 book referenced above, he pronounced:

> We warn the North, that every one of the leading Abolitionists is agitating the negro slavery question merely as a means to attain ulterior ends, and those ends nearer home. They would not spend so much time and money for the mere sake of the negro or his master, about whom they care little. But they know that men once fairly committed to negro slavery agitation—once committed to the sweeping principle, 'that man being a moral agent, accountable to God for his actions, should not have those actions controlled and directed by the will of another,' are, in effect, committed to Socialism and Communism, to the most ultra [Left-wing] doctrines of Garrison, Goodell, Smith and Andrews—to no private property, no church, no law, no government,—to free love, free lands, free women, and free churches. . . .
>
> Socialism, not Abolition, is the real object of Black Republicanism [that is, Left-wing abolitionists, then members of the Republican Party—which was Liberal at the time]. The North, not the South, the true battle-ground. Like [Frances] Fanny Wright, the author [founder] of American Socialism, the agitators of the North look upon free society as a mere transition state to a better, but untried, form of society. The reader will not fully comprehend the ideas we would convey, without reading *England the Civilizer*, by Miss Fanny Wright. It is worth reading, not only as far the best history of the British constitution, but as the most correct and perfect analysis and delineation of free society—of that form of society which all Socialists and all thinking men agree cannot stand as it is. The Abolition school of Socialists like it because it is intolerable—because they consider it a transition state to a form of society without law or government. Miss Wright has the honesty to admit, that a transition has never taken place. No; and never will take place: because the expulsion of human nature is a pre-requisite to its occurrence.
>
> But we solemnly warn the North, that what she calls a transition [to socialism, and afterward communism], is what every leading Abolitionist is moving heaven and earth to attain. This is their real object—negro emancipation [is] a mere gull trap.[33]

New York socialist Gerrit Smith, known deceptively as an "abolitionist" in mainstream history books.

THE GREAT SLAVERY SCAM

As you peruse the following pages, keep the above facts firmly in mind. They will play a large and significant role in your understanding of the topics encompassed in this book. They are part of what I call "The Great Yankee Coverup," and its offspring, "The Great Slavery Scam"; the latter a 300 year old plot in which Old England and New England brought domestic African slavery into North America, then later, when Liberal Yankees found it financially unprofitable and racially uncomfortable, forced it onto the Conservative South. Finally, they used the institution as a weapon to hurt Dixie economically and to inaugurate a political war against Conservatism, Western tradition, and the U.S. Constitution.

Although this a 19th-Century illustration of a boatload of African slaves on their way to market, it could just as easily have been created today, for every year thousands of black Africans continue to be kidnaped and enslaved by fellow black Africans, then sold at profit to other black Africans.

My book *Everything You Were Taught About American Slavery is Wrong, Ask a Southerner!* lays out the historical foundations of The Great Slavery Scam. This book, *The Bittersweet Bond*, provides the evidence of its results.[34]

We have noted the words of Lincoln's future Chief Justice Salmon P. Chase, who was voicing the general opinion of the Liberal North (which included thousands of Yankee socialists and communists), when he said: "I do not wish the slave emancipated because I love him, but because I hate his [white Southern] master."[35] For those who still cling to the now thoroughly refuted fairy tale that the Victorian Left and the modern Left were or are truly concerned about either slavery or black people, consider the following: According to the Global Slavery Index, at present there are nearly 10 million slaves in Africa, making it the continent on which "modern day slavery is most prevalent."[36]

Thus Africa currently possesses nearly three times as many black servants as the Old South did. Yet not one of these modern native African bondsmen was enslaved by a white person or has a white master. This is indigenous African slavery: Black Africans kidnaped, abused, sold, worked, and sold again by and to other black Africans. As a historian and slavery scholar, I have spent much of my life reading, researching, and writing on these topics. Never once have I come across a single Left-wing organization, or even a Left-wing individual, that has spoken out against either early or modern domestic African slavery.

This absolutely confirms the validity of Chase's 155 year old statement, as well as the bold fact that the Great Slavery Scam is alive and well to this day, irresponsibly promulgated in our children's schoolbooks as "factual history."

WRITING ABOUT SOUTHERN ETHNIC STUDIES IN 2022

☞ Though modern readers may find some of the material in this book "white supremacist" in tone, in order to avoid presentism and its inevitable distortion of history, one must learn to read it through the lens of Victorian Southern whites who lived before, during, and shortly after the War for Southern Independence. Only then, as a product of its own time and place, will this material be truly understandable. Let us examine this matter more closely.

The Left is today promoting the idea that everything connected to whites, the American South, and particularly the Confederacy, is inherently "racist." To have any hope of convincing the public of these absurdities Liberals first had to change the original definition of the word racism from "the belief held by an *individual of any race* that one race is superior to another," to "the belief held by a *white person* that the Caucasian race is superior to all others."

Charles Anderson Dana, personal friend of radical communist Karl Marx and an editor who worked for socialist newspaperman Horace Greeley. Dana was a revolutionary socialist who served in the Lincoln administration as Assistant Secretary of War. Why? My books explain.

The world will never accept the Left's infantile attempt to redefine the word racism, and for good reason. The idea that only whites are racist is not only scientifically untenable, it is demonstrably false. Throughout history there have been countless examples of black supremacist individuals and organizations, Asian supremacist individuals and organizations, Latino supremacist individuals and organizations, and Native American supremacist individuals and organizations. As just one example, black supremacy was so widespread during the mid 20th Century that at least one popular black leader, Martin Luther King, felt the need to publicly condemn it.[37] Nor is the concept of black supremacy a phenomenon of the modern era. Numerous black supremacy movements, headed by vocal black racist activists, are known to have flourished during the 19th Century.[38]

THE LEFT TRANSFORMS BIOLOGY INTO RACISM

Were there white racists and white supremacists in the Old South? Of course, and some of their words appear in the following pages. It is important to bear in mind, however, that many if not most of the blacks who worked as servants in white Southern homes were Africans by birth, or first generation Americans (born in the U.S. of native African parents), with no knowledge of European American culture, customs, language, foods, clothing, or religion. Already enslaved by fellow black Africans, then purchased by Yankee slave traders on Africa's West coast, the former group arrived on our shores as what appeared to early white Americans as godless, naked illiterates, "semi-savages,"[39] as some white Southerners referred to them in the 1700s and 1800s.

To fit into their new way of life, newly arriving Africans had to be Europeanized, and more specifically Americanized and Christianized. Many white Southerners likened the expensive, difficult, complex, and time-consuming process to socializing young children in preparation for adulthood. Before condemning the whites of the Old South, one must understand the perspective of an 18th- or 19th-Century European American in this situation, and how, for that time and place, he or she might assume a feeling of racial superiority, or, in other words, of "white supremacy."

Slavery was once integral to many indigenous American peoples, a number who not only enslaved fellow Indians, but owned Caucasian and African slaves as well. In this 19th-Century illustration, a group of Native Americans has kidnaped a white woman and enslaved her. She will be worked for the rest of her life under harsh conditions, suffering all of the indignities and tortures typically experienced by most female slaves around the world. Why does the Left continue to ignore the realities of early Native American slavery? To the educated the answer is obvious.

The Left also likes to call this xenophobia, and defines the word as "the fear of foreigners," which they, in turn, loosely interpret to mean the "fear of people of other races." This is another example of progressive word twisting, however, for xenophobia is Greek for "stranger fearing"—with no connection whatsoever to race. To be precise then, I will use the term racial xenophobia, the "fear of (unknown) people of other races," a type of reactive impulse that has its roots, not in true racism (the idea of racial superiority) as the Left claims, but in biology.

Anthropological studies reveal that racial xenophobia is actually a neurally hardwired, sociobiological survival mechanism: simply put, by shunning outsiders, the safety of a band, group, or tribe is enhanced, helping ensure its survival.⁴⁰ In this sense, its biological sense, there is nothing nefarious or racist about it; and in fact, primatological studies show that it is also found in nonhuman primates.⁴¹ In humans specifically, racial xenophobia typically manifests as one race (or human type, variety, or color) believing it is superior to all others. In ancient Africa, for instance, native blacks believed they were superior to non-blacks; in ancient China native Asians believed they were superior to non-Asians; and in ancient America indigenous peoples believed they were superior to non-Native Americans.⁴²

Yankee newspaperman and socialist Horace Greeley, another personal friend of the founder of modern communism Karl Marx. Big government Liberal President Lincoln wrote Greeley a letter in 1862, stating that he was not interested in "destroying slavery," and only wanted to "save the Union"—even if it meant not freeing any slaves.

It should come as no surprise then that much of the so-called "racism" displayed by 17th-, 18th-, and 19th-Century Southern whites had its roots in biology—not racial hatred. For just as it benefitted Native Americans experiencing the arrival of the first Europeans, racial xenophobia helped Southern whites understand and manage what they viewed as "alien newcomers"; the "strange, black-skinned pagans" who had recently disembarked from Yankee slave ships, fresh from the shores of the "Dark Continent." This is hard science, free from the revisionism of political correctness, gaslighting, and presentism.

Caucasian xenophobia, or white supremacy, was not just a phenomenon of the Old South. There were also millions of white supremacists in the Old North, among them President Abraham Lincoln (see Appendix B), as well as most of his administration and soldiery. The following excerpt, from a public letter he wrote to socialist Horace Greeley in 1862, is just one example of many hundreds that could be given demonstrating Lincoln's true sentiments concerning slavery and African Americans:

> As to the policy I "seem to be pursuing," as you say, I have not meant to leave any one in doubt. I would save the Union. I would save it in the shortest way under the Constitution. The sooner the national authority can be restored the nearer the Union will be "the Union as it was." If there be those who would not save the Union unless they could at the same time save slavery, I do not agree with them. If there be those who would not save the Union unless they could at the same time destroy slavery, I do not agree with them. My paramount object is to save the Union, and not either to save or destroy slavery. If I could save the Union without freeing any slave, I would do it; and if I could save it by freeing all the slaves,

I would do it; and if I could do it by freeing some and leaving others alone, I would also do that. What I do about slavery and the colored race, I do because I believe it helps to save this Union, and what I forbear, I forbear because I do not believe it would help to save the Union.[43]

WHY DID SOUTHERN BLACKS OVERWHELMINGLY SUPPORT THE CONFEDERACY?

Another question is often asked of the Southern historian regarding race relations in the Old South: "Why did nearly all Southern black servants willingly remain loyal to their white owners during the War, and even volunteer to serve in the Confederate army and navy, when the South sought their ongoing enslavement?" This is easily answered by three important facts:

1) Southern blacks knew that the war was not over slavery; and they knew this because not only had both Confederate and Union soldiers told them so, more importantly both C.S. President Davis and U.S. President Lincoln had emphatically said so during their public speeches.

2) Southern blacks understood that slavery would be abolished whether the South won or lost the war.[44] How? They had learned that white Southerners had been seeking a benign method of abolishing slavery since the 1700s, and were, in fact, in the middle of testing various emancipatory procedures when Lincoln illegally and unnecessarily invaded Dixie in April 1861.

3) Would you turn against someone who nurtured, clothed, fed, housed, doctored, employed, and cared for you (often from birth to old age) because a foreigner advised it? This was the question facing black Southern servants beginning in 1861. Most said no and remained with their white families. Even after legal emancipation (Dec. 1865), over 90 percent continued to live and work for their now former owners.

Confederate Major John Cussons.

While naturally these vital facts have been suppressed by the Left, in this work they will be emphatically repeated again and again in the personal eyewitness accounts of 19th-Century white and black Southerners.

OUR HISTORY BOOKS ARE WRITTEN BY BIASED SOUTH-HATERS

Sadly for the Truth, nearly every mainstream book is written by an uninformed, or informed but malicious, South-loather, both types of writers characteristically operating on the far left of the political spectrum (though one will also find uneducated Conservatives among these biased propagandists), each one posing as a "neutral" historian.[45] Upon reading or reviewing these types of arrogant, hate-filled works, however, intelligent people all have the same reaction, one similar to the following 1912 report by a Confederate veteran, A. H. Lankford, concerning Henry William Elson's 1904 multi-volume work, *History of the United States of America*—certainly one of the most slanted, error-filled "histories" ever penned, particularly its section on Lincoln's War. "We find," begins our Southern critic, Elson's book

> to be most unfair and untruthful; a most ingenious and cunningly devised work, shaded all through with a sympathetic, hypocritical respect for the South, tinged with some make-believe of affection for the whites of the South, yet an uncontrollable love for the colored race.... The [socialist-leaning] author favors through the entire work from the earliest days of the government a strong central government based upon the most extreme and ultra plans offered by the extreme Federalist [Left-winger], who but for [Conservative Thomas] Jefferson would no doubt have succeeded in organizing a centralized [that is, socialized] government.... His description of the war shows a mind ignorant of the facts or so full of hatred that it would not permit him to write the truth....[46]

This gentleman's Confederate veterans' camp thereby resolved:

> That we enter our most solemn protest and condemnation of the use of the book in any Southern school, even in the colored schools. Recognizing the cunning ingenuity and the great effort to arouse the sympathetic feeling for his colored brother and to prejudice the mind against everything in the South but the said colored brother, we regard it as the most dangerous and hypocritical work before the rising generation of our beloved Southland. In this connection we earnestly call upon those whose duty it is to select educators for all Southern schools of whatever grade to elect no teacher who will for one moment teach this or any other such book. We further enter our protest against the custom of employing Northern teachers, by whom it is almost impossible to avoid showing a preference for their much-loved negro brother and prejudice against the Southern whites, and we further appeal to those who have charge of this duty

Miss Emma George Hemmingway, of Carrollton, Mississippi, Confederate Sponsor for the Army of Tennessee Department.

to employ only teachers who exhibit patriotic [that is, Conservative] principles . . ."⁴⁷

In the long run this noble effort by my early 20th-Century Southern comrades failed. In 2022, some 110 years later, these types of heavily slanted revisionist books, filled with the overtly fake history of socialists and communists, continue to be used in our public schools, where they poison Southern children against their own heritage, unnecessarily agitate members of all races, and infect the Northern populace with a lifelong abhorrence of everything Southern. Of course, this is the purpose of such works, not impartial education. As is quite clear from the statements above,

> the history of the war between the sections of the Union has been written largely by Northern men, and everything that could bring discredit on the South, as to the cause and the conduct of the war, has been sought out and generally exaggerated.⁴⁸

Little wonder that Left-wing Yankee businessmen, that is, postwar carpetbaggers, were variously known in the South as the "scum of the human race," the "refuse of the North,"⁴⁹ and the "hyenas of the North," and were often detested even more than Union soldiers.⁵⁰ As traditional Southerners described carpetbaggers, they "acted more like cannibals and savages than human beings."⁵¹ One outraged Old South writer asserted that during so-called "Reconstruction," the Left had "so altered free America as to make it the foremost province of his Satanic Majesty."⁵²

VICTORIAN LEFT-WING PLOYS

When it comes to the age-old fight between good and evil, the Right and the Left, conservatism and liberalism, there is truly nothing new under the sun. Victorian radical Leftists, that is socialists and communists, were engaging in the same nefarious tactics in the 1800s that they employ today. Such early schemes included using minorities as political pawns, gaslighting the public concerning Lincoln's War, rewriting school textbooks to reflect only the Left's viewpoint, demonizing and

Southern black mammies cared for white children as if they were their own, even breastfeeding them if and when necessary.

New England poet and South-hater, James Russell Lowell, enjoyed publicly defaming the South, the resulting unhistorical misconceptions which continue to unfairly damage Dixie's image, reputation, and honor.

suppressing the works of Conservative Southern authors, banning the display of the Confederate Flag, stuffing ballot boxes with fake and thus illegal votes for Left-wing candidates, persecuting and threatening Conservative blacks, and indoctrinating non-whites with communist ideologies then inciting them to crime, racism, and violence. In at least one known case (described in this very book), Lincoln and his progressive sycophants even staged a fake "pandemic," then forced toxic (often lethal) vaccines on Southerners. Countless hundreds of Confederate soldiers were permanently crippled as a result, many even dying from the U.S. government's intentionally poisoned "medicine."

Another standard communist maneuver used by the Civil War era Left was the divide-and-conquer strategy, which involved fabricating a fake race war, a fake socioeconomic war, and a fake gender war. And let us not forget, as discussed earlier, the Left's notable linguistic chicanery: altering the definition of words and names to hide facts, such as referring to the War Between the States as the "Civil War" and calling the continued postwar punishment and humiliation of the South "Reconstruction." Such deception was purposeful: confused, despondent, victimized, angry, and distracted people are more amenable to governmental manipulation.

Though these radical progressive ploys and tactics were instigated some 150 years ago, they will be familiar to modern day readers. Why? Because they continue to be used by their political descendants.

LIBERALS PREDOMINATELY RUN AMERICA'S SCHOOLS
Unhappily, censorious Leftists still openly run our education system, using dictatorial (read *unconstitutional*) powers to control what our children think. Again, this is not new. The ink on Lee's terms of surrender had not yet dried before Liberals (then the Republicans) were sending Yankee teacher-activists into the Southern states to take over our schools. One Southerner made the following observation after a lifetime of studying Northern Leftists:

> I have noted an intolerance of opposition, an assumption of infallibility in judgment, a self-confidence which would

denounce the Almighty if he differed from the Puritan [that is, Yankee] idea, a willingness to deny or to pervert and misrepresent facts, to sustain a theory which have led to persecution and oppression in order to establish a certain theory or course of conduct.[53]

In 1914, the Schuyler Sutton Camp, United Confederate Veterans, of San Angelo, Texas, objected to the educational literature that had recently been "furnished the school children of that city":

> Some six years ago this Camp made public protest against certain books in the library at Central School, of the city of San Angelo, in which the South and some of her patriots were represented in an unfair light, and some of such books, if not all, were removed. Lately we have discovered that insidiously No. 30 of the "Riverside Literature Series," by [Boston's] Houghton, Mifflin & Co., has crept in and is used as literature, especially in a certain grade at Central School.
> The following quotation from James Russell Lowell, on page 82 of No. 30, is particularly obnoxious:
>
> "I pity mothers, tu, down South,
> For all they sat among the scorners;
> I'd sooner take my chance to stan'
> At jedgment, where your meanest slave is,
> Than at God's bar hol' up a han'
> Ez drippin' red ez your'n, Jeff Davis."
>
> This Camp expresses its profound contempt for the distorted mind that evolved such rot, and condemns the publishing company that would foist it upon an unsuspecting public, and also criticizes the management of the school for carelessness and indifference in permitting its use and requests its extirpation at once for all time. — Stephen Elmore, Commander.[54]

HOSTILITY BETWEEN SOUTH & NORTH

Likewise, 19th-Century South-haters routinely referred to the South's beloved Confederate First National Flag, the Stars and Bars, as "the emblem of slavery, secession, treason, and bitterness."[55] In return, Confederate veterans labeled Yankeedom "the intolerant, heretical North."[56]

The Battle of Gaines' Mill.

This intense sectional animus has never ceased, and continues to this day; a politically based vitriol that prevents Liberals, and non-Southerners in general, from recognizing what all Victorian Southerners, both white and black, knew, understood, and believed regarding "the true spirit of affection and understanding that exists between the white people of the South and the negro. . ."[57]
This is where my book comes in.

THE LOVE BETWEEN WHITE MASTER & BLACK SERVANT

The depth of the intense familial love between black servants and their white owners can be seen in the kinship nicknames that the latter often bestowed upon the former; terms of endearment like "uncle," "aunt," "grandma," and "grandpa," and the popular Southern favorite, "mammy"—a name that carried with it the most profound respect and even veneration. This interracial warmheartedness is also evident in the many racially inclusive terms used by Old South whites for Old South blacks, affectionate phrases such as our "colored brother"[58] and "my brother in black."[59]

How tragic that all of this was interrupted by "that fearful conflict which . . . overthrew the Constitution of the United States adopted by the fathers,"[60] along with the postbellum farce known as "Reconstruction," at which time "wicked and corrupt men duped [that is, communized] the black people,"[61] as my Southern ancestors rightly opined.

POSTWAR BLACK WEALTH & ECONOMICS

Noted author and member of the Daughters of the Confederacy, Decca Lamar West, Sponsor for Texas Division, United Confederate Veterans.

Early Yankee historians were well-known for "their usual disregard of truth,"[62] creating records that "were doubtless like Northern histories, untrue in statement of matters pertaining to the South and her people. . ."[63] One area where this was particularly true was the economic status of Southern blacks in postbellum Dixie. Did newly freed blacks exist in "abject poverty due to entrenched white racism," as Liberal mainstream historians continue to boldly assert?

Though at least one entire book has been devoted to this subject, the immense material success of Old South Africans is seldom if ever acknowledged by the legacy media or our Liberal-run school system. Why? Because it does not fit the Left's fabricated narrative about the "white supremacist South." But facts are facts. Fortunately for us, some of these were preserved during the late Victorian Era, before our venomous unlettered foes could revise or suppress them.

For example, from one source we learn that as of the year 1895, "the [combined postwar] wealth of the Negroes in the several *Southern States* is as follows":

- Alabama, $9,200,125 [$325 million in today's currency, L.S.].
- Arkansas, $8,010,315 [$283 million in today's currency, L.S.].
- Florida, $7,900,400 [$280 million in today's currency, L.S.]
- Georgia, $10,415,330 [$368 million in today's currency, L.S.].
- Kentucky, $5,900,010 [$208 million in today's currency, L.S.].
- Louisiana, $18,000,528 [$636 million in today's currency, L.S.].
- Mississippi, $13,400,213 [$474 million in today's currency, L.S.].
- Missouri, $6,600,345 [$233 million in today's currency, L.S.].
- North Carolina, $11,010,635 [$389 million in today's currency, L.S.].
- South Carolina, $12,500,000 [$442 million in today's currency, L.S.].
- Texas, $18,000,500 [$636 million in today's currency, L.S.].
- Tennessee, $10,400,200 [$367 million in today's currency, L.S.].
- Virginia, $4,900,000 [$173 million in today's currency, L.S.].[64]

Logic tells us that the freed Southern slaves—the majority of them uneducated and untrained—could not have amassed this spectacular wealth (some $5 billion in today's currency) in a single generation without external assistance. Where did this help come from?

As we shall see, according to the post Reconstruction testimonies of both blacks and whites, it came mainly from thousands of white ex-slave owners, who gave encouragement, business advice, property, and even financial aid, to their former African servants; all in an effort to help ease them through the difficult transition from servitude and dependency to capitalism and independence.

Another Left-wing myth dead from factual causes.

A SECRET NO MORE

It has been said that "history is a secret," and as a historian I can testify that there is a kernel of truth to this old maxim. For no one knows exactly what relations were like between whites and blacks in the Old South—except those who actually experienced them. This book, *The Bittersweet Bond*, is their story.

LOCHLAINN SEABROOK
Nashville, Tennessee, USA
July 2022
In Nobis Regnat Christus

"Books invite all; they constrain none."
Hartley Burr Alexander (1873-1939)

CHAPTER ONE
1893-1896

THE ANTE-BELLUM SOUTHERN WOMAN
☞ Since the day of exploded ideals has arrived, when William Tell and George Washington's little hatchet—yea, even the all-pervading Puritan who dominated our school histories—one and all have been dethroned from their sure seats, it seems as if the traditional Southern woman of the old plantation life might be allowed to descend from the cross where she has been [unfairly] nailed for generations.
   This graceful bul lackadaisical effigy of the imaginary "Southern Princess" who alternately lolled in a hammock in slothful self-indulgence, or arose in her wrath to scourge her helpless dependents, is the creation which our neighbors [i.e., Yankees] have been pleased to call the "typical Southern woman."

Varina Anne "Winnie" Davis, "Daughter of the Confederacy."

How different was the real housemistress who, on the great river properties, before the war, ruled the destinies of her family with gentle and wise sway. To us who know her in her old age it seems inexplicable that her place has been so long usurped by the figure fashioned by a hostile sculptor.
   What a blessing this woman is to the "New South," the South of struggles and poverty—even the bitterest of her detractors must acknowledge, now that the clouds and smoke of battle begin to clear away and under the sun of peace reveal her true self.
   What she was in the larger and more complicated sphere of her old life is known only to those who took part in it, or to the younger generation who feel the beneficent influence of her character. Had the women of the plantations been the lazy drones of the popular fancy, dreaming away their aimless lives in an atmosphere heavy with the odors of yellow jasmine, magnolias and roses, she would not have been vanquished by the conditions over which she has been victorious.
   When war, pestilence, famine settled on her country the Southern woman, armed cap-a-pie with her heredity of good housewifery, self-control and patience, sprung uncomplaining and cheerful to her place, and vanquished her difficulties with a manly vigor and a womanly grace, the memory of which is very precious and sweet savored to those with whom she dwelt.
   Old-fashioned Virtues and Taste: She probably did not understand

the higher mathematics, but her arithmetic sufficed for household accounts and to gauge her expenses.

Her family practice in the hospital of her plantation made her the best of nurses.

Although her ideas of modern philosophy may have been of the vaguest, gentle and sincere piety breathed through all her arduous life, and made of her the best model for the half-civilized souls [blacks] intrusted to her care, and also exerted refining influence over the men of her family. If among the Hebrews each man was a priest to his own family, among our people every woman officiated as priestess in the isolated corner where she dwelt with the man toward whom "duty was pleasure and love was law," to whom "for better or worse" until death should them part. With her whole heart she gave her best energies to his service. It was her mission to counsel and comfort the weak-hearted and succor all those who were desolate and distressed, were they of her own or of the subject race. She was the mediatrix, the teacher, and, in short the mother of her people; and to her, if to anyone, the negro owes his present civilization and moral culture.

Black family, Stone's River, Middle Tennessee.

The prejudices of her male relatives were arrayed against publicity of any kind for her—even the homage due to her virtues seemed an invasion of the sanctity of home. Thus *the record of her deeds has been suppressed, and she blossomed, bore noble fruit, and faded behind a screen so thick that it has obscured to the outside world the gracious lines of her personality, and her works alone praised her "in the gates," but her children now rise up and call her blessed.*

How the Southern Woman was Trained: To understand the so-called "New South," it is necessary to comprehend the actual duty of her mothers and the social relations which brought forth a race of people honorable, kindly, faithful and recklessly brave, yet adaptable in the highest degree.

These positive virtues are not generally associated with adaptability to new conditions, yet the Southern people in their bitter experience of defeat have given evidence of this power in its full significance.

The men and women of our country had, during the slave-holding period, fulfilled so many varying and incongruous duties to their slaves that they were in a measure fitted for any labor. *The first lesson that a little Southern girl learned, in preparation of her duties as mistress of a plantation, was her association, usually developing into a warm friendship, with the [black] maid of her own age, who was generally given by the mother of the negro to "be some sarvice to little missie," a sort of counterpart to the [adult] "body servant"* whom the recent dialect stories have made so familiar to our non-slaveholding neighbors. Although the peculiar relations of things made this intimacy less close between master and man, *the love which began in their early youth ripened generally into a hearty affection which usually was lifelong, beginning, as it did, with their childish games in the negro quarter.*

The Negro Quarter: It is doubtful if there was ever a *terre defendus* so attractive to a child as this same "quarter," a collection of small dwellings built on each side of a street, and inhabited by children of a larger growth who were prodigal of stories flavored by the faith of the *raconteur*. There were friendly yellow dogs; chickens, ruffled, muffled and duck-legged, which answered to names, with callow broods racing after them, and wonderful hens' nests full of eggs in unfrequented corners; fires in the open air with fat sweet potatoes roasting in their ashes; doll baby gardens planted and torn up at once by a multitude of little coffee-colored playmates who scampered about "little missus" in a frenzy of delight.

Mistress and maiden confided everything to each other, and their mutual affection stood the mistress in good stead in her after life and enabled her often to penetrate the interesting but bewildering tangle of "tergiversations" which the plantation negro calls his thoughts. Experience taught her the habit of their minds, and opened to her the genuine dialect of a thousand idioms which she would afterward have to use in instructing her slaves. It also initiated her into the African standards of right and wrong, by which she gauged the depth of the offender's culpability.

There, too, she learned the potentiality of sarcasm in dealing with a race so alive to a sense of the ludicrous that an appeal to its risibles will often answer the purpose better than punishment.

An instance of this kind is given of a Southern woman who cured her negro marketman of bringing the family a turkey daily for dinner because he had speculated in them and they were cheaper than other meat. She invited him to "stand on the gallery and gobble a little." This ludicrous performance deterred him from a repetition of the offense when more serious remonstrance had proved fruitless.

How She Absorbed Housewifery: The little [white and black] girls were present at all the milkings, churnings, and even the grinding of meal on the place, and so became familiar with the minutiae of these industries.

Confederate President Jefferson Davis.

When the young [white] mistress was married the superintendence of these duties devolved upon her—the curing of the meat, which was to form the staple fund of *the white and black family* throughout the year, the recipes for which were handed down from mother to daughter for generations. As there were no markets, chickens and turkeys and ducks and geese must be reared in plenty; butter must be churned; a good vegetable garden sedulously cultivated; the fruit trees and berry vines persuaded to bear fruit after their kind; to overlook the weaving-room, where the cotton cloths as well as woolen used to be made, was also her duty; and in all these things our grandmothers and mothers were as proficient as the chatelaines of the Middle Ages. Much of these arts the Southern child absorbed without special instruction. Also a part of her education was the cutting and sewing of all kinds garments, the cooking and serving of all sorts of dainties, and the intelligent care of the sick.

Well-read Plantation Women: This practical education went hand in hand with the elementary and theoretical one under governesses, or in the little schools composed of the children of the neighboring places. Whether this method of mixing the actual with the ideal was peculiarly beneficial to their minds, or that the loneliness of their lives drove them into more serious studies, *it is remarkable how many well-read women there were on these river places whose familiarity with the classics was close enough to be loving, and whose skill in the tinkling music of their day was of no mean proficiency.*

So well was their capacity and attainments recognized that the distinguished American historian of this century, [Yankee scholar] Mr. [George] Bancroft, declined a wager with a Southern lady about a literary question saying: "I have been told to beware of the plantation woman—she reads so many books she will prove me in the wrong."

As the Southern woman developed into maturity, dividing her time between her studies and observation of the busy life around her, she read in the daily practice of her elders the constantly repeated lesson of her duty to her sable dependents.

Photo taken 1860-1870, Bundy and Williams, photographers, Middleton, Connecticut.

On the plantation it was not a question of cottage visiting, such as is common in English and New England country life. It was the actual care of an irresponsible family, large and often refractory enough to dampen the zeal of the most philanthropic.

There were clothes to be made for the [black] babies and little [black] children, and as well for the [black] "orphans," the shiftless [black] bachelors and motherless boys and girls who would not sew if they could. Then the [black] seamstresses who were to do this work were to be trained from the manner of holding a needle and scissors through all the various kinds of stitches to be taken up to dressmaking.

There were [black] waiters, waitresses and dairy maids to instruct and cooks to superintend. Also there must be many of these skilled [black] servants, because, *without exception, they all had families* [all emphasis, L.S.], and if one of these should be taken ill another servant must be taken out of the field to supply the parent's place in the house, so that the child might be properly attended and the mother's heart at ease.

The fallacy that those darky servants grew like blackberries on the briers belongs to that land of Cockagne where roasted pigeons fell from the sky. Certainly these self-producing prodigies did not exist for our mothers. It will be only after a long and careful course of training, with mutual forbearance and patience, that the free negro will make as accomplished a servant as our slaves were.

Truth About Whippings and Sellings: The extreme penalty of whipping was reserved for such offenses as stealing and other crimes. As the negroes could not be "discharged without a character,'" the mistress was not armed with the terror always in the hands of the modern housewife, but she had to make the best of her husband's negroes as she found them, trusting to her own powers as educator to form of the young ones such servants as she would like to have about her.

To sell one of the negroes "born on the place" was an evidence of the direst poverty of the master or of the most heinous conduct on the part of the slave.

Such peccadilloes as insubordination, untidiness or stupidity formed no reason to the mind of either [white] mistress or [black] maid in the Old South for a dissolution of their mutual relation; nor could a tormented mistress find relief by giving a useless servant her freedom.

There is an authentic story of one who tried, during a visit to the North, to thus rid herself of a drunken maid whose taste for Madeira had tempted her to run up a score on her mistress' account at the neighboring drinking shop. When the mistress remonstrated the negro answered her that being a "quality darky" she could hardly be expected to get drunk on whisky "like poor white trash," and that as far as her "free papers" were concerned she would have none of them. There was no use talking, she was "master's nigger," and he would have to support her as long as she lived. There was no recourse but to submit, and the aid continued to follow her own sweet will until her freedom was forced upon her by the war. This was no singular or isolated case. . . .⁶⁵

MISS VARINA ANNE "WINNIE" DAVIS, DAUGHTER OF PRESIDENT JEFFERSON DAVIS

GIVE THE OLD SLAVE A HOME

☛ It is consistent with the spirit of the *Confederate Veteran* magazine to introduce and advocate a measure which will surprise, but I trust please, our best people. It is to *give homes to the old negroes who were slaves for twenty years*. This project has had earnest consideration. It has been submitted to friends who have frowned and smiled alternately, the frown coming first. Its scope widens upon reflection, and the good that would come of it, while being much more beneficial to the South than the North, would hardly bring a tithe of benefits, in a sectional sense, to what has been enjoyed on the other side. The pensions annually are now about $190,000,000, and distributed in large proportion at the North. This act of benevolence toward a people whose bondage existed for twenty years or more, would be a tax upon the Government of say $60,000,000, but it would be once for all. The plan contemplates an appropriation of $200 to be expended for land and $100 with which to build a residence for every male and female who served as a slave for twenty years previous to Lincoln's emancipation proclamation, Feb. 22, 1865, provided he or she has never been pensioned and has never held any position under the pay of the

Confederate monument, Greensboro, Georgia.

Government.

The suggested conditions of this benefaction are that the $200 be expended for land so cheap that it will buy not less than ten acres. It may be as low as they can find it. The right to sell said land should be denied them for ten years. These sums should be invested through white commissioners not interested in the lands, and should he selected by the county courts, or similar authorities, to serve without compensation, the presumption being that good men would cheerfully and faithfully render these services gratuitously. The beneficiary should, of course, in all cases, have the option as to details of investment. Where these ex-slaves own homes, if they reside upon the land they should be allowed to invest the residence appropriation of $100 in additional land.

The foregoing is in brief the plan commended. Meditation will show, in an amazing degree, the benefits of such benevolence on the part of the Government. True, the benefits would inure specifically to the Southern people, white as well as black. On many a country place interests are largely identical. The white folks having maintained these old black people, and would do so anyhow. It would enable many whites to provide more liberally for them than they ever have done. It would induce many darkies to remove from dingy suburbs of cities and towns to the open and healthier atmosphere of the country. It would tend to increased respect of the younger negroes for their ancestry, thereby strengthening one of the commandments.

Betty Bormer, former black servant, Ft. Worth, Texas, 1937.

A plea for our old black people is deservedly pathetic [that is, pitiable]. Who among us does not feel genuinely kind to the old darky on whose lips "Massa" and "Mistis" are still heard with musical euphony? Who among us, passing that period of their lives when many of them had hard task-masters, does not recall with an everlasting gratitude that, during the four years of war, thousands of them were loyal, to the last degree, to the dependent members of the family whose protectors were in the war? Why, if the great Government to which we all bear should refuse them the benevolence herein suggested, it would be fitting for the Southern people, themselves, robbed by the Government of billions of money in holding them as lawful property, to undertake a provision of this kind [all emphasis, L.S.].

Republicans [in 1893, still the Liberal Party],[66] on the other side, cannot afford to oppose this measure. Their partisan representatives, years ago, before the Southern people had recovered from the great disaster to their estates, promised "forty acres and a mule" to these identical persons.

The principles of Democracy are not observed in this plea, but the peculiar exigencies of the ease should excuse the digression. It is a broad charity to a class whose simple, unfailing faithfulness, though not strict as to chicken roosts, merits the unstinted liberality of the American people. A distinguished Tennessean, and Democratic [in 1893, still the

Conservative Party] official, who limps from the effect of a federal [Yankee] bullet, said, "If not Democratic it is Confederate." [That is, if one does not wish to consider the proposal strictly Conservative, then it may at least be viewed as traditionally Southern in tone and purpose." L.S.]

Two articles have been furnished [below] on this subject by request—one by Wm. M. Green, whose father, Rev. Dr. A. L. P. Green, though a man of large means, owned but two slaves, and bought them to gratify them, as he had quibbles about slavery, and the other by Mr. Edward E. Young, whose father gave up his life for the cause of the South, and who is now engaged in the material development of Tennessee.[67] — *CONFEDERATE VETERAN* MAGAZINE

THE OLD NEGROES & THE GOVERNMENT

☛ I have been thinking for a long time—I may say for years back—as to the feasibility or practicability of governmental assistance for the old slaves of the South. Now, I do mean this, not as a fancy or wild philanthropy, but an even, properly balanced, long delayed dispensation of justice—not an empty honor or a vapid promise, but some actual bread and sop from the great bowl of the Government for the patient but hungry black freedman. Can the present administration afford such a venture? If it should its history will be glorious. The old planter says, "I am in favor." The Confederate soldier says, "Let it be done." The Federal [Yankee] soldier says, "I cannot consistently object." The bones of Abe Lincoln and Jeff Davis cry aloud. "Be just to the old slave." The Government has poured its millions and billions into pensions; has paid the Indians for imaginary titles more than a hundred millions. The truth is, the red man, as a roving savage, has never been the friend of his white benefactor; has done nothing in converting the wild forest into a garden—has actually impeded the march of civilization. He works not, suffers no solicitude, and pays no taxes. I have reference only to those tribes that are the wards of the Government. On the other hand, *the negro has been the friend of the white man; has been living with him and working for him in North America more than two centuries.* He has stood by his white brother in conquering the wilderness, in building cities, in building railroads. With his black hands he has furnished rice, sugar, corn, tobacco and cotton to the millions in America and Europe. He prefers to remain near the habitation of the white man, and will never leave unless by force or deception. He realizes his dependence, and, under the direction of the white man, is industrious and religious; but, when set off to himself, becomes a barbarian and a bond. His freedom was thrust upon him, and with it came many a sorrow that he knew not of in a state of servitude. Besides, *there is a cruel disposition upon the part of some strangers* [that is, Yankee socialists and communists] *to keep him disquieted and restless; for men, who*

Mrs. Edwin G. Weed, President United Daughters of the Confederacy.

are merciless and mercenary, tempt him into ill-starred expeditions to Eldorados of the North and West, and laugh at his discomfiture as he returns penniless, starved and in rags. Without trenching upon his liberty, cannot the state Legislatures protect him from a vicious Moses and an imaginary Canaan? He is a good laborer, but would have been much better than he is if he had been shielded from his Godless and money-loving [that is, greedy] friends.

The old, polite ante-bellum darkie still stands with his hat off and says with a grin of expectancy, "At your service, Mass William." Especially in the interest of this class I am writing. I propose, with some exceptions, that every ex-slave who had been in a state of servitude for twenty years at the date of President Lincoln's emancipation proclamation, be furnished from the United States treasury with a sufficient amount of money to purchase twenty acres of ground in some rural district of the South, in or near his place of habitation. I would shut out from this benefit all negroes, male and female, who are pensioners, or who are in any way employed by the Government, assuming that these classes are already provided for. I would have a bill, embodying the above propositions and exceptions, prepared and presented by some Congressman who was himself, or his father, a slaveholder. I regard it as eminently fitting and opportune that a Democratic [then Conservative] administration should take the initiative in this racial benefaction; for certainly a proposition to ameliorate the condition of a Helot would have come with more grace from a native Spartan than a Roman.

Confederate General Thomas J. "Stonewall" Jackson.

I arrogate to myself the inherent right of making the above proposition: e.g., my mother, my father and grandfather were slaveholders. By descent I am a Democrat [Conservative], as my grandmother was a near relative of Thomas Jefferson. However, at this present my party fealty is a little shriveled, as I have a disposition and tendency to wring the alcohol out.

The proposition that I have made is in crude form—only the general drift or gist of a bill is given. I have not so stated, but it would be necessary to incorporate in the bill certain guards against land-sharks [that is, real estate swindlers] and pot-house politicians [that is, bibulous bureaucrats]. Hoping that this philanthropic bird may be joined by others of stronger and swifter wing, I turn it loose.[68] — WM. M. GREEN, NASHVILLE, TENN.

MORE SUPPORT FOR GOVERNMENT SPONSORED HOUSING FOR FORMER BLACK SERVANTS

☛ What a spectacle the consummation of this plan would present! The greatest Republic the world has ever known—symbolized by a perfect Anglo-Saxon figure would, from the golden-wreathed chariot of universal liberty, dispense to 150,000 ex-slaves the sacred vestments of a permanent home. These bowed and dusky forms would once again stand erect, if only to shout a welcome to their benefactor, and reach their hard mahogany hands to their wrinkled brows to ascertain whether this "is a sho' 'nuff somefin' or jes a dream."

From Maryland to Texas and from Kentucky to the Gulf these new tax-payers would be distributed. Their joy and good fortune would be shared by the entire American-African race. Instead of millions of shiftless, discouraged tenants, the South would have thousands of colored families living in their own homes, cultivating their own soil, and feeling that they are at last in reality, what they have so far been largely in theory, citizens of a Republic whose laws make no distinction "for color or previous condition of servitude."

They would thus naturally take an interest in whatever concerned the welfare of their own community, and from family relations up to the responsibilities of state, would act thoughtfully and for the best interests of the country at large.

Miss Elizabeth E. McClain, Chief Maid of Honor, West Virginia Division, U.C.V.

In Philadelphia, where there is a larger percentage of home owners than elsewhere in America, they have never yet had a strike. The spectral spirit of discontent, which applied the torch to railroad cars in New York and precipitated bloodshed at Homestead, can find no lodgement in a community where everyone owns his own home and is not only content and happy but constitutionally and unalterably opposed to whatever is against the peace and dignity of society and that would tend (as all agitation does) to increase his own personal taxes, in order to meet the extra expense of the State caused by the violation of the law.

The industrial problem of the South is yet to be solved. Materially speaking, it is full of promise; but who can tell the importance of intelligent caution at this point? In the great mechanical and industrial activity that is sure to come in the near future, does any thinking mind doubt that it would be well for the South to have thus permanently set at ease the minds of many thousand adults who belong to that class which experience has shown are always the most dangerous in times of civil or political excitement?

In one of the greatest speeches of his life, delivered at Dallas, Tex., Oct. 26, 1888, on "The South and Her Problem," Henry W. Grady said:

"All this is no unkindness to the negro; but rather that he may be led in equal rights and in peace to his uttermost good. Not in sectionalism—for my heart beats true to the Union, to the glory of which your life and heart is pledged. Not in disregard of the world's opinion—for to render back this problem in the world's approval is the sum of my ambition and the height of human achievement. Not in reactionary spirit—but rather to make clear that new and grander way, up which the South is marching to higher destiny, and on which I would not halt her for all the spoils that have been gathered unto parties, since

Catiline conspired and Caesar fought. Not in passion, my countrymen, but in reason; not in narrowness, but in breadth; that we may solve this problem in calmness and in truth, and, lifting its shadows, let perpetual sunshine pour down on two races walking together in peace and contentment. Then shall this problem have proved our blessing, and the race that threatened our ruin, work our salvation, as it tills our fields with the best peasantry the world has ever seen. Then the South, putting behind her all the achievements of the past and in war and in peace they beggar eulogy—may stand upright among the nations and challenge the judgment of men and the approval of God, in having worked out, in their sympathy and in his guidance, this last and surpassing miracle of human government."[69] — EDWARD E. YOUNG

A COLUMBUS, MISSISSIPPI, DARKEY
☛ There is living near Columbus, Miss., a colored man named Richard Franks, who is *well known to many of us. He has been a consistent Democrat [that is, a Conservative] ever since he had his freedom*. He is the father of thirty-one children, and all living; has been married twice, and his second wife is the mother of twenty children. His thirtieth son is named for Grover Cleveland. He does not look like an old man yet. He farms, and also sells charcoal to many in this place. *He will live and die in Dixie* [all emphasis, L.S.].[70] — *CONFEDERATE VETERAN* MAGAZINE

THE OLD VIRGINIA TOWN, LEXINGTON
☛ This writing is from memory of an only visit made there [to where Gen. Robert E. Lee and Stonewall Jackson are buried], July 21, 1891, an account of which was written at the time but never published, and the copy lost.

The Lees were all at home and cordially interested in honoring the memory of Gen. Thos. J. Jackson. It was the greatest day in the history of old Lexington, for the attendance was much larger than that when the formal presentation of the recumbent figure of Gen. Lee occurred.

L-R: Anderson Edwards, Minerva Edwards, former black servants, Marshall, Texas, 1937.

A superb colossal bronze statue of Stonewall Jackson had been provided, and his body had been removed from the original family lot to the central circle in the old cemetery of the town, and the bronze figure (it is also by Mr. Edward V. Valentine) was in position.

The principal ceremonies were had under the broad shades of the [Washington and Lee] University campus, some half a mile away, at the conclusion of which the great procession, numbering perhaps 20,000, passed through the main streets and *near the old church, where Jackson taught his Negro Sunday-school*. The military—infantry, cavalry and artillery—passed by the cemetery and formed on an adjacent slope in rear.

. . . Every old soldier present must have wished that he had served under Stonewall Jackson. The negro men of the town who had the honor of being taught by him in his Sunday-school, when boys, were proud of it [all emphasis, L.S.].[71] — DR. J. WM. JONES

BLACK YANKEE SOLDIERS AT THE BATTLE OF THE CRATER
☛ The Alabamians [Confederate] made a grand charge under a terrible fire, reaching the crest of the "Crater" without faltering, and here a short struggle ensued. They tumbled muskets, clubs, clods of earth, and cannon balls into the excavation on the heads of the enemy with telling effect. This novel warfare lasted only a few minutes, when [Union Gen. William F.] Bartlett ordered up the white flag, and about five hundred [Yankee] prisoners marched to our rear. The [Yankee] negroes among them were very much alarmed, and vociferously implored for their lives. One old cornfield chap exclaimed: *"My God, massa, I never pinted a gun at a white man in all my life; dem nasty, stinking Yankees fotch us here, and we didn't want to come fus!"*

Miss Etta Hardeman, Gainesville, Georgia, and the flag she gave to the Georgia Cavalry, U.C.V.

 . . . Next morning was a bright and beautiful Sabbath, and nothing of moment occurred. At least three thousand of the Federal dead were still on the field, putrefying under the scorching rays of the sun. *I remember a negro between the lines, who had both legs blown off, crawled to the outside of our works, stuck three muskets in the ground, and threw a small piece of tent cloth over them to shelter his head from the hot sunshine. Some of our men managed to shove a cup of water to him, which he drank* [all emphasis, L.S.], and immediately commenced frothing at the mouth, and died in a very short time afterwards. He had lived in this condition for nearly twenty-four hours.

On Monday morning a truce was granted, and the Federals sent out details to bury their dead between the lines. They dug a long ditch, and placed the bodies crosswise, several layers up, and refilled the ditch, and thus ended the tragic scenes of three days in and around the "Crater."[72]
— CONFEDERATE LT. COL. WILLIAM H. STEWART

CONFEDERATE HUMOR: HOW MANASSAS, VIRGINIA, GOT ITS NAME
☛ After the battles of Bull Run and Manassas it was the writer's privilege to stand picket at the farm-house of a good old Mrs. Taylor, a few miles east of Fairfax Station. It was there I learned the true meaning of the word Manassas, and how it originated. A faithful old negro man belonging to Mrs. Taylor met a neighboring brother, and addressed him about as follows: "Uncle Willis, kin yer tell me how dey got dis name Manassas fur dis place down dar whar dey has all dem big guns?" "I dunno, Brer Ephriam, cep'ing tis we is de man, and dem Yankees whar cum down here is de asses; dats how we gets de name Manasses, I speck."[73] — F. M. BURROWS

THE BLACK MAN WHO REFUSED TO JOIN JOHN BROWN

☛ T. L. Patterson, Esq., of Cumberland, Maryland, whose good wife sent many subscribers soon after *Confederate Veteran* magazine was started, asks for a list that she may procure renewals. The thought is commendatory. These venerable people have grown grandchildren, and although almost under the shadow of Pennsylvania Mountains, they manifest such zeal for the cause of the South as makes Confederate veterans prouder of their record than they would be of all things that could be bought with money. Mr. Patterson was Government Engineer, and located at Harper's Ferry when [radical Left-wing socialist] John Brown "started the war." The people in that quiet village were as much astounded by the event as were those of any section of the country. Mr. Patterson's family were witnesses. *They well remember the killing of a faithful darkey who would not join the Brown party* [my emphasis, L.S.].[74] — CONFEDERATE VETERAN MAGAZINE

WAR INCIDENT AT ATHENS, GEORGIA

☛ . . . Mrs. James Rutherford. . . was a remarkable woman. She was sister of Gens. T. R. R. Cobb and Howell Cobb, two names that will forever be a part of the history of our Empire State. While the struggle for independence was in progress she took up every carpet in her house but one and made them into blankets for soldiers, and she openly declared her willingness to go into the fight. Her personal courage was illustrated in a memorable event near the close of the war: The Federals had pulled down the fence to a little field of young corn just back of her garden and turned a multitude of mules in it. She called a negro man, ordered him to drive them out and put up the fence, but he said, "No, Mistis, dem Yankees would kill me." "No," she said with emphasis, "I'll go with you, and they will not resent us." Sure enough the soldiers stood astounded upon seeing the lady and the negro clear the field, and when the negro had put up the fence they gave three cheers. *Moreover, they never disturbed her premises again* [my emphasis, L.S.].[75] — CONFEDERATE VETERAN MAGAZINE

Former black servant, circa early 1900s; original caption: "Mammy going to market."

OUR SOUTHERN WOMEN IN WAR TIME

☛ The women of the South did not shrink from the prospect of great and painful economies; they also appreciated that their own patriotic duty was, as cheerfully as possible, to bid farewell to the men of their family who must go to the front, perhaps never to return. Sometimes hope buoyed them up, and they looked on the sunny side and believed that their dear ones would be spared because their cause was righteous. They did shrink, however, affrighted from the prospect of being left alone with a multitude of ignorant negroes who might he instigated to rebellion, without physicians to attend their children or priests to bury them if they died. These horrors oppressed them.

Many a woman, buckling on her husband's sword, asked him to show her how to load and shoot a pistol, adding, "not that I am afraid of any thing, but in case of need." Her next problem was how to handle that pistol, which was an object of almost as great dread as would be the foe it was to repel.

Good Conduct of the Negroes: *All Southern women acknowledge with pride the good conduct of the rank and file of negroes on the breaking out of the war. They generally remained true to the families left in their charge, and protected the women and children to the best of their ability. In short, their course was a powerful testimonial to the life-long kind and just exercise of their masters' power over them* [my emphasis, L.S.].

However, the crops failed frequently. The negroes grew to partake more or less of the excitement which pervaded the whole country, and this interfered with the needful routine of their labor. Then again, the work horses were levied upon for the use of the [Confederate] Government. Thus were the means of cultivation narrowed. The fallow land grew impassable with weeds, the fences and levees fell, the fields which had waved with corn and the cotton blooms became a tangle of vines and bushes, "unprofitably gay with the blue flowers of the destructive morning glory, the execrated tie-vine."

Moreover, all large balances of cash lay out of reach, invested, so that there was little wherewith to buy from the neighboring towns or cities; and as the prosperity of these centers was dependent upon the grain and cotton sent in from the plantations, want came upon all.

Confederate President Jefferson Davis and his wife, First Lady Varina Howell Davis.

The very poor suffered in the absence of their breadwinners. Necessarily those better provided for gave of their surplus, and when they became sorely pressed themselves they shared whatever could be spared by their families; as the poorer classes expressed it, they "had a divide."

. . . The harbors were closed by the blockade. No supplies of clothing could he imported. The time came when the stock of cloth, shoes, medicines, machinery—indeed, of almost every thing necessary to civilized people—was nearly exhausted. The South had proved agriculture to be the most profitable employment, and had never fostered manufactures; besides, her operative classes were not suited to the care of machinery. Now the people found themselves confronted with new problems which they must learn to solve. All these needs must be supplied by the women.

The store each family possessed themselves, of quinine, and such other drugs as were needful for the diseases of a warm climate, was gradually relinquished for the use of the soldiers. Replenishment was impossible. Quinine had been proclaimed by the [Yankee] blockaders "contraband of war." The [Confederate] women turned, undaunted, to the indigenous *materia medica*. Decoctions of willow bark, of dewberry root, orange flowers and leaves, red pepper tea and other "tisanes" took the place of the drugs.

One heart-broken woman wrote to her husband: "Twenty grains of quinine would have saved our two children. They were too nauseated to drink the bitter willow tea, and they are now at rest, and I have no one to work for but you. Do not think of coming. I am well and strong, and am not dismayed. I think day and night of your sorrow. I have their little graves near me."[76] — MRS. VARINA H. DAVIS, WIFE OF CONFEDERATE PRESIDENT JEFFERSON DAVIS

"MISTIS"

☞ Of all extraordinary myths and illusions over cherished, the popular idea of those in the North and East of the case and luxurious idleness of Southern women is the most delusive.

Not of the "new" South do I write, but of the antebellum days of slavery.

The most painstaking, indefatigable workers, mental and physical, the world ever knew were the wives and daughters of the Southern planter.

This statement may sound paradoxical nevertheless it cannot be gainsaid.

Take, for example, a cotton plantation of four hundred slaves, the master had his [black] assistant or overseer, whose duty was to superintend the outdoor work of the field hands; but the [white] master was no sluggard, he arose at dawn, and sometimes steadily pursued his work of general superintendence far into the night.

The [white] mistress had more exhaustive duties still. She was the head and front of business. In her hands lay a heavy and a fearful responsibility. She was at once at the head of the sanitary and commissary departments.

Miss Charlie Scott, Sponsor for Forrest Cavalry Corps, Birmingham Reunion.

The master filled the large square smoke-house with provisions. "Mistis" carried the key. No planter's wife ever surrendered that scepter of power, the smokehouse key. It was she who saw that provisions were plentifully and justly dealt out. *She saw that her people* [black servants] *were well clad as well as well fed, and otherwise made comfortable.*

Think of the amount of clothing required for four hundred people, and not a garment bought ready made and not a sewing machine in the land!

The material was bought by the bale, cut into shape and made up. The planter's wife had to superintend, ofttimes cut, arrange and sew. No one could teach negro seamstresses but "mistis." Every detail, every preparation, and always the button holes, were left for her tired hands.

Outside of this responsibility and monotonous labor it was "mistis" who was called up at midnight to minister to some sufferer in the [servants'] quarter. If not moved by that beautiful charity so inherent in the hearts of women, another very important impetus urged careful attendance upon sick slaves—*negroes were not neglected*. Losing a "field hand" was equivalent to losing fifteen hundred or two thousand gold dollars [in today's currency $50,000 to $70,000], therefore medical attention was prompt and efficient. A physician was often miles away, therefore "mistis" sometimes practiced medicine—her store room was also her drug store. Blue mass and quinine were her favorite medicines, though paregoric, Epsom salts and "number six" played quite an important part. Lard and molasses was her infallible remedy for croup and bad colds. On the intelligence, energy and benevolence of "mistis" much depended.

"Mammy."

The plantation was altogether one vast family. The only seeming drone in this busy hive was the black mammy, who, though she toiled not with her hands, she, too, had her responsibilities, for to her were confided the children of her master. To her loyal heart this trust was as beautiful as it was sacred. The children were taught to respect and obey her, and she in turn gave her whole life to their welfare and happiness. I know of one Southern statesman whose home holds many rare and valuable pictures, but the most appreciated of all is the life size crayon of a withered, black face—his mammy, whom he now cares for with a son's devotion.

On the plantation the slaves had comfortable dwellings in the quarter in sight and hearing of the planter's residence. The quarter was two long streets crossing each other midway. Each dwelling boasted a flower yard in front and vegetable garden in the rear. The plantation church stood a little way back, and all were required to attend services on Sunday. There was very little friction on a well-ordered plantation. Well-fed negroes are usually contented; their careless temperaments, reckless of to-morrow's weal or woe, are easily satisfied.

The "mistis" of the quarter, the medical and clothing departments, was also "mistis" of the kitchen. The secrets of culinary success were taught by that inexorable teacher, experience; for verily there's no royal road to the mysteries of the successful concoction of dainties.

The purest and best training for boys and girls was on the ante-bellum plantation. From the teachings of a well-chosen governess, or from neighborhood schools, they had first a solid literary training—though still under mammy's argus eye.

Within the home circle "mistis" reigned supreme. With the refining influence of her social jurisdiction, with books and music and flowers, with carefully chosen companions, she developed the character of her daughters and sons into the beauty and chivalry of the South. Her life was concentrative in its aim's and efforts, and every one within the radius of her influence was the better for it.

Plantation life, with its hearty, open-handed hospitality, the old-time Southern "mistis" entertaining with gentle grace and dignity, are things worthy of remembrance.

"Mistis" was the authority, the oracle of the plantation. It was she who was appealed to for favors, she who praised or scolded, she who stood between the offender and the [black] overseer's wrath.
Ask some old-time plantation darky who, in slavery times, was his best friend. My word for it, his dim old eyes will brighten as, in a flash of memory, he sees the crowning joy of the old home, and he will answer, with a smile, "Mistis" [all emphasis, L.S.].[77] — MRS. C. C. SCOTT, IN THE *ARKANSAS TRAVELER*

SOMETHING OF SLAVERY AS IT EXISTED

☞ I am a Southerner, 55 years of age. *I was familiar with the "institution" of slavery, for my father owned quite a number of negroes—men, women and children. Being forced to pay two large security debts, he was reduced to the alternative of selling his land or his negroes. The latter begged so earnestly not to be sold that the land was sold [instead] and all the negroes were held until, at the fall of the Confederacy, they were set free.*

To my mind there was much beauty as well as happiness in the relation of the old Southern owner and his slave, when both "acted up" to their duties under such relation, just as there is, under similar circumstances, in the other family relations, of husband and wife, parent and child. *"At our house" the white children were made to "behave" respectfully to the old negroes, and were punished for any breach of respect reported by black "Uncles" and "Aunties," as we were taught to call them.* In a few homes that I knew impudence of the white children to the old negroes was not checked, but in other respects this shortcoming was more than counterbalanced, especially by *the invariable kindness of their white parents.* I have also known families—but very few, I am thankful to say—in which the negro slave was treated in a very cruel and barbarous manner. In such cases both [black] man and [white] master were frequently to blame. In some cases the vice of the master seemed to beget its like in the slave, just as, *in many cases, the virtue and gentle breeding of the master and mistress were assumed by the negro. In dignity and courteous demeanor negro coachmen and dining-room servants were very agreeable company.* The author of *In Ole Virginia* [Thomas Nelson Page] has drawn pictures of the old negro that were very true to nature.

A 130 year old illustration of Gen. Stonewall Jackson (center) and his staff.

After the question of slavery had been thrust into politics a large amount of rhetorical fireworks were set off in abuse of it and in the praise of freedom. For years it was impossible for two persons from the different sections of our country to speak dispassionately on this matter. Now, after almost thirty years have elapsed since the abolishment of the institution, I believe it may be approached from both sides more calmly than was ever possible heretofore.

Whatever its effect may have been on the whites I do not think any one will deny that it has done much for the negro. We may dwell on the horrors of the voyage in the [Yankee] *slave-ship until we forget that it was thus that the poor savages providentially rescued from the worse fate of being roasted to feast their cannibal conquerors. Their lives as slaves had, on an average, no more bitterness than fell to the lot of each one of us during our minority* [under the age of 18, that is, minors]. *Our hearts bled for them when, after the death of "Ole Marster and Mistis," they were sold from the auctioneer's block or divided among the heirs, separating parents from children and husbands from wives. But such separations were not peculiar to slavery. We still experience the same sad scenes whenever the children of the poor are cantoned out, at the death of their parents, in homes so widely separated that they may never meet again.*

Minerva and Edgar Bendy, former black servants, Woodsville, Texas, 1937.

Brutal masters beat their helpless slaves [illegal in all Southern states]; *brutal husbands and brutal parents beat their helpless wives children* [also illegal in the South]. *The lewd master compelled his unwilling maid-servant to gratify his lust* [illegal]; *the lustful brute still assaults the helpless woman that falls into his power* [also illegal].

If the facts were known it would appear that negro slavery [white and red slavery also existed in early America] *in the United States was a most humane state of pupilage by which a lot of savages from Africa were trained up in the arts of civilization and in the knowledge of Christian duty, thus fitting them to take part in our government, the grandest in the world. I can think of no better plan by which such an amount of good work could have been done. Both England and the United States established colonies in Africa by which to educate and christianize the natives* [all emphasis, L.S.]. They have accomplished little or nothing more than to render assistance to the natives in hampering the [domestic African] slave trade on the [African] coast. The interior [African slave] trade is still carried on [and continues as of 2022], but does not afford a sufficient market, and the [African] conquerors have again resorted to the "sacrificial feast" on their prisoners as a means of disposing of them.[78] — OMIKRON KAPPA, LOUISIANA, MISSOURI, MAY 29, 1893

FROM A LETTER TO *CONFEDERATE VETERAN* MAGAZINE

☞ . . . our opponents [that is, Yankees, liberals, socialists, and communists] have published tons of literature giving the dark side of slavery. We have little telling of its bright side. . . . I was born during slavery times and was old enough before its abolishment to appreciate its existence. . . . Let each issue of your paper contain something telling of the bright side, of the corn shuckings, the quiltings, the barbecues, the big meetings, the weddings, etc., showing that *the slaves enjoyed life and were not eternally skulking in dark corners dodging the whip of the brutal overseer, or quaking with terror at the bay of a blood hound* [my emphasis, L.S.]. You advocate the building of monuments to our heroes. I tell you that unless something is done at once, and done persistently, to counteract the influence and misrepresentation of [the purposefully disinformational anti-South novel] *Uncle Tom's Cabin* and the like, our children will look upon those whose memory those monuments are intended to perpetuate as objects of pity, if not of contempt. For the past eight years I have been living in St. Paul, Minnesota. I have talked with children there on the subject of slavery, and the poison is doing its work, and doing it effectually. Even at this day a man who owned slaves is looked upon as little, if any better, than a slave trader, a pirate, or a brigand, who held prisoners for a ransom. I am not talking theory, but actual experience. As soon as those who were the actual owners of slaves have died out in the South this feeling will gradually work its way into [the South] our own country [his prediction has come true, L.S.]. For God's sake do something to prevent the great names of our ancestors being the theme for a jest and the subject for taunts. Please pardon this long letter and tirade, but I feel deeply on this subject. I think something should be done to counteract the growing sentiment. I believe that the *Veteran* is the medium through which it can be done.[79] — MANLY B. CURRY, LOUISVILLE, KY.

SLAVERY WAS NOT THE CAUSE OF THE WAR

☛ . . . Twenty-eight years have passed since the close of our civil war. Since then a majority of the adults living in those years have been called home, and almost a new generation has taken their places on the farm and plantation, and in the counting-room, shop and office. Time, I trust, has healed the wounds of war, but with the revolving years the causes and events of that terrible struggle seem to be forgotten, or if not forgotten, considered as unimportant events of history. And even *the history of those events, and the causes that led to that struggle, are not set forth fairly and truthfully.* It is stated in books and papers that Southern children read and study that all the blood-shedding and destruction of property of that conflict was because the South rebelled without cause against the best government the world ever saw; that although the Southern soldiers were heroes in the skillfully massed and led, they and their leaders were rebels and traitors, who fought to overthrow the Union, and to preserve human slavery, and that their defeat was necessary for free government and the welfare of the human family.

As a Confederate soldier and as a citizen of Virginia I deny the charge, and denounce it as a calumny. We were not rebels; we did not fight to perpetuate human slavery, but for our rights and privileges under a government established over us by our fathers and in defense of our homes. The South loved the Union. Her interests were identified with it. Her statesmen had aided in its creation and development. Her warriors had fought under its flag, by sea and by land, and shed their blood in its defense. *To the South the Union was a temple dedicated to American constitutional liberty—to the principles of a liberty approved by great*

Thomas Jefferson.

thinkers and consecrated by the blood of martyrs; a liberty that was designed to protect the individual man in all that was right, and to prohibit him from doing that which was wrong. Not a liberty for one class of people or section of country to prey on any other people or other section. Not a liberty for the majority to invade the rights of the minority, and to use the powers of the government to the aggrandizement of the former and the injury of the latter, but *a liberty guaranteeing equality of right and privileges to each section and each State.* But when the [Left-wing] priests that ministered at the altars of this temple sought to teach new theories of liberty, such as had not been taught by the [founding] fathers, and which were destructive of the principles of the Constitution, and fatally injurious to the rights of the States, and especially to the Southern States, then the cotton and sugar Southern States determined to abandon the temple and erect one, where they could worship according to what they understood to be the faith delivered by the fathers, who in the belief of man's capacity for self-government, and in prayer to God, had built our political temple.

Battle scene, American Revolutionary War, 1775-1783.

In determining to separate, those States thought they were sustained by the teachings of the Declaration of Independence, which declared in immortal words that "all governments derive their just powers from the consent of the governed," that when any form of government becomes destructive of these ends it is the right of the people to alter or abolish it, and to institute a new government, laying its foundations on such principles, and organizing its powers as to them shall seem most likely to effect their safety and happiness. They also thought that the powers granted to the general [central] government, by virtue of which it alone controlled the States, were delegated powers, which could be revoked at any time by the party delegating. They read in the resolutions of some of the States adopting the Constitution of the United States an express reservation of this power. Our own State, especially when she adopted the Constitution of the United States, declared that the powers granted to the United States could be resumed when perverted to her injury or oppression.

Those Southern States believed that the powers granted to the federal government had been used to their injury and oppression, and therefore they decided to abandon the Union. In taking this step, slavery was not the cause, but the occasion of the separation. It might as well be said that tea was the cause of our separation from the government of Great Britain in 1776. The government of Great Britain, prior to that date, claimed the power to tax the colonies, although they were not represented in the parliament. That power the colonies denied; they claimed they were British citizens, and as such were entitled to all the rights of every other citizen of that kingdom; that because separated from the island that contained the capital, they were not less citizens of that kingdom; that it was a principle dear to a Briton that no money should be taken from him in the form of taxes except by consent of his representatives, and as they were not represented in parliament England had no right to tax America. Notwithstanding the protest of the people of this country, England taxed America by putting a tax on tea. Hence the Boston tea party, the war of the revolution of 1776 and its results.

The Southern States claimed they had exactly the same right in the Union as the Northern States; that her soldiers had fought in the war for independence, in that of 1812, in the Indian wars and in the Mexican war; that her statesmen had contributed to the adoption of the Constitution of the United States, the development of American institutions and the enlargement of the territory of the Union; that the common government should be administered for the benefit of all the people, and not to develop one section to the injury of the other sections; not to tend the social and moral views of one part of the country to the disadvantage of another part of it. *They* [the Southern states] *claimed that when the Union was formed slavery existed in all of the States; that it was recognized in the Constitution of the United States, and because it had become unprofitable in one portion of a common country* [that is, the North], *and therefore had ceased to exist in that section, the slaves of the North having been sold South, the powers of the general government should not be used to the injury of the South.*

I would not do justice if I did not state just here that there was a section of people at the South and at the North in the early days of the republic and since opposed to slavery on moral and economic grounds. Perhaps at our revolutionary period the anti-slavery sentiment was stronger in Virginia than in New England [this is correct, L.S.]. Massachusetts [where both the American slave trade and American slavery got their start] was at that time engaged in the slave trade, deriving profit from the use of her ships in that traffic. It was not until after the great difference of opinion between the statesmen of the country as to the powers of the general government that the sectional differences on the subject of slavery became so decided and marked. With the increase of this difference of sentiment as to governmental powers grew the difference on the subject of slavery. In this State, about 1832, there was a most powerful anti-slavery party, headed by such men as James McDowell, one of the most eloquent and cultured of our Governors, and by Charles J. Faulkner, father of the distinguished United States Senator of that name from West Virginia.

But it was not until the failure of those who claimed large powers for the general government on the subject of a national bank, international improvements and a protective tariff to obtain control of the government, that the anti-slavery party assumed any considerable importance. A combination was made in the North and Northwest by those who claimed the aforementioned powers for the general [that is, central] government with the anti-slavery men. The [primarily Left-

Boston Tea Party.

wing] combination claimed for the general government, on the subject of slavery:

    1. Power to abolish slavery in the District of Columbia.
    2. Under the power to regulate commerce, the power to prohibit the carrying of slaves from one slave State to another slave State.
    3. The right to prohibit slavery in the territory of the United States.

    You will observe, first, that all of these matters related to slavery, but the principle, under all this claim for power, like that in regard to the taxation of tea, was far deeper than appeared on the surface. It involved the integrity of the Constitution of the United States and the equality of the people of the Southern States. The District of Columbia contained the capital of the United States. Southern members of Congress came to Washington to discharge their duties, bringing with them their wives and children, and if by hostile legislation their servants—the maids of their wives and the nurses of their children—were to be liberated by act of Congress as soon as they trod the soil of the District, that city was no place for Southern Senators and Representatives.

Slavery was recognized by the original U.S. Constitution.

    2. As to the commerce between the States, as stated before, slaves were recognized as property when the [U.S.] Constitution was adopted. The Constitution of the United States contained a provision for their rendition when they escaped from one State to another; also, for the continuance of the slave trade until 1808. To interdict the selling of slaves from one State to another would have been, in effect, to deprive the citizens of our Southern States of the right to migrate to another. Also to deprive him of the use of what had been considered property from the foundation of the government.

    3. To prohibit slavery in the territory of the United States would virtually exclude the Southern citizen of the United States from the common territory. The territory of the United States, about the settlement of which this controversy culminated, was obtained as the result of the war with Mexico, and to exclude the citizen with his slaves was, in fact, to deliver the territory purchased by the money and by the blood of all to one section of the country, to be organized into such political form as to give political power to one section of the country, and thereby give effect in legislation to all the views of the [Liberal] North on the subject of governmental powers. The [Conservative] South claimed an equality of right in all the territories, in the District of Columbia, and in the trade and commerce of the country, and to deny her rights was practically to make her people hewers of wood and drawers of water to the more prosperous and populous section. Notwithstanding the objections and even protests of her statesmen and people, the territory acquired from Mexico was organized so as to

exclude slavery, and therefore the South from settlement therein. Not only was this done, but a sectional [Left-wing] President [Lincoln] was elected by a sectional majority [the Republicans, then the Liberal Party] on a national platform of party principles.

The South then seceded, not in a body, but separately. The Constitution of the United States had been adopted by States, each State acting by itself and for itself. Our own State, Virginia, seceded in April, 1861. I would like to tell about the action of the Gulf States, and of the views of their great thinkers and statesmen, but I have not time to do so. I am sure, however, you will indulge me for a short time, while I recall some things about Virginia, even if I repeat myself, connected with the part she took in the transactions of that period, and in those of our revolutionary days and since, which will present her to you as the grandest figure of any State in the records of time.

Richard Henry Lee.

In every period of her history Virginia has stood up for the right, as she understood it, against her seeming interest and against power. Settled by English speaking people, she inherited from them the love of truth and liberty, and devotion to right, that has distinguished the inhabitants of Great Britain from the days of her Alfred to our revolution. When the clash of opinion arose as to the rights of the British colonies in America, Virginia, against the seeming interest of her people—certainly against that of her leaders—took the side of the weak in favor of the right, and against the strong and wrong. Her Patrick Henry, by his Demosthenean eloquence, moved the hearts of his countrymen to resistance, as the storm moves the sea. Her George Mason, amid the throes of revolution, gave to his State and the world Virginia's great bill of rights and her first constitution—the first written constitution the world ever saw. Her [Thomas] Jefferson, with his pen, recorded in memorable words the rights of a free people and the wrongs of America. Her [George] Washington led the armies of the rebellious colonies to victory, peace and independence. The war over, the colonies that had been united in defense against Great Britain formed a Union [one that Washington called a "confederate republic"], under what are known as the Articles of Confederation.[80] Then, in order to strengthen that Confederation and promote the common welfare, Virginia ceded to the Confederacy all of her magnificent territory northwest of the Ohio River, now the abode of a great population and the center of wealth and political power.

The Articles of Confederation proving inadequate, a convention of the States was called, and that body gave to the world the Constitution of the United States. That instrument was largely the work of Virginia. The convention that formed it was called chiefly through Washington. Her [James] Madison and Edmund Randolph and Henry Lee, its chief defenders in Virginia, against the opposition of such men as Patrick Henry, George Mason, Thomas Nelson, Jr., and Richard Henry Lee, who opposed its adoption by their State without amendment, for reasons which, had they been heeded then, would in all probability have averted our civil war. Some of the writings and utterances of these distinguished objectors, in the light of recent events, seem to be as prophetic as the words of the great Jewish prophet, Isaiah.

The Constitution was adopted, George Washington was made the President of the United States. He put the Federal government in operation, organized the great departments of the government, recommended and approved appropriate legislation, and laid the foundation upon which has been built this great republic. The third President was Thomas Jefferson. Under his administration we obtained from the great Napoleon [Bonaparte] for $15,000,000 [about $360 million in today's currency] title to the territory known as Louisiana, which comprised not only the State of Louisiana, but Missouri, Arkansas, Iowa, and parts of Nebraska, Kansas, Minnesota, and the Indian Territory. Jefferson was succeeded by another Virginian, James Madison. Under his administration war was declared against Great Britain, which brought that power to respect our flag and the rights of our sailors. To another Virginia President, John Tyler, are we chiefly indebted for the State of Texas. Although it was annexed during the administration of James K. Polk, yet the credit of its acquisition is due to John Tyler's administration.

After this came another war, in which our Winfield Scott planted the flag of the United States on the halls of the Montezumas, in the city of Mexico, and thereby obtained peace between this country and Mexico; and as a result of that peace all the territory of the United States, bounded by the Mexican frontier on the south, and the Louisiana purchase on the east and north and northwest, and by the Pacific on the west, was added to this country.

In the Mexican battles Virginia and the South bore their full part. No sooner was the territory acquired than the controversy arose as to its settlement between the sections of our country; one claiming that it should be kept open and free to the people of all the country, whether the North or the South; the other that it should be dedicated to freedom; that the national soil should be like the enchanted ground of an Eastern story, upon which all that entered, no matter how clad, were immediately arrayed in garments of light and beauty—so every slave, as soon as he trod the national soil with his master, should stand clothed in the robes of freedom. Apparently this seemed like the earnest protest of the lovers of freedom against slavery, but in reality it was but a scheme to exclude the South from the occupancy of the newly acquired territory.

Napoleon Bonaparte.

The student of the political history of the period will discover that it was not so much opposition, in the decade of 1850-60, to slavery as the desire to get political control of the country, in order that the vast powers of the general government might be yielded to aggrandize one section at the expense of the other. In the furtherance of that scheme it was important to exclude from the newly acquired territory Southern men [that is, Conservatives] and their influence in order that the views of the opposite school [that is, Liberals] might take root and obtain power and control. No more effectual method than the exclusion of slavery, and thereby the Southern slaveholder, could have been devised. The Southerner was accustomed to slavery and slave institutions in his home and on his farm and plantation, and if prevented by law from taking his slaves to the territory of the United States he therefore was virtually excluded. He would either have to forego the advantages of purchasing cheap lands or leave his labor and his domestic habits behind him. Therefore this scheme, however fair to the eye, was in effect a denial to the Southern slaveholder [that is, Conservatives] of any participation in the common territory, and was equal to a deed of cession of all that territory to the Northern States [that is, Liberals].

It was the determination of the Northern States to adhere to that policy, by the election of a President pledged to such views, that caused, as heretofore stated, the separation of the Gulf States from the Union. Virginia, however, did not then secede. Her patriotic Governor, John Letcher, called an extra session of the Legislature to meet January 7th, 1861. That Legislature convened a delegated convention of the people of the State, which assembled at Richmond on the 13th of February, 1861. That convention was composed of some of the most distinguished, *conservative and patriotic* citizens of Virginia. Among them A. H. H. Stuart, John Janney, Robt. E. Scott, John B. Baldwin, Geo. Y. Summers, and your fellow-citizen, Hugh M. Nelson, whose name graces yon monument—all Union men, as were the majority of that body. That convention chose for its president that eminent citizen of London, John Janney. He belonged to a Quaker family, loved peace and the ways of peace. I doubt not that this had something to do with his selection. It was designed to show that Virginia was for peace, and not for war. Previous to that her Legislature had sent a commission composed of four of Virginia's distinguished sons, viz.: John Tyler, Geo. W. Summers, William C. Rives and James A. Seddon, to Washington to attend what was called a Peace Congress, that convened upon her invitation or suggestion. That Congress failed to accomplish any good results. On the 8th of April, 1861, the Virginia convention sent a commission, consisting of William Ballard Preston, A. H. H. Stuart and Geo. W. Randolph, to see President Lincoln and obtain information as to his views, purposes and policy in regard to the seceded States. The report of that committee was not satisfactory.

After this the affair of Fort Sumter took place. It fired the Northern heart. President Lincoln called for his army of 75,000 men, and on Virginia for her quota. After this Virginia seceded, she did this chiefly because she was called upon to contribute her share of force to coerce the seceding States. As valuable as the Union was to her, as much as she loved it because of her part in its construction and maintenance, she held it was not an end, but the means to an end—personal and political

Children's Auxiliary, U.D.C., South Pittsburg, Tennessee, displaying the Confederacy's First National Flag.

liberty, State equality and sovereignty; that *the Union established by the fathers was one of consent, love and affection, and not of force*; that whether it was wise on the part of the Gulf States to separate was not a matter for her to determine, because *in her judgment they clearly had the right to separate, and those wielding the powers of the government of the United States had not the right to force them back into the Union, and that to force them back into the union, and that to compel them by force to return, would be to trample underfoot the teachings and principles of the fathers, therefore, with sad heart and tearful eyes, she passed, in April, 1861, her ordinance of secession.*

I have made this brief reference to the foregoing facts in regard to Virginia's contributions to the cause of American liberty, and to the Union, and to her course in the early days of 1861, to show how dear to her was the Union, how she yearned for peace, and that it was not slavery that induced her to separate from the then government of the United States, but her love for the Constitution and the Union, as established by the [founding] fathers.

. . . Human institutions have their uses and their limitations. They are the scaffolding to the building, a means to an end. *Although African slavery was not the cause, it was the occasion of our war. It was useful and valuable in its day. It lifted a people who, in the land of their nativity, were savages, out of barbarism and animalism to such a plane of Christian civilization as to qualify them, in the judgment of the Conquerors of the South, to participate in the government of the great republic. What a tribute to the much abused South! What a monument to Southern Christian men and women! Match me if you can out of the record of missions subsequent to the days of the Apostles and the early teachers of Christianity any work among the heathen that can compare with it in results, when viewed from the standpoint of those who have given the African the ballot.*

But in the plan of the Great Ruler, doubtless the time had arrived for African slavery to pass away. So far as we can see, it could not have been gotten rid of in this country except by the means used. *Mr. Lincoln did not by his war proclamation intend to destroy slavery in the States. Its destruction was an evolution of the war—a war measure, consequent upon the events and result of war.*

Moses, the world's great law-giver, commanded his people to teach the laws he had been directed to give them unto their children, in the house and by the wayside, to bind them as a sign upon their hands, and as frontlets between their eyes. *May we not, in imitation of the great law-giver, tell our fathers, mothers, daughters and teachers to teach the children committed to their care and instruction the principles of American liberty, State and national, not as taught by the precept and example of the multitude* [today known as the mainstream media], *but as delivered by the fathers of the republic, and for which our comrades died that fell in battle. To tell and teach them that the dead, in honor of whom this monument has been erected, were not traitors, but true citizens, who gave their lives in defense of the truth, as they understood it, and of their altars and their*

Patsy Moses, former black servant, Waco, Texas, 1937.

homes; that [Confederate officers] *Lee, Jackson, Stuart, Ashby and Hill, and their soldiers, were not rebels, nor traitors, but patriots, loving God and their fellow-men, and that they did their duty to their country* [all emphasis, L.S.]. Teach them also to look upward to the Great Ruler of all things, truth and untruth, and forward to the duties in life that may be before them; to do their duty as our brave soldier did; to do it under all circumstances to themselves, to their country and their God—and then come what may, success or failure, they will receive the plaudits of good men, the approval of their own consciences and the approbation of their God.[81] — AN ADDRESS BY COL. RICHARD HENRY LEE, OF VIRGINIA, AT THE DEDICATION OF THE CONFEDERATE MONUMENT AT OLD CHAPEL, IN CLARKE COUNTY

THE SOUTH DID NOT SECEDE OVER SLAVERY

☞ . . . *We* [Southerners] *cannot be placed in the false position of having fought to hold men in slavery. The South never made a free man a slave, and never took from the dark land one human being to shackle him with servitude. The race of Southern men inherited the institution* [from the North, the birthplace of American slavery], *which was put on us by the cupidity of* [British] *slave traders against the protests of our colonial fathers. Eight millions of Caucasians and four millions of Africans—the first masters, the last slaves. That was the problem we inherited. Shall they remain slaves and how long? or be at once emancipated? and then be put into possession of equal power with the white man to direct a common destiny? Shall our constitutional power, our inherent natural right to regulate this special interest, be wrested from us and vested in aliens to that interest, to be exercised by them to create social and political relations never known in the history of civilized man, and for the right regulation of which no prophecy could forecast a law, and our sad experience has been unable to devise a remedy? To put it forensically, the South did not plead to the issue of slavery or no slavery, but to the jurisdiction. To create the jurisdiction was to give up self-government.*

If we resisted the government, we defended the Constitution; we supported the sovereignty which ordained the supreme law of the land, though we opposed by force the usurpations of the delegated agent of the sovereignty.

We failed—were defeated—came back to the Union, yes, but to the Union under the Constitution—and though amended—in substance the same old Constitution. The rents in its sacred parchment are healed; the blood-stains are obliterated.

Confederate Lieut. Col. William H. Stewart, 1860s.

Virginia greets the daughter of North Carolina, a younger sister in this great Union. Let us labor to perpetuate this galaxy of commonwealths, bound by the gravitating forces of commercial, geographical, social and political interest, and of common aspirations, as

the inheritors of the free institutions of the Anglo-American race. Let us co-operate to save the Union from the maelstrom of a centralized paternalism, and to anchor our liberty and right in the safe harbor of ancient constitutional polity. God preserve and perpetuate the union of these States on the solid rock-bed of the Constitution of our fathers.[82] — HON. JOHN RANDOLPH TUCKER, FROM A SPEECH GIVEN AT VANDERBILT UNIVERSITY, NASHVILLE, TENN., JUNE 1893.

IN DEFENSE OF THE SOUTH

☛ The South planned first the co-operation and consolidation of the Colonies; Patrick Henry sounded the key note of Independence; Thomas Jefferson wrote the Declaration; a Southern Colony emblazoned first on her standard, "Virginia for Constitutional Liberty." A Southerner led the armies of the Revolution to victory, and it was Southern intellect and patriotism that planned the Federal Constitution, and finally brought about consolidation. To the South is due that Texas is not now a hostile government; that Louisiana is not a French republic, and that the majestic Mississippi is all in our own land. The old South led in the council chamber, in the and to battle. How can the Northern people bring charges so infamous against such a record of loyalty and patriotism?

Miss Katherine Howell, Russellville, Arkansas, Maid of Honor for Arkansas Division, U.C.V.

The South was not responsible for slavery nor eager for its perpetuation. The first nation on the civilized globe to protest against it as monstrous was a Southern Colony. Virginia twenty-three times protested to the [British] Crown in public acts of her Assembly, and in 1778 passed a law absolutely forbidding the further importation of slaves.

On the other hand, slavery received its first legislative sanction by the Commonwealth of Massachusetts.

The prohibition of the slave trade was finally brought about through the influence of President Jefferson and the active efforts of the Virginians.

The North led with plans of gradual emancipation, because slavery was not profitable there; but in the South as well, societies for abolition and colonization were organized. Naturally the South moved slowly, for to her people the problem was a vital one, the number of slaves in Virginia alone being seven times as great as in the entire North.

Civil war was the result. The North had the backing of the resources and sentiment of the world, besides overwhelming odds in battle; and for four years the South baffled an army that could have withstood the universe.

The war left the South exhausted to the last degree. The ragged, half-starved Confederate soldier, crushed with defeat, returned to his once happy and beautiful home to find his house in ruins, his farm devastated, his slaves free, his stock killed, his barns empty, his trade destroyed, and his money worthless.

The North took advantage of this helpless condition, and under the euphemism of reconstruction made an attempt to destroy the South. She was dismembered, disfranchised, denationalized, and turned into military provinces. Besides the war having rendered to the torch and sword three billion dollars' worth of property, she had been robbed from her poverty of a billion dollars in twenty years to pension Northern soldiers. *Thomas Nelson Page is reported to have made this strong statement:* "It was intended that the South should be no more." But God called her forth with the old spirit; she resumed her youth like the eagle, fixed her gaze upon the sun, and once more spreading her pinions, lifted herself for another flight.

Steps must be taken to preserve from oblivion, or worse, from misrepresentation, a civilization which produced, as its natural fruit, Washington and Jefferson, Lee and Jackson. Their stories must be told and their deeds must be sung through the ages—not what its enemies thought it to be, but what in truth it was.

We are not willing to be handed down to the coming generation as a race of slave-drivers and traitors. So let the North lay aside her prejudice and hatred, and seek the truth instead. She should reveal that the [Southern] Cavalier, as well as the [Northern] Puritan, was on the continent from the earliest days, and has been the most conspicuous element in its progress and its freedom. She should admit that the South has a heart of feeling and honor, and is worthy of justice [all emphasis, L.S.].[83] — ARTHUR MARSHALL, SPRINGFIELD, MO.

Some of the South's finest musicians could be found among her black population.

MAMMY SUSAN & HER WHITE MISTRESS

☛ One day mistis sent for me, an' she say—

"Susan, you've been a kind, faithful servant all your life, and I'm goin' to ask you to make me a very solemn promise."

"What is it, mistis?" I say, jes as well as I could, 'cause I never see dat look on mistis' face before, and dat lump in my throat was a-chokin' me so. She say—

"I'm going to heaven to-day, Susan, and I want you to take care of my children when Im gone."

I jes' fell down an' take her white hand in my two black ones, an' den she put her udder hand on my nappy head, an' I see her lips a-movin'. I knowed she was a-prayin', an' I couldn't talk 'cause I was a-cryin' so; but somehow I make out to say—

"Yes, mistis, 'fore de Lord, I'se gwine to take care of dem chilluns long as I live."

An dat's de reason I'se here now, chile. All de horses in A'merst county can't pull ole Susan off dis plantation long as de Lord keep bref in dis body.[84] — MAMMY SUSAN, BLACK SERVANT, VA.

LIFE IN A CONFEDERATE CAMP

☛ Our life in camp was one round of fun and gaiety. George Christian's yellow boy, Jess, did the cooking and stealing for our mess, and Gus McClellan's pop-eyed negro Tip, with his assistants, kept up the corners for the couriers, fed his Mars Gus' horse, blacked his boots, washed his clothes, and brightened his sabre and spurs. Gus himself was a character. He was a brother of the great Alabama writer, "Betsy Hamilton." He could sing a song, tell a good story, dance "Lucy Long," and would light the devil, and "give him the go." Never did old Talladega send to the war a braver soldier than Gus, or a more faithful negro than Tip. Gus is dead, and Tip was caught by a bright-eyed dusky damsel about Petersburg and returned to Alabama to visit "Old Marster and Mars Gus," after twenty years' of hard work, thinking and dreaming of "old Talladega, Alabama." Alas! his homecoming was sad in the extreme! He went at once from the station to the old plantation, through the fields, over the well-known foot-path straight to "Old Marster's room." He would see him that night, and his brothers the next day. When he knocked on the door he was answered by a stranger. He called, "Old Marster, it's me, your boy Tip what went with Marse Gus to the war; I made money nuf to come back, and I is here. Open the do', please sir!" But the place was in the hands of strangers. "Old Master" was under the marble, "Marse" Gus dead too, and the others scattered in different States. But his mistress, "Betsy Hamilton," has told this story and placed it where it will live and be dramatized when she, too, shall have been gathered with the sleepers under the oaks.⁸⁵ — H. W. MANSON, ROCKWALL, TEX.

SOUTHERN BLACK MAN HELPS CONFEDERATE VETERAN

☞ I was the Chaplain of the Forty-fifth Mississippi Regiment. I saw Captain Sloan on the field of Chickamauga, Sept. 20, 1863. Four surgeons pronounced his case hopeless. . . . The shell made a gash from the outer edge of the right eye to the corner of the mouth. From Sunday noon until Tuesday about 2 P.M. no relief was given him—not a drop of water could be given him. I obtained private physicians from Ringgold, Ga. They [repaired his extremely severe injuries as best they could]. . . . An old physician who had served in the Mexican war, and who saw him, said that he knew of only one man similarly wounded on record. Captain Sloan was frightfully mutilated. For over thirty years he lies down supine three times a day on two chairs and is fed as a child. I have made several efforts for relief in his behalf. . . . The first response came from Hon. G. F. Rowles, of Natchez—a negro—a representative of Adams County. He sent $25. . . .⁸⁶ — REV. CHAS. H. OTKEN, SUMMIT, MISS., JAN. 4, 1894

Children of the Confederacy.

CONFEDERATE GROUP PROTECTS BLACK MAN

☞ Thomas D. Ransom, Commander Stonewall Jackson Camp at Staunton, Va., recently called a meeting of its members to protect from mob violence a negro under trial during popular excitement. He appointed a committee and charged it with the duty of aiding the authorities of the county and city in the preservation of order, as representatives of the Camp, and of giving immediate notice to all members of the Camp accessible to them, of any emergency calling for its further action.⁸⁷ — CONFEDERATE VETERAN MAGAZINE

WHAT ACTUATED SOUTHERN SECESSION

☛ I am not one of those who, clinging to the old superstition that the will of heaven is revealed in the immediate results of "trial by combat," fancy that right must always be on the side of might, and speak of Appomattox as a judgment of God. I do not forget that a [Russian Gen.] Suwaroff [that is, Aleksandr Vasiliyevich Suvorov] triumphed, and a Kosciusko fell; that a Nero wielded a sceptre of empire, and a Paul was beheaded; that a Herod was crowned, and a Christ was crucified; and, instead of accepting the defeat of the South as a divine verdict against her, I regard it as but another instance of "truth on the scaffold, and wrong on the throne."

Appomattox was a triumph of the physically stronger in a conflict between the representatives of two essentially different civilizations, and antagonistic ideas of government. On one side in that conflict was the [Conservative] South, led by the descendants of the Cavaliers who, with all their faults, had inherited from a long line of ancestors a manly contempt for moral littleness, a high sense of honor, a lofty regard for plighted faith, *a strong tendency to conservatism*, a profound respect for law and order, and *an unfaltering loyalty to constitutional government*.

Confederate General John B. Gordon.

But, it was not to perpetuate slavery that they fought. The impartial student of the events leading up to the civil war cannot fail to perceive that, in the words of Mr. Davis, "to whatever extent the question of slavery may have served as an occasion, it was far from being the cause of the conflict." That conflict was the bloody culmination of a controversy which had been raging for more than a generation, and the true issue in which, as far as it pertained to slavery, was sharply stated by the Hon. Samuel A. Foot, of Connecticut, when, referring to the debate of the admission of Missouri to the sisterhood of States, he said: "The Missouri question did not involve the question of freedom or slavery, but merely whether slaves now in the country may be permitted to reside in the proposed new State, and whether Congress or Missouri possessed the power to decide."

And from that day down to 1861, when the war-clouds burst in fury upon our land, the real question in regard to slavery was not whether it should continue in the South, but whether the Southern man should be permitted to take his slaves, *originally purchased almost exclusively from Northern slave-traders*, into the territory, which was the common property of the country, and there, without interference from the general Government, have an equal voice with his Northern brother in determining the domestic policy of the new State. *The question was not whether the negro should be freed or held in servitude, but whether the white man of the South should have the same privileges enjoyed by the white man of the North. It was not the desire to hold others in bondage, but the desire to maintain their own rights that actuated the Southern people throughout the conflict* [all emphasis, L.S.]. . . .[88] ―
CONFEDERATE VETERAN, REV. R. C. CAVE, ST. LOUIS, MO., MAY 30, 1894

YANKEES ADMIT THE WAR WAS NOT OVER SLAVERY

☞ I had an interview with [Union] Gen. [Ulysses S.] Grant in Memphis, Tenn., in 1862, and he said to me that the war had no reference to slavery. It was to keep and save the Union. The freedom of the negro was the one and only result of the war. Therefore the North seeks to cover and keep out of sight the awful horror of its wicked war of conquest under that one accidental good. . . . The North lost by the war 279,376 men. The South lost 133,821, making in all 413,197 men killed in wicked battles, or by disease that was the direct outcome of the war. . . . The object of the Southern Woman's Historical Society is to keep the truth before the public, and correct the errors that are made with regard to the causes of the war. And another object of our society is to teach our children the truth regarding that series of battles. We don't want to have them taught in the schools that their parents and grandparents were rebels. We want them to understand the situation as we understand it, and as it really was [all emphasis, L.S.].[89] — MRS. MINOR MERIWETHER, PRES. OF THE SOUTHERN WOMAN'S HISTORICAL ASSOCIATION

SOUTHERN WHITES WANT MONUMENTS HONORING BLACK SERVANTS BUILT ACROSS DIXIE

☞ For some reason there comes a spontaneous disposition in honor Southern women. Men may become lukewarm in their patriotism and neglect to do their duty, but women never. Said a veteran the other day: "We ought to build monuments to our Southern women, and to the negroes who were so faithful as slaves during the war." A lady who was present illustrated the merit of the negroes by telling that an uncle of hers went to market early one morning in Nashville, was "bayoneted to death" and left in a stable, and that *the family servants took charge of five young girls, whose mother had died previously, worked for and maintained them until after the war, when the eldest married a wealthy Kentuckian, who educated them all.* . . .

Black servant women and their children in the "negro quarter."

It seems opportune now to erect monuments to the negro race of the war period. The Southern people could not honor themselves more than in cooperating to this end. What figure would be looked upon with kindlier memory than old "Uncle Pete" and "Black Mammy," well executed in bronze? By general cooperation models of the two might be procured and duplicates made to go in every capital city of the South at the public expense, and then in the other large cities by popular subscriptions. Who would not be glad to see typical representatives of these kind old servants in their little cabin homes preserved by the Southern people—aye, even if hen roosts were occasionally bare? Let the Women take it up; the men will help.

> There is not of record in history subordination and faithful devotion by any race of people comparable to the slaves of the Southern people during our great four years' war for independence [all emphasis, L.S.].[90] — *CONFEDERATE VETERAN MAGAZINE*

WHY SLAVERY WAS LEGAL IN THE 1860S

☛ . . . During colonial times in this country the political authorities of Great Britain, Spain, and France, and the Dutch merchants planted African slavery in all the North American colonies. At the time of the declaration of American independence, 1776, African slavery existed in all of the thirteen colonies. At the date of the adoption of the Federal Constitution, 1787, African slavery existed in all of the States except one. The commercial reason for the planting of African slavery in this country was no doubt stimulated by the hope of ease and gain. *It was at the same time justified by the Church on the ground that the negroes were taken from a condition of heathenish barbarism and cannibalism and brought to where they could be taught the arts of civilization and industry, and where they could be instructed in the doctrines and practices of the Christian religion. I am not discussing the question now as to whether this practice and these views were correct; I am only telling you what was done and thought to be right by our ancestors and by the great governments of the world.* When the Constitution of the United States, the compact of union, was adopted it recognized the right of property in African slaves. The African slave trade was then still being carried on, and the Constitution of the United States provided that it should not be prohibited by Congress prior to the year 1808, twenty years after the adoption of the Constitution. It also provided that slaves escaping from one State into another should not be discharged from service or labor, but should be delivered up to the owner. There were differences of opinion as to the rightfulness of slavery among the men who formed the Constitution. Subsequently, and before 1861, a number of the Northern States, where *slave labor was not thought to be profitable*, abolished that institution, and by degrees a strong prejudice grew up against slavery, first among philanthropists and religionists, and then in a number of states it became a political question. The agitation of this question was not at first entirely sectional, but it became so subsequently. Its agitation, *as early as 1820*, threatened the perpetuity of the Union. The agitation went on until it resulted in civil war and bloodshed in Kansas. This was followed by the invasion of Virginia by John Brown and his deluded followers for the purpose of inaugurating civil and servile war in that State [that is, the initiation of a fabricated race war, to this day a political ploy still used by the Left]. And when he was executed for his crimes Northern churches were draped in mourning, and their bells tolled in token of their sympathy with him and sorrow for his fate. In the Thirty-fifth Congress, when the agitation was threatening the peace of the country, thirty-odd propositions of compromise were made for the

John C. Calhoun.

purpose of averting the danger of disunion; all of these, without exception, were made either by [Conservative] Southern members or Northern Democratic [then the Conservative Party] members. And every such proposition which was presented in the House of Representatives was received by the Republican [then the Liberal Party] members with hooting and expressions of derision, and the Southern members were often told that they had to submit to the will of the majority. The [U.S.] Constitution was denounced by some of the [Left-wing] agitators as a league with hell and a covenant with death, and *the agitators claimed that there was a higher law* [known today as "social justice"] *than the Constitution* [all emphasis, L.S.]. In the campaign of 1860 the Republicans [Liberals] nominated as their anti-slavery ticket both their candidates for President and Vice President from the Northern States, a thing which had not occurred before that time, except in the election of Gen. [Andrew] Jackson as President and Mr. [John C.] Calhoun as Vice President, both from Southern States, in 1828, when there was no sectional issue. . . .[91]

— HON. JOHN H. REAGAN (FORMER CONFEDERATE POSTMASTER GENERAL UNDER PRESIDENT JEFFERSON DAVIS), APRIL 1894

WILLIAM ROSE: NOTABLE BLACK CONFEDERATE

☞ One of the best known freedmen in Columbia, S.C., is old William Rose, who has been messenger for the Governor's office under every Democratic [that is, Conservative] administration since 1876. His history is worthy a space in the *Confederate Veteran*. He is now eighty years of age, but is still active and vigorous enough to be at his post of duty every day, and *nothing delights him more than to take part in any Confederate demonstration.*

Confederate Gen. Maxey Gregg.

William Rose was born in Charleston in 1813, and was a slave of the Barrett family of that city. He was brought to Columbia when only twelve years old and was taught the trades of carpenter and tinner. In his younger days he went out to the Florida War as a drummer in Capt. Elmore's company, the Richland Volunteers, an organization which is still in existence, and which has made a proud record for itself in three years. Subsequently he went through the Mexican War as a servant for Capt. (afterwards Col.) Butler, of the famous Palmetto Regiment.

But the service in which he takes the greatest pride was that in the days of the Confederacy. He was the body servant of that distinguished Carolinian, [Confederate] Gen. Maxey Gregg, and as soon as he heard that his beloved master had fallen on the field of Fredericksburg he rushed to his side as fast as a horse could take him, and remained with him until the end came. His description of the death of Gen. Gregg, of his reconciliation with Stonewall Jackson, and his heroic last message to the Governor of South Carolina are pathetic [that is, sad] in the extreme and are never related by the old man without emotion.

William saw [Grover] Cleveland inaugurated, and was present at the unveiling of the [Confederate] *soldiers' monument at Richmond, and at the recent grand Confederate reunion at Birmingham. From the latter he returned laden with badges which he cherishes as souvenirs of the occasion.*

For sixty years he has been identified with the Richland Volunteers, and they never parade without him. About two years ago he presented a gold medal to the Company, which is now shot for as an annual prize. He never forgets [Confederate] Memorial Day, and no 10th of May has passed by since the close of the war without some tribute from him. . . [being] placed on the Gregg monument at Elmwood. Recently he has been given a small pension by the United States for services in the Florida War.

Old "Uncle" William is of a class fast passing away. They will not have successors, but all the world may witness benefactors in Southern whites until the last of them crosses the "dark river" [all emphasis, L.S.].[92] — C. M. DOUGLAS, PRESS, COLUMBIA, S.C.

LOUISIANA BEFORE & AFTER LINCOLN'S WAR

☛ Twenty years ago, and even ten years, St. Mary, [Louisiana,] under the old system, which Abolitionists [socialists and communists] painted in such horrid colors, was an Eden compared to its present situation.

Then our white people were prosperous and happy, and our black people well fed, well cared for and contented. Our fields smiled, and the autumnal harvests were rich and abundant.

The smoke of a hundred and seventy furnaces, over which a thousand huge sugar kettles foamed and boiled, ascended to greet the blue autumnal skies.

The corn song of the negroes, the loud laugh, the cheerful voices and happy faces of the colored race, the dance and fiddle at the quarters, were indications, not merely of peace, but of lively enjoyment.

Cheerfulness at the cabins, and hospitality at the house of the planter, were the order of the day all over St. Mary's Parish, La.

When ever the negro and the white man met on the road, the respectful touching of the hat, the friendly nod and kind voices, showed how kind were the relations that existed between the two races in this delightful and happy land.

And when the abundant sugar crop was ready for market, our bayous, lakes and bays were enlivened by twenty puffing and smoking steamers, from the two-horse towboat up to the fine passenger steamer, whose tables were always loaded with all the luxuries of the land, and whose cabins were cheered by ladies and gentlemen of refinement, wealth, and a high order of intelligence.

William Green, former black servant, San Antonio, Texas, 1937.

Our colored population were then well clothed, abundantly fed, nursed in sickness, and kindly cared for. Behold them now in rags, dissatisfied, unhappy, the pliant tools of [Left-wing] *strangers who wish to use them, and then throw them aside!* [all emphasis, L.S.]

Our roads were then well worked and were graced by hundreds of fine horses and splendid carriages. Look at them now! Who has profited by this melancholy change? Madness rules the hour!⁹³ — THE FRANKLIN BANNER, OCTOBER 31, 1895

BOOKER T. WASHINGTON ON BLACK ADVANCEMENTS

Booker T. Washington.

☛ I am exceedingly anxious that every young colored man and woman should keep a hopeful and cheerful spirit as to the future. Despite all of our disadvantages and hardships, ever since our forefathers set foot upon American soil as slaves [Important note: many early blacks came to America as free men and women, L.S.], *our pathway has been marked by progress. Think of it. We went into slavery pagans; we came out Christians. We went into slavery a piece of property; we came out American citizens. We went into slavery without a language; we came out speaking the proud Anglo-Saxon tongue. We went into slavery with slave chains clanking about our wrists; we came out with the American ballot in our hands* [my emphasis, L.S.].⁹⁴ — BLACK EDUCATOR, PROF. BOOKER T. WASHINGTON

VICTORIAN EVIDENCE OF DOMESTIC AFRICAN SLAVERY
☛ [Here is just one example of the many African tribes still involved in indigenous African slavery and slave trading as of 1895.] The Pessehs, who are located about 70 miles from the coast, and extent about 100 miles from north to south, are entirely pagan. They may be called the peasants of West Africa, and *supply most of the domestic slaves for the Veys, Bassas, Mandingoes, and Kroos* [my emphasis, L.S.].⁹⁵ — JAMES T. HALEY

THE GOOD OLE ANTEBELLUM DAYS
☛ Well, it was in the good old antebellum days when every white boy and nigger on the plantation had pop-crackers and popped 'em. The coming home of negroes who were hired out by the year as tanners, blacksmiths, carpenters and shoemakers, and whom we never saw at any other time, was a great pleasure to me and to them, and as they never failed to bring me "sump'n good" and made "a heap o' fuss" over me. It made me happy. Then, too, it was a time when I could enjoy the companionship of those whom I preferred. The white boy was good enough to play with at school, but he was inclined to have his way, and if I opposed any proposition made by him to play a certain game, he or I would have to give in or fight it out. But *the negro boys looked up to me* [my emphasis, L.S.], *and whatever was my will was theirs, and they obeyed me in all things and followed wherever I led*.⁹⁶ — MR. POLK MILLER, RICHMOND TIMES

VISITORS TO NATHAN BEDFORD FORREST CAMP
☛ Many pleasing things occurred during the [Chickamauga National Military] Park dedication. Of the many thousands of the old soldiers, the Union soldiers largely predominated. Many of them visited our [Confederate Veterans] Camp and exchanged friendly greetings. *Only the kindest feeling prevailed*. Over seven hundred registered at our Camp,

while many neglected to do so through oversight. Company A, Confederate Veterans from Memphis, attracted more attention, perhaps, than any part of the military in the great parade on the 20th, and were cheered all along the line of march. Tender memories crowded upon many of the spectators, and many hearts filled with emotion as these [Confederate] veterans of many bloody fields passed in the great procession. They were commanded by their gallant [Confederate] Capt. [William Watts] Carnes. A large floral wreath, presented to them by a lady, was carried in the parade. *An old negro man, evidently not expecting this feature, as the company came opposite him, was carried away with enthusiasm. Throwing up his hat he shouted, "Them's our boys! Them's our folks!"* [all emphasis, L.S.][97] — J. W. WILLINGHAM, SERGT.-MAJOR; CHATTANOOGA, TENN.

CONFERATE VET RECEIVES HERO'S WELCOME

☛ June 12th, 1865. We beat the [end-of-the-war] party home at least three weeks. My dear old mother threw her arms around me and wept. Old "black mammy," and other darkies who remained at home, rushed up and hugged me, and old Henry, *the faithful servant who had taken care of my mother through the war, with its maelstrom-like swirl of fire and persecution, got a bottle of whisky and was soon "gloriously" drunk.* My faithful dog Carlo, that gave the alarm which kept my mother and sister from burning up, seemed as if he realized the situation and would go crazy with delight. For a moment I forgot the gloom of surrender.

I had reached home in time to join with mother in meeting her absent ones. One by one my [Confederate] brothers came in—Maj. J. S. Ridley, of [Gen. Carter L.] Stevenson's Division; Capt. George C. [Ridley], and Lieut. Charles L. Ridley, of Gen. Ben [J.] Hill's Staff, and Dr. J. L. Ridley, Surgeon in [Gen. George G.] Dibrell's Cavalry, and then our little sister, a refugee at Lagrange. Ga., returned, and next came my venerable father from across the mountains on his little mule. *Last of all, my servant Hannibal to whom I am indebted for bringing home the diary from which this journal was written. Old "black mammy's" joy upon Hannibal's return may be imagined.*

Confederate Gen. Alexander Peter Stewart.

[Confederate] Gen. [Alexander P.] Stewart and family were back home at Lebanon, and we at home at old Jefferson, Tennessee, within a few miles of the battlefield of Murfreesboro. Two dwellings had been laid in ashes by Federals, and my oldest sister had died from fright created by these fires.

"The old home" was not what it used to be, "yet there was no place like the old place.". . . In a short time everybody went to work to drive "the wolf from the door;" all was gone but the wallet and staff. I went off to school to supplement my broken education, interrupted by war's dread alarm. One day in April, 1866, I received from Gen. Stewart a letter that made me so happy—"just as proud as a big sun flower that nods and bends to the breezes." I copy it here as a family heritage. It is a beautiful tribute to the Confederate soldiers who "fought the good fight and kept the faith":

> Lebanon, Tennessee, April 13, 1866. My Dear Bromfield: —I hope you have a good school and that you are making the best possible use of your time and opportunities. You have passed creditably through the scenes of the great struggle for constitutional liberty, and I hope will be prepared to pass with distinction through the still more stirring scenes which are before you. . . . Remember me very kindly to your father and mother, when you write them, and believe me always very sincerely, your friend, Alex P. Stewart.[98] — BROMFIELD L. RIDLEY

SLAVERY & THE TRUE CAUSE OF LINCOLN'S WAR

☛ . . . In nothing has the South suffered so much at the hands of [malicious South-hating] writers of school history as in the treatment of the subjects of State sovereignty, nullification, slavery, and secession. Since the success of the northern [that is, Liberal] resources over southern [that is, Conservative] arms in the Civil War, it has been the practice of northern writers to isolate the period of the war and either uphold the specific acts of the South in withdrawing from the Union as a political crime, using as a term of reproach the term of rebellion, or to infer from the fact that southern independence was not maintained that secession was morally wrong. The facts of American history rob the reproach of its sting when it shows that the foundation of our present government was laid in secession, the states moving in the matter virtually seceding from the perpetual union under the articles of confederation; that the structure of American Independence was upreared in rebellion; that subsequently every section of the country has at some time threatened to secede.

Miss Grace McCulloch, Major Gen. Missouri Division, U.D.C.

In reference to the question of nullification it was not one of the southern states that alone proposed it, but it originated in the North, where many of the states, by legislative enactment, nullified the Constitution of the United States, especially with respect to the fugitive slave law; "that the whole country, and not the South alone was responsible for slavery, the system prevailing in the North as long as it was profitable; that the slave trade was made possible only by New England vessels, manned by New England crews."

The true cause of the war between the states was the dignified withdrawal of the Southern States from the Union to avoid the continued breaches of that domestic tranquility guaranteed, but not consummated by the constitution, *and not the high moral purpose of the North to destroy*

slavery, which followed incidentally as a war measure.
   As to the war itself and the result thereof, *the children of the future would be astonished that a people fought so hard and so long with so little to fight for, judging from what they gather from [the biased and historically inaccurate Yankee] histories now in use, prepared by writers from the North, they are utterly destitute of [truthful] information as to events leading to the war. Their accounts of the numbers engaged, courage displayed, sacrifices endured, hardships encountered, and barbarity practiced upon an almost defenseless people, whose arms-bearing population was in the army, are incorrect in every way.*

African servant and child.

   A people, who for four long years, fought over almost every foot of their territory, on over two thousand battlefields, with the odds of 5,864,272 enlisted men against their 600,000 enlisted men, and their coasts blockaded, and rivers filled with gunboats, with 600 vessels of war, manned by 35,000 sailors, and who protracted the struggle until over one-half of their soldiers were dead from the casualties of war, had something to fight for. They fought for the great principle of local self-government and the privilege of managing their own affairs, and for the protection of their homes and fire-sides [all emphasis, L.S.]. — THE HISTORICAL COMMITTEE ON SOUTHERN SCHOOL HISTORY

ONE OF DIXIE'S MANY WEALTHY BLACK SLAVE OWNERS
☛ *The richest colored man in Georgia is Mr. Harry Todd, of Darien. His personal property and real estate are valued at $500,000* [equal to about $18 million in today's currency]. *When a youth his* [white] *"master" died, giving him his freedom. He was kept by the family on a fair salary as assistant overseer. This money was invested in real estate,* slaves [all emphasis, L.S.], *and Confederate bonds. When the downfall of the Confederacy came he lost all except his lands. He has made his money raising cotton. He has an interesting family, five children, all well educated and highly respected. He has a summer resort in the mountains and is altogether comfortably situated.*[100] — JAMES T. HALEY

TRIBUTE TO A FAITHFUL BLACK CONFEDERATE
☛ *"Uncle Jim" Bate, a colored man who lived and died in Sumner County, had quite a history. He was brought from Huntsville, Ala., to Sumner County before the war by* [Confederate] *Gen.* [William B.] *Bate, being a part of the inheritance of Mrs. Bate from her grandfather, Benjamin Pope. "Uncle Jim" was devoted to the family to which he belonged. He was an accomplished cook and house-servant, and was serving the family as such when the war began. He accompanied Gen. Bate to the army and remained with him as a faithful servant during the entire war. He nursed the General, while wounded, with a constancy and devotion characterized by the deepest sympathy.*

   "Uncle Jim" came from the Confederate Army in 1863 to his home

in this neighborhood, then in the Federal lines, and took South with him, at their own request, his family and other servants, fifteen or twenty in all, belonging to Gen. Bate. *They were furnished homes and cared for in the South by their owner, and at the close of the war they were brought to their old home or wherever they desired to locate. Some of them are still with the family.* "Uncle Jim," wishing to live in Gallatin, was provided with a comfortable home where he had his every want supplied by his former owner and members of the family, until he died recently nearly eighty years old. The "boys" who knew him during the war were fond of him. He often prepared [a special] diet for those who were sick in camp. *The battle did not demoralize him, and it was his boast never to have lost anything that was under his care on a retreat.* When the Confederate lines were broken and overrun at Nashville, in December, 1864, the division headquarters' wagon, in which were the army papers of Gen. Bate and camp equipage of the mess, was under a heavy fire and likely to be captured. The white driver jumped off the saddle mule and ran away, leaving the wagon. *Jim abused him for cowardice and, mounting the mule, drove the wagon from under fire, thus saving it and the papers of the division. After the war Jim was kindly remembered and treated, especially by those who knew him in the army.*

The white family to which he had belonged and the ex-Confederates who knew him followed "Uncle Jim's" remains to the grave. It was an object lesson to those who fought on the other side, and to Northern [that is, Left-wing] philosophers. He now sleeps under the shade of a beautiful oak in the Gallatin Cemetery. Peace to the ashes and honor to the name of "Uncle Jim" Bate! [all emphasis, L.S.].[101] — CHAS. B. ROGAN, OF GALLATIN, TENN.

CONFEDERATE MAJ. J. W. SPARKS, OF TEXAS RANGERS

☛ Major. Jesse W. Sparks was born at Nacogdoches, Texas, January 1st, 1837, and died at Piedras, Negras, Mexico, August 1st, 1896. From September, 1857, to March, 1861, he was a student of Union University at Murfreesboro, Tenn., when he left college and joined the Confederate Army and made fine record as a soldier. After the war he returned to Tennessee and married Miss Josephine Bivins of Rutherford County, in 1866. For twelve years he was Clerk and Master of the Chancery Court. He was elected State Senator subsequently and was in the practice of law when in 1893 he was appointed by. . . [Democrat, then a Conservative, U.S. President Grover Cleveland, to the position of] American Consul to Mexico, stationed at Piedras Negras. His death at his post of duty was a great shock to his family and friends, although he had been in ill health for some years and was a dreadful sufferer at times from a bullet which never could be extracted. *Major Sparks shared liberally his income with the poor and needy of both races.* He was so unstinted in his benevolence that he was generally and forcibly popular. *A conspicuous deed of his while Consul to Mexico was his*

Confederate Major Jesse W. Sparks.

fearless action in behalf of a large number of negroes who had been persuaded to go from the United States into Mexico. They had become diseased with smallpox, were almost literally naked and were starving when they undertook to return home. The authorities on the other side refused permission for them to cross the Rio Grande, but Consul Sparks, the *Southern white man*, assumed all responsibility. He got on the engine by the engineer and required him to open the throttle and run the train across despite all other authority. Then he took the responsibility of supplying food until his acts were approved at Washington.

One of the most beautiful of a multitude of floral designs at his funeral was contributed by the colored people. They subsequently held a public meeting and passed resolutions, one of which reads:

"That we deeply deplore the death of Major Jesse W. Sparks, by which *we and our race have lost one of our best and truest white friends* [all emphasis, L.S.], and mankind a benefactor."

Another prominent characteristic of Major Sparks was his great interest in Indians, and he had a large collection of very fine Indian relics. Sitting Bull was to him a most interesting character.[102] — *CONFEDERATE VETERAN MAGAZINE*

POWHATAN TROOP MONUMENT DEDICATION

Confederate Powhatan Troop monument on dedication day.

☛ August 20, 1896, was a memorable Confederate day at Powhatan, Va. It was the occasion of dedicating a monument to the Powhatan Troop, which though organized in a time of peace with "Guard of the Daughters of Powhatan" inscribed on its banner, the gallant command went forth to battle for the cause of the South in 1861... . With a membership of a little more than 100, the killed and wounded of the Powhatan Troop numbers forty-six. *The music of the day was by the Belle Meade Brass Band from a colored college* [my emphasis, L.S.].[103] — *CONFEDERATE VETERAN MAGAZINE*

PROOF THAT THE NORTH DID NOT FIGHT OVER SLAVERY

☛ When Mr. Lincoln was on his way to be inaugurated, and also in his inaugural address, he denied any desire to interfere with slavery in the States, and *his Proclamation of War against the South was not because of her acceptance and endorsement of slavery, but because of her effort to dissolve the Union*. It was this call to save the Union which thrilled the heart of the North from Maine to the Pacific. If these thousands had been called to blot out negro slavery there would never have been a Union Army. Even after the war was under full headway and the Federal Army had crossed into Kentucky, there was no evangel in its front, proclaiming the emancipation of the negro, and there was not a day in the year 1862 when a Kentucky slave-holder, who was raising a regiment to save the Union, could not have sold his own negroes on the block without molestation. Mr. Lincoln, in his first annual message, asked Congress to pass an Act for the abolition of slavery in the year *nineteen* hundred [1900], each slave-holder to be compensated for his slaves. This he thought would save the Union. He closed this message with a paragraph that all the loyal of the South "should be compensated for all losses, by acts of the United States, including losses of slaves."

In the first part of this message, Mr. Lincoln was in favor of *paying for all slaves emancipated*, brought about by the United States Army, in addition to the value of the slaves. Mr. Lincoln in his Emancipation Proclamation did not offer to *every* slave the guerdon of freedom, as he excepted [that is, he excluded] *thirteen counties in western Louisiana, the City of New Orleans, all of West Virginia, and several counties in old Virginia. The fact that he did not offer freedom to the slaves in this territory is proof conclusive that any man or set of men who were enlisted in the War for the Union had the legal as well as the moral right to hold their slaves. To every mind capable of a logical deduction of this, it meant at that time the moral obligation of slavery depended on the loyalty of the owner to the Union* [all emphasis, L.S.].[104] — JOHN SHIRLEY WARD, LOS ANGELES, CAL.

SAMUEL DAVIS: BOY HERO OF THE CONFEDERACY

☛ The grand sacrifice of his life by [the Confederate boy soldier] Sam Davis was not induced by his desire to sustain his reputation as a great officer or a great public man, for he was neither, but only a private soldier and a mere country boy. It was not induced by his desire to save wife or child, or his mother or his father, or any of his kindred, or even his friend, as none of them were involved. *The person involved was a lowly negro boy, whom he had persuaded to secure the papers from* [Union] *Gen.* [Granville] *Dodge's desk. Davis was caught with the papers and condemned to be hanged as a spy. He was offered both life and liberty on condition that he would betray the negro* [named Coleman]. *The negro had absolutely no claim on him, except the moral obligation of good faith.*

Sam Davis, "Boy Hero of the Confederacy."

Sam Davis held steadfastly to this obligation of good faith, and refused to betray the negro, even at the cost of his liberty and his life [all emphasis, L.S.]. No greater exhibition of unselfish heroism can be found in history or romance, and every American should feel proud to honor the memory of Sam Davis. [Note: The 21 year old was executed by Yankee soldiers at Pulaski, Tennessee, on November 27, 1863.][105] — T. S. WEBB, ESQUIRE, KNOXVILLE, TENN.

JOHN PROCTOR: TRIBUTE TO A KIND & LOYAL SERVANT

☛ Early on Christmas morning of the year 1864 a meeting between an old slave and his young master, then in camp, is worthy of record as showing the faithfulness of the negro to the Confederate soldier. This is the incident: As a member of the Beaufort (S.C.) Volunteer Artillery, a boy of 17, I was camped in Fort Coosawhatchie, on the line of the Charleston & Savannah Railroad. Just across the river a part of Sherman's army was stationed, and back of the army was the old plantation, "Cedar Grove," my old playground, where in childhood I was happy. To reach me, a circuit of some fifteen miles had to be made. *On Christmas morning of 1864, John Proctor, a faithful servant of my father, brought me a large case of cooked rice and a fine duck already prepared. He said he knew his young master was in camp, and had slim rations to eat, and he brought him the duck and the rice for one good meal and to remind him of the old days on the plantation.*

This kindness I have never forgotten. Old John is still living in Beaufort, South Carolina. He is 90 years old. I write this. . . as a tribute to him [all emphasis, L.S.].¹⁰⁶ — WILLIAM M. HUTSON

CHATTANOOGA NEGROES COMPLIMENT A CONFEDERATE

☞ W. P. McClatchy, Commander N. B. Forrest Camp, Chattanooga, Tennessee, has been *honored by the negro men of that city.* They presented him with a gold-headed cane. *Addresses were made by J. W. White and J. G. Burge, negro lawyers there.* Comrade McClatchy held the office of City Recorder (Judge of the City Court) last year, and at the expiration of his term he was greatly surprised when these men presented it as a token of their friendship and esteem, and for *the just and impartial manner in which he had dealt with their race.* He asked them why they had "U.C.V. 1861-65," engraved on it, and they replied that *they wished to emphasize that while he was a Southern man, and a Confederate soldier, he had administered the law justly and impartially.* The N. B. Forrest Camp hearing of this compliment to its commander, by a rising vote thanked the donors for their expression of confidence in and esteem for a Confederate soldier, and a Southern Democrat [then a Conservative] who had "administered the law, in wisdom, justice and moderation."

The daily life of Southern black servants was the opposite of what is taught in modern mainstream history books.

The inscription reads: "U.C.V., 1861-1865, J. W. and J. G. to W. P. McC., 1895." Which stands for United Confederate Veteran 1861 to 1865, J. B. White and J. G. Burge to W. P. McClatchy, 1895.

In a note the comrade [McClatchy] says: *"I never had a present in my life that I appreciated any more than this. Every true Southerner understands and appreciates a good negro, while the negro understands that the Southern man is the best friend he has. But for the meddling of people* [mainly Liberals, at the time going by the party name Republicans] *who really care nothing for the negro, but who are prejudiced against the South, there would be no friction between the races"* [my emphasis, L.S.].¹⁰⁷ — CONFEDERATE VETERAN MAGAZINE

BLACK SERVANT GIRL DEFENDS WHITE CONFEDERATE OWNERS AGAINST MARAUDING YANKS

☞ . . . One morning, about 8 o'clock. . . some forty or fifty [Yankees] in number. . . surrounded. . . [our] house. . . . I was standing in the hall arranging some letters to be sent off South, when Joe, from the gallery, saw glistening bayonets in the hands of men double-quicking up the avenue. He ran in to report it and to hide the gun. He crossed the hall just as they got opposite the hall door. Seeing him, they cried out, "There goes the rebel!" and with the vilest curses cried: "Shoot him! shoot him!" Two of them rushed by me, one pulled Joe out, and the other leveled his gun and fired. Just as he did, I threw the gun up and the ball went through the ceiling. He then, with the glare of a demon, placed the gun against my temple and with a vile oath said he would blow out my rebel brains—I was not the least frightened then, though I shudder now at the thought. I said, "All you are fit for is to frighten children." The other demon pulled Joe out and was beating him with his gun when [my] sister Mary ran in and threw herself over Joe to protect him. *A negro girl took up a chair and said, "You strike Marse Joe again and I'll break dis chair over yo head." That enraged the [Yankee] brute who had pinioned me and he let go to strike [what he called] the "damned nigger"* [my emphasis, L.S.]. Mary and I got Joe into a corner to ward off their blows; seeing one man with the badge of an officer, she said, "You are an officer. Can you not protect this boy? He has done nothing to you." Two or three were pounding him over our shoulders until he was covered in blood, as was our clothing. The man replied: "I'm no officer, and if I were I would not stop them." I said, "Oh, Mary, don't ask anything of him. Look at him! Don't you see he was born a brute?" He cursed us. They [the Yankee troops] went through the house, [and in clear violation of the Geneva Conventions] turned every bed and piece of furniture into heaps in the middle of the floor, threw everything out of the kitchen and turned the stove upside down. My dear, sweet, gentle mother did all in her power to appease their wrath, but she got only the vilest of curses for it. An Irish girl, who had been as housekeeper and maid, took up a turkey they had left the night before, tied with the cord and tassel off one of their hats, threw it into the wagon when they put their dead comrade in, and said: "There, take all your dead. We want none of them." They left and took Joe with them, telling us we would never see him again. . . .¹⁰⁸ — MRS. W. H. SEBRING, MEMPHIS, TENN.

Mrs. W. H. Sebring.

THE POSTWAR SOUTH BENEFITS BY HAVING TWO RACES

☞ . . . [The] glorious South is still on its native heath, with unimpaired faith in itself, and intent on hospitable purpose and patriotic plan. It rejoices in nature's rich resources: soil and sunshine. The waterflow to deep sea and waterfalls on the way; the iron, the coal, the marble, the stone, the salt, the forest, the mountains, the vales, the flocks and herds, cotton and corn, cereals and sugar cane, grass and grapes, fruits and fish, *generous men and lovely women*; children, promising and plentiful; *and all this with the extraordinary advantage of having a population of two colors: black and white. There is no "negro problem" at the South. That mysterious race whose*

Confederate General Clement A. Evans.

origin is in darkness, whose history is blank until it begins with enslavement by the first infamous traffic in human flesh on the ships of foreign and Eastern [that is, Yankee] speculators, whose slavery in the South was the only elevating force which lifted them to civilization and freedom—that people's presence among us betokens not evil, but good, to both races. Separate, distinct, yet in mutual aid, the lines of progress can run on in harmony. It is a weakness for 60,000,000 whites to entertain dread of 10,000,000 negroes. It is cowardly to fear their aggression; it is cruel to deny them the chance to prosper; it is criminal to prostitute them to the uses of [political] party [all emphasis, L.S.]....[109] — CONFEDERATE GENERAL CLEMENT A. EVANS

THE LOYALTY OF THE BLACK SOUTHERN SERVANT

☛ In regard to the loyalty of the slaves, be it said to their eternal credit, no race was ever more loyal and helpful than they, during those four years of bloody strife. They took special pride in the feeling that they were the only protectors of the mistress at home during the absence of her natural protector and guardian.

A certain lady was told that her negroes were holding nightly meetings in her kitchen, and it was suspected that they were making arrangements to desert [to] the [Northern] enemy. One night, a low, earnest sound was heard from that locality. Creeping softly along to hear what the conspiracy might be, the mistress found the entire group of negroes on their knees, while one of them was offering up an earnest petition to the "Fader in Hebben," and praying Him to "bress missis and de chillun, an pertickler de young masters in de wah."

A ten dollar Confederate bill is now kept as a memento of an old [black] nurse who, after the war, brought it to her mistress to "he'p 'er ter git along."

An old negro man [named Tom] who had been his master's body-servant, brought a store of provisions and laying it before his former owner, said: "Marster, it mos' breaks my heart to see yo' an' ole miss in dis yere shanty, but 'would break 'tirely to know yo' was hongry an' couldn't git nuffin to eat."

His master, brushing the tears from his eyes, said: "Tom, I can't take these things from you and leave you and your children to starve."

The faithful old man replied: "No danger o' dat, Marster; Tom is used to helpin' hisself, but you an' ole miss nebber could do dat."

The master, greatly touched by this show of affectionate gratitude, said: "Tom, we have fallen upon evil days, but perhaps I may live to repay you for your kindness."

"Lord, Marster," replied the old man, "You's done dat time an' agin fur all dese years, an' I'se sho' it's my time to tek keer o' yo' an' ole miss" [all emphasis, L.S.].

The negresses would sell any of their home products for finery. A veil with these dusky dames would bring any amount in butter, eggs or chickens; the blacker the skin, the more ardent the desire to "dress like de white folks."

When the Federal Army was leaving Columbia, [South Carolina,] a number of the negroes followed, some of them going in their Masters' carriages. One old dame thus seated, dressed in all the finery she could lay her hands on—including a white lace veil—and fanning herself vigorously with a huge palmetto fan, although it was February, was met by an acquaintance, who hailed her after this fashion, "Hello, Aunt Sallie, whar yo' gwine?"

Nodding her head with a patronizing air, she answered, "Lor', honey, I'se gwine back inter de Union." And she got there. In less than six months afterwards, word came back to Columbia that she was "doing time in a prison for pilfering from her Northern mistress."[110] — MRS. F. G. DE FONTAINE

N. B. FORREST & HIS KINDNESS TOWARD BLACKS

☛ . . . [The Battle of] Okalona was fought on an open plain, and Forrest had no advantage of position to compensate for great inferiority of numbers, but it is remarkable that he employed the tactics of Frederick [the Great] at Leuthen and Zorndorf, though he had never heard these names. Indeed, his tactics deserve the closest study of military men. When asked to what he attributed his success in so many actions, he replied, "I got there first with the most men." . . . I doubt if any commander since the time of lion-hearted Richard [I], has killed so many of his foes as Forrest. His word of command was unique, "Move up, and mix with 'em!" While cutting down many a foe with [his] long-reaching arm, his keen eye watched the whole fight and guided him to the weak spot. Yet, he was a tender-hearted, kindly man. *The accusations of his enemies that he murdered his prisoners at* [the Battle of] *Fort Pillow and elsewhere are absolutely false. These negroes told me of Forrest's kindness to them* [my emphasis, L.S.].[111] — DR. JOHN A. WYETH, CONFEDERATE VETERAN

A proposed statue to Confederate General Nathan Bedford Forrest.

U.S. GOVERNMENT PROMOTES ANTI-WHITE RACISM DURING RECONSTRUCTION

☛ . . . With all our pride on account of the qualities exhibited by our [Southern] people during the war, perhaps the most striking illustration of their capacity for self-government is shown by their conduct since it ended. Their county desolated by the war; their wealth and resources exhausted; tens of thousands of their best men filling honorable graves on the fields of battle; their social and domestic institutions destroyed; their local governments annulled under the policy of reconstruction; denied the blessings of civil government; the military made paramount to the civil authorities; the right of the writ of *habeas corpus* suspended; arrests without affidavits of guilt and without warrant; citizens liable to be tried by drum head military courts; *freedmen's bureaus established everywhere, under the control of the military and a set of lawless camp followers of the army, stimulating the negroes to hostility to the whites* [my emphasis, L.S.]; with an alien race made dominant who were unused to the exercise of the duties of citizenship, and unqualified for self-government, with no security for life, person, or property. Overwhelmed by all these calamities, that the people should have been able to reorganize society, and to re-establish civil government, revive the ordinary industries of the country; and, in less than thirty years, reach the condition of general prosperity which now prevails throughout the Southern States, furnishes the strongest possible proof of the capacity of our people for the preservation of social order and self-government, and cannot fail to secure for them the good opinion of the civilized world.[112] — HON. JOHN H. REAGAN, TEX.

John Henninger Reagan, of Tennessee (later Texas); Confederate States Postmaster General under President Jefferson Davis.

TRIBUTE TO A SOUTHERN SERVANT, BLACK CONFEDERATE, & TRUE FRIEND
☛ [What follows is a tribute to]. . . the memory of [George,] *a faithful* [servant] *man in black who followed me through from First Manassas, Leesburg, where he assisted in capturing the guns we took from Baker, to the Peninsular, the Seven Days before Richmond, Fredericksburg, the bombardment of the city December 11, and the battle, two days after, at Marye's Heights; to Chancellorsville, the storming of Harper's Ferry, and the terrible struggle at Sharpsburg (Antietam now), and last, Gettysburg.* Here he lost his life by his fidelity to me— his "'young marster" and companion. We were reared together on "de ole plantation" in "Massippi."

I was wounded in the Peach Orchard at Gettysburg on the second day. The fourth day found us retreating in a cold, drizzling rain. George had found an ambulance, in which I, Sergeant Major of the Seventeenth Mississippi, and Col. Holder of that regiment (still on this side of the river), and an officer of the Twenty-first Mississippi, whose name escapes me, embarked for the happy land of Dixie. All day long we moved slower than any funeral train over the pike, only getting eight miles—to Cashtown. When night came I had to dismount from loss of blood and became a prisoner in a strange land. On the next day about sundown faithful George, who still clung to me, told me that the Yankees were coming down the road from Gettysburg and were separating the "black folks from dar marsters;" that *he didn't want to be separated from me and for me to go on to prison and he'd slip over the mountains and join the regiment in retreat, and we'd meet again "ober de ribber,"* meaning the Potomac. We had crossed at Williamsport.

I insisted on George accepting his freedom and joining a settlement of free negroes in the vicinity of Gettysburg, which we had passed through in going up to the battle. But he would have none of it; he wanted to stay with me always. I had him hide my sword, break it off at the hilt and stick it in a crack of the barn (that yet stands in the village) to the left of the road going away from Gettysburg, where I, with about thirty other wounded, lay. I can yet see that faithful black face and the glint of the blade as the dying rays of that day's sun flashed upon them. A canteen of water and some hard tack was the last token of his kindly care for me.

In the spring of 1865, I saw a messmate from whom I was separated on that battle and he told me the fate of poor, faithful George. He had gotten through the lines safely and was marching in the rear of our retreating command, when met by a Northern lady, who had a son in our command, whom George, by chance, happened to know. He was telling her of her son, who was safe as a prisoner, when *some men in blue came up. George ran and they shot and killed him*. He was dressed in gray and they took him for a combatant. The lady had him buried and then joined her son in prison. She told my messmate of this and he told to the boys in camp the fate of *the truest and best friend I ever had. George's prediction will come true—I feel we will meet again "over the river"* [all emphasis, L.S.].[113] — CONFEDERATE OFFICER C. C. CUMMING, FORT WORTH, TEXAS

FAITHFUL SERVANT BRINGS HIS MASTER'S BODY HOME

Confederate Gen. Simon Bolivar Buckner.

☛ . . . a young man named Brock, of Hawkins' Sharpshooters [CSA], [Simon B.] Buckner's Division, was killed by a Yankee over a mile away. Brock and the Yankee, only, were firing just previous to the battle of Perryville. Brock finally exposed himself carelessly and bit the dust. The battle was just opening, and soon the death grapple commenced.

[I speak]. . . *feelingly of Brock's faithful servant who had "promised ole Marse to fetch that chile to him and ole Mistis." Hearing of his young master's death, he made his way to the front line while the battle raged, and safely bore the body to the rear.* How this faithful servant succeeded in passing, with Brock's dead body, out of Kentucky, through Tennessee, and to South Mississippi, is not known. But he did, and brave young Brock's grave was watered with the tears of *a loving family* [my emphasis, L.S.].[114] — HON. WM. AMISON, OF THE FORTY-FOURTH TENNESSEE, C.S.A.

Confederate medal commemorating the founder, editor, and publisher of *Confederate Veteran* magazine, Sumner Archibald Cunningham (1843-1913). One of the many heroes of the Battle of Franklin II, Cunningham served as a Confederate sergeant, Company B, 41st Tennessee Infantry.

Wes Brady, former black servant, Marshall, Texas, 1937.

CHAPTER TWO
1897-1900

THE SOUTH IS NOT RESPONSIBLE FOR AMERICAN SLAVERY
☛ [Yankee orator] Mr. [Edward] Everett taught us to believe that Massachusetts was always anti-slavery. He maintained that her opinions on that point had never changed. He affirmed that the South and the North had once coincided in their views, and that what ever modification had taken place, had been in the South, which had become more and more pro-slavery, because of her growing interest in the production of cotton. But Massachusetts had always been true to her pristine faith. [Author George H.] Moore, [Librarian of the New York Historical Society, and a corresponding member of the Massachusetts Historical Society,] destroys that very delightful New England delusion. "Massachusetts had always carried herself with prudish dignity in the family of States." Mr. Moore disclosed her doings years ago, and "the pretty pranks she played when a girl."

[American slavery] began in Massachusetts with the enslaving of captured Indians in the Pequod war. Through fear of their escape and consequent revenge, many of them were exported to Bermuda, the worthy Puritans finding that traffic very profitable. Governor [John] Winthrop mentions, that "through the Lord's great mercy," a number of them had been taken, of whom the males were sent to Bermuda, and the females distributed through the Bay towns, to be used as domestic servants. There is something very amusing in the coolness of these proceedings. Captain [Israel] Stoughton, who assisted in the work of exterminating the Pequods [Indians], after his arrival in the enemy's country, wrote to the Governor of Massachusetts [Winthrop] as follows:

Children of Confederate General Benjamin Franklin "Frank" Cheatham.

> "By this pinnace you shall receive forty-eight or fifty women and children; concerning which there is one, I formerly mentioned, that is the fairest and largest that I ever saw among them, to whom I have given a coat to clothe her. It is my desire to have her for a servant, if it may stand with your good liking, else not. There is a little squaw that Staward Calacut desireth, to whom he hath given a coat."

The expatriation of the Indians led to the commencement of the African slave trade. A vessel, the *Desire*, of 120 tons, [built in [Massachusetts in 1630,] was used for that purpose. A letter to the Governor states: "Mr. [John] Endicott and myself salute you in the Lord Jesus. We have heard of a division of women and children in the Bay, and would therefore be glad of a share, viz: a young woman or girl, and a boy if you think good. I write to you for some boys for Bermuda."

The Salem slave-ship *Desire* brought negroes in exchange for Indians, from the West Indies. [Emanuel] Downing, in a letter to his brother-in-law, Governor Winthrop (1645), writes:

"A war with the Narragansetts [Indians] is very considerable to this population, for I doubt whether it be not sin in us, having the power in our hands, to suffer them to maintain the worship of the Devil, which their powwows often do. Secondly—if, upon a just war the Lord should deliver them into our hands, we might easily have men, women and children enough to exchange for Moors [that is, blacks or Africans], which will be more gainful pillage to us than we conceive, for *I do not see how we can thrive until we get a stock of slaves sufficient to do all of our business, for our children's children.* . . . And I suppose you know very well how we shall maintain twenty Moors cheaper than one English [European American, that is, white] servant. The ships that shall bring Moors may come home laden with salt, which may bear most of the charge, if not all of it."

This lighthearted black field servant, like all other types of Southern "slaves," could have purchased her freedom any time she desired. She, along with the vast majority of her fellows, chose to remain in bondage for reasons explained in this book.

The [Yankee] colonists tried their hands at slave breeding. Mr. Moore gives an amusing but unsuccessful instance of this kind in the case of Mr. Maverick's negress. As a result their increase was found unprofitable. It did not reimburse the incidental loss of service. Little negroes "when weaned, were given away like puppies." The master might deny baptism to his slaves. They were advertised in the Boston newspapers for sale in this way: "Just arrived and for sale, a prime lot of negro boys and girls."

By the laws of Massachusetts slaves were not permitted to be abroad after nine o'clock at night; *they were prohibited from improper intercourse or contracting marriage with whites.*

They did not have quick conscience against separation of families. Here is an advertisement: "A likely woman about nineteen years of age, and a child of about six months, to be sold together or apart."

Commenting, the *Commercial-Advertiser* [book reviewer] says: "Ah! Boston, Boston!—'[together] or apart'—and the mother only nineteen years old!" These advertisements continued to appear in the newspapers until after the Declaration of Independence.

The same arguments continued into the Seventeenth Century. Judge [Samuel] Sewell argued: "The niggers are brought out of a Pagan country into places where the Gospel is preached. The Africans have wars with one another, and our ships bring lawful [enslaved] captives taken in those wars. Abraham had servants bought with his own money, and born in his house."

Thus sustained, the slave trade long continued in Massachusetts [all emphasis, L.S.]. Mr. Moore gives a copy of instructions of a mercantile firm to the captain of one of their slave ships, in 1685, directing him to make the best of his way to the coast of Africa, and invest his cargo in slaves. They show him how to proceed in a critical inspection of the negroes before paying for them; and what he must do for the preservation of the health of his cargo, since on that the profits of the voyage depended. His compensation among other things, is to be four slaves out of every hundred, and four at the place of sale. The prohibition of the slave trade was at length effected in Massachusetts in 1788.[115] — CONFEDERATE VETERAN MAGAZINE CITING AN ANONYMOUS BOOK REVIEWER/CRITIC FROM THE NEW YORK COMMERCIAL-ADVERTISER

Miss Mary Kennon Jones, Gonzales, Texas; Maid of Honor for Charleston, Texas, 1899.

BLACK FIDELITY TO THEIR WHITE FAMILIES

☛ Some six years' ago I was in Salisbury, Maryland, and in talking with old citizens about war times, the question of the negroes' fidelity to the families in which they had been slaves was mentioned, and this incident was related to me:

A gentleman of family at Salisbury went into the Confederate Army, leaving his wife and children at home. One of the servants, a negro man, became the reliance about the house for protection and general oversight. Like the great body of the slaves of the South during the trying times of the war, he was devoted and true, having in him the very soul of honor. He felt that his master had left everything—"ole Miss," the children and "the place" in his care. The soldier fell in the war, and so the negro felt all the more his duties and increased obligations.

The negro's devotion was quite provoking to some of the people [that is, mainly Maryland Liberals], white and black, and many efforts were made to get him away from that family. They tried to get him to enlist in the Federal Army with promise of a bounty, but he steadfastly declined, giving as his reason that he must stay with his master's people and take care of them. They pleaded and urged, but in vain. At last they plied him with drink, and while under the influence of whiskey, he enlisted in the Federal Army. As soon as he was sufficiently sobered to realize what he had done, he was heartbroken, and he knew not what to do.

He was marched away to join the army with other recruits. *At his first opportunity he deserted and returned home*, and told all to his master's family, but they could do nothing to relieve him. He was soon arrested [by U.S.

military authorities] as a deserter and sent to prison. *Overcome by shame at the thought of having deserted the best friends he had in the world, he cut his blanket into strips and hanged himself in jail. That simple negro's death was infinitely more honorable than the life of many a proud man, and it told of a noble work done by that family who instructed and influenced the poor slave cast upon their hands and hearts by conditions which they could not control.*

In the fall of 1894 I was the guest of a typical Southern family in Athens, Alabama. The venerable matron upon whose head more than seventy years had left their frosts; she was a queenly woman of culture and piety. During an evening's conversation I told the above incident, and I saw this precious woman's face glow as I talked. When I finished she told me of what had happened in her own family.

During the war they were living at Huntsville, Ala. The father was dead—perhaps he died in the war. During those years somehow the negroes of the family were sold. This mother of the house was greatly troubled about their sale, and though every indication pointed to the certainty of the early emancipation of all the slaves, she said to her son that she intended to buy them back again. They urged prospective freedom, and that if the parties who owned them learned her purpose, they would know it was merely a matter of sentiment and would make her pay well for it. But she could not rest and went to the men who held them. Sure enough, they demanded full price, and that in gold. This did not daunt her, and, making great sacrifices, she procured the gold, and brought the three negro men home.

Mary Armstrong, former black servant, Houston, Texas, 1937.

Soon they were all free and the war was over. This good woman was living with her children in Huntsville; the three negro men were living in the country near by and doing well. *One morning they all came to the house where she was living with her son, and asked to see her privately. When she came in, the oldest one, speaking for the three, said to her, "Ole Miss, you've been mighty good to us; we love you, and specially we can't forget how you bought us back to the old home jes befo' the war was over. Now, we've come to try to do something for you. We're all doing well—making more'n a good livin', and we want to take care of you as long as you live. We'll rent you a good house, and we'll furnish you all the money you need—so much every month, and you shall be perfectly comfortable till you die."*

They meant all they said, and were able to do it, but she nor her children would let them do it, but the spirit was as true and noble as ever prompted an honorable white man to gratitude.

These incidents show something of the relations which have existed for long generations in Southern homes between master and slave, and their name is legion, for they are many. How little do even the least prejudiced people of the North know of this side of slavery! Does not this account for the unparalleled behavior of the whole negro race in their Southern homes during the war which they knew to be for their emancipation? [all emphasis, L.S.].[116] — REV. J. C. MORRIS, D.D., NASHVILLE, TENN.

THE FAITHFULNESS OF THE SOUTHERN NEGRO

☛ [I would like to] mention a few faithful characteristics of a negro boy that attended me during the war. Willis was of pure African blood. He and I were brought up together. *When I decided to enlist in the Confederate States Army my father insisted that this boy should attend me.* Willis remained true and faithful throughout the war. He would always bring the results of his foraging to me before gratifying his own capacious appetite. He was wonderfully brave—when the enemy was at a distance but was sure to be lost for two or three days after a battle. After the surrender of my command, at Washington, Ga., we made a tiresome march to Chattanooga. While there Willis addressed me as "Master" in the presence of some Federal soldiers, one of whom chided him for calling me master, saying: "He is no longer your master. You are as free as he is."

Willis straightened himself up and replied: "He is my master, and will be until one of us dies."

His speech made my heart tingle.

We were sent together to Nashville, Tennessee. There I decided to part with Willis, at least for a time. I divided equally with him the $26 in silver [the equivalent of about $800 in today's currency] which I had received at Washington, Georgia, as final remuneration, and advised him to stop in Nashville, where he could ply his picked-up trade of barber, and he did so. Later on in life some stolen goods were found in Willis's house, which he said had been left there by another negro. He was tried and convicted as a party to the theft, and sentenced to the penitentiary. When I heard of it I made every possible effort to get him pardoned, visiting Gov. [DeWitt Clinton] Senter (at that time in office), and employing an attorney in the effort. The poor fellow sickened and died, as I believe with a broken heart, soon after all hope for release disappeared.

Six Confederate veterans pose proudly with the Confederate Battle Flag.

A pathetic story of a slave's loyalty is told in the *New York Sun*, and the *Sun* says "it's so." Dr. McReynolds, in the long ago, having the "gold-fever," *left his wife near Harrisonville, Missouri, and, taking his servant, Asa, went West, and had secured $10,000* [about $300,000 in today's currency] *in gold, and was about ready to return when he sickened and died. Faithful Asa undertook to reach home with the gold, but had many discouraging adventures. While on the way he was captured by Indians, but he managed to bury the treasure. They might have treated him badly had he not posed as a doctor, there being a scourge among them at the time. After his release he gathered the gold and succeeded in getting home and delivering it to Mrs. McReynolds. She gave him his freedom and part of the money, and in the end he had a burial like white folks, near his mistress* [all emphasis, L.S.].[117] — BURGESS H. SCOTT, PADUCAH, KY.

REFERENCE TO A LARGE CONFEDERATE "NEGRO FORCE"

☛ . . . [Sometime during Lincoln's War,] by direction of [Confederate] Gen. Braxton Bragg, [Confederate Colonel Nathaniel Rives Chambliss] . . . reported to [Confederate] Gen. Josiah Gorgas, at Columbus,

Mississippi, who made him Superintendent of the Mining Bureau at that place. Next [Confederate] Gen. [Simon Bolivar] Buckner, commanding Selma, Alabama, created it a military post, and appointed Col. Chambliss commandant, with orders to fortify the place. Very soon, *with a large negro force* [my emphasis, L.S.], he surrounded the town with a cordon of fortifications worthy of [French military engineer Marquis de] Vauban. . . .[118] — FROM A SKETCH OF COL. CHAMBLISS BY MRS. ELIZABETH BURGESS BUFORD OF CLARKSVILLE, TENN.

THE SOUTH'S "GREATEST VICTORY"
☛ Many Southern people—old soldiers, as also younger men—have come to believe that in our defeat we met our greatest victory; *that the freeing of the negro freed the white race also, in a larger sense* [my emphasis, L.S.]; and as the ruin then seemed "never before so overwhelming, never was restoration swifter."[119] — GEORGE E. PURVIS

EMANCIPATION BIRTHED TRUE SOUTHERN INDEPENDENCE
☛ We have found out that *in the general summing up the free negro counts more than he did as a slave. . . . Above all, we know that we have attained a fuller independence for the South than that which our fathers sought to win in the forum by their eloquence or compel on the field with their swords* [my emphasis, L.S.]. . . .[120] — HENRY WOODFIN GRADY OF GEORGIA

FAITHFUL SERVANT ON THE BATTLEFIELD
☛ Observing in recent issues of the *Confederate Veteran* mention of the fidelity of negro servants during the war, I give you my experience.
Returning to my command near Richmond in the winter of 1864-65, after a short leave spent in Lynchburg, I took with me a young [black] man named Alfred. I had gone to school on the plantation where Alfred was born and had known him as a child and afterwards, but never well; and, as he was of unprepossessing demeanor, did not suspect his worth. In camp and on the march he was an excellent servant. On my going into action at Five Forks, as usual unmounted, he took charge of my horse,

Captured Confederate cannon on the battlefield of Chickamauga.

which, in view of the disastrous defeat there, I had the best reason for expecting never to see again. Alfred appeared, however, next day, horse and man both safe, and I was assured by men in the regiment who saw him leading the animal through thickets and brushwood within the Yankee fire that he had *saved my property at the risk of his life* [my emphasis, L.S.].

I was captured at Sailor's Creek April 6, but was detained prisoner only a week. Shortly after my return to Lynchburg Alfred presented himself one day, bringing what he considered the most valuable of the few effects that I had left in a valise in our headquarters wagon, with which he remained on the retreat until its contents were destroyed by our own people to prevent their falling into the enemy's hands. He told me somewhat sheepishly when he handed them over that they were all the things he could save "when dey was spikin' de baggage." I had no idea of ever recovering them.[121] — MR. L. M. BLACKFORD, OF ALEXANDRIA, VIRGINIA, FORMERLY ADJUTANT OF THE TWENTY-FOURTH VIRGINIA INFANTRY

NEGRO PARADERS AT CONFEDERATE REUNION

☛ . . . But the parade itself, what shall we say of it? First of all, there was not a young man in it; and there could not be, for it is more than thirty-two years since [Confederate Generals Robert E.] Lee and [Joseph Eggleston] Johnston surrendered. Secondly, there was not a discontented or seditious man in it. The utmost good humor prevailed from one end of the line to the other. A few of the companies and divisions carried arms, and kept the military step; a good many, though without arms, were uniformed in gray jackets; but the majority wore citizen's clothing. Here and there a detachment was mounted, but by far the larger part trudged along on foot. Once in a while we caught sight of an old fellow on a wooden leg manfully trying to keep up with his comrades. *At long intervals a black face might be seen, wearing a look of conscious elation. One venerable colored man in particular wore a battered silk hat, and bowed right and left to the spectators* [my emphasis, L.S.]. The young ladies who were sponsors and maids of honor for the different states rode in tallyhoes or carriages, except the thirteen who constituted a guard of honor to the commanding General and were all on horseback. Among the new flags, Federal and Confederate, a few of the "tattered standards of the South," rent with bullets and shells, and worn with age, were held aloft, and were everywhere greeted with cheers. All the bands played "Dixie," nothing but "Dixie," but none grew tired of it. The various commanding officers, from Gen. [John Brown] Gordon down, were saluted thousands of times as they rode along the streets. Gen. [Clement A.] Evans, who was at the head of the Georgia contingent, looked like a cross between a cavalry commander and a Methodist circuit rider. The rank and file were greeted with as many demonstrations as the superior officers. It was a glad, great day. . .[122] — DR. E. E. HOSS, NASHVILLE REUNION

John Barker, former black servant, Abilene, Texas, 1937.

LOYAL BLACKS HELPING CONFEDERATE SOLDIERS

☛ . . . The remarkable story is known of how Sam Davis emphatically refused to give information which would have saved his life. . . . A proposition was made to give him his freedom if he would tell where Coleman [Sam's 19 year old black friend and servant] was, which he could easily have done. Had he yielded to this and gone free, all of us [in our company] would have been caught; but he firmly refused to reveal any information.

Another man, a negro, deserves all honor for his faithfulness. He was a servant of old man Tom English, and brought information from [Union] Gen. [Granville] Dodge's office. He got the information in this way: Gen. Dodge ordered his secretary to make out the usual monthly report in regard to his entire army, its strength, etc. He made it out in pencil and submitted it to Gen. Dodge, who ordered it copied for official signature. The secretary finished it after working all night, but left the old pencil copy on the table. This office porter was supposed to burn all waste paper, but his quick insight discovered in this something valuable. So he carefully laid the document away, and next morning brought it to our [Confederate] headquarters. At night about three o'clock Bob Owens and I got in to our quarters. Sam Davis had that report. It named the forces at Nashville, Murfreesboro, and Shelbyville, as well as Pulaski. After the capture of Davis they sent an army to scour the country. One day just before dawn, while all were asleep, this same negro appeared and told us to move, for the Federals were within one hundred and fifty yards of us. He said that he came with the Federal army to get to us, and then fell in a branch [creek] for an excuse to get away. He got wet through and through. While Squire Schuler was getting quilts and blankets our old black friend disappeared, and the next seen of him was his feet as he went headlong into a brush-heap to dry off. Several days later they captured all our forces except Bob Owens and myself.

Rufus Hollis and wife.

It is a general mistake that we had to disguise ourselves to procure information for our army.[123] — MR. ALFRED H. DOUGLAS, CONFEDERATE VETERAN, NASHVILLE, TENN.

SOUTHERN SERVANT SAM & A YANKEE VETERAN

☛ A [white] gentleman was passing by
An old farmyard one time—
'Twas on a verdant mountain high
In Georgia's sunny clime.

While strolling thus, absorbed in thought,
He saw a faithful [black] slave
Standing near a marble slab
Which marked his master's grave.

The old [black] man saw him drawing near,
And made a graceful bow.
"My dear old friend, why stand'st thou here?
Thy heart is sad, I trow."

He lifted up his hoary head,
A tear coursed down his face.
"O gent'man, sah, ain't yo' dun hea'
De his'try ob dis place?

'Twuz on dis spot, long time ago,
One pleasant summah day,
De Yankees shot po' Massa Joe,
En dis am whar he lay.

Yo' see Mars Joe wuz comin' home
To see his maw and paw,
'Cause he be'n fightin' fo' de Souf
Since fust de 'gin de wah.

W'ile he wuz wa'kin' lazy like,
His face towa'ds de ground,
He thought he heared de bushes crack,
En' tu'nin, looked aroun'.

Law bless ma soul! w'at he see den
Among dem cedah trees
Wuz 'nough to meck de blood ob e'en
De bravest sojer freeze.

De Yankees swaumed all th'ough de woods,
Like bees aroun' de hive;
W'ere e'er you'd look a sojer stood—
De place wuz jes alive.

Po' massa dun fell in a trap,
But 'twasn' none his fault;
He did'n' see no Yankees dere
Till some one called out: 'Halt!'

'Good mawnin', gents!' Mars Joe den say,
Wile passin' by de ranks.
Den he tu'ned en' run'd away—
Close 'hind 'im run'd de Yanks.

Da run'd en' yelled en' shot at him,
But he did'n' min' none dat.
De bullets went all th'ough his coat.
En' one tuck off his hat.

Mrs. Herbert M. Franklin of Tennille, Georgia, President of the Georgia Division, U.D.C.

He run'd right straight on pas' his dooh —
He knew to stop meant deaf—
But jes' ez he got neah de woods
He fell, all out' er breaf.

Quick ez a thought da had 'im bound,
En led 'im pas' his dooh.
He looked so sorry at his home
He neber saw no mo'.

Den come his pooh ole feeble maw
To beg fo' his release;
But dey jes' tole 'er he mus' die,

His noble life mus' cease.

Pooh massa hear, den tu'ned en' say:
'Den, men, ef I mus' die,
Release me from dese cruel bonds,
En' please mah hands untie.

Confederate women's home, Fayetteville, North Carolina.

Yo' all well knows de Southe'n men
Will light yo', one en' all.
Gih me a swo'd, no murder's noose;
Wile fightin' let me fall.'

Dey only laugh en shake dey heads.
'No, Reb, yo' knell am rung.
Yo' hab yo' choice: will yo' be shot?
Or maybe yo'll be hung?'

'No sahs; ef I'm to lose ma life,
I choose a sojer's deaf.
Long lib de Souf! I'll always cry,
E'en wid mah dyin' breaf.'

Dey led 'im to dat big ole tree.
Po' massa called me dere.
'Good-bye, ole Sam; gib lub to maw.
I place 'er in yo' care.'

Jes' den de cap'n called out, 'Load!'
Den, 'Aim!' en 'Fire!' he cried.
An awful bang—de smoke clar'd off,
En' dar's w'ere massa died."

He [Sam] pointed to the little grave
Beneath the sad old oak.
"It wuzn't long 'fo' missus died;
Her po' ole heart wuz broke."

The [white] gentleman was silent for awhile;
He seemed absorbed in thought.
His mind went back to scenes of war,
Of battles he had fought.

"I feel much touched," at length he said [to Sam],
"And all you say is true.
O God forgive me for that sin.
I led those boys in blue."[124] — AS TOLD TO JOHN KNOWLES BISHOP BY SAM, "AN OLD DARKY WHO WAS A [SOUTHERN] SLAVE DURING THE CIVIL WAR"

SKETCH OF A BLACK MAMMY BY HER WHITE MISTRESS

☛ . . . It must be said that the whole [Tennessee] plantation prospered under the steady rule of Aunt Dice [our new black mammy, who came to us from Virginia in 1834]. No sooner was she domiciled by her broad cabin hearth than she began to enlarge her borders. Her two years' experience as a hired underling held her in good stead: she understood her master's needs, the merits and demerits of his slaves. Her second coming was an era of greater importance. The negroes, from venerable Uncle Amos to the smallest pickaninny, realized that *she held a certain amount of power—how much, she herself did not stop to question; she only knew that she was grateful to a kind master, and she proved her gratitude with the remainder of her long life. For her, too, the change was wholesome; whether from her comfortable surroundings, or the kindly treatment of a new and much-loved master, it is hard to say, but certain it was that the frail, sickly negress gained new strength as the years passed on, until the neighboring slave owners reluctantly acknowledged her "the likeliest nigger on the whole creek." Certainly she was the hardest worker: she often said there was not a lazy bone in all her body. Not only did she help to tend and rear the children, but she was the ruling spirit of all the "hum and hustle" of each busy day. Her first duty was to sound the long, wild call of the hunting horn from the back gallery, and dole out to the slaves their morning "drams" from the rum barrels in the cellar before the day's work began.*

Black mammy with one of her white children.

It was here that she commenced her discipline. The long row of rollicking laborers filing up the path from the quarters hastened to a quickstep under her searching glance. Not that she disapproved of merriment. "Light hearts make light work" was a proverb at Riverside. But she received no laggards at her early drink offerings. Uncle Jack knew to a nicety how long to hold his inverted position, his usual obeisance to his morning dram. Aunt Dice heard complacently the rhythmic "pitapat" of merry feet, the back steps knocked out on the graveled walk, or the jokes which were "swapped" in bantering tones and high good humor—a form of greeting that varied little from morning to morning.

"Hi, dar, nigger; stir yo' stumpers!"

"I takes no slack jaw dis mo'nin'. I walks right ober you 'reckly."

"Huh! ef yo' sasses me, I slams yo' down, chile, and puts my foot on yo' haid. What's de kon'squence ob dat?"

"A daid nigger! Dar'll be de kon'squence," is the cheerful response, while a succession of calls, "hoorahs," and cries of "Hear dat nigger now!" "Ain't he a steppin'?" sounded clear and vibrant on the still air.

On they came, Uncle Amos quietly in the lead, baring his head to Aunt Dice's courteous "Good mo'nin'," Uncle Silas following with his usual plea for a "leetle drap mo' for de mis'ry in de back," and the sharp response, "Step on, Silas; I want yo' room."

"Come, boys, be lively; daylight's burnin'." And the dusky column moved on with boisterous shouts and musical calls, startling the sleepy cocks from the barnyard roosts, and echoing across the river, which lay aflush under the eastern skies.

Aunt Dice, though supervisor, scorned an idle hour. It was she who prepared the well-cooked meals for the master's table; who ordered provisions for the quarters; overlooked the butter-making, the spinning and weaving, the cutting of garments, and the plain sewing for the numerous slaves; never resting her weary feet until the last laborer went back to the fields after the midday meal. Her master sometimes gently interfered: "Two hours' rest at noon, Dice. Man and beast should rest in the heat of the day."

So when the songs of the laborers rang out from the fields, and the music of wheel and loom went merrily on within, Aunt Dice went out to her cabin to take her well-earned rest and enjoy a quiet smoke, her only indulgence. Her clean, fragrant pipe, used in unobtrusive hours, was never offensive.

The master smiled over his purchase. He had made no mistake. Conscious of his trust, she soon assumed control of the slaves—in a way. Respectful they certainly were; man, woman, and child were under her imperious sway, and well she ruled. Aunt Dice believed in discipline; while one and all liked

Center: Mrs. Julia Jackson Christian, wife of William Edmund Christian and only child of Confederate General Thomas J. "Stonewall" Jackson. Child on left: Julia's son Thomas Jonathan Jackson Christian; child on right: Julia's daughter Julia Jackson Christian Preston.

and admired her, she thought it best to instill into this liking a little of fear, to make it wholesome. A lazy negro was her special detestation. She delighted in scattering a crowd of dusky forms, basking, lizard-like, in the sun. Few of the laziest could stand the curious sidelong glance of her sharp eyes, and many a step quickened under that searching look.

How far her rule extended even the master did not question, nor the mistress [the author of this sketch], *who began to lean upon her and trust to her guidance in the manifold duties of a southern matron. The rule of the house—its domestic duties—it was hers to order. Her judgment was supreme, her counsel never lost. The mistress, who as "Lady Bountiful" dispensed a wide charity, had only to say to her, "Aunt Dice, our neighbor is sick; she needs help." Aunt Dice packed a full basket and started on her errand of mercy, ministering to the poor in a way well fitted to heal a mind diseased. She fed and nursed, she cleaned and swept, until the bare, rude homes of the poor whites shone bright with the sick faces.*

The master found himself referring to her wisdom: "Dicy, shall we kill hogs this week?"

"They's eatin' they heads off, Mos William, an' fat as mud."

The hogs were slaughtered.

"Is it time to plant potatoes, Dicy?"

"'Pears to me the groun's waitin' fur' em."

But Aunt Dice was also learning. Within her wholesome surroundings she found much to edify, to help her. The nobility and upright character of her quiet master; the influence of the mistress, a woman of kind speech and gentle manner; the pure atmosphere and well-ordered household; a house whose God was the Lord, the Bible the most honored book in the quaint old bookcase; not a home of pretentious superiority, but one of comfort and solid standing, of quiet, far-reaching charity and Christian excellence—all these elements were unfolding within the stunted soul of the slave an inherent germ of rare worth and beauty. Her observant eyes lost nothing that could serve to strengthen or uplift her. Her hungry soul was feeding [all emphasis, L.S.]. . . .[125] — NINA HILL ROBINSON, RIVERSIDE PLANTATION, SOUTH AFTON, TENN., 1897

WHY FORCED ABOLITION IN THE SOUTH WAS WRONG

☞ . . . When the constitution of the United States was formed the institution of slavery existed in every one of the states, though emancipation had been begun in New England. Found to be unprofitable as an economic organization, it was rapidly eliminated from the Northern society, which was and is based on the idea of profit and loss.

Confederate Vice President Alexander H. Stephens.

Profitable in the South, it developed and prospered. It produced an enormous expansion of material and consequently political power. It developed a society which for intelligence, culture, chivalry, justice, honor, and truth has never been excelled in this world, and it produced a race of negroes the most civilized since the building of the Pyramid of Cheops [or Khufu] and the most Christianized since the crucifixion of our Lord. The Southern race ruled the continent from 1775 to 1860, and it became evident that it would rule it forever as long as the same conditions existed. The free mobocracy of the [Liberal] North could never cope with the slave democracy of the [Conservative] South, and it became the deliberate intent of the North to break up institutions so controlling and producing such dominating influences. Slavery was the source of political power and the inspiration of political institutions, and it was selected as the point of *attack. The moral question was subordinate to the political and social one. The point of the right or wrong of slavery agitated but a few weak-minded and feeble men. The real great dominating and controlling idea was the political and social one, the influence of the institution on character and institutions. There was forming in the South a military democracy, aggressive, ambitious, intellectual, and brave, such as led Athens in her brightest epoch and controlled Rome in her most glorious days. If that were not destroyed, the industrial society of the North would be dominated by it. So the entire social force—the press, the pulpit, the public schools—was put in operation to make distinctive war upon Southern institutions and Southern character, and for thirty years attack, vituperation, abuse, were incessant.*

It was clear to the states of the South that there could be no peace with them [Liberal Yankees], and there grew up a general desire to get away from them and live separate. . . .

I repeat and reiterate that the war waged upon the South was an unjust and causeless war of invasion and rapine, of plunder and murder; not for patriotism nor high motives, but to gratify ambition and lust of power in the promoters of it, for contracts and profits by the supporters of it. I do not deny enthusiasm for the Union to the gallant young Americans who died for their flag, but I do insist that the Union would have been smashed to smithereens and the flag gone to pot if there had not been fat contracts for shoddy coats and bogus boots to preserve the one and to uphold the other. The sentiment would not have lasted thirty days if the people behind had not been making money. The war of the South was a war of self-defense, justified by all laws sacred and divine, of nature or

Confederate monument, Arlington, Virginia, dedicated June 4, 1914.

of man. It was the defense of the [traditional Conservative] *institutions of marriage, of husband and wife, of parent and child, of master and servant. Not one man in a thousand in the Confederate army had any property interest in slavery. Every man had a home and a mother. If the stronger section had the right to overturn the institution of servitude maintained by the* [Old Testament] *patriarchs and sanctioned by the apostles, which had in all time been the apprenticeship by which savage races had been educated and trained into civilization by their superiors, it would have precisely the same right to overturn the institution of marriage and establish its system of divorce laws, by which the ancient institution of concubinage could be restored and maintained. If one section could impose its will in another, the one was master and the other was slave, and the only way to preserve liberty was by armed resistance. I insist that the South did not make war in defense of slavery; slavery was only the incident, the point attacked. The defense was of all* [traditional] *institutions—marriage, husband and wife, parent and child—as well. But the instinct of the great mass of this* people, that instinctive perception of truth which in this race is as unerring as a mathematical proposition, understood, grasped, appreciated, at once that the question was a question of race domination, and they understood, too, the fundamental fact that in all trials of strength—strength of body, strength of will, strength of character—the weakest must go to the wall, and the great, manly, just, humane heart of the master race pitied the inferior one.

The great crime of the century was the [economically and socially premature] emancipation of the negroes. They are an affectionate, trustworthy race. *If the institution of slavery had been left to work itself out under the influence of Christianity and civilization, the unjust and cruel incidents* [that arose after full abolition in December 1865] *would have been eliminated* [all emphasis, L.S.]*, just as they have been in the institution of husband and wife. . . . Now* [for example] *under the law of Virginia, the married woman is the equal in all legal and property rights with her husband, and in all others she is his superior.*

Institutions and society change by the operation of the law of justice and love, of right and charity, and by its influence the negro would have been trained and educated in habits of industry, of self-restraint, of self-denial, of moral self-government, until in due time he would have gone into the world to make his struggle for survivorship on fair terms. As it is, against his will, without his assistance, he has been turned loose in America to do the best he can in the contest with the strongest race that ever lived. . . .[126] — BRADLEY T. JOHNSON, BALTIMORE, MARYLAND

BLACKS & THE REBUILDING OF THE POSTWAR SOUTH

☛ It is a rare privilege . . . to have had part, how humble, in this work. Never was nobler duty confided to human hands than the uplifting and upbuilding of *the prostrate and bleeding South . . . beautiful in her suffering, and honest, brave, and generous always.* In the record of her social, industrial, and political illustration we await with confidence the verdict of the world.

But what of the negro? Have we solved the problem he presents or progressed in honor and equity toward solution? Let the record speak to the point. *No section shows a more prosperous laboring population than the negroes of the South, none in fuller sympathy with the employing and land owning class. He shares our school fund, has the fullest protection of our laws and the friendship of our people. Self-interest, as well as honor, demand that he should have this. Our future, our very existence, depends upon our working out this problem in full and exact justice. . .*

The relations of the Southern people with the negro are close and cordial. We remember with what fidelity for four years he guarded our defenseless women and children . . . . To his eternal credit be it said that whenever he struck a blow for his own liberty he fought in open battle, and when at last he raised his black and humble hands that the shackles might be struck off, those hands were innocent of wrong against his helpless charges, and worthy to be taken in loving grasp by every man who honors loyalty and devotion. Ruffians have maltreated him, rascals have misled him,

Henry Woodfin Grady.

philanthropists established a bank for him, but the South, with the North, protests against injustice to this simple and sincere people. To liberty and enfranchisement is as far as law can carry the negro; the rest must be left to the conscience and common sense. It must be left to those among whom his lot is cast, with whom he is indissolubly connected, and whose prosperity depends upon their possessing his intelligent sympathy and confidence [all emphasis, L.S.]. *Faith has been kept with him, in spite of calumnious assertions to the contrary by those who assume to speak for us or by frank opponents. Faith, will be kept with him in the future, if the South holds her reason and integrity.*[127] — HENRY WOODFIN GRADY

EVIDENCE OF "THOUSANDS" OF BLACK CONFEDERATES

☛ *I reported at Jackson the acceptance of the detachment making up the full complement of the* [Confederate States cruiser] *Arkansas. Of course we must remain at Jackson until the departure of the Arkansas for Baton Rouge, 4*[th] *of August, being held in readiness by the commodore, subject to the call of* [Confederate] *Gen.* [John Cabell] *Breckinridge, against that city, and I then returned to Yazoo City, and within three days was aboard the St. Mary patrolling the river. Lieut. Shepperd's Mobile was placed on the stocks for ironcladding. We made Greenwood, one hundred and sixty miles north, at the junction of the Tallahatchie and Yallabusha. A fort was shortly to be located at this junction, to bear the name of* [Confederate] *Gen.* [John Clifford] *Pemberton, a compliment justly won.*

Confederate officer George S. Waterman.

Our Confederate right was a series of batteries or forts twenty-three miles from the Mississippi on the Yazoo, at the first bluff, called Haines Bluff; our left, the fortified city of Vicksburg, and our line connecting these was nearly fourteen miles in extent, and was a natural fortification, strengthened by a year's labor of thousands of negroes [my emphasis, L.S.], *directed by the finest engineering talent of the Confederacy.*[128] — GEORGE S. WATERMAN, CONFEDERATE STATES NAVY

LOYAL SOUTHERN BLACKS

☛ *I was wounded at Perryville, Kentucky, October 8, 1862, imprisoned at Louisville and Cairo, and exchanged at Vicksburg, Mississippi, December, 1862. I then joined the Sixth Alabama Cavalry, and was again captured at Bluff Springs, Florida, March 25, 1865; was imprisoned on Ship Island under* [Yankee] *negro guards, and paroled at Vicksburg May 6, 1865.*

It seems like a long, long time since 1861-65. We old Rebels—bless the word!—have had a rough, tough time since then. I am, if anything, stronger in the [Conservative] *principles for which we fought than ever, having thought and read a good deal. There is nothing I am prouder of than the glorious record made by the immortal six hundred thousand,* while I believe the thoroughbred Southerners are the best fighters on earth.

Perhaps we will have a history after a while—a plain statement of facts as to the causes of the war, numbers on each side, the record made by each side, the civilized or uncivilized mode of carrying it on, including treatment of prisoners and citizens by each.

My old army servant, Jim, now blind, is yet with me. He has not only proved a faithful servant, but a true friend. When I was wounded he went on the battlefield to bring me off, and came near being killed. A shell, with the "string" [fuse] still burning, fell by his horse's feet. He said he "didn't stay there long." In speaking of the fighting, he said: "Our men stood still and shot, they moved forward and shot. It was just like a shower of rain moving." He brought my horse, pistol, etc., home, and delivered them to my family. I have never known Jim to tell a lie or to be dishonest.

Rachel, my old cook from Virginia, is now dead. "Mama," as the children called her, had a poor opinion of freedom [emancipation]; she had a poor estimate of the negroes themselves. When I told her that she was free she commenced crying, and asked if I wanted to get rid of her. Afterward the old [black] nurse came to see me again, lamenting her hard lot, and said that she "used to have a backer," but had "no confidence in these new-issue negroes" [all emphasis, L.S.].[129] — A. J. PUCKETT, HECTOR, ALA.

LIBERAL NORTH USES BLACKS AS POLITICAL WEAPONS

🖎 . . . The South has exhibited as much, if not more, regard for the integrity of the Union than the States of the North. . . . Her devotion to the republic established by the efforts of [Virginians George] Washington, [James] Madison, and a host of [other] venerated [Southern] patriots and statesmen was dearer to her than even her own section; and for ten long years, patiently hoping against hope that a sense of right and justice would prevail, she witnessed State after State in the North trampling the laws of the country in the dust. She saw abolition [that is, radical Left-wing] fanaticism whetting its sword and thirsting for the blood of her citizens. She submitted to this same abolition fanaticism [that is, John Brown and his gang] invading her territory with cutthroats and desperadoes *armed to kill the whites and incite the blacks to bloody insurrection*. She endured published slanders, scattered broadcast over the world by this fell fanaticism, *some of this incendiary stuff, indorsed by prominent* [Left-wing] *Congressmen, going to the extent of urging the negroes to rise by night and butcher their masters and families; and, if that were not practicable, to poison the waters and kill them thus by stealth* [my emphasis, L.S.].

Lewis Jones, former black servant, Ft. Worth, Texas, 1937.

Why did the South so long endure all this and not accept [Yankee] Mr. [Daniel] Webster's decision that the compact [of the Union] was at an end? It was her devotion to the Union. And not until this abolition fanaticism, feeding upon sectional hate [that is, the Liberal North vs. the

Conservative South], grew to a strength that enabled it to obtain the advantage of Federal position and, in 1861, to inaugurate the John Brown raid on an enlarged and extended scale did the South accept the fact and act upon it. So long as the treason against which that distinguished statesman inveighed was confined to the local governments of abolition States, she was willing to abide by the Union; but when [Yankee] Mr. [Salmon P.] Chase, who spoke for the then incoming [Left-wing] administration of Lincoln, declared that this same treason was to be practiced by the Federal government, there was nothing left for her [the South] but to accept the fact that the Union was dissolved and to exercise the right of a free people to form a government to their own liking. . . .[130] — HON. JOHN N. LYLE, WACO, TEX.

SOUTHERN BLACKS INSULT YANKS BUT NOT CONFEDERATES

☛ . . . In a letter to his wife from Nassau, April 6, 1864, Mr. [Thomas] Sharp [a Confederate spy originally from Pennsylvania] states: "We left Wilmington about 3 P.M., and went down Cape Fear River, reaching Fort Fisher, at its mouth, about sundown. There were fifteen Yankee blockade vessels lying off the bar. At dark we started out. It was quite stormy. We passed within one hundred and fifty yards of the Yankee war vessels in the storm unperceived. The storm got worse, and we could hear our ship twisting in every timber. The cotton on deck floated round in the water." In this letter he gave at length a thrilling description of the storms and an interesting account of the people at Nassau. *The customs officers were "all negroes, who were civil to Southerners, but didn't hesitate to insult Yankees"* [my emphasis, L.S.]. In Nassau he found that he must go to England and to France instead of Canada, where he started originally. . . .[131] — CONFEDERATE VETERAN MAGAZINE

FAITHFUL SERVANT UNCLE DAVE HATCHER

☛ Dave's master was James Hatcher, Esq., of Edgefield County, South Carolina, and *Dave, in slavery times, was his "driver"*—head man of the plantation when no overseer was employed. Dave had the confidence of the white family, for when the body of the young master was brought home from the terrible battlefield of Chickamauga he mourned with them, for "de only boy had done gin up his life a fitin' fur de Souf." When Dave's fidelity was tested, he stuck by "de fambly"; and during the reign of terror [Reconstruction], when noble men of the South acquiesced in the doings of the Ku Klux Klan to strike awe and fear to the hearts of the newly enfranchised [blacks] and their carpetbag leaders, Dave was still faithful and true.[132] When his master was to be arrested as one of the Klan, Dave carried the news to him, having learned of it from other negroes. When secure in his retreat, Dave was the bearer of news, etc., to him from home. This fidelity caused his arrest, and at the headquarters of the Federal garrison he was hung up by the thumbs for a long, long time, that the authorities might extort from him the whereabouts of the fugitive; but they

"Uncle" Dave Hatcher.

did not know Dave, for he said: "I was jes agwine to die hung up befo' I would tell on 'im." Dave was let down at last and turned loose, but to this day does not like that blue uniform, and wonders why "our young sodger people wear it instid of de gray" [all emphasis, L.S.]. Dave still holds his own, has reared a "likely set of chillun," and has acquired a little property. He has forgiven the United States government for its indignity of long ago sufficiently to accept a branch of the Star Mail Route, which he faithfully runs, although his "fumbs are a little bit crooked and weak yit."[133] — CAPT. B. H. TEAGUE, AIKEN, S.C.

SOUTHERN BLACK SERVANT CALLS YANKEE TEACHER "WHITE TRASH"

☛ I remember . . . when they began to have the first freedmen schools around Memphis in 1864. Several Massachusetts tutors were teaching the freedmen the new doctrine of political equality. The negroes, you know, can never separate political equality from social equality; so when the [Yankee] teacher said, "We are all born free and equal," Clarissa Sophia [a former Southern servant] broke in, "Wa' dat yo's sayin' now? Yo say I'se jes as ekal as yo is?" "Yes," said the teacher; "and I can prove it." "Ho! 'tain't no need," replied the lately disenthralled [black woman]. "Reck'n I is, sho' nuff. But does yo say dat I'se good as missus, my [white] missus [that is, mistress]?" "Certainly you are, Sophia," said the teacher. "Den I'se jes gwine out yere rite off," said Sophia, suiting action to word. "Ef I'se good as my missus, I'se goin' ter quit, fer I jes know she ent 'soshiatin' wid no sich wite trash as you is."[134] — MELVILLE D. LANDON, UNION SOLDIER

MORE FORREST MYTHS THOROUGHLY DEBUNKED

☛ [I was intimately associated with Bedford Forrest before the War for Southern Independence. Here are my observations pertaining to his dealings with black servants]: *Forrest was kind, humane, and extremely considerate of his slaves. He was overwhelmed with applications from a great many of this class, who begged him to purchase them. He seemed to exercise the same influence over these creatures that in a greater degree he exercised over the soldiers who in later years served him as devotedly as if there was between them a strong personal attachment. When a slave was purchased for him his first act was to turn him over to his negro valet, Jerry, with instructions to wash him thoroughly and put clean clothes on him from head to foot. Forrest applied the rule of cleanliness and neatness to the slaves which he practised for himself. In his appearance, in those antebellum days, he*

Confederate General Nathan Bedford Forrest.

was extremely neat and scrupulously clean. In fact, so particular was he in regard to his personal appearance that some were almost inclined to call him foppish. The slaves who were thus transformed were proud of belonging to him. He was always very careful when he purchased a married slave to use every effort to secure also the husband or wife, as the case might be, and unite them, and in handling children he would not permit the separation of a family [my emphasis, L.S.].[135] — AS TOLD TO JOHN A. WYETH BY COLONEL GEORGE W. ADAIR, ATLANTA, GA.

SOUTHERN BLACK LEGISLATORS CONTRIBUTE TO BUILDING CONFEDERATE MONUMENT

Original caption: "Southern beauties who represented states at the Birmingham Reunion, U.C.V."

☛ An association of ladies was formed at Columbia [South Carolina] in 1869 for the purpose of erecting a monument to the memory of the Confederate dead. The State being under Radical [that is, extremist Left-wing] rule, it was decided not to place the monument on the Statehouse grounds, but on a high hill overlooking Sydney Park. Before much progress had been made the ladies were informed that the weight of the monument was too great for so small an area near the edge of the hill. The granite base was then erected in Elmwood Cemetery, in a prominent location reserved for Mexican soldiers. In September, 1875, the marble shaft, statue, etc., which had been wrought in Italy from the famous quarries of Carrara, were safely landed in Columbia; but as the full amount was not in hand, it was determined to allow them to remain in the boxes until they could be claimed as the property of the association.

In 1876 the State freed itself from the "coils of the deadly serpent" [that is, Reconstruction], and [former Confederate Gen.] Wade Hampton became our successful leader in the endeavor. An application to the Legislature to erect the monument on the Statehouse grounds of course met with approval, the men themselves contributing. *Among the contributors were two colored members* [my emphasis, L.S.].[136] — CONFEDERATE VETERAN MAGAZINE

DEBUNKING THE LIES IN YANKEE HISTORY BOOKS

☛ ... We were in error in supposing our work done [of cleansing Southern school books of malevolent Yankee myths and absurd anti-South fairy tales]. We are not altogether rid of false teachings, whatever may be said of the purposes of our teachers. Because of newly aroused thought, the opinions alluded to are less prevalent than they were; but they are still heard from young men who, during the last thirty years, have been misled as to the characteristics of our people and the causes of the "war between the sections," from some who, "looking to the future," as they phrase it, foolishly ignore the lessons of the past, and from others who, thinking themselves impoverished by the war and being greedy of gain, have neither thought nor care for anything nobler. There are a few older men who think that the abandonment of all the principles and convictions of the past is necessary to prove their loyalty to the present. There are some who dare to tell us that "the old days are gone by and are not to be remembered;" that "it is a weakness to recall them with tender emotions." To these we reply: "Put off the shoes from off your feet, for the place whereon you stand is holy ground." Young or old, these men are few, but they are ours, and *their children inherit their errors.*

Those not already aware of it will be surprised to learn that *there are teachers in the South—high in position but, as we think, very ignorant of our history—who accept the Northern theory that "slavery was the cause of the war,"* and must accept the dishonoring consequence that its preservation was our sole object in that struggle—the favorite position of the Northern advocate and the last support of his cause. This position they take in spite of the fact that *the quarrel between the North and the South began when slavery existed in all the States.* That writers or readers should ignore the proofs of this is surprising. We cite, for instance, [George] Washington's stern order issued to the army before Boston in 1775, promising exemplary punishment to any man who should say or do anything to aggravate what he called "the existing sectional feeling." For *that feeling in that day we cannot find cause in slavery, for the good people of New England shared our Southern guiltiness.* Nor is it to be explained except as springing from the old jealousy of Puritan and Cavalier, and the resentment of the Virginians against the New Englanders for failing to help them in the Indian war; whence, according to some authorities, the epithet "Yankee" sprang.

. . . We return to the most offensive doctrine of the [mainly Yankee-authored] books that we condemn: the charge that the Southern soldier fought for slave property. If this charge be just, let the truth be taught. It is false. The answer to it is on every page of our history, and *the books that make it should not be used in our schools.*

Confederate Gen. Robert E. Lee with some of the army's subordinate officers.

We all remember how many Virginians of 1861, knowing that the blood thirst of [the English civil war battles of] Naseby [1645] and Marston Moor [1644] was unslaked, yet weary of the blood feud that had antedated the Revolution; tired of sectional strife recurring with every question of general interest; simply weary of quarreling; convinced by the election of [big government Liberal] Lincoln that the quarrel never would end—went into the war [for Southern Independence] in hope of conquering peace, and *before going gave their negroes leave to be free if they chose.* The attitude of one or two prominent fighters with respect to slave property will be sufficient for our purpose. *The Campaigns of Stonewall Jackson*, by Col. G. F. R. Henderson, of the British Staff College, Chamberley, England, should be read by every man, woman, and child in the South. It would help the Northern people to a knowledge of the truth. [Among the pages of] . . . of that great book, we find the following extract from a letter of Gen. Robert E. Lee:

"In this enlightened age," wrote the future general in chief of the Confederate army, "there are few, I believe, but will acknowledge that slavery as an institution is a moral and political evil. It is useless to expatiate on its disadvantages. I think it is a greater evil to the white than to the colored race, and while my feelings are strongly interested in the latter my sympathies are more deeply engaged for the former. The blacks are immeasurably better off here than in Africa—morally, socially, and physically. The painful discipline they are undergoing is necessary for their instruction as a race, and, I hope, will prepare them for better things. How long their subjection may be necessary is known and ordered by a merciful Providence. Their emancipation will sooner result from the mild and melting influence of Christianity than from the storms and contests of fiery controversy. This influence, though slow, is sure. The doctrines and miracles of our Saviour have required nearly two thousand years to convert but a small part of the human race, and even among Christian nations what gross errors still exist! While we see the course of the final abolition of slavery is still onward, and we give it the aid of our prayers and all justifiable means in our power, we must leave the progress as well as the result in His hands who sees the end and who chooses to work by slow things, and with whom a thousand years are but as a single day. The abolitionist must know this, and must see that he has neither the right nor the power of operating except by moral means and suasion; if he means well to the slave, he must not create angry feelings in the master. Although he may not approve of the mode by which it pleases Providence to accomplish its purposes, the result will nevertheless be the same; and the reason he gives for interference in what he has no concern holds good for every kind of interference with our neighbors when we disapprove of their conduct."

Litt Young, former black servant, Marshall, Texas, 1937.

On the same page Col. Henderson quotes from the lips of Mrs. [Mary Anna Morrison] Jackson like opinions held by her husband. These are opinions expressed before the war. Do they indicate that Lee and Jackson fought to preserve slave property? I myself know that *at the beginning of the war Gen. Lee, wise and far-seeing beyond his fellow-men, was in favor of freeing all the slaves in the South, giving to each owner a bond, to be the first paid by the Confederacy when its independence should be secured; and that Stonewall Jackson, while believing in the scriptural right to own slaves, thought it would be politic in the white people to free them.* He owned two. One was a negro man, whose first owner, being in financial difficulties, was compelled to sell. *The negro asked Gen. Jackson to buy him* and let him work until he accumulated the money to pay the General back. He was a waiter in a hotel, and in a few years earned the money, gave it to Jackson, and secured [that is, purchased] his freedom. The other was a negress about to be sold and sent away from Lexington. *She asked Jackson to buy her*, which he did, and then offered to let her work as the man had done and secure her freedom. *She preferred to stay with the General and his wife as a slave*, and was an honest, faithful, and affectionate servant. Gen. Joseph E. Johnston never owned a slave.

Dr. Hunter McGuire.

How much of the fighting spirit and purpose of the South were in the breasts of Lee, Johnston, and Jackson? Do the facts recited indicate that the desire to retain slave property gave them nerve for the battle? *Does any man living know of a soldier in this State who was fighting for the negro or his value in money? I never heard of one.* The Stonewall Brigade of the Army of Northern Virginia was a fighting organization. *I knew nearly every man in it, for I belonged to it for a long time, and I know that I am within proper bounds when I assert that there was not one soldier in thirty who owned or ever expected to own a slave* [all emphasis, L.S.]. "The South fighting for the money value of the negro." What a cheap and wicked falsehood![137] — DR. HUNTER MCGUIRE, VIRGINIA CONFEDERATE VETERANS

CLOSE BONDS BETWEEN SOUTHERN WHITES & BLACKS

☞ In your February number you published a poem entitled "Dem Yankees," and failed to give credit due its author, Irwin Russell, of Mississippi. He was the first man to write poems in the true dialect of the Southern negro. *Like all young Southerners whose parents were wealthy, he had a strong affection for the negroes owned by his father*, and through his dialect poems, published by the Century Company, of New York, he has given to the world characteristics of the negro which are as true to life as possible. It was he who attracted widespread attention outside the South to *the fidelity and loyalty of the slave to "old marster," and to the love of the whites for the faithful old servant of bygone days* [my emphasis, L.S.]. Russell died at the age of twenty-six years, but his writings—with those of Thomas Nelson Page, "Uncle Remus," and others who have taken up the pen to portray "old times down South"—tell the true status of master and slave before the war, and explain the meaning of [black servant] Uncle Dan, when he is heard to sing:

No mo' will I hunt for de 'possum an' de coon,
Or set about dat sweet ole cabin doh,
For de cruel war has ruined my happy Southern home,
An' I never specks to see de like no mo'.[138] — POLK MILLER, LETTER TO *CONFEDERATE VETERAN* MAGAZINE

BLACK SERVANT BOY SAVES CHURCH FROM DESTRUCTION

☛ *Confederate Veteran* is pleased to present herewith several pictures of interesting points in and about [Charleston, South Carolina,] the "City by the Sea." Among these is St. Philip's Church, whose early history is identical with that of the far-famed St. Michael's, and dates back as far as 1681. In that year a wooden building was erected there, the parish being designated St. Philip's. In 1711 the congregation built a new church "of brick," as the legal permit specifies, on the east side of Church Street, between Queen and Cumberland Streets. This was regarded as one of the finest churches in America. It was destroyed by fire in February, 1835. An incident in the burning of this magnificent building—the most valuable, historically, in Charleston, perhaps in the whole South—gave the motif for the historic poem called "How He Saved St. Michael's," in which *the hero, a negro boy who was a slave, saved the church from destruction by climbing on to its steeple and plucking therefrom a firebrand which had alighted there. For this act of bravery he received his freedom* [my emphasis, L.S.].[139] — CONFEDERATE VETERAN MAGAZINE

St. Philip's Church.

BLACK CONFEDERATE ON THE START OF LINCOLN'S WAR

☛ Jes' set down dar, Marse Charley, on dat ole time har cloth char,
Hit's mighty saf' an' easy, 'twas a present from yo' Mar [white mistress].
Bles' heaben for her goodness, caze she was mos' kine to me—
Her face was like a angel, an' her eyes was like de sea,
So blue an' deep. You could not fine de bottom ob dem eyes,
Dey look like some 'eflection ob de Savior from de skies.
Her words was like dat manna dat de anshunt Isrulites
Foun' on de mornin' pastur, what de angels spread o' nights.
O, she was good to all ob us, white fokes an' niggers too,
An' nar a sole libbed on dis place dat didn't lub Miss Sue.
"Ole Miss" we called her in dem days. We lubbed to say "Ole Miss,"
Hit was a sign ob 'fection, jes' de same thing as a kiss.
I members well dat lone, sad day when she took sick an' died,
I went down in de lowgroun' pines an' cried, an' cried, an' cried.
De sweetes' life had lef' dis lan', de sweetes' voice was still;
De ole plantation changed dat day, an' 'neber, neber will
Be like hit ust er be. Set down Marse Charley on de char.
I hope you is a righteous chile ob yo' sweet, righteous Mar.
You want me to tell you ob de time when young Marse Ran' got kilt?
'Twas awful hard to bar Sar, but 'twas what de good Lord wilt.
Hit 'tis a sadsome story, but I'll tell you ef I can—
My memory is gwine fas', but I cuarn't forgit Marse Ran',
Nor how he libbed, an' lubbed, an' laffed, an' rid, an' fit, an' died;
Now how I prayed so long dat day, an' when I quit I cried.
Hit 'twas a turble battle, but we fit hit as we mout,
I b'lieb hit was de hardes' fight dat in de war we fout.

But ef I'm gwine to tell you den I spec' I'de bes' begin
Wid when we yeard about de war fo' he an' I went in.
In ole Amelia, we was here, when news dar comes to us
About de war arisin', an' I think 'twas May de fus'
In eighteen hundud sixty one an' Nannie Domino.
Dat was de year de lowgroun's had de dreadful oberflo'.
De corn crap hit 'twas ruint, an' de Appomattox riz
Untwell hit cotched de cow pen an' drowndid our bes' cow, Liz.
De taters warn't no good dat year, an' wheat was mighty bad—
Hit seemed we had de wustes' luck dat we had eber had.
I don't kno' much 'bout who got mad, or what dey got mad for,
But bofe sides got to sassin', an' dat sassin' 'fotched de wor.
I'se yeard sence den dat 'ligion is mos' gin'rally de cause
Ob all dis rumpass an' a killin' what we call de wors,
But in dis case 'twas diffrunt an' de niggers made de muss
Dat brung a tribulation an' a fightin' on to us.
De Yankees sade dey's suf'frin', an' we'll sot de niggers free.
De Cornfed [Confederate] sade, you shet up, an' jes' let our niggers be.
De niggers warn't complainin' an' dey lubbed de cabin life,
In dat ole time of comfort for de man an' chile an' wife.
De vict'als was abundant, an' our close was spic an' span,
An' den we libbed jes' like we would in dis bles' Suddern Lan'.
Wid watermillions ripe an' sweet down on de ice house flo',
An' possums in de simmon trees, what else did we want mo'?
De niggers warn't complainin', an' dey neber sade a word
About a bein' unhappy Sar, as eber I is yeard.
De gempman was de marster, but de gempman was our frien'.
An' we didn't want dat frien'ship to bust up Sar, an' to en'.
But startin' to Virginny, whar we sade dey should not come
To gib us any trouble in our ole Virginny home,
We got to fight de battles ob de Souf Cornfidrit [Confederate] wars,
An' dat's 'bout all I knows Sar, in de matter ob hits cause.
But you ought'r seen our fokes den when dey foun' de news was true
Dat 'vasion was a comin' Sar. De air was black an' blue.
I neber yeard sich langwidge from ole marster fo' dat day;
He cuarried on in what seemed like a mos' unchristian way.
I b'lieb 'cept for dat 'ligion dat hilt holt on mos' on us
He would a broke completely an' los' hesef' an' cuss.
Ezactly like de men de ladies too got mad you kno',
An' sade so much a quar'lin' dat you almos' thought dey swo'.
De chilluns eben dey got mad an' made deir leetle fuss
You scace could fine a single sole dat wasn't fit to cuss.
De gempmen jined de comp'nies, an' mos' eb'ry single man
In ole Amelia county an' her sister Powhatan
Was jinin' an' a gwine, I clar, untwell when dey was done,
Ob all de men in dese here parts dey hardly lef' a one
To take care ob de place, or ten' a crap, or blow a horn.
Dey was mo' scacer den a measly nubbin' in our corn.
Yo' Pa he jined de Richmon' Blues, an' den my young Marse Ran',
He jined de hoss-back troop dey raised across in Powhatan.
Deir captin was Marse Charley Ole—a good one to be sho',
An' deir leftenant was, you kno', Mis' Hobson' young son Joe.
De sargent was Marse Harty, Mister Willyum Hair' son's son.

An' Marse Joe Gibbs, our mess's cook, he was anodder one.
Den dar was young Marse Lewis Harvie, an' Marse Jimmie Werf—
As fine a lot ob cabilmen [cavelrymen] as rid upon dis erf.
In dis here worl' no braver men no wars ain't neber see,
An' all de men ob dat ole troop was brave as dey could be!
Dey lubbed to git to fightin' as mos' fokes do lub to eat,
An' dey didn't hab no notion 'bout a time for a retreat.
When dat ole troop got started dey was gwine some whar dat day,
An' 'twarn't no use for Yankees to git crosswise in de way,
For dey was gwine I tell you, gwine a bubblin, to dat spot
Like gravy in a skillit dat ole Nat had made red hot.
Dar warn't no way to hender dat ole resky Powitan troop;
You ought'r seen 'em chargin', an' you ought'r yeard 'em whoop.
'Twas like a great big pac' ob houn's a openin' wid deir cry
Behin' a fox a runnin', but who knowed he had to die.
Marse Ran' he rid de sorrel colt, an' I, I rid ole Nade,
An' way we went one day to whar de war would be dey sade.
But fus' we marched to Richmon' town, an' dat was only fun,
Becaze, you kno', de time for fightin' hadn't as yit begun.
But hit was comin' slo'ly, an' dat sojer play didn't las'
For mo'n a week or month befo' de mis'ry come to pas'.
In Richmon' hit was nelegent. De vict'als was de bes',
An' not a thing had we to do but jes' to eat an' res',
Dey mounted guard a mornin', an' had eb'nin' dress perade,
All dressed up in deir finery an' lots ob golden braid.
De ladies come mos' all de time to see de sojer boys,
An' life in camp was jes' a great big passel full ob joys.
So dey was geth'rin an' geth'rin' untwell dar come a day
When buglers blowed de bugles an' we had to march away.
De ban's dey sot to playin', an' de drums begun to beat,
De cannons rumbled loudly 'long on wide, rock paved Broad street,
De banners was a flyin', an' de sojers look so glad,
Dat we begun to feel dat war was what we wished we had.
De sight we made was splendid, an' de hosses mos' kep' step,
An' ladies waved deir kerchiefs, an' smiled, an' laffed, an' wep'.
An' some was gwine to glory, Sar, an' some was gwine to die,
An' soon dem praisin', smilin' ladies dar was gwine to cry.
Our gin'ral was de gin'ral dat mos' eb'rybody love.
He was so han'some dat he mout a drapped down from above,
A angel gone to sojerin' upon dis sorry worl',
But dat he lubbed to be a singin', chirpy as a girl.
He'd sing away a mornin', an' he'd sing de same at night,
Nare shadder crossed his countenance, dat face was always bright.
You'se yeard ob him Marse Charley, Gin'ral [Jeb] Stuart was de man,
De fines' calvry gin'ral dat we had in all de lan'.
I hear him now a singin' 'bout de ole hoss dat was gray,
A comin' out a wildernes' an 'warn't gwine long to stay.
I almos' see dem golden spurs he wore upon his boots,
An' graceful wabin' ob his han' tow'ds ole Sweeney Toots,
His drab, saft hat an' feadder cotched up wid a star ob gole
Ole Marster [God] when he made dat gin'ral sho'ly broke de mole.[140] —
SERVANT "UNCLE ISAAC", SERVED UNDER CONFEDERATE
GEN. JAMES EWELL BROWN "JEB" STUART

DO YOU REMEMBER?—AN OLD TIME DARKY

☛ Did you ever think how little we live in the present? It is almost appalling when we consider that the present is only an instant, and that constantly we are being either hurled into the future or living in the past. Some say we should keep straight ahead, and never look back; but even if our past has been unprofitable and mean it is well to look back profiting by our experience; then when it has been bright, happy, full of precious memories, how much of the sweet and good of life we should miss were we deprived of the power of reviewing these receding years, with their joys and sorrows intermingled. In no people is this power of recollection more clearly or more beautifully developed than in our old-time slavery darkies. Events that with us would pass unnoticed are with them memorable. From them they reckon time; of them they tell their children with pride and satisfaction.

I was sitting by the bedside of a sick friend who was just convalescent when an old negro woman appeared on the scene. "Good mornin'," she said, as she approached the bed. "Is you sick?"

"I am not well," was the reply.

"Y-e-s-'m. Is you bin sick long?"

"For several weeks," said my friend.

"Y-e-s-'m. Something like cholera morbus?"

"No, I have had fever, which has impaired the action of my heart, and am now suffering from heart depression," said my invalid, beginning to be somewhat amused.

"Well, honey, my ole moster usted ter be pestered wid dat very same thing," she said, respectfully seating herself at some distance, and continuing: "You knowed my ole moster? He was well knowed all round dis here country. He was a good man, my ole moster wuz—used ter think er heap o' his niggers, an' treat 'em good, too. I tell you, honey, we didn't wan't fer nothin'—had plenty to eat and plenty to wear. We had good houses, and our doctor bills all paid. O, I'll tell you, honey, I wuz the white folkses' pet nigger baby in my time, I wuz! My ole mistis jes' taught me how to work till I could do anything. But things is changed now, and, honey, dis is de hardest resperence I is ebber had. No halfway white folks didn't raise me—no, ma'am, dey didn'!"

"Who was your master?" my friend at last ventured to ask.

"Why, honey, my ole moster wuz ole Gen. Tom Brown, an' he lived right out here 'bout er mile an' a half, whar de orphan 'sylum is now."

"That is where my father took refuge with his family during the war. Do you remember Col. Scott?" asked my friend, becoming more interested in the queer old darky.

"Why, l-a-w y-e-s, c-h-i-l-e. I 'members jes' as well dat fine black horse he give Miss Bobbie, when he lef our house!"

"Then perhaps you remember me, as little Sarah Scott?"

Ellen Butler, former black servant, Beaumont, Texas, 1937.

"Law, honey, is dat you?" falling down upon her knees beside the bed. "I is had you in my arms many an' many a time, and kissed your little fat hands, and baked you patties. W-e-l-l, dis here is a treat ter me, chillun, show! Dis is sorter like a Christmas present! Fore God, I's glad I happened round! Honey, does you 'member ole Uncle Matt Bradshaw, de carriage driber? Why, he wuz jes' as polite as a basket o' chips. Kin you ricollect dem parrots an' dem cedar buckets right ober yonder in de cellar filled wid butter an' eggs an' zerbs, an' all de jellies and pickles and cordial and wines? Why law, chile, you ain't got nothin' up an' down dese streets I ain't seed, and dese here town niggers can't fool me. We had hen houses all lathered good nuff fer anybody ter stay in, but I'll tel you, honey, things is disappearin'. Why, we is thowed away more'n dey ebber had. Our dinner tables use ter look better dan de party tables do now. Dey jes' think now ole-time niggers don't know nothin' jes' cause dey can't read an' write, but dis is one thing I does know: de niggers now ain't got no manners like de ole-timers, an' you don't never see none o' de ole-timers in jail. Niggers whut's bein' brought up now wuz brought up by air, dey wuz! Dey ain't had no raisin'. De buzzards laid 'em, an' de sun hatched 'em, dey did. I'll tell you honey, plenty o' dese here folkses say de sun don't shine on 'em, but chile, de sun shines on me cause I jes' lays right on de white folks' hips, an' dey is 'bliged to carry me. I say, honey, you ain't got a single child as pretty as you. Miss Liz ain't neither. Miss Liz wuz de puttiest bride dat ebber wuz in dis here town. She looked jes' like er angel drapped down from heaven. When Miss Liz moved way off somewhar to live I went to cook for her. I stayed right smart little time, but couldn't stand it no longer, so I jes' told 'em I had come back to de ole home agin.

Mrs. Lulu B. Epperson.

"Miss Liz had seed a lot o' trouble and had a heap o' chillun, and she wuz all broke up, but I told her jes' to pick up her heart and de good Lord would help her. Why, whar Miss Liz went to live, honey, I never seed a lady dat didn't have somethin' de matter wid her system, but I tell you, chile, whar dey drawed up water in a little candy bucket dat wus so hard dat it eat up de tin and de zinc, it wuz jes' bound to eat up dar insides, but I ain't goin' to talk much, cause I'll cry. I's done forgot now dat I am here to git a little washin' to do; dem good ole days is gone, and I don't know whar we is all a comin' to. *My mistus show loved her servants* [all emphasis, L.S.]. Why, I tell you, honey, she wouldn't let Aunt Sooky drink brown sugar in nothin' she eat, she wouldn't! I don't know what dey is all a comin' to, but I is ready for de chariot to swing low an' carry me home whenever the good Lord gits ready. All my people is gone 'cept one chile, an' he is married, livin' way off yonder. My hair is gittin' gray, and I know my time's most out."

"But," my friend interrupted, "you must not talk so sad. You are good for a long time yet, and my daughter wants a good cook. How would you like to go and live with her?"

"Well, I would like that, show! I is comin' to see' you ag'in, but I'll tell you, honey, ef you want me to cook good things you musn't give me nothin' to cook, cause I can't cook dat. Dis here is a treat to me, chillun, show! sorter like a Chrismus present!"[141] — LULU B. EPPERSON

WHITE & BLACK UNDER THE OLD REGIME

☛ . . . *When fond memory carries me back to my childhood's happy days, these colored friends on the old plantation occupy a very important place.* I recall the commodious carriage, the bay horses, and old Uncle Abram seated on the driver's seat to take us, the children, through the beautiful woods, to make a visit to the old "maumers" down on the plantation. Our mother taught us to respect age in whatever position we found it, and we always called the older [black] women "maumers" as marks of respect due their years. How dear these scenes are to us even now!

Every slave family possessed a garden, truck patch, chicken house and a lot of hens, and, from these sources, always had something nice to present to us, their young "misses." We cherished these humble presents, peanuts, fresh eggs, and the like, as though they were of intrinsic value. Their little cottages were arranged so as to form streets. After making the round of visits, not slighting any, but going in to see every one at home, sitting and chatting with all, we usually finished our calls at Uncle Sam's house. *He was the foreman on the plantation, and had a more pretentious home. His wife, maum Flora, would entertain us most royally with bread and milk under the grand old oaks that sheltered the space around the door. These two humble friends would express much sincere delight at our accepting their generous hospitality.* I have spent many happy hours with these good people in the long ago. The old [black] man [Uncle Sam] was a Methodist preacher, and close by his house stood a neat little building, in which he gathered all the children on Sunday morning to teach them their duty to God and man. Later in the day the adults assembled for worship. Frequently a visiting preacher would assist Uncle Sam in ministering to these people on a Sunday. The old man could read the Bible, but his education did not extend much beyond that and weighing the cotton as it was gathered from the fields, and putting down the weights for my father's inspection. *Uncle Sam was, I believe, a good Christian man, and these people looked up to him with almost reverence. My father was a kind, indulgent master, and I think I have never in the world met with happier people than were these simple uneducated blacks* [all emphasis, L.S.] . . .[142] — VICTORIA V. CLAYTON

FIRST ABOLITIONIST U.S. PRESIDENTIAL CANDIDATE WAS A SOUTHERNER

The Weeden home, Huntsville, Alabama.

☛ The handsome old residence at Huntsville, Alabama, now owned by Miss [Maria] Howard Weeden, the author of *Shadows on the Wall*, has a history. It was built by [Kentuckian] Mr. James G. Birney [born in 1792] who was then a resident of that city, and who was *the first abolition candidate for President of the United States*.[143] He was a contemporary of [Alabama] Gov. C. C. Clay [Clement Comer Clay], Judge Hopkins, Judge Kelley, and others of that day.

... At that period [that is, the antebellum period] of our national life slavery was not considered morally indefensible, but was regarded as right and warranted by Scripture, *and while so regarded by these people they yet desired to do away with it gradually.*

Mr. Birney was himself the owner of slaves at Huntsville, but sold them and went to Ohio, where for the violation of the fugitive slave law he was indicted, and *Gov. Salmon P. Chase, the Secretary of the Treasury in Mr. Lincoln's Cabinet, gained a national reputation in his defense* [all emphasis, L.S.].[144] — CONFEDERATE VETERAN MAGAZINE

AMONG JEFFERSON DAVIS' PERSONAL BELONGINGS ...

☛ [In early 1899, Mrs. Varina Jefferson Davis, wife of the late Confederate President, bequeathed "twenty-one cases and packages" of containing some of her husband's "dearest" personal items to the Louisiana Historical Association. Among the many sacred articles packed in "this noble gift" were President Davis'] "dress coat, vest, pants, white gloves, black necktie, pair of shoes, pair of slippers, two pairs of socks worn by Jefferson Davis, last hat (derby) worn by him, envelope full of his hair, gold watch worn by him at the battle of Monterey, a gold-headed cane, a carved cane, field glasses—all used by him; a cup and saucer used by him in prison at Fortress Monroe; his paper weight; . . . [and] *a pen receptacle, made by his old slave, which article he kept on his desk,* . . . [and] *an engraving of the bust of Albert Sidney Johnston, in a frame made by Jefferson Davis' old slave, Robert Brown* [my emphasis, L.S.] . . ."[145] — GEN. J. A. CHALARON, NEW ORLEANS, LA.

Confederate President Jefferson Davis.

MORE PROOF THAT UNION SOLDIERS OWNED SLAVES

☛ [Written by a Yankee veteran:] The First Regiment, Eastern Shore Maryland Volunteer Infantry [U.S.], was organized at Cambridge, Dorchester County, Md., in the fall of 1861, and was commanded by James Wallace, Esq., an attorney at law and farmer. *He owned nine slaves, and had some of them in camp with him as servants.* Capt. John R. Keene, of Company C, also had slaves with him, *his father being the owner of about sixty. Other officers of this regiment had slaves in camp with them.* The regiment was organized for home service—at least many of the men were enlisted with this understanding, so that when ordered out of the State into the two counties of Eastern Virginia there was much dissatisfaction. Company A (Capt. John C. Henry, of Cambridge) was mustered out of the Federal [Union] service, and many then went South and enlisted in what I believe was the First Maryland Volunteer Infantry of the Confederate army. In the battle of Gettysburg we met and fought this regiment and wounded and captured one of our old men of Company A, who informed us that Capt. Henry and several of our old comrades were directly in our front fighting us. This on the Federal right

Maj. Luzerne Todd of Co. D, 23rd New York Infantry Regiment posing with one of the many black slaves who served in the Union army.

near the base of Culp's Hill. Previously Company B, when ordered into Delaware, had laid down their guns and refused to do service outside the State, but at Gettysburg they served loyally. Company K, Capt. Littleton Long, also had trouble, and the records show that a large majority of the company was dishonorably discharged. The regiment was never treated by the Federal government as were other Northern regiments. It was held back. *There were so many slaveholders in the command that the enlistment of their servants during the absence of the owners from home, and consequent loss of service, caused great dissatisfaction. The slaves of these loyal men, who lost their property while away from home fighting for the Union, were never paid for, though a record of each slave is kept at the county seats of Eastern Maryland. The* [U.S.] *government had agreed to respect the right of property in slaves on the part of owners who remained loyal to the Union, but nevertheless while away from home fighting for the Union these same slaves were enlisted and freed* [all emphasis, L.S.]. I suppose there were similar experiences in regiments of other border States.

Our regiment served three years, and was honorably discharged, many of the men "veteranizing" into the Eleventh Maryland Volunteer Infantry.[146] — JOHN E. RASTALL, ADJUTANT 1ST REGIMENT, EASTERN SHORE MARYLAND VOLUNTEER INFANTRY, U.S.

NINETY BLACK CONFEDERATES RECEIVING MILITARY PENSIONS WITHIN A FIVE-MILE RADIUS

☞ In sending my renewal for the *Confederate Veteran* I am proud of the opportunity to express full indorsement of your leader in the December number on national dignity and Confederate honor, every line of which rings of the true metal. Of pensions to the truly meritorious (although I still believe the North misguided in coercing the South), I have no protest to offer. But the dispensing of such is evidently very lax. *I am reliably informed that over ninety negroes within a radius of five miles of this place are on the pension roll, and I doubt that half a dozen of the number are disabled in any particular* [my emphasis, L.S.].[147] — DR. H. W. HILL, MOORESEVILLE, ALA.

VICE PRESIDENT STEPHENS' BLACK SERVANTS MOURN HIS DEPARTURE & HIDE HIS WHEREABOUTS FROM YANKS

☞ [In November 1864, after hurriedly packing a few important personal items, Confederate Vice President Alexander H. Stephens was quickly ushered from his home by a friend, Confederate soldier Robert Reed, at the announcement that some of [Union Gen. William T.] Sherman's men were on their way to his home, Liberty Hall, to arrest and seize him.]

The slaves had gathered in the hallway, and as Mr. Stephens came down the steps, beaver on, valise in hand, pitiful sobs broke from the dusky group. Mr. Stephens lifted his hand, but no words came.

"O, my Marster!" old Silas clasped him in his arms, and those were the only articulate words that rose above the sobs of a broken-hearted circle. No potentate e'er received richer homage than the tears that fell on his hands and feet.

"Silas," Mr. Stephens laid his hand on the bowed gray head, "you and Ned bring the homespun and jeans, and let me give it out. You will find the thread and buttons too. Go with them, Aunt Chloe, and show Silas and Ned where the things are. Aunt Chloe, bring the flannel also; you may need it before I get back to you." At this intimation of a prolonged absence, the weeping broke out afresh.

The three returned with full arms, and as a patriarch bidding farewell to his household, he divided among them his possessions. There was many a low-spoken "Bless you, my marster!" as turbaned mammies received the year's apparel for them and theirs; and pickaninnies peeped from behind their mothers' skirts to see the bright new cloth.

"Silas, you have the smokehouse key; give them their weekly rations as usual. Mr. Allen will let you have all you need at the store."

[Just then Reed declared:] "Mr. Stephens, we must be many miles from here by sunset." In the young soldier's voice rang a note of sympathy that every slave's quick ear caught and understood. With a kindred touch, they turned to him: "De Lord bless you, Mars Robert, fer takin' our good marster from de Yankees!"

"Yes, Reed, you are right; we must go. But I hate to leave these people: I hate to leave them. They have been so true to me." He was o'ermastered for a moment, and the brave man wept. Gently Robert Reed took his arm and led him toward the door; and had it been the dead body of their master being borne forever from their sight, more distressed mourning would not have filled the hall. They followed him

At the time of this photo, circa 1875, former Confederate Vice President Alexander H. Stephens was a popular U.S. politician. The always frail American statesman is pictured here being assisted by an unnamed former black servant. Stephens, like nearly all other 19th-Century white Southerners, loved and respected Southern blacks and was loved and respected by them in return—as the accompanying article demonstrates.

to the door, down the steps, to the front gate; watched him board the train; watched till the train flashed beyond vision; then turned back, a sad procession, to the deserted hall.

It was just about sunset when a line of [Yankee] horsemen rode up before Liberty Hall. "Here! open the gate!" yelled one to an old negro woman crossing the yard.

"Good ev'nin', sah," low curtsied the dame. "Is yer huntin' fer anybody?"

"Yes; we are hunting for your owner, Alexander Stephens."

"Well, I declar', sah; I'se mighty sorry. Marster's done gone out fer ter take a little ride. Will yer light, sah, tell he come home?"

"Yes, old woman; you just open the door, and we'll make ourselves at home. See here, we want a rousing good supper."

In less than an hour Aunt Chloe stood back of the captain's chair, waiter in hand, as she was wont to stand behind "Mars Elick" [that is, Master Alick, Stephens' nickname] while he took his solitary tea. Jocular remarks were passed upon the scarcity of forks and spoons, more intelligible to their sable hostess than her self-invited guests imagined.

"Yes, sah," she explained deferentially; "Mars Elick ain't, fer common, had so much comp'ny, an' we ain't zackly pr'ared. Jes' him an' us is here mos' de time."

Old Silas chuckled behind the pantry door as he thought of a hollow log filled with [their] silver [hidden] away down in the woods. He plucked at Chloe's sleeve as she passed through for hot cakes: "What's dat you tole 'em? What de Lord gwine say ter you [on Judgement Day]?"

"Humph! You reckon de Lord hold me 'sponsible fer dat? No sah, nigger. De Lord knows who's I'm dealin' wid. He knows Ise jes' he'pin' Mars Elick; no lie fer him ain't gwine ter count."[148] — JULIA B. REED

ONE THOUSAND CONFEDERATE "NEGRO LABARORS"

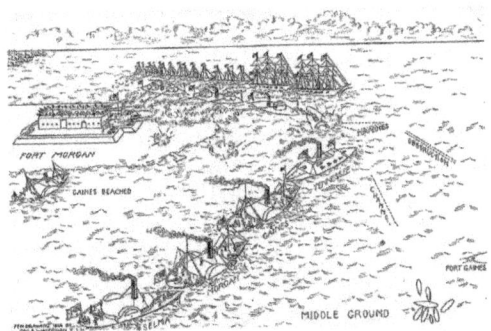

Pen drawing of the Battle of Mobile Bay, August 5, 1864, by George S. Waterman, C.S.N.

☞ . . . I shall always remember the wonderful engineering lavished upon the defenses of Mobile. There were three continuous lines of earthworks around the city. The first was constructed by Capt. C. T. Lieurner in 1862 at an average distance of three miles out from the main streets, with fifteen redoubts; and when Vicksburg fell, in 1863, Mobile felt that her day was coming, and [Confederate] Gen. Danville Leadbetter built the second line of works, nearer the city—in fact, running through the suburbs and inclosing sixteen redoubts; then, in 1864, the third line was projected by [Confederate] Lieut. Col. V. Sheliha about midway between the two lines already built, and it included nineteen heavy bastioned forts and eight redoubts. So that Mobile had as bulwarks fifty-eight forts and redoubts, with connecting breastworks. The parapets of the forts were from fifteen to twenty-five feet thick, and ditches through which tide water flowed about twenty feet deep and thirty feet wide—rendering the defenses so formidable that it had been estimated a garrison of ten thousand effective men could hold the city six months against a besieging army of forty thousand. It was garrisoned by about nine thousand men, including the troops on the east side of the bay and *a thousand negro laborers* [my emphasis, L.S.] subject to the command of the engineers. During the summer of 1864 [Confederate] Maj. Gen. Franklin K. Gardner was in charge, and he was later succeeded by [Confederate] Gen. Dabney H. Maury. Then, in the fall, [Confederate] Lieut. Gen. Dick Taylor commanded the entire department until the end.[149] — GEORGE S. WATERMAN, CONFEDERATE STATES NAVY

HOW COUNTLESS WHITE CONFEDERATE SOLDIERS SURVIVED THE WAR

☛ Benjamin Franklin White was born in New Berne, North Carolina, and finished his education at the Western Military Institute, at Nashville, Tennessee. Immediately after the declaration of war, in May, 1861, he resigned his position as Assistant Secretary of the Memphis Gas Company and raised a company of infantry, the Tennessee Guards, by whom he was elected captain. This company left Memphis in [Confederate] Col. Neely's Regiment, of [Confederate] General [Gideon] Pillow's command. After serving in the infantry for some time, Capt. White joined the cavalry under [Confederate] Gen. [Nathan Bedford] Forrest, who detailed him to raise a company of light artillery. This he did, and commanded it until the battle of Chickamauga, when he was promoted on the field and given command of a battalion of artillery in [Confederate] Gen. [Joseph] Wheeler's Cavalry. Capt. White took part in every fight in which his company was engaged, but was never wounded, though he had several horses shot under him and numerous bullet holes made in his clothes. He was captured at the battle of Murfreesboro, but was so ill from rheumatism that he was placed in a private house under guard. From this place, *with the aid of his faithful negro servant* [my emphasis, L.S.] he made his escape.[150] — CONFEDERATE VETERAN MAGAZINE

Benjamin F. White.

AFFECTION NOT OWNERSHIP

☛ The civilization of the ancient regime in the South was a picturesque civilization. A feudalism there was, it is true, and projected into the nineteenth century, but a feudalism stripped of those conditions, which, making it cruel, had exiled it from the older countries, and now so modified by that spirit of gentleness which makes everything great that it furnished the unique opportunity for that life in the Southern States which charmed all who touched it. Ruling in this feudalism, *the Southern people were a refined and hospitable people, and their land was quiet, content, and happy.* Whether then it were right or wrong this feudalism produced that which is gone and may never return, a picturesque life filled with romance and peace. In those days there was a knight errantry as gallant and as true as when the lady's glove was caught in the steel headgear of the cavalier, and the winning graces of the lady were a stateliness of generous courtesy that compelled a willing respect as it made plain a genuine cordiality of welcome hospitality. And when those days were departed, they had well-nigh buried the cavaliers. Their generation was also of the past. Their social system and their notion of the sovereignty of government they believed ideal. But whether or no that was true, what fetched so beautiful a life could not then have been all wrong.

Touch those times and you have touched a high impulse of humanity. Go back to them and you breathe in an atmosphere of gentle refinement. Few can recall a fair cheek then mantled with shame, and rare was the man, the gentleman, who at sometime had not found an inspiration to chivalry in the gentle character and sweet purity of the Southern maiden. Like the music of birds, we believe, was the life in the Southland.

There were vassals [servants], but the vassal was loved by the lord of the manor. The lady so refined and gentle that the caste feeling was forgotten, met and touched and spoke to those who must come and go at her bidding in such manifest friendship that the tie which bound them one to the other was that of affection rather than that of ownership. On the plantation there was an esprit du corps which was as strong among the one caste as among the other. This feudalism, which, in large part made the South characteristically the South, was a poetic thing, without tyranny, and working no wrong, save where men were bad, and bad men will be, and bad men will disturb any relationship. Perhaps, doubtless the institution of slavery was an error lingering in the land. Its time of correction had not come, and in so far as that was true it was still doing a good work. But was it an error? *The rationale of history rather persuades us to believe it a factor in a progressing civilization, disappearing when its task was done.*[151] Regard it as you will, *it was, in these days of which we think, a factor in the process of development of the [black] people, who are made the subject of much pity, pity which they did not either seek or appreciate, and for which they knew no occasion. Strange as this may appear, it is true. It had taken them out of the crassest moral turpitude, separated them from barbarism, and placed them in the school of civilization, with all its possibilities of destiny before them. It may have been one of the "growing pains" of humanity's upward struggle. But, be it what it may, it gave the slave his opportunity now in full fruition, and it was a potent factor in the old life of the South* [all emphasis, L. S.].[152] — WILLIAM DUDLEY POWERS

In early America black children were often referred to as pickaninnies. Modern Left-wing presentists have decided this word is "offensive." But its early Spanish roots prove otherwise. Of mid 17th-Century origins (circa 1653), pickaninny derives from the Old Catalan word *pequenino*, meaning "very little."

A CONFEDERATE SOLDIER'S LOVE FOR HIS BLACK SERVANTS
☞ My Dear Mother: Ed Friend will leave in the morning for Athens on furlough. I did not know until a few minutes ago that he was going,

therefore my letter will be short. I will keep Clara supplied with money. Do not have any uneasiness on her account; I will be her guardian.... Our rations are very short indeed, but I am willing to live on acorns for seven years or longer to gain my freedom and independence. Our army is in fine health and in good spirits, and we are determined, with the help of God, to be free [of the North's Left-wing tyranny]. God alone can chastise us. We adopt for our motto an old saying of one of the Revolutionary fathers of '76 that "Resistance to tyrants is obedience to God." I hope the people of Athens will not despair or give up. You must encourage the desponding and vacillating; tell them to trust to our valor and to God. You must write to me whenever you can. Tell grandma to write. *Give my love to all the children and servants. Tell* [our servants] *Jack and Cesar that my confidence in them is unbounded, and I expect them to take care of everything.* I want some *of Aunt 'Bitha's bread* [my emphasis, L.S.]. Your affectionate son, Rob.[153] — CONFEDERATE MAJOR ROBERT DONNELL, FROM A LETTER DATED AUGUST 5, 1863, AT CHATTANOOGA, TENN.

BLACK SERVANT PROTECTS WHITES FROM YANKEES

☛ In the April *Confederate Veteran* is mentioned the death of [Confederate] Capt. Nathan S. Boone, of [Confederate] Gen. [Nathan Bedford] Forrest's escort. Forrest fought Wilson's raiders stubbornly at an old Baptist church called Ebenezer (since called the battle of Ebenezer), between Maplesville and Plantersville, Alabama. They made the next stand in Selma, where there were breastworks, and another battle was fought. The Confederates were scattered, and the Yankees came on down as far as Cahaba. We lived on the main road leading from Cahaba to Linden, Ala. About dark, one of my neighbors notified me to be on my guard, as the Yankees would certainly be there that night. I was alone except for my five sleeping little ones and *an old* [black] *servant who had volunteered to do all in his power to protect us* [my emphasis, L.S.]. I placed lighted lamps in the rooms, and seated myself on the front porch to wait. About eleven o'clock I heard the clatter of horses' feet crossing the bridge, the clanking and jingling of sabers and spurs, and quickly they were at the gate. With the first "Halloo" my heart gave a bound, for I knew they were our men. It was Capt. Boone who addressed me: "Well, madam, are you frightened to death?" I replied: "No, sir; but I am so glad that you are not Yankees. Was Gen. Forrest killed? We heard today that he received a severe saber cut over the left ear." He said: "No, madam; Gen. Forrest was well this evening. I am the man who has the saber cut." His head was bound in a large towel. Soon a courier came inquiring for Gen. Forrest's horse that was wounded and had been ordered to my

Horace Overstreet, former black servant, Beaumont, Texas, 1937.

house. I told him we had sent the horse to the house of a neighbor, and I called a negro to accompany him there. When they reached the house the horse had been sent farther for safe-keeping, and to this day I had never heard of the horse or the courier or the captain of Gen. Forrest's escort until the interesting article appeared in the *Veteran*. Gen. Forrest left a glove at Plantersville, and it is now in possession of Mr. Perry McGhee, Stanton, Ala.[154] — MRS. MARY A. HAMMER, MAYHEW, MISS.

MONUMENT TO SOUTHERN SLAVES AT FORT MILL, SOUTH CAROLINA

☛ Before the war Fort Mill was a mere railway station in the northeast corner of York County, South Carolina. The depot, in a depression, was contiguous to a smithy, a store, and three or four residences of neighboring planters on adjacent hills. In this little hamlet during the fall of 1860 the prominent young men of the community organized, it is believed, the first company in the South enlisted for the vindication of the States. This company was offered to the State, but on account of some technicality was not accepted. Afterwards John M. White, its captain, went to Montgomery, Alabama, and offered his company to the Confederate authorities in that city, but the same technicality prevailed. It was not long, however, before these same young men were forming and commanding companies that did excellent service in four years of bloodiest war.

Monument to "Faithful Slaves," Fort Mill, South Carolina.

On the historic ground where this first company mustered now stand three monuments in a small triangular park. One commemorates the heroes of the civil war; another, the women of the Confederacy; and the third, the faithful slaves of the war times. Much of the credit of erection is due to Capt. Samuel Elliott White, brother of Capt. John M. White, commander of the first company, who was ably and willingly aided by the Spratts, L. N. Culp, Rev. James H. Thornwell, and many others.

. . . [The Monument to Faithful Slaves is described as follows:] Four steps of masonry support a marble pedestal, on which is a square shaft for inscriptions.

On the south side is inscribed:

1860.
Dedicated to
The faithful Slaves
who, loyal to a sacred trust,

Toiled for the support
of the army with matchless
Devotion, and with sterling
Fidelity guarded our defenseless
Homes, women, and children during
the struggle for the principles
of our "Confederate States of America."
1865.

On the east side, in a receding panel, appears a log under a shade tree, whereon rests one of the faithful slaves, his hat on the ground, shirt open in front, with a scythe and at rest. Before him are shocks of grain. On the north side is the following:

1895.
Erected by Samuel E. White,
in grateful memory of earlier
days, with the approval of the
Jefferson Davis Memorial Association.

There are added names of some faithful slaves.
On the west side, in a receding panel, appears a farmer's mansion, and on the front steps sits an old black mammy with a white child in her arms, both of whom are in loving embrace, while in the foreground are the baby's wagon and other playthings. Above this square shaft is a tall obelisk of pure white marble.[155] — A COMRADE OF CAMP 920, U.C.V.

MORE EVIDENCE OF THE BLACK CONFEDERATE

☞ [Confederate] Gen. [Leonidas] Polk being ordered to assume command of the Mississippi Department, with headquarters at Demopolis, Alabama, we bade farewell to the Army of Tennessee, whose fortunes we had followed so many months. Preparatory to locating at Demopolis, we were some weeks at Enterprise, Mississippi, a station on the Mobile and Ohio Railroad, distant some thirty or forty miles south of Meridian, Miss., where the railroad crosses leading from Jackson eastward to Selma. A military family attached to a general officer is generally composed of one or more messes, who for convenience's sake appoint one of the mess the custodian of cash funds, who also acts as caterer for all concerned. *My own particular mess was composed of Lieut. William M. Polk, youngest son of the Lieut. Gen. commanding, who had been a cadet with me at the Virginia Military Institute, and Lieut. Sam Donelson, of Nashville, Tennessee. I owned a colored boy, Tom, of my own age, who had been given me by my father, and who was a good cook. We were the youngest members of*

Confederate Gen. Leonidas Polk.

the staff, and congeniality had bound us together [my emphasis, L.S.]. as is apt to be the case under such circumstances, and the older members of the staff had dubbed us the "infant mess."[156] — MERCER OTEY, SAN FRANCISCO, CAL.

TRIBUTE TO A FAITHFUL SERVANT & BLACK CONFEDERATE: WILLIAM JOHNSON

☛ While the race problem creates serious concern for the welfare of both races and for the country, it behooves *the* [white] *Southern people, who are, and ever have been, their* [that is, blacks] *best friends*, to be on the alert for opportunities to influence all classes for the general good. The *Veteran* improves its opportunities *to pay tribute to faithful slaves, and it bespeaks the cooperation of our people in sending concise contributions to the honor of those who have ever been faithful*. Two illustrations are here given.

William Johnson (colored) lives by Nolensville, Tennessee, near his birthplace. He was a slave, and the property of Mr. Ben Johnson, as was also his mother.

In 1862 a part of the army commanded by [Confederate] Gen. [Nathan Bedford] Forrest was stationed at Nolensville, and young William Johnson (fifteen years old) drove one of the wagons with provisions for the army. [Confederate] Capt. B. F. White, who had been assistant adjutant general on the staff of Gen. Forrest, had been detached, and was in command of a battery of artillery captured at Murfreesboro. Seeing the [black] boy William, he liked him, and proposed to buy him. Mr. Johnson sold him to Capt. White for $1,200 [about $36,000 in today's currency], and *he went with Capt. White in the regular field service*.

William Johnson: Faithful Southern servant, brave Confederate serviceman.

Soon after his purchase of William, the great battle of Murfreesboro was fought; and while on the battle during the battle, Capt. White was attacked suddenly with inflammatory rheumatism. His servant William was with the wagon train, and did not reach him until the next day. The day following, the Confederates retreated, and the Federals, who also had been falling back, retraced their movements and occupied the area in which Capt. White was left in that painful and awful predicament, attended only by his servant William. For three months Capt. White was guarded by the Federals in a house on Thomas Butler's plantation, near the village of Salem. One bitter cold night the guard went to his camp some distance away, when the Captain asked William if he couldn't get him away from there. It was soon arranged for him to take a spring wagon and a broken-down army horse on the Butler farm. He put his charge in the wagon, and by a circuitous route got away without apprehension. *Late in the night the horse so nearly gave out that William walked in water and ice over his boots, and would lift the wheels of the vehicle out of the mire, and moved on until they were safe in the Confederate lines*. A better horse was procured, and the afflicted officer was taken to Shelbyville [Tennessee], and from there he was permitted to visit Mobile, where he recuperated, William of course going with him. *This faithful servant remained with Capt. White, who went back into field service,* but his health failed, and when his constitution gave down he was put on post duty, and at the end of the war he was paroled at Albany, Georgia. He brought William back to Nashville, leaving him with an uncle when he left to reside in Memphis. He afterwards moved to California. They never met again.

When the notice of Capt. White's death appeared in the December *Veteran* for 1899, *William saw it, and asked to pay tribute to his memory.* That desire becomes the occasion for the *Veteran* to pay just and well-merited tribute to William Johnson. He resumed his original name after the war.

William has lived all these years in the neighborhood of his birthplace, and has maintained a reputation as an honest, upright man—such as will ever have the devoted friendship of the white people, and who will prove it if later in life misfortunes should render him unable to support himself [all emphasis, L.S.].

During the time of Capt. White's confinement in the Federal lines he allowed William to carry three young [white] ladies through the lines to Shelbville. They were Misses Sallie J. McLean and Lizzie and Julia Lillard. After his return from that trip, Capt. White gave him permission to visit his mother, at Nolensville, before they escaped to the South.

Comrade James W. Hill writes of these ladies going to Shelbyville, and that Miss McLean was his "best girl," that "she was and is the fairest rose that ever bloomed in Tennessee."[157] — *CONFEDERATE VETERAN MAGAZINE*

TRIBUTE TO A FAITHFUL SERVANT: "UNCLE NED" HAWKINS

☛ Comrade C. L. Kalmbach, of Cobb's Legion (Georgia), procured through Samuel L. Richards, a nephew of Uncle Ned's mistress, a sketch of his labors in the sixties. The scouts generally of the Northern Virginia Army [C.S.A.] knew him, and will gladly recognize his kindly face after these many years. The data furnished is as follows:

Living on the banks of the Rappahannock [River], in the county of Culpeper, is a venerable old colored man, known by all near him as "Uncle Ned." His fidelity to his old mistress, his loyalty to the Confederacy, and his devotion to our soldiers were truly remarkable. He risked his liberty and his life more than once for the safety of our citizens and soldiers. On one occasion some of our scouts called at the house of his mistress—knowing they were always welcome there—and while she and her sister, assisted, of course, by "Uncle Ned," were busily engaged in preparing for them a much-needed breakfast, the dreaded cry was heard: "The Yankees are coming!'" They were *guided by the ever-faithful "Uncle Ned"* to the pines near by, and he returned to the house. After the Yankees left, he took the breakfast in an

Uncle Ned Hawkins: Loyal Southern servant, outstanding Confederate soldier.

old haversack, with a few ears of corn on top, and told our scouts if all was right when approaching them he would raise his hat and scratch his head, and if not, his hat would remain on his head; and should he meet the Yanks, with those ears of corn, his excuse would be that he was hunting his sheep. *Many, many such acts he did for the safety of our soldiers, and now he and his aged companion are struggling hard for a living; and—O that some brave Confederate could assist them in their good old age!* [all emphasis, L.S.]. He is certainly worthy of notice.[158] — *CONFEDERATE VETERAN* MAGAZINE

CAUSE OF WAR WAS NOT SLAVERY

☞ *If it will stimulate other survivors to put on record personal experiences, which I think can with perfect propriety be written, I will be satisfied, because the historian of the future will be able, using such material, to form a true idea of the motive which actuated the soldiers of the Confederacy. They fought, as we know, for a high ideal, not for human slavery, because not one out of five of those who stood in the ranks owned property in slaves or were interested in such property* [my emphasis, L.S.]. *They fought to establish an independent government of the* [Conservative] *Southern States, feeling that under the constitution they had this right, and that it would be better for those States to be disassociated from their* [Liberal] *neighbors to the North.*[159] — JOHN ALLAN WYETH, *CONFEDERATE VETERAN*

GEN. BRAXTON BRAGG'S OLD SERVANT

☞ *The following tribute of respect from Leonidas Polk Bivouac, No. 3, and William Henry Trousdale Camp, 495, of Confederate Veterans, truthfully portrays the feeling that exists between the Southern people, especially the Confederate Veterans, and the old and faithful Southern negroes:*

Whereas the faithful old negro man, Braxton Bragg, died in Columbia, Tennessee, Wednesday morning, January 17, 1900; and whereas Bragg was the body servant of [Confederate] Gen. Braxton Bragg, and *was true to his Southern friends and principles through life*; therefore be it

Resolved that a page in our minutes be set apart in honor of Braxton Bragg, the negro, who died here at an advanced age; that our thanks are hereby extended to *our comrades, Daughters of the Confederacy, and citizens generally who were so kind to Bragg during life and in his last sickness;* also to our comrades who made the funeral arrangements.

Confederate Gen. Braxton Bragg.

The following comrades served as pall bearers: H. A. Brown, H. G. Evans, W. J. Whitthorne, J. T. Williamson, H. L. Hendley, and A. N. Akin. Revs Baker P. Lee and W. T. Ussery, conducted the funeral services. Although the weather was inclement, the funeral was largely attended. The Columbia newspapers and the *Confederate Veteran* are requested to publish these proceedings.[160]

— W. A. SMITH, J. M. HODGE, B. S. THOMAS, COMMITTEE

BLACK SERVANT HELPS WHITE FAMILY TRICK THE YANKS

☛ ... When the Federal officers had gone [from the house] the girls rushed in to ask what stories the "horrid old Yankees" had told. When the sad news was announced they refused to believe it; they would not admit that their hero, [Confederate General Turner] Ashby, was killed. But they could only wait in their anxiety. "Cupid would soon come," and they would "know all." *Cupid, a tall negro man, was the body guard of Capt. Hilary and his brother. He had cared for them since their babyhood. He had taught them to ride and hunt and swim, and when Charles entered the army as captain Cupid went too, as his cook.*

Night came, but they could not sleep. Piling pillows upon the floor, they gathered around "Grandma," who tried to soothe the frightened girls, while "Uncle Douglas" prayed that these awful times might soon cease and his beloved country once more be at peace. They sat in darkness, lest they arouse the suspicions of the Yankee sentinel, whose tread could be heard as he paced to and fro on the street below.

Confederate Gen. Turner Ashby.

A tap at the back door was answered by Uncle Douglas, and in a moment Capt. [Charles] Hilary [painted in blackface, disguised as a black servant] held his sister in his arms. "Thank God!" she whispered. "O my boy! is Temple safe? Is Cupid with you?"

"Yes, yes, dear; we are all right, but nearly starved."

The girls gathered eagerly around their daring visitor, *while Cupid, stationed near the door to guard against surprises*, was at once supplied with pies, cheese, and biscuit— "Valley fare."

The young people spoke in whispers. As the tallow candle flickered it cast strange shadows, and as one ray fell upon the blackened face of [Charles] the young captain the girls laughed hysterically. Nellie whispered: "O Charlie, that is so dangerous! You might be caught, and they would call you a spy."

"O, no fear! We are [pretending to be] two runaway slaves. Don't look so scared, little girl. *You ought to hear Cupid boss the Yankees. They always let him pass with any 'brudder' he may have along"* [all emphasis, L.S.].[161] — MRS. DANGERFIELD, LEXINGTON, KY.

YANKEE NEWSPAPER INTERVIEWS JOHN BROWN'S SISTER

☛ Interviewer: "Don't you think that a great State like Virginia might have been more lenient toward such a small and powerless force [as your brother John Brown and his band of men]?" she was asked.

[Martha Davis] replied: "No. John and his comrades were not lenient toward Virginia and her institutions, and I never blamed the State, as many have. According to the national and State constitutions, John was wrong. No nation or State can tolerate the depredations of marauding bands of men, no matter what their purpose is. We would not tolerate it to-day. A band from an adjoining State attempting to overthrow our *local institutions would be captured, prosecuted, and probably executed as John and his men were. No doubt we [Northerners] have wronged the South in many ways. In the old days we [Yanks] thought that the only thing to be secured was the emancipation of the slaves, and we did not consider the condition the slaves would be in when they became free. Several wars ago, in conversation with a Southern lady who had been a slaveholder, I became enlightened. Great tears streamed down her face as she portrayed to me the destitute condition of the negroes. Many of them who before the war had always had overseer and master and cabin and food after the war immediately found themselves with nothing, and without even a means of livelihood"* [my emphasis, L.S.].

Mrs. Davis, never very tall, is now somewhat bent with her sixty-eight years and the burden [of her brother's reputation] she has borne.[162]
— MRS. MARTHA DAVIS, SISTER OF YANKEE MADMAN JOHN BROWN, FROM AN INTERVIEW IN A YANKEE NEWSPAPER (*SUNDAY TIMES-HERALD*, CHICAGO, ILL.)

BLACK CONFEDERATE IS FATHER FIGURE TO YOUNG WHITE MASTER

☛ . . . The division was bivouacked in a beautiful wood just north of Chambersburg [Pennsylvania], and there remained two or three days. It was a delightful rest. There we wrote our last letters to the loved ones at home. We had left the war-wasted and battle-riven Old Dominion, and had come to the land of corn and wine, flowing with milk and honey. Everything indicated prosperity and abundance. It was at a season of the year when the trees drooped with ripening cherries, and in every direction you could see these trees filled with Confederate soldiers helping themselves to that most luscious fruit. For a few miles around the camp the men had liberty to observe the country, always under instructions to do no mischief. Just how far they observed instructions is not known. *A comrade had a negro servant named Ned that was a good fellow and very much attached to "Marse Joe," for whom he cared as a father might care for a son* [my emphasis, L.S.]. Having a black skin, we thought the people would like to do something for Ned, and so he was sent out with as many canteens as he could carry and such other means of foraging as we had. Ned returned late in the afternoon with every canteen full of milk. These canteens had been captured, as well as our muskets, from the Federal Army; in fact, Lee's Army appeared to be equipped from the Federal Army. . . .[163]
— CONFEDERATE CAPT. W. C. WARD, BIRMINGHAM, ALA.

L-R: Tildy Moody and her husband Andrew Moody, former black servants, Orange, Texas, 1937.

LOYAL BLACK SERVANTS DURING BATTLE OF BRICE'S CROSS ROADS

☞ . . . Friday, the eventful 10th of June [1864], a negro man came in and reported that the Yankees had camped the night before at Stubbs's farm, seven miles from us, in the direction of Ripley. Some scouts had called at Mr. J. O. Nelson's during the night, and warned them of the impending danger. It was not known whether they would go by the Baldwyn or the Guntown road.

I took charge of my father's mules and horses, and with some negroes to help care for them and a little brother thirteen years old, went into a dense thicket a mile and a half southwest of our home, where we hoped to hide our stock and save them from seizure by the Federal troops if they came our way. My father hid in the woods north of his dwelling, where he remained safely till the day after the battle. The anxiety with which we watched and listened can be imagined. From our hiding place we heard a mysterious roaring noise made by the advancing Federal army. Not long after, one of our own negroes, who came skulking through the woods, told us that the Yankees were then at my father's home; that the yard was "black with Yankees"; that they had taken everything we had to eat, and that about fifty wagons were in the road in front of the dwelling; also that there were thousands of negroes with the Yankees. We listened intently, and anxiously awaited developments. Soon a volley of small arms was heard—the first shots of the day. The advance guard of Sturgis's force had encountered a squad of Confederate cavalry. This occurred in Dry Creek bottom. . . .[164] — REV. SAMUEL A. AGNEW, D.D.

Mrs. Helen J. Plane, U.D.C., Atlanta, Georgia.

RECOGNITION OF THE "FAITHFUL OLD CONFEDERATE NEGROS SERVANTS"

☞ . . . While there is no bitterness, but the kindest of feeling [among Confederate veterans], toward the Union soldier, it must be remembered that the Federal armies were composed, like almost all the armies of Europe, of young men who enlisted as a *dernier ressort* ["last resort"] and for the pay; whereas the Confederate armies were composed of the best material of our land, not for the pay, but for principle. Our ranks were filled with young gentlemen of education and refinement, many of them leaving homes of wealth and luxury to enlist as privates.

I am glad to see you [*Confederate Veteran* magazine] begin to do justice to the *faithful old Confederate negro servants*. We have three or four in our [Confederate Veterans] *Camp* [my emphasis, L.S.].[165] — R. K. CHARLES, DARLINGTON, S.C.

POSTWAR SOUTHERN BLACKS SEE SOUTHERN WHITES AS "THEIR BEST FRIENDS"

☞ . . . The purpose of this writing is to plead that our people stand together for the good of our common country. Race issues demand this, even should the people become lukewarm in the associations whereby *we* have been so constantly and universally sympathetic through more than three decades. The severity and bitterness of the long years of reconstruction may have had greater compensation than we realized through the devotion of the Southern people to each other. Those attachments should continue as long as there be memories to revere of sacrifice in a common cause. No issues having pecuniary consideration should ever cause a breach among our people. All lines of patriotic life were above that so long that the surrender would lower our political morality below what we can afford. The people of the Southern States should meet in convention, if necessary, to maintain the solidarity of the section. "Solid South" is a term used [by the radical Left] to discredit the people of the [Conservative] South, but results have caused that sentiment to be a benefit to the section, and thereby a blessing to the nation. In this connection *the most hopeful sign of the race problem is the action of prominent negroes in publicly advocating the wisdom and the justice of their race, looking to the white people of the South as their best friends* [all emphasis, L.S.].[166] — CONFEDERATE VETERAN MAGAZINE

MARY ABERCROMBIE, WIFE OF CONFEDERATE GENERAL FRENCH SAMUEL G. FRENCH

☞ On the 12th of January, 1865, Mary was married to Gen. S. G. French, Confederate States army. In September [six months after Lee's surrender] she left her father's home and went to Greenville, Mississippi, with her husband, to live on his plantation. What a change! She, who had no knowledge of plantation life, who had never seen a chicken killed, nor a dog in the house of her father, had now to confront plantation life amidst freedmen under the horrors of reconstruction, and nobly she did more than her part. *At her bidding the idle negroes would plow till the dusk of evening, or gather the crop in the dew of the morn; but for her and no one else would they work. All were devoted to "Miss Mary," for in sickness she visited them and gave them medicine, and in many ways administered much for their relief* [my emphasis, L.S.] . . . .[167] — CONFEDERATE VETERAN MAGAZINE

Mary, wife of Confederate Gen. S. G. French.

"UNCLE WILLIAM" ROSE, FAITHFUL BLACK CONFEDERATE SOLDIER

☞ . . . Although an earnest lawyer, [Confederate] Col. [Maxey] Gregg was also thoroughly posted in military matters. Responding to the call from the State, he immediately enlisted and served his country gallantly and efficiently until his death, in 1862, at Fredericksburg, Virginia. He was then only forty-seven years old, although he looked much older. He was mortally wounded while gallantly repelling [Union Gen. George G.] Meade's charge. He was a brave and fearless soldier, and a noble gentleman. After he was mortally wounded he lingered for many hours in terrible pain, which he bore with uncomplaining patience and Spartan bravery. *I heard his old body servant, "Uncle William" Rose, who was his faithful friend until the end,* tell with streaming eyes of his sufferings and untold

Christian fortitude. *This old servant has never forgotten his former master and general, and it is a touching sight every year on memorial day to see him with tottering steps and shaking hands lay a wreath of flowers on Gen. Gregg's monument in Elmwood cemetery. The old man is truly a veteran, having served in three wars—the Mexican, Florida, and Confederate. Nearly ever since the war, no matter who is Governor, "Uncle William" has been porter to the Governor's office, and sits at the door day after day in his comfortable chair, and happy in the possession of Gen. Gregg's watch, which he gave him on his deathbed, and a gold-headed cane presented to him a few years ago by the Legislature* [all emphasis mine, L.S.].[168] — MRS. A. G. ROBERTSON, COLUMBIA, S.C.

SKETCH OF MRS. J. M. KELLER

☞ One of the most interesting and forceful women in the Montgomery Convention, U.D.C. [United Daughters of the Confederacy], was Mrs. J. M. Keller, of Hot Springs, Arkansas, President of the Arkansas Division, U.D.C, and wife of Dr. J. M. Keller, President of the Association of Confederate Surgeons. Mrs. Keller was Miss Sallie Phillips, of Jefferson County, Kentucky, and a descendant of the Botts family, of Virginia. Although it is within a year of their golden wedding, she is as physically and mentally active and bright as most women of half her age.

Mrs. J. M. Keller, President of the Arkansas Division of the U.D.C., circa 1900.

When the war began her home was in Memphis, Tennessee, and she at once became very active in establishing and organizing hospitals for Confederates, and, under instruction from her husband, filled the place of the first matron of the Overton Hotel-Hospital, supervising its furnishing and attendants, without pay, until its perfect organization. The position was then given to a poor woman on a salary.

Mrs. Keller prides herself on the honor of having been the first woman banished from her home at Memphis by [Yankee] Gen. W. T. Sherman, after he captured the city, and carefully preserves his order as a souvenir. She, with her two baby boys, Irvin and Murray, five and seven years of age, *accompanied voluntarily by faithful "Old Black Daddy"* [my emphasis, L.S.], were put across the Mississippi river into the swamps of Arkansas, several miles from any house, where they remained for several days until friends sent a guide and took them to a point on the river several miles above, and out of sight of Memphis, where the steamer *Von Pool* landed contrary to orders, at night, and secretly took her little party to Cairo, Illinois, whence she went by rail to her mother, in Jefferson County, Ky. There she remained, although frequently arrested, until joined by her husband after the surrender in July, 1865, without having seen him from May, 1862.

She devotes her life to charity and efforts to produce a true history of the war and its causes, and the care of poor Confederate veterans.[169]
— *CONFEDERATE VETERAN* MAGAZINE

CHAPTER THREE
1901-1904

WHITE SOUTHERN WOMAN CARES FOR SOUTHERN BLACKS
☛ Years ago, when in social prominence, [Mrs. Pattie Buford of Lawrenceville, Virginia] . . . *abandoned the gaieties of life and took up the care of suffering negroes in "the black belt."* She appealed to the people at large, and by their aid she built a hospital for the aged and afflicted. Endowed with spirit and genius, she thrilled the charitable, built a hospital, and then an orphanage, caring for a multitude in that way and giving medicines and food through a dispensary that she had provided. *It is believed that she accomplished more than has any other person with the means at hand* [my emphasis, L.S.].[170] — RICHMOND TIMES

CHILDREN OF BLACK SERVANTS CELEBRATE 25 YEAR FRIENDSHIP WITH WHITE SOUTHERN FAMILY

P. Cunningham.

☛ An illustration of *the friendly relations existing between the best element of the colored people and the whites in the South* is given by a small photograph—a print from which is here given—*which has been preserved with pride, through friendship, for twenty-five years* in the [African American] *family of* William H. Key, *and presented recently to the* [European American] *father of* . . . Paul Davis Cunningham [chief engineer of the U.S. Boundary Commission]. Key and family are of a later generation than the [earlier] slave generation, but were nurtured in the spirit of those who were. In many ways it is demonstrated that *the relation between the whites and the blacks of the South is of ready adjustment, and there is mutual interest in the welfare of each other* [all emphasis, L.S.].[171]
— CONFEDERATE VETERAN MAGAZINE

CONFEDERATE VETERANS PRAISE BOOKER T. WASHINGTON
☛ . . . No man of his race has so established himself in the esteem of white and black alike as Booker T. Washington. His counsel has been wise among his people, and *he has grown splendidly in the estimation of whites, South as well as North* [my emphasis, L.S.]. . . .[172] — CONFEDERATE VETERAN MAGAZINE

OUR FAITHFUL SLAVES OF OLD
☛ . . . An article in the *Confederate Veteran* by Mr. A. N. Edwards, of Strawn, Texas, about a few faithful negroes, reminds me to mention an old negro of ours, "Uncle Chap." He was certainly as true and faithful a negro as ever lived. *He guarded our home and an aunt's, who was left without protection save her negroes, who, by the way, were faithful, as thousands were all over the Southland. Only those who owned the slaves and were among them know how to appreciate their faithfulness during those dark and fearful times.* This old

negro worked with his arms [guns] by his side through the day, and guarded our homes at night, and was never too tired to start at any moment to warn the people through the country of approaching danger.

When my mother's father, who was very aged, was taken to Fort Pickens, he was put under a guard of negroes. All save one were very kind. They seemed to understand that he was a slaveholder and a Southern gentleman. . . .[173] — R. H. A.

LOYAL BLACK SERVANTS RECALLED

☛ I am glad to see that the *Confederate Veteran* is giving space to the "Black man," a multitude of whom were most faithful and true to "ole marster and mistis" during those terrible days of war and destruction in our loved Southland.

There lives in Nashville an old [black] man, now nearing the bright and happy shore, together with his wife, worthy, industrious people, a sketch of whose life it is a pleasure to write.

Aaron Owens, nearly fifty years ago, married a girl by the name of Fanny, belonging to my father, Felix Compton. After Lincoln's proclamation freeing the slaves was issued, Aaron, unlike the other servants on the plantation, said to his old master: "I know I is free, but you needn't think I is gwine to do like de rest of de niggers, steal away in de night, fur I ain't gwine to leave you and ole Mistis as long as you will let me stay wid you and de chillun;" and he kept his word most faithfully, running many risks, and doing much for those who needed his help.

In the early part of 1862, not long after the occupation of Nashville by the Federals, many Southern soldiers who were captured in Nashville hospitals owe their escape from Federal lines, in part, to Aaron's assistance.

Former black Southern servants reminiscing on the old farm.

The soldiers would come to my father's house from the hospitals, and he would start them on their way to Southern lines, furnishing them horses and sometimes money, *with Aaron as a guide*, to places of safety. At one time my mother got an old lady, living about ten miles from us, to weave her forty yards of jeans, out of which to make pants for loved ones then in the army. It so happened that she had not sent for it before [Confederate Gen. John Bell] Hood's army camped in front of Nashville.

One day she said to Aaron: "Get the buggy ready to go with me for my jeans."

They had but little trouble passing Confederate pickets, for our home was inside their lines, but when they reached the Federal lines it took some arguing, some bribing, and much begging to pass, but Aaron would plead so pathetically, "Please, Mister, jest let my Mistis go see her friend, we won't be gone long; she brung me wid her, fur she knowed you wouldn't say no to a poor colored man"; so on they went till the goal was reached. They got the jeans and returned home safely, when busy hands went to work, and much comfort was rendered thereby to

Capt. James Mernaugh, Paris, Kentucky.

Confederate heroes, among the number [Confederate] Gen. [James Ronald] Chalmers, whose headquarters were in the house.

Now one word about faithful Fanny, for she too did her part. During the two days' fight [at the battle of Nashville], December 15 and 16, 1864, our house was a Federal hospital, to which over one hundred and fifty dead and wounded soldiers (mostly Confederates, who were captured on the battlefield) were brought. When the fight began the smokehouse was filled with meat, being cured, besides cans of lard, etc.

The Yankees, in wanton destruction, broke open the door, took bucketful after bucketful of dirt and ashes from the floor and, using sticks, their bayonets, or anything they could get, stirred it into the lard; took all the meat, and, literally, left our family with nothing to eat.

For three days Fanny would go to the kitchen, where the [Yankee] officers meals were being prepared, and beg and take from the pots and kettles food, which she would bring to her mistress and master, and then get more for her own little family.

Old "Marster" has long since passed into that sweet and peaceful rest that comes ever to the faithful, old "Mistis" is living in a distant Southern city, and the "chillun" are scattered; but *never, while memory lasts, will Aaron and Fanny be forgotten* [all emphasis, L.S.].[174] — ANONYMOUS

CONFEDERATE CAMP MAKES BLACKS HONORARY MEMBERS

☛ At the second meeting of our [Confederate veterans] Camp, James A. Jackson, No. 1508, we received a number of new members. We are now eighty-three strong. *We also admitted five faithful old colored servants as honorary members. They followed their masters through the war. When sick or wounded they nursed them. They want to go to Memphis* [Confederate reunion], *and they will go. Some provision ought to be made for all such, and a general invitation extended to them to attend the great reunion. The Brownsville (Tennessee) Camp carried several of their old servants to the Nashville reunion, in 1897, and, as the boys used to say, they had "a hog-killing time"* [my emphasis, L.S.].[175] — REV. E. C. FAULKNER, MONTICELLO, AR.

FAITHFUL NEGRO WHO WAS A SLAVE: FED ARDIS

☛ [Accompanying this article] . . . is a good picture of Fed Ardis, who was the property of Mr. Isaac Ardis. Fed is now living in Texas, and is about seventy-five years old. He was given to Mr. Ardis's wife when he married her in Russell County, Alabama, 1841. *Fed was a good boy, and won the confidence of his master and mistress, and as the family increased and grew he was a great favorite with the children because of his kindness to them.*

When the war came on Mr. Ardis made Fed his foreman, and intrusted all his farm business to him, which he managed very faithfully and successfully. Toward the close of the war the deserters became very troublesome in Southeast Alabama, and to protect themselves the old men of Dale County organized a small company of themselves and elected Mr. [Isaac] Ardis captain. He was a resolute, vigorous man, and made it so warm [uncomfortable] for the deserters that he incurred their bitter enmity. *When away from home he trusted his business, his property, and his family to Fed and other faithful negroes on the place. His mistress would intrust her money and other valuables to Fed to keep them from falling into the hands of the enemy.* Occasionally Mr. Ardis would come home for a day or so to see how everything was getting on. On one occasion he came home to stay all night, but by some means the deserters found it out and planned to kill him. After supper Fed went to the lot to see about the mules, as was his custom, and in passing the front of the house he saw two men standing by the yard gate with guns. He went by whistling as though he had not seen them, and passed around to the back of the house and called

Fed Ardis.

his master to the window and told him not to go out, as there were men around to assassinate him. They closed the front door, blew out the lights, and Mr. Ardis passed out the back way. *Fed went back to the negro quarters and got several other negro men with their axes and went back to the house, and placed them as guards around the house, and said to his Mistress:* "Now, Miss Lizabeth, you go to sleep. If anybody gets in this house to-night, they have got to kill us first."

Fed was always very religious, and he was very able in prayer. During slavery he and other old faithful negroes would attend church and take their places in a cut-off portion of the church, just back of the pulpit, which was provided for them in erecting churches. Strange as it may sound to some people at the North, Fed was frequently called on to pray, especially during prayer meeting services.

He was a very sensible man, and his prayers were very effectual. After the war he obtained some education, and got license to preach, and soon became a "big preacher" among the negroes in Southern Alabama. He became a presiding elder in the Methodist Church.

A few years ago he [Fed] came to Texas, and Dr. Ardis, of Greenville (who had been his young master), sent him money to come on. He has just lately returned from a visit back to his old Conference in Alabama, the negroes there having written him if he would visit their Conference they would pay his expenses.

Soon after he went to preaching, my wife, who was his young mistress [that is, pupil], sent him a fine Oxford Bible, which he appreciates highly.

Fed is doing well, and will have a good home on Dr. Ardis's place as long as he lives, and I very much believe will have a far better one when he crosses over "the Jordan" [all emphasis, L.S.].[176] — A. N. EDWARDS, STRAWN, TEX.

FAITHFUL BLACK CONFEDERATE: HANNIBAL ALEXANDER

☛ *Hannibal Alexander was a slave belonging to Parker Alexander. He went with his young master, Sidney Alexander, to the war, and did his duty faithfully.* "Ham" died recently in Monroe County, Mississippi. He and his wife Delia by industry made a good living and accumulated a competence, ever having the confidence and friendship of the white people about their lifetime home.

In the army he was cook. He was in the siege of Fort Donelson. He was captured there, and went to Camp Douglass as a Confederate prisoner. He answered roll call all the time as a white soldier. Being a bright mulatto, he was brought to Vicksburg and exchanged with the others, and again went with his young master into service.

The Federal sergeant that called the roll was somewhat suspicious as to "Ham" (as he was called by the boys) being a slave, but he was told that living in Mississippi he was sunburned and that made him dark.

Hannibal was a very intelligent negro, and knew if he left his master he could go free, but he elected to stay with him among the white men he had been raised with, and preferred to suffer with them.

I knew Hannibal for more than forty years as slave and freeman, and he was ever polite and friendly to all his former owners. In the old days I went on many a hunting and fishing expedition with Sidney, with "Ham" to wait on us [all emphasis, L.S.].

His old master with whom he went in the army is yet alive, but in poor health.[177] — W. A. CAMPBELL, COLUMBUS, MISS.

JEFFERSON DAVIS'S FORMER COACHMAN

☛ The faithful, venerable [black man] Lewis Alexander, who has for so many years been a genial and active messenger in the Treasury Department, died in Washington, D.C., January 8, at the advanced age of eighty years. Alexander was long in the service of Jefferson Davis as coachman, and he later went abroad and acted in the same capacity for the Belgian Minister.[178] — *CONFEDERATE VETERAN* MAGAZINE

TWO OF THE 65 BLACK CONFEDERATES IN FORREST'S COMMAND

Confederate Capt. John W. Morton, Chief of Artillery under Gen. Forrest.

☛ With the batteries of [Confederate] Capt. John W. Morton, Gen. Forrest's chief of artillery, there were two negroes, Bob Morton, a cook, and Ed Patterson, the hostler for the captain, both of whom served with the artillery throughout the war. Ed Patterson, whose fidelity and loyalty stoutly withstood the test of battle and even of capture, still survives. He is a respected householder and property owner, near Nashville, and delights to recall the time when he wore the gray in Morton's Battery. Everybody in the artillery service of Forrest knew and liked Ed. He took good care of the horses, and performed his duties with unflagging good humor [my emphasis, L.S.].

On one occasion it was feared that Ed was lost to the battery. In the terrific fight at Parker's Cross Roads, when Morton's men, behind the guns, were almost overwhelmed by superior numbers of the enemy in a sudden charge, about twenty members of the battery were run over and captured. Ed was among them. He was missed, notwithstanding the confusion of the disaster, and the temporary reverse of the almost invariably successful artillerists was regarded by them as aggravated by the loss of their diligent hostler. Capt. Morton particularly mourned his absence. One morning, a few days after the battle, he rode into the camp of the battery, mounted upon a superb horse, whose caparison denoted it the property of an officer of no mean rank.

"Hallo, Ed! Where did you come from?" was the artillery chief's greeting.

"I des come f'om de Yankees," responded Ed complacently, as he dismounted and stood proudly eying the steed.

"How did you get away, and where did you get that horse?"

"Wall, sah; dey taken us all along. When we got out o' sight o' y'all, I notice dat dey didn't 'pear to notice me, an' when dey get to whar dey was gwine into camp, I sort o' got away. De Yankees des seed me ridin' 'roun', an' I 'spec' maybe dey thought I was waitin' on some o' de officers. I des went on th'ough de woods. I seed a heap o' dead men wid blue coats on, an' a heap of 'em what was 'live, too. D'rectly I come to a big road. I seed one o' our boys walkin' what 'ad done los' his horse. I axed him which er way Marse John went. He knowed me, an' said de artillery done gone down dis road. I kep' on, an' passed a heap o' our men walkin'. I axed 'em which er way de artillery done gone, an' de said, "Down dis road." I kep' on an' kep' on 'til I got here; an' dat's why I'm here, Marse John. Dey took yo' horse away f'om me, but I done got you a better one, sho. No, sah; dey didn't 'pear to notice me at all. When I was comin' on I seed some mighty nice-lookin' hosses tied in de bushes, an' ez dey wan' nobody noticin' I tuck 'n' pick me out one, an' des got on dis 'n' and rid him to hunt y'all. I seed a blue overcoat layin' on de groun', an' I took 'n' put it on. An' it's a good one, too, Marse John."[179] — CONFEDERATE VETERAN MAGAZINE

SOUTHERN BLACKS DURING RECONSTRUCTION

☛ [With the end of the War for Southern Independence and the beginning of Reconstruction in the Spring of 1865, we] . . . did not fully understand what the negroes would do, or how they would act. *The North had brought them from Africa in their ships, and had sold them in the South, and now proposed to release them and place them in power over the white people of the South. This must have been prompted by the blindest prejudice and a most malignant heart or ignorance of the true philosophy of the situation. The South had done more for the negro than all the North put together. We had civilized and Christianized 4,000,000 of that race* [my emphasis, L.S.]. Be it said to the honor of the women of the South: They had looked after the physical and spiritual welfare of the negro, and had so Christianized him and so attached him to his home that he was true and faithful in the hour of our greatest need, and many anticipated evils did not come.[180] — JUDGE H. H. COOK, FRANKLIN, TENN.

Miss Nellie Duncan, Sponsor for Camp at Talbott, Tennessee, Dallas Confederate Reunion.

CONFEDERATE INDIAN COLONEL SPARES A REGIMENT OF BLACK YANKEE SOLDIERS

☞ Col. Sim Folsom, an honored [Confederate] Choctaw Indian veteran of civil war fame, died at his old home near Docksville, Choctaw Nation, Indian Territory, in December, 1900. "Col. Sim," as he was called, was a man of fine character and with a remarkable career. He was a half-breed Indian and a ranking member of one of the largest and most highly respected families of the Choctaw tribe, the Folsoms. At the outbreak of the war between the States he was about thirty years of age, and was among the first of his countrymen to offer his services in defense of the Sunny Southland.

In the organization of the volunteer forces of the Choctaw Nation that flocked to the standard of the Southern Confederacy, Sim Folsom was commissioned colonel, and placed in command of the Second Choctaw Regiment of Cavalry [C.S.A.]. The entire forces of the Choctaw and Chickasaw Nations were formed into one brigade, and the command given to [Confederate] Brig. Gen. Douglas H. Cooper, who was prior to the precipitation of war an Indian agent in the service of the United States government. This brigade engaged in nearly all the campaigns and battles of any note in the Trans-Mississippi Department, and its aged members down to this day exultingly boast that they never surrendered. Even now in the twilight of a long life the white-haired old [Confederate] Indian veterans of Cooper's Brigade proudly tell of heroic deeds under their revered old paleface chief when [Confederate Gen.] Sterling Price led them to victory. It was the fortune of Col. Sim's regiment to come forth from this unequal struggle with a bright record in arms. The opportunity to do patriotic duty was presented to him and his regiment more frequently than to their comrades, and right well was it performed. At Wilson's Creek "Col. Sim" rallied his broken squadrons time after time on that sorrowful day when [Confederate Gen.] Ben McCulloch nobly yielded up his well-spent life for his country's sake at Elk Horn tavern. *Col. Sim's war paint was well smeared when his revengeful "bucks" measured muskets with [Union Lieut. R. L.] Phillips's Kansas regiment of fugitive negroes at Poison Springs, Arkansas, and it is said that he with the flat of his sword checked the indiscriminate slaughter of the ebony-skinned Yankees on this memorable occasion, thus saving many nappy heads from being scalped* [my emphasis, L. S.].

Cherokee leader and Confederate officer, General Stand Watie.

. . . At the close of the war Col. Sim refused to give himself up to the authorities, and amidst the turmoil and discontent that immediately followed the surrender he quietly withdrew to private life, from the solitude of which he never again emerged. A widow and several children survive him.[181] — VICTOR M. LOCKE, ANTLERS, INDIAN TERRITORY

STONEWALL JACKSON'S BLACK CONFEDERATE COOK ATTENDS CONFEDERATE VETERANS REUNION

☛ The Richmond *Times* gives an interesting report of the reunion of Virginia Veterans at Petersburg on October 23-25. It was the fourteenth annual gathering of the Grand Camp. Ex-Gov. W. E. Cameron delivered a grand welcome on behalf of the A. P. Hill Camp, and a fitting response was made by Capt. T. D. Ransom. Those addresses ought to be in the *Veteran*, but were received too late for this number. The Sons of Veterans were on hand, and contributed to the success of the meeting, while the sponsors and maids of honor added to the joy of the occasion. The attendance from Richmond was large, the R. E. Lee and George E. Pickett Camps attending in bodies, and the sixty-three veteran beneficiaries of the Soldiers' Home at Richmond were also present. The Richmond companies of the Seventieth Regiment, some two hundred and fifty strong, made a fine appearance.

Confederate General Thomas Jonathan "Stonewall" Jackson.

The main feature of the second day was the great parade, and it was practically a holiday. Nearly all the business houses were closed, and *almost every building in the central portion of the city was richly decorated with Confederate and national flags*, some of the decorations representing great cost. It is estimated that there were about twenty-five thousand people along the line of march. Col. William H. Stewart, the eloquent orator, made an address upon Matthew Fontaine Maury.

A grand concert at night was given in honor of the Grand Camp. It consisted mainly in the singing of old, familiar songs. The chorus was made up of Frank Cunningham and Polk Miller, of Richmond, and a picked choir from Petersburg. Among the songs were "Bonnie Blue Flag," "My Maryland," "How Can I Leave Thee?," "My Old Kentucky Home," "Tenting on the Old Camp Ground," "Auld Lang Syne," and "Dixie." Several solos were also sung. An entertainment was given by Mrs. Preston L. Roper in honor of Miss Lucy Lee Hill and Mrs. H. P. Bailey, of Newport News.

Jefferson Shields, of Lexington, an old-fashioned negro, who was the cook for Stonewall Jackson during the war, received much attention [all emphasis, L.S.]. . . .[182] — CONFEDERATE VETERAN MAGAZINE

BLACK CONFEDERATE VOLUNTEER SHEDS TEARS AT SEPARATION FROM WHITE MASTER

☛ . . . One other experience in my army life of something more than a year may not be without interest. About midnight of April 2, 1865, we were aroused by the beat of the long roll. Lee's lines around Petersburg had been broken, and his starved army was on the retreat, endeavoring to effect a junction with [Confederate Gen. Joseph E.] Johnston in North Carolina. President [Jefferson] Davis and his Cabinet had fled from Richmond to Charlotte, North Carolina, and we were ordered to spike our guns, get what rations we had—this was irony, indeed, for not a particle of meal or flour, or even a piece of bread, did we have—and be ready to march in thirty minutes. We crossed the James [River] on a pontoon bridge a few miles below Richmond, and about two o'clock in the morning we rested a little while on the Manchester Hills, almost in sight of Richmond, and from there saw a scene that I shall never forget—Richmond in flames.

We hurried on, with the enemy harassing us from front, rear, and flank; weary and foot-sore, with nothing to eat except a little corn. Still we marched on, fighting, starving, dying. On the afternoon of the 5th it seemed to me a physical impossibility to keep up with my company. Pettit, Lasseur, *and faithful negro Ben, who voluntarily had shared with me the hardships of camp life during the entire time I was in the army*, and myself "fell by the wayside." We lay down in an old broom-sedge field. The night was chilly, and we had no covering, yet we were so completely worn out that our slumbers were as peaceful as though we had lain on a bed of down. We awoke the next morning early. It was lovely springtime. We could hear the continued booming of guns in the distance in almost every direction. The four of us held a "council" to determine whether we should return to our homes, then only about twenty-five miles away, or push on and endeavor to catch up with our command. Pettit said go back, Lasseur said go back, Ben said go back; but I said no. *We separated, negro Ben shedding tears when good-byes were exchanged* [my emphasis, L.S.]. . . .[183] — CONFEDERATE VETERAN R. S. ROCK, EVANSVILLE, IN.

Will Adams, former black servant, Marshall, Texas, 1937.

GEN. STONEWALL JACKSON: SUNDAY SCHOOL TEACHER AT HIS OWN ALL BLACK CHURCH

☛ . . . But, while vividly recalling many of these battle pictures, I prefer to think of Stonewall Jackson as the humble, devout Christian, the "soldier of the cross," and to recall him as he appeared in that attitude, the deacon of his Church who "had no time to attend to anything else" when his duties demanded his attendance at a deacon's meeting, the Church collector who got a contribution from every one on his list, *the teacher of the negro Sunday school so devoted and true* [my emphasis, L.S.], the man of humble prayer, and the diligent student of God's Word . . . .[184]
— CHAPLAIN J. WM. JONES

MEMORIES OF MY MOTHER, HER BLACK SERVANT, & YANKEE WAR CRIMES

☛ On the 31st of December, 1862, her old home, standing on the banks of the beautiful Rappahannock, Culpeper County, Virginia, occupied by herself and an older sister, was fired upon by the vandals in blue [Yankee soldiers], and she was painfully wounded, and lay upon a bed of suffering for weeks. Her sister was greatly alarmed, and asked aid of a surgeon from among the enemy. Mother was in quite a critical condition, yet she told the surgeon she preferred death to his touching her. While on crutches she would tell them of their many, many mean deeds and cruelties to Southern people.

She, with the exception of a sister in East Tennessee, is the last of a once large and influential family, whose forefathers owned their old homestead for more than a century. Her only brother was hunted like a wild beast, and driven from his comfortable home to find shelter in our glorious Rebel army. He was too old to enter the service. I shall never forget how a number of Yankees dashed up, pistols in hand, and surrounded the house to capture "one feeble old man." Two of them, claiming to be officers, came up to the door and inquired for my father. When told by my poor, weeping mother that he was not there, such oaths [cursing] followed as I scarcely ever heard. They said if they found him they would hang him to a large oak standing just in front of our dear old home—long since in ashes. Then number two said: "No, we will scalp his damned old bald head just here at the door." They said they had orders to search the house, and, with pistols in hand, sabers clanking, spurs rattling, said mother must accompany them, pretending to be so scrupulously honest, while at the same time those out of doors were in every place, breaking every lock, and carrying off all they found, whether of use to them or not. *I can see my dear old mother now ascending the stairs with trembling limbs and tearful eyes, followed by Mary, the faithful house servant, who was ever true to her mistress in time of trouble.* These are only a few trials borne by our family.

In the Old South, black servant families were made legal members of their white owners' families at the time of purchase—a fact rigorously censored by modern mainstream historians.

We were deprived of every comfort, and at times scarcely had the necessaries of life. Then poor mother would ask them not to leave us to starve, that she could not communicate with her friends. Their reply was "We are acting upon [Union Gen. John] Pope's orders." *That was truly their mode of warfare, waged against old men, helpless women and children* [all emphasis, L. S.].

Some wish to bury the past. I should like to attend a reunion of thorough Confederates, but if one single bluecoat is to be there, I prefer to stay away.

When the green grass waves over my grave, just as it does now over my dear old father's and mother's, and my children stand by and view mine as I do theirs, they can say, as I can, she never forgot how they were treated by the Yankees. But there is a comfort in knowing that God is just, and all will be well some day.[185] — ANONYMOUS FEMALE

LOYAL BLACK SERVANT & CONFEDERATE

☛ *I now look back and am amazed at the fidelity of our slaves during the trying times of those days, surrounded as they were by temptations and inducements to abandon us.*

I told my [black servant] boy Tom on several occasions that Mr. Lincoln's proclamation of January 1, 1863, pronounced him free, and at any time he was at liberty to go North, and I should put no obstacles in his way. I can never forget the expression on the face of *this faithful and loved companion of my youth*, as he candidly avowed his devotion to me, saying, "Why, Marse Willie, you don't suppose I'm going to leave you; didn't I promise old miss and old marster to always stay with you?" and *he never did desert me through the whole war; but was always the warm-hearted, faithful creature under all circumstances. He was only a year younger than I, and we had grown up together with no distinction that his yellow skin could claim from my white; together we had been taught the prayers and catechism at my father's hearthstone, and morning and evening we daily worshiped in the family circle. If he or any other of the house servants were ill, they claimed as much care and comfort as my sisters. If I had a dollar, Tom could always claim half of it.* After the war closed he and I drifted away with the great stream of struggling soldiers who were scattering here and there, seeking to earn their daily bread. *Whether the honest fellow is now alive or not I do not know*, but, God knows, he could always share my crust and cot [all emphasis, L.S.].[186] — MERCER OTEY, SAN FRANCISCO, CAL.

Miss Anna Maud McGowan, Nevada, Missouri.

TRIBUTE TO AN ALLEGIANT BLACK CONFEDERATE: ANDERSON MCALLISTER

☛ . . . Doubtless all of the surviving members of Company E [Second Mississippi Regiment, C.S.A.], especially McDowell's messmates, will be pleased to know that *Anderson McAllister, my* [black] *war servant, is still living. He is getting on quite well; has a comfortable home, and plenty around him, and is respected by all the good people who know him* [my emphasis, L.S.].[187] — A. H. MCALLISTER, NEW ALBANY, MISS.

BLACK SERVANT SEEN AS MORE IMPORTANT THAN WHITE OWNER

☛ . . . Anne Chalmers was an independent young woman. She followed the dictates of an imperious will, and at the death of her parents assumed control of her own and her young sister's destiny. Having inherited beauty, her views on matrimony were exasperating to suitors who came to the house where she lived with [the family's black servants] Amy and Jude. Jude had been "body servant" to [Confederate] Col. Chalmers before the war and coachman in his family for a period of eighteen years afterwards, and so thoroughly was Miss Chalmers imbued with the idea of his importance that it was *years before she gained her own consent to thrust him into the background. Indeed it was not until old age weakened his intellect that she held undisputed reign at Oakwood* [Mansion] [my emphasis, L.S.]. . . .[188] — NANCY LEWIS GREENE

WAY DOWN IN LOUISIANA
☛ Way down in Louisiana, not many months ago,
There lived a lively darky—his name was Peter Snow;
He played upon de banjo, likewise de tambourine,
An' he was de han's' most nigger ebber to be seen.

Chorus
In de Louisiana lowlands, lowlands, lowlands,
In de Louisiana lowlands, low.

Down on de Chickahominy, you ought to seen dis nigger!
When de fight begin he cut a comic figger;
Killed a thousand Yankees, captured ebry gun,
An' buried dem in de lowlands at de settin' ob de sun.

Chorus
In de Louisiana lowlands, lowlands, lowlands,
In de Louisiana lowlands, low.[189] — ANONYMOUS

MORE EVIDENCE OF THE BLACK CONFEDERATE SOLDIER
☛ [The writer] . . . expects to have in Dallas [where the next Confederate veterans reunion will be held] a tent at the Fair Grounds with the sign, "Headquarters Quirk's Scouts, [Confederate Gen. John Hunt] Morgan's Cavalry, C.S.A.," where *he hopes to "meet every man, white or black, who may be there that ever served with Morgan"* [my emphasis, L.S.]. He will also have a register in which to record their names and post offices.[190] — J. N. GAINES, TRIPLETT, MO.

BLACK SERVANT BURIED WITH WHITE FAMILY
☛ In Maury County [Tennessee], about six miles from Columbia, on the road leading to Mt. Pleasant, in a grove of majestic and towering oaks, may be seen a neat brick church [St. John's Church, at Ashwood, Tenn.] of simple gothic architecture; its interior plain and appropriate and capable of seating five hundred persons. It has just been completed, and is the result of the joint liberality of Bishop Polk and three of his brothers, who with a spirit worthy of commendation and imitation have thus devoted a portion of the wealth with which God has blessed them to his service.

St. John's Church, Ashwood, Tennessee. I have visited here many times (L.S.).

. . . *In the cemetery lot, near this church, of George W. Polk and family there is a grave of the "black mammy" in the midst, giving her name and stating that she assisted in rearing the eleven children in that family* [my emphasis, L.S.].

Prominence is given this church, however, especially because it was the burial place after the carnage at [the battle of] Franklin [II] of so many officers and other gallant Confederates. Hardly a more beautiful spot of earth can be found than is in this vicinity.[191] — CONFEDERATE VETERAN MAGAZINE

BLACKS ASK TO ATTEND CONFEDERATE VETERANS REUNION
☛ The A. P. Hill Camp, Confederate Veterans, Petersburg, Virginia, sends out "General Orders, No. 211," with the following in gilt border and under the Confederate battle flag and that of the State of Virginia: The veterans of A. P. Hill Camp would be recreant to their duty, regardless of their own pleasure and untrue to themselves, if they should fail to give public expression to their appreciation of the favors showered upon them in their efforts to suitably entertain the Grand Camp of the State on the occasion of its recent session in this city. From the Chief Executive of the State *to the humble colored men who asked that we accept their gratuitous service* [my emphasis, L.S.], all classes vied with each other in aiding us to do honor to our guests. To enumerate those who have shown us marked kindness, would be unseemly and impossible in this order. But the camp has prepared such a list for preservation among our records, and to all our friends we can say that there are not wanting veterans among us who maintain that each single act of kindness was the factor that made the occasion the grand success that it was. . . .[192] — CONFEDERATE VETERAN MAGAZINE

Officers of Kentucky Division, United Confederate Veterans.

MISSISSIPPI'S BLACK CONFEDERATES RECEIVING PENSIONS
☛ . . . We have quite a number of *colored servants who deserve and receive* [Confederate military] *pensions* [my emphasis, L.S.]. . . .[193] — ROBERT E. HOUSTON, ESQ., ABERDEEN, MISS.

KENTUCKY WOMEN OBJECT TO THE PLAY *UNCLE TOM'S CABIN* BEING PERFORMED IN THEIR CITY
☛ The Lexington, Ky., Chapter [of the] Daughters of the Confederacy created a sensation recently by requesting the manager of the local opera house "never again" to book [the anti-South Yankee play] *Uncle Tom's Cabin* as an attraction. The petition was indorsed by the whole chapter representing the most influential and exclusive circles of the blue grass region. The women of the South are very much in earnest about having a just representation in history, and rightfully object to the portrayal of an exaggerated and sensational coloring of events as found in Mrs. Stowe's [fictitious and malicious] book. The Lexington Chapter is to be

commended for its decisive, fearless, and earnest action in demanding the suppression of such misleading [left-wing indoctrinating] productions and have won the admiration of their associates in every state.

The [opera house] manager's [snide] reply that "the war had been over thirty-six years," serves as a forcible reason that it should no longer be kept up in such plays. The true purpose for producing this drama—for it has degenerated into such a purpose—is to catch the hard-earned wages [and minds] of the negro, for few besides now patronize it, especially in the South. They are excited and embittered by it, and for this reason alone, if for no other, it should be suppressed.

The Lexington Daughters of the Confederacy in asking that it should be excluded entirely in the future give as good reasons that *the best citizens and old families living in and about the city were once slave owners, as a heritage, not of their own choosing. That the incidents of Uncle Tom's Cabin are not typical of slave life in the South, but of isolated cases, that the production of the play and its being advertised with bloodhounds and pictures of an old negro in chains and a slave owner with a whip in his hand, give a false idea of the history of the times to the children of the city* [my emphasis, L.S.], *and is disrespectful to Southern gentlemen and good citizens.*[194] — *CONFEDERATE VETERAN MAGAZINE*

Left-wing Yankee novelist, agitator, and indoctrinator, Harriet Beecher Stowe, author of one of the most damaging and historically inaccurate anti-South books ever penned.

SOUTHERN VS. NORTHEN PERSPECTIVES

☛ . . . *The [Liberal] North and the [Conservative] South, differing in religion and in public policy, though of the same race, and with different climates, developed along different lines. The North became chiefly commercial, the South agricultural. The North, as its commercial spirit grew, inclined more and more to nationalism. The regulation of commerce was one of the powers delegated to Congress. Actuated mostly by its own interests, the North came to believe that one of the main objects of government is to aid private enterprise by bounties, subsidies, and protective tariffs. Naturally, then, it fostered the idea of a strong central government, which it expected to control. And so it adopted a loose construction view of the Constitution.*

The South, on the other hand, clung to the idea, as enunciated in the Declaration of Independence, that government is instituted to protect men in life, liberty, and the pursuit of happiness. It adhered also to the original theory of our government, as understood by the framers of the Constitution, as understood by the people when the Constitution was adopted, and as understood by a majority of the people of both sections for more than a generation afterwards.

The South held to conservative views, and believed, then, in a strict construction of the Constitution. It sought no government aid in private enterprise; it was opposed to class legislation, and all undue restrictions of trade. Above all, the South insisted on limiting the Federal Government to its distinctly delegated powers, for, as it believed, it was only by a strict construction of the Constitution that the rights of the States could be preserved.

Such were the fundamental differences between the two sections. Such were both the cause and the effect of the different lines of development. The North grew move rapidly in wealth and population than the South did. Foreign emigrants settled mostly on Northern soil. Largely ignorant of our institutions, and unimbued with the spirit of government as developed among the early colonies, they were, as a rule, national in sentiment.

Col. John W. Gray.

Slavery was a pretext, and not really the cause of the Civil War. The causes of that war lay deeper than slavery. But *slavery was used to intensify sectional feeling, and to prepare the minds of the people of both sections for the clash of arms that, sooner or later, had to come.* For whatever of sin there was in the institution of African slavery in this country New England was no less responsible than the Southern States, and old England most of all. But while some of us may be unwilling to admit that slavery, as it existed in the South, was a sin, but few, if any of us, will deny that it was an evil, that it retarded the development of the South, and intensified sectional feeling. We must never forget, however, that *originally, slavery was forced upon the South, until by reason of the large increase in the number of slaves it became a political necessity. It was not so much a question of the abolition of slavery as what to do with the negro if emancipated* [all emphasis, L.S.]. Self-preservation is the first law of nature, and the majority of the Southern people believed, as far back as [Thomas] Jefferson's time, that life and property would be unsafe if the negroes, semi-savages as they were then, were set free and turned loose in their midst. Nor must one forget that slavery had a legal status, that it existed in all the thirteen original States, and that its protection was guaranteed by the fundamental law of the land.[195] — MAJ. WILLIAM A. OBENCHAIN

MORE EVIDENCE OF BLACK CONFEDERATES

☛ . . . Albert W. Traylor was born at "Winterpock," Chesterfield County, Virginia, where his direct lineal ancestors had lived six generations. He married in Chesterfield County January 19, 1848, Mary Elizabeth Acree Adams, who died in 1888. In the Confederate service *he was in charge of the slave laborers used in the construction of the earthwork fortifications at Drewry's Bluff* [my emphasis, L.S.], subsequently detailed for service in the management of the interests of Lewis D. Crenshaw & Co. at Midway Mills, in Nelson County, when they were filling large contracts for the Confederate government, and he later did actual service in the field as a private in Company E, Twenty-First Virginia Regiment of Infantry, Terry's Brigade, Gordon's Division, A.N.V. . . .[196] — *CONFEDERATE VETERAN* MAGAZINE

CONTRARY TO WHAT IS TAUGHT IN THE SOUTH BY YANKEE EDUCATORS . . .

☛ . . . [Southern] children should be taught that the Constitution was not adopted until nearly six years after the conclusion of the [American] Revolution, and then only after months of much dissension and many concessions. That Virginia, New York, and Rhode Island signed with the proviso that they might withdraw when it was for their best good. That Massachusetts did in 1804 prepare to secede, and New England in 1814. That New England did not lend a helping hand in the war of 1812. That *after the first Dutch importation, New and Old England imported slaves, and that the slave trade was continued twenty years because New England capital was invested in ships for the slave trade. That the North sold her domesticated slaves to the South, because slavery was not profitable, and after she sold them she thought slavery wicked. That John Brown was an anarchist.* That the Southern States were forced to secede, and that in claiming the forts, they claimed only the return for securities which they had put into the pool of States. That the Northern army outnumbered the Southern nearly four to one. That the Confederates surrendered because they had not food to eat, clothes to wear, nor men to fight [and not because the South finally came to accept the Left-wing policies of Lincoln and the Liberal North]. They should know of [Union Gen. Philip H.] Sheridan's order in the [Shenandoah] Valley [that is, to destroy all supplies and food and drive the populace out], and [Union Gen. Benjamin F.] Butler's in New Orleans [which ordered that all Southern women who disrespected Union officers would be legally regarded as prostitutes]. They should be told [the truth] of the reconstruction period.[197] — MISS ANNA CAROLINE BENNING, CHAIRMAN OF THE TEXT-BOOK COMMITTEE

Miss Regina E. Rambo, Sponsor for Georgia.

MORE EVIDENCE OF FORREST'S BLACK CONFEDERATES

☛ Preston B. Coleman died at his home in Union County, Kentucky, January 21, 1902, aged seventy-nine years. He enlisted in the Confederate service in 1862, Company F, organized by Capt. J. J. Barnett at White Sulphur Spring, of the First Kentucky Cavalry.

. . . While under [Confederate Gen. Nathan Bedford] Forrest, Comrade Coleman was wounded in a stockade fight in Tennessee, the ball entering the front of thigh and passing through same. He rode in the ranks a whole day by placing one hand on pommel of saddle and the other on back part of same. Reaching McMinnville, Tennessee, *(where Forrest lost his negro boy* [my emphasis, L.S.], *and baggage wagon in the charge)* he insisted on keeping his place in line of charging column, although unable to handle a weapon, but was finally persuaded from doing so. In any perilous detail work he was usually one of the number selected. After the war was over he returned to his home in Union County, Kentucky, and engaged in farming. He was a man of strong impulses, a staunch friend, true as steel. He left his wife and daughter a good farm.[198] — *CONFEDERATE VETERAN MAGAZINE*

WHITE SOUTHERN BUSINESS SUPPORTS BLACK INTERESTS
☞ For the occasion of the Negro Young People's Christian and Educational Congress, Atlanta, Georgia, August 6-11, the Southern Railway will sell tickets to Atlanta and return, August 4 and 5, at a rate of one fare for the round trip, plus fifty cents, from points within a radius of three hundred miles. Final limit for return of all tickets fifteen days from date of sale. For further information, call on any ticket agent of the Southern Railway.[199] — ADVERTISEMENT IN *CONFEDERATE VETERAN* MAGAZINE, 1902

BLACK SERVANT PROTECTS CONFEDERATE FAMILY FROM YANKEES

Andrew Goodman, former black servant, Dallas, Texas, 1937.

☞ In the early spring of 1857 this young couple [Dr. James McDonald Keller and Mrs. Sadie Phillips Keller], with their two boys, Irvin and Murray, moved to Memphis, Tennessee, where the Doctor rapidly gained a lucrative practice, and his wife became at once universally popular. Soon secession and the war came on, and both became active and eminent participants. The Doctor, a "fire eater," gave up all private practice, and in May received an appointment as surgeon in the Confederate army, with orders to organize and control such hospitals as occasion might demand, and in this important work Mrs. Keller was his most valuable aid, giving her entire time to the arranging of the hospitals and caring for the sick and wounded. At the battle of Shiloh Dr. Keller was ordered to report for operative duty at Corinth, and immediately after that fearful conflict was ordered to report as medical director to [Confederate] Major General [Thomas Carmichael] Hindman, then of [Confederate] General [Braxton] Bragg's army. Mrs. Keller was banished with her two little boys across the Mississippi River into the swamps of Arkansas, with only two trunks and *no protector except a faithful old negro servant, "Black Daddy," who remained true and faithful through the war and up to his death several years later* [my emphasis, L.S.]. Memphis friends, horrified at such treatment, secretly arranged to get the captain of a steamboat to land above and out of sight of the city at night to take them up as far as Cairo.

Thence by cars they went to Louisville, where they remained until 1865, when the Doctor, whom she had not seen since 1862, reached her, having surrendered with [Confederate] General [Nathan Bedford] Forrest at Gainesville, Alabama.[200] — ANONYMOUS "CORRESPONDENT"

BLACK CONFEDERATE VETERAN, JERRY MAY, READS & SHARES CONFEDERATE MAGAZINE

☞ I have been for years a subscriber to the *Confederate Veteran*, and it is a source of keen regret to me that I have not preserved its issues. Generally they have gone to [former] Confederates around me who are not subscribers. *Of late a negro, Jerry* [W.] *May, who went through the war with the Baldwin Blues, of Milledgeville, has been getting them, and I may assure you that he is the most faithful of all your readers. Jerry informs me that when he finishes the copies he sends them to a Confederate widow who was kind to him a long time ago* [my emphasis, L.S.].[201] — HARRY STILLWELL EDWARDS, POSTMASTER, MACON, GA.

THE INTEGRAL ROLE OF THE BLACK MAMMY

☞ . . . On [Confederate] Gen. [Felix Kirk] Zollicoffer's departure from Nashville for the seat of war, the five young children were left in care of their oldest sister, Mrs. James H. Wilson, their mother having died several years before. Mrs. Wilson removed with them to her husband's plantation, "Harpeth," sixteen miles from Nashville, where she nobly supplied a mother's place until ill health and a growing family of her own caused the duties of her position to fall by degrees on the youthful shoulders of [Ann] Maria [Zollicoffer, the General's daughter], who gradually became, in turn, the head of the band of orphans. At an age when girls are usually thinking chiefly of pleasure, her time and thoughts became engrossed with the problems of the nursery. *After the battle of Fishing Creek, whereby the children were doubly orphaned, they also suffered the loss of the good old "black mammy" who had from their infancy nursed and bathed each of them, rocked them to sleep, and tucked them in bed* [my emphasis, L.S.], motherly offices which thenceforth devolved on the devoted young sister.[202] — *CONFEDERATE VETERAN* MAGAZINE

Miss Ann Marie Zollicoffer.

FORMER SOUTHERN SLAVES OFFER TO WORK FOR FREE TO HELP BUILD CONFEDERATE VETERANS' HOME

☞ [To J. M. Falkner, Esq.] Dear Sir: In writing to you the other day in reference to the philanthropic work at Mountain Creek for the Confederate veterans, I neglected to say that we should be proud to assist you in your laudable enterprise if you should desire us. We can furnish you at any time ten or fifteen carpenters, painters, blacksmiths, and others who might be useful in building up your soldiers' home. We should be glad to work a week or ten days without money and without price. Our shoe department will be glad to furnish you with at least a dozen pairs of shoes a year for those grand old men who followed Lee's tattered banners down to Appomattox, leaving their bloody footprints

over the snow-covered hills of Virginia.
    Although I came up from the other side of the flood [Africa] and drank of the dregs of the cup of slavery, still I honor those gray-haired veterans, and I feel that, when they pass away and when their old slaves have passed away, in a measure the power of the balance wheel of Southern society will be gone. The propriety of this offer on my part may be called into question by those who do not measure slavery as I do. *I feel that the slaves got more out of slavery than did their masters, in that the slaves were helped from the lowest state of barbarism to Christian citizenship of the greatest government the world ever knew* [my emphasis, L.S.].[203] — W. H. COUNCILL, BLACK INDUSTRIAL SCHOOL TEACHER, HUNTSVILLE, ALA.

WHITE SOUTHERNERS DESIRE PENSIONS FOR FORMER SOUTHERN BLACK SERVANTS

☞ The columns of a country newspaper are but a small forum in which to speak of so large a subject; nevertheless we must use the opportunities at hand until better offer.
    [Ohio] Senator [Marcus A.] Hanna has introduced a bill in the United States Senate looking to the pensioning of the old slaves of the South. He did it apologetically, and no doubt hypocritically. He had no idea and no desire that it would ever become a law. Yet one of these days he may be taken by surprise. He has opened a vent through which Southern voices may be heard.
    We [Southern whites] all want to see the old slaves pensioned—not for policy's sake, but for humanity's sake; not for the negro vote, but for the suffering around us; not for spite against the North, but for pity toward poor, helpless creatures, whose patience and sufferings are ever before us.
    If I remember aright, the Confederate Veteran, *published by a Confederate soldier* [Sumner A. Cunningham], *and the official organ of all Southern patriotic societies, was the first and only paper in the United States to come out boldly and advocate honestly the pensioning of our old slaves.*
    When I think of the vast sums that are given by Northern philanthropists for educating the negroes beyond their need and beyond their good, and then turn about and see the hundreds of poor old slaves around me suffering with cold and hunger, my heart grows faint. When I see them silent and patient, waiting for God to release them from a bondage worse than a master's hand, and then think of those who are living on government bounty, I am disgusted.

Marcus A. Hanna, U.S. Senator.

    Every year the Christian Herald *and other religious papers at the North collect vast sums of money for famine sufferers in India and Norway and Mexico; but not one dollar for a poor, old, starving Southern negro. Rockefeller, the Pious, last year gave more than five millions to Sunday schools, Christian associations, and negro colleges; but not one farthing to help feed, clothe, and shelter the poor old slaves of the South!*

The home of Confederate President Jefferson Davis after Richmond, Virginia, was made the capital of the Confederacy. In 1916, when this photo was taken, it had become a Confederate museum.

Let's see. How many cases can I recall on the instant right here before me? There is blind Nelson, an old paralyzed Squire, begging from door to door. There is old Zeke in his hut down on the river, kept alive by the charity of a few people. There is old blind Ann Plummer, kept from starving by the kindness of two white women, on neither of whom she has the slightest claim. About a year ago old Eliza West was found dead and alone in a cabin in the country. The coroner held an inquest, and the verdict was: "Died from natural causes." If slow starvation and cold and neglect can be called "natural causes," then the verdict was correct. And several years ago an old negro man, Watson Knox, was found dead, lying across the path where he had started to town to beg for the little pittance that had kept him alive thus far. I know all about this case, for Watson was a slave of my father. I had taken care of him for years. *A more faithful, grateful, honest negro never lived.* He had those of his own blood and bone around him, yet he died of cold and hunger, and the only tears that were shed over his dead body were those I shed, and they were tears of remorse because I might have done more and did not.

But it is useless to multiply instances—they flock to my mind like ghosts, and everybody in Wilkes County [North Carolina] who reads this can recall as many more. *I have tried to tell the story through Northern newspapers and magazines, but they will have none of it.* No! they want to hear of "education" and "progress" and "uplifting" of the race. They listen with insatiable eagerness to tales like Booker Washington has to tell, but stop their ears to tales of crime and suffering. *How a people who were so hysterical over slavery can be so callous now, I can't conceive. How a people whose hearts were wrought up to the pitch of war and bloodshed by* Uncle Tom's Cabin *can now scoff at the idea of want and crime among these same old slaves gone masterless, I can't conceive. How a people who erect, at a cost of thousands of dollars, marble fountains for dumb beasts to drink at can refuse to give a cup of cold water to Southern negroes, I can't conceive.*

But they do it. And they do it because they are Southern negroes. If they lived at the North, and this pension money flowed into Northern avenues of trade, they would pension them. Or if it was to "uplift" and place them on an equality with the whites of the South, they would pension them [all emphasis, L.S.].

But no! They live hidden away in hovels on Southern soil. They have no vote; they have no voice. The world will never know how they died. But Senator Hanna has opened a breach in the wall, he has lighted a torch that he little dreamed of, and by its light the world will begin to see and know. And the negroes themselves will begin to see and know. They will soon find out, Senator Hanna, whether it was pity or policy that induced you to offer a bill "by request"' for pensioning the old slaves of the South.[204] — MRS. M. T. GREEN, *WASHINGTON CHRONICLE* (GEORGIA)

PENSIONED BLACK CONFEDERATE SOLDIER LOYAL TO THE END

☞ Frederick Pouncey, colored, was the property of Mrs. Martha Cone, Strata, Montgomery County, Alabama, before and during the War between the States. Capt. Ben Hart made up his company of the best material in Montgomery County. *"Uncle Fed" went with his young masters of that company whom he had nursed and watched over from boyhood to young manhood.* The company became a part of the Twenty-Second Alabama Volunteers. Will Henry, now, I believe, a resident of Kentucky, was first lieutenant.

"Uncle Fed" was born March 25, 1825, and died August 15, 1902, aged seventy-seven years. *On account of his loyalty to the Confederate cause, he was highly respected by more white people than any negro who ever lived in Montgomery County. Following his young masters on every battlefield where they fought, he at the end returned to "Ole Missus" with but one of those committed to his care in the beginning of the war.* He was for a long while a physical wreck, until death claimed him.

During the fight at Shiloh this negro began to collect relics taken from the Yankees, and January 8, 1902, he made a will in which he bequeathed to the Sophia Bibb Chapter. No. 26, U.D.C. of Montgomery, Ala., an artilleryman's sword, a Yankee canteen, and other articles of minor value. *In closing his will he said: "I do this because of the love I have for the boys who wore the gray."*

When the old man saw that his days were numbered, he sent for the writer of this sketch and gave him the will and relics, and made an earnest request that he see its provisions carried out to the letter. *So implicit was the confidence of the* [Confederate] *veterans in the old man that they asked the County Board to place his name on the pension roll many years ago, after which time he drew the pittance appropriated on equal terms with disabled white veterans. He was a thorough Democrat* [that is, a Conservative], *and voted the ticket despite the taunts of his race* [most of who tended to vote for the then Liberal Party, the Republicans]. When the time came to register in 1902 "Uncle Fed" was the only negro given a life certificate in Beat 15, Montgomery County, Alabama.

On the left a white mistress cards wool fibers, while on the right one of her black servants weaves rolled yarn. Nineteenth-Century white and black Southerners developed the most powerful bonds of affection, trust, and respect that have ever existed between two races.

He died in the faith of the Primitive Baptist Church. He never went off after any new religion, but remained steadfast to the end among his white brethren in full fellowship, where he was accorded every privilege belonging to the Church. He neither sought nor desired social equality. Many of his white friends stood about his grave when his body was laid to rest. Penciled on a rude headboard were these words: "A Christian and a soldier."

A marble slab should mark the old man's last resting place, and I am willing to help buy one. I knew him for more than fifty years, and I never heard his moral character attacked by any one. After he was made a "freedman" he clung closer to his white friends than while he was a slave, because, said he, "The white folks here where I was born is all the friends I have" [all emphasis, L.S.].²⁰⁵ — J. R. MCLENDON, NAFTEL, ALA.

LOYAL BLACK CONFEDERATE BURIED IN CONFEDERATE UNIFORM

☛ The just tribute to the faithfulness of a negro, Frederick Pouncey, by J. R. McLendon, of Naftel, Alabama [above], furnishes an example worthy to be remembered of the real relationship of the master-and-slave period. Once before this I attempted to give you an account of my boy, Reuben May, black in all but heart and faithfulness, but the effort fell so far short of the deserts of Reuben that I desisted. *In him there is an example for faithfulness that cannot be excelled.*

For generations Rube's ancestors had belonged to my father's family. He was born a few years after I was, brought up a house boy, his mother the cook, *his father the foreman on the plantation.* When the war broke out Rube was taken along as a servant. He soon became well and favorably known in the regiment, and was with it in all its campaigns, even into Maryland and Pennsylvania. During the battle of Gettysburg he possessed himself of a piece of gingham, of which he gave me enough to make two shirts. I asked him no questions as to the manner of obtaining it, remembering the words, "Eat what is set before you, asking no questions."

The actual love this good boy bore me was exemplified after each battle by his greeting me with outstretched hands and with tears streaming down his cheeks. When I was wounded at the battle of the Wilderness, Reuben's anxiety was intense until he found out it was not serious. Often in camp, when our rations were scarce, he would come to me and propose that he go out "foraging." I would hand him my purse with no thought of counting the money, and sometimes he would be gone a week. But my faith was strong, and *he never failed me. After the war he followed me home as best he could, and went about his business as he had always done, never mentioning price or pay.*

I had hired the other negro men to cut and split wood to sell to steamboats. After this a certain order was issued by a certain [Yankee] officer of the Freedman's Bureau at Selma, Alabama, that all people hiring freedmen should enter into a written contract, signed by both parties, which was to be submitted to said officer for approval, the officer to be paid one dollar. In conforming to this order I called up the men, stated the nature of the order, wrote the contract, and all signed it but Rube, who sat off a little way with bowed head. I was chagrined that my faithful boy should fail in this extremity and not enter into what I thought was good for them and good for me, but said nothing until all had left, when I asked: "Rube, what was the matter?" He raised his sad eyes to me and said: "Mas' William, ain't I free?" "Yes," said I. *"Well, if I am, what have the Yankees got to do with it?"* I explained as best I could, appreciating the boy as never before. "Well," said he, "no contract for you

and me. I am going to live where you live as long as I live unless you drive me away from you. I have lived with you all my life without a contract, and don't want one now."
    Faithful creature! He so lived, he so died. On his deathbed, the last time I went in to see him, I sat down beside him. He crawled closer and put his head on my leg and seemed satisfied. The next day he died. *He was buried in my* [Confederate] *uniform. His loyalty and faithfulness is a sad but sweet memory. Can such another example be presented?*
    [Appended note from *Confederate Veteran:*] It is a fact that since the adoption of the new Constitution the checkrein of both (Southern) white and black seems to have been let down, and *more good feeling exists than at any time since the war* [all emphasis, L.S.].²⁰⁶ — CONFEDERATE CAPT. W. H. MAY, COMPANY G, THIRD ALABAMA INFANTRY, MARION, ALA.

BLACK CONFEDERATE SERVES THROUGHOUT ENTIRE WAR
☛ The [accompanying] photograph represents Mr. E. B. Mobley, Rock Hill, South Carolina, Company F, Sixth South Carolina Infantry, and *Hampton Stratford, aged seventy-eight, who was his faithful body servant during the entire war* [my emphasis, L.S.]. Mr. Mobley says of his army career:

E. B. Mobley and his servant, black Confederate soldier Hampton Stratford.

    "At the breaking out of the war I was a member of a Chester County (S.C.) cavalry troop, and did not leave home with the regiment with which I was afterwards identified—the Sixth South Carolina Infantry [C.S.A.].
    "After waiting for nearly two months, we became impatient, and nine of us, accompanying Capt. W. P. Crawford, went to Summerville and joined the command mentioned. That regiment proceeded to Richmond about the middle of July. We remained there several days, and reached Manassas Junction about noon of the day of the first battle. After a short delay, we went on the but the Yankees had left for Washington. On our way to the field we met a man on horseback carrying in front of him the body of Col. Fisher, of North Carolina, who was killed that day.
    "I was with my regiment in most of its engagements—and it saw hard service—being wounded at the battle of Second Manassas. The regiment left Chester on the day I was twenty-one years old, and I spent my twenty-fifth anniversary as a prisoner at Appomattox. Out of the ten of us who left the cavalry and joined the Sixth Infantry, only two returned home with it."²⁰⁷ — *CONFEDERATE VETERAN* MAGAZINE

PREDOMINANT SOUTHERN WHITE SENTIMENT
☛ . . . *the negro race has no more real, sincere, and honest friends in the world than the* [white] *people of the Southern States, and, in fact, there are more*

instances *of genuine and affectionate friendship between white and black people in that section than anywhere else on earth. . . . . [The] South has a place for the negro, and knows him, and is his true friend* [my emphasis, L.S.].²⁰⁸ — BISHOP THOMAS F. GAILOR

BLACK PREACHER DEFENDS THE SOUTH
☞ [During a 1903 speech before the African Methodist Episcopal Church in Brooklyn, New York, black preacher Rev. R. D. Stinson] declared that mass [anti-white, anti-South] meetings in the North, agitating for the negro of the South, did the masses in the South great injury; that the negro in the South was all right; that he was owning homes, educating his children, and did not demand social equality, and that *as far as he was concerned he would rather live in the South than to be a millionaire in New York.*

"The sooner the great mass of our people entertain a good opinion of the South the better it will be for us," said the speaker. "There is as much ignorance, bad feeling, and prejudice existing in the North as in the South. *The South is the place for the negro. You have no place for us in the North* [all emphasis, L.S.]. The negro is going to stay in the South and make the best of his condition. I am not saying this because I want the favor of any one. I am not crouching."²⁰⁹ — AFRICAN AMERICAN PREACHER, REV. R. D. STINSON, ATLANTA, GA.

SOUTHERN BLACK MAN WRITES LETTER TO PRES. THEODORE ROOSEVELT
☞ [African American J. B. Raynor addressed the following letter to the president via the *Houston Post.*] Should the chief executive read it, he will learn something to his advantage. The colored man states correctly the Southern white man's attitude in the matter. Explaining who the Southern man is, this negro says that "he is the true American, the son of the patriots of 1776, and he is brave, proud, dictatorial, and loves and honors his women and home with a devotion which makes him superior to all other races of mankind. Again, the [white] Southerner feels his superiority, because he knows it, and he will not submit to be ruled by any inferior race. Again, the [white] Southerner is the most generous of men, and is charitable to a fault, and cares nothing for wealth, but loves honor with a devotion sublime. Again,

Future U.S. President Theodore Roosevelt, 1885.

the [white] Southerner is the only man in the world who truly knows negro idiosyncrasies, and he knows how to treat and handle the negro. *The Southerner is the negro's best and only friend, and has done more, and will do more, for the negro than any other man living. All the land that the negroes own in the South they bought from the [white] Southerner, and the worthy negro is just as secure in his political rights in the South as a worthy white man is in New England*" [my emphasis, L.S.].²¹⁰ — CONFEDERATE VETERAN MAGAZINE

CONFEDERATE GEN. W. H. JACKSON BELOVED BY WHITE & BLACK

☞ Surrounded by his devoted children and other nearest relatives, [Confederate] Gen. William H. Jackson fell peacefully asleep on the night of March 31, [1903] at historic Belle Meade [Plantation], the fairest of all the Southland's fair homes, made beautiful by a combination of early traditions and nature's choicest endowments.

Confederate Gen. William "Red" Hicks Jackson.

. . . Up to the time of his death Gen. Jackson kept alive the spirit of ante-bellum days, and *white and black alike, from the President of the United States down to the humblest negro, appreciated the quality of welcome that went with his firm grasp of the hand and deep-voiced assurance, "I am glad to see you!"* [my emphasis, L.S.]. There must be glad welcome from the shores of eternity for the spirit of one who has cheered the stranger within his gates and given shelter to those who have craved his bounty and with confidence sought his help.

The funeral of Gen. Jackson was conducted by his warm personal friend and associate in arms, [Confederate] Col. David C. Kelley, now an eminent minister of the Methodist Church and at the head of Forrest Cavalry Corps of Veterans.[211] — *CONFEDERATE VETERAN* MAGAZINE

CONCERNING SLAVERY . . .

☞ Hon. B. G. Humphreys addressed the people of his old home at Port Gibson, Mississippi, on behalf of the Sons of Confederate Veterans in a memorial service. He showed a spirit worthy of his sires. After noting some remarkable statistics of Mississippians in battle, he said concerning slavery:

"I would not, of course, have the institution back again if I could; but it is my fixed opinion, judging the negro who grew to manhood in slavery and the negro who has grown to manhood in freedom, that as a race *he reached his zenith in all those qualities which make for civilization and Christianity under the old regime*. Forty years in the history and development of a race is but a short while indeed, but in that time the finger of 'Ole Massa' and 'Die Missus,' which always pointed heavenward, has been unobserved, and the course of the great body of the younger [Southern black] generation, I regret to say it, has been almost headlong in the opposite direction.

"The songs that have come down to us from the old plantation are not the songs of the caged bird; there is no wailing of the soul crying out to its God for deliverance; there is no story of brick without straw. Many and many is the time that I sat as a child and looked into the black and wrinkled face of the freedman and noted the light that does not lie illumine his face as he recounted the happy days back on the old plantation.

"If proof were needed that the story of Uncle Tom's Cabin was a figment of the imagination, the war itself furnished it. Left at home to work the field and make the crops that were to support our armies, the negro had it in his power at *all times to strike the blow that would have brought the Confederacy to its knees. The first blaze of an insurrection, the first scream of a murdered mistress, would have dissolved the ranks of the Confederate armies, and every soldier 'would have brooked the eternal devil' to make his way back to his home and his loved ones. Yet in all those long and bloody years never a torch was lighted, never a hand was raised"* [all emphasis, L.S.].

> 'The slave who wore no cross nor crown
> With shackled feet trod freedom down,
> Knew that each rebel soldier slain
> Broke one link in his iron chain,
> Yet fought his way through the whirlwind's breath,
> Rode on the storm to conquer death,
> Reckless of what might mar or make;
> Only to die for his master's sake.
> Waterloo, Trafalgar, Salamis,
> Marathon, show us a page like this.'

"Let me read you a piece of poetry that must forever give the lie to the calumnies heaped upon our [Old South] fathers, a poem which, whenever read, will, I sincerely hope, rekindle the dying embers of the old-time feeling we once entertained for the negro. No such story as is told in this poem was ever founded on fiction."

Old Mose at Gettysburg

Rushing from shelter far in the rear,
"My master wounded?" is that what I hear?
Forth to the rescue rushed the slave,
Into the battle to succor and save.
"Master, O Master," he cried aloud.
Breaking a path through the battle cloud,
Fighting his way through friends and foes;
"Answer me, Master; here's Ole Mose.
You know when we left Ole Missus said,
'Fotch him back, Moses, livin' or dead.'
I promised, O Master!"— but more and more,
Louder and fiercer the cannons roar.
"Master!" again the tempest rose—
"Answer me, Master; here's Ole Mose."
The valleys trembled again, and then
The mountains reeled like drunken men.
"I done told Missus, O Master dear,
Ole Mose is comin'; can't you hear?"
Through hurtling death and fire and smoke,
What arm wards off the fatal stroke?
What, judged by human, finite sense,
Could shield, but the arm of Providence?
'Twas Heaven's own mercy, tender and sweet,
The angel spirit in his feet,
That led Ole Mose through the crimson tide
To stumble and fall at his master's side.
"Dear Mose, is it you?" as soft and slow
The wave of life ebbed to and fro.

"Tell mother—God bless you, dear Old Mose"—
His life went out on the storm that rose.
Sheltered in arms that were strong to save,
In the brave black arms of the faithful slave,
Borne back, back over rock and ledge,
Over the battle's perilous edge,
Borne by this martyr, this more than man,
Southward across the Rapidan—
Back to the dear old homestead where
White doves float in the crimson air.
Stood by the grave where his master slept,
For the first time turned aside and wept.
Is it strange that his future seemed dark and dim,
And dark to us as it was to him?
He had fought for his master, had gladly died.
Shall we not help him in paths untried?
All over the South one prayer arose:
"God forget us who forget Ole Mose."[212] — CONFEDERATE VETERAN MAGAZINE

WHITE OWNED NEWSPAPER AIDS BLACK CONFEDERATE VETERAN

☞ The *Osceola Democrat* (Missouri) *raised money to send "Uncle" George McDonald, of St. Clair County, a colored Confederate veteran . . . to the Confederate reunion at Columbia last month. "Uncle" George went with the Confederates from St. Clair County, and fought in several engagements. At* [the battle of] *Wilson's Creek a Minie ball plowed through his hip and a buckshot struck him in the face* (my emphasis, L.S.).

George lay groaning upon the ground when he was found by Owen Snuffer, lieutenant of his company. Snuffer stooped down, examined the black man's wounds, and stanched the flow of blood from them. "For God's sake," cried the suffering negro, "give me a drink of water." Snuffer's canteen was empty, but midway between the firing lines was a well. To reach it the lieutenant was to become the target of sharpshooters, and it meant almost certain death. But with bullets falling around him like hailstones he pushed forward until the well was reached. And then he discovered that the bucket had been taken away and the windlass removed. The water was far down and the depth unknown. The well was old-fashioned—stone-walled. Owen pulled off his long cavalry boots, and, taking one in his teeth, he let himself down slowly, hand over hand, until the water was reached and the boot filled, and then he climbed up, straddling the well and clutching with hands and feet the rocky walls. Reaching the surface again, he picked up the other boot and safely made his way back to the

Zek Brown, former servant, Ft. Worth, Texas, 1937.

Confederate lines.

Returning from the war, "Uncle" George settled near Monegaw Springs, and has reared an intelligent, honest, industrious family. One of his children educated himself, graduated at the Smith University, in Sedalia, and is now in charge of a Church in Kansas. Another is waiter at the Commercial Hotel in Osceola, and is known for his strict integrity.[213]
— *CONFEDERATE VETERAN* MAGAZINE

BLACK SERVANT BRINGS TEARS TO A CONFEDERATE GENERAL'S EYES

☞ We heard of a little incident that may profit some of our Northern foes, should this paper fall into their hands, and they will take the trouble to peruse it. [Confederate] Gen. Joe [E.] Johnston was receiving friends at the Lamar House. He was surrounded with many gallant officers who had called to pay their respects, when there came a smart rap at the door. An officer, shining with stars and gold lace, opened the door, and there stood a venerable negro woman with a coarse sunbonnet on her head and a cotton umbrella under her arm. "Is this Mr. Johnston's room?" asked the old woman. The glittering officer nodded assent. "Mr. Joe Johnston's room?" Assent again being condescended, she said: "I want to see him." In she marched, and tapped the great military chieftain on the shoulder. He turned and clasped her ebony hand in his, while she for a moment silently perused his features. At length she spoke: "Mr. Joe, you is getting old." The General affectionately held his old nurse's hand, and answered her artless inquiries, while large tears rolled down his soldierly cheeks. The venerable negress who made the commander of the armies of the West "cry like a baby" was Judy, slave of Dr. Paxton [and Gen. Johnston's childhood nurse], who had "toted" Joe in her arms when he was a baby.[214] — KNOXVILLE *REGISTER*, 1860s

Two famous Confederate generals postbellum. Left, Joseph E. Johnston; right, Robert E. Lee; circa 1870.

WARTIME HEROISM OF SOUTHERN WHITE WOMEN & BLACK SERVANTS

☞ In a late issue of the *Veteran* I notice an account of the trials and dangers undergone during the war by a noble Confederate woman in reaching her afflicted husband. Say what we please about the heroism of our Southern men, all that we endured is far eclipsed by the heroism of Southern women. I need not dwell upon the risk they ran while alone they remained at home surrounded by thousands of slaves, nor of their hardships and labors in feeding and clothing themselves and children. *In these respects their heroism is equaled only by the devotion of their faithful slaves, who deserve the greatest credit for their loyalty to their owners.* Such a record as was made by our noble women and faithful slaves is unparalleled in the annals of history [my emphasis, L.S.]. Let our children and children's children have these lessons deeply instilled into their hearts and minds.[215] — GEORGE W. L. FLY

LEE PROVES THAT THE CONFEDERATES FOUGHT TO PRESERVE STATES RIGHTS NOT SLAVERY

☛ . . . Patriots they were in very deed and truth, fighting with as lofty spirit and as worthy motive as ever filled the breasts of courageous men; patriots even when you set the highest standard of patriotism, which can be no other than the struggle for human liberty. *The soldiers of the South did not fight for slavery; they fought for freedom. The right of a Church to be free made the wars of [Oliver] Cromwell. The right of a colony to be free made the war of the Revolution. The right of a State to be free made the war for Southern independence—the right of a State to be free [that is, self-governed]. The world has never known, nor will it ever know, a loftier patriotism than the patriotism of the soldiers of the South.*

The C.S.A. was a Conservative confederate republic that fought to preserve the original U.S. Constitution. This makes the South "the Heart of America" (the original caption of this Victorian illustration).

. . . Therefore, when in April, 1861, Francis Preston Blair [Sr.], the authorized agent of President Lincoln, offered [Robert. E. Lee] . . . the command of the Union forces with the words, "I come to you on the part of President Lincoln to ask whether any inducements that he can offer will prevail on you to take command of the Union army"; Lee answered, "If I owned the four million slaves [in the South], I would cheerfully sacrifice [that is, emancipate] them to the preservation of the Union; but to lift my hand against my own State and people is impossible."[216] — REV. J. A. B. SHERER

BLACK CONFEDERATE & SERVANT ATTENDS HIS WHITE OWNER'S FUNERAL

☛ [From an obituary concerning the death of Confederate Major Charles H. Smith, known to readers of the *Atlanta Constitution* as "Bill Arp":] *"Tip," a faithful man born a slave in Mrs. Smith's family, who served the Major faithfully through the war and afterwards, who moved him from Rome to the farm near Cartersville, and then went from Rome to move the family into town, was present at the funeral* [my emphasis, L.S.].[217] — *CONFEDERATE VETERAN MAGAZINE*

ACCOUNT OF FAITHFUL BLACK SERVANT BOB BEAVERS

☛ Bob, or as he sometimes, when a slave, liked to be called, "Col. Robert," was the slave, the carriage driver, and general all-round helpful servant of the late Hon. Warren Akin, ex-member of the Congress of the Confederate States. From the beginning of the War between the States he was keenly interested in all that occurred, so much so that some persons thought he was eagerly looking for freedom. His master did not think so, and trusted Bob implicitly to care for his family during his absence from home and to care for his property as far as he could. Bob always expressed and showed the utmost interest in the Southern soldier; so much so that when boxes of home-made comforts were sent to our soldiers he always put in his contribution of well-knit gloves, knit with a needle like a crochet needle that was of his own make. Soldiers in Virginia often sent thanks for the gloves that added to their comfort. When Stoneman's raiders came through Oxford, Georgia, by Bob's warning and management his master barely escaped to the woods as they entered the village. Their first inquiry was for Col. Akin.

Mrs. E. C. Pendleton, of Richmond, Virginia.

Bob was offered $500 in gold if he would secure his capture. He was not even tempted to betrayal. The offer was raised to $1,000. He told me: "I had to tell a heap of lies, but I said nothing about Marster." At that time he was much excited, and, with his ax held behind him, followed a Federal soldier who was plundering the house. I was alarmed, and, calling him aside, asked what he was doing with that ax. He replied: "Why, Miss Mary, if that man insults you, I will kill him." With a warning for him to be quiet, I took the ax away and hid it.

During Col. Akin's "hide out" Bob carried his food to him and protected him in every way possible. When told he was a free man, he seemed depressed, and remarked: "I don't want to be free; I don't know what to do with myself. I don't know how to support my family." It was a large family, and he was the only one who seemed to have any conception of what it was to support them. His master made arrangements for him to get back to Bartow County, bought for him a cow, a horse, some few hogs, and went security for his year's supply. But he was extravagant, and could not understand the necessity for economy. After many changes of place, he finally settled down at Cassville, where he had lived from boyhood, and just said: "Master, you will have to help me." Then the master died, and Bob became dependent on the sons. *He worked hard, was honest and respectable, was always cheerful and gay, with perfect confidence in the "Akin boys" to care for him.* He joined the Methodist Church several times, and at last settled down into a devout and pious life. After a long illness he seemed to recover his health, but was suddenly stricken with paralysis, and after a few days' silent suffering he died. He was seventy-three years of age. When a negro has lived long as slave and as a freedman, has been faithful in what he considered his Christian duty, without even making any attempt at social equality with the white race, has always been cheerful and hopeful, even under adverse circumstances, it seems right to me that some notice should be taken of that man's life, and after death he should be remembered with grateful hearts by those he served; and it is thus Bob Beavers is remembered by the wife and children of the man he so faithfully served.[218] — MRS. M. F. AKIN, CARTERSVILLE, GA.

ANOTHER VIEW OF THE PATRIOTISM OF LEE & THE CONSERVATIVE SOUTH

☛ . . . it is clearly shown that [Union Gen.] George H. Thomas [a Southerner from Virginia] did intend to cast his fortunes with his native State, and was prevented from doing so by the influence of his wife or other considerations which could not be called "patriotic" by any stretch of language. As for Robert Edward Lee, he was the son of "Light Horse Harry" [Henry Lee III] a Virginian of the Virginias, and a patriot to the very core. He was not an "original secessionist" (as was Thomas), and clung to the Union with filial devotion, but he never doubted the right of a State to secede from the Union, and held most emphatically that "a union pinned together by bayonets" would be no union at all. When President Lincoln, through the Elder [Francis Preston] Blair, offered him the supreme command of the United States armies in the field called out to "suppress the rebellion," he promptly declined the tempting offer, saying: *"If the four millions of slaves in the South were mine, I would free them with a stroke of my pen to avert this war. But I cannot take up arms against my State, my home, my children."* He fought for his home, his native State, and the God-given "inalienable rights" of his people. *He always called the war "our great struggle for constitutional freedom"* [my emphasis, L.S.]., and never regretted the part he took in it. He said to his great lieutenant, Wade Hampton, in 1869: "We could have taken no other course without dishonor; and if it were all to be gone over again, I should act in precisely the same manner." [Yankees and Liberals claim that] Thomas [was] a patriot and Lee a traitor! Well, this will pass into history as true when it is established that "the Tories" of the Revolution and Benedict Arnold were patriots, and George Washington and "Light Horse Harry" Lee were traitors, when "might makes right" and truth becomes falsehood.²¹⁹ — DR. J. WILLIAM JONES

Confederate States steamer *Gaines*.

FORMER BLACK SERVANTS INVITED TO CONFEDERATE REUNION

☞ Preparations for the Confederate reunion appear to be, progressing very slowly, and a little information as to what a company of cavalry is doing may interest the readers of the *Veteran*. Harvey Scouts, attached to Jackson's Cavalry, have rented the third floor of 116 Exchange Alley, in which they have placed wire cots, mattresses, pillows, sheets, mosquito bars, and other conveniences. Here the veterans can sleep and refresh themselves. The privileges of the place will be extended to the members of the company, free of charge. *An invitation has been sent to the negroes who went out as servants to the boys* [my emphasis, L.S.]. Should all Camps accept the course inaugurated by the Harvey Scouts, a fuller attendance would be insured.[220] — THE HARVEY SCOUTS, CONFEDERATE VETERANS, NEW ORLEANS, LOUISIANA

ELAM & SAM

☛ The late Elam Alexander, of Macon, Ga., founder of Alexander's Free School and one of nature's noblemen, perpetrated a grim joke while making his last will and presumably near his end on his favorite negro "body servant," Sam, who had been his faithful attendant for many years. Mr. Alexander, feeble and suffering, was lying in bed, his lawyer sat at a table and wrote down the various bequests, while Sam bustled about the room, deeply sympathizing with his suffering master, anxious as to his own future, and keenly curious as to the disposition to be made of the large estate. The sick man, besides leaving the fund for founding the school in Macon that bears his name, had generously provided for his kindred and all of his old negroes except Sam. When he could stand the suspense no longer, Sam slipped behind the lawyer and softly whispered, "See what Marse Elam gwine ter do fur me," and then noiselessly left the room, leaving the door ajar so he could hear what was said. The lawyer called Mr. Alexander's attention to the fact that he had made bequests to all of his old servants except Sam. The feeble testator turned his head on his pillow, sighed, and said: "Sam has been a mighty good negro." "Bless God!" came in fervent tones from the delighted Sam, whose hopes were raised by this praise, through the partly open door outside of which he was listening. "I believe I will take him with me," continued Mr. Alexander. This was too much for Sam. He burst into the room, threw himself on his knees by his master's bed, and cried: "For God's sake, Marse Elam, don't do dat." The sick man smiled at his joke, *and made Sam happy with a generous bequest* [all emphasis, L.S.].[221] — *CONFEDERATE VETERAN* MAGAZINE

Miss Marie Estelle Patillo, Decatur, Georgia, Latina Maid of Honor to Sponsor for Oklahoma Division.

WOUNDED CONFEDERATE CAPTAIN SAVED BY FAITHFUL SERVANT

☛ *Not often have I come in contact with relations more beautiful than existed in some cases between young Southern masters in the service and their slave attendants.* These latter belonged for the most part to one of two classes; either they were mature and faithful men, to whose care the lads' parents had committed them, or else they were the special chums and playmates of their young masters' boyhood days and perhaps had attended and waited upon them in college.

My first cousin, William Henry Stiles, Jr., captain in the Sixtieth Georgia Infantry, of which his father was colonel, was wounded late in the evening of the battle of Fredericksburg; but the casualty was not generally known, probably because the surgeons finding him on the field, after a hurried examination, pronounced his wound mortal and added,

"We are sorry to leave you, Captain, but we have all we can do," to which he replied: "Certainly, gentlemen, go and attend to the men; but you are mistaken about me. I haven't the least idea of dying."

They left him. Neither his father nor any member of his company was aware of his locality; *but there was one faithful soul to whom he was more than all the regiment. If his master continued missing, the world was empty to him; and so in cold, darkness, and sadness he searched every foot of the ground the regiment had fought over till at last he found him. Then the faithful slave wandered about until he got from the bodies of the dead blankets enough to make a warm, soft bed, carefully lifted his master onto it, and covered him snugly. He then managed to start a fire and got water for him, and finally, most important of all, he got from the body of a dead Federal officer a small flask of brandy and stimulated him carefully.*

About daylight the doctors came again and, surprised to find the captain alive, made a more careful examination and found that the ball had passed entirely through his body just between the upper and lower vital parts, but that *he would have died from exposure had it not been for the faithful love that refused to be satisfied until it had found and provided for him* [all emphasis, L.S.].²²² — CONFEDERATE MAJOR ROBERT STILES

TRUE CAUSE OF THE WAR

☛ It has been to a large extent assumed that negro slavery was the cause of that war. This is not strictly true. It was the occasion of the war, but not the principal cause of the war. The real cause of the war was sectional jealousy, the greed of gain, and the lust of political power by the Eastern States [that is, Yankee Liberals]. The changing opinions of civilized nations on the subject of slavery furnished the occasion which enabled [Left-wing] political demagogues to get up a crusade which enabled them in the end to overthrow, in part at least, the Constitution of the United States [a Conservative document], and to change the character of the Federal government [in the direction of socialism] by a successful revolution.²²³ — HON. JOHN H. REAGAN (FORMER CONFEDERATE POSTMASTER GENERAL UNDER PRESIDENT JEFFERSON DAVIS), APRIL 19, 1903

Miss Julia Velma Enslen, of Birmingham, Alabama, Maid of Honor to Alabama's Sponsor at Charleston.

WHITE CONFEDERATE VETERAN WISHES TO RECONNECT WITH "FAITHFUL NEGRO"

☛ Our [Confederate] Capt. N. B. Roberts and Lieut. G. E. Thomas were from Columbus, Georgia, and better soldiers or braver men never lived. Lieut. Tom Granbery was idolized by the entire company. The noble and brave Lieut. Sam McLeary fell at my side on July 18, 1864, at Kennesaw Mountain, with a bullet through his brain. I sent his body to his wife in Harris County, Ga. *I would be glad to see her if she still lives, and also the faithful negro servant, Lairy, who accompanied the body home* [my emphasis, L.S.]. . . .²²⁴ — CONFEDERATE VETERAN MAGAZINE

A EUROPEAN VIEW OF BLACKS, GRANT, & THE NORTH

☞ ... [Union Gen. Ulysses S.] Grant was a man of tremendous, indomitable will power: cold, determined, sober-minded, and practical. The resoluteness that marked his every action and *his apparent disregard for human life, particularly that of the negro, for whom the North was pretending to fight, characterize him as a man preeminently fit for his position* [my emphasis, L.S.].[225] — BARON VON FREYTAG-LORINGHOVEN, GERMAN HISTORIAN

BLACK CONFEDERATE HELPS CAPTURE A COMPANY OF YANKS

☞ Judge Harris, of Memphis, who was a Mississippian prior to his removal to Tennessee, told *a unique story during the [Confederate] reunion of the capture of an entire Federal company by one man of his command, the Seventeenth Mississippi, who was aided by a negro* [my emphasis, L.S.]. The man was John Lake. The negro who aided him was known as Sandy. Lake, who was in Company F, sighted the soldiers, who were in camp. Instructing Sandy and sending him to flank them, he boldly walked up in front with drawn sword and demanded their surrender. The Yankees sprang for their arms, when the negro yelled out: "Shall we open fire, Captain?" Thinking that they were surrounded, the Yankees laid down their arms and were marched off to the main body of Confederates.[226] — *CONFEDERATE VETERAN* MAGAZINE

NO APOLOGIES, SAYS CONFEDERATE GENERAL

☞ I hold that the action of the Southern people was legally, constitutionally, and morally right. The Southern people were devoted to the Constitution and laws of the country, and never violated either. They never encroached upon the rights or property of the people of any section, and were entirely content in the enjoyment of those rights that were guaranteed to them by the Constitution. *They did not create the institution of slavery nor introduce the negro into this country, and have no occasion to apologize for the existence of the one and the presence of the other, nor for their action in 1861-65* [my emphasis, L.S.].[227] — CONFEDERATE GENERAL ALEXANDER PETER STEWART

Confederate General Alexander Peter Stewart.

LEFT-WING NORTH WAGES AN IMMORAL WAR ON THE RIGHT-WING SOUTH

☞ ... The sectional agitation that began with the formation of the government and continued with but slight intermission for nearly three-quarters of a century came to a culmination when at last the leaders of the dominant faction of the [Liberal] North, appealing to the angry passions of men, raised a moral and political issue that divided the country by a geographical line, and, under the pretext that *African slavery, which their own fathers, by bargain and sale, had transplanted in the South,* was an unpardonable sin, that there was an "irrepressible conflict" between

Miss Edmonda Augusta Nickerson.

the two great sections of the country, and that the Union "could not endure half slave and half free," they commenced those unlawful aggressions against the constitutional rights of the [Conservative] South that destroyed all social and religious intercourse between the sections, marred their political welfare, dissolved the fraternal Union, and at last deluged the whole land in blood. They conspired to do this, and did do it, in order to extend their [Left-wing] political power and *establish a sectional empire that would be dominated for all time to come by a majority of the State and the people of the North. They organized a mighty military and naval force, and sent it to invade the Southern States by sea and land, to inaugurate against them a ruthless and bloody war, to destroy their sovereignty, and to subjugate their people to the domination of an unconstitutional power* [all emphasis, L.S.]. . . .[228]
MISS EDMONDA AUGUSTA NICKERSON, WARRENSBURG, MISSOURI

GEN. STONEWALL JACKSON'S BLACK SERVANT CHEERS AS HE MARCHES IN CONFEDERATE PARADE

☛ [At the reenactment of the battle of the Crater, Petersburg, Virginia, November 6, 1903:] The parade through the streets of Petersburg was the most imposing and picturesque seen in the city since Lee's army marched out of it. But the climax of all was when the wavering lines of Mahone's old Crater Legion, made up from members of all the Camps, marched by, bearing aloft the battle flag presented to them by Portsmouth Chapter, U.D.C. A shout from ten thousand throats greeted them, mingled with tears of women. *A grizzled old negro, clad in Confederate gray, with his army canteen over his shoulder, the observed of all observers, was lustily cheered as he marched in the procession, for he was well known as Stonewall Jackson's cook and servant* [my emphasis, L.S.].[229] — *CONFEDERATE VETERAN* MAGAZINE

LOYAL BLACK CONFEDERATE LEADS FUNERAL HORSE OF DECEASED MASTER, CONFEDERATE COL. JOSEPH B. BIBB

☛ . . . No body of men ever reflected more honor upon the State than the brave soldiers of [Confederate Gen. Edmund Winston] Pettus's Brigade. No regiment ever made a finer record than the dear old Twenty-Third Alabama under the devoted patriot and heroic soldier, Col. J. B. Bibb. His influence over his men was marvelous, and his personal magnetism was always on the side of right and justice. It has truly been said of him that "no knightlier soldier ever drew blade in defense of his native land."

. . . He was wounded at the battle of Nashville and borne from the field with bleeding lungs, which were never healed. Besought by his officers and surgeon to leave the service, he refused, saying: "The Confederacy has need of all her sons, and death is preferable to defeat."

. . . Col. Bibb was buried in his Confederate uniform, which had been preserved at his own request for that purpose. *His riderless army horse was led by his faithful army servant as his old comrades bore him to his last resting* place in *Oakwood cemetery* [my emphasis, L.S.]. As the cortege passed on, tears fell from eyes unused to weeping, for one of the bravest and noblest of men had pasted from earth to join the host invisible: "To live in hearts we leave behind is not to die."[230] — MRS. J. M. P. OCHENDEN

CONFEDERATE SOLDIER BIDS A FINAL FAREWELL TO HIS BLACK SERVANTS

☛ J. Wesley Choate, of the Wayne County, Tennessee, Rangers, died in the hospital at Nashville during the war, September 18, 1861. He was of the first in his section to enlist. While on a brief visit home in August he seemed to have a presentiment that he would never return. *In this depressed spirit he called the servants to tell them good-by* [my emphasis, L.S.].

Confederate Col. J. B. Bibb.

In turning to his mother at the last, he said: "Must this parting be forever?" In less than six weeks his father was summoned to his sick bed, but ere he reached Nashville he met an escort taking him to his home for burial. Young Choate was a noble, generous-hearted youth, and his death created widespread sorrow.[231] — *CONFEDERATE VETERAN* MAGAZINE

A BLACK SKIN, BUT WHITE SOUL

☛ The loyal old Southern plantation negroes, like their friends and former masters, the Confederate veterans, are fast passing away. One of these, "Uncle" Jim Gass, recently died in Bonham, Texas, and Comrade W. T. Gass, editor of the Hopkins County *Democrat*, whose slave he was, pays this tribute:

"The announcement of the sudden death of this faithful and honest old man was a cause for tears and sorrow to the writer. The faithful negro carried us around in his arms and on his sturdy back and shoulders in infancy, and as we grew older taught us to swim, to fish, to hunt, and to ride. He was black, but he had a whiter soul and purer life than hundreds of boys and men we have known with white skins. When the war clouds of 1861 came, although but a boy of fifteen, I enlisted in the Confederate service. Jim came to me and said: 'Marse Will, I want to go wid you to de war. I'll stay wid you and never leave you.' My mother was a widow, father having died a short time before, and I explained to Jim that we both couldn't leave home at once; that one of us would have to stay to care for her and four brothers and sisters younger than myself. The argument was unanswerable. 'Dat's a fact, Marse Will; I specks I'm de one to stay.'

"Looking back through the mist and tears of forty-one years, it is a melancholy pleasure to testify to the faithfulness of our trusty old slave and companion of boyhood, for he was as true to his trust as was any Confederate soldier true to his flag during all those four years of war, blood, fire, and blockade. And when, in May, 1865, I returned home, I found Jim still at his post of duty. With two horses and a wagon he had been making numerous trips to Shreveport, taking down flour and trading it for sugar and molasses, helping my widowed mother to keep the wolf from the door, Jim being her mainstay and chief purveyor of the commissary department. Peace to his ashes!" [all emphasis, L.S.].[232] — W. T. GASS

"CLOSE RELATION & LOVE" BETWEEN WHITE & BLACK CONFEDERATES

☞ . . . We knew that surrender was inevitable, yet feelings of deep depression came over us when we were ordered to "stack arms." Being [Confederate] Gen. [John Clifford] Pemberton's escort, we were allowed to retain our side arms, but some of our servants who wanted to go out with us were not allowed to do so. Mine came to me and gave me his watch and all the money he had, $2.50 in silver, and told me to keep it for him, and if they would not allow him to pass out with us he would join us the next day outside the lines. *How faithful! and how my heart was touched by it! On a former occasion, when I was left in a sick camp, he remained with me; and at night, when everything was still, I heard his voice lifted earnestly in prayer of supplication that his young master might fix his heart on things above, and that a kind Providence would protect and preserve his life. Imagine at this day* [1904] *the close relation and love that existed between master and slave! His contact with the Southern white man gave him a moral training that was the wonder of the world. While our men were out in the field of battle, what kept the [black] farm hands growing meat and bread to feed them? Was it fear of his master, who was away in the army? What enabled our refined women to remain at home for four years of the war, surrounded by a throng of blacks, without a thought of fear, but a feeling of protection?* [my emphasis, L.S.].

My first night out from Vicksburg will long be remembered. I left the city with three small pieces of jerked mule meat, and a little sugar in my haversack. We camped on a large plantation, and I got an old negro woman to cook me something to eat. She brought me a thick pone of corn bread and a panful of clabber, and I then partook of the most sumptuous repast I ever enjoyed. My messmate, A. B. Jayroe, told me the next morning that his supper the night before was twelve ears of green corn. I did not doubt his statement, as neither of us could hardly travel that day.

I arrived at home to enjoy for a short time, under my parole, the love and association of family and friends, and, above all, the sweet smiles of a rosy-cheeked, brown-eyed little [white] maid—"the girl I left behind me"—whose picture I carried with me through the hurtling fire and smoke of battle for four years, and who, at its close, linked her fortunes with mine, and has shared with me life's sunshine and shadows for nearly forty years.[233] — CONFEDERATE LIEUTENANT C. S. O. RICE, COMPANY M, SEVENTH TENNESSEE CAVALRY

UNDERPRIVILEGED BLACKS LOSE "THEIR BEST FRIEND"

☞ January 1, 1904, was a sad day for Vicksburg [Mississippi], and the usual greeting of Happy New Year was forgotten, for as friend met friend the only words heard were: "Dr. [T. G.] Birchett is dead." . . . He was sixty-eight years of age at the time of his death.

He went into the War between the States as surgeon for the Warren Light Artillery [C.S.A.], but soon rose to be surgeon of Hardee's Corps, which position he held throughout the war. He was ever at the front and true to the Confederate cause to the end of his life. After he returned home, at the close of the war, he renewed the practice of medicine, and no man

Dr. T. G. Birchett.

ever did more to relieve the afflicted than he. His kind heart would never let him refuse a call, regardless of the hour, weather, or remuneration; and *the poor of the city, both white and black, have lost their best friend* [my emphasis, L.S.]. All city offices were closed out of respect for the dead, and the flag on the city hall lowered to half-mast. . . ."²³⁴ — *CONFEDERATE VETERAN* MAGAZINE

NEARLY 20,000 BLACKS VOTE FOR FORMER CONFEDERATE GENERAL HAMPTON

☛ [When his 1876 election was contested and blocked by radical Left-wingers, Conservative Gen. Wade Hampton appeared on the steps of the State Capitol and addressed his angry white and black followers with these words:] "I pledge you my honor that all will be well. I have been elected Governor of South Carolina by the votes of 75,000 white and *17,000 colored citizens* [my emphasis, L.S.], and by the help of God I will take the office and honestly discharge its duties."²³⁵ — *CONFEDERATE VETERAN* MAGAZINE

LOYALTY OF "BLACK MAMMY" & "UNCLE JEFF"

☛ In the spring of 1878, when I was twenty-three years old, I was making a business trip on horseback to Velasco, Texas, following the course of the river. Being in a hurry to overtake a steamer, then on its way to Galveston, I did not stop except to eat and sleep, and did most of the latter in the saddle. Arriving one afternoon about three o'clock at Brazoria, I stopped to let my pony drink and blow and was off again, intending to ride all night and make Velasco the next day.

As I was about leaving Brazoria I heard a cry behind me and, looking back, saw an aged negro gesticulating and calling to me. I stopped, not knowing who it could be, as I had left Brazoria, my native place, seventeen years before. The old darky came up almost out of breath and said: "Say, Marse, don't you know me?" On my replying in the negative he burst into tears, and it was some time before he could talk. "Marse Louis, I am your old Uncle Jeff." I then

A black mammy and her young white charge, daughter of the mistress of the house. The original caption of this photo is "Please Mammy."

recalled that he married my old black mammy, Aunt Winnie, and that in 1859 my father, who owned both of them, gave them their freedom [seven years before Lincoln issued his illegal "was measure," the Emancipation Proclamation]. *I got down from my pony and could not but feel affection for the old negro who was so grieved because I did not at once recognize him.*

He begged me to go and see old Black Mammy, and, while it was inconvenient, I did it. He took me to a fine large building, and when we got there insisted on lifting me from my pony and carrying me into the house. As an old gray-haired black woman came looking on in surprise, he said: "Winnie, the good Lord be praised, our own Marse Louis has come to see you."

Winnie was conducting a hotel. Her guests were all white and of the better class, but, *leading me by the hand as she did many times when I was a little toddler*, she took me into the sitting room and spoke to those about her: "Say, you white folks, I'se run dis house many years an' I always treated you right, but I want you all to git out, for ma boy, Marse Louis, is gwine to stay here to-night, and no one else gits nothing when he is here."

There was nothing to do but stay, and I want to emphasize it when I say that *no monarch could have been treated better than I was that night*. When I sat down to supper they said, "Marse Louis, de place of us black folks is behind our Marster's chair," and there they stood.

I left them next morning, and with a feeling that our black mammies never forget us. To all who are still living I say: "God bless them!" [all emphasis, L.S.].[236] — LOUIS L. J. KOCH, NASHVILLE, TENNESSEE

OUR BROTHERS IN BLACK: AN ADDRESS OF THE SOUTH TO THE NORTH

☞ Hark you, my Puritan critics!
Forget you the Cavalier's pride?
And know you the black Ethiopian?
The leopard—the spots on his hide?

You sold us the African chattels,
You tempted our ease and our greed;
And then you got zealously righteous
And warred on the law and our need,
While we made the savages Christians
And paid for the sins of us both.
Now, counting the good and the evil,
We blush not, and nothing are loath.
We forged, too, a bond of affection,
More firm than the title you gave—
The weal of the served and the serving,
The love of the master and slave.
We sucked the breasts of their mammies—
They fed from the fat of our store,
And, called to the far field of conflict,
We left them on guard at our door.

We bowed to the God of the battle—
We own he was wiser than we—
And patiently took up the burden
Of teaching the bond to be free.
For wronging—if wrong was committed—
The rod had been laid to our back;
Yet, stricken, we knew it was ours
To guardian our brothers in black.

And you in your heedless ambition—
Forgetting the Cavalier's pride,

Forgetting the rule of the Saxon,
For which you yourselves would have died—
With bricks without straw you endeavored
To fashion new pillars of state,
And seal up the house of our fathers
With sectional, partisan hate.

Instead you made wreckage of Statehood;
You loosed us the terrors of race,
And only our God and our virgins
Know what we were called on to face.
At last by the right of the Saxon,
By strength that was bred in the bone,
By law that is higher than statute,
We came in the end to our own.

Confederate division (right) under General Samuel G. French, storming the Yankee stronghold (left) at the Battle of Allatoona (Georgia), October 5, 1864.

Again we gave cheerful compliance—
We took up the burden with care,
We give them the blessings of learning;
We pay—they receive, share for share,
And full opportunity opens
To black man and white man the same
To follow the bent of his genius
To fortune and culture and fame.

By parallel lines they are treading
The highways all people have trod,
But socially there is a chasm
Dug deep in the wisdom of God.
To span it were death to both races;
But, drunk on your meddlesome brew,

They reel to the doom of the foolish
Or madden on wormwood and rue.

We know them—they know us. Between us
Is knowledge you never can know.
We know, for the centuries taught us;
They know, for they learned it in woe.
So, hands off! The burden is ours;
And, faithfully plodding along,
We'll move through the night to the morning,
And answer to God for the wrong.

Go, ponder this rule of the ages.
Writ large on the scroll of the skies:
The white man will govern with wisdom,
And chaos will reign when he dies.[237] — CLARENCE OUSLEY, PRINTED IN THE *HOUSTON POST* (TEXAS)

BLACKS MOURN THE LOSS OF CONFEDERATE OFFICER
☛ [Confederate] Capt. R. B. Mason, after a long illness, died suddenly of heart failure at his residence, in Athens, Alabama. He had a host of friends, for his warm heart and genial disposition had endeared him to many. . . . The funeral services were held in St. Timothy's Protestant Episcopal Church, the rector, Rev. Horace Weeks Jones, reading the burial service. The outpouring of people, both from town and country, in respect to the memory of the noble dead, was such that the church could not half hold them. *There was a large attendance of colored people.* Capt. Mason was greatly loved and respected by them. *Some fifty or seventy-five of these colored people came up from the old plantation at Brown's Ferry to gaze, through their tears, for the last time on the kindly face of their dead friend, and during the funeral services at the church they occupied space in the vestry rooms on each side of the chancel* [my emphasis, L.S.].[238] — *CONFEDERATE VETERAN MAGAZINE*

Confederate officer R. B. Mason.

A FAITHFUL NEGRO: "UNCLE CLAIBORNE"
☛ Rapidly the old slaves and the old slave owners are passing away. In a few years not one will be left. *The bonds of affection and duty between very many of them were strong.* This has been *a conservative influence* in the South, and has undoubtedly often prevented the relations between the races from becoming acute. The future must take account of the elimination of this wholesome factor. *Not only as an office of love, but to help to impress upon the minds and hearts of the younger generation the lesson taught us by those, white and black, who, amid all of the racial turmoil of the years subsequent to the Civil War, lived together in unbroken peace and friendliness, discharging mutual offices of duty and affection even unto the grave, I write to commemorate the*

Col. John Overton and his wife Harriet V. Overton.

character of Claiborne Hines, a full-blooded negro, who at the age of seventy-nine, at Travelers' Rest, in Davidson County, Tennessee, the historic home of the Overtons, which had been his home uninterruptedly for forty years, passed away amid the honor and affection of all who knew him.

He was "Uncle Claiborne" to every one but Col. John Overton, who was the only person, white or black, that called him Claiborne. If truth, honesty, faithfulness in the discharge of every duty, large and small, and undeviating daily practice of the faith of a simple Christian make a soul white, then never did there appear at the bar of final judgment a whiter soul than that which went up from that pure-minded negro. Col. and Mrs. Overton trusted all of his words and acts with implicit confidence. I have often heard both of them say that they never knew him to say or do anything but what was right. This is the concurrent testimony given by Miss Mary Maxwell, a sister of Mrs. [Harriet Virginia Maxwell] Overton, and all who knew him. There was a strong bond of affection between Uncle Claiborne and that family down to the third generation, and nothing ever occurred to weaken it.

As long as Col. and Mrs. Overton lived he never went to bed without, of his own accord, tapping at their window and saying, "Marse John" or "Miss Harriet"—as the case might be—"do you want anything?" The answer was almost invariably, "No, thank you, Claiborne," or "Uncle Claiborne," and then the mutual "Good night," but his practice never varied, for he felt in his loyal heart that he must have his dismissal.

After Col. Overton died and Mrs. Overton sickened and it was determined that she should go on that trip to Florida whence she never returned alive, Uncle Claiborne went to her door and, brushing the tears from his eyes, entreated her not to go, saying: "Stay with us, Miss Harriet. We will take care of you and help b'ar you up." A thousand instances could be recalled of his constant and loving care. No wonder that they all loved him. No wonder that Mr. Overton's son, who succeeded to the home place, felt it a privilege to support him in his old age, a privilege for which there would have been rivalry from other members of the family but for the fact that he preferred to pass his last days at his old home; and no wonder the family felt that it was right that his funeral should take place in the old mansion, from which had been borne his old master and mistress, who loved him and whom he loved so tenderly.

There may be some who will have no sympathy with this tribute, but they will not be found among those who cherish the best sentiments and traditions of the South [all emphasis, L.S.].[239] — HON. JACOB MCGAVOCK DICKINSON, CHIEF COUNSEL FOR THE ILLINOIS CENTRAL RAILROAD, CHICAGO, ILLINOIS; PRINTED IN THE NASHVILLE AMERICAN

Jacob McGavock Dickinson.

FAITHFUL SLAVE, GOOD FRIEND, CONFEDERATE SOLDIER (TWO TOURS OF DUTY), & "CONFEDERATE HERO": WILSON CARTER

☞ Wilson Carter was born a slave of William H. Mitchell in Morgan County, Georgia. He is now sixty-six years old, and has been in the service of the family all of his life. He was a humble, obedient slave until "set free," since when he has been a circumspect, law-abiding citizen, and commands the sincere respect of his whole circle of acquaintance, the white people, especially, being counted his friends.

In early life Wilson was a consistent member of the Presbyterian Church. After his marriage in 1867 he joined the Methodist Church through courtesy to his wife. All these years he has led a most exemplary life, and in consequence has secured for the comfort of his old age more than a competency, for he owns a comfortable home and has money at interest, to which he adds his monthly salary. He has never served other than the family in which he was born, and to-day is the honored, trusted gardener and coachman, carrying the keys, etc., for young William H. Mitchell, who accords "Uncle" Wilson every indulgence, which beguiles him into feeling his importance as "general supervisor" of the domestic matters of the home.

Confederate veteran Wilson Carter.

In the beginning of the War between the States Wilson accompanied his young master, W. T. Mitchell, who went out with a volunteer company from Columbus, Ga., and was in active service mainly in the Army of Tennessee, following the hardships and severe fighting consequent to "Sherman's bloody march," including the dreadful battle of Chickamauga, where his young master gave up his precious life on the battlefield. Wilson, true to his trust as body servant, was near by, and after the fight he made his way alone, recovered the lifeless body, prepared it with all the care and tenderness possible, wrapped it in his blanket, dug the grave, buried it himself, marked the place, then took his weary, desolate waiting until some chance to make his way home to the stricken family, which chance came with the wounding of young Willis Banks, a brother of Dr. E. A. Banks, to whom the Veteran paid tribute a year or so ago. Only those who witnessed these heartbreaking scenes can conjecture the agony of such a home-coming.

In the course of six months a call was made for recruits, and boys sixteen and eighteen years old voluntarily rushed to fill the places and avenge the death of their loved ones. Then it was a younger son, Frank H. Mitchell, brother of the brave boy who fell at Chickamauga, volunteered to leave home and risk all for his country, and again faithful Wilson, with all the horror of his first experience fresh in his mind, expressed his willingness to accompany the second son, which he did, and *remained in service until honorably discharged* at the sad and final surrender.

Doubtless the desire to accompany "Mars Frank" was stimulated by the fact that he had nursed him in his childhood, and realized his ability now to care for him as he would be exposed to the rigor and hardships of war. What a proof of this noble negro's loyalty and affection! *Any Southern heart can well understand why this faithful servant should continue to occupy in this family a prominent place of trust, tenderness, even sacred affection, which prompts full confidence in our daily intercourse, yet with never a tinge or suspicion of familiarity on his part. All the little niceties of his early training are punctiliously practiced, even to the leaving of his hat outside the door when he enters the house.* He is the bearer of all important letters, notes, and documents of every description, and worthily supports the acknowledged title of "Faithful Wilson." In all probability this and much more will be recorded of Wilson when with him "time shall be no more," but *I think it a fitting tribute now, and it will certainly be very gratifying to him to feel assured that we recognize his solid virtues, and there could be no greater proof of our appreciation than that he should see it published in your patriotic, loyal Veteran, thereby constituting him a "Confederate hero"* [all emphasis, L.S.].[240] — UNNAMED VICE PRESIDENT OF THE LADIES' MEMORIAL ASSOCIATION, ROME, GEORGIA

A MONUMENT TO THE FAITHFUL OLD SLAVES

☛ As the President of the North Carolina Division, U.D.C., I heartily indorse the following letter from Mrs. Aston, and hope the Daughters will take some decisive action in the October convention looking to the erection of this monument. The letter is addressed "to the Daughters of the Confederacy and all the women of the South." — Mrs. Fred A. Olds

Mrs. Aston's Letter—*My Dear Sisters: Will not every one of you raise your voice with mine in making amends for a long-neglected duty in rearing a monument to our faithful old slaves?*

Of all people that dwell upon the earth, I think these deserve the grandest monument. Soon all this generation will have passed away. Let us hasten with the work while some of us still survive.

Confederate veterans have for some time been speaking of raising a monument to the Southern women. We appreciate this, and thank them for their remembrance of our self-denials and hardships which tried women's souls; but what else could have been expected of us when our dear ones were at the front? While this was the case we felt we were enduring this for sacred ties of kindred and country. How different with the faithful slaves! *They did it for love of masters, mistresses, and their children. How nobly did they perform their tasks! Their devotion to their owners, their faithfulness in performing their labors and caring for us during these terribly disastrous years, and their kindness at the surrender, while we were powerless and helpless, have never been surpassed or equaled.*

"Confederate Soldier's Diploma," awarded to Confederate veterans who were considered camp members in good standing.

One of the youngest Confederate soldiers in the War, Robert S. Shreve enlisted at the age of 13, joining Gen. Forrest's Cavalry at Port Gibson, Mississippi, on August 17, 1862.

At the time of the surrender we were entirely defenseless. Our noble, famished, ragged patriots were still away from their homes, and among us was a band of robbers [Left-wing Yankee soldiers] *who were bad counselors to our slaves. Their kindness and their devotion to us was the most beautiful this earth has ever witnessed.*

From the Mason and Dixon line to the Gulf and from the Atlantic to the Gulf there was not a massacre, house-burning, or one of those unmentionable crimes which are now so common in the whole country. Think of this; 'tis wonderful. Our gratitude to God and love for the old-time servants should be boundless.

Who will say they do not deserve the greatest monument that has ever been erected? This acknowledgment from us to them of our appreciation of kindness and devotion shown by them to their former owners would be in their last days a beautiful thought. To those of their race of the present generation it would verify the character of the Southern people, their former owners, and also show the true relation that existed between master and servant [my emphasis, L.S.].

Would it not be an act of justice for the women of the South to ask our noble men if we may not be permitted to turn this monument over to those who, if not more deserving, are equally so with our Southern sisters? I would suggest that when it is erected a tablet might be inserted bearing this inscription: "*Given by the Confederate Veterans as a memorial to the women of the South, and given by them in memory of the faithfulness of our former servants*" [all emphasis, L.S.].[241] — MRS. C. GILLILAND ASTON, 49 CHURCH STREET, ASHEVILLE, NORTH CAROLINA

SOUTHERN HISTORY INCLUDES BLACK CONFEDERATES

☞ [Excerpted from a review of the book, *History of the Doles-Cook Brigade, Army of Northern Virginia*, by Henry W. Thomas:] In every family in this State which cherishes with pride the record made by the gallant sons of Georgia in the tremendous conflict that shook this continent and filled the world with wonder, the graphic description of marches and battles herein contained will be read with pleasure and profit.

There is a sketch of each regiment composing the brigade, prepared by a member of such regiment, and a complete roster of the officers and privates of each company, with a record of the services of each. *Nor did the author forget the faithful slaves, who followed their masters to the war and were true to the last* [my emphasis, L.S.] . . .[242] — COL. JOSEPH T. DERRY, ATLANTA, GEORGIA (See following entry.)

BLACK CONFEDERATES AS RECORDED BY THEIR WHITE COMRADES

☞ . . . Members of the brigade have requested that a chapter in this history be devoted to the negroes who acted as body-servants for the officers and men of the various regiments composing the Doles-Cook Brigade, during the "war between the States." Sufficient data is not at hand to authorize sketches of all who shared the hardships of the march and camp life with us. While on this subject, the life, habits and treatment of the good and honest old-fashioned negro will be discussed, and the part he played during the stormy war period, and the relation he bore to the white people before that time. *Before this period the negroes of the South were the happiest and most contented race of people in the world; they had no cares or responsibilities of any kind to make them miserable.*

Their houses, clothing, provisions and everything they needed to make them comfortable and happy were furnished by their owners. When sick they had the most careful nursing and the best medical attention that the country afforded, and delicacies suitable for sick and convalescent were prepared for them until restored to health. When death invaded their ranks they received decent and Christian burial from their owners. The majority of the negroes were kindly and humanely treated, for mutual ties of friendship existed, and common sympathy and pecuniary considerations alike prompted this course. Few owners were guilty of cruelty to their slaves, and such were always regarded by their neighbors with loathing and contempt.

Many instances could be cited where suitable clothing was furnished and large wedding suppers given slaves by their owners when they married, and on such occasions the ceremony was witnessed by large numbers of whites and blacks, and all partook of the bountiful repast prepared for the occasion, and all had a merry time.

Nearly all of the farmers gave their [black] hands patches of land to cultivate, and often assisted in its cultivation in order to encourage and furnish them with money to use as they deemed proper. Christmas week was the happiest and jolliest period of the year, and all looked eagerly for its coming. During that time no work that could possibly be avoided was required of them. They visited, danced, frolicked and lived sumptuously. Their owners purchased and distributed presents to each of them, and all were happy and contented.

Eva Martin, former servant, Beaumont, Texas, circa 1937-1938.

Hog-killing time was another big event. The boys delighted in blowing up bladders, frying melts and sweet-bread on the hot stones, then indulged in eating brains, chitterlings, sausage, souse spare-ribs and backbones with plenty of meat on them; later on hogs-heads and feet were enjoyed the negroes sharing in all these luxuries. These were indeed happy days, but they are gone forever. The Yankee, Western farmer, and what is termed the "New South" have done away with these luxurious and delightful times. A new order of things has risen new ideas, new methods, and new people have supplanted those of the past. But have all of these changes brought greater or more lasting happiness, or are the people more honest, more industrious or better citizens? No doubt a very large majority of the older people of the South, both white and black recalling ante-bellum times would promptly answer, no.

Corn-shuckings, house-raisings and log-rollings (of which this generation is ignorant) were notable events, in either of which both whites and blacks would travel miles to assist their neighbors. In husking corn sides were chosen each with its captain or leader the pile of corn divided the leaders placed on top of their parts and walking continually from one end to the other shouting with stentorian voice some of their accustomed "corn-songs," as they were called, to which the whole crowd of huskers would respond in like manner. They would work until midnight, then quit and commence to dance, sing and eat, the dancing and singing usually lasting until daylight. The great body of negroes seen at night by the glare of numerous lightwood fires made a weird and picturesque spectacle. Their shouting could often be heard four or five miles away. The corn when husked was thrown to the front and the shucks to the rear, and to behold the clean white corn flying through the air was a sight never to be forgotten. As a general rule a drink of good, pure old corn juice was given to every one present, and then no more until they had finished their work. Every one went home happier and more contented, and looked eagerly forward to the next frolic. The older set understand and appreciate negro character better than the younger generation; they know their habits, peculiarities, weakness and dependence, and overlook many of their faults and shortcomings, for they were nursed by them played with and visited their humble but comfortable cabins at night, listened for hours to their weird songs, enjoyed their clog or breakdown dances, hunted rabbits, coons and "possums" with them, ate potliquor and corn pones out of the same vessel, listened to their folk-tales and frightful ghost stories until they were afraid to go home alone for fear of meeting hobgoblins of which they had heard so much.[243] They deserve and should receive the gratitude of the Southern people for their good and exemplary conduct while all of the adults who were fit for military service, and most of the schoolboys who had reached the age of fifteen were in the Confederate army. *No disorder or disaffection of any kind occurred in any portion of the South during all those dark and trying days.*

They were kind, gentle and obedient to the orders of the old men who were unfit for service, and to the women and children who were striving and using every means within their power to sustain themselves and the armies in the field battling for the independence of the South. The negroes were kindly disposed toward these defenseless people, yea, their devotion, fidelity and loyalty was indeed wonderful and beautiful. The old men women and children in the country were absolutely at their mercy. They could have burned their houses, destroyed property of all kinds, committed the darkest and most heinous crimes known, and murdered them in cold blood. Did they do it? No, but on the contrary protected them and looked after their comfort, safety and interests.

Where on earth will you find another race of people situated as they were, who would have acted and conducted themselves as these good-hearted and ignorant [that is, uneducated] *slaves did? The negroes of that day and time were, as a rule, kind, gentle and considerate, and with few exceptions would have remained the same obedient and trusting people if it had not been for the teachings of the* [Left-wing Yankee] *adventurers who came South soon after the surrender and fired their hearts with hatred for their best and truest friends* [a fake race war].

Mrs. T. J. Latham.

The solution of the Negro problem even at this date could be quickly solved to the satisfaction of all concerned, and the two races adjust themselves if the Yankees would quit meddling with them for each to a certain extent is dependent upon the other. *When in trouble or distress they invariably apply to the Southern man, and not to their Yankee friends.*

W. H. Councill (colored), President of the Alabama Agricultural and Mechanical College at Normal, Ala., says: *"I have found the white people of the South at all times unstinted in their support of all institutions for the moral, religious and industrial development of the negro race. . . . An appeal to the Southern heart for any character of aid for the negro always meets with the warmest encouragement . . ."*

The slaves were allowed to attend divine service on Sundays, and were not only comfortably but well dressed. In some instances the negroes owned their own churches, but as a rule all of the churches belonging to the whites were provided with galleries for their use, and often certain seats in the rear of the church were set apart for their use. Their children attended Sabbath-school, and they were taught in the Sunday-school by the best ladies and gentlemen of the community. It is a matter of history that General "Stonewall" Jackson was Superintendent of a negro Sabbath-school at Lexington, Virginia, previous to the war.

While it is true that we have some bad negroes amongst us who commit heinous crimes and terrible acts of violence, *it is also true that the great majority are law-abiding, good citizens who deserve and enjoy the respect and friendship of their white neighbors.*

When the war commenced Colonel Benjamin Camp, a planter of Campbell County, Gaeorgia, *owned a negro man by the name of Will, who was foreman on the plantation*, and which bad been given to his wife on the date of their marriage. Lieutenant-Colonel Thomas C. Glover, of the Twenty-first Georgia, married a daughter of Colonel Camp, and when Glover was wounded at Sharpsburg, Maryland, September 17, 1862, this negro was sent to Virginia and brought him home. Before the fall of Atlanta in 1864, a raiding column of Federal cavalry crossed the Chattahoochee River at McCoy's Ferry, two miles below the Camp farm. The Federals remained three or four days just across the river from the Camp plantation, and during that time Will dug a hole four feet square

Samuel H. Deane, Confederate veteran.

and six feet deep in the stable, in which he buried feather beds, clothing, silverware, and numerous articles of value, then covered it up with boards and a heap of stable manure on top of them, and a mule stood over the buried articles. He next went to a remote part of the plantation dug a hole in which he placed three large wooden boxes which he filled with over a hundred bushels each, of corn and wheat. The next day the Yankees crossed the river, went to the residence of Colonel Camp and arrested him. Will saw the Yankees as they approached the house and made a break for a skirt of woods about fifty-yards back of the house. The Yankees soon ran him down and carried him to the house. The cause of his being captured was that he had badly sprained one of his ankles in moving the wheat, and in making the sprint he again hurt it. The road and yard were crowded with cavalrymen when he was taken to the house, and a major in command of the advance had the old gentleman a prisoner on the front porch and his wife, who was a stout lady, was giving the officer a piece of her mind. Soon after Will was brought into his presence. This officer was rude and ungentlemanly enough to curse the old lady. As soon as he did so the negro instantly struck the ruffian a terrible blow with his fist under the burr of the ear and knocked him headlong off the porch and half way to the gate. The enraged major arose, drew his sword and started to cut Will down, but at that moment the colonel in command rode up. Colonel Camp gave him a Masonic sign which he recognized and honored and at once ordered him released and placed a guard around the premises to prevent all pilfering by the soldiers. The only mule left on the place was taken when they left, and Will was ordered to mount it and go with them as a guide. They asked him many questions, among them what he had been hauling away from the plantation. He replied, nothing; but had started to go to the mill two or three times that morning, but every time he made the attempt heard that they were coming and turned back. To all questions about the country and route to various places he professed profound ignorance, pretending that he had been so closely confined at home that he knew nothing of the surrounding country. After going two miles and finding him to be such a consummate ignoramus he was ordered to get off the mule and go back home. They then took a negro belonging to a neighbor of Colonel Camp for a guide; while he was mounting the mule Will whispered to him, "know nothing." Will started back home limping, but had gotten only about half way when he met [Confederate] General [Lawrence Sullivan] Ross' Brigade of Texas Cavalry on the Yankees' trail. He told Ross what he knew of the raiders, their probable number and where they intended going. He told him that they were making for Fairburn and Fayetteville, but in order to reach these places would have to go to Campbellton, and turn at right angles to Fairburn. He also told the general that he could guide the command by a settlement road which would enable it to get ahead of the Federals and ambush them. Ross had one of his men take him on his horse and, under his guidance, got ahead of the Federal cavalry and placed men in ambush on either side of the road that they would have to travel. They came in a short time, and when the head of the column was well nigh through the Texans fired into them and among the first killed was the major who had so cowardly cursed a lady.

After the battle was over and they were gathering up the Yankee dead, and the dead body of the major was found, Will exhibited every symptom of delight and danced with all the vim that his sprained ankle would permit.

Confederate monument, Albany, Georgia.

George Wallace served through the entire war as a body-servant of [Confederate] Captain Howard Tinsley, and was at the surrender of Lee's army. He rode [Confederate] General [Philip] Cook's famous war-horse "Old Whitey" home and turned him over to Mr. Winship, a brother-in-law of the general, as he was still in prison. At the battle of Winchester he was shot down and so stunned that it seemed that he would die. General Cook called one of his staff and asked him to shoot the horse, as he did not wish him to suffer or fall into the hands of the enemy. A bullet was fired into his head but it seemed to revive him, for he at once got upon his feet and went to the rear. The next day a member of the brigade who knew the horse took him away from a soldier who was riding him to the rear, and returned him to General Cook, who continued to ride him until the close of the war. Old Whitey lived for twelve or fifteen years after the surrender, and whenever driven to Americus [Georgia], if the brass-band happened to be playing, he would become very much excited and would get as near the music as possible. When he died he was buried in a coffin which General Cook had made expressly for him. The general was greatly affected by the death of his old war steed.

Confederate veterans from the Sixteenth Confederate Cavalry Regiment, circa 1904.

George became a politician and was elected to the State Senate during the Bullock regime. He now holds a position in the post office in Macon, Ga.

"Pete" was the carriage-driver of [Confederate] Colonel Tim M. Furlow, of Americus. "Pete" went to the war with his young master, the gallant William L. Furlow, captain of Company D, Twelfth Georgia Regiment. Captain Dawson was captain of Company A, and W. H. Turpin was first lieutenant. These officers were under "Stonewall" Jackson. In the battle at McDowell, Virginia, on the 8th of May, 1862, these three gallant and brave officers fell. Distance from the railroads, difficulty of transportation, decided those in authority to bury the three Georgians in Virginia's soil. But Pete, fond of the folks at home and devoted to his young master, would not consent. So persistent was he that the colonel of the Twelfth Georgia finally agreed to help the negro.

They aided him in getting coffins for the three; and Pete, having the money of Captain Furlow hired an ox-cart and hauled the bodies sixty miles to a railroad station; and, suffering delays, by sheer persistence got the remains on the cars and finally brought them to Americus. *The faithfulness of the negro appears all the brighter when he could have so easily deserted and gone with Milroy's troops.* Pete himself was a sacrifice to the hardships of war and was never again strong and robust. *Thinking of the strong ties that existed between the old owners and their domestics, it seems a thousand pities that these ties should have been so ruthlessly severed and broken by those [liberal, anti-white, racist Yanks] who came South to organize the negroes into a "black man's party" and teach them to distrust those whom they honored and respected and among whom they had to live.*

Ab Lee went to Virginia with [Confederate] Lieutenant, afterwards Captain, A. S. Reid, of the Twelfth Georgia Regiment, as his body-servant, and remained with him until the surrender. *He is an honorary member of the Confederate Veterans' Association of Putnam County, and also of the Doles-Cook Brigade Survivors' Association.* He is now living in his old home at Eatonton, Georgia.

"Hugh T. Morton Jr., snug in his baby carriage." In the South we begin teaching our children the facts about the War and the Confederate Cause from birth.

Dick, the body-servant of R. H. and W. F. Jenkins, Company G, Twelfth Georgia Regiment, was a good-hearted and handy man always in a good humor and very obedient. At the battle of Chancellorsville, on Sunday morning after the Yankees had been driven some distance, Dick went on the battle-field to rob dead Yankees. He soon came upon one with an elegant pair of boots, which he concluded to appropriate to his own use. He took hold of his foot and commenced to pull at the boot, but the supposed dead man spoke in a feeble voice and asked him to please give him a little water. This speech so frightened Dick that, instead of complying with the dying man's request, he fled precipitately.

Isham, commonly called "Smut" because he was so black, was the body-servant of [Confederate] Lieutenant Stephen B. Marshall, of the Putnam Light Infantry, Company G, Twelfth Georgia Regiment. He was the liveliest and rarest darkey in the regiment. Always in trouble but never out of humor, every one picked at him and had some joke to tell on him. Lieutenant Marshall was an officer in a volunteer company before the war. On one occasion it went into camp at the Oconee Spring in Putnam county. While on this trip the officers gave a dinner and invited a number of ladies. Amongst that number was the lady to whom Lieutenant Marshall was engaged, and afterward married. Isham was the cook and had orders to smother a chicken. Finally dinner was announced but the chicken was not brought to the table. After becoming impatient on account of the delay, Isham was called and asked if he had smothered the chicken. He answered yes, but said he did not know whether he was dead or not, but that he ought to be, as he had tied it up in a bag, put it in a box, and the box under the bed. When the assembled crowd heard this they roared with laughter, while Marshall was mortified and angered beyond expression.

At the battle of Allegheny Mountain a shell exploded near Isham, when he immediately mounted a bare-back mule, his face toward the tail of the beast, and the mule was rapidly driven to the rear by the use of Isham's heels and a pole; both the mule and negro were missing for two or three days. When he returned Marshall asked him why he left, when he promptly answered: "Because, 'a good run is better than a bad stand,' for had I remained and received a wound or been killed, I could not have served you as I promised old master I would."

Isham went to his reward several years ago, and it is hoped that he reached a better and happier home beyond the skies.

Morris, the [black] body-servant of H. W. Thomas [the author of this entry] of the Putnam Light Infantry, Company G, Twelfth Georgia Regiment, was a good true and faithful man ever ready to perform any and all duties required of him. He never crossed the Potomac; would always get permission to remain in Virginia when our army invaded Maryland and Pennsylvania for fear of being captured, but came promptly to camp and reported for duty as soon as the army returned to Virginia. Whenever bullets commenced to fly and shells to whistle he invariably sought the rear. When asked why he did not remain with or near his white friends who had to face the enemy, he would reply, "You are white and I am a negro and can't stand the racket." *He was at the surrender and walked every step of the way home with his master, and remained with him until advised to hunt a job and look out for himself. He was universally liked by the good people of Eatonton because he was polite, accommodating* and knew his place. He died with consumption about eight years after the surrender, and the writer hopes that the change was a happy one.

Old South plantations were run in a leisurely manner, with native African folk songs and instruments often filling the air.

It is to be regretted that *a complete list of the many negroes who went into the army as cooks and body-servants* [all legally considered "Confederate soldiers" by Yankee military authorities] *with the various members of this brigade cannot be obtained.*

It is nothing but simple justice to give each one due credit for services rendered their owners during the war, for the majority of them were good and faithful servants. Those who survived the war, and who attend our annual reunions are treated with the kindest consideration and mix and mingle with the boys in the most cordial manner, and seem to enjoy the meetings fully as much as their white comrades. Several of them yet attend such meetings, and are honorary members of our association and take seats in our convention hall. All of the survivors of this brigade feel kindly toward them, for they were constantly together for the greater part of the war, and each was known by sight if not personally. There is not one of them that the members of this brigade would not help out of any difficulty or assist financially if within their power [all emphasis, L.S.].²⁴⁴ — HENRY W. THOMAS, CONFEDERATE VETERAN

TWO REASONS THE CONFEDERATE MILITARY STRUGGLED TO ENLIST BLACKS

☛ . . . [In early 1865, in] the Confederate Senate I remember listening to an animated discussion in regard to enlisting negro troops in the army. It was urged by some of the [Confederate] Senators that we should enlist and arm fifty thousand negroes, of course with a pledge of freedom.

I knew we could not possibly arm five thousand. The ordnance department was exhausted. One company of negroes was formed, and I witnessed the drill in the capitol square, but I understood that as soon as they got their uniforms they vanished in one night.

. . . As the spring of 1865 approached the officers often discussed the situation. We knew that Lee's lines were stretched to breaking, we knew the exhausted condition of every department, and we knew the end was near.²⁴⁵ — WILLIAM LE ROY BROUN, CONFEDERATE LIEUTENANT COLONEL

BLACK CONFEDERATE AT THE BATTLE OF SHARPSBURG

☛ [From the obituary of Mrs. Nancy Haywood (née Blount) Branch:] Mrs. L. O'B. Branch, widow of the famous North Carolina brigadier general [Lawrence O'Bryan Branch] who gave his life for the Confederacy at Sharpsburg, passed peacefully away at her home in Raleigh on November 9, 1903.

Mrs. Branch had been in declining health for several months, and had almost reached the advanced age of eighty-six years. She was the daughter of Gen. W. A. Blount, one of North Carolina's distinguished men, and her mother was the daughter of Sherwood Haywood, Esq., of Raleigh. In 1844 she was married to Gen. Lawrence O'B. Branch, who represented his district in Congress for several terms, and during that time his family lived in Washington City. At the outbreak of the war he went to the front and was made brigadier general. He lost his life while

Mrs. Nancy Branch.

leading his brigade in the battle of Sharpsburg, September 17, 1862; *and his body was borne from the field by his faithful negro servant, Wiley* [my emphasis, L.S.]. After forty-one years of patient watching and waiting, his devoted wife is again with him. . . .²⁴⁶ — *CONFEDERATE VETERAN MAGAZINE*

BLACK TENANT LAMENTS DEATH OF WHITE LANDLORD

☞ I am compelled to say that my all and all is gone. He has been the friend for his negroes. Now he is gone and we are lost. There is no man like him for his negros, and I hope the angels will meet him, and I hope that heaven will crown him. God save him, for he has fought a good fight. Save my Marster.[247] — BILLIE YARBROUGH, FORMER AFRICAN AMERICAN SOUTHERN "SLAVE"

HEARTBROKEN SERVANT HELPS BURY HIS DECEASED MASTER, A CONFEDERATE SOLDIER

☞ On one of the loveliest days of last June a sweet little girl of ten summers knelt in a field of daisies, gathering the flowers she loved. Acres of daisies whitened the hill slope all about her, and she gathered handful after handful till her arms held a great sheaf. Looking up with a sudden thought, she said: "I will gather more and put them on the soldier's grave."

A little later the rays of the setting sun touched a low mound in the village cemetery decorated with flowers gathered by the hands of a little child, born long years after "the soldier" had been laid there to rest.

It was the grave of George Blaine, of the Seventh Texas Regiment, who was killed at the battle of Franklin [II]. On the eve of the battle, far from his Texas home and the sister who prayed for him there and watched for the brother who would never return, he told his negro servant [Nick Blaine] that he had a cousin, the wife of Dr. Aaron C. White, living at Spring Hill [at "White Hall"], twelve miles from Franklin. He wished to be taken to their home if killed or wounded in the battle. He fell never to rise again, and the heartbroken servant took him to Spring Hill.

The writer was one of the three small children of the home who saw him for the first time in the calm majesty of death. It made an indelible impression, and the pathetic burial at the village cemetery the following day is still vividly remembered. There were no military honors, no minister to conduct a religious service, and no crowd to follow him to his last resting place. *Only three little children looked on in awed silence while their father helped the faithful servant lower the body into the grave and fill in the earth, but the frame of the latter shook with sobs and the tears rained down his face as he bent to the task which hid forever from his sight the loved form of his young master.*

There was mourning in every house in the village that day: the churches were turned into temporary hospitals filled with wounded and dying soldiers, and all were too busy ministering to those yet living to do honor to the dead.

"Uncle Nick" was sent on his way with his master's horse and watch, a lock of hair, etc., and later the sister wrote from Texas that he had reached her safely with these last tokens. She spoke of having her brother's

The death of "Uncle" Alfred Jackson (above), a family servant of President Andrew Jackson, was announced in *Confederate Veteran* magazine, 1902.

body removed as soon as days of peace came, but she too died, and he was left to slumber on here.

The years slipped swiftly and silently away, and almost forty had been numbered with the past when the postmaster at Spring Hill received a letter inquiring for Dr. White or some member of his family. *It was from "Uncle Nick" Blaine, the faithful servant of the young soldier, asking about the grave of his master. He wrote after receiving the desired information and sent some pressed cedar to be laid on "master's grave"* [all emphasis, L.S.].

The grave has never been marked by a stone, but a wild cherry sprang up near the spot and grew into a tree. Mocking birds build their nests there and sing requiems above his sleeping dust.[248] — MR. WHITE, SPRING HILL, TENNESSEE

Noted deaf and blind author, lecturer, and Swedenborgian Helen Keller, daughter and granddaughter of Confederate officers.

More factual history that has been left out of our history books: Both white and black servants, from adolescence to retirement age (mid 60s), served both white and black families in the Old South. This photo, one of countless numbers that have survived, shows Isaac, a black "slave" boy (on the left), and Rosa, a white "slave" girl (on the right). Both worked in New Orleans, Louisiana, during the War for Southern Independence. Photo taken circa 1863 by "Kimball" of New York City.

CHAPTER FOUR
1905-1908

WHITE REVIEW OF THE 1904 BOOK *THE OLD SOUTH*
☛ I think the little book appealed to me so strongly just now because for some time my thought has been running on the Old South and the negro. On December 18 I heard Bishop Goodsell preach to the colored M. E. Conference. . . . I have often thought of our colored people and wished we were helping them.[249] — MRS. M. D. WIGHTMAN

BLACK REVIEW OF THE 1904 BOOK *THE OLD SOUTH*
☛ I was borned in the Old South. Your little book was the only Christmas present I received. I have read it through three times, and cried over it.[250] — "AUNT'" MIMA MITCHELL (COLORED)

SUPPORT FOR SOUTHERN "MONUMENT TO THE BLACKS"

Miss Maude Burwell Stockton, New Orleans, La.

☛ In the hearts of the mighty fallen is deep rooted the feeling of inextinguishable gratitude to the loyal slaves to whose care the women and children were intrusted during the entire period of the War between the States. It is a sentiment that still remains smoldering in the souls of those who owned them. To those slaves who watched the fireside, tilled the soil, helped spin, weave, and make raiment for the master and sons on the battlefield—to those slaves who protected and provided for the families at home is due a monument that will tell the story to coming generations that cannot be taught the lesson of self-sacrifice and devotion of the slave in any other way. If a time is ever ripe for a noble deed, now is that time, for the grand, courteous Southern slave owner is fast passing away; and to erect the monument would be to hand down to posterity an open book, in which our Southern children can learn that every negro is no "black fiend." The [Liberal] North would not understand the sentiment. Of course not.

Erecting this monument would influence for good the present and coming generations, and prove that the people of the South who owned slaves valued and respected their good qualities as no one else ever did or will do. It would bespeak the real conception of the affection of the owner toward the slave and refute the slanders and falsehoods published in Uncle Tom's Cabin.

There did exist in the days of trial and hardship not only a perfect understanding but the kindest sympathy, and in thousands of plantations and homes where every white male on the place able to bear arms would go to the battlefield the helpless families of women and children were left entirely to the care and protection of the trusted slaves.

This monument would have great effect as a proof of the feeling of gratitude that centers the hearts of Southern people from the sixties to the present day, and would link ages of the past to the coming years, when our grandchildren and theirs in turn would stop to inquire the meaning of it and the motive that prompted its erection, learning therefrom truths in the history of the Southern States and from a truthful source.

The "Monument to the Blacks" would not only tell the traditions, romance, poetry, and picturesqueness of the South, but would speak the pathetic [that is, poignant] scenes enacted in many grand old Southern homesteads. *No one who was rocked to sleep by the sweet lullaby of the faithful black "mammy," listened to her weird ghost stories, nursed at her breast, or played about her cabin door would ever be willing to have these tender memories die out. There is the side of sentiment, the side of gratitude, that those who have felt the touch can never give up, nor can they forget the debt due the faithful "ten per cent of slaves that remained with their masters after freedom."*

Dr. A. A. Faris, Confederate veteran.

If "this is not the time for erecting monuments to the old slaves," one will never be erected, for the [white] men and women who hold them in tender remembrance will ere long be called to a greater reward, and they alone can fully understand the motive of such a work and *the necessity to leave a mark by which their children's children may perpetuate the heroic deeds of the slaves who were devoted and true to their ancestors in times of deadliest peril.* Erect the monument; it will result in much good, as it will tell future generations that *the white men of the South were the negro's best friends then and that the men of the South are the negro's best friends to-day.*

Instances portraying the fidelity of the slaves might be told to fill endless volumes, and would recite the sweetest stories of heartfelt devotion, the most unselfish acts, prompted by pure love; *self-forgetting, they would sacrifice comfort—yea, even go hungry—and with a smile serve those to whom they felt an undying fealty. They could not express all they felt, but for mammy's "girl" or "boy" they could work and suffer and teach a blessed lesson of endurance and glorified fortitude* [all emphasis, L.S.]; for, as Miss Dromgoole so sweetly expresses it:

> Her face is as black as ebon
>   Wrinkled and seamed and old;
> But her heart, I know, is as white as snow,
>   And true as the rarest gold.
>
> Her brown hands, old and feeble
>   With touch of the passing years,
> Would banish each trace of care from my face
>   And brush from my heart the tears.

Mammy and friend, I loved her,
  Humble and all unfamed;
But I love to trace in her love the face
  That robber years have claimed.

Her face is as black as ebon,
  Her soul is as fair as the day;
And her prayers, I know, wherever I go,
  Will follow me all the way.[251] — MISS MARY M. SOLARI, J. HARVEY MATHEWS CHAPTER, U.D.C., MEMPHIS, TENN.

FROM THE OBITUARY OF CARRIE MCGAVOCK

☞ Died, at the home of her son-in-law, Mr. George L. Cowan [of Forrest's Escort], near Franklin, Tenn., on the 22nd of February, 1905, Mrs. Caroline ["Carrie"] E. W. McGavock, in the seventy-sixth year of her age.

Mrs. Carrie McGavock of Carnton Plantation, Franklin, Tennessee.

Caroline Elizabeth Winder was born near Natchez, Miss., September 9, 1829; but in her infancy she was removed with her parents to their plantation in Louisiana, west of New Orleans, where she was brought up. Her mother was a daughter of the Hon. Felix Grundy, the great lawyer and Senator of Tennessee. She ever enjoyed the advantages of wealth and high social position, and she received the best intellectual and moral training according to the ideals and standards of the Presbyterian Church, of which the family were members.

On December 6, 1846, she was united in marriage to Col. John [W.] McGavock, of Franklin, Tenn., and came to his home, "Carnton" [Plantation] where she spent the remainder of her life, nearly sixty years. This fine old home, under her care, was for half a century the center of the most lavish and generous hospitality. She and her husband were true types of the old-time Southerners, warm in heart, genial in manner, refined in sentiment, abundant in kindness.

It was around Carnton that the dreadful battle of Franklin [II] was fought, November 30, 1864, and the grand old home was filled with the wounded, to whom Col. McGavock and his wife ministered with all their resources. On the morning after the battle five Confederate generals lay dead on the wide gallery of the house. For weeks these good Samaritans nursed the wounded, cared for the dying, and buried the dead.

When the war was over, Col. McGavock gave the beautiful cemetery, in which are gathered the bodies of the heroic soldiers who fell on that fatal field. The care of this resting place for heroism was a sacred duty to Mrs. McGavock until the end of her life. The Confederate Veterans can never forget her.[252]

. . . An expression of gratitude that so many people attended the funeral was made to a venerable lady, who responded "Ah me! Everybody loved her." *One of the sincerest of all the mourners present was an intelligent colored woman who was bought for Mrs. McGavock in her girlhood—in 1849—by her father. Through all the years this faithful woman had been present with the family in its every affliction* [my emphasis, L.S.].²⁵³ — REV. JAMES H. MCNEILLY, D.D., CONFEDERATE VETERAN, NASHVILLE, TENN.

MORE SUPPORT FOR A MONUMENT TO SOUTHERN SERVANTS

☞ I have just read Miss Mary Solari's grand sentiments in the March *Veteran* in regard to a monument to the faithful blacks of the South. Being in full sympathy with her in all her views, I wish to emphasize her idea that right now is the time to begin the noble work, and I would esteem it an honor to be among the first to begin working for the cause.

A few instances from my own life will show why my heart should dictate such a step. My mother died when I was four years old, leaving three little girls, myself the oldest, and *it was an old black mammy who cared for us till the new mother came to take the place of the lost one. My baby sister's crib was placed in the cabin by mammy's bed, and it was an old black hand that tenderly rocked it for many a night, and we lisped our prayers at a black mammy's knee.*

During the war, while my father was in the army, my mother and four children lived on the plantation, a mile from any other white person, and were protected by a faithful old negro man, who was father's foreman. There were

Plantation families, both white and black, considered themselves members of each others' kinship group, and shared in one another's daily joys and sorrows.

about seventy-five negroes on the place, and he superintended everything and made the crops. After the surrender, he remained our "right hand" until death claimed him.

My father died in 1879 of sporadic yellow fever, and his sudden death caused one of those dreadful panics that we can remember only with horror. The white people fled; but our negroes were there, faithful to the very last, and they formed the midnight funeral procession that carried my honored father to the cemetery. Do you wonder that I should be glad to give a proof of gratitude for such heroic devotion? I know there are thousands of men and women in the South whose experience has been similar to mine [all emphasis, L.S.]. Will not some one start the movement for a monument and give us the opportunity of assisting in the work?²⁵⁴ — MRS. KATE W. MOORE, OAKLAND, MISS.

HE SERVED UNDER TURNER ASHBY: AFRICAN CONFEDERATE "BLACK HAWK"

Rev. Dr. J. B. Avirett and "Black Hawk."

☞ A letter received from Camp Rest, Buena Vista, Va., July 17, 1905, states that the accompanying photograph is that of the Rev. James Battle Avirett, chaplain of the 7th Virginia Cavalry, Army of Northern Virginia, C.S.A., and that of *John, the colored cook of the mess connected with Chew's Battery of Horse Artillery, belonging to the Ashby Brigade of Cavalry*, at the head of which the brilliant cavalry officer, Gen. Turner Ashby, was killed June 6, 1862, in the very wonderful campaign of "Stonewall" Jackson in the historic Shenandoah Valley.

This old chaplain, by virtue of the date of his commission (June 17, 1861), is the oldest chaplain of the Confederate service, and now lives in his old age at Buena Vista, Va., a retired clergyman of the Protestant Episcopal Church. He is the author of the life of his general, entitled *Ashby and His Compeers* . . . His last book, entitled *The Old Plantation*, is richly descriptive of Southern life before the War between the States. *The old cook of the mess, commonly called "Black Hawk," was the faithful depositary of the officers' watches and money when the fight was on. Highly respected and as trustworthy as he was during that fearful struggle, "Black Hawk" still ministers as a trusted servant in the family of the late Gen. James H. Williams, of Woodstock, Va.* [all emphasis, L.S.] . . .[235] — *CONFEDERATE VETERAN* MAGAZINE

THE TRUTH ABOUT SLAVERY & LINCOLN'S WAR

☞ If our fathers [that is, Confederate veterans] have buried their resentments, their sons cannot do less by remembering the good and forgetting the mean things of that historic conflict. But there is one duty that the Southern son owes to his father as well as to his nation, and that is to insist persistently at all times and upon all occasions that the history of the war shall be truly written, that its causes shall be asserted, and that we may proclaim and posterity know that *the soldiers of the South fought for principle and honor and the preservation of that construction of the Constitution which was given by the men who made it.*

The preservation of facts and actual experiences in the memory of the living is of immediate necessity that there may be proper material for the writing of this true account. There was enough of glory for both, enough of heroic acts and noble sacrifices to satisfy the zeal of the bitterest partisan, and *there can be no excuse for a Southerner writing a history which does not deal truly with the situation. Certainly the Northern historian should be sufficiently gratified with the victory of the Northern armies not to feel compelled to make false record of the causes that led to the unhappy conflict. If, in preserving history, it becomes necessary to speak the bold truth, there should be no complaint, and there will be none except by those who have something to conceal. The South has nothing to hide, and asks the printing of unvarnished facts, nothing more.*

While Appomattox settled all disputes on the State Rights Doctrine as well as the slavery question, it should not prevent the story of what came before being truly told. The dispassionate historian of the future will write that *slavery was not introduced in America at the solicitation of the men who settled the South. The first American slave ship was fitted out by the Pilgrim Colony, and the first statute establishing slavery was enacted in Massachusetts* [all emphasis, L.S.].[256]

The War between the States was not started for the emancipation of slaves, nor did Lincoln and Grant go into it for that purpose, but to preserve the Union of States. Lincoln said, in his inaugural address of March 4, 1861: "I have no purpose directly or indirectly to interfere with the institution of slavery in the States where it now exists. I believe I have no lawful right to do so, and I have no inclination to do so." And again: "I did not at any time say that I was in favor of negro suffrage. I declared against it. I am not in favor of negro citizenship." *Emancipation came as an incident of war.*

The first American Confederacy to recognize slavery by law was the United Colonies of New England. Its original disappearance from the North was due less to morals than to climate. [Thomas] Jefferson protested against it before Lincoln and Davis were born. Southern States, by legislative enactment, stopped its growth before the Federal enactments of 1808. The North did as much as the South to put the black curse upon our land, and then made the South pay the entire cost for the sins of both. . . .[257] — MR. HARRY B. HAWES, OF ST. LOUIS, MO.

BLACK CONFEDERATE: "UNCLE" JERRY PERKINS

☛ Charles Perkins enlisted at Brownsville, Tenn., under Capt. H. S. Bradford, who was afterwards Col. Bradford, of the 31st Tennessee Infantry. He was killed in the battle near Atlanta July 22, 1864. *The [black] boy Jerry went with him as a body servant* [my emphasis, L.S.]. Before leaving, Charley's mother told Jerry that he must bring his "Marse Charley" back to her, and he promised that he would do it; that he would take him back alive or dead.

On that fateful July 22 young Perkins was killed; and when the regiment fell back to bivouac for the night, Jerry was alarmed not to see Marse Charley, and, upon being told that he was dead, said, "Here's your supper. I'm going to find Marse Charley," and away in the darkness he went. In a short while he returned, carrying the dead body of his young master on his back. He carried it a mile or so farther to a farmhouse, got some plank, borrowed a saw, hatchet, and nails, made a box, dug a grave, and buried him in the farmer's yard. *He walked from Atlanta to Brownsville, Tenn., and reported the sad news.* He was supplied with a farm wagon and a metallic coffin, went back to Georgia, disinterred the body of Charley Perkins, and hauled it home to Brownsville.

"Uncle" Jerry Perkins.

Jerry is a favorite with the [Confederate heritage group] Hiram S. Bradford Bivouac, and attends all of their Reunions.[258] — J. W. MCCLISH, BROWNSVILLE, TENN.

SOUTHERN BLACK BOY PREFERS CONFEDERATES TO YANKS
☞ While at Holly Springs Vandorn's Cavalry [C.S.A.] went to the enemy's rear and captured that place one morning about daybreak. A negro boy was making his way out, and, being dressed in blue and in the early twilight, I took him to be a Federal and halted him. *After finding that he was only a negro boy, I would have let him go on, but he wanted to go with me for protection, and, picking up an old mule, I put him on it and let him go with us.* He said he was thirteen years old and was waiting on an artillery officer, Maj. Mudd, I think. The boy said he lived near Huntsville, Ala., and went with the Federals from there to Memphis.

Three extraordinary American Conservatives. L-R: Confederate Generals Stonewall Jackson, Joseph E. Johnston, and Robert E. Lee.

After taking Holly Springs, our command continued to go north, and, crossing Little Hatchie at Davis's Bridge, we had quite a skirmish with the enemy in getting across the river. The lame horse crowd being in the rear and one of my neighbor friends being the crowd, I let the little negro stay with him. They got cut off from the command and went home, in Tipton County, Tenn., and the boy went with him. After getting home, the boy went to my father's and remained there during the war. *Although the Federals were frequently at my father's after that, he never wanted to go with them, but stayed at home and would help to hide the stock. On one occasion he got one horse back from them after they had it in their possession. After I got home from the war, he lived with me for several years* [all emphasis, L.S.].

He was a bright boy, and *I taught him to read and write.* He took a great interest in learning and progressed rapidly, finally becoming a Methodist preacher. He got a country circuit, and after three or four years was made presiding elder. Since that time I have not known much of him, but think he has quit preaching and is running a large farm in Arkansas. He was always Democratic [before 1896, the Conservative Party] in politics, and would sometimes take an active part in trying to gel the negroes to vote for some of his white friends. He has always gone by the name of Jim Battery. I do not remember who he belonged to before emancipation.[259]
— W. H. STRANGE, GIFT, TENN.

BLACK SERVANT PROCURES A PENSION FOR HIS FORMER WHITE OWNER
☞ An interesting figure at the [recent Confederate veterans'] Louisville reunion was Jerry W. May, colored. Jerry is a mail carrier at Macon, and has been in the service for over twenty years. *Each year when the time for the Confederate Reunion rolls around Jerry asks for his vacation and accompanies Camp Smith to the rendezvous of the old Confederates.* This is the fourteenth

Reunion he has attended.

During the war Jerry was the body servant of William Wynn, of Georgia, who enlisted and served throughout the long contest as a private. His master was a member of the 7th Georgia Regiment of Harrison's Brigade. After the war, his master, who had lost everything by the ravages of the Federal army, moved to Prescott, Ark., leaving Jerry in Macon. A few years later he died, and his widow was left alone with nothing on which she might rely for a support. *Jerry began the task of securing a pension for her, and after several years of hard work he was successful. Through his efforts she was enabled to live comfortably.*

The *Veteran* wrote to Jerry in regard to the above, and he responded promptly, stating: "My old master, William Wynn, was born and reared in Monroe County, Ga. He enlisted in the 7th Georgia Regiment, as stated, Company D. He took me as body servant; and after the war, everything was lost to him—even I myself came near being lost to him, but not quite. After the war, he moved to Prescott, Ark., and began farming; but he was quite old and feeble, so he could do but little at it. Later he wrote me that he could get a pension under the Arkansas laws, but he was too feeble mentally and physically, and he wanted me to do it for him. *I replied that I would do anything in my power on earth for him and his wife as long as they lived.* I went at once to Gen. C. M. Wyley, the Ordinary [that is, judge] for Bibb County, got application blanks, took one to every member of the old company that I could find, got them signed with affidavits before proper officers, made oath myself, and had seals put on where seals could be found. Sad but true, he died just before I got the papers ready. I then went back and got other blanks, and did the same work for his widow. *I paid every cent of money necessary without any cost to her.* I sent all the papers for him and her both, and the committee put her on the pension list. *She wrote me her sincere thanks for what I did, and said she was all the more grateful because I had been one of her slaves."*

Jerry W. May, Macon, Georgia.

These are sincere suggestions to young negroes as to how they may ingratiate themselves into the good will of white people. It would be well for them to consider how they can best advance their highest interests. Those [blacks] of the South should not forget that the element of their color at the North are no credit to the race as a class, and that the result is fast creating far bitterer prejudices against them in that section than has ever existed in the South. If young negroes at the South would accept conditions that cannot be overcome and steadfastly avoid impolite, not to say impudent, methods, they would speedily find friendships among them that would be as lasting as it is with their parents. It is for the good of all and more for the inferior race that general friendly relations exist. [Note: As explained in my introduction to this book, this sentiment was common at the time—among blacks as well as whites. Lincoln himself, for example, repeatedly referred to

African Americans as an "inferior race."][260] Let any of them try it, and they will not regret it. *The Southern people remember the amiable dispositions of the race, and will be diligent to aid them if they will adopt the only method possible for friendly relations.* This advice is in as friendly spirit as it is possible to write, and it is meant to emphasize the advice to negroes. *If they will maintain the rule of due politeness to white people, they will find among them stanch friends who will see that they are justly treated under all circumstances* [all emphasis, L.S.].[261] — CONFEDERATE VETERAN MAGAZINE

SOUTHERN SERVANTS IN NORTHERN PRISONS

☛ [Many black servants went to prison with their white Confederate owners rather than accept the so-called "freedom" offered by the Yanks. One of these patriotic Southern Africans was named Dick, the servant of Confederate Capt. R. M. Hewett.] . . . . [Dick] was *faithful and loyal to his master to the end. The Federal officers at Johnson's Island offered all kinds of inducements to get Dick to leave Capt. Hewett and take service with them, but he stoutly declined, preferring to remain in prison and share the hardships with his master. They refused to issue him any rations, but each of us divided our own meager supply, which gave him a portion equal to ours. Dick was exchanged with his master only a short time before the surrender, and Capt. Hewett died soon after reaching Dixie.*

Confederate Gen. Pierre G. T. Beauregard.

There was another faithful slave in Johnson's Island named John, who belonged to [Confederate] Capt. J. R. Wilson, now living in Florence, Ala. *He also went through the hardships of prison with his master rather than accept his freedom and remunerative service from the Federals. John went out on exchange with his master, and lived for some years after the war, until his death, on the plantation of Capt. Wilson, in Mississippi. It is needless to say that John never wanted for anything his master could supply* [all emphasis, L.S.].[262] — CAPT. A. O. P. NICHOLSON, COLUMBIA, TENN.

THE CONFEDERATE SOLDIER DID NOT FIGHT FOR ENSLAVEMENT, HE FOUGHT FOR LIBERTY!

☛ . . . If it is charged that slavery was the cornerstone of the Southern Confederacy, what are we to say of the Constitution of the United States? That instrument as originally adopted by the thirteen colonies contained three sections which recognized slavery.

But after all that may be said we are told that slavery was the cause of the war and that the citizen-soldiers of the South sprang, to arms in defense of slavery.

Yes, my comrades, *calumny, masquerading as history*, has told the world that that battle flag of yours was the emblem of slave power, and that you fought not for liberty but for the right to hold your fellow-men in bondage.

Think of it, soldiers of Lee! Think of it, followers of Jackson and

Stuart and Albert Sidney Johnston! You were fighting, they say, for the privilege of holding your fellow-men in bondage! Will you for one moment acknowledge the truth of that indictment? *Ah, no! that banner of the Southern Cross was studded with the stars of God's heaven. You could not have followed a banner that was not the banner of liberty! You sprang from the loins of freemen! You drank in freedom with your mothers' milk! Your revolutionary sires were not inspired by a more intense devotion to liberty than you were!*

Tell me, were you thinking of your slaves when you cast all in the balance, your lives, your fortunes, your sacred honor, in order to endure the hardships of the march and the camp and the peril and suffering of the battlefield? Why, it was but a small minority of the men who fought in the Southern armies—hardly one in ten—that were financially interested in the institution of slavery [all emphasis, L.S.].

There is, however, a court to which this contention may be referred for settlement—one whose decision all men ought to accept. It is composed of the three men who may be supposed to have known, if any man knew, the object for which the war was waged—Abraham Lincoln, Jefferson Davis, and Robert E. Lee. And their decision is unanimous. Mr. Lincoln always declared that the object of the war was the restoration of the Union, and not the emancipation of the slaves. Mr. Davis as positively declared that the South was not fighting for slavery, but for independence. And Robert E. Lee expressed his opinion by setting all his slaves free January 8, 1863, and then going on with the war for more than two years longer.

Rev. R. H. McKim.

— REV. RANDOLPH H. MCKIM, NASHVILLE CONFEDERATE REUNION[263]

UPLIFTING SOUTHERN BLACKS

☛ [Editor's note: Just as we find today (2022), and even as far back as Lincoln (1860-1865), in the early 1900s, socialist and communist agitators were employing race-baiting, fear, crime, violence, gaslighting, and socioeconomic and racial division to weaken traditional American society, with the ultimate goal of destroying it. Conservative Southerners then, as now, fought against this insidious evil through numerous means, an example of which, at the beginning of the post-Victorian Era, is given in the following article. L.S.]

There is an industrial college for negroes at Conroe, Tex., known as the Conroe-Porter Industrial College, which ought to become a great institution. The property consists of eight acres of land paid for, one four-story building with twenty-three rooms and two more buildings, and enough lumber on the ground to erect another commodious building. The college has about forty boarders and one hundred other students.

The object of the school is to teach young negroes these lessons: (1) The science and art of politeness; (2) how to obey law, and respect for public sentiment; (3) how to resist temptation and be virtuous; (4) that idleness is sin, all labor is honorable; (5) that a good character is the greatest wealth; (6) that *the white people in the South are the negro's best friends*; (7) that Christianity means love and service.

The Houston *Post* says: "An institution like this deserves encouragement not only for the great good which will accrue to the negroes who learn these important truths, but for the welfare of the white people among whom the negroes have to live. A negro who is polite, law-abiding, virtuous, honest, and industrious will never lack for friends in the South; and if the Southern people could have their way, all the negroes would live up to the standard of this school at Conroe. There are many such negroes in the South, and *negroes of character are respected and treated with cordial consideration by the white people.*

"There is no negro problem in which the self-respecting, honest, and industrious negroes are concerned, and there will not be. The problem comes of the presence of a constantly growing number of idle, lawless, and vicious negroes, many of whom [provoked by radical, anti-American, Left-wing groups] *are continually clamoring for social equality and treatment that is not even extended to white people who are similarly idle and vicious.*

Miss Mary Adean Wilkes, Confederate sponsor for Tennessee.

The *Post* hopes that the trustees of the Conroe School will meet with generous encouragement at the hands of the while people. *The institution is under the control of an advisory board of white men,* who are endeavoring to acquire more land and erect other needed buildings."

In commending this institution the integrity of the management is presumed through the indorsement of the Houston *Post*. The Southern people have been so tried on these "educational" lines that it is difficult to consider this subject without prejudice. If this industrial school, or "college," is conducted on the lines indicated, *our white people should give it hearty encouragement* [all emphasis, L.S.]. Let its maintenance be by our own people, entirely free from Northern missionaries [that is, communist activists and propagandists]. An institution properly conducted on these lines would rapidly prove a blessing to both races. It would be just such a monument to the South's regard for well-behaved [that is, socialized] negroes as would be universally satisfactory."[264] ―
CONFEDERATE VETERAN MAGAZINE

MORE PROOF THAT THE CONFEDERATE MILITARY WAS DISCUSSING GOVERNMENTAL AUTHORIZATION OF BLACK ENLISTMENT AT THE BEGINNING OF 1865

☛ . . . The propriety of taking the negro as soldiers is being discussed more or less by the army; have not heard as yet sufficiently to form an opinion as to whether it be popular with the army, but *am sure that some prominent officers who were bitterly opposed to it eighteen months since are now advocates for the plan* [my emphasis, L.S.]. . . .[265] ― CONFEDERATE GEN. ROBERT CHARLES TYLER TO CONFEDERATE MAJ. W. J. SLATTER, FEBRUARY 1865

LINCOLN SUPPORTED COMPENSATED EMANCIPATION & MAINTAINED THAT YANKEES WERE AS RESPONSIBLE FOR SLAVERY AS SOUTHERNERS

☛ *Mr. Lincoln said he believed the people of the North were as responsible for slavery as the people of the South*, and if the war should then cease, with the voluntary abolition of slavery by the States, *he should be in favor, individually* [that is, himself personally], *of the government paying a fair indemnity for the loss to the owners* [all emphasis, L.S.]. . . . But on this subject he said he could give no assurance—enter into no stipulation [without the agreement of the U.S. government].²⁶⁶ — CONFEDERATE VICE PRESIDENT ALEXANDER H. STEPHENS QUOTING ABRAHAM LINCOLN AT THE HAMPTON ROADS CONFERENCE, FEBRUARY 3, 1865

MORE EVIDENCE OF BLACK CONFEDERATES

Noted French American author, Miss Edna Sidonie de la Houssaye, Sponsor for Confederate Camp No. 2, Army of Tennessee Association, New Orleans, La.

☛ . . . [Confederate Brig. Gen. Henry Lewis] Benning's Brigade, consisting of the 2nd, 15th, 17th, and 20th Georgia Regiments, was stationed at Newmarket, about three miles lower down the James River, in front of and watching the command of [Union] Gen. [Benjamin F.] Butler ("Spoons"). Being in command of the 17th Georgia, I was ordered to Fort Harrison, and with some two hundred penitentiary convicts and *three hundred negroes* [my emphasis, L.S.] then at Fort Harrison, to proceed to strengthen the works. With seven companies, three companies being left on picket duty, I arrived at the fort late in the evening of the 28th of September, leaving orders for the three companies to rejoin the regiment as soon as relieved from picket duty. . . .²⁶⁷ — CONFEDERATE MAJ. JAMES B. MOORE, CAMERON. TEX.

BLACKS PAY HOMAGE TO CONFEDERATE SOLDIER

☛ On the afternoon of July 16, 1905, the soul of [Confederate] Gen. Bryan M. Thomas, of Dalton, Ga., "passed over the river to rest under the shade of the trees" in the realms of the eternal camping ground. . . . As he lay in his casket, clad in his uniform of gray and surrounded by beautiful flowers, many people, including the hoary-headed veteran with his iron cross, the youngest school child, the business man wearing his insignia of Masonry, and *the humblest negro, paid tribute to his worthy memory* [my emphasis, L.S.]. . . .²⁶⁸ — *CONFEDERATE VETERAN* MAGAZINE

FAMOUS INFLUENTIAL CONFEDERATE VETERANS PREPARED TO ATTEND FUNERAL OF BLACK CONFEDERATE SOLDIER

☛ The *Constitution* [newspaper] prints an interesting story of Amos Rucker, a noted old negro of Atlanta. *An accepted "street rumor" that Amos was dead created widespread expressions of sorrow. There was good reason for the esteem in which the old negro was held.*

In the beginning of the war, in 1862, [Confederate] Col. [Edmund Winchester] Rucker and a son went to the war, and *with them went Amos.*

"Somehow, it mattered not how the commissary was depleted, Amos was ever ready to serve a meal to his masters and to his masters' friends. Never in those days when freedom was only a few hundred yards away, just across the divide between the two armies, did Amos forget he was a negro except when fighting was going on. Then taking up a gun dropped by a soldier who had died fighting, he took that soldier's place in the battle line and did his best. A crippled leg and a red scar in his left breast now bear testimony to the fact that Amos Rucker was a soldier, tried and found to be brave.

"When rumors reached the city that Rucker was dead, initial steps were taken for his funeral. Pallbearers were selected and orders were issued for the Veterans of the city to attend the funeral in a body Wednesday afternoon. The pallbearers selected were ex-Gov. [Allen D.] Candler, Gen. A. J. West, F. A. Hilburn, member of the City Council; J. Sid Holland, member of the Aldermanic Board; Judge W. Lowndes Calhoun, ex-Mayor of Atlanta; and Dr. Amos Fox, a member of the Board of Police Commissioners and ex-postmaster—*each being a Confederate Veteran*. Dr. Holderby was to have preached the funeral. *The body was to have been escorted to South View by the Atlanta Camps of Confederate Veterans* [all emphasis, L.S.].

"The only hitch in the arrangements was that Amos was not dead. When the driver of the undertaker's wagon, which had been sent to Rucker's home, near Atlanta University, was approaching the home the driver almost dropped from his seat when he observed just in front of him Amos Rucker walking into the city."[269] — *CONFEDERATE VETERAN MAGAZINE*

Gen. Edmund W. Rucker, close cousin of the author-editor, who descends from the Ruckers.

MORE PROOF THAT THE CONFEDERACY WAS A CONSERVATIVE GOVERNMENT

The Confederacy's First National Flag, sketched in 1905 by Jessica Randolph Smith.

☞ [According to *Confederate Veteran* magazine, Orren Randolph Smith, of Louisburg, North Carolina, was the designer of the First National Flag of the Confederate States of America.] . . . The idea of the flag was taken from the Trinity ("Three in One"), for the three wide bars represented Church, State, and press. The first bar (red) represented State, legislative and executive; the second (white), the Church, Father, Son, and Holy Ghost; the third (red), freedom of speech, liberty of the press, freedom of conscience, bound together by a field of cerulean blue, the heavens over all, with a star for each State in the confederation. The seven white stars were placed in a circle all the same size, showing that each State had equal rights and privileges, irrespective of size or population. The little flag was about a foot

long and about eight inches in width. With this flag was sent the suggestion that a star be added for each State that joined the Confederacy.
[In response to a public "Flag Wanted" advertisement put out by Confederate authorities seeking designs for a flag to represent the new C.S.A., Smith's] . . . flag was packed and sent to Montgomery, and on its journey it had many companions, for a number of designs were sent to the [Confederate] Committee on Flags; and a varied assortment they proved to be, from every known color and device to "the lone star of Texas" and "the rattler and palmetto of South Carolina."

The Confederate Congress adopted the flag sent by Orren Randolph Smith, and *it is now honored over all the world as the flag that floated over the bravest and hardest to conquer soldiers that this world ever saw—the stars and bars.* This flag was used officially by the Confederate States of America until after the second battle of Manassas, when a change was made [that is, the creation of the Confederate Battle Flag], owing to the fact, as has often been published, that the stars and bars resembled so forcibly the stars and stripes, especially when limp. . . .²⁷⁰ In 1844 when [Liberal] Henry Clay made his great speech amidst a great assembly, as he rose [Left-winger] W. G. Brownlow, of the Knoxville *Whig*, [disrespectfully] shouted, "Hands on your pocketbooks, gentlemen; there is a Democrat [then a Conservative] present"; and [Smith,] the man who designed the first flag of the Confederacy was present, *one of the most devoted followers* [of archetypal Conservative] *Thomas Jefferson ever had* [all emphasis, L.S.].²⁷¹ — JESSICA RANDOLPH SMITH, HENDERSON, N.C.

Orren Randolph Smith.

ONLY ELEVEN YEARS AFTER THE PUBLISHING OF *THE COMMUNIST MANIFESTO* RADICAL LEFTIST JOHN BROWN USES MARXIST & RACIST TACTICS TO DESTROY THE SOUTH
☙ At Leavenworth, Kans., 1856-57, in the turbulent [antebellum] days of "bleeding Kansas," when proslavery and antislavery were fighting for the mastery in two conventions for and against "free soil," both sides importing delegates and members, and heard that [Yankee Rev. Henry Ward] Beecher was preaching in Plymouth Church with a Bible in one hand and a rifle in the other, "Passage paid, redeem Kansas and be saved," the South was preaching and teaching, "No Mason and Dixon's line, no Wilmot proviso binds us in prison bonds; on to Kansas!"
Out of this conflict came [Left-wing revolutionary] John Brown ("Old Ossawatomie") in 1859, who, with his helpers, captured Harper's Ferry arsenal in a night attack, *to arm the negroes, kill all the whites, and let the negroes have possession of the country* [all communist strategies; my emphasis, L.S.]. Many in the Republican party [then the Liberal Party], sympathizing with him in his murderous attack upon innocent citizens, called him "St. John Brown, whose soul is marching on to glory."²⁷² — JESSICA RANDOLPH SMITH, HENDERSON, N.C.

BLACK CONFEDERATE SAILORS WORK ON STEAMER THAT SUPPLIES FORREST WITH PROVISIONS

Capt. C. S. Peak.

☞ [Confederate] Capt. C. S. Peak died on the 8th of March, 1905, after a short but severe illness. He was born in Meigs County, Tenn., in August, 1839, the son of Maj. Jacob Peak, who was a wealthy farmer and slave owner. Maj. Peak served four years under [Conservative] Gen. [Andrew] Jackson in the Creek Indian War, in which he won the rank of major for gallant service.

When the war clouds gathered in 1861, young Peak was in the steamboat business on the Tennessee River; and when East Tennessee became the theater of active operations, he owned and commanded the steamer *Tennessee*, operating between Decatur and Knoxville. *The deck hands were negroes from his father's plantation. The boat and negroes were tendered* [that is, offered to] *the Confederate government, and accepted by* [Confederate] *Gen.* [Edmund] *Kirby Smith, who commanded the East Tennessee Department. Comrade Peak was commissioned as captain and placed in charge of the department of transportation, in which capacity he kept the armies of* [Nathan Bedford] *Forrest at Kingston and Smith at Knoxville bountifully provisioned from the rich bottom lands of that section* [my emphasis, L.S.]. When the Confederates were retiring from East Tennessee, Capt. Peak was ordered to destroy his boat, as the enemy was about to capture it. After this, he became a member of a company of the 3rd Confederate Cavalry, under Col. Hart, of Georgia, and served in the ranks as a trooper till the close of the war . . . .273 — *CONFEDERATE VETERAN MAGAZINE*

CONFEDERATE CAPTAIN & HIS FAITHFUL INDIAN SERVANT BOY

☞ Mrs. Evans, Dear Madam: It has fallen to my lot to inform you of the melancholy fate of your lamented husband, and may God help you and give you fortitude in your bereavement.

[Confederate] Capt. [Mark L.] Evans was ordered into the battle of Perryville [Kentucky] on the 8th inst. to charge a battery, which he did most gallantly. But he received a fatal wound in the head by a Minie ball which fractured his skull. He was brought to my home, where he had good attention until the 18th inst., when at forty minutes past six he expired. He lay in a drowsy state all the time, and never opened his eyes; he talked very little, and his talk was like a man who is very drowsy. His Masonic brothers helped to get his coffin and to bury him. He and Col. McDaniel, of Georgia, were buried at the same time. Their bodies now lie in the Masonic grounds, where they can be removed.

Confederate officer Mark L. Evans.

Anything that you would desire me to do shall be done with pleasure. Most truly your friend, B. Mills.

Note.—*The Indian boy* [Capt. Evans's body servant] *attended him most faithfully* [my emphasis, L.S.]. *My wife has his clothes, a ring, and a lock of his hair, which will all be kept for you. His brother and some friends remained with him for three days, when the enemy came and they left him in my charge.* B. Mills.²⁷⁴ — FROM A LETTER BY B. MILLS TO MRS. MARIA EVANS CLAIBORNE, THE WIFE OF CONFEDERATE OFFICER MARK L. EVANS

BLACK CONFEDERATE LISTED AT HOPKINSVILLE CEMETERY UNDER "CONFEDERATE DEAD BURIED IN KENTUCKY"
☛ *Washington Hall, man of color. Hill's Co., Grigg's Regt., Tex. (no date; this old man was a faithful servant to his master, and died much beloved by his company)* [my emphasis, L.S.].²⁷⁵ — MRS. SOPHIE FOX SEA, HISTORIAN KENTUCKY STATE DIVISION, U.D.C.

WHITE CONFEDERATES CONSIDERED THEIR BLACK SERVANTS FAMILY MEMBERS
☛ . . . Now, Daughters, I have nothing but pleasant things to say of the members of my Division. Therefore, in justice, please hear me patiently, and you will know, better than you ever knew before, how happy, loyal, peaceful, and good we are; for I want to tell you that we care for your living far from their earthly home and your dead, whose souls have reached their heavenly home—therefore from this platform it gives me infinite pleasure to state that between the storm-tossed waters of the Atlantic, as they bathe the feet of that majestic goddess, "Liberty," at New York, and the sun-kissed waters of the Pacific, as they pass through the Golden Gate at San Francisco, there is a State called "Ohio," where there too are also brave, loyal [Confederate] women who love to keep alive the memories of home, and who, though staying at home in the sixties, *were protected by the faithful darkies who loved them and were called members of their household, and who guarded them with their humble love, thus making it a little easier for the brave of that time to go forth and fight for love of home and to maintain State rights* [my emphasis, L.S.].

These women have banded themselves together and loyally work under the rules of the General Order, the title of the Ohio Division, United Daughters of the Confederacy, and who send you this greeting to-day. . . .²⁷⁶ — FROM A SPEECH TO THE UNITED DAUGHTERS OF THE CONFEDERACY, BY MRS. FLORENCE TUCKER WINDER, ST. LOUIS, MO., CIRCA 1905

Mrs. Florence Tucker Winder.

A FAITHFUL NEGRO: "UNCLE" GEORGE YOUNG
☛ ["Uncle" George Young, though now free] . . . was a faithful servant; and when it was said that if [Grover] Cleveland should be elected [U.S.] President the negroes would be reenslaved George said he was "not afraid, but would go right back to [his master] Mars Elic."

George was strictly honest, and was never known to be guilty of an intentional wrong. He was a member of the M. E. Church, South, and a faithful Christian.²⁷⁷ — BETTIE A. CALHOUN, LIBERTY, MO.

WHITES ARRANGE FUNERAL FOR BELOVED BLACK MAMMY "AUNT" MARY MARLOW

Rose Fay, former black servant, Bracketville, Texas, 1937.

☞ *An old "black mammy" past ninety-three years of age died at Milledgeville, Ga., in January, 1906, and was buried by white people. Young gentlemen whose parents and grandparents were objects of her care in their childhood were pallbearers and walked by the hearse to the cemetery. The procession was headed by the pastor of the Presbyterian Church. The Atlanta Constitution states: "'Aunt' Mary Marlow said that when she was a girl about twelve years old she was on a fence near Richmond, Va., seeing a procession go by that was honoring [Marquis de] Lafayette, when she was stolen from the fence and brought to Georgia by slave traders and became the property of Hon. Francis V. DeLauney. She nursed his children and his children's children and some of their children, and it was some of these children that she had so tenderly nursed that to-day bore her to her last resting place and followed her to her grave. In the procession were other white citizens, who were perfectly willing to show the world that here was one who had lived a life worthy of public recognition and whose hearts had been so touched by her gentle, faithful acts that forty years of ever-changing conditions had not shaken or destroyed the tender memories that bound them to this old woman"* [all emphasis, L.S.].²⁷⁸ — *CONFEDERATE VETERAN* MAGAZINE

THE OLD PLANTATION DAYS

☞ . . . *[The white Southern speaker] . . . said he loved the old-time negro, the black mammies and the uncles, and declared that [because they were still largely uneducated] giving these people immediate liberty was all wrong and giving them the franchise was a crime. Then he said it was the duty of all Southern men to uplift the negro. He declared that Booker Washington was doing no new thing, excellent as his work is; but that before the war the South taught the negroes to be carpenters and blacksmiths and bricklayers and that the work had been interrupted by the war* [my emphasis, L.S.]. . . .²⁷⁹ — F. HOPKINSON SMITH, ANNUAL ROBERT E. LEE DINNER, WALDORF-ASTORIA HOTEL, NEW YORK CITY, NY.

WHITE SOUTHERN ARTIST-POETESS CAPTURES TRUE ESSENCE OF WARTIME BLACK SERVANTRY

☞ It was my great pleasure to meet and know personally Miss [Maria] Howard Weeden, who dedicated her pen and brush to that page of literature that remembers with undying devotion the Old South and ante-bellum institutions. Joel Chandler Harris, Thomas Nelson Page,

Maria Howard Weeden.

John Fox, Jr., James Lane Allen, and a host of others of equal renown have created a distinctive school of literature, chaste in conception, deep-tinted with romance, spirited as a cavalier ballad, and all bathed in the pathos of the War between the States. In this memorial literature the ex-slave has place and part. Dignified by his fidelity, unconsciously humorous, he, with the shadowy pageantry of "the storm-cradled nation that fell," has become the heritage of "song and story."

What many have achieved in literature, Miss Weeden has accomplished with her brush—preserved a type, illumined an era. She made a specialty of negro heads [portraits], little masterpieces that commanded instant recognition in the world of art and letters. These heads have reached the public as illustrations of three volumes of poetry, shyly humorous, quaintly modest verses that attract us by a homely phrase and haunt us like regret for something loved and lost. Her verses, for all their dainty charm, are in line with the writings of many others; but as an artist she enjoys the unique distinction of standing alone, a specialist, in a field of rich poetic and humanic interest.

. . . The more I see of the ex-slave through the kindly vision of Southern genius in art and literature, the more am I convinced that the South understands the negro at his best. I half suspect that the "colored brother" so much patronized by the excitant [Liberal] legislators of the North is the picturesque creation of romance that deals tenderly with "things past and gone." I am quite persuaded that the negro of the New England era of literature who shone forth so pathetically through the vision of [James Russell] Lowell, [Henry Wadsworth] Longfellow, [John Greenleaf] Whittier, and others who stimulated the war was not a negro at all, but a finely organized, painfully sensitive, delicately complex creation of the poet's frenzy. No wonder the North went into chimerical schemes of legislative philanthropy over a Mrs. [Elizabeth Barrett] Browning, a Charlotte Bronte, a Lowell, painted black and quivering in agony under the lash of cruel slavery. The negro and the mule are valuable industrial factors, but they are not the ethereal manifestations that vex the statesman of New England with insistent demands for social equality [all emphasis, L.S.].

I found Miss Weeden not a great while before her untimely death in Huntsville, Ala., a town tenacious of the olden times. Her lifetime residence, Weeden Place, is just the environment for the talents she developed. It is a colonial mansion set in deep shadows, asleep, as it were, under the spell of ancientry. Here is an abiding presence of restfulness, simple hospitality, a something of noble permanence to which old associations climb and cling and blossom. like the moonflower, in the starshine of memory.

"The Mystic," by Miss Maria Howard Weeden.

Personally, Miss Weeden was a lady of high respect, retiring almost to shyness, yet serenely poised, as if she had no need to fret and fume and hurry and slur her life work to meet the fierce commercial greed of the hour. Three volumes of poetry and portraits attest her answer to the high call of art, which yields nothing of excellence save to the rapt meditations of genius and industry. That her inspiration was the humble folk about her, models that lacked sensuous beauty of form and the splendid radiance of thought, detracts in no wise from her unique place in the world of art and letters. She wrought modestly in clay, and realized in truths that may some day aid the historian to explain how a wise and beneficent Providence tempered the outworn institution of slavery with affection and mutual good will.[280] — MARY BRABSON LITTLETON, CHATTANOOGA, TENN.

Weeden Place, home of Miss Maria Howard Weeden, Huntsville, Ala.

HOW VICE PRESIDENT STEPHENS & HIS BLACK SERVANTS REACTED TO HIS POSTWAR ARREST & DEPARTURE

☛ . . . The leave-takings were hurried and confused. *The servants all wept. My grief at leaving them and home was too burning, withering, scorching for tears.* At the [train] depot there was an immense crowd—*old friends, black and white* [all emphasis, L.S.]. They came in great numbers and shook hands. That parting and that scene I can never forget. It almost crazes the brain to think of it. . . .[281] — EXTRACTED FROM THE DIARY OF CONFEDERATE V.P. ALEXANDER H. STEPHENS

THE JIM LIMBER INCIDENT: YANKEE SOLDIERS KIDNAP ADOPTED BLACK SON OF CONFEDERATE PRESIDENT JEFFERSON DAVIS & HIS FAMILY

☛ At about three or four o'clock the *Clyde* put out to sea. Before leaving Mrs. [Jefferson] Davis addressed a note to [Union] Gen. Saxon [correct name: Rufus Saxton], who had charge of colonization [that is, black deportation], in confiding to him the little orphan mulatto boy [named Jim Limber] she had with her. The parting of the boy with the [Davis] family was quite a scene. He was about seven or eight years old, I should think. He was little Jeff's [Jefferson Davis, Jr., a son of Jefferson Davis] playfellow; they were very intimate, and nearly always together; it was Jeff and Jimmy between them. When Jeff knew that Jimmy was to be left, he wailed, and so did Jimmy. Maggie [a daughter, Margaret Howell Davis] cried, Varina [a daughter, Varina Anne "Winnie" Davis] cried, and the colored woman cried. Mrs. [Varina Howell] Davis said the boy's mother had been dead a number of years, and this woman had been as a mother to him. As the boat that was to take Jimmy away left our side he screamed, and had to be held to be kept from jumping overboard. He tried his best to get away from those who held him. At this Jeff and Maggie and Varina screamed almost as loud as he did. Mrs. Davis also shed tears. Mrs. Clay threw Jimmy some money, but it had no effect.

Some one on the deck of his boat picked it up and handed it to him; but he paid no attention to it, and kept scuffling to get loose and wailing as long as he could be heard by us.

After all, what is life but a succession of pains, sorrows, griefs, and woes! Poor Jimmy! He has just entered upon its threshold. This will hardly be his worst or heaviest affliction, if his days be many upon this earth.[282] — EXTRACTED FROM THE DIARY OF CONFEDERATE V.P. ALEXANDER H. STEPHENS

BLACK SERVANT WRITES RESPECTFULLY OF FIRST WHITE TEACHER OF NEGRO SCHOOL: A CONFEDERATE VETERAN

☛ Hon. Joel T. Bledsoe, tax receiver of Macon County, Ga., died at his home, in Montgomery, Wednesday night, February 21 [1906?]. He was a worthy Confederate veteran.

[The following] notice was sent to the *Veteran* by S. J. Chalmers, *colored*, of Altonia, Tex., who writes of him: "Joel Bledsoe went to the war when little boys were being received. The child came home at the close with but one leg. *He taught the first negro school in that section. He was my first teacher, but I was twenty-four years old*" [all emphasis, L. S.].

Chalmers also writes that his master was James Williamson, of Georgia, whose two sons, William Alan and Person, served through the war.[283] — *CONFEDERATE VETERAN* MAGAZINE

BLACKS ATTEND FUNERAL OF BELOVED WHITE CONFEDERATE VETERAN

Capt. J. G. Morrison, C.S.A.

☛ [Confederate] Capt. Joseph Graham Morrison died April 11 [1906], after a lingering illness, in Charlotte at the home of his sister, Mrs. Gen. T. J. ["Stonewall"] Jackson [Mary Anna Jackson]. He was buried in Lincoln County in the graveyard of old Machpelah Church, near his own home, where he had been a member and a ruling elder for years.

. . . The whole countryside had gathered to pay the tribute of affection to one whom they honored. One of the strong men who helped to fill the grave declared with moistened cheeks that, out of a personal acquaintance with Captain Morrison running over thirty years, he had come to regard him as one of the very best men he ever knew. That remark crystallized a testimonial in which hundreds were ready to join as they stood around the new-made grave.

Old soldiers wept for the loss of a comrade who had gone to rest, Church members wept because this day they put out of their sight a Christian brother whom they loved and trusted and an elder whose wise counsel and devoted leadership had guided the little congregation through many a dark and trying day in its checkered history. Neighbors, too, without regard to Church ties, were carrying their own burdens of sorrow as they covered the grave of their beloved friend with a profusion of floral offerings of exquisite beauty. *White-haired negroes—men and women—also stood with bowed heads about that grave, and realized that they were the poorer for the death of this ever-faithful friend of the black people, the last link that held many of them to the better, happier day of long ago* [my emphasis, L.S.].[284] — REV. DR. A. T. GRAHAM

THE CONFEDERATE MAMMY
☛ . . . A colored woman supporting her lame mistress to a comfortable chair, and then tenderly ministering to her wants, carried me back to the black mammy days. *"She is a Confederate,"* exclaimed one of the party from Marshall, Mo., *"and proves her by her works. Washes and irons to keep her almost helpless charge comfortable."* "One left!" I exclaimed, "of the many faithful"; and *my mind flashed back to childhood days, when six motherless children, one in the arms, the others clinging to Mammy's skirts, looked up into her kindly black face for sympathy and mother-love, and she gave it freely and truly* [all emphasis, L.S.].²⁸⁵ — ANONYMOUS

☛ STONEWALL JACKSON HONORED BY NEGROES
News from Roanoke, Va., July 29 [1906] is reported as follows: "A handsome memorial window of Gen. Stonewall Jackson was unveiled in the Fifth Avenue Presbyterian Church (negro) to-day. *The window was erected by the* [African American] *pastor, Rev. L. L. Downing, the money for its purchase coming wholly from the negroes. The exercises were largely attended by both races*, the Confederate Camps of Roanoke and Salem and the Chapters of the Daughters of the Confederacy of the same place being well represented. The chief addresses were by leading white citizens of Roanoke. *Downing's father and mother were members of a Sunday school class of negro slaves taught by Jackson at Lexington before the war, and to-day's exercises marked the realization of an ambition Downing has had since boyhood to pay fitting tribute to the Confederate commander* [all emphasis, L.S.]. The picture presented on the window is that of an army camping on the banks of a stream, the inscription underneath being Jackson's last words: 'Let us cross over the river and rest in the shade of the trees.'"²⁸⁶ — *CONFEDERATE VETERAN* MAGAZINE

The great "Stonewall."

BLACKS MOURN THE DEATH OF CONFEDERATE VETERAN
☛ This heroic soldier [Confederate Capt. J. D. Smith] in war and model citizen in peace passed away at his home, in Houston, Miss., on June 28, 1905. He deserves a place in the gallery of dead heroes in the *Veteran*, that modest temple of fame where privates as well as generals are admitted.
. . . The writer of this brief memorial, O. C. Brothers, and Captain Smith were as brothers during the war—not only brothers in arms but as brothers by blood. We ate, slept, marched together, constant companions and chums, till Captain Smith was transferred to the cavalry; and amid the fierce onset and the roar of battle the writer's thoughts followed with intense anxiety his chivalrous friend and messmate, because he always led where the fight was hottest and most desperate. Around the camp fire he was a noble companion—bright, joyous, genial, gentle as a woman, and as loving as a child, he was indeed a most lovable man; but in battle he knew not fear, and seemed to court death itself by his heroic dash and superb bravery.

After the war Captain Smith was called by the people of Chickasaw County to many important offices of trust, such as chancery clerk, assessor, treasurer. *In all he served with honor and credit, and all the people, both white and black, mourned his loss* [my emphasis, L.S.]. He was seventy-two years old. May he sleep in peace![287] — O. C. BROTHERS

WISE COUNSEL TO SOUTHERN BLACKS

☛ Notwithstanding your success in different lines, you have not done what you could. You could have made greater advances. The opportunities have been open to you for years. In this country all are born free. The inalienable rights under the constitution are life, liberty, and the pursuit of happiness. *These should be guaranteed to all, white and black, and the white people of the South will not limit you in these respects. They are and always have been your friends. They are glad to see your industrial advancement.*

Mose Hursey, former servant, Dallas, Texas, 1937.

... *The avenues of industry are open to you, and it depends on you as to whether or not you mount the highest rung of the ladder.* ... Right here in this city men [Yankees] who were brought here from the North to work on the First National Bank building refused to work because negroes were employed on the building. Southern men had worked on the building with these negroes and there had been no friction. All that you have to do is to put your hands to the plow, and without looking back work out your salvation. The basis of all nobility is purity of heart and rectitude of conduct.... *If you yourselves have no ancestry to which you look back with pride, you can bequeath to your children such an ancestry. The future of your race depends entirely upon the character of the different individuals composing it.* As did Moses to the children of Israel, I have this day set before you good and evil; *you can choose* [all emphasis, L.S.].[288] — MAYOR B. W. GRIFFITH, VICKSBURG, MISS., FROM AN ADDRESS TO THE NEGROES AT THE OPENING OF THE STATE FAIR

MORE EXAMPLES OF SOUTHERN BLACK FIDELITY TO WHITE OWNERS

☛ ... The kindliest relation that ever existed between the two races in this country, or that ever will, was the ante-bellum relation of master and slave—a relation of confidence and responsibility on the part of the master and of dependence and fidelity on the part of the slave.

Two instances of slave fidelity which came under my personal observation are still so fresh in memory that I deem them worthy of record, especially as they furnish such forcible illustration of *the tender relations existing between the two races under the old regime.*

In the late spring of 1864, while I was a [Confederate] prisoner of war in Fort Delaware [a Union prison], a fresh batch of [Confederate] prisoners was brought in one day—men who had been captured at

Miss Agnes Clifton Jones, Athens, Georgia, Sponsor for Troop Artillery Camp.

Spottsylvania—and among them was an old negro man. No one knew, not even the old negro himself, why he had been brought there for confinement in a Federal prison. His story was that he was the slave of old Dr. Chancellor, who lived near Fredericksburg; and that meeting some Federal soldiers in the road, they began to ply him with questions about the movements of Lee's army. Failing to give them satisfactory answers, they arrested him, and he was finally landed in Fort Delaware. He was a respectful, well-behaved old darky. He was assigned to a corner bunk on the lower tier in the Virginia barracks, and his deportment was all that could be expected under the peculiar circumstances. One day along in the fall season he was called out and taken up to headquarters, when he was informed that he was to be released, but as a preliminary to his release it was necessary that he should take the oath to the United States government. At this he hesitated, saying he did not understand the nature of the oath. One of the officers read it over to him carefully, but he still hesitated. Then the officer, in his plainest manner, undertook to explain to him the purport of the oath, and closed by asking him if he now understood its meaning. The old darky, after a moment's reflection, replied: "No, sah, I don't rightly understand it yit; but let me ask you one question; Is it something old master would take if he was here?" The officer frankly told him it was not such an oath as his old master would want to subscribe to. "Then I'll not take it," promptly responded the old negro. "I'll never do anything to bring disgrace upon old Master or the family name." Upon his fit refusal to take the oath, the faithful old slave was remanded to prison, where he died about six weeks later, a martyr to his fidelity to the old master whom he loved better than his own life.

  The next incident came to my attention in the winter of 1875 on a trip to Florida. We were going down the Coast Line and were passing through the rice plantations above Charleston. Traveling facilities were not so good on railroads then as now. We had a sleeper, but there was no smoking compartment. After breakfast I had gone forward into the smoking car to enjoy my cigar. At a little station *a very well-dressed negro man came aboard*; but as there were some white gentlemen in each seat, mostly Northern tourists, he did not offer to sit down by any of them. After he had been standing awhile in the aisle I moved over and invited him to have a seat by me. At first he demurred, saying he did not like to intrude upon white gentlemen; but upon my insistence he finally sat down, remarking, "You must be a Southerner." *I asked him why he thought so. His reply was that he did not believe a Northern man would invite a negro to sit by him.* In the conversation I interrogated him as to his past history, and will tell his story, as he told it to me, in my own language.

Before the war he had been the driver or foreman on the plantation owned by his young master, who lived in the big house up on the hill, where he employed his time with his horses and hounds, after the easy fashion of the old-time Southern gentleman. When the war came, the master went with the Carolina troops to Virginia, and *left the plantation in the care of the faithful driver.* The master survived the war, and after Appomattox returned home to a scene of desolation. He called up the driver and told him to continue to run the plantation as best he could with hired labor, and to *keep half the earnings for himself,* and to pay over the other half to him. A succession of good crops, with fairly remunerative prices, yielded profits. The driver continued to boss the plantation, while the master devoted his time to the sports of the field. It so happened that an old mortgage on the plantation had not been taken care of; and the creditors, growing tired of waiting, finally foreclosed. At the public sale bidders were few, and, owing to the scarcity of money in that region at the time, the bids were not high. From having stored away his half of the earnings [contrary to Yankee myth, like this black servant, a majority of Southern "slaves" earned an income] the negro driver was enabled to buy in the plantation and became the owner in fee.

Jefferson Hayes Davis (1884-1975), grandson of Confederate President Jefferson Davis. Originally named Jefferson Addison Hayes, at age six the youngster's name was legally changed in order to carry on the Davis family name.

When he had concluded his story, I said to him: "What of the master? What became of him?" His face lighted up as he replied: "O, Master still lives up in the big house on the hill and keeps his horses and dogs. He still gets his half, and always will. He doesn't know that the plantation has been sold."

I will add, by way of explanation, that the impression I got from the negro's recital of his story was that the master was not in absolute ignorance of the fact that the plantation had been sold, nor was he indifferent to *the kindness of his former slave* [all emphasis, L.S.]. What the negro meant to convey was that the master was being so well provided for and his position so much respected that he scarcely realized the change in ownership. The master's confidence in his former slave was still supreme, while the latter's fidelity to the erstwhile master could have been surpassed only by the ties which knitted David and Jonathan together [see 1 Samuel 18:1].[289] — GEORGE H. MOFFETT, PARKERSBURG, W.VA.

GEORGE BOYNTON: A SELF-DESCRIBED "CONFED NIGGER"

☛ [During the Confederate Veterans' Reunion at Dallas, Texas, April, 1902, the][. . . veterans at the Fair had a good time. There were seated on the platform of the large auditorium [Confederate] General [William Lewis] Cabell, [Confederate] General [Richard Montgomery] Gano, Judge C. C. Cumming, Historian of the Division, and others.

As the initial notes of "Dixie" came from the silvered instruments applause swept over the large auditorium and finished in a wild shout, at which the veterans and some of the ladies stood in their seats waving canes, hats, and handkerchiefs. Following "Dixie" was given [that is, played] the "Bonnie Blue Flag." This brought the second demonstration of the afternoon, in which *George Boynton, an aged negro living in Dallas,* with [his] *front bedecked with badges, pins, and pictorial buttons (the latter of* General [John Brown] *Gordon), jumped to the stage and, waving a tattered Confederate flag, danced from one end of the stage to the other. Over his shoulder was swung a haversack, from the top of which protruded a chicken's head. Boynton was introduced as "the colored man who went to war with his master, Lieutenant Boynton, of the 64th Georgia Infantry, and remained with him until he was killed."* Boynton was immediately the center of attraction. He told the veterans that he was taken along to "look out for chicken." He had the honor of entertaining General Gordon at breakfast one Monday morning. It consisted of young pig, fried chicken, yellow yams, and "cawn" bread "what ain't be'n sifted." General Gordon afterwards told Lieutenant Boynton that he would never have his regiment searched for forage again. "So long as you folks come together I'm comin' too," was the way the old darky put it; "and I hopes de good Lawd will let it be often, for I's a Confed nigger." There was much cheering when the negro finished; and as the band played "Old Black Joe," many of the old fellows pitched coins [in] to the negro's hat on the stage [all emphasis, L.S.].²⁹⁰ — *CONFEDERATE VETERAN* MAGAZINE

Confederate General John Brown Gordon.

RAISING A HAT TO THE OLD SLAVES

☞ ... In concluding this article would that suitable language were at command to *express my admiration of the loyalty of the old slaves of that era—equally applicable to the slaves of Tennessee, Mississippi, Alabama, Georgia, and South Carolina*—with whom the writer was more or less thrown during "those times that tried men's souls!" There was little difference among them as to their loyalty to their old masters and their families. With every incentive to go wrong, with every opportunity in the presence of Federal soldiers to take revenge for real or fancied wrongs inflicted on them by their old masters, I never heard of one instance of an advantage being taken of their power, but have heard of many instances where their influence was for the protection of the families of their old masters. All such incidents would go back very quickly to the father, husband, or son at the front. By the conscript law one white man was exempt from military service to twenty slaves. With this small per cent of white men, *these faithful slaves worked year after year, raising corn and oats and hogs, very generally managed by the wife of the husband at the front. Had these slaves shown the least restlessness, the least disposition to insurrect; had one of those outrages on women been reported as to-day are met with such summary vengeance, the soldiers in the armies could not have been held back from their mothers and wives and sisters.*

There are a few of these old slaves left, and as they pass around I feel like raising my hat. There were a few at the Nashville Reunion who could be *recognized by the kindly light that glinted from their eyes and the doffing of the hat as they recognized the Veteran's badge.*

What higher *proof of the kindly feeling existing between master and slave* could be found than their conduct toward each other during those times that, indeed, "tried men's souls."

What stronger testimony could be brought forward in *refutation of the slanderous charges that are promulgated for political purposes during each presidential campaign* [all emphasis, L.S.], through *Uncle Tom's Cabin* and other such plays, against the old slaveholders? These slanders are put forward by the very [Left-wing] men whose [Yankee] forefathers years ago fitted out ships and sailed from their rock-ribbed shores, asking the blessings of the Almighty for a prosperous voyage. The destination of these ships was the west coast of Africa, where were loaded on to them the forefathers of these old slaves whose praises have been sung and transported in chains to the Southern tier of Colonies of His Brittanic Majesty in North America.[291] — WILLIAM D. PICKETT, LEXINGTON, KY.

MEMORIAL WINDOW TO THE FAITHFUL SLAVES

☛For more than forty years the women of the South have been struggling to perpetuate the names and mark the resting places of her men who fought and fell in behalf of their principles and homes during the Civil War. The work has been necessarily slow. Impoverished, with devastation, desolation, and ruin on every side, this spark of determination was nevertheless kindled, and is now glowing with the hope that their work will wring from the future a proper meed of justice to their soldiery.

While honoring others, a great desire of the hearts of these women has been to memorialize, in some fitting way, *the fidelity of the slaves during the period of stress and trial, to those who were faithful at home* lo "ole miss' and the chillun," *and to those old heroes who followed the fortunes of the young master on the fields of conflict, through shot and shell, through suffering unto death, and to the grave; and then back home to those in waiting with the sad tidings of the loved and lost. These faithful compatriots who bivouacked with* [Confederate Generals Robert E.] *Lee,* [Joseph Sidney] *Johnston,* [Nathan Bedford] *Forrest,* [Benjamin Franklin] *Cheatham, and* [Sterling] *Price are held in grateful remembrance; and welded with our memories of those dark days is their fidelity, unequaled in the annals of history by any other race in bondage. They stood loyally when freedom opened a vista of dazzling promise* [my emphasis, L.S.]. The Daughters of the Confederacy, while honoring others, desire also to honor these by placing in the Battle Abbey of the South a memorial window. They hope to accomplish this before that generation passes away—showing their recognition and appreciation of their faithful service. We appeal to all Southerners for indorsement and help, to honor a people who were "tender and true."[292]
— MRS. BELLE KELSO ALLISON, WINONA, MISS.

Confederate General Benjamin Franklin Cheatham.

THE CONFEDERATES WERE CONSERVATIVES FIGHTING TO PRESERVE THE CONSTITUTION

☞ . . . I am not here to-day to cast one slur at the gallant men who wore the blue, but to give due praise and honor to the splendid soldiers who wore the gray. I would not wish one star less within the blue field of the stars and stripes, the banner of our common country; but I will not hide in shame one inch of the flag which we followed under solemn conviction through weariness and suffering, blood and defeat, the stars and bars. *The men who went forth to battle under this flag were not actuated by hate, by desire for conquest, or to maintain the institution of slavery, but battled for what they believed to be a great fundamental doctrine, a foundation principle in a government founded upon the consent of the governed* [my emphasis, L.S.].

Battle of Fort Sumter.

Beginning with this great ground of their action, let us pause to consider who these men were and from whence they came. They were the direct descendants of the [Conservative] men who led the colonies in the conflict with England in the great struggle for liberty and the men who shaped the constitutional foundations of the young republic.

George Washington, a [Conservative] son of the South, led the colonial forces through seven years of conflict to final victory. The fertile brain of [Conservative] Thomas Jefferson, a son of old Virginia, conceived and his deft hand wrote the Declaration of Independence, while [Nathanael] Green, [Francis] Marion, and the stalwart sons of the South gave bloody emphasis to it upon many a hard-fought field. . . .[293] — DR. W. T. BOLLING, MEMPHIS, TENN.

CONFEDERATE GENERAL REPORTS 500 BLACK CONFEDERATES AT THE SOUTH'S ANDERSONVILLE PRISON

☞ On August 25, 1864, [Confederate] General [John H.] Winder reported to [the Confederate Capitol at] Richmond: "There are 29,400 prisoners, 2,650 troops, *500 negroes* [my emphasis, L.S.] and other laborers . . . ."[294] — *CONFEDERATE VETERAN* MAGAZINE

"VENERABLE NEGRO" AT THE FUNERAL OF MRS. JEFFERSON DAVIS

☞ News of the death of Mrs. Varina Jefferson Davis is too wide-spread for any formal notice herein to be worthwhile, but the *Veteran* will seek to pay a worthy tribute to her honored memory.

After her death in New York and a service there, a guard of honor furnished by the United States government and a message to Mrs. J. A. Hayes from President [Theodore] Roosevelt and wife (from whom was also received a magnificent floral offering) were conspicuous tributes among the many from all sections of the country.

The editor of the *Confederate Veteran* attended the services in St. Paul's Church, Richmond, and the funeral as one of the honorary pallbearers, and escorted with the Lee and Pickett Camps the remains from the railroad station to the church. Veterans removed the casket from the car, carried it to the hearse, and then carried it into the lecture room of the church, where it remained under a guard of honor by the Veterans until three o'clock, the hour for the service. The usual burial service of the Church was followed, supplemented by Chaplain General Dr. J. William Jones, who announced the hymn "How Firm a Foundation, Ye Saints of the Lord," stating that it was "the favorite hymn of Lee and Jackson."

. . . At the conclusion of the ceremony at the grave there were three shots of cannon, followed by three volleys from small arms, concluding with taps.

[Confederate] Gen. Stephen D. Lee was marshal of the funeral procession. There was a [Yankee] delegation from the New York Camp of Veterans, under Commander Owen, and a large attendance of representative Daughters from New York and various sections of the South.

The casket was elegant but plain, having no ornamentation save the handsome plate that contained the words: "Varina Jefferson Davis. Born May 7, 1826. Died Oct. 16, 1906. At Peace." The casket was covered with the Confederate battle flag and the last flag of the Confederacy until removed at the grave.

Confederate General Stephen Dill Lee.

A *venerable negro from Raleigh, N.C., long the coachman of the family, was in attendance, and was treated with most cordial consideration. He had attended the burial of* [Confederate] *President* [Jefferson] *Davis also* [my emphasis, L.S.].[295] — *CONFEDERATE VETERAN MAGAZINE*

BLACK SERVANTS WILL NOT ALLOW THEIR MISTRESS TO DO MENIAL TASKS

☛ During the dark days of 1861-65, a sewing society for the benefit of our brave boys was kept up at my old home, "Warthen," in Greenville County. We met every Monday afternoon, ladies coming in from all directions for miles in their buggies, on horseback, or walking to aid in this good work. Large boxes were filled as fast as the clothing was prepared and shipped principally to Virginia, wherever most needed, often to Fairfax and Orange C. H., Richmond, and other points. My experience of those days has proven invaluable to me since the freedom of our slaves, for I learned to sew, knit, and even to spin thread, much to the chagrin of our old servants, who protested against their "young missus" doing any menial service, even to the making up of a bed. "Chile, for pity sake stop dat. What is me here fur?" Another would say: "Now, Miss Tannie, you bother me too much foolin' with dat wheel. I got my task to do—will tell your par." O the reeling was just fine if any of the old negroes would allow us to hold the broaches for them to see the thread going into hanks, rapidly rolling off from the broaches. . . .[296] — MRS. P. A. MCDAVID, GREENVILLE, S.C.

APPRECIATION FOR A LOYAL BLACK CONFEDERATE SERVANT
☞ . . . Before closing this brief and imperfect sketch of my military career *I wish to put upon record my appreciation of the services of my body servant, George White, whose fidelity and care for my welfare during the whole time of my army life was something wonderful. His watchful care and thought for my comfort and well-being is worthy of a green spot in my memory. He often went hungry himself that I might have something to eat* [my emphasis, L.S.]. Though his skin was black, he had a heart possessed only by the great and good of earth.[297] — CONFEDERATE OFFICER GEORGE REESE

CHARLES THOMPSON: BLACK CONFEDERATE
☞ . . . Sumner County [Tennessee] undoubtedly never witnessed a simpler nor a better attended funeral. St. Peter's Church did not admit nearly all that came to the service there; and none could have failed of interest in the noble, simple, and sincere ceremonies at the grave by Donelson Bivouac, U.C.V., and by the King Solomon Lodge, No. 99, F. and A. M. *One of the most grieved of those in attendance was Charles Thompson, colored, who followed all the fortunes of the 2nd Tennessee Volunteers as a servant of the three Thompson brothers, of Castalian Springs* [my emphasis, L.S.].[298] — FROM THE OBITUARY OF CONFEDERATE CAPT. SAMUEL ROBERT SIMPSON, OF GALLATIN, TENN.

SOUTHERN WHITES DISCUSS THE POSTWAR "NEGRO PROBLEM": BLACK & WHITE RACISM

Caroline Douglas Meriwether Goodlett, founding President of the United Daughters of the Confederacy.

☞ *We all like the old negroes, and those of the fast-decaying remnant of ex-slaves are still faithful and loyal to the families of their former masters. The same instincts are much more prevalent among their offspring than is generally realized. While the Associated Press flashes a horrible account of a fiendish deed by one negro, ten thousand others are going quietly about their business as law-abiding and worthy of consideration as could be expected of them. . . . Let us confront the problem honestly. The negro did not come among us of his own accord, and they can't all get away. If proper tact were exercised, it would be quite sufficient. Let the white people of the South revive the old rule of kindness, and never, anyhow in their presence, speak ill of the negro race* [all emphasis, L.S.].[299] — *CONFEDERATE VETERAN* MAGAZINE

CONFEDERATE VETERAN LEAVES INHERITANCE TO BLACK SERVANT
☞ Ralph Benjamin Sandiford died in Oxford July 17, 1906. He was born on St. Helena Island, S.C., July 1, 1837. He entered the Confederate service with the Oglethorpe Light Infantry of Savannah, which became Company B, 8th Georgia Volunteers, and served in the Army of Northern Virginia. This, it is said, was the first company in all the South that offered its services to President Davis for the war. It was mustered into

service May 21, 1861, and surrendered at Appomattox, having taken part in forty-one battles.

. . . He was married April 23, 1877. at St. Mary's, Ga., to Jennie G. Burns. After the mother of his children died, he devoted himself entirely to the work of rearing them properly, and he acted the part of both father and mother. He led a quiet Christian life, knew no town gossip, was very charitable in word and deed. He was always prompt in meeting his obligations. *He left a small legacy to the colored woman who had served the family faithfully for some years* [my emphasis, L.S.].[300] — CONFEDERATE VETERAN MAGAZINE

BLACK SERVANT CARES FOR WHITE MOTHER & DAUGHTER DURING THE WAR

☛ My husband, Judge Burnett, had been in the South about two months when I joined him in Richmond, Va., in December, 1861. I went through the lines with my little baby girl, Mary, with great difficulty, and soon found myself in the war most truly. I crossed the lines eight times and was a prisoner four times.

In March, 1862, I was in the Trans-Mississippi Department when the battle of Oak Hills or Elkhorn was fought, was at Van Buren, Ark., near enough to the battle to hear the cannonading, and was there when the Confederates camped near the place after the battle was over. . . . Our next stop was at the healthful little town of Cartersville, Ga., where we remained for a few weeks, the Judge going on to his duties at Richmond. *We were cared for by black Sam, a negro man that my mother had raised* [my emphasis, L.S.].[301] — MRS. THEODORE L. BURNETT, LOUISVILLE, KY.

"MANY COLORED PEOPLE" ATTEND FUNERAL OF CONFEDERATE VETERAN

☛ Lawrence Aylett Daffan was born April 30, 1845, in Conecuh County, Ala. His father, John Warren Daffan, was born and reared in Westmoreland County, Va. His mother, Mary Jones Daffan, was born and reared in Caroline County, Va. In 1849 the family went from Alabama to Texas, living first in Montgomery County, and in 1860 went to Navasola.

His first employment was carrying the United States mail from Montgomery to the old town of Washington, in Washington County.

In 1861, age sixteen years, Lawrence Daffan enlisted in the Confederate army as a private and went to Virginia.

. . . Colonel Daffan was a Knight Templar, a member of the Shriners, and a charter member of the Houston Lodge, Benevolent and Protective Order of Elks. *Among those who paid the last tribute at his grave were the many colored people, men and women, to whom he had been a friend* [my emphasis, L.S.], and the city was in mourning, the stores were all closed and the schools were closed as a tribute of respect and love to an esteemed and well-beloved citizen, whose place cannot be filled.[302] — CONFEDERATE VETERAN MAGAZINE

Confederate Colonel L. A. Daffan.

COMMUNIST AGITATION IN THE SOUTH, 1906

☞ . . . The people of the Old South were homogeneous. Some of our Southern people are inviting foreign immigration to the South. It will be well for us if immigration shall not be more rapid than assimilation. Other portions of our beloved country have gotten more than they bargained for in this matter of immigration. The anarchists and unbelievers [that is, socialists and communists] of many lands and many tongues have come in multitudes. The power of assimilation has been overtaxed, and the consequences are not satisfactory to the parties immediately concerned. Let us take warning. *The old white South got along pretty well with the old black South, all things considered* [my emphasis, L.S.]. Conditions have changed somewhat, but we understand one another, and with less assistance from abroad that we do not ask for, and the exercise of a reasonable degree of common sense, every square mile of this Southern land would bloom in bountifulness and beauty.[303] — BISHOP O. P. FITZGERALD

THE AMERICAN ABOLITION MOVEMENT BEGAN IN THE SOUTH

Left, Miss Elizabeth "Bessie" W. Washington; right, Robert E. Lee III, grandson of Gen. Robert E. Lee, 1897.

☞ . . . For the purposes of this occasion we care not how the African slave first placed his unhallowed foot on Southern soil. Suffice it to say that, although the South had at one time no inconsiderable career of maritime adventure, "no ship or shipmaster of hers was ever in a single case implicated in the illicit African slave trade." Her greatest men always maintained slavery to be the most dangerous element in the country. From the beginning the statesmen of the South scented danger in the great race problem with which they were being saddled, and the question that was uppermost in their minds was, What shall be done with the emancipated serf? "Much as I deplore slavery," says Patrick Henry, "I see that prudence forbids its abolition." Henry Clay asserted that "the evils of slavery are absolutely nothing in comparison with the far greater evils which would inevitably follow from sudden, general, and indiscriminate emancipation." And again he says: "If we were to invoke the greatest blessing on earth which heaven in its mercy could bestow on this nation, it would be the separation of the two most numerous races of its population and their comfortable establishment in distant and distinct countries." Mr. [George] Mason, of Virginia, went farther in declaring: "The traffic is infernal. To permit it is against every principle of honor and safety." Mr. [John C.] Calhoun was of the opinion that the existing relations between master and servant "cannot be destroyed without subjecting the two races to the greatest calamity and the section to poverty, desolation, and wretchedness."

Virginia in October, 1778, and Georgia in 1798, passed acts prohibiting the importation of slaves. The former act provided for a penalty of one thousand pounds, and also that every slave imported contrary to the true

Rev. M. B. Havner and his wife.

intent and meaning of this act shall upon such importation become free. Thus, *to the everlasting credit of the South, upon whose devoted head the vials of holy wrath have been so unjustly and brutally poured out for propagating, nourishing, and harboring slavery, she led the world in an earnest attempt to prevent the very thing of which she is accused.*

During the fight of 1820-21, which resulted in the Missouri Compromise, slavery had hardly become a political question, and as proof that the Southern States had not at that early period banded together in support of the system, *the States of Virginia, Kentucky, and Tennessee were earnestly engaged in practical movements for gradual emancipation of their slaves; and this good work continued until it was arrested by the abolitionists* [that is, radical Left-wingers], *who "insisted upon convicting as criminals those who were so well disposed to bring about the very result at which they themselves professed to aim."*

"Promised emancipation refused to submit itself to hateful abolition." Under the guise of philanthropy and humanity, and notwithstanding the fact that England had liberated four hundred thousand slaves at the cost of twenty million pounds paid to their owners, *the abolitionists* [that is, socialists and communists] *demanded the uncompensated freeing of the slaves, the great majority of which were in the South. Such a wholesale attack on private property by the Sate has no parallel in history;* the nearest approach to it is the suppression of the monasteries by Henry the VIII, and [French clergyman Charles-Maurice de] Talleyrand's famous measure for the spoliation of the Church during the French Revolution under the sophistical plea that it belonged to the nation.

Finally scheming politicians, *"invincible in peace, invisible in war,"* took advantage of the unfortunate state of affairs [that is, the growing sectional hatred between the Conservative South and the Liberal North] and adopted slavery for their slogan and a vehicle for their selfish ends.

Mr. [George] Lunt, of Massachusetts, says: "*Self-seeking and ambitious demagogues, the pest of republics, disturbed the equilibrium, and were able at length to plunge the country into that worst of all public calamities—civil war. The question of morals had as little as possible to do with the result. Philanthropy might have sighed, fanaticism have howled for centuries in vain, but for the hope of office and the desire of public plunder on the part of men who were neither philanthropists nor fanatics.*" Thus slavery was the occasion and not the cause of the revolt, "*just as property is the cause of robbery.*" Slavery was the South's calamity, and not her crime. Two most significant facts remain in this connection. First, there was incorporated in the organic law of the Southern Confederacy [that is, the C.S. Constitution],[304] made wholly by slave States, an absolute prohibition of the foreign slave trade. The final act was the emancipation of the slaves by the votes of the Southern States.

Mr. Lincoln's proclamation of January, 1863, was legally absolutely void and ineffective. The negroes were freed by the thirteenth Amendment to the Constitution. When this was adopted, the Federal Union was composed of thirty-six States. The fifth article of the Constitution provides that no amendment to the Constitution shall become part thereof until "ratified by the Legislatures of three-fourths of the States." Therefore it required twenty-seven votes to ratify the amendment. On the 18th of December, 1865, the Secretary of State reported twenty-seven States having so ratified. Sixteen of these were Northern States. Nine of those States refused to vote for the measure, and the remaining eleven required to make up the two-thirds were the Southern States. *The much-maligned, slave-tortured South became the liberator of the serf. It is one of the ironies of history that the South, which had done so much to prevent and stamp out the black terror, should be called on to be sacrificed on the altar of the opinions of those who were in a large measure responsible for the existence of the African within her borders* [all emphasis, L.S.]. . . .[305] — FROM AN ADDRESS BY ROBERT E. LEE III, GRANDSON OF GEN. ROBERT E. LEE

THE PECULIAR INSTITUTION & THE WAR FOR SOUTHERN INDEPENDENCE

☛ . . . there is this remarkable fact in connection with slavery and its relations to the war, which we have not seen elsewhere referred to, and which is to our mind *a conclusive refutation of the charge that the continuation or the extinction of slavery had any influence whatever on the conduct of the Southern people, and especially that of the Confederate soldier in that war.*

The writer belonged to one of the three companies in the army, the personnel of which is so vividly described by the author of *Four Years Under Marse Robert*, in which there were serving as privates many full graduates of the University of Virginia and other leading colleges both North and South. In these companies a variety of subjects pertaining to the war, religion, politics, philosophy, literature, and what not, were discussed with intelligence and often with animation and ability, and yet *neither he nor any of his comrades can recall the fact that they ever heard the subject of slavery or the relations of the slaves to the war, referred to in any way during that period.* . . . We have inquired of comrades of various other commands about this, and with the like result. *Do men fight for a thing or a cause they never speak of or discuss? It seems to us that to ask this question is to furnish the answer.*

Not only is the foregoing statement true, but with the exception of the steps taken to send negroes to help erect fortifications, employing them as laborers, etc., but little consideration seems to have been given them or of their status to the war either in the Congress or the Cabinet of the Confederacy. The reasons for this are manifest to those of us who lived in those days, but a word of explanation may be necessary to those who have since come on the stage of life. In the first place slavery, as it existed in the South, was patriarchal in its character; *the slaves (servants, as we called them) were regarded and treated as members of the families to which they severally belonged; with rare exceptions, they were treated with kindness and consideration, and frequently the relations between the slave and his owner were those of real affection and confidence.* As Mr.

Henry Edward Wood, Confederate veteran.

[George] Lunt, the Boston writer . . . says: "The negroes were perfectly contented with their lot. In general they were not only happy in their condition, but proud of it."

Their owners trusted them with their families, their farms, and their affairs, and this confidence was rarely betrayed—scarcely ever, unless they were forced to violate their trusts by coming in contact with the Federal armies, or were beguiled and betrayed themselves by mean and designing white [Left-wing] men. The truth is, both the white and the black people of the South regarded the Confederate cause alike as their cause, and looked to its success with almost, if not quite, equal anxiety and delight. A most striking illustration of this and of the readiness of the slaves to fight even, if necessary, for the Confederate cause is furnished by the following incident: *In February, 1865, when negro troops had been authorized to be enrolled in the Confederate army*, there were employed at Jackson Hospital, near Richmond, seventy-two negro men. The surgeon in charge, the late Dr. F. W. Hancock, of Richmond, had this men formed in line; and after asking them "if they would be willing to take up arms to protect their masters' families, homes, and their own from an attacking foe, *sixty out of seventy-two responded that they would volunteer to go to the trenches and fight to the bitter end.*"806

Miss Alleen Smith, Maid of Honor Forrest's Cavalry.

At the date here referred to we know that the life of the soldier was one of the greatest hardship and peril, and *the fact that five out of every six* [about 84 percent] *of these negroes were then ready to volunteer and go to the trenches showed conclusively how truly they regarded the Confederate cause as their cause as well as that of the white people of the South.* Indeed, we doubt if a larger per cent of the whites in any part of the country would have volunteered to go to the front at that stage of the war. If, then, it were true, as alleged, that the white people of the South were fighting for slavery, does it not necessarily follow that the slaves themselves were ready and willing to fight for it too? One of these propositions is just as true as the other.

We think we have shown then that even if we admit that slavery was, as falsely charged, the "cause of the war," the South was in no way responsible for the existence of that cause; but *it was a condition forced upon it, one recognized by the supreme law of the land, one which the South dealt with legally and justly as contemplated by that law,* and history shows that in every respect, and in every instance, the aggressions and violations of the law were committed by the North. Mr. Lunt says: "Of four several compromises between the two sections of country since the Revolutionary War, each has been kept by the South and violated by the North." Indeed, we challenge the North to point out one single instance in which the South violated the Constitution or any of the laws made in pursuance thereof; whilst, on the contrary, the fourteen of the Northern States passed acts nullifying the fugitive slave law, passed by Congress in obedience to the

Constitution, denounced and defied the decisions of the Supreme Court, and Judge [Jeremiah Sullivan] Black, of Pennsylvania, says of the abolitionists [that is, socialists and communists]: "*They applauded John Brown to the echo for a series of the basest murders on record. They did not conceal their hostility to the Federal and State governments nor deny their enmity to all laws which protected white men. The Constitution stood in their way, and they cursed it bitterly. The Bible was quoted against them, and they reviled God the Almighty himself*" [all emphasis, L.S.]. . . .[307] — JUDGE GEORGE L. CHRISTIAN, RICHMOND, VA.

SLAVEOWNER'S SON DESCRIBES PLANTATION LIFE
☛ . . . I am the son of a former large slaveholder of Mississippi who had from one hundred and fifty to two hundred slaves. Though a small boy when the war began, I was thoroughly familiar with plantation life. I lived on the plantation during the war and during the dark days of reconstruction. Prior to and during the war and after it I was thrown in daily contact with the negroes on our own plantation and others.

Miss Mildred Lewis Rutherford, author, teacher, and Historian General of the U.D.C.

I cheerfully admit that during the war there was scarcely a plantation in the South where the mistress and her children were not left alone at the mercy of the slaves a great part of the time, and that the record shows unswerving loyalty on their part. This happy condition was the result of years of training until it had become an inherited tendency. No thought of social equality, and the vile thought inevitably incidental thereto [that is, black supremacy—an idea that grew in popularity throughout the 1800s], ever entered the heads of the negroes. *The discipline of the plantation was firm but kind, and the relation between the owner and owned took on a paternalistic character, the owner feeling as he might toward a lot of children and the slaves looking up to him as a superior whom they held in highest respect. There naturally grew up an affection, a bond of sympathy, and a mutual feeling of interest that was as beautiful as a poem*, whatever may be said about the institution of slavery as a whole. (And I wish to say just here that none of the old slaveholders nor any of their descendants would restore the institution if they could.) [all emphasis, L.S.]. . .[308] — E. H. HINTON, ATLANTA, GA.

YANKEE INTERFERENCE & SOUTHERN BLACKS
☛ . . . The intervention of the [Liberal] North in religious and educational matters, together with conditions prevailing at the close of the Civil War, produced an alienation between the negro and the [Conservative] Southern people which has proved very unfortunate for both races. At the beginning of his career of freedom the negro needed sympathetic guidance at the hands of those best acquainted with him. Instead, he became "a bone of contention" between the two sections embittered by the Civil War. . . . [Having been Christianized, the Southern black man] . . . is incalculably the better off for the results of his enslavement. In an important sense "*the South of 1860 was the victim rather than the master*" of her slave population" [my emphasis, L.S.].[309] — REV. DR. GROSS ALEXANDER

TENNESSEE CONFEDERATE VETERANS VOTE TO BUILD MONUMENT & GIVE PENSIONS TO "SLAVES" WHO SERVED IN THE WAR

☛ The Tennessee Division, U.C.V., met at Covington on October 9, 1907, with a large attendance of delegates, and there were many visitors there at the time. . . . [Confederate] Gen. George W. Gordon [founder of the original Ku Klux Klan, 1865-1869, a Conservative, non-racist, pro-Constitution organization that has no connection to the modern KKK—which was founded in 1915][310] offered the following preambles and resolutions, which were unanimously adopted:

"Whereas there has ever been and still is a ready recognition throughout the Southern States of the faithful and praiseworthy course and conduct of the slaves toward their then owners and their many unprotected families during our interstate war, from 1861 to 1865; and whereas we deem it just and due to the good faith and good name of said slaves, as also to their former owners and to history, that this highly instructive and most significant fact be promulgated and perpetuated; therefore be it

Confederate General George Washington Gordon.

"Resolved, That it is the sense of the delegates and representatives of the Tennessee Division of the Federation of United Confederate Veterans here assembled that *a stately and durable monument should be erected at some central and appropriate site in the South to the faithfulness and praiseworthiness and to the fidelity and of the slaves to their owners and to their families during the great American war mentioned.*

"Resolved, That the Secretary be, and hereby is, instructed to prepare a copy of these preambles and resolutions to be offered for adoption at the next Reunion of the General Federation of United Confederates, at Birmingham, Ala., in 1908.

"Resolved, That *it is the sense of the delegates of the Tennessee Division of United Confederate Veterans that the negroes who faithfully served as attaches, employees, or servants in the Confederate army till the close of the war should be pensioned by amendment to the pension laws now in operation in this State"* [all emphasis, L.S.].

The following officers were elected for the ensuing year: George W. Gordon, Major General, Commanding the Division; John M. Brooks, Clay Stacker, John H. McDowell, Brigadier Generals, Commanding respectively the First, Second, and Third Brigades; John P. Hickman, Adjutant General and Chief of Staff.

Hearty thanks were extended for the bountiful hospitality of the people of Covington.

The Division then adjourned to meet in Nashville on the second Wednesday in October, 1908.[311] — CONFEDERATE VETERAN MAGAZINE

BLACK SERVANT FIRST TRAINER & RIDER OF "TRAVELER," GENERAL LEE'S WARHORSE

☛ The readers of the *Veteran* are just now especially interested in Traveler, General Lee's war horse. A history of him has been published several times, but the first man who ever rode him has not yet been mentioned. The photograph here presented is a good likeness of Frank Page, as he was known to the people of Lewisburg, W.Va., when he was performing the duties of janitor at the school building and bank. He was born in 1846 a slave, the property of Mr. A. D. Johnston, near Blue Sulphur Springs, Va. (now West Virginia); and when quite a lad, he broke the colt "Jeff" which afterwards became the favorite Traveler of General Lee. This servant handled horses with much skill, and "breaking the colts" was his business. So he came to have the honor of being the first rider of Jeff (Traveler), and trained him for exhibition at the Lewisburg Fair in 1860.[312] — *CONFEDERATE VETERAN* MAGAZINE

Frank Page.

N.C. CONFEDERATE VETERANS VOTE TO GIVE PENSIONS TO SERVANTS WHO SERVED IN THE WAR

☛ . . . Resolved: 2. That L. O. B. Branch Camp, No. 515, U.C.V., in the belief that some recognition should be given the worthy negroes who followed the fortunes of the Southern Confederacy as faithful servants, who in many cases put aside opportunities for freedom on account of love for their own white folks, also that such residents of this State who served as servants in the Confederate army, rendering true and faithful service to their owners or others, shall be entitled to a pension on proof of such service [my emphasis, L.S.].
3. That a copy of these resolutions be sent to the General Assembly of North Carolina, with the request that provision be made for said pensions by adding a fifth clause to the Pension Act.
A bill has already been presented to the General Assembly and referred to the Pension Committee.[313] — J. C. BIRDSONG, RALEIGH, N.C.

"GOD BLESS THE OLD FAMILY NEGROES!"

☛ . . . I had an audience with [Confederate] Secretary [of War, John Cabell] Breckenridge, and he gave me a commission, transferring me from General [Joseph] Wheeler to General Forrest. I had been in service with General Forrest before, and was anxious to get back to him. I surrendered with him at Gainesville, Ala., and still have my parole of honor, which I prize very highly. I was allowed my horse and sidearms, and took up my route home in company with Col. David C. Kelley and D. C. Seales of Nashville, Tenn. All were glad to see me when I got home. *Even the negroes who had been raised up with me, who had hunted rabbits and fought yellow jackets with me in childhood days, seemed to be as glad over my return as my own dear family. God bless the old family negroes! I shall always love them* [my emphasis, L.S.] . . .[314] — CAPT. FRANK BATTLE, TENN.

PRESIDENT DAVIS' BLACK SERVANT DEBUNKS YANKEE MYTH

☞ For some unknown reason, probably for no better excuse than to deny the absurd story of the next day, some of the Northern newspapers have revamped the old rumor about President Jefferson Davis, of the Confederate States, having been disguised in the garb of a woman at the time of his capture. This story has been so often refuted that further denial is unnecessary; but one of the most interesting facts brought out by the more recent discussion is that the government has the garments worn by Mr. Davis when he was captured carefully preserved at Washington.

These articles are in the original box in which they were sent from Georgia to [Union] General [John M.] Schofield by the officers making the arrest. They consist of a shawl, a rain-proof coat without cape, and a pair of spurs. The shawl is such as is worn now by men of advanced years to protect the throat and shoulders. It is, in fact, a large muffler. Sometimes a shawl of this pattern is worn by women; but the customary use is as a man's muffler, either with or without an overcoat.

The rain coat is a man's garment. It is short with broad shoulders, and, with allowance for the change of mode, is a commonplace waterproof coat. It is of soft gray material, and it worn now by a middle-aged man on a rainy day would not attract any special notice on the streets at Washington.

... Mrs. [Margaret "Maggie" Addison] Hayes [daughter of President Jefferson Davis] ... sends a letter from Jim Jones, the negro coachman who faithfully served the family of Mr. Davis and accompanied them after the evacuation of Richmond until his capture. She says: "It was he who aroused my father and notified him of the approach of the enemy. He is employed in the Stationery Department of the United States Senate, Washington." The letter is as follows:

"My Dear Miss Maggie: Your very welcome letter of June 25 reached me in due time, and I was truly glad to hear from you all.

"I had not heard anything about the lady and the flowered dressing gown, but know that neither your father (Hon. Jefferson Davis) nor his wife [Varina] had any such gown either on them or in their immediate possession the morning of his capture in Georgia in May, 1865, and have tried to make that plain in the affidavit inclosed. Please have Mr. [Joel Addison] Hayes [Jr.] read it over and let me know if I have covered all the ground he thinks necessary. I am anxious to tell the whole truth about Mr. Davis's capture and to protect any Southern society from imposition, particularly if that imposition places Mr. Davis in a false light.

"The old story about Mr. Davis's trying to make his escape attired in woman's clothes is entirely wrong, and does Mr. Davis a very great wrong; for, except for [the presence of] his wife [at the scene], he would

Confederate President Jefferson Davis.

have made a bold effort to unhorse the Federal cavalryman, mount his horse, and ride away in the darkness. He never had any inclination to disguise himself; and if he had formed any such idea, he had nothing at hand with which to disguise himself. Yours most respectfully, James H. Jones."[315] — *CONFEDERATE VETERAN MAGAZINE*

MORE PROOF OF BLACK CONFEDERATES
☞ . . . The 10th Alabama Regiment [C.S.A.] was the best in the army. This thought with all the regiments made the Southern army the best the world ever saw. *In our regiment we had judges from the bench, lawyers of high rank from their offices, merchants of wealth from stores, farmers of large plantations, and numerous negroes who served through the war as privates* [all emphasis, L.S.]. To give an idea of the morale of the 10th Alabama, we had in Congress at one time after the war four members—William H. Forney, John H. Caldwell, Taul Bradford, and Tod Hewitt—and at the same time Rufus Cobb was Governor of Alabama. The first four, also General Forney, have crossed over.[316] — W. W. DRAPER (MAJOR 10TH ALABAMA REGT.), ATLANTA, GA.

Miss Mildred Ray Harrison, Sponsor Pacific Division, Richmond Reunion.

BLACK SERVANTS IN THE COLONIAL SOUTH
☞ . . . Annie Kendrick Walker . . . gave an interesting story of "Hayslope," a noted home near Russellville [now in West Virginia], some twenty miles from Tazewell C. H., the home of Hugh Graham. Hayslope was presented by Mr. Graham to his daughter, Louise, who became the wife of Theophilus Rogan. This place was founded by Col. Thomas Roddy, commissioned colonel through his gallant service in the battle of King's Mountain [American Revolutionary War]. Colonel Roddy had an esteemed servant, "Harry," whom he bought from [Southern] General [Francis] Marion and whom the General had captured from a British officer. *Colonel Roddy was a devout Baptist; and when he said "grace" at meals, the dining room doors were thrown open, so that the blessing sought was to benefit the servants in the kitchen as well as the family* [my emphasis, L.S.] . . .[317] — *CONFEDERATE VETERAN MAGAZINE*

THE TRUE SLAVE HISTORY OF TENNESSEE
☞ The old-time [Southern] Presbyterian mother was a great Bible student. She was a Bible oracle. These mothers in Israel exerted great influence not only in their own families but in the community. Almost without exception they detested slavery, and to them, perhaps more than to any other cause, is to be attributed the advanced position of Tennessee in early days on emancipation. *Under the Constitution of 1796 free negroes voted. In 1801 Tennessee enacted a law favoring voluntary emancipation. In 1824 there was formed at Columbia "The Moral and Religious Manumission Society of West Tennessee;" and in 1827, of the one hundred and thirty-five antislavery societies in America, one hundred and six were in the South and twenty-five of these were in Tennessee. Three-fifths of her people were in favor of*

slave emancipation before it was thought of in Boston.

Shortly after the Tennessee Manumission Society memorialized Congress to prohibit internal slave trade the citizens of Ohio, after selling land to three hundred negroes, freed by the will of John Randolph, of Roanoke, raised an armed force and refused to let them take possession.

When the liberty-loving Tennesseans were striving for the freeing of Southern slaves, Illinois was passing her law fining any free negro fifty dollars who stayed in that State ten days with the intention of remaining; and if the fine and costs were not paid immediately, the negro was to be sold to any one who would pay them. And Philadelphians were burning African churches, and in New York negroes were terrorized and slain by the vengeful mob. But for all this, when Tennessee saw the [U.S.] Constitution of our fathers denounced [by Liberals] as a "league with hell and a covenant with death," and she to be dragooned into unconstitutional views of the government they had established, 115,000 of her sons leaped to arms. But that conflict is ended; and now, turning our backs upon the past, save its imperishable glories, fully realizing that old things have passed away, save the memory of knightly deeds and deathless fame, renewing loyal to the flag of the indissoluble Union of indestructible States, we earnestly address ourselves to the new conditions that confront us all and the new problems that press for solution; yet we must be allowed to rejoice in the conviction that those sorry historians who impugn the motives of gentlemen and traduce the deeds of soldiers will sink into forgetfulness, and that posterity will vindicate us as the only defenders of the Constitution of 1776, to establish which all our fathers fought, and to maintain which in its integrity ours taught us to fight, and we did.[318] — HON. C. W. HEISKELL, MEMPHIS, TENN.

White slavery coexisted side-by-side with black slavery in early America. The young Caucasian slave girl pictured here, Fannie Virginia Casseopia Lawrence, was purchased from her owner in Virginia, then taken north where she was baptized in Brooklyn, NY, by Yankee clergyman Henry Ward Beecher, a sibling of New England novelist Harriet Beecher Stowe.

CONFEDERATE OFFICER GOES IN SEARCH OF FORMER BLACK SERVANT

☛ On the evening of the 23rd of February last [1908] Major [Joseph] Vaulx [of the First Tennessee Infantry] went out in a carriage to visit an old man slave, once his own servant, who had been reported to him to be in a state of destitution. Death came to him before finding the object of his search, but it will always comfort his friends to know that he died on a mission of mercy....[319] — JAMES D. PORTER

GEN. ROBERT E. LEE & SLAVERY
☞ . . . Several years before the War between the States, when he decided for himself that slavery was not right, he did not try to find some one to whom he could sell his slaves, put the money in his pocket, and then cry out against slavery; but he—R. E. Lee—freed his slaves and was himself the loser financially. This man, "great in victory but greater in defeat, great in war but greater in peace," will go down in history as one of America's greatest men.[320] — MRS. TENNIE PINKERTON DOZIER, FRANKLIN, TENN., HISTORIAN TENNESSEE DIVISION, U.D.C.

A LIBERAL YANKEE'S ESTIMATE OF SOUTHERN BLACKS
☞ The following is from a February 24, 1834, letter by young [Bostonian, Charles] Sumner [later to become a Massachusetts senator] to his parents while making the journey [south] from Baltimore to Washington. Had he lived longer, [the Yankee congressman] . . . might have expressed his appreciation of what the South did to develop the slaves: *"For the first time I saw slaves, and my worst preconception of their appearance and ignorance did not fall as low as their actual stupidity. They appeared to be nothing more than masses of flesh unendowed with anything of intelligence above the brutes. I have now an idea of the blight upon that part of our country in which they live"* [my emphasis, L.S.].[321] — *CONFEDERATE VETERAN MAGAZINE*

New England progressive Charles Sumner, circa 1860.

YANKEES SOLD THEIR SLAVES TO SOUTHERNERS THEN LABELED SLAVERY A "SIN"
☞ . . . The right or wrong of slavery we need not discuss or attempt to determine who was most responsible therefor. The institution is dead beyond the possibility of resurrection, and *the whole nation is glad. The later geographical limitation of slavery in the United States were determined not by conscience, but by climate. It was climate at the North and the cotton gin in the South that regulated the distribution of slave labor. I have scant respect for a conscience too sensitive to own certain property because it is immoral, but without compunction will sell the same to another at full market value. Had the [Yankee] slaveholders of the North manumitted their slaves and not sold them [to the South] because their labor ceased to be profitable, there would have been more regard for their subsequent abolition zeal* [my emphasis, L.S.]. . . .[322] — BISHOP CHARLES B. GALLOWAY, JACKSON, MISS.

OUR BLACK MAMMY
☞ Prior to 1865 the [wealthy] Southern people were "plantation folk," living with their servants on large estates. There was among them a freedom from restless change because of the fixedness of their possessions. They were content and the happiest people on the face of the globe. Each proprietor felt himself a king. He was master of all he

surveyed. The practical lives of our ancestors were such as to challenge and hold our loving respect.

At no time in the history of our race has there ever been a peasantry so happy and in every way so well-to-do as the negro slaves of America. The civilized world stood amazed at the social conditions in the South during the eventful period from 1861 to 1865. The slaves during that time guarded with loving fidelity the homes of their masters.

Among the most faithful were our black mammy. She was the most loved and by all odds the most privileged "pusson on the plantation." *No one, not even "missus," opposed her.* Though born in a lowly station, she wielded a scepter. She held in her arms the joy of the home—the little one given to make life beautiful, he who in coming time would be king in his father's place. It was young master! Or maybe the little one was "Meh Layde," the future queen and mistress.

Mrs. William Hume.

Ah! history has no parallel to the faith kept by the negro in the South during the Civil War. Often five hundred negroes were found to one white man on these plantations, and yet through these dusky throngs the beloved women and children walked in safety. The unprotected home rested in peace.

. . . Among the noblest and most devoted of all surely may be classed our black mammies. Being in the house altogether with the master, mistress, and children, they had fine opportunities for improving themselves in every way. No instance can be given of one of these faithful ones proving aught but the loving and devoted friend of the home, and black mammy would die for her [white] baby—the baby in her charge [all emphasis, L.S.]. Not only in monumental praise but in "song and story should our black mammy receive a part of the dues we owe her memory." (Mrs. Hume had with her a picture of the black mammy of her family who had served them twenty-seven years.)[323] — MRS. WILLIAM HUME, NASHVILLE, TENN.

HOW MANY SOUTHERN BLACK SERVANTS RESPONDED TO FREEDOM

☛ It was in August, 1865, and we had long since received the sorrowful news of Lee's surrender. The struggle was over; the dreadful loss of life and property had not availed us. My husband had been in the Confederate army, and I was now in Alabama, far from the Tennessee home from which I had been ordered in the third year of the war by [Union] Gen. Gordon Granger [after whom Fort Granger, Franklin, Tenn., was named], under suspicion of being a spy for the Confederate army I had left with my children three days after receiving the order, and since that time I had wandered through many of the Southern States and suffered much privation. At present I was boarding in the home of a Southern planter whose negroes, numbering over a hundred, were now set free, and were as helpless and lost as children in their unaccustomed freedom. Provisions were very scarce in the South, and we had often suffered with hunger.

. . . The day before we left, Mr. Oliver asked us to go out on his back veranda and witness the contracts he was going to make with his former slaves. When we were all ready, the horn was blown for the negroes to assemble from the quarters, and soon the yard was filled with the dark-hued crowd. Their attire was very scanty, the climate was hot, and our long sojourn there had accustomed us to the sight. The grown women wore only one long garment, a "shift," the men cotton shirts and trousers, and all the children under twelve years of age, both boys and girls, were clad only in their own dark skins. Mr. Oliver was an old man, and the negroes waited in respectful silence.

"I have already told you," he said, "that the war is over and the Yankees say you are free. If you want to go away and leave me, I have no right to keep you. But I am not compelled to feed and clothe you as I have done; you must now learn to make enough to feed and clothe yourselves. That is what freedom means—a little more work. My crops are still growing in the fields, and I want hands to work them and women to cook and wash. I would rather hire my own negroes than others. Now those of you who want to hire to me step up one at a time and tell me."

Since, by law, a servant's "slavery" service did not begin until around the onset of adolescence, black children spent their entire early childhood in complete freedom.

They came forward slowly, hesitating, as yet, to think and act for themselves; all but one man. . . . Some who came [forward] he refused to hire. Turning to us, he said: "They have only been burdens to me; and if freedom has come to them, it has also come to me." One of these was Emmaline, a [black] woman who before her freedom had been valued—with her expected child—at one thousand dollars [$18,000 in today's currency, 2022]. *Negroes always took a great pride in the price at which they were held by their masters, and Emmaline had often boasted of her worth.* Later, when the hiring was over, she came to me, weeping bitterly, and said: "Miss Martha, master don't want me; he won't keep me, and mistis says she don't want me neither! I wish to de Lord dem Yankees had done let me 'lone. Den I was worth a thousand dollars, an' now I ain't worth nothin', an' can't even hire myself. O what will I do when master sends me 'way?" I was sorry for her, for her case was a hard one; but I could find no words of comfort. Freedom had come, to her, even if it was unwelcome, and the poor woman went away wringing her hands and bitterly lamenting [my emphasis, L.S.].[324]
— SALLY ROYCE WEIR

GRANT'S CRIMES & LINCOLN'S ILLEGAL EMANCIPATION

☛ What Col. W. H. Stewart says in a complimentary way of [Union] General [Ulysses S.] Grant in the December *Confederate Veteran* [1907] is quite true as far as it goes. I feel very grateful to him for his kindness to our army in 1865 at Appomattox, etc.; but those orders he issued in August, September, November, etc., 1864, to his subordinate generals, [David] Hunter, [Philip H.] Sheridan, [Wesley] Merritt, etc., we cannot forget. These orders are enough to paralyze the most forgiving and knightly Christian hero in the world. These orders are to be found in the "Official Records," War Department, at Washington.[325] They are in strange contrast with [Confederate] General [Robert E.] Lee's Order No. 73, issued at Chambersburg, Pa., when he entered the State, June 27, 1863.

General Grant recommended to [Union] General [Henry W.] Halleck that the destruction in the Valley of Virginia should be such that "crows flying over it for the balance of the season (July 1864) would have to carry their provisions with them."

He wrote to General Sheridan: "We want the Shenandoah Valley to remain a barren waste."

Union Gen. Henry W. Halleck.

To General Hunter he wrote: "Take all provisions and stock for use of your command; such as cannot be consumed, destroy."

To General Merritt he wrote: "Carry out my instructions. Destroy all mills, grain, and forage. You can drive off or kill all stock. Leave the valley a barren waste."

We may forgive, but can we forget the above orders? Are they such as to draw out our best feeling of commendation?

Napoleon [Bonaparte] could have burned Moscow, but even his severe combativeness dictated a more humane course. These orders were as uncivilized as Mr. Lincoln's proclamation setting free the unprepared negroes of the South. It was without [legal or constitutional] authority and in violation of his own recorded convictions. (See his first inaugural address, March 4, 1861.)[326] — E. H. LIVELY, ABERDEEN, WASH.

HUMOROUS INCIDENT BETWEEN A BLACK CONFEDERATE & A YANKEE SOLDIER

☞ . . . Another incident, probably not in print: [Confederate] Col. C. C. McKinney, of the 8th Tennessee Infantry, had as a body servant during our retreat from Dalton, Ga., to Atlanta a negro named Sam. Sam was apt in catching on to phrases often used by Colonel McKinney, one of which was: "I casually remarked." On a certain occasion in that campaign Colonel McKinney furnished Sam his horse and sent him out foraging. The Federals were on our flanks, and Sam got too close to them before discovering the enemy. Sam wheeled his horse and made for tall timber, with a Federal cavalryman right after him; but Sam finally reached camp with eyes protruding like young moons, and proceeded to narrate his adventure. A man of the 8th asked him what the Yank said to him, and Sam replied: "He said, 'Halt, halt,' but I casually remarked, 'I never halt.'" "But, Sam, didn't he shoot at you?" "No, sah; he was a very bold-looking man; but I don't think he had anything to shoot with."[327] — JOHN T. GOODRICH, FAYETTEVILLE, TENN.

RADICAL RECONSTRUCTIONISTS IN ALABAMA EMPLOY COMMUNIST TACTICS, SUCH AS EXPLOITING BLACKS IN ATTEMPT TO DESTROY THE CONSERVATIVE SOUTH & THE U.S. CONSTITUTION

☛ A history of the stirring times of the city of Montgomery and of the State of Alabama has never been written. It is the purpose to write it now, while there are yet living witnesses to verify every statement. It is written too that it may be preserved for the education of our coming generations and for the vindication of Southern honor before the civilized world.

In tears and the agony of disappointment because of surrender and that the stars and bars had gone down in defeat to rise no more the Confederate veteran made his way from North Carolina and Virginia afoot, riding when he could, inspired by the hope of being soon at home with his loved ones. He thought surrender was the end of the long years of his griefs and sorrows and a renewal of his to the stars and stripes. He could not believe that free America would employ any policy or measure that did not promise sweet peace and the harmony and prosperity of a reunited country.

Union Gen. Ulysses S. Grant.

At the gate of his home, in smiles and gladness, he greeted wife and children with kisses and embraces. All along his way home were standing [U.S.] armies at every turn. Fortunately and pleasingly the United States regimental forces, both officers and privates, were polite, affable, and disposed to do anything comporting with the health, happiness, or prosperity of his fallen foe. Busy with his home interests, his energies were concentrated in his best efforts to make it what it was before grim-visaged war had defaced or destroyed its beauty and peace. He stopped the holes in his roof, filled up crevices through which the chilly winds of winter came, repaired his barns, remade his fences, and was in utter ignorance of the infernal fires being kindled [by Liberals, socialists, and communists, members of what was then a Left-wing Republican Party] at the National Capital.[328]

When it was made known to him that Mr. [Jefferson] Davis was held a prisoner, bound with chains and fetters, his blood grew warm with the spirit of resentment.

Not content with the cowardly cruelty of incarcerating Mr. Davis and others, their venom rankled against even Gen. Robert E. Lee, who would have been their fellow-prisoner and fellow-sufferer had not [Union] General [Ulysses S.] Grant stood an impassable barrier, a wall of fire between them and him.

Jealousy, envy, malice, and the direst poison of hate gathered in the halls of Congress, growing into a mighty and consuming fire until our constitutional compact became only ashes, and the accursed spirit of reconstruction had so altered free America as to make it the foremost province of his Satanic Majesty. Then came swarms of locusts, clouds of vultures, and countless beasts of prey, each commissioned with authority to invade the sanctity of home, to look into all places, and to appropriate jewels, plate, gold or silver coil, cotton, or other things of value.

When that fire of Inferno had grown into its utmost proportions, all governments of Dixie, State, county, and municipal, were dissolved and an election ordered. *Negroes in their ignorance, the contemptible scalawag who had turned his back on his country in her hour of need, and the carpetbagger glorying in freedom and singing of the "bottom rail on top" migrated from county to county, town to town, and wherever there was a ballot box deposited a handful of illegal votes, unable to understand what their votes meant.* "They obeyed the word that was saunt." Great haste was made in the inauguration of State, county, and municipal governments and the installment of officers. Stealage became their order of procedure, and so continued until there was no money [left] to defray daily needs and darkness overspread their skies. In this emergency, on the suggestion of their [Left-wing] white pilots, resort was had to the issuance of State, county, and city bonds, which were divided among those in power and by them bartered at any price in the markets of the North.

Alabama was bankrupt, being hopelessly involved in a bonded debt of nearly $35,000,000 [$640 million into today's currency, 2022], and having neither money nor bonds in her treasury. [Indoctrinated] negroes became insolent and rapacious, with tendencies toward riot and disposition to appropriate the little left by the war upon which the wives and children of the old [Confederate] soldiers were subsisting.

This U.S. propaganda lithograph, created by artist Augustus A. Tholey and published in Philadelphia, Penn., in 1867, is disingenuously entitled "Reconstruction of the South." Like nearly all disinformation artwork, it was designed to gaslight the public. In this particular case we are being overtly indoctrinated with the Left-wing view that Lincoln's War was a "noble cause," one whose primary goals were to "emancipate the enslaved black man," "eradicate white supremacy," and "civilize the barbaric South, then rebuild it into a copy of the righteous North." The facts in this very book, relayed by reliable eyewitnesses, thoroughly refute all of these claims.

Such was the aspect of our political horizon when our people, without regard to gender or age, firmly resolved, to resist the yoke of oppression at any cost.[329] In conference it was proposed and agreed to outvote them in the ensuing city election, and so wrest from the dirty [progressive] hordes the power they had usurped.

Organizations were perfected, fellow-soldiers and their sons were called from our own and adjacent counties, and they came unbidden from other States; so that when the auspicious day came, in 1872, we were all at the polling places and in force, equipped with carefully correct lists of citizens who were legally entitled to suffrage.

That day the sun rose upon the heavens in beauty and splendor. [Left-wing indoctrinated] negroes were in swarms and militant, coming from other counties and towns to exercise their American freedom; nor were the hungry carpetbaggers or scalawags wanting.

Balloting was both rapid and continuous amidst imprecations and uncivil expressions of speech as some negro belonging anywhere outside of Montgomery County was challenged.

Miss Myra Smartt, Chattanooga, Tenn., Sponsor for Tennessee Division, Nashville Reunion.

The writer found it necessary on that day to absent himself from the polls of Ward 2, going to Dexter Avenue. On his speedy return he was accosted by [former Confederate] Col. H. C. Semple, who informed him that he was just from an investigating trip to the capitol; that he had found recorded in the *House Journal* a bill which had become a law prohibiting the punishment of repeating or other illegal voting. This information was manna falling to us from heaven. The efficient, good work of Colonel Semple was utilized at once, being conveyed to other polls, where our good people saw the dire necessity of driving the [indoctrinated] negro and his white [Left-wing] friends from all the voting places, of which they had taken possession, and permitting only Democratic [that is, Conservative at the time] ballots to go into the box.

A [Conservative] *negro* came to the writer wanting to vote with the white people, the Democratic [that is, Conservative] ticket. He was pursued to the very polls by a pack of howling devils, yelling: "Kill him! Kill him! This 'nigger' is here to vote the Democratic ticket."

The fury and noise was so great as to be deafening, so that it was next to impossible to understand anything said to each other. Sticks, clubs, knives, and pistols were ready in hand for use, when Mr. "Billy" Ray, then an old man, jerked off his coat, threw it on the ground, and exhorted the boys, saying: "Now is as good a time to die as any. Let the fight begin."

Stonewall Jackson's invincibles never obeyed order to charge with more alacrity. The fight did begin in earnest. The Metcalfs in one place, the Caffeys in another, the Westcotts close by—all around old soldiers and boys who were too young for service when our country needed them were battling with great, burly [unregistered] negroes to drive them from the voting place. This determined effort was not without fruit. Messages were quickly sent to the other polls of what we had accomplished. Before the hour of 12 m. [midday] the enemy were routed, head, neck, and heels, and the polls were ours without dispute; but continuous and industrious work had to be kept up that we should have a majority of votes in the count at 8 P.M. Counting the ballot was enormous work, but its footings were honest and a righteous vindication of the good people of Montgomery.

Alabama Governor George Smith Houston.

Our good people rejoiced, and congratulations seemed to come from the civilized world. This signal triumph was quickly followed by a new city government and the speedy removal of the debased herd of vultures from every place of trust or honor.

Holding the polls for ourselves only, voting thirty, fifty, one hundred times each, and cramming the boxes, was an invincible process; but it was inaugurated and made law by the Mongrel Legislature for its perpetuation, and without our knowledge Colonel Semple brought us the information necessary to our great triumph.

This election was an education to our county and State; so that when elections came later, Alabama's fetters were broken and she was herself again. Negro, scalawag, and carpetbag [that is, Left-wing] politicians ceased to be a menace to our city or an offense to our people.

[Conservative] Governor [George Smith] Houston was elected in 1874, and each county chose its own members of the General Assembly and its own county officers. But when attempt was made to oust the culprits from their usurpations, it looked again like bloody war. But the carpetbagger, scalawag, and ignorant, impudent [indoctrinated] negro gave way to the inevitable, and sweet peace came to Alabama. The dust of battle was dissipated.

Our Governor was inaugurated, the Legislature met, and at once began looking into *the unclean work of reconstruction*. A true state of facts was presented to them in an empty treasury and evidence recorded in treasury books of $35,000,000 bonds sold or divided between such of them as had footing in or access to power.

Bankruptcy! repudiation! was heard in all our realm. Our stanch old Governor and his wise men applied themselves to the task of scaling or compromising for less than $8,000,000. They utterly refused to allow that Alabama was responsible for one dollar; but rather than have our State's good name dishonored by such association, this compromise was agreed to. All of Dixie came into line with Alabama. *Thus were broken the shackles riveted upon our homes by that unrighteous convention of Satanic spirits calling themselves "The Congress and Senate of Free America." So did Heaven thwart and bring to naught their wicked designs and cause the sun of liberty to roll in glory as it came to us from our Revolutionary fathers* [all emphasis, L.S.].

The writer assures the Christian world that every statement in this history is the truth and calls the living participants of that fearful, uncertain time as witness.330 — JAMES W. POWELL, MONTGOMERY, ALA.

THE TRUE SOUTHERN CAUSE: CONSTITUTIONAL GOVERNMENT, A CONSERVATIVE CONCEPT

☛ On the field of Sharpsburg a monument should be erected to the memory of the dead of Hood's Texas Brigade. They were sacrificed for the want of proper support, but their spirits rise like white clouds in the sky and tell us that *they died for a just cause. The cause for which they fought is not a "lost cause." I repudiate and contemn that phrase. They were not fighting to destroy the Union, but for the perpetuation of the principles upon which the Union was formed. The right of local self-government, the sovereignty of the States, is the seed of the Union, and is steadily growing in strength and vigor. Their struggle was for constitutional government, the corner stone of national union. They were not rebels, nor were they traitors; they did not die for secession and slavery, but in vindication of constitutional sovereignty, without which constitutional liberty would be only a memory.*

William H. Fairfax, Confederate soldier.

Many who once condemned the South and denounced us as rebels and traitors have raised the veil of prejudice, and now accord to us the highest tribute of patriotic courage and manly devotion to the great principle upon which this government was founded [that is, the Conservative concept of self-government, or home rule or states' rights, as it is also variously known]. *Looking back after the lapse of nearly half a century, the terrible losses sustained on all the red fields from Big Bethel to Appomattox throw a halo around a "just cause" which grows brighter as the years roll on, and which should nerve the heart and inflame the speech for the sovereign principle of "home rule"* [my emphasis, L.S.].[331] — W. HAMBY, 4TH TEXAS, AUSTIN, TEX.

TEACHING SOUTHERN CHILDREN THE TRUTH OF HISTORY

☛ . . . [The truth] . . . *will be very valuable, especially to our young people, who know so little about the causes of the war, and have been told so repeatedly in Yankee books that it was a fight to destroy the Union and perpetuate slavery on the part of the "Rebels," so that many are growing up to believe these falsehoods, and do not appreciate that on our part it was a fight for the God-given principles of self-government and the defense of our homes and firesides against unjust invasion* [my emphasis, L.S.].[332] — CONFEDERATE VETERAN MAGAZINE

WHITE SOUTHERNERS ONLY PEOPLE TO TREAT BLACKS WITH "REAL KINDNESS"

☛ . . . *The Southern States have their own problems, which they desire to solve for the common good. It is true also that there are other questions not exclusively Southern in which the people of the South are concerned equally with all citizens; such, for instance, as the general questions of the just relations between the States and between any State and the general government. But even this problem was made local as to the Southern States and became acutely sectional in the years between*

1850 and 1861, when the circumstance that African slavery had become an institution was used to create a dangerous Southern problem.

After many unsuccessful expedients, the States in the South fled for refuge to secession; and that being denied, they were forced to fight; and having failed in that, they surrendered without any settlement by negotiations or war. Hence the old disturbing presence in our country of a people of African descent became more serious than ever because the problem was loaded from 1865 with new and insupportable conditions. These negroes in the Southern States were merely turned loose with nothing but the power to vote and hold office without qualifications. *They were not offered homes anywhere except in the South, and they fell as a load on the Southern people. But the South assumed the burden, and the assertion is here made that no body of people in any age of the world has treated this negro race with real kindness except the people of the Southern States* [all emphasis, L.S.].

Former servants attending "Old Slave Day" at Southern Pines, North Carolina, 1937.

All nations have enslaved them, and not one has trained them into that physical, intelligent, moral manhood which is the indisputable qualification of a valuable population. For example, consider the negroes in Africa under European rule. The Southern States have over six millions of this race to care for, and the Southern people are qualified to execute the trust justly, benevolently, and for the general welfare. It is, therefore, insisted that the [Left-wing] hindering intermeddling with the purposes to righteously solve this problem shall cease; for whatever the motive may be, such interference is misdirected, hurtful, and often open to suspicion as being accompanied with insincerity, selfishness, or ignorance of Southern conditions. . . .[333] — CONFEDERATE GEN. CLEMENT A. EVANS, CHAIRMAN OF THE COMMITTEE

MORE PROOF THAT THE UNION CAUSE WAS NOT ABOLITION

☛ *You propound the question whether the present war in the United States is to emancipate the negroes from slavery. I say this is not the intention of the Federal government, but to put down rebellion, etc. You have lived in the United States, and you must have observed what a dreadful calamity it would be to throw at once upon the South, in looseness, four millions of slaves* . . . [my emphasis, L.S.].[334] — J. W. QUIGGLE (AMERICAN CONSUL TO ANTWERP), IN AN 1861 LETTER TO ITALIAN SOCIALIST GIUSEPPE GARIBALDI, WHO HAD BEEN OFFERED A UNION MILITARY COMMAND BY LINCOLN

BLACK CONFEDERATE SEEKS OUT HIS OLD MASTER

☛ The Colored Baptist Association of Kentucky held its annual meeting in Hopkinsville recently, when the [African American] Rev. James K. Polk called to see [Confederate] Capt. C. F. Jarrett, whom he served in the Confederate army until the surrender of General [Nathan Bedford]

Forrest at Gainesville, Ala. It was a joyous meeting. They had not seen each other for forty three years. There were many pleasant reminiscences as well as sad. *"Jim" was a faithful friend and servant. He never shirked a battle, and was always near enough to share his haversack or lead up a new horse. He is now a servant of the Great Master of all, and will doubtless prove true and faithful to the end. In accounting for a change of name in connection with "Jim," Captain Jarrett notes the fact that nearly all the negroes with freedom took another name, and this darky, proud of Tennessee, sought to honor her only native President* [all emphasis, L.S.].[335] — CONFEDERATE VETERAN MAGAZINE

AMERICAN ABOLITION BEGAN IN THE SOUTH
☛ [Yankee historian George Lunt of Massachusetts writes that long before the start of War Between the States, the] . . . States of Virginia, Kentucky, and Tennessee were engaged in practical movements for the gradual emancipation of their slaves. This movement continued until it was arrested by the agitations of the abolitionists.[336] — RANDOLPH H. MCKIM, D.D.

White Victorian Southern artists portrayed Old South black servants as they usually were: tender, gentle, respectful, and loving, a depiction in stark contrast to what typically came from the pencil or paintbrush of Yankee artists: wholly inaccurate, and often laughably ridiculous, political images intended only to foment anger and bitterness toward the white South. The picture above, entitled "Me and Mammy," is by the former type of artist, Dixie poetess and illustrator Miss Maria Howard Weeden of the Yellowhammer State. Of this poignant portrait Mary Brabson Littleton writes: "[The Mammy,] . . . the typical nurse, is positively lovable in the spirit of kindly sympathy and natural goodness that oozes from her rough features. The world of [white] childhood might be intrusted to her care without fear of any greater harm to them than overkindness and indulgence in their whims and fancies. The face [in the above drawing] wears a smile that belongs to the whole [black] race—indescribably warm and young and sweet."

The cover of *Confederate Veteran* magazine, December 1901, Vol. 9, Issue No. 12.

CHAPTER FIVE
1909-1912

BLACK MAMMY HAPPILY GREETS RETURNING CONFEDERATE SOLDIERS

☞ . . . We marched to Irvine, the county seat of Estill County, Ky., that night, much of the time in a torrent of rain, arriving there early the next morning, where we captured a small garrison and valuable government stores, including a quantity of McClelland saddles, together with United States bridles and halters that had never been unpacked. I appropriated a saddle, bridle, and halter from Uncle Sam's stores.
. . . At Crab Orchard I remember an old gray-haired black mammy was out in a yard clapping her hands and shouting: "Glory to God, the Rebels is come back! And have you come to stay?" "Yes, Auntie," we assured her, "we are going to stay this time" [my emphasis, L. S.]. . . .[337] — J. N. GAINES, BRUNSWICK, MO.

Black mammy with her "babies."

CONFEDERATE VETERAN ADMIRED BY BLACKS

☞ . . . Judge Jeremiah R. Morton died at his home, in Lexington, December 18, 1908, without a moment's warning. At the usual hour in the evening, about 6:30, he returned from his law office to his home, on East Short Street, seemingly in fine health and spirits after an unusually busy day in the court room and in his office, took up an evening paper to read the daily news, as was his custom, when the hand of death struck him, and in a moment the vital spark was gone forever.
Soon the sad news spread throughout the city, and there was deep sorrow in many homes, for *he was known and beloved by all, rich and poor, male and female, white and black. He was a Confederate veteran* [my emphasis, L.S.], a Freemason, and one of the oldest, ablest, and most popular members of the Lexington bar; and as a token of love for their comrade, their brother, and their associate and of appreciation of his many noble qualities, the members of each of these organizations attended his funeral in a body. . . .[338] — MILFORD OVERLEY, LEXINGTON, KY.

MORE EVIDENCE OF KINDLY MASTERS, SLAVE MARRIAGE, & LIFELONG WHITE & BLACK FRIENDSHIP

☞ A few years before the Civil War *the negro Jim who was my nurse when a child*, became enamored of a dusky damsel [named Viny] belonging on a plantation some miles across the Tennessee River. *My father*, notwithstanding he *was a very kind and humane master, considerate of the happiness and well-being of his negroes*, didn't want to take the chances of a thousand-dollar negro being eaten by fishes in the blue waters of the Tennessee [River]; so he told Jim to call off his passion from the other side of the river, feather a new dart, and let fly at some one of the dusky beauties on his own or neighboring plantations. But this proved to be a case where love laughs at locks, rivers, and all other barriers. My father, knowing Jim to be quite shrewd, notified Mr. Hill, the owner of the dark beauty, not to permit the marriage for the reason stated above.

All this diplomacy occurred without my knowledge, yet I had often written Jim passes to cross the river and visit plantations on Sunday, all without my father's knowledge. In fact, *I was so much attached to Jim, having my life interwoven with his from babyhood up to that time at least, I* considered *no sacrifice too great and no risk too hazardous to make for him. In fact, while I was the nominal master, Jim was the power behind the throne.* Besides, Jim was a diplomat; and when some risky favor was asked, he became very assiduous in his attention to me. He would plan and assist me in my boyish pranks and escapades. He had taken special care of the horse my father had allowed me to claim and use. It was Henry's business to look after, feed, and curry the horses. Jim would frequently in my presence accuse Henry of neglecting my horse, which more than once brought on a difficulty.

"Slave" weddings were common, legal, joyous, much anticipated events on plantations across the Old South, and were celebrated by both black and white families.

Finally Jim concluded he would go over a certain Saturday night and be married to the girl on Mr. Hill's place. He didn't know that my father had headed him off by his order. So when he made his appearance, armed with a pass with my father's name signed to it, Mr. Hill informed him of my father's order, and of course forbade the interesting ceremony. Jim returned wiser, but more determined than ever.

By this time the case had become complicated and assumed a serious aspect for Jim and his affiance, and it called for more diplomacy. After the proper preliminaries, Jim unbosomed himself to me, yet keeping me entirely ignorant of my father's opposition. The order of my father to Mr. Hill and the tangle he got into were all wisely kept from me. He "jes' wanted me to write him a little order to Mr. Hill and say, 'I'ze 'cluded to let Jim marry Viny if you'se got no 'jections to it.'"

So I readily complied, and Jim, armed with the order and other passports necessary, all bearing my father's name, in due time made his appearance at the mansion house of Mr. Hill, accompanied by his best man. With the politeness of a Chesterfield and the dignity of a Choate, he presented his passport and "letters of credit," and was kindly informed by Mr. Hill in his usual calm and quiet way that he was glad indeed that his master had reconsidered the matter and permitted him to have the woman of his choice. The Rev. Mr. Hamer united the two hearts that wanted to beat as one.

. . . In after years the secretary was orderly sergeant of Company H, 49th Alabama Regiment, was made prisoner of war, and on the way to Camp Chase spent one night in the Nashville penitentiary before he was twenty-one years old. *Jim was never separated from Viny. The last time he saw Jim, in the seventies, he was a prosperous pastor of a Colored M. E. Church in Nashville, Tenn. He came to see me in Alabama at his old plantation home, brought me a fine shaving set, and said he and Viny had twelve children, all living* [all emphasis, L.S.].[339] — F. A. HAMER, DARDENELLE, ARK.

THE "POLITENESS & CIVILITY" OF THE OLD "SLAVERY DAYS"

☞ . . . Senator Bob Taylor, of Tennessee, has proposed a monument symbolical of slavery days carved from a single block of Southern marble, in the center *a courtly old-time Southern planter high-born and gentle with a kindly face*, on the right the old plantation negro "uncle" and slave, and on the left the shiny-faced black "mammy," the helper of every living thing in the big house of the white folks and in the cabin of the "pickaninny."

I hope the monument will take form. I should crave the privilege of inscribing it. Under the central figure, the old master, I would carve the word "honor;" under the slave, the old faithful Uncle Remus, I would carve the word "homage;" under the black-faced, broad-bosomed mammy, *whose breasts often succored the children of the whites*, I would carve the word "humanity."

Miss Fereba Grier, Charlotte, N.C., Sponsor for Mecklenburg Camp, U.C.V., at Louisville, Ky.

There is nothing in the history of the South before the war more interesting than the ties of affection and respect that bound the slave to his master and master to slave. Neither prosperity nor ruin, decay nor disaster has changed this feeling. Find them where you will, they will bear witness to this statement. Hunger and want never disquieted the slaves' constant good nature. Good humor and laughter distinguished their lives. The politeness and civility of the Uncle Remus of slavery days was only outdone by his master. . . .

. . . There were no vast fortunes in the South of those days accumulated by processes tolerated now. There were no law-defying corporations. The wealth of the people was in the land, and this descended from father to son, as did the customs and habits of their domestic lives.

Piety and patriotism were the dominant trails in the make up of the people. Their churchgoing and reverence spread an atmosphere of religion over all. Even the dusky slave felt its influence. Every Church had its black worshipers—in the same church, mind you, black and white worshiping together [all emphasis, L.S.].[340] — A. G., COLUMBUS, OHIO

SOUTHERN CHRISTMAS INCLUDED ALL RACES

... *Christmas cheer comes but once a year in these prosaic days* [1909], *but it was Christmas cheer all the year in the* [antebellum] *days of the Old South.* Christmas began a week before the calendar date, and they forgot the date of its ending in so far as cheer was concerned.

... The Christmas I refer to was in 1860, a few months before the beginning of the Civil War. We all went back to the old home—to grandfather's—to celebrate Christmas. That old stone house was the Mecca for all the relations of the family. ... At three o'clock in the morning we were all up, creeping stealthily along the wide hall, knocking on each door, shouting, "Christmas gift!" and were always welcomed from within. Father pretended to scold that we awakened the household. Mother got up, although pretending to protest. The entire household was up, the big dining room was crowded, the big table full of presents. *Every one was remembered, white and black alike* [all emphasis, L.S.]....[341] —A. G., COLUMBUS, OHIO

HOW THE SOCIALIST & COMMUNIST NORTH PROPAGANDIZED THE WORLD & HELPED LAUNCH LINCOLN'S WAR

☞ Historians have been busy assigning causes for the terrible war of 1861-65, which desolated the southern section of the United States and destroyed an institution which had become a part of its domestic life. The war is attributed to ignorance of each other in the two sections of the Union, to sectional prejudice, to conflict of economic interests, to different interpretations of the Constitution, to ambitious rivalries for supremacy in the government.

Confederate General William Brimage Bate.

No doubt each of these factors contributed to bring about the final outbreak of hostilities and to the bitterness of the struggle. But in reality it was a war of conscience against conscience—a conflict of moral ideals. Each side believed it was contending for righteousness against iniquity. The [Liberal] North thought it was fighting against an order of society unjust and oppressive; the [Conservative] South believed it was fighting for a social order in the main kindly and beneficent. The North fought for a theory of human rights; the South for a condition, the best conserver of actual rights of two races widely different yet forced to live together.

It is frequently said that *if the Northern people* [Liberals] *had known the actual condition of the slaves in the South* [Conservatives] *and the kind feeling which in general subsisted between master and slave, then all bitterness of feeling would have disappeared and the radical demands of the abolitionists* [that is, socialists and communists] *would have been so modified that the questions could have been settled without war.*

But the chief obstacle to settlement was that these abolitionists, with their active [communist] *propaganda, would not accept any fact that would controvert their theory of human rights. Intensely prejudiced and partisan* [Left-wing]

writers with very limited opportunities to know all the facts went through the South to observe conditions. They reported the exceptional cases of cruelty and oppression, and their statements were accepted as gospel, which no amount of evidence could invalidate as to the terrible condition of the slaves and the tyranny of the masters. Thus the conscience of the Northern people was aroused against a system for which they felt the nation was responsible. At the same time the conscience of the Southern people resented what they felt was an injustice to them and a false judgment of their institutions.

When conscience is involved in any great question, compromises are only temporary. At length it has to be settled by force, the appeal to arms, that *ultima ratio regum*. Although the result of the appeal is not necessarily just and righteous, *war never settles the right or wrong of anything. It often only establishes some giant wrong. One of the mightiest agencies of oppression and injustice in this world has been a perverted conscience. Our Saviour warned his disciples that their persecutors would think they did God service. And the horrors of the Inquisition were inflicted by conscientious ecclesiastics.* No doubt many of those who accomplished the emancipation of the slaves in the South at such fearful cost of blood and treasure, of life and suffering have the approval of their own consciences, and congratulate themselves on their success as agents of God's righteousness. Yet *we of the South, who were the victims of that conscience, believe that it was blinded, perverted, and unjust. And our consciences do not reproach us for having resisted to the utmost of our power.*

States.	Inmates of Homes during 1915.	Appropriations for Homes during 1916.	Pensions Paid, 1916.	Annual Pensions to Veterans and Widows.	Veterans on Pension Roll.	Widows on Pension Roll.	Expended for Pensions and Homes to Jan. 1, 1916.
Virginia (A)	289	$ 60,000	$ 572,000	$ 33	8,122	4,793	$ 7,277,000
North Carolina (A)	150	35,000	500,000	32	8,708	6,326	6,500,000
South Carolina	71	17,000	282,000	36	3,670	4,868	3,907,000
Georgia	115	36,000	975,000	60	10,000	7,695	18,725,000
Florida	28	5,040	775,000	120	2,486	2,649	7,289,000
Alabama (B)	98	14,700	950,000	64	7,436	7,436	11,668,000
Mississippi	230	50,000	475,000	40	4,519	4,670	5,979,000
Louisiana (B)	125	25,000	550,000	96	3,185	2,728	4,117,000
Texas (C)	352	91,830	1,350,000	67	7,379	10,241	7,650,000
Arkansas	136	48,000	650,000	62	5,274	5,275	6,150,000
Kentucky	208	42,000	348,000	120	1,744	1,208	1,333,000
Tennessee	98	25,000	940,000	120	4,552	3,360	8,440,000
Oklahoma	98	17,500	20,000	120	644	356	630,000
Missouri (D)	281	55,850	100,000	120	11,811		1,105,000
Maryland	pays no pensions.	15,000	Maryland pays no pensions.			Provides Home only.	
West Virginia provides no Home and pays no pensions.							
Total	2,354	$512,920	$8,487,000		69,530	61,605	$90,970,000

(A) Virginia, North Carolina, and Texas have separate small Homes for women. Alabama, Mississippi, Louisiana, Arkansas, Oklahoma, and Missouri admit wives with husbands into Homes. South Carolina, Georgia, Florida, Kentucky, Tennessee, and Maryland do not admit wives or widows.
(B) Pension varies; provided by special tax. Men and women on pension roll said to be about equal; no separate list kept.
(C) Pension varies; special tax. Six hundred and ninety-seven negro servants of veterans are pensioned.
(D) Missouri does not pension widows.

1916 registry of pensions paid by the Southern states to Confederate veterans. Note "C" in list at bottom: In Texas alone pensions were paid to 697 "negro servants of veterans." Today, by legal definition, these African Americans are considered Confederate soldiers.

It was essentially the Puritan [Left-wing] conscience which forced on the war. And inasmuch as the Southern [Conservative] conscience was as firm in its conviction as to the duty of resistance, the war was inevitable. *My observation of the Puritan [Yankee Liberal] and my reading of his history leads me to think that when he has made up his mind as to what is right no amount of fact is allowed to interfere with his course.* Every one must admire his stern devotion to principle as he sees it, his firmness of purpose, his self-sacrificing zeal, his energy, his independence of thought, and his brave assertion of that independence at any cost.

But on the other hand *I have noted an intolerance of opposition, an assumption of infallibility in judgment, a self-confidence which would denounce the Almighty if he differed from the Puritan idea, a willingness to deny or to pervert and misrepresent facts, to sustain a theory which have led to persecution and oppression in order to establish a certain theory or course of conduct.* So in the early days of New England Baptists and Quakers were banished because their consciences could not conform to those of the Puritan.

In the course of nearly half a century as a minister of the gospel I have had various illustrations of this peculiarity of the Puritan [Liberal] conscience which will not accept any fact that would contradict its moral ideals. And let it be said that *the Puritan has been so masterful in the realm of higher thinking that he has molded and controlled the ideals of the whole northern section of our country. He has claimed liberty to his own opinions, also liberty to force them on others.*

Starting my ministerial life with the highest admiration for the Puritan, I fear I shall close it with a feeling of utter revolt against his [Left-leaning] character as an enemy of true liberty of conscience. This feeling applies only to the English Puritan, from [Oliver] Cromwell down, until I sometimes wonder whether to class the great Lord Protector as hypocrite or saint.

But my purpose in this paper is to give some illustrations of *that stubborn prejudice in the* [Liberal] *North which misrepresented and misjudged the* [Conservative] *South and which refused to listen to any facts that might correct or modify opinions that rested on theory and not fact.*

The theory was that all slavery was wrong, a violation of inalienable rights; that it must necessarily oppress and maltreat the slave, and also it must brutalize the master and make him cruel; therefore Southern slavery must be a system of cruel oppression, and that any facts to the contrary were only exceptional. So the system was denounced as "the sum of all villainies," and *conscience was invoked and cultivated to destroy it.* The abolitionist [socialists and communists] gloried in the war of emancipation as a righteous war. *The true Southerners* [Conservatives] *looked upon it as an unrighteous* [Left-wing] *attack upon a social order which was forced on them largely by the Puritan* [Yankee Liberal] *and whose overthrow would bring dire consequences.*

Col. John W. McGavock.

The first illustration I shall give was related to me by the late Col. John McGavock, of Franklin, Tenn. [owner of Carnton Plantation].[342] He was a typical gentleman of the old school, brave, gentle, upright, scorning a lie or any hypocrisy with utmost contempt. In his boyhood days he spent a good deal of his time in Washington with his relative, Hon. Felix Grundy, Senator from Tennessee. He heard frequently the discussions in the Senate between the great leaders, Clay, Calhoun, Webster, Benton, and their peers. It was my privilege to enjoy the friendship of Colonel McGavock for a number of years before his death, and his reminiscences of those days were exceedingly interesting. As he sat in his great arm-chair, which had belonged to

General [Andrew] Jackson, and talked of those old days of strenuous debate, I felt that his memories ought to be recorded as a valuable contribution to the history of the time.

Among other things, he told me that several years before the war a prominent United States Senator visited Tennessee and was the guest of Gen. W. G. Harding at Belle Meade,[343] the celebrated stock farm near Nashville. He spent several days observing closely the life of the place, and all were pleased with his agreeable manners and his brilliant conversation, revealing the treasures of a wide culture. He asked General Harding if there would be objection to his talking with the negroes on the place, as he wished to know the facts of our Southern life. He was told to make himself perfectly at home and to speak any of them freely on any subject he chose. Of course it was understood that he wished to hear the slave's version of his condition. The guest was a gentleman, and had no such thought as stirring disaffection among the slaves. He went into the quarters and saw them at their meals and on to the farm and saw them at work. He talked with [black] men and women.

Southern black servant families posing outside their homes. Well clothed, well fed, well housed, and well cared for, all of a Southern servant's needs were provided for from birth to death by their white owners.

He was impressed with the intelligence and answers of one especially, who became afterwards the noted "Uncle Bob," in charge of the thoroughbreds. He suspected that Bob knew who he was and that he had been posted as to his answers, so he said after a long talk: "Do you know who I am?" Bob answered promptly [though incorrectly]: "Yes, sir; you are Marse Pony Cheatham"—a man whom Bob had seen at Belle Meade and who bore some resemblance to him.

When his visit ended, Mr. S. was very cordial in his thanks to General Harding for the opportunity of seeing for himself the life of a large Southern plantation. Colonel McGavock, who had it from General Harding, said that the guest remarked in substance: "Well, sir, the institution is entirely different from what I had supposed. Sir, this is really the old patriarchal system of the family, like that of Abraham."

Yet this man went home and, disregarding his own observations, was induced to listen to the statements of [Left-wing] partisans, and was driven by the exigencies of party to become the most bitter in his denunciations of the South and its institutions. His [largely socialistic and communistic] theory of the wrongs of slavery must be maintained.

Two Southern black youngsters, photographed between 1860 and 1870 by John D. Heywood, at New Berne, N.C. This old albumen print is often cited by ill-informed enemies of the South as evidence of "the poor conditions black Southern slaves were forced to live under." To begin with, pre-adolescents did not serve as "slaves." Second, there is no information in the original source (the Library of Congress) to indicate whether these were the children of *slaves* or of *free blacks*. Third, this image may have been taken years after slavery was officially abolished in the U.S. by the Thirteenth Amendment in Dec. 1865. In any case, as this very book demonstrates, and as I have shown in my numerous books on American slavery, generally speaking, all Southern black families possessed both the ability and the freedom to raise or lower their own standard of living quite independently of the economic state of their white owners. Thus, just as under capitalism, industrious free and bonded blacks could advance in life, while indolent free and bonded blacks were more likely to regress economically. It is possible, even probable, then that these boys were the offspring of the latter.

Another illustration of this [biased] peculiarity of the [Liberal] New England mind was given to me by one of my teachers in college.

In the years 1854 to 1856 I was a student at Jackson College, in Columbia, Tenn., which was [illegally and unnecessarily] burned by the Federal forces in 1864. I was fifteen years old when I entered. The students were assigned rooms in the college building—four to a room—for study by day; and as the rooms were all occupied, the professor of Latin and Greek took me to room with him. He was an old bachelor, and treated me as a son. He was a native of Maine, a graduate of Bowdoin College, the *Alma Mater* of Longfellow, Hawthorne, and Franklin Pierce. He was a man of broad and *liberal culture*, who bought and read many books. One day in the late fall, when we had begun to have fire in our room, he came in with a new book and sat down to read. After a while he got up and thrust the book into the grate. Of course I was surprised, and asked why he did it. He said: "That book is Mrs. Harriet Beecher Stowe's *Sunny Memories of Foreign Lands*. I thought I had a book of travels, which I know Mrs. Stowe could write well. Instead, it is only an abolition document." I afterwards learned his experience of abolitionism, which was in substance that after his graduation he determined to be a teacher. So he looked for a place which would yield him a living. There was a better prospect in the South then than in his own home [state]. Although he was against slavery and was prejudiced against the South, yet for the sake of the salary he swallowed his prejudices and came to Pulaski, in Giles County, Tenn., where he secured a select school of boys, twelve or fifteen sons of the neighboring planters. He thought he could stand it for a few years until he could make enough money to return to God's country, and there spend the rest of his life as a teacher amid congenial [Left-wing] surroundings. After a little while, as he became acquainted, he was invited nearly every week to go home with one or other of the boys to stay from Friday evening until Sunday morning, when the family came to the town to church. At the end of six months he wrote home to his people in Maine, telling them that *they were mistaken as to slavery; that it was not the cruel system they imagined it was.* They answered that he had not had a chance to see the dark side. At the end of a year he wrote again, urging them to revise their judgment. They replied that the slave holders, knowing that he was from the North, had concealed the cruel features of their treatment of the slaves, and that he did not know the real conditions.

He then concluded to write no more on the subject, but to take utmost pains to inform himself on the general treatment of negroes by white masters. At the end of three years he expected to return to Maine, and then in personal talk with his family and friends he would convince them of their error. But he was sadly disappointed. He went back to spend three months before returning to Tennessee, where he had made up his mind to spend the rest of his life. He had been at home only a short time when the subject of slavery was brought up. He told them simply what he had seen, not concealing the occasional cruelties nor apologizing for the real evil of the system. *He told of the contentment of the slaves, their freedom from care, the provision for food and clothing, the attention in sickness, the kind feelings of master and slave for each other.* He only asked that they recognize facts and the difficulties in the way of carrying out their theories.

Margaret "Maggie" Howell Davis Hayes, Daughter of Confederate President Jefferson Davis.

His friends were impatient with his story, and finally intimated in plain terms that he was in the pay for the [slave] holders, hired to make false statements; that they knew that conditions were different from his representations.

At the end of three weeks he had enough of Maine, and he packed his trunk and came back to Tennessee. I understood that he never went back to his old home until after the war, when he married and took his bride to see his people.

He did what he could for the Confederacy, serving in hospitals and in such positions as his strength would permit. His last years were spent in the ministry of the gospel.

Another incident involving two ministers of the gospel will show how thoroughly this prejudice existed in the Churches of the North. It was related to me several years ago by the late Mrs. Mary Thompson, the mother of the Hon. John Thompson, Commissioner of Agriculture of Tennessee, and of Mr. Joseph H. Thompson, a prominent banker of Nashville. She was one of the loveliest and saintliest characters I ever knew, and also most charitable in her judgment of everybody.

The General Assembly of the Presbyterian Church met in the First Presbyterian Church in Nashville, Tenn., in May, 1855. Dr. Edgar, the pastor, and his committee of entertainment received two letters, one from a minister in New England, the other from a minister in the West.

These men were brothers, who had not met for twenty years, being in such widely separated fields. Each was appointed a commissioner to the Assembly. They asked that if possible they be assigned to the same home during the Assembly's meeting.

Mrs Thompson's husband, Mr. John Thompson, was very much interested in these letters, and asked that the brothers be sent to his home. He lived on a large plantation a few miles from the city. He promised to put a comfortable buggy and a gentle horse at their disposal, so that they could go and come at their pleasure.

On the afternoon before the meeting of the Assembly Mrs. Thompson went to meet her guests and brought them to her home. It was a pleasant May day, and they were delighted with the freshness and beauty of the country. While they were sitting in the parlor for a few minutes before going to their room the [black] house maid came in to make some inquiry or announcement, and she and her mistress had some little talk aside. As she left the room the ministers looked after her with evident surprise. At length one of them said to Mrs. Thompson: "She didn't seem to be afraid of you." Her reply was: "Afraid? Why should she be afraid of me?" He said: "Why, we had understood that the black people do not dare to speak to the whites without permission, and they usually get down on their knees." Of course Mrs. Thompson ridiculed his foolish and false ideas.

The work on the plantation interested them very much. It was the season of planting, and everybody was up early and everything was moving from morning until night. The ministers were busy too, seeing as much as they could in the intervals of the Assembly's sessions.

The Overton House, also known as Travelers' Rest, Nashville, Tenn. Confederate General John Bell Hood headquartered here prior to the Battle of Nashville, Dec. 15-16, 1864.

When the Assembly adjourned, Mr. Thompson invited them to remain with him as long as they could, that they might see more of Southern life and the condition of the slaves. They gladly accepted his invitation, and spent several days in going over his place and in visiting the neighboring plantations. They were shown the storerooms with bales and bolts of cloth to make up into clothing for the negroes, with boxes of boots and shoes and hats and caps; the work rooms, where Mrs. Thompson directed the sewing women; the smoke-houses, with the great supply of cured meats; the mills for grinding the corn; the nursery for the babies while the mothers were at work; the cabins in which the negroes lived, each with its garden spot; the barns and stables and tool houses—in a word, all the necessary equipment of a large plantation, with its many slaves forming a village in itself, clustered about the "big house" of the "white folks."

They visited Colonel [John] Overton's and General [William G.] Harding's plantations ["Traveler's Rest" and "Belle Meade" respectively] and several of the farms of the neighborhood. *They seemed much surprised at the general air of content and happiness which prevailed among the negroes,* to whom they spoke freely, asking many questions.

Mr. Thompson told them that several of these gentlemen owned plantations in Arkansas and Mississippi, where they raised cotton and where the life was much the same as here, under the direction of a trusted overseer and his family. He told them that what they had seen was a fair sample of the treatment of the slaves generally by their owners; that, *while there were no doubt cruel masters, they were the exception, and public opinion as well as [the law and] self-interest restrained them from excess of harshness.*

The brothers were very thankful for the attentions which they had received, and said to Mr. Thompson: "We have had our eyes opened. Now how can we repay your kindness and show our appreciation?" He replied in substance: "Gentlemen, I foresee great trouble for our country in the near future to come from the agitation of this question of slavery. *Your people are denouncing us with great bitterness as the oppressors of a helpless race. They do not know the actual condition and treatment of the slaves nor the difficulties that beset their demands. This is with us not a question of a theory of human rights, but of actual facts with which we have to deal, and we are trying to give the negroes all the rights which they are fit to exercise. Surely if your people but knew the truth, they would cease their agitation of a question which they are incompetent to deal with. The Southern people cannot be expected to submit patiently to abuse which they feel to be unjust.* Now I ask of you gentlemen that when you go home, one to the East, the other to the West, you tell your people just what you have seen of the treatment of the slaves. Use your position and influence to get facts before them. I do not wish you to apologize for us nor to cover any unfavorable facts which you have noted. You have seen a fair example of the way the large proportion of the negroes are treated. You also can judge of the difficulty in the way of freeing such a mass of an utterly different and inferior [in other words, as yet still largely uneducated] race from the restraints of slavery and having them live among us. And you might at least help to stop this agitation."

Liberal Victorian Yankees knew almost nothing about how Dixie's authentic servant system operated—and, tragically, they seemed little interested. As this photo of Mississippi cotton pickers shows, farm work was not the exclusive realm of black field slaves. On plantation after plantation across the Old South, whites and blacks worked together in the fields, the white owners and their children often sharing in the labor.

Mrs. Thompson heard the whole conversation of which I have given the substance. She said that as her husband ceased speaking both ministers threw up their hands and said: "Mr. Thompson, *if we were to tell our people exactly what we have seen just as we have seen it, we could not keep our* pulpits a month. We would be set down by public opinion as liars, bribed by the slaveholders. Our people are so set in their views of slavery that they would not believe a word we spoke and would refuse to hear us preach."

Mr. Thompson loved the Union with his whole heart. His father was one of the pioneer settlers of Tennessee. He bade his guests "good-bye" with a heavy heart, feeling that if they judged their own people aright there was no escape from a bloody conflict of the sections.

Several years ago I spent some weeks in Edinburgh [Scotland] and Belfast [now Northern Ireland], and met some of the most intelligent and fair-minded Scotchmen and Irishmen. Of course they asked me about the life of the South, and seemed astonished that Christian people could defend the institution of slavery. I became convinced that for years the abolitionists [that is, socialists and communists] of the North had systematically carried on a propaganda of misrepresentation and falsehood for the purpose of prejudicing the minds of the European peoples against us, and to a large extent they had succeeded. I was enabled to correct some of these false impressions. But while some were willing to hear our side, others refused to believe me. These two classes of foreigners were represented directly after the war by two different delegations that visited this country.

The circumstances were given to me by the Rev. Dr. Thomas V. Moore, for many years pastor in Richmond, Va., and afterwards pastor of the First Presbyterian Church in Nashville, where he died, and by the Rev. Dr. E. T. Baird, Presbyterian Secretary of Publication. Two or three years after the close of the war a delegation from the Free Church of Scotland, consisting of the Rev. Drs. Patrick Fairbairn and Edgar, visited this country, to bear greetings to the Presbyterian General Assembly North. Dr. Fairbairn was a distinguished professor and author, and had edited in Scotland a volume which Dr. Moore had issued in this country.

Confederate General Nathan Bedford Forrest at the head of his cavalry, moving to attack the Union right.

On landing in New York, some days before the meeting of the Assembly, they were cordially welcomed, and in their speeches they were effusive in congratulating the pious North for its glorious work in breaking the fetters of four millions of bondmen. They were equally effusive in condemning the South for her effort to rivet those same fetters more firmly. As there was time to spare, they visited Richmond, as Dr. Fairbairn wished to visit his friend, Dr. Moore. They wished to see something of how the negroes lived in slavery. Drs. Moore, Moses Hoge, and Baird took pains to show them some of the old homes around Richmond and visited several of the old plantations down the James River. They pointed out the negro quarters, with their cabins and gardens, and also the various buildings in which provision was made for their comfort. They told of the life and work not only on the large plantations but on the smaller farms and in the villages and cities and in the homes of the masters. They told of the religious instruction of the slaves, of the buying and selling of them, and of their family life. The whole story was told honestly, not concealing the harsher features.

Fort Sumter in 1861, with Confederate First National Flag on display.

When the delegation was received by the General Assembly, the effort was made to have them repeat their speeches made on their arrival. But they evaded the subject of slavery and emancipation, and their references to the war were slight and guarded. Dr. Fairbairn intimated that he had found that they did not know enough to talk wisely on the subject.

After his return to Scotland, Dr. Fairbairn wrote letters to Dr. Moore expressing deep sympathy with the Southern people and Churches in the very difficult problems forced upon them by emancipation. Especially did he deplore the giving [of] the ballot to the negro. Dr. Moore gave me two or three of these letters, but in moving my library I have lost them.

Now for the other class of foreign critics. The next year another delegation came from Scotland on a similar mission. It consisted of Dr. James McCosh, afterwards the distinguished and able President of Princeton University, and Dr. William Arnot, a minister and author of great talent and learning. They also went to Richmond, anxious to see for themselves the conditions. They received the same courteous treatment from the same gentlemen, who took them on a steamer running to Norfolk, that they might see something of the old Virginia mansions. But Dr. Baird told me that the response to these courtesies, especially by Dr. Arnot, was so rude as to be positively insulting. Whenever any statement was made indicating that the negroes were well treated and happy, Dr. Arnot would dispute it in the most offensive manner: "No, sir! I know better than that; you can't deceive me. I have investigated this matter, and know that there was not a redeeming feature in the system." This in substance was his reply to anything that did not conform to his opinions, until at last Dr. Hoge, the most courteous of men, lost his patience and said to them: "As you seem to have no confidence in us as Christian gentlemen, we shall leave you to yourselves." So the Richmond gentlemen withdrew into the boat and had no more to do with the visitors. Dr. Baird said that he could not explain such boorishness in men of such unquestioned ability and high position except on the ground of *inveterate prejudice with boundless self-conceit*. I suppose all who know anything of Dr. McCosh know how profound was his confidence in his own opinions. I was told that when the visitors returned to Richmond they were entertained by a prominent negro family. If it were so, I can't see how any Southern man could attend Princeton under his presidency.

These incidents show how difficult it was to get the facts before the Northern and the British people. In Great Britain the anti-slavery sentiment expressed itself in self-righteous glorification of English freedom in contrast with the slavery-darkened United States. It was their boast that as soon as the foot of a slave touched English soil one breath of English air made him a free man. They sneered at our flag as having stars for the white man, but stripes for the negro. These complacent censors seemed utterly oblivious to the terrible conditions of large sections of their [own] laboring population held in bondage to an oppressive service far more exacting than a Southern slave ever knew. They seemed also to forget that negro slavery was imposed on this country by the British government, which was ably seconded by the traders of New England trading rum to Africa for slaves to be sold in America.

We are told that our Civil War was the result of ignorance of each other in the two sections of our country. But there was no chance to relieve the ignorance when prejudice so intense and inveterate was cultivated in the North by pulpit and press—a prejudice which was founded on conscientious devotion to a theory and which refused to believe anything contrary to the theory.

Miss Ella Clingan, Jackson, Miss., Sponsor at Louisville Confederate Reunion for Robert A. Smith Camp.

The abolitionist [socialist/communist] thought he was doing "God's service" by his crusade against an institution which he regarded as the "sum of all villainies." And so he demanded "an anti-slavery constitution, an anti-slavery Bible; and an anti-slavery God." It was not the first time [nor would it be the last] that conscience has trampled on justice in the name of religion.

The war was bound to come. The abolitionist [socialist/communist] won the victory. To-day he boasts of the achievement as a glorious triumph of righteousness. *No Southern man would restore the institution of slavery.* But the end is not yet. We are confronted by the most difficult problem that ever a nation had to solve. Can the relations, social, political, economic, of two races as widely differing as Caucasian and negro living under the same government be so adjusted as to give justice and proper development to both races? Thus far we have had only an experiment. It remains to be seen whether emancipation has been a blessing to our country, and especially to the negro, or has introduced evils that in the end will be more terrible than slavery.[344] — REV. JAMES H. MCNEILLY, D.D., CONFEDERATE VETERAN, NASHVILLE, TENN.

CUBAN CONFEDERATE SOLDIER, & HIS THREE SISTERS WHO SPIED FOR THE CONFEDERACY

☛ . . . Long before the War between the States Mauritia Sanchez left the West Indies and settled on the east bank of the stately St. John's River, opposite Palatka, Fla. His ill health, which had caused his removal from Cuba, continued to grow worse till when the war broke out he was a feeble man, worn and aged. His family consisted of an invalid wife, *a son* in the Confederate service and three attractive daughters, who were only prevented by their womanhood from also joining the army. In lieu of this they gave every aid and assistance possible to the cause of the Confederacy [my emphasis, L.S.].

Information concerning the Yankees percolated through the lines and reached the Confederates, and after watching closely the Yankees decided that Mauritia Sanchez was its source, and the feeble old man was arrested as a spy and dragged off to prison in what was then called San Marco, and is now Fort Marion, St. Augustine.

This left the three girls, Panchita, Lola, and Eugenia, unprotected, for their invalid mother was their care, not their guard. Often in the night their place was surrounded by Yankee troops, both whites and blacks, and the house searched for concealed spies; for the information still reached the still reached the Confederates, and the Yankees did not suspect the truth—that the girls themselves were the informers.[345] — L. H. L.

WHY A BLACK CONFEDERATE WAS ACQUITTED OF MURDER

☛ The story is told that a negro under the charge of murder was being tried in a Georgia court. Much testimony had been taken, and it seemed to be very serious for the defendant, whose plea was self-defense. An old man in the court room arose and, addressing the court and jury, said: "Please your honor and gentlemen of the jury, years ago my only brother [Augustus Gabriel Toombs, a Confederate soldier,] fell wounded on the battlefield of Gettysburg. He lay there bleeding to death, with no one to help him. Shot and shell, the fierce, fiery stream of death were sweeping the earth about him. No friend dared go to him, no surgeon would approach him. The singing of bullets and the wild music of shells were his only requiem. *My brother had a body servant, a negro man, who waited on him in camp. The negro saw his master's danger, and straight out into that hell of battle and flame and death he went. A cannon shot tore the flesh from his breast; but on he went, and gathering my brother in his arms, the blood of the man mingled with the blood of the master, he bore him to safety and to life.* Jim, open your collar." He did so, and the jury saw on his breast long, jagged scars where the shell had ripped its way. Continuing, [Confederate] General [Robert Augustus] Toombs said: "Jim's skin is black; he is a negro; but the man that would do what Jim did for my brother has a soul too white ever to have killed a man except in defense of his own life." Jim was cleared.[346] — *CONFEDERATE VETERAN* MAGAZINE

Confederate Gen. Robert Augustus Toombs.

BLACK CONFEDERATE SOLDIER AMOS RUCKER BURIED IN HIS GRAY UNIFORM WITH MILITARY HONORS

☛ There is an underlying note of tenderness in every heart, and it vibrates to the touch of real pathos, as a violin does to its bow. The story of Amos Rucker, the old negro [Confederate] veteran of Atlanta, carries its own moral. *Amos belonged to the Rucker family, of Colbert County, Ga., belonged in a wider sense than as a mere human chattel that the slaves were said to be, for every joy or sorrow in "ole Marster's" family touched its sympathetic chord in his heart. The children he watched grow up were as dear to him as his own, and "ole Miss" was always the pinnacle of all that was good in his eyes.*

Amos was a young man at the time of the war; and when "Marse Sandy Rucker" went to the front, Amos went too, just as proud as was that young soldier of his "marster's" gray uniform and brass buttons.

In all those long, hard years the 33rd Georgia Regiment bore its part in the bloody struggle, and there was no braver member than Sandy Rucker, and shoulder to shoulder with him fought Amos, as though he too was an enlisted man. He took part in every engagement, and, gun or bayonet in hand, stood ready to "close up" whenever there was a vacancy in the line. The cause of the Confederacy was his, because his master had espoused it first; then it was his from the love he came to bear the flag, and no truer, more loyal heart beat under the gray than that of Amos Rucker.

Confederate veteran Thomas W. Colley of Abingdon, Virginia, at age 59, circa 1896.

He joined the [Confederate veterans'] Camp of W. H. T. Walker, and there was no more loved nor respected member than the black, whose bowed form and snow-white hair showed the passing of the years so plainly. He attended every meeting till the one before his death, when he sent word to the Camp that he was too ill to attend, and added: "Give my love to the boys."

He went to all the Reunions whenever possible, and here he attracted much attention. He was very proud to show off a wonderful feat of memory, for he could call the roll of his old company from A to Z, and he would add in solemn tones "here" or "dead" as the names left his lips.

The people who had had his lifetime devotion took care of both the old man and his wife. As he said: "My [white] folks give me everything I want." At his death in Atlanta in August, 1909, there was universal sorrow. His body lay in state, and hundreds of both white and black stood with bared head to do him honor. Camp Walker defrayed all burial expenses, buying a lot in the cemetery especially for him, so that the old man and his wife could lie side by side. The funeral services were conducted by [Confederate] Gen. Clement A. Evans, the Commander in Chief of the Veterans, and his volunteer pallbearers were ex-Gov. Allen D. Candler, Gen. A. J. West, ex-Postmaster Amos Fox, F. A. Hilburn, Commander of Camp Walker, J. Sid Holland, and R. S. Osbourne. Very tenderly they carried the old veteran to his grave, clothed in his uniform of gray and wrapped in a Confederate flag, a grave made beautiful by flowers from comrades and friends, among which a large design from the Daughters of the Confederacy was conspicuous in its red and white.

A simple monument will be erected to the faithful soldier by the white comrades of his Camp and from contributions from his many friends in Atlanta [all emphasis, L.S.].[347] — CONFEDERATE VETERAN MAGAZINE

PROOF LINCOLN'S WAR WAS NOT OVER SLAVERY

☛ It is plain to all thoughtful men that the institution of slavery, mild, benignant, and fraternal as that institution was as it existed in the South prior to the days of [radical Left-wing Yankee William] Lloyd Garrison and gentlemen of *his cult*, was already doomed, and would have fallen in a few years anyhow, even if it had not been drowned in the blood of half a million victims in the most momentous struggle of modern times. It has been so in Brazil, in Cuba, in all the South American republics, and that within twenty years after the close of our Civil War. Some one, commenting on our Civil War, has remarked that the South was unlucky; and truly has she been unlucky, before the war, during the war, since the war—before the war in that the inevitable institutional revolution which must have been plainly patent to the thinking men of that day could not have been allowed to progress peacefully instead of eventuating in a fratricidal strife which cost her the lives of thousands of the flower of her young manhood, only to end in a miserable fiasco, for

Plantation hostler. As white Southerners had been trying to find a humane and efficient way to abolish slavery without widespread socioeconomic and psychological damage since the late 1600s, it is clear that the institution would have gone extinct on its own had the South been left alone, as Confederate President Jefferson Davis and millions of other white Southerners had requested.

the negro problem, which it sought to solve, is as far from solution now as then. *The public opinion of the Christian world as well as the fast-gathering force of a strong and growing and thinking minority in the South itself would have compelled emancipation in a few years, whether or not the War of Secession had ever been fought or whether or no that war had ended in her triumph or defeat* [all emphasis, L.S.]. . . .[348] — WATKINS LEIGH, MONROE, LA.

MORE PROOF LINCOLN'S WAR WAS NOT OVER SLAVERY

☛ . . . *I believe if the Confederate States had succeeded the result would have been to accomplish all the benefits the Union forces fought for, but without the attendant evils that are now upon us!* It is legitimate to inquire, in view of the facts in the case, what would have been the result upon our condition and our institutions if the Confederate States had established their independence. I can only give my opinion. *There would have certainly been the emancipation of the slaves.* First, the sentiment of the civilized world was opposed to slavery; and though our system was misunderstood, yet no nation can hold out against a universal moral sentiment. Second, *there was a feeling all through the South favorable to emancipation as soon as it could be done without danger.* If the abolitionist propaganda had not aroused opposition by its bitterness and misrepresentations, *the border States would have brought about the freedom of the slaves several years before the war.* Third, the conduct of the slaves during the war entitled them to freedom, and all the South thought so. General Lee freed his slaves in 1863, and all the other slave owners would have followed, and the freeing would have been brought about in such a way as to have avoided the evils that have resulted from emancipation. The slave would . . . have been given liberty . . . and the right to develop the best that was in him, and he would have received the hearty help of every Southern white man [all emphasis, L.S.]. . . . ³⁴⁹ — REV. JAMES H. MCNEILLY, D.D., CONFEDERATE VETERAN, NASHVILLE, TENN.

PRO-SOUTH SPEECHES AT THE TENN. STATE FAIR BY U.S. SEC. OF WAR & ALSO GEN. ULYSSES S. GRANT'S SON, 1909

☛ . . . Returning to the city [Nashville, Tennessee], the party [of the committee of the Tennessee State Fair Association] was met by [U.S.] Secretary of War Judge [Jacob McGavock] Dickinson at Greenwood Park, where the negroes were having their annual fair. J. C. Napier, President of the Fair, and other officials were in readiness to extend every courtesy. After viewing the handiwork of the negroes and their beautiful [live] stock, there was a meeting in the pavilion and speeches were made by Judge Dickinson and General [Frederick Dent] Grant [son of Union Gen. Ulysses S. Grant].

They were remarkable talks. Judge Dickinson spoke to them [the black audience] as a Southerner and a Confederate, giving them practical advice. He told them that if they wanted to succeed in life they must be industrious and diligently economical in saving their earnings. *He referred to their freedom and how it came about, declaring that the war was not waged for their freedom, but that it was simply an incident of the war* [my emphasis, L.S.]. He told them that the one time General Lee left the army during the war was to go to his home and formally give freedom to his slaves [owned, not by Lee, but by his wife's family]. General [Fred] Grant in his address spoke kindly to them and of his pleasure in seeing their prosperity. He had known their race all of his life. His family owned slaves until they were freed by Lincoln's proclamation, and he said that after the war their old servants maintained an interest in the family, and in all the intervening years they had not failed to make known their needs, which had been heeded. It was a remarkable record that in the latter years of the war Lee fought on with no interest in slavery, while [U.S.] Grant held his until freed by the "exigencies of war. . . ."³⁵⁰ — *CONFEDERATE VETERAN* MAGAZINE

Group at Nashville Fair grounds. Front row, left: J. M. Dickinson; front row, right: Fred Grant; back row, from left to right: W. W. Harts, G. W. Goethels, Frank Ewing, and Sumner A. Cunningham, the editor of *Confederate Veteran* magazine.

A TRUE HISTORY OF SOUTHERN ABOLITIONIST SENTIMENT

☛ . . . There is another charge made against Mr. [Jefferson] Davis and the South, and that is that the object of the Civil War was not to assert and protect the rights of the States, but to perpetuate the institution of

African slavery. That this is not true, you veterans of that day know. Not one in five of the men engaged in that war owned a slave or had any interest in them. *You and your comrades, slaveholders as well as nonslaveholders, went out to defend your State against invasion and to protect the assertion of a right reserved when the Union was formed.*

The people of this commonwealth [Virginia] *from the dawn of its colonial existence down to the fanatical agitation of the slavery question on the part of the* [Liberal] *North recognized that slavery was an evil, and but for that* [Left-wing] *agitation there is little doubt that there would have been a gradual emancipation of slaves in this State without the shedding of a drop of blood, and in a manner which would have redounded to the interest of both races. This is made clear from her history.*

During her colonial life the Virginia House of Burgesses passed twenty-three acts, running through a hundred years, seeking to prohibit and exclude from her borders the Africans who were being brought to her shores by New England and Old England slave dealers, and all the efforts of our ancestors were vetoed and thwarted by the [English] king [George III] and Parliament of Great Britain, without whose assent our Legislature could make no law upon the subject. When this colony declared her independence in 1776, one of the first acts of her Legislature was to pass a law forbidding the African slave trade, and *that was the first act ever passed by any State or nation prohibiting it.* She was the advance guard of the nations in putting an end to that cruel wrong.

The indignation which the State of Virginia felt toward the British government for forcing African slavery upon her people can be seen from the first constitution of the State, in which it is declared as one of the detestable and insupportable acts of tyranny on the part of the British king that "he was prompting our negroes to rise in arms among us, those very negroes whom by an inhuman use of his negative he had refused us permission to exclude by law."

When, in order to induce the smaller States to agree to form a more perfect union after the Revolutionary War, this State ceded to the United States her interest in the great Northwest territory, covering what is now the States of Ohio, Indiana, Illinois, Michigan, and Wisconsin for the most part, won by the genius and valor of [Gen.] George Rogers Clark [of Virginia], one of her most distinguished sons, she favored excluding slavery from that territory forever, and it was done.

When the Constitution of the United States was framed, she sought to have prohibited at once the African slave trade to any part of the Union; *but the States of New England, whose people were engaged in the trade,*

"His Most Excellent Majesty," King George the Third, British ruler at the time of the American Revolutionary War. Nearly a century later, Southerners would fight the "Second American Revolutionary War," this time against another autocratic tyrant, big government Liberal Abraham Lincoln.

with the aid of other States, were able to continue the nefarious traffic until 1808, or for twenty years longer [all emphasis, L.S.].

In the early [eighteen] thirties a bill was offered, and came near passing the Virginia Legislature, for the gradual emancipation of slaves, and would no doubt have passed then or a few years later but for the Nat Turner insurrection and the fanaticism which encouraged if it did not cause it. . . .[351] — FROM AN ADDRESS BY JUDGE JOHN A. BUCHANAN, MEMBER OF THE VIRGINIA COURT OF APPEALS

EIGHT FORMER BLACK SERVANTS OF CONFEDERATE VETERAN SERVE AS HIS PALLBEARERS

☛ Since the death of this celebrated soldier, statesman, philanthropist, journalist, and financier much has been written of him and much may still be written, for it is indeed hard for mere words to do justice to such a man.

Miss Olivia Saunders, a Maid of Honor for North Carolina, Atlanta Confederate Reunion.

Joseph Bryan was the eighth child of John Randolph Bryan and his wife, Elizabeth Caulter Tucker. He was born August 13, 1845, at Eagle Point, his father's plantation in Gloucester County, Va.; and died at his country seat, Laburnum, near Richmond, November 20, 1908. Through both father and mother he was connected with the highest aristocracy of the State whose proud boast is that it has a native nobility inferior to none in this country or in the Old World. This "gentle blood" dominated his entire life, and his every act was influenced by its refining touch.

. . . His charities were very widespread and unostentatious. It is said that he gave thousands of dollars to the [Confederate] veterans who were in need and thousands more for Churches and schools without distinction to sects. He loved to assemble around him in gracious hospitality his many friends, and his intimates held his home as their own. Fond of a joke, he delighted in the badinage and the quick play of wit and repartee. Having seen only the best aspect of slave life, he was still opposed to slavery, and only the fact that he thought his care to be for their good kept him a slave owner, for on his plantation the master was the friend, supporter, and defender of his servants. It was from these servants that his pallbearers were selected, and eight of them bore him to the grave [my emphasis, L.S.].[352] — FROM THE OBITUARY OF JOSEPH BRYAN, CONFEDERATE VETERAN MAGAZINE

CONFEDERATE GEN. BUCKNER & SHELBURN

☛ [In 1909] Marmaduke B. Morton visited the last surviving lieutenant general of the Confederate army, Simon Bolivar Buckner, at his residence ["Glen Lily"], near Munfordville, [Hart County] Ky., for a historic interview.

. . . The day with Simon Bolivar Buckner, one time a captain in the regular army of the United States, one time a lieutenant general in the army of the Confederate States of America, one time Governor of Kentucky, one time candidate for Vice President of the United States, will never be forgotten.

As his guests were seated the General handed around the pipes and cigars. One of the party who had some former acquaintance with General Buckner's tobacco took a pipe. The General mixes his own tobacco—the famous Hart County Yellow Pryor, a little light Virginia and North Carolina leaf, and a dash of Turkish to give the finishing touch. He generally says he has "missed it a little in the mixture," but the smoker would never find this out from the smoking.

One of the visitors asked about a picture of General Buckner and an old negro man hanging on the wall. Mrs. Buckner, who had just entered the room, explained that the old negro belonged to General Buckner's father and was reared with the General. "Shelburn was one of the most sturdy, respectable, gingerbread old negroes you ever saw. You got acquainted with him and were good friends at once. He had been living in Arkansas for many years and wrote that he would like to come to see the General, and we arranged for him to make the trip" [my emphasis, L.S.].

Right: Confederate Gen. Simon B. Buckner; left: "sturdy and respectable" Shelburn.

Mrs. Buckner said she expected that the meeting between the two old friends would be quite demonstrative and that they would want to talk to one another all the time, but to her astonishment nothing of the sort happened.

"So Shelburn came, and they sat for about an hour on the porch and smoked and looked at one another. Both were rather quiet. Once Shelburn said: 'Young Marster, do you remember what we used to call one another when we were children?' The General replied in the affirmative. Then they would smoke along for a while, and the General said: 'Shelburn, do you remember Jack, the old dog we used to have?' 'Yes, sir,' replied Shelburn."

She said they were the most unvivacious pair she ever saw, yet they seemed to enjoy one another immensely.

"Shelburn spoke of the General's father, Colonel Buckner, as 'Old Marster;' he spoke of the General as 'Young Marster;' but he did not know what to call young Simon Bolivar. He would get terribly mixed on his various masters. After Shelburn went home, the General sent him one of the pictures of themselves taken together. The old negro wrote and thanked him for it and said: 'I think I is the best-looking.'"...[353]

CONFEDERATE VETERAN MAGAZINE

MORE EVIDENCE OF BLACK YANKEE SLAVES IN THE UNION ARMIES

☛ . . . About ten days afterwards we were at Strasburg on picket, and then advanced in front of [Confederate Gen. John Brown] Gordon in his memorable night attack at Cedar Creek, October 19, 1864, where we drove the enemy from their camp down to and below Middletown, capturing many prisoners and much camp equipage, *including* [Union] General [Philip H.] Sheridan's *servant* [my emphasis, L.S.] and milch cow and [Union] General [William H.] Emory's horse. . .[354] — FROM THE RECORD OF THE 5TH VIRGINIA CAVALRY, BY COMRADE P. J. WHITE, OF ROBERT E. LEE CAMP

White Union soldiers posing with a working black camp slave (lower left), circa 1863. Yankee-slanted sources, such as the Library of Congress, refer to blacks in Union photos as "servants," while referring to blacks in Confederate photos as "slaves." This is the opposite of reality, however. Originally Yanks called bonded Africans "slaves"; Southerners, as noted in this book, never thought of them as slaves, and so did not call them by this name. The so-called "slavery" system in antebellum Dixie was actually *a mild form of indentured servitude*, which is why Southerners generally referred to them as "servants."

"THE NEGROES' TRUEST FRIENDS"

☛ . . . We ex-Confederates want this government to be the best in the world. Our homes are in it, all our interests are here. We would resist interference of foreign nations; our loyalty cannot be questioned. *No people were ever truer to [constitutional] principles and convictions than the Southern people. None of us regret what we did—just the reverse. I am prouder of my four years' service in the Confederate army under [Stonewall] Jackson than of all else in life.* We were overwhelmed by numbers and resources, but our spirits are unconquered. We had to submit to [anti-South] constitutional amendments passed at the close of the war when [Left-wing] prejudice ran high. *They forced humiliation on the South; they antagonized the races* [communist tactics still used by the Left today] . . . There is only one remedy: annul the fourteenth and fifteenth amendments. *The negroes' truest friends are in the South and will treat them right* [[all emphasis, L.S.]. . .[355] — JAMES H. HENDRICKS, SHEPHERDSTOWN, W.VA.

THE SOUTHERN VIEW OF "THE GREAT EMANCIPATOR"

☛ The centenary of Abraham Lincoln! What a flood of eloquence, encomium, and praise it has brought forth from pen, pulpit, and after-dinner speech! He has been set upon a pedestal and clothed with attributes that make him little less than divine. [George] Washington has been made to step down from his long-approved pinnacle of greatness, while one enthusiast in his blind fanaticism has compared him most favorably with Jesus Christ himself.

He has been placed so far above the ordinary mortal that we feel justified in our curiosity to know how big he really was and if all these attributes of greatness have been thrust upon him or do they accord with facts that history has made indisputable?

. . . He took the oath of office "to preserve, protect, and defend the Constitution," and yet he did not hesitate to violate its principles whenever it suited his policy to do so. Though "devoted to the Union," yet he took the initiative (utterly disregarding the usages of war among civilized nations) and precipitated upon the unprepared South a war unequaled for cruelty and barbarism in all modern history.

He is called "The Great Emancipator." Yet in his inaugural address in 1861 he said: "I have no purpose, directly or indirectly, to interfere with the institution of slavery in the States where it exists. I believe I have no lawful right to do so, and I have no inclination to do so." His subsequent actions showed how little regard he had for this pledge. Like [Charles-Maurice de] Talleyrand, the most unscrupulous of men, he "used words to conceal his thoughts."

[Lincoln's] . . . admirers have laid special force upon his great heart, pulsating with throbs of justice, kindness, and humanity. Did his heart pulsate with these noble qualities when, disregarding all the rules of civilization and humanity, he declared martial law in the States of the South, flooded the country with violence and bloodshed, and legitimatized the most atrocious form of irregular warfare?

He was commander in chief of the [U.S.] army. Yet was he ever known to set his seal of disapproval upon the actions of his generals in their conduct of the war? [Union] General [Benjamin F.] Butler's treatment of the people of New Orleans was horrible almost beyond belief. "Peaceful and aged citizens, unresisting captives and noncombatants, were confined at hard labor with chains attached to their limbs, were held in dungeons and fortresses, and Union soldiers were encouraged to insult and outrage the wives, mothers, and sisters." But Lincoln allowed him to remain at that post until the "French emperor threatened to recognize the Confederate States unless Butler was removed."

American monarch, big government Liberal Abraham Lincoln. Supported by diehard socialists like Charles A. Dana, encouraged by entrenched communists like August von Willich, and endorsed by zealous radical European revolutionaries like Karl Marx, this dictatorial Left-winger dragged America into its only fratricidal war, one that came at the cost of millions of lives and billions of dollars in damages. In 2022 the Conservative South has still yet to fully recover.

Destruction and devastation became synonymous with [Union Gen. William T.] Sherman's march through Georgia to the sea, then the Carolinas; while [Union Gen. Philip H.] Sheridan over a hundred miles through the beautiful Valley of Virginia so obeyed the cruel and inhuman orders of his superior general that in truth "a crow flying through its desolated wastes would have to carry its provisions with it." This is but an incomplete picture of the cruelties inflicted upon helpless noncombatants. *These atrocities were never checked by a word or command from the President of the United States. His emancipation of six millions of slaves, his exciting them to insurrection, his placing guns in the hands of negroes to murder their former masters exceeded in atrocity and cruelty the tyranny of any despot in any age. His giving the ballot to ignorant negroes who had no more knowledge of the rights of suffrage than so many mules is but in keeping with the* [radical Left-wing] *policy pursued by him from the beginning* [all emphasis, L.S.]. . .

Was Mr Lincoln a man of high ideals? Was he a lover of the sublime, the beautiful? Was he a Christian, a gentleman? Facts compel us to say: "He was a hypocrite in religion, a vulgar buffoon, indecent in his anecdotes, and cruel in his instincts." What, then, has been the basis of all this fictitious greatness? What has been the cause of thus raising him to the very pinnacle of fame accorded no other American, not excepting even the great Washington himself? We answer: "Assassination." Assassination placed the crown of the martyr upon his brow. Henceforth "all things unclean became divine."356 — MRS. M. P. SHEPARD

U.S. PRESIDENT TAFT ON THE SOUTH & THE "NEGRO QUESTION"

☛ At a dinner given by the North Carolina Society of New York Hon. William H. Taft, then President elect, made a speech on the subject of "The South and the National Government." This was so forceful, logical, and of such wide research into existing Southern conditions that Andrew Carnegie had it published for circulation in pamphlet form, for he felt that it would do much to enlighten the South as well as the North as to their respective duties toward each other and aid in bringing about a stronger allegiance between all good citizens who are desirous only of what they believe to be the best good of the nation as a whole.

Mr. Taft is a man of large heart, of warm sympathies, but cool brain, of sound judgment and lofty purpose, and his speech was a polished and brilliant address. He handles the negro question in the South with eyes open to conditions as they are, as they were, and as they are represented at the North. He says: "It is to no purpose to point out that early in the history of the country the North was as responsible for bringing the slaves here as the South. We are not concerned with whose fault it was that there was such an institution as slavery; nor are we concerned with the probability that had the Northerners been interested in slaves they would have viewed the institution exactly as the Southerner viewed it, and would have fought to defend it because it was as sacred as the institutions of private property itself."

William Howard Taft, 27th President of the U.S.

. . . Mr. Taft says: *"Nearly five million slaves were freed. Only five per cent of these could read or write, and a much smaller per cent of them were skilled laborers save in the agricultural field. They were but as children in meeting the*

Frances Halliburton Luna, Mascot of the Texas Division, U.C.V.

stern realities of life as free men, and as such they had to be absorbed into and adjusted to Southern civilization. (How could they have any knowledge of responsibilities? Hitherto they had been cared for and protected, and never had to plan what they should eat nor where withal they should he clothed, for as children the master regarded them and provided for them.") [This problem was just one of many which made it difficult to abolish slavery in the South. L.S.]

Farther on in his able speech Mr. Taft says: "The fear that in some way a social equality between the races shall he enforced by law or be brought about by political measures really has no foundation in fact. *The Federal government has nothing to do with social questions, and the war amendments do not declare for social equality. All that the Constitution attempts or can attempt to secure is equality of opportunity the law in the pursuit of happiness and the enjoyment of life, liberty, and property. Social equality is something that grows out of voluntary concessions by the individual forming the society.*

. . . It is because of the courteous sympathy of Mr. Taft's full comprehension of the South's view-point that he says: "The Southern people are high-strung, sensitive, and outspoken, and considerations of sentiment are frequently quite as strong as those of some political or economic character." He then adds in another part of his speech: *"The Southern people are homogeneous and preserve their traditions. They are of the purest American stock, and the faith of the father is handed down to the son almost as a sacred legacy."*

. . . Reverting to the negro question. Mr. Taft says: "I believe that the solution of the race question in the South is largely a matter of industrial and thorough education. *I believe that the best friend that a Southern negro can have is the Southern white man,* and that the growing interest that the Southern white man is taking in the best development of the negro is one of the most encouraging reasons for believing the problem is capable of reasonable solution. The hope for the Southern negro is in teaching him to be a good farmer, how to be a good mechanic, in teaching him how to make his home attractive, and how to live more comfortably and more according to the rules of health and morality.

. . . The South is infinitely reasonable; and if the policy of Mr. Taft is at all commensurate with his speech, there will be little of the restiveness under *Northern rule, Northern misunderstanding, and Northern coercive measures that has marked many previous administrations* [all emphasis, L.S.]. The wise Greek Socrates said: "Measure no senator till he be dead, lest a morrow find that measure cut short by acts." Mr. Taft begins his administration to a good "measure," and the South unites in the wish that four years from now "that measure" will not be "cut short by acts."357 — *CONFEDERATE VETERAN* MAGAZINE

PRESIDENT JEFFERSON DAVIS & HIS BLACK SERVANTS

☛ . . . In his domestic life Mr. Davis stands as an example for all people. A gentleman from Massachusetts, a special friend of Mr. Lincoln, told me that he knew James Jones, the body servant of Mr. Davis, in Washington, and it was difficult for him to understand the devotion of that slave to his master—long after the war was over *an affection that impelled him if possible to attend the funeral service of Mr. Davis and to honor the memory of the old master whom he loved. This was also embodied in the resolutions of the servants of the Davis family, and this relationship of faithful servant to kind master in the South suggests the appropriateness of a monument, the opposite of that in Boston, where Mr. Lincoln is striking the shackles from the hands of a slave, on whose face is the expression of despair. We want in our Southland the figure of Mr. Davis sitting at his desk with pen in hand looking up kindly at his servant, whose face is wreathed in smiles, awaiting directions for the day*—this servant whose one thought while free from care is the protection of the widow and orphan of the Southern home; a slave whose emancipation would have taken place in the natural course of events in the South in accordance with the judgment of Christian gentlemen [all emphasis, L.S.]....[358] — REV. JAMES R. WINCHESTER, D.D., DELIVERED AT THE MEMPHIS CONFEDERATE REUNION

Confederate President Jefferson Davis at age eighty.

FIFTY-EIGHT YEAR FRIENDSHIP BETWEEN CONFEDERATE MASTER & BLACK SLAVE

☛ [Former Confederate] Capt. William [T.] Smith is well known and beloved around Christianburg, Va., and almost equally well known is his old servant "Jack." *The two have been close friends and comrades for fifty-eight years* [my emphasis, L.S.], *though the line between master and man is well preserved. They have been pictured in the papers. Captain Smith is proud of his war record, and is never tired of telling thrilling stories of the sixties.*[359] — *CONFEDERATE VETERAN* MAGAZINE

BLACK SERVANTS CONTRIBUTE MONEY TO BUILDING OF ARLINGTON CONFEDERATE MONUMENT

☛ [Receipts:] ... Mrs. Lillie F. Worthington, Director for Mississippi, $40. Contributed by J. S. C. Blackburn, Governor Canal Zone, $10; Mrs. Lillie F. Worthington, Wayside, Miss., $10; Dr. T. Flournoy Worthington, Wayside, Miss., $5; W. W. Worthington, Wayside, Miss., $5; Miss Lucy Dancy, $1; Dr. Gill, $1; "Little Lillie E.," $1; *"Eugenia, Cora, Pink, and Harry," house servants of Director (each fifty cents), $2* [my emphasis, L.S.]; Stonewall Jackson Chapter, No. 975, U.D.C. Swan Lake, Miss., $5....[360] — WALLACE STREATER, TREASURER, FROM HIS REPORT FOR THE MONTH ENDING APRIL 30, 1909

BLACK "GOOD SAMARITANS"

☛ Memphis was in the hands of the Federals, and a cordon of pickets were around it on every side. My sister-in-law [Jennie] from Panola, Miss., had been in Memphis for some time, and was very anxious to get back to her home and family; but we did not know exactly how to manage her going. Finally it was decided that I should go with her, and the next question was our mode of conveyance. The Yankees had taken every decent carriage or horse on the place, and the only attainable thing to carry us was a dilapidated buggy with rattling wheels and holes in the top big enough to thrust your fist through. To draw this elegant equipage we had a flea bitten gray mule badly wind-broken and so thin that every bone showed. We started next morning early . . .

. . . It rained all that day, and we missed our way trying to take a short cut, and by dark we were entirely lost. Trying to ford a little creek, our buggy wheel stuck tight. I did all I could to get it out, but could not. I then stepped on the off wheel to see if my weight would not help, but missed my footing and lay [fell?] down in the creek. It was cold, and the water was filled with floating bits of ice. *I called and called, then Jennie and I called together, and soon we heard a dog bark, then a crash of footsteps through the underbrush and "Who dar?" in unmistakable negro tones. I begged him to come to our aid, and he said he would go and get a light. When he returned, his wife was with him. They proved to be caretakers of a large house whose master and mistress were away. The old darkies opened the house, made a big fire, supplied us with dry clothes from the mistress's wardrobe, and prepared us a delightful supper.* I never enjoyed anything more than I did that night's sleep in the four-post bed, so high we had to climb into it on steps, and piled up with feather beds halfway to the ceiling, it seemed to me.

Those darkies were genuine good Samaritans. She cooked us a good breakfast and sent us on our way with many smiles and courtesies and good wishes. He said he "would go wid you past dat long hill on de road, for dar is sho some pow'ful bad places dar in it." It was well he went, for halfway up the hill—crack, and our buggy broke half in two. The front part stayed on the hillside, fastened to a very much astonished mule. The back part, with Jennie and me sitting up in it, went rolling down the hill, and bumped right into a tree! Our good Samaritan went off across the field to the house of a neighbor, who came back with him, each armed with cotton rope. By the time they finished tying up that mud-spattered buggy with white rope it was a sight that would have made a sphinx laugh. Taking together the ties our first escort had made in the harness and the knots our last escort made in the buggy, there was not much of our outfit that was without its decorations except the mule's tail, which he needed to flap. This he did constantly, except when he got it over the reins, when I had to lean over the dashboard and lift it to freedom. This interesting proceeding occurred every mile or two, and effectually prevented any monotony.

. . . [After numerous other adventures we finally made it to] Jennie's

James W. Joplin and family. Six of his sons were Confederate soldiers.

home, in Panola. We had been five days on the road, and *were certainly glad when we heard the noisy welcome of dogs, darkies, and children when we turned into the long lane that led "home"* [all emphasis, L.S.].³⁶¹ — MRS. EMILY S. LEDYARD

WHITE YANKEE RACISM ALIVE & WELL IN 1910

☛ The Supreme Court of *Iowa has recently decided that "private business concerns can legally refuse to serve negroes."* This decision is very significant of the feeling engendered by a personal knowledge of the African race. Only a few years ago the North was rampant for the equality of the black brother, many of the most fiery orators actually claiming that the bar against intermarriage should be removed. This decision of the Iowa Supreme Court shows the Northern tendency now. Following fast on this decision, which came about through a suit brought because a negress was refused service at a pure food exhibit, comes another from the Supreme Court of New York, equally a guidepost to the present equality questions in the North, for *New York rules that a private school may legally refuse entrance to a negro*. In theory the negro is the social and racial equal of the white, and this ruling that the word "private" to business enterprises or schools can be used to bar them promises "future development."

Apropos of the negro question, it is well to call attention to the statements made by various Northern [that is, Left-wing] newspapers that

Mammy and her "pet."

the negroes were not receiving their full share of school appropriations, but were being denied in Southern States their legal educational rights. *Atlanta, Ga., makes official reports that the negro girls' college has three times the endowment fund for negotiable property that the eleven white girls' schools of the State have all together* [all emphasis, L.S.].³⁶² — CONFEDERATE VETERAN MAGAZINE

"MY OLD BLACK MAMMY"

☛ She was lovely to me in her colored bandana
With which she turbaned her head.
Her songs were far sweeter than flute or piano
As she put me to sleep in my bed.
Her soft, crooning voice I can never forget.
Like an angel in dreams she comes to me yet.³⁶³ — COLONEL JAMES "JIM" [P.] GORDON, OF MISSISSIPPI

GEORGIA MEMORIAL TO THE BELOVED BLACK MAMMY RECEIVES FULL SUPPORT ACROSS THE SOUTH

☛ S. F. Harris, who is one of the foremost *negro educators in the South*, has started in Athens, Ga., a memorial to the old black mammy, *loved of all Southern hearts*, which is meeting with hearty success [my emphasis, L.S.]. This takes

the form of an industrial and cooking school, which will be located on ten acres of land just outside of Athens. The necessary funds for this school have so readily been subscribed [mainly by white Southerners] that Professor Harris thinks it will be in full operation by fall.³⁶⁴ —
CONFEDERATE VETERAN MAGAZINE

OBITUARY OF A BLACK CONFEDERATE SOLDIER: PRESS ROBERTS
☞ Old Uncle Press Roberts is dead. No longer will the faithful old darky be seen trudging along with shuffling gait behind the gray-clad ranks of Company A. Never again will the black hand of the faithful old slave be raised in salute to "de colonel" or "de cap'n" at a Confederate Reunion, for old Uncle Press has joined the phantom ranks of gray on the other side of the river.

William Lowndes Yancey.

Although he was seventy-two years old, he was tilling his field near Germantown when he was overcome by the heat, and after lingering several days died.

When the war broke out, Uncle Press followed "massa" into the thick of the battles. He stuck with the Confederate army until the end; and when the news of the surrender came, he felt as badly as any gray-coated soldier. After the war he rarely missed a Reunion, attending to the baggage and looking after the comfort of the members of Company A.

During the four years that Col. Edward Bourne was commander of the Tennessee Regiment of Veterans Uncle Press was his body servant, and *there was no more faithful man in the regiment. Many white friends attended the funeral* [all emphasis, L.S.].³⁶⁵ —
CONFEDERATE VETERAN MAGAZINE

MORE ON PRESS ROBERTS
☞ [Personal note appended to the entry above: "Uncle" Press Roberts] . . . *was one of the faithful old darkies who followed and served his master in the Confederate army throughout the war, and ever since had loved the Confederate soldiers and the cause for which they fought. At all times he voted as he understood they wanted him to vote. He rarely missed any large gathering of Confederates in this section, and was always cheerful and ready to serve the old soldiers. He served me faithfully over four years* [all emphasis, L.S.].³⁶⁶ —
COLONEL EDWARD BOURNE, IN THE *MEMPHIS APPEAL*

RADICAL LEFT-WING *NEW YORK POST* SPREADING ANTI-SOUTH PROPAGANDA IN 1910
☞ The *New York Evening Post* [now the *New York Post*, founded in 1801 by big government Liberal Alexander Hamilton] in its splenetic way maintains that the erection of a statue to Robert E. Lee in the national capital "cannot free him from the reproach of having chosen to lead the forces that battled for human bondage."

The *Baltimore Sun* stingingly rebukes the *New York Post*: "The Post is sufficiently intelligent to know that Lee never did this. He was not in favor of human bondage, as he proved by manumitting his own slaves. The *Post* knows that Lee took command of the Southern army, not to support human bondage, but to repel the invasion of his native State. The *Post* knows that when Lee took command of the army slavery was not the issue, and Lincoln had given the distinct assurance that it was not the purpose of the North to interfere with slavery, but to preserve the Union, and that alone. *The South was fighting for the right to leave the Union, and the North fought to prevent it* [my emphasis, L.S.]. *Emancipation had no official indorsement when Lee took command. . . .*"[367] — CONFEDERATE VETERAN MAGAZINE

PROVEN FACTS ABOUT LEE, LINCOLN, THE WAR, SLAVERY, & ABOLITION

☛ . . . On January 1, 1863, Lincoln issued his emancipation proclamation, and for the first time slavery entered as a war issue, and it was forced in by the [Liberal] North. The true significance of this proclamation has never been properly estimated. *The President of the United States of America has more power than any constitutional monarch on the globe, and in nothing has this power been more flagrantly abused than in this proclamation.* The [Conservative] South was gaining in strength and the anti-war feeling was increasing in the North, and the supremacy of the war party of the North depended upon a crippling blow to the South by other means than arms, and *the deadliest method was the destruction of the labor source of the South*, thereby crushing all industries of whatever kind; still worse, cutting off the possibility of food supply *and, more heinous still, arming the slaves against their owners.* "Therefore, I, Abraham Lincoln, President of the United States, by virtue of the power vested in me as commander in chief of the army and navy of the United States"—so runs the language of this document—issued a proclamation freeing the slaves in the Confederate States of America, disposing of the property of another nation with its own established government, and so acknowledged by all civilized nations. *This blow, intended for the South alone, was in reality a treasonable attack upon the foundation of the entire fabric of American governing institutions and an open defiance of international law.*

Abraham Lincoln did not free the slaves of the South. *The proclamation in itself had no more weight or value than a like proclamation issued by him freeing the serfs of all the Russians. The power to issue such a proclamation was not vested in him as President; in that capacity his act was autocratic, unconstitutional, treasonable.* But it was not even in his office as President that he issued this proclamation; it was as "commander in chief of the army and navy" that he issued it, thereby as subordinate usurping powers specifically delegated to the executive and legislative branches of government and arrogating to himself power forbidden those branches. *The Constitution oi the United States in guaranteeing the "inviolable rights of the free, independent,*

William Henry Seward.

sovereign States" permits and defends the institution of slavery. The Constitution of the Confederate States opposed slavery, and forbade the importation of slaves. The last cargo of slaves brought to America came in a ship built in a Maine shipyard, owned by a Massachusetts company, commanded by a Massachusetts captain, and manned by a Massachusetts crew. The only Southerners in any way connected with the transaction were the crew of the Confederate vessel commanded by a Confederate lieutenant, who captured the slaver and returned the negroes to Africa. General Lee, the Confederate commander in chief, was not a slave owner. General Grant, the Federal commander in chief, through his wife owned four slaves. The Republican party [then the Liberal Party] in power, having consented to Lincoln's autocratic proclamation as a means to cripple the South, was in consequence compelled to indorse it after the fall of the Southern Confederacy. Whether the power Congress conferred upon itself in the Thirteenth Amendment is valid is a question to be settled in the future.

The anti-war feeling at the North became intense, and it grew more difficult to secure troops. Accordingly on June 20, 1863, Lincoln violated Article IX of the Constitution by seizing a large part of Virginia's territory and railroading it into the Union as the State of West Virginia. William H. Seward called attention to there being no law to sanction the seizure. "But," said he, "we have the power, and might makes right." The Northern anti-war feeling making it well-nigh impossible to obtain fresh troops, on August 19 of the same year Lincoln [unlawfully] suspended the privileges of the writ of *habeas corpus* throughout the Union. As the years wore on, the impoverished, exhausted South could not withstand the overwhelming, well-supplied forces of the North. Yet so gallantly did Lee's starving, ragged veterans hold off the enemy—the whole line of defense averaging one man to the mile—that Lincoln sharply inquired of his commander in the field "if he couldn't break through. Such a long, slim animal must have a weak point somewhere." Grant replied that he was "hammering away." So the hammer swung and the rapier parried and thrust till *the memorable 9th of April, 1865, when surely was enacted the strangest scene known among nations—the victor laid down arms to the vanquished. The South won in its fight for the preservation of the Constitution and lost in the armed struggle with a superior force. The North lost in its fight against the Constitution and won in the armed struggle with an inferior force. Principle versus brute strength. Brute strength won the battle. Principle vindicated itself, and so triumphed. Both won, both lost.* Yet so formidable was the ragged gray line that half an hour before it laid down its arms it drove the Union army before it. Lee knew the end was inevitable. *To prolong the struggle was to wipe out the "seed wheat of the South." This great general was never greater than in the hour of defeat.* General Grant in his hour of victory, great in his magnanimous treatment of a vanquished foe, rose to nobler heights in forcing his government to keep faith and respect the terms of surrender.

Miss Metamora K. Hurley.

Forty-five years have passed since that 9th of April marked the close of an epoch in history, and the victorious North, intoxicated with power, has not yet learned to temper power with justice. *Robert E. Lee fought for the preservation of the Constitution and all it involved, and he saved the Union, though defeated in arms.* Article III, Section 3 of that Constitution says:

> "Treason against the United States shall consist only in levying war against them or in adhering to their enemies, giving them aid and comfort. No person shall be convicted of treason unless on testimony of two witnesses to the same overt act or on confession in open court. The Congress shall have power to declare the punishment of treason; but no attainder of treason shall work corruption of blood or forfeiture except during the life of the person attainted."

This plain language admits of no ambiguous construction, yet the United States government has persistently and deliberately violated it. *The charge of treason was never legally brought against General Lee, for the simple reason that the North knew there was no basis upon which to prefer such a charge or secure conviction. Yet Congress in direct violation of Article III, Section 3, and of Amendment V, forcibly confiscated General Lee's beautiful estate of Arlington, and refuses to make any compensation therefor to his heirs* [all emphasis, L.S.].

Robert E. Lee was never arraigned by court-martial or Congress; but he was tried before the world's tribunal, and the verdict was: "Gen. Robert E. Lee—Christian gentleman without reproach, soldier without peer."[368] — MISS METAMORA KINGSLEY HURLEY, BEDFORD CITY, VA.

Monument to Confederate General Robert E. Lee, Monument Avenue, Richmond, Virginia.

WHITE TENNESSEANS GIVE "SUBSTANTIAL" FINANCIAL ASSISTANCE TO HELP BUILD RETIREMENT HOME FOR FORMER BLACK SERVANTS

☛ A large gathering of ex-slaves and their descendants was held in Memphis, Tenn., in February [1910], at which it was decided to build a substantial home for the dependent old [black] people. *Many of the prominent white citizens of Memphis are cooperating in this movement, giving encouragement by substantial assistance* [my emphasis, L.S.]. Committees were appointed, with L. W. Wallace as chairman and H. H. Hume secretary, to solicit funds and carry out plans.[369] — *CONFEDERATE VETERAN* MAGAZINE

YANKEE BECOMES CONFEDERATE SOLDIER AFTER EXPERIENCING THE REAL SOUTH

Burr Bannister.

☛ Your letter found me at home, having met with an accident by a fall on an icy walk. I was born October 19, 1836, in Brockport, N.Y., and received my education in Rochester and Lima, N.Y. In 1853 I went to Michigan, then to Tennessee. There I studied dentistry at Shelbyville and made my residence in Richmond, and obtained practice in surrounding towns and the country, which I enjoyed. My practice often took me to the homes of your people, the simple life and novelty so different from Northern society that I expected to find. *I soon learned to unlearn many wrong impressions I had of Southern people. In the North no sermon, lecture, or song was popular unless some* [negative] *impression was made on our younger minds such as would be drilled into our ears by the song, "The poor old slave way down in Tennessee," who I found to be a most happy and contented being* [my emphasis, L.S.] . . .[370] — FROM A LETTER BY FORMER CONFEDERATE ORDERLY SERGEANT BURR BANNISTER, 2ND TENNESSEE FIELD BATTERY, DATED DECEMBER 27, 1909

A SOUTHERN MONUMENT FOR FORMER SLAVES

☛ General Orders, No. 6, under date July 30, 1910: [The following] resolutions [were] adopted at the Birmingham Reunion, held June 9-11, 1908:

Whereas there has been and still is a ready recognition throughout the Southern States of the faithful and praiseworthy, the peaceful and lawful course and conduct of the slaves toward their owners and their many unprotected families during our interstate war, 1861 to 1865; and whereas we deem it just and due to the good faith and good name of said slaves, as also to their former owners, and to history, that this highly instructive and most significant fact be formally promulgated and perpetuated; therefore be it

Resolved, That it is the sense of the delegates and representatives of the United Confederate Veterans that a stately and durable monument should be erected at some central and appropriate site in the South to the quietude and praiseworthiness and to the fidelity and of the slaves to their masters and their families during the great interstate war of 1861 to 1865.

Only those familiar with the beautiful patriarchal life on the Southern plantations previous to 1865 know of the devotion of the slaves to their owners and the children of the family. They were reared like members of a large household. The children of the owners and of the slaves associated most intimately together, and enjoyed alike the pleasures of the home, all receiving the care and attention of the heads of the family, who had a tender feeling for these dependents [my emphasis, L.S.].

When during the war the men of the South were at the front and no others at home but women and children, these slaves attended with the usual care to the

duties *of the plantation and looked after the comfort and well-being of the defenseless family with fidelity and devotion. Then, too, the negro boys were with the young men in the army. They accompanied them on their hazardous expeditions, shared their dangers, cared for them when sick or wounded, and occasionally bore their bodies from the field of battle, and finally carried the precious remains to the sorrowing ones at home* [my emphasis, L.S.].

Can any man or woman at the South think of these things and not feel the deepest, interest and the highest pride in the behavior of these loyal slaves? The men and women of the South—the U.C.V., the U.D.C., the U.S.C.V., and the C.S.M.A.—owe it to themselves to see that some evidence is given to the world of their appreciation of the faithfulness and affection of this devoted people. The General commanding hopes that steps will at once be taken to remedy the neglect that has existed so long.[371] — *CONFEDERATE VETERAN* MAGAZINE

The Battle of White Oak Swamp.

FIGHTING FOR STATES' RIGHTS NOT SLAVERY

☛ Reading in the October *Veteran* the comment on "Suppose the South Had Succeeded," it brought to my mind Mr. [Jefferson] Davis's speech while on a visit to the Army of Tennessee [C.S.A.] just before its start under [Confederate] General [John Bell] Hood into Tennessee [Note: Hood took command in July 1864]. Our division, [Henry DeLamar] Clayton's, [Stephen Dill] Lee's Corps, was drawn up in a square around the platform on which the President and Gen. Howell Cobb addressed the division. Mr. Davis's speech was a masterful effort to enthuse the soldiers for future deeds of valor. What he said that particularly struck me and has stayed in my memory to this day was:

> "They are going to have an election up North. It lies between [Conservative Union Gen. George B.] McClellan and [big government Liberal U.S. President

Abraham] Lincoln. You would naturally think that General McClellan as a Democrat [the Conservative Party at the time] would suit us very well if he could be elected; but I think, however, that if McClellan should be elected there will be a division or another secession between the East and the West. There would be an Eastern and Western as well as Southern Confederacy. The West, on account of the Western rivers which would flow to the sea through our land and those by the highway of commerce, might think it advisable to join hands with us; but we would not accept their offer of a union with them. We would tell them it was impossible; that there had been too much blood spilled between us, but that the rivers would and shall be free for our common commerce."

Union General George Brinton McClellan.

These words left an impression on my mind that I have not forgotten. They were the very words our President spoke; therefore if the South had succeeded by the secession of the West from the East through McClellan's election, one of the things that would have happened, according to Mr. Davis, would have been the free Mississippi River. The other question, States' rights, would also have been settled for good in the way we believe it was intended it should. The third, slavery and slaveholding aristocracy, would certainly have continued for a time; but Russia's first abolishing the slavery of the serfs, Brazil emancipating slavery, the West India Islands following suit, *an anti-slavery movement in the South*, would have become an immense lever against them, to which they would have had to yield or have the world against them.

There were too many nonslaveholding soldiers (called [by the black racist term] "white trash" by the slaves) that fought for States' rights bravely, but not for the perpetuation of slavery [all emphasis, L.S.]. It was supposed in early days that no white labor could raise cotton, sugar, rice, etc., on extreme Southern plantations; but this idea has long since been exploded by actual facts, which further make the South generally more prosperous than in olden times.[372] — J. C. HARTMAN, SHIPPINGPORT, PA.

SOME HISTORICAL TRUTHS

☛ . . . Nearly two hundred years after the discovery of this continent there came to the bleak shores of New England a colony of men calling themselves the Pilgrim Fathers, or Puritans. They came, they said, seeking religious liberty and freedom from persecution, but in course of time as they grew strong *they grew bigoted and intolerant*. They persecuted other religious bodies and drove them out of the colony; they burned innocent men, and women, and little children as witches. *The* [Northern Left-wing] *descendants of these witch burners are the same men who many years after attempted to set up a moral standard for the balance of the world.* They passed what are known as the "blue laws," some of which were the most absurd imaginable, among which was one that a man was not allowed to kiss his wife on Sunday and many others as ridiculous. Not many years afterwards a [Yankee] ship sailed for Africa and kidnaped a shipload of natives, and this was the first link in the chain of events which brought on the most stupendous war since the dawn of time. It drenched this continent in fratricidal blood, and the end is not yet. . . . I am no apologist for slavery; but *Northern men commanding Northern ships introduced slavery into this country, and after trying slave labor and finding it unprofitable sold the slaves to the South, and then held up holy hands in horror at the enormity of slavery.*

The State of Georgia held a State convention to protest against the importation of slaves; but after the invention of the cotton gin by Eli Whitney, who, by the way, was not the inventor of the gin, Joseph Watson antedating Whitney by several years, *the culture of cotton became profitable and the slave trade was acquiesced in.* At this point I will state that the first steamboat ever operated was by Judge [James] Longstreet [Sr.], father of Confederate General [James] Longstreet. Anaesthesia was discovered by Dr. Crawford W. Long, of Georgia, and the first sewing machine was invented by a Mr. [Frank] Goulding [of Georgia].

In the course of time there sprang up an abolition party [a group of radical Left-wingers later closely associated with socialists and communists] in the [Liberal] North with the sole object of freeing the slaves of the South, notwithstanding the Constitution recognized slaves as property. The abolitionists said: "The Constitution is in league with hell and a covenant with the devil, and slavery should be abolished."

The history of American slavery in two sentences: In the 1600s Yankee, not Southern, ships began sailing to Africa's West Coast, where they purchased Africans who had already been enslaved by their African neighbors. When, later, slavery was deemed unprofitable in the Northeast (due to the short growing season, harsh winters, and rocky, sandy soil), New England's African slaves were pushed onto a reluctant Dixie, at which time Victorian Liberals began to use them as political pawns in their ongoing socioeconomic war against the Conservative South.

[Liberal Yankee novelist] Mrs. [Harriet Beecher] Stowe wrote *Uncle Tom's Cabin*, which was *an infamous slander upon the people of the South*, and [scalawag and anti-South activist Hinton Rowan] Helper wrote a volume entitled *The Irrepressible Conflict*. While there were many books written against the South, the two mentioned inflamed the [Liberal] Northern mind more than any others. In 1858 Lincoln ran against [Yankee Conservative Stephen A.] Douglas for the United States Senate, and in a speech at Freeport, Ill., he made the statement that this country could not exist half free and half slave; that it must be all free or all slave. About this time [radical Left-wing Yankee] John Brown, with some other fanatics [socialists], seized Harper's Ferry and tried to incite a servile insurrection and murder the men, women, and children of the South. In 1860 Lincoln was elected President by the Northern people on a sectional platform, *not getting the electoral vote of a single Southern State*.

Many people said the South was too hasty; they ought to have waited for an overt act. What were the speech of Lincoln, the books of Mrs. Stowe and Helper, and the John Brown raid? The South struck at the only time it could before its hands were tied, and it struck a knightly blow!

. . . The Federal government mustered into service 2,800,000, besides 34,000 seamen; the South mustered 600,000 all told. You matched us man for man and then had 2,200,000 more. What men could do we did, but the odds were too great and we were overwhelmed. There were 200,000 Germans, 200,000 negroes, and 400,000 men of the Southern States against us.[373]

Well, Appomattox came and with it came the end of the war. These disasters were followed by a reign of terror worse than war. It was the carpetbaggers' era. The [Southern] white people [that is, Conservative Southern Caucasians], the soldiers who defended their homes and firesides, were disfranchised and their former slaves were given the ballot. It was said this was done to punish them—punish them for what? Men who would not fight under such circumstances would be despicable.

. . . I have referred to the days of Reconstruction. If it had been left to the gallant fellows who faced us on so many bloody fields, we would have been spared such horrors, for "the bravest are the tenderest, the loving are the daring;" but it was the [progressive Yankee] politicians of the [radical Left-winger] Thad Stevens type who were too cowardly to fight but persecuted us after we were down.

Radically Left, South-hating, Yankee busybody, Thaddeus Stevens.

. . . I cannot close my address without paying a tribute to the faithfulness and loyalty of the slaves. There was a bond of sympathy and affection existing between master and slave that was sublime. I had a happy childhood. I had no young brothers and sisters, and my childhood playmates were slaves. We played, hunted, and fished together, and a happy, joyous life we had. Good slaves were rarely ever punished. Now and then you would find a cruel master, as now cruel, brutal, drunken husbands who abuse their children and whip their wives. If they were the unhappy, discontented people they were pictured, why did they not rise when their masters were in the army? Instead they toiled patiently to keep us in food and took loving care of the women and children left to their care. I love the memory of old slave times; I love the old family slaves as I do my own kindred. The South is going to raise a monument, towering high above the earth, to their memory [all emphasis, L.S.]. . . .³⁷⁴ — DR. R. S. WARD (CO. C, MORGAN'S SQUADRON), CLARKSON, KY.

VICTORIAN LIBERALS REVERSED THE FACTS & GASLIT THE AMERICAN PUBLIC

☛ . . . The South accepted the defeat of her armies in the utmost good faith, and not one man in ten thousand would change the result if he could; and I feel that I voice the sentiment of every Confederate soldier when I salute the stars and stripes as the flag of our country, the only flag and the only country to which we owe allegiance, but that does not mean we fought for a "lost cause." *The soldiers of the Confederacy rebelled against Federal power, but they were not traitors.* Those who still call us traitors and rebels think treason is the child of the South and that it was conceived in the sin of slavery and was born in the iniquity of secession. They overlook the fact that *treason, slavery, and secession are all children of New England. The first of all the colonies to legalize traffic in human slavery and to pass laws for the regulation and control of trade in African slaves was Massachusetts. The first speech ever made in favor of the dissolution of the Union was made by a Congressman from New England. The first convention ever held on American soil to consider the question of secession was held in New England, and was participated in only by representatives from New England States. They did not then think that secession and the right of local self-government were treasonable heresies* [all emphasis, L.S.]. . . .³⁷⁵ — GENERAL HAMBY

United Confederate Veterans' uniform button. The Confederate Cause was Americanism, or what we now call conservatism. Therefore, it was not a "lost cause." It was and is an *eternal cause*, one that is more vigorous today than ever before in American history.

TRIBUTE TO A BLACK CONFEDERATE, FRIEND, & LOYAL SERVANT

☛ A strict and steadfast loyalty is a true and tried patriotism; and when this matchless type of loyalty shows itself in crucial test, it should be acknowledged, whether emanating from the heart of a white or black man.

Recently I noticed where a U.C.V. Camp attended the funeral of an old negro man who had served throughout the war with a member of the Camp, and afterwards had attended all their meetings, always fearlessly asserting his allegiance to our cause.

I wish now, over forty-five years since my man-servant, John Bull, left with me, a lad of sixteen years, for the Southern army, to pay tribute to his unswerving loyalty and rigid honesty. John was a St. Johns, S.C., negro, being reared on a plantation about forty miles north of Charleston.

Many Confederate soldiers had their servants with them in the army. My father furnished me one of the best servants on the place. John Bull served me most

Elijah Cox, former black servant, Texas, circa 1937-1938.

faithfully before Sherman's army on the coast of South Carolina from the battle of Honey Hill to Charleston and then throughout the North Carolina campaign to the surrender on April 26, 1865, at Greensboro, N.C. His loyalty to me was proverbial, and he soon became so well known that his spare time was put in doing washing for officers who had no servants, and all were glad for him to make his pocket money—to forage with, for he was a hustling provider for our camp.

The battles of Averysboro and Bentonville were fought within two days of each other, so that I was away from my servant and camp for about three days. When I started into the battle of Averysboro, I handed John a wallet, made out of oil matting (now called linoleum), containing about $500 [$15,000 in today's currency], saying to him that if I should not return he could use it and make his way home the best he could.

After the first day's fighting, we met a courier, who had brought us some white fat bacon and corn bread, knowing that we had nothing to eat with us. To my surprise, he said to me: "We had to threaten to arrest that man [servant] of yours last night." But when I asked what was the trouble, his reply filled me with pride. He said: "When night came on, John insisted on going on the battlefield to look for you, saying, 'I can't 'go home an' tell Missis I don't know where Mars Samuel is.'" Well, I was naturally very glad to know of his loyalty and concern.

After the battle of Bentonville, I returned to camp. The first man I met was John Bull. His radiant face told me more forcibly than words could possibly have done his delight at seeing me as he came forward to take my horse. The first thing he said was, "Well, sir, I'se had bad luck while you'se gone; de camp ketch fire an' nearly all de clo's an' washin' bu'n up, but I save, dis," and he hauled out of his pocket my wallet of money, all safe, but with the matting around it so burnt and charred that I could just break it off. His pants, in the pocket of which it was put away, were burned up, and my washing and that of the other officers was entirely destroyed. How easy it would have been to let the money go too; but he did not, and returned every cent of it untouched. That was not only loyalty but a well-tried and tested honesty as well [all emphasis, L.S.].

After [Confederate Gen. Joseph E.] Johnston's surrender at Greensboro, N.C., I had one horse and most of the same money. I took the horse and gave John the money for the second time, and told him to make his way home by offering to pay on railroads, wagons, or any way he could get a ride. He beat me and my horse to Aiken, S.C., about three hundred miles, just twelve hours, and to my surprise opened the gate for me on my arrival, wearing that same look of joy on his darkly tinted but brightly honest face.

I have often told this as an example of an old-time negro's loyalty and honesty.[376] — SAMUEL W. RAVENEL, BOONVILLE, MO.

BLACK CONFEDERATES MENTIONED IN THE OBITUARY OF MRS. ELLA PALMER

☞ ... Prior to the battle of Shiloh, in 1862, while at Chattanooga [Mrs. Palmer's] ... interest in the work [of systematic nursing] was aroused by the sick and dying [Confederate] soldiers who had contracted pneumonia in the wet trenches at Forts Donelson and Henry. These men were taken to Chattanooga and put into an old academy and other vacant buildings. At that time the hospital corps, in addition to a large number of surgeons and physicians, consisted of men detailed from the army to act as nurses, cooks, and such other positions as were necessarily filled about the hospitals. Of course these men had no previous experience. Negro men and women, principally field hands from the surrounding plantations, were also utilized [my emphasis, L.S.] ...[377] — CONFEDERATE VETERAN MAGAZINE

SOUTHERN BLACKS PLAYED MANY IMPORTANT ROLES IN THE WAR

☞ At a meeting of the Magruder [Confederate Veterans] Camp, Galveston, Texas ... Comrade [Col. James P.] Gordon told several interesting stories of the part the [Southern] negroes played in the war, of their devotion to the mistresses left alone by the men being in the army, of the faithful following of a soldier master by his negro servant, also their loyalty in times of trouble [my emphasis, L.S.]. ...[378] — CONFEDERATE VETERAN MAGAZINE

OBITUARY OF BILL KING: BELOVED BLACK CONFEDERATE

☞ Bill King is dead. Members of the 20th Tennessee (Battle's) Regiment will remember him. *No more faithful negro ever served a cause than did Bill King serve the boys of the old 20th.* He went into the war as the body servant of the sons of Mr. Jack King, of Nolensville, Tenn., but *he became the faithful servant of every member of this regiment.* He went with the brave boys into the heat of battle, he nursed and cared for them in sickness, and assisted in burying the dead on the battlefields. *He was as true to the cause of the South as any member of that gallant band* under the intrepid leadership of Col. Joel A. Battle. In Shiloh's bloody affray Colonel Battle was captured, and the leadership fell to young Col. Thomas Benton Smith.

When one of his young masters was killed in battle, Bill was one of the escort which tenderly bore the body back to his mother and father.

Since the war Bill King had been classed as an unreconstructed Rebel. *He was a true and loyal Confederate until his death.* He affiliated with old soldiers, attending every gathering within his reach. He was a member of Troop A, Confederate Veterans, Nashville. He lived on his old master's farm, near Nolensville; but he died in Nashville at Vanderbilt Medical College, where he underwent a serious surgical operation.

Mr. William Waller, an undertaker, took the body back to Nolensville for burial. *The body was clad in the Confederate uniform which he had during the past few years worn on all reunion occasions, according to his request.* The funeral

Miss Margaret Anderson, Maid of Honor, Chattanooga Reunion.

service was conducted in Mount Olivet Methodist Church (white) by the pastor, Rev. H. W. Carter [all emphasis, L.S.].

Bill King was seventy-three years old, and leaves a wife and ten or eleven children. He was a Baptist; but as there is no church of this denomination near his home, his friends decided to have the funeral in the Methodist church. He was buried in the Nolensville Cemetery.[379] — *CONFEDERATE VETERAN* MAGAZINE

CONFEDERATE CAPT. "BILLY" SMITH & HIS LOYAL BLACK CONFEDERATE SERVANT JACK

☛ Captain William ["Billy"] T. Smith of Montgomery County, Virginia, whose death occurred suddenly at his home, the Meadows, February 7, 1910, was a prominent and popular farmer and one of the most gallant officers of the Confederate army.

. . . He was ardently loved by his men, and was accounted the handsomest man in the regiment [Company F, 14th Virginia Cavalry]. He always rode a fiery horse, and *was accompanied to the war by his body servant, "Jack," who never left "Mars Billy" from the day he was born till he followed his lifeless form to the grave, driving "Mars Billy's" old sorrel at the head of the long funeral procession. Captain Smith never believed in negro slavery, and when the war broke out gave Jack his freedom; but the negro has remained true to his white folks through all these years. "Mars Billy" was his idol, and so completely did he imitate his voice that members of the family often mistook one for the other* [my emphasis, L.S.].[380] — *CONFEDERATE VETERAN* MAGAZINE

THE SOUTH IS & ALWAYS HAS BEEN THE LEADER IN AMERICA'S DEVELOPMENT

Charles Cotesworth Pinckney.

☛ It is a fact that the greatest actors on the stage of the Revolutionary War were [Conservative] Southerners. They were leaders in battle and council. Twenty years before a shot was fired Patrick Henry, of Virginia, was denouncing the oppressions of the British in the colonies both in the courts and on the hustings.

Thomas Jefferson wrote the Declaration of Independence, and a year before that the Mecklenburg Declaration of Independence was proclaimed in North Carolina.

[George] Washington was commander in chief of the armies in the field, the Corypheus [that is, the leader] that led them to victory at Yorktown.

Richard Henry Lee, the other Lees, Masons, Pendletons, and Randolphs were peerless orators and statesmen in council. [James] Madison is called the "Father of the Constitution," but Charles Cotesworth Pinckney, of Charleston, S.C., more than any other man contributed to its formation and adoption—all Southerners.

The [Conservative] *Southerners ruled the republic successfully and happily till* [big government Liberal Abraham] *Lincoln came with war, havoc, and desolation such as the annals of nations have never disclosed of any other people. Cruelties and outrages unprintable were in Sherman's march through Georgia and* the Carolinas. *The fathers of the republic planned better things for their descendants.* Now [1910] *the outlook for the South promises results that will be an honor to this great country and to the cause of civilization. Happily the negro problem is becoming eliminated, as the negroes must see that their best friends are Southerners* [all emphasis, L.S.], *and cotton will be the balance in moneyed powers.*[381] — WILLIAM G. HORSLEY, GREENVILLE, TEX.

IT WAS NOT ABOLITION BUT THE MANNER OF ABOLITION THAT MATTERED TO WHITE SOUTHERNERS

☛ My Dear Lankford: Your kind favor of July 27 [1885] contains that which is well calculated to cause one's thoughts to revert to the good old days *when we were battling against the world for our independence. We failed, but we (the South) have the satisfaction of knowing that no people on the earth endured or fought more from patriotic desires. We were overcome by the hirelings of the world, who were ignorant of our people, devoid of honor and patriotic duty. As we all surrendered, it behooves us to abide by the terms imposed. Nobody cares that slavery is obliterated. It was not the loss of slavery we so much objected to, but the manner of its abolishment.* . . .[382] — FROM A LETTER BY CONFEDERATE GEN. JOHN ORVILLE SHELBY TO GEORGE W. LANKFORD, AUGUST 2, 1885

EXPERIENCES OF WHITE & BLACK FAMILIES DURING THE SHELLING OF FREDERICKSBURG

☛ . . . On the 9th of December [1862] the mother of Mrs. Goolrick was awakened by some one tapping at her window, and her nephew told her he had just returned from the Federal camp, where he had gone in disguise, and he knew that Fredericksburg would certainly be shelled at daylight, and that the family must escape at once. There was no one to help them get away and no horses or wagons. At four o'clock [A.M.] they were awakened by a crash which seemed to tear the earth asunder, and which was quickly followed by another crash of a shell that exploded right in the yard.

Hastily seizing whatever clothing they could, the family fled to the cellar, where the house mother had previously sent some chairs and a sofa for just such an emergency. *The negroes huddled in the cellar also. The fat cook, Aunt Sallie, had her little pickaninnies* [children] *with her, and slapped* [them] *right and left if they made their*

Between 1861 and 1865, the Liberal North wreaked untold death and destruction across the Conservative South. This photo, taken in April 1865, shows the ruins of the Petersburg Railroad Depot at Richmond, Virginia. No intelligent person believes that the cause of abolition was behind such mindless violence.

presence known by a squeal of fear or a jump as the shells broke all around the place. The widow remembered her husband's picture in the room above; and though shells were flying every moment, she left the cellar in pursuit of it. She could not reach the picture string from a chair, so she put the chair on a sofa and lifted it down. With the picture in her arms, she was only halfway to the door when a shell broke through the wall, splitting the chair and sofa into kindling wood.

"Uncle Charles" was a bright and shining light among the negroes; and while the fury of the shells made hearing even difficult, the old man was on his knees beseeching the throne of grace for mercy on "ole miss and de chillens" as well as on his wife and little ones. Then as a big shell burst right at the door of the cellar he fell flat on his face and howled: "It's done come now sho nuff."

The Union attack on Fredericksburg, with buildings burning in the background. Pencil and ink drawing by Alonzo Chappel, December 1862.

Later the shelling ceased, and the family went upstairs, to find the place a mass of shattered woodwork, plaster, and furniture, with toppled chimneys added "to make confusion worse confounded." They found some food and went back to the cellar, when the shelling began again. Finally it ceased altogether, and they went out to a scene of such utter desolation that words were inadequate to describe it.

[Confederate] General [Robert E.] Lee gave orders that every one should leave the town of Fredericksburg, as it might become necessary to fire the place at any moment, and a bombardment from the Confederates was imminent. The family, wrapped in whatever they could find, began its exodus, carrying not even their jewels or valuables in their hurried leaving.

The walk through the melting snow was very hard upon the women, and they were glad to reach Refugee Camp, where they remained for weeks, enduring every discomfort. Finally the women and children were permitted to leave camp and return to what had been their home. They had to cross the battlefield, and here the little boy picked up a bayonet which he afterwards used to toast bread upon as well as a means of stirring the fire.

They cleaned out one room as well as they could, and from all over the house brought any article of furniture that was too badly broken. They had a little rusty stove which served both for heating and cooking purposes. *The first night the little family were domiciled in this caricature of their old home a faithful negro from town came with a pitcher of milk and a loaf of bread as a gift, and these offerings he brought every day while the cold weather lasted* [all emphasis, L.S.]. In the spring, through the kindness of friends, the family moved to Danville, Va., where they remained till the end of the war, when they returned to their desolated home.[383] — AS REMEMBERED BY MRS. FRANCES BERNARD GOOLRICK (U.D.C.), THEN A CHILD

LOYAL BLACK CONFEDERATE TAKES UP ARMS AGAINST THE YANKS

☛ ... While ... [at home on leave] the question would arise as to what was man's first duty, to his family or his country. If I lost all that life holds dear, what is my country or any country to me? And so through the long, sad hours of that night and day these thoughts surged through my mind, until the fateful moment for me to leave had come. My little darling clung to me with the tears streaming down her wan face, begging me not to leave her. But had I not given [Confederate] General [Patrick Ronayne] Cleburne my soldierly pledge that I would return before the expiration of my leave, or die in the attempt? And so I left, but with a broken heart and the sad, despairing little face looking into mine with every sorrowful step I made toward camp.

My father-in-law, Col. Matt Stratton, and Capt. Tully Craig, with *my faithful negro Ned, accompanied me on my return*. After crossing Sand Mountain and as we approached Wills Valley, we were told by parties we met that the valley swarmed with Federal soldiers; and as our route took us down the valley some distance and then across it, we kept a sharp lookout for the enemy. We had just descended the mountain and gained the valley when we saw some hundreds of yards off and approaching us six mounted soldiers. We could not discern at that distance whether they were Federals or Confederates, but supposed they were Federals. They evidently had seen us too, for they were unslinging their guns and getting ready for the expected fray. As they approached slowly I suggested that we had best determine whether we should fight or run. I reminded the gentlemen that as my leave of absence would shortly expire I must force my way, and *I felt sure that we would win, only six to four, if Ned would fight. I turned and asked: "Will you fight, sir?" Ned answered promptly: "Yes, sir, I surely will."* ... [all emphasis, L.S.].[384] — CAPT. H. J. CHENEY, NASHVILLE, TENN.

Confederate Gen. Patrick Ronayne Cleburne.

WHITE CONFEDERATE VETERANS WANT PHOTOS OF BLACKS AT CONFEDERATE REUNION

☛ While taking pictures at the Mobile [Confederate] Reunion there were *several veterans who wished to secure pictures of the old negroes there* [my emphasis, L.S.]. Unfortunately I lost the list of names. One gentleman paid for a picture. If those persons still desire the pictures, same will be sent them.[385] — MRS. RUTH EVANS DENISON, MARSHALL, TEX.

BLACK CONFEDERATE: ANDREW WALKER

☛ ... I was superintending the men under me in tearing up the flooring of the large foot bridge to prevent the enemy from passing over with their cavalry and heavy ordnance, as [Confederate General Pierre G. T.] Beauregard was thought to be rapidly pursuing this part of [Union Gen. James H.] Wilson's command. Here the noble young [Lieut.] McKnight was killed, and he was on leave of absence from "Leed's Light Horse," New Orleans. *My servant, Andrew Walker, received a slight flesh wound* [my emphasis, L.S.], but from his wild expression, showing so much of the white of his eyes, it was evident that he "thought that his time had come." Mr. W. C. Camp, proprietor of the hotel, who left the bridge for the fort to report, had both eyes shot out. So sad! Lieutenant Lee, of Tennessee, was anxious to help out; but his horse was killed, and he could not reach the fort. ...[386] — S. F. POWER, NATCHEZ, MISS.

BLACK SERVANTS PARTICIPATE IN WEDDING OF WHITE COUPLE

Mrs. Olivia Moore O'Neal.

☛ Olivia Moore was born in Murfreesboro, Tenn., in 1819; but in her infancy was taken to Huntsville, Ala., where she grew into a brilliant girlhood. While in the bloom of her early teens she met and married Edward Asbury O'Neal [later to attain the rank of brigadier general, C.S.A.], a handsome youth, even then distinguished by his intellect and keen grasp of facts and their relative significance. This marriage took place in Huntsville on April 12, 1838, and was an event of great social interest. There were eight bridesmaids and attendants, and it was followed, as the fashion of the day, with many entertainments and feastings. Relatives of both families vied with each other in the brilliancy of their entertainments, and the "infare," as these wedding festivals were called, lasted for several days. The wedding guests went from one house party to another equally as brilliant, till all the near relatives who lived near enough had done honor to the young couple. *The darkies were conspicuous in connection with these wedding feasts, for they felt that the marriage of their "young missis" was something that touched their family pride, and they were anxious to add to the general merry-making; so the sound of the banjo and stamping of the "pigeon wing" came from the cabin as an accompaniment to "Money Musk" and "Sir Roger de Coverley" in the "big house"* [my emphasis, L.S.]. The marriage was very happy. The two were close friends and comrades always, the wife's aid being given in all the questions of importance in her husband's rapid upward career. ...[387] — CONFEDERATE VETERAN MAGAZINE

WHITE MISTRESS IN SEARCH OF FORMER BLACK SERVANT

☛ Wants to Find an Old Family Servant: Miss B. B. Brewster, of Corpus Christi, Tex., *desires to know the fate of an old family servant named Sylvia Byrd, as she wishes to assist in taking care of her* [my emphasis, L.S.]. Miss Brewster formerly lived in Greenville, Tex.[388] — CONFEDERATE VETERAN MAGAZINE

SEEKING MILAN COOPER, SERVANT OF JEFFERSON DAVIS

☛ I am trying to locate *Milan Cooper*, an old darky who claims to be *one of the last and faithful servants of* [Confederate President] *Jefferson Davis* [my emphasis, L.S.]. It is said that he lives in Dade County, near Miami, Fla. I should like very much to secure data pertaining to this old darky and his merits. If he really served Mr. Davis faithfully, I want to bring him to our city. Information will be appreciated.[389] — A. W. CORBETT, ST. AUGUSTINE, FLA.

FROM THE OBITUARY OF CONFEDERATE GEN. GEORGE DOHERTY JOHNSTON

☛ Following Dr. Snedecor's address, the Rev. Dr. D. D. Little delivered an eloquent tribute to the man who had been a great help and inspiration to him in his own work in behalf of the negro. Dr. Little said that General Johnston was preeminently a man of the Old South, the embodiment of all the honor, chivalry, and hospitality preserved in romance and tradition. He referred to the exemplary character of the deceased, and declared that if he had been surrounded by all his friends his last message to them would have been: *"Be true to the Old South and its ideals, be good to the black man in our midst, and keep faith in God"* [my emphasis, L.S.].[390] — *CONFEDERATE VETERAN MAGAZINE*

YANKEE'S SPEECH TO A "GREAT GATHERING OF NEGROES" AT FISK UNIVERSITY, NASHVILLE, TENN.

☛ . . . We can better understand the anti-slavery agitation in its bearings on the development of our national history when we remember that in the formation of the [American] Colonization Society, of which Henry Clay [Abraham Lincoln's "beau ideal"] was President, the conscience of anti-slavery men, both at the North and South, found a most effective opiate in the doctrine of gradual emancipation and deportation of the slaves to Africa. [Lincoln himself was a leader in and a lifelong member of the A.C.S.].[391]

Henry Clay.

So as we look back upon the war it ought to have for us no sting or bitterness, but every angry thought should be stilled in presence of a great sorrow. On both sides were men of the highest principle and the noblest intention, giving themselves up in heroic devotion and self-sacrificing bravery to what they thought was true.

Sometimes the question is asked *"Were not the slaves better off under slavery than they are now under freedom?"* I think a candid answer to that question demands us to say that some were better off under slavery than they are under freedom. The abolition of slavery acted on the colored race like a wedge, forcing some down and some up. Those who were fit for freedom, prepared to embrace and make the most of the opportunities offered them as free men, rose. But some were not fit for freedom. Now that is no reflection upon the colored race. We have a very large proportion of the white race that is not fit for freedom. We have innumerable numbers of men and women that we are compelled to confine in institutions and keep as wards of the State, or they destroy themselves and everybody else.

If slavery was an unutterably evil institution, with no alleviating features, how are we to account for the fact that when the Confederate soldiers were at the front fighting, as thought, for their independence, the negroes on the plantations took care of the women and children and old people, and nothing like an act of violence was ever known among them? I have seen in Charleston, S.C., a monument erected by former slaveholders and their descendants in grateful acknowledgment of the fidelity of those slaves who remained upon the plantations and cared for their women and children while they were at the front, and I understand that the Confederate veterans are also to erect another such monument.

Certainly such kindly feeling between master and slave shows that there must have been something good in the institution of slavery. Certainly that is the plain implication of *Uncle Tom's Cabin*, for the very noblest characters in the book, Mrs. Shelby, Eliza, Uncle Tom, St. Clare, and little Eva, were all the offspring of the institution of slavery and nourished on its breast, and certainly an institution that in itself was essentially wicked and diabolical could not have produced such noble characters. So we should not look back upon slavery as a reign of unalleviated wickedness and horror, but remember it had within itself, in spite of its many abuses and intolerable horrors, much that was good.

The abrupt emancipation of millions of Southern servants in December 1865, was much harder on black slaves than on the North's originally intended target: white Southern slave owners. Millions were immediately forced into abject poverty and homelessness, surrounded by crime, filth, and disease. It is estimated that at least one quarter of freed black Southern servants eventually died as a direct or indirect result of sudden abolition—a horror the South had long tried to prevent.

. . . It is an unfortunate thing, to my mind, that the color line has been so drawn as it has been drawn, and that the attention of both the races is of necessity so concentrated upon the fact of color. But that is inevitable. It cannot be otherwise. *To my mind the only solution is that your people should develop their own peculiar culture, their own peculiar race pride, and remove prejudice, not by protest, but by doing away with all worthy cause of such prejudice. That comes through thrift, economy, education, intelligence, and work of character* [all emphasis, L.S.]. It is a difficult problem that is before you for solution. I believe you are solving it, and upon you educated young men and women who go forth as teachers, leaders, and inspirers of your own people rests a great responsibility, but with that responsibility a mighty opportunity for good.[392] — DR. CHARLES E. STOWE, SON OF HARRIET BEECHER STOWE

WHITE RACISM & ANTI-ABOLITION SENTIMENT IN THE NORTH

☞ [Left-wing Northern history books have been lying to the public for so long about so-called "Southern racism and slavery" that it is worthwhile resuscitating the following facts:]

1. In 1843, fourteen years after the Missouri controversy, "leading abolitionists were brutally attacked and their dwellings, together with a number of churches, schoolhouses, and negro homes in various parts of the country, were destroyed; Philadelphia had a three nights' riot in which the mob assaulted nearly fifty houses inhabited by negroes;" and Arthur and Lewis Tappan, natives of Massachusetts, noted abolitionists in the city of New York, were mobbed, the dwelling house of the latter and its contents being destroyed.

Radical Left Yankee meddler, Massachusetts socialist William Lloyd Garrison.

2. In the later months of 1835 "attacks on negroes and abolitionists were of daily occurrence." Such agitators as William Lloyd Garrison and George Thompson, abolition missionary from England, were mobbed in Boston, the former . . . by "gentlemen of property and respectability."

3. In 1835 an angry crowd broke up the school of Prudence Crandall in Canterbury, Conn., because she admitted negro children as pupils, destroyed valuable property, and had her imprisoned in the town jail.

4. In 1835 Thompson, the English missionary, wrote to the Leeds (England) *Mercury* that "rewards were offered for his abduction and assassination;" that "New England had universally sympathized with the South;" and Senator Isaac Hill, of New Hampshire, stated that Thompson "had escaped from Concord in the night and in woman's clothes."

5. In 1837 Rev. Elijah P. Lovejoy, publisher of an abolition newspaper in Alton, Ill., was killed by a mob, and his printing establishment was destroyed.

6. In 1838 the Pennsylvania Hall, belonging to the abolitionists of Philadelphia, was attacked by a mob and burned, the shelter for the colored orphans was fired, and the negro quarters were attacked.

7. In 1838 [Quaker poet] John G. Whittier, now famous for his calumnious "Barbara Frietchie" and his "Astraea at the Capitol," faced an enraged mob in Philadelphia, which destroyed his printing office, where his abolition newspaper, the *Pennsylvania Freeman*, was published.

8. In September, 1841, in angry crowd in Cincinnati destroyed several houses belonging to abolitionists.

9. Far into the [eighteen] "fifties" . . . Wendell Phillips delivered his abolition addresses "in the face of threatened attacks of mobs;" and was . . . "ostracized in Boston and rotten-egged in Cincinnati."[393] — COL. B. F. GRADY, CLINTON, N.C.

JOHN BROWN WAS NOT AN ABOLITIONIST "SAINT" BUT A RADICAL LEFT-WING AGITATOR & MURDERER

☛ John Brown—Sir: Although vengeance is not mine, I confess that I am gratified to hear that you were stopped in your fiendish career at Harper's Ferry, with the loss of your two sons. You can now appreciate my distress in Kansas, when you entered my house at midnight and arrested my husband and two boys, took them out of the yard and in cold blood shot them dead. This was in my hearing. You can't say you did it to free slaves; we had none and never expected to own one. You made me a disconsolate widow with helpless children. While I feel for your folly, I trust you will meet your just reward. O how it pained my heart to hear the dying groans of my husband and children.[394] — LETTER FROM MAHALA DOYLE TO JOHN BROWN, CHATTANOOGA, TENN., NOV. 20, 1859 (JUST DAYS BEFORE BROWN WAS CONVICTED & HANGED ON DEC. 2, 1859)

CIVILIZATION OF NEGROES IN THE SOUTH

☛ Slavery is now a part of American history which began in twelve of the American colonies, which subsequently formed the American Union of States. As a recognized institution of the government it was carried into the Southern States as they were admitted to the Union. The importation of Africans as slaves was prohibited by law in 1808. *The African, coming from a barbarous state and from a tropical climate, could not meet the demands for skilled labor in the factories of the Northern States; neither could he endure the severe cold of the Northern winter. For these reasons it was both merciful and [good] "business" to sell him to the Southern planter, where the climate was more favorable and skilled labor not so important. In the South the climate, civilization, and other influences ameliorated the African's condition, and that of almost the entire race of slaves, which numbered into the millions before their emancipation. It should be noted that their evangelization was the most fruitful missionary work of any modern Christian endeavor. The thoughtful and considerate negro of today realizes his indebtedness to the institution of African slavery for advantages which he would not have received had he remained in his semibarbarism waiting in his native jungles for the delayed missionary.*

Permit me to refer to a native African owned as a slave by my father. He left Africa when a youth, and brought a knowledge of affairs which existed in his native country. He would take me on his knee and recite for my entertainment the customs of his people in their native land. He became a very devout and consecrated Christian, and was withal a man of more than average intelligence for one of his race. *I often heard him*

Victorian Conservative Southerners considered him "Satanic": radical socialist outlaw and murderer John Brown. Though fellow Yankee socialists, like Henry David Thoreau, portrayed Brown as a "Christlike" figure, in Dixie his villainous legacy lives on.

express thanks to his Heavenly Father for the institution of African slavery, for on account of it he had learned of the true God and of his Son Jesus Christ. "But for it I would have been left in the darkness of superstition and heathenism."

Philanthropy and beneficence characterized the great majority of Southern slave owners. Besides, there was too much money invested in a slave to allow abuse that disabled him from labor. His health and strength were linked after as a matter of profit. Likewise were food, raiment, and shelter provided.

As to the spiritual consideration, *it was common for master and servant to worship together in one audience. On many plantations the servants were assembled for religious service, and often on Sunday morning a Sunday school was held for their special instruction.* It was through these that the colored "parson" got his knowledge of the Bible, of which they were wont to say: "I b'lieves it from kivver to kivver, and follows my Lawd down into de ribber."

Indeed, the Christian master was interested in the physical and spiritual welfare of his slaves, as was the Centurion who besought Jesus to heal his servant. Concerning the faith of this Roman slave owner the Saviour exclaimed: "I have not found so great faith; no, not in Israel." Could not such faith have been exercised by an American slave owner? *That unkindness, and by some masters cruelty, was inflicted none deny; but such was the exception and not the rule. In every clime and in every institution may be found "one whose brute feeling ne'er aspires beyond his own mere brute desires."*

Dred Scott and his wife Harriet.

Commendation is due the officers of Massachusetts and Boston for returning the fugitive slave, Anthony Burns. . . . By doing so they honored the Constitution, the compact between the States. The decision in the Dred Scott case verified the return as constitutional. Every State and Federal officer had taken oath to obey, to support, and to defend the Constitutions of their respective States and of the United States. The same oath-taken obligation rested on every white man by virtue of his citizenship. Another notable precedent for returning a fugitive slave is given by Paul, the apostle fo the Gentiles, who recognized both law and expediency in returning the fugitive slave, Onesimus, to his master, Philemon, who himself was a Christian and a slave owner. Paul was a great example as a Christian patriot.

Let the historian justly consider the men and causes that brought on the Civil War. *The Southern States entered the Union as slave States, so cannot be charged as having held slaves without the consent of the Union.* This union was entered into by the States "for better for worse," as the combined strength was needed to oppose the mother country. *The [Conservative] South sought to maintain the Constitution and the rights of the States to police State rights. The [Liberal] North interfered with State affairs which existed in the formation of the Union. The South contended for the Constitution, the North for the Union.* Slavery being the issue, malignancy was freely indulged in by both sides. It was not American to endure passively. Then followed

Southern secession against *Northern rebellion*. The Constitution was lost; the Union was saved. Millions of lives were directly and indirectly sacrificed, billions of dollars expended, and the results are not yet recorded. *The war was not justifiable. If the nation had heeded the teachings of Southern statesmen prior to the [eighteen] sixties, without war slavery would eventually have been abolished, the emancipated slaves colonized, and the Union preserved without the shedding of blood. The leaven of emancipation had found place in Southern minds, and would have quietly leavened the whole lump, had not abnormal ferment been injected, which precipitated resentment. Not to resent would be to consent that contumelies were deserving. The South was beaten but not broken.* If the South had forseen defeat, she might have exclaimed as did Demosthenes: "I say, if the event had been manifest to the whole world beforehand, not even then ought Athens to have forsaken this course, if Athens had any regard for her glory or for her past or for the ages to come."

"The past is irrevocable; the future is improvable." This was the home cry and hope of the returned Southern soldiers. New lines must be run. With no precedent or experience as a compass to guide, never did people survey more wisely the unexplored regions of both social and civil embarrassments than the people of the South. The scars of war remained, and the sore places, often bruised, would bleed afresh; but in their zeal they looked not to present comfort, but to future welfare. Thus they showed that "noble souls, through dust and heat, rise from disaster and defeat, the stronger."

The South gave to history heroes that class with the heroic of any age. The world sings their praises and destiny takes care of their honor. The South has sworn allegiance to the new Union and to the amended Constitution, and will prove as loyal as in the days of [George] Washington, [Andrew] Jackson, and [Zachary] Taylor, and as heroic as when led by [Confederate Gen. Robert E.] Lee [all Conservatives]. *The South has no apologies to offer for her course*, however much she deplores any cruelty or injustice by either section. Let the reunited nation say, peace to the past, cooperation for the present, "one and inseparable now and forever."

U.S. President Andrew Jackson.

In the funeral oration of the great [Daniel] Webster in memory of [Southern Conservative] Mr. [John C.] Calhoun, believing that the same mutual confidence and respect exist in the minds of both Northern and Southern men, he said: "He (Calhoun) had the indispensable basis of all high character: an unspotted integrity and unimpeachable honor. There was nothing groveling or low or meanly selfish that came near the head or heart of Mr. Calhoun. Whether his political opinions were right or wrong, they will descend to posterity under the sanction of a great name. He is now a historical character. We shall indulge in it as a grateful recollection that we have lived in his age; that we have been his contemporaries; that we have seen him, heard him, known him. We shall delight to speak of him to those who are rising up to fill our places. And when, one after another, we shall go to our graves, we shall carry with us a deep sense of his honor and integrity, the purity of his private life and exalted patriotism."

U.S. Vice President John C. Calhoun.

It is a deplorable fact that after more than forty years of civil liberty by the Africans in America so many of them are untrustworthy [having been indoctrinated by the radical Left to hate white people and white culture]. In former days the planter without fear intrusted his wife and daughters to "Uncle Tom" and his sable sons. *Uncle Tom's Cabin* was a fort of protection for the family. Mr. Tom's sons [that is, the new post-war generation] are terrors to the Anglo-Saxon woman. She once could visit her neighbors without fear; but not now. The Southern people are censured because of mobs. Mobs should be discouraged in all righteousness everywhere. The mobocrats do not all reside in the South; and it is safe to say that mobbing will usually follow the "nameless crime." There is an innate law in all consciences against "forceful abduction." It is the duty of all civilization to educate and restrain against such unnamable crimes without condoning the crime or criminal.

Would it not be just for you in this series of sermons to state the examples of cruelty to slaves as exceptions and by no means the rule? "Uncle Tom's Cabin," *missed the benefits of African slavery, for the slaves were being lifted from barbarism to civilization and Christianity. The crimes committed in the name of slavery were far less than the ills that befall strikers and other laborers.*

The sword of the South is her plowshare and pruning hook now. Let the stars that represent the Southern States on the flag shine in their true light.

(Appended note from *Confederate Veteran* magazine: Dr. Burress enlisted in the 19th Mississippi early in the war, and served with it for two years in Virginia. He was commissioned a lieutenant in the Provisional Army, C.S.A., and reported at Enterprise, Miss., where he served ten months. He was then commissioned to raise a company of boys for General [Nathan Bedford] Forrest. He served with his boy company to the end of the war, surrendering at Columbus, Miss. When commissioned as captain of his company of boys he was twenty years old. His boys averaged from fifteen to seventeen years, and he says: "As brave as the bravest and worthy of a better captain.")[395] — L. R. BURRESS, BROWNSVILLE, TEX., IN AN OPEN LETTER TO REV. N. DWIGHT HILLIS, D.D., PASTOR PLYMOUTH CHURCH, BROOKLYN, N.Y.

SOUTHERN BLACKS FAR & WIDE MOURN THE DEATH OF CONFEDERATE PRESIDENT JEFFERSON DAVIS

☛ . . . When the end came at the advanced age of eighty-two in December, 1889, in the city of New Orleans, a wail of genuine sorrow went up from every part of the Southland, from Maryland to Texas, and the hearts of his people mourned for him as no man was ever mourned for. Hundreds of the leading men from every State of the South went to New Orleans to be present at the funeral ceremonies and pay a loving tribute of respect and esteem to the South's idol. Even his former slaves, who resided in distant parts of the South, attended with sorrowing hearts, and dropped their tears upon his bier. Strange as it may seem, even the negro population of the South showed their respect and love for this wonderful man by many tokens of genuine sorrow [my emphasis, L.S.]. In every State of the Old South there was a house of mourning. . . .[396] — FROM THE OBITUARY OF JEFFERSON DAVIS, BY JUDGE SAMUEL WHITE, PORTLAND, OREGON

BLACK MAMMY SUPPORTS THE CONFEDERACY & READS *CONFEDERATE VETERAN* MAGAZINE FROM COVER TO COVER

☛ Of the many who read the *Confederate Veteran*, no one is more interested perhaps than *an "old mammy,"* named Easter Partee Brownlee, who looks forward to its monthly visits with the keenest anticipation. She is a servant in the family of Mr. Samuel A. Pepper, of Memphis, Tenn., and *has been a faithful friend to his children for twenty-three years.* The enclosed picture was taken with the eldest of the children. The little girl is now grown and married, and "Mammy" lives with her, nursing the second generation. She came to Memphis from Aberdeen, Miss., having lived as a child in the family of Judge Locke Houston. *She knitted socks for the Confederate soldiers and helped to make the homespun dresses worn by the Southern ladies during the Civil War. She was never a slave,* her mother having been freed by Mr. Jimmie Jones, who moved to Mississippi from South Carolina; and her mother's children were also freed. When this Jones family moved to Columbus, Miss., Easter was left under the guardianship of Judge Houston. She lived in the Houston families of Mississippi until going to Memphis, her last home there being with the late Capt. Robert E. Houston, a well-known lawyer of Aberdeen. Soon after her arrival in Memphis, Easter entered the family she has remained with ever since, and her devotion and loyalty to its members has frequently been commented upon with well-deserved praise. *She is educated, and reads everything in the Veteran, learning from its pages of many white friends who will no doubt remember her. She sheds many a silent tear as she learns of the death of old time friends.* I suppose that she is one of the very few negroes who read this magazine, and as such I thought *her little history might prove of interest to those good Southerners who*

Easter Partee Brownlee (left) and unnamed Pepper child (right).

all love and honor our dear and faithful old mammies of the antebellum times [all emphasis, L.S.]. It is sad to realize that their tribe cannot increase the relation that is beneficial to both races. May all such find their reward when the day of judgment comes!³⁹⁷ — MRS. ALAN PEPPER SPEED, MEMPHIS, TENN.

TRUE HISTORY THE NORTH WILL NOT PUBLISH

☛ . . . *He who has spent much time in studying human nature as it appears in the records of different countries and different generations cannot hope to find in the writings of most of the authors of so-called histories of the United States many evidences that these authors were able to do justice to the people of the Southern States.* Here is what [one of these false histories] . . . says: "At the close of the recent war with England the South was more favorable than the North to a protective tariff. One cause of this was, it is asserted, that the South at first expected to work its own cotton, but this it could not do. Slave labor had not the intelligence to manufacture, and white labor could not flourish by the side of slave labor."

Yankee slave ships unloading their African human cargo at the docks in Washington, D.C. The U.S. Capitol can be seen in the upper right.

. . . *This is all misleading.* This act was to be in force for only three years, so as to compensate capitalists for the necessary losses which changes of occupations would entail; and as to the attitude of "the South," public records show that New England gave seventeen yeas and ten nays; that the Middle States, including Maryland, gave forty-four yeas and ten nays; and that Virginia, North Carolina, South Carolina, and Georgia gave fourteen yeas and thirty nays.

Hence the slap at slave labor and the disposition of "the South" must be considered as due to that sectional blindness which can [only] see the misdeeds of the "slave power" and deal blows to the "rebels."

According to [a more accurate history] . . . a great many Indian slaves were shipped to the West Indies and exchanged for negroes, a trade in which, as every one knows, the West Indian was cheated. In 1638 the Salem [Massachusetts] ship, the *Desire,* was sent by the Colonial [Yankee] authorities to Africa and brought back a number of negroes for whom purchasers were easily found. In 1643 the four New England colonies formed a confederation among themselves, mutually binding themselves to surrender fugitive slaves; and for a century or more, up to the [American] Revolution [1775], as "negro children were considered an encumbrance in a family" . . . they "when weaned were given away like puppies."

As slaves were not fit for seamen, slavery soon became worthless in New England; but what became of them? The normal rate of increase of colored people in the United States from 1880 to 1890 was 13.5 per cent; and, applying this rate to the colored people of Massachusetts, we find that 606 of them were carried out of the State in the decade closing with 1810, and that 916 were carried away in the decade closing with 1820.

To all this it is interesting to add that *all New England voted in the affirmative when a motion was made to substitute 1808 for the 1800 which had been agreed to in the convention which framed the Federal Constitution, and it is more interesting to add that during the period ending with 1808 there were shipped to the United States something over 143,000 slaves. Who brought them?* We may not err greatly if we suppose the answer to this question can be seen in the following statement made by the Duc de La Rochefoucauld-Liancourt, who came over to the United States in 1795. In his *Voyage dans les Etats-Unis* he says that *"nearly twenty vessels from the harbors of the Northern States" were busy shipping negroes from Africa "to Georgia and the West Indies."* And if this is not satisfactory, all doubt must be considered removed when we find in President Lincoln's message of December 3, 1861, this statement: "Five [Yankee] vessels being fitted out for the slave trade have been seized and condemned. . . . One [Yankee] captain, taken with a cargo of Africans on his vessel, has been convicted, etc."

. . . [Thomas] Jefferson's draft of the Declaration of Independence contained a bitter denunciation of George III because, as it said, *"He has waged cruel war against human nature itself, violating its most sacred rights of life and liberty in the persons of a distant people who have never offended him, captivating and carrying them into slavery;"* but when he submitted his paper to John Adams, of Massachusetts, Benjamin Franklin, of Pennsylvania, Roger Sherman, of Connecticut, and Robert R. Livingston, of New York, *this denunciation was stricken out.*

While Southerners like Thomas Jefferson were trying to abolish slavery as soon as practicable, Yankees such as John Adams (above) were voting to keep the slave trade open for as long as possible. Most Northern-slanted historians have removed these facts from their books.

. . . fifteen or twenty years earlier, when a prominent member of Congress who afterwards became a member of a presidential cabinet was coming out from a heated sectional debate, he was asked . . . : *"Will you tell me what is the real reason why Northern men encourage those petitions (for the abolition of slavery)?"* The reply was: *"The real reason is that the South will not let us have a tariff, and we touch them where they will feel it."*

[We also have] . . . a statement made in 1859 by Salmon P. Chase, a native of New England, who was then Governor of Ohio, and after serving in Lincoln's cabinet was appointed Chief Justice of the Supreme Court. Talking to W. D. Chadwick, he said: *"I do not wish to have the slave emancipated because I love him, but because I hate his master."*

When John Brown came into Virginia to "free the slaves by the authority of God Almighty," Gov. John A. Andrew, of Massachusetts, was one of his chief supporters, *the hope of the Massachusetts abolitionists being that the appearance of Brown and his little band would excite the slaves to rise up and murder the white people.* But in September, 1862, when [Union] General [John A.] Dix proposed to remove a number of escaped slaves from Fortress Monroe to Massachusetts, this Governor objected, saying, "I do not concur in any way or to any degree in the plan proposed," and he added: "Permit me to say that [due to entrenched white Yankee racism] the Northern States are of all places the worst possible to select for an asylum [for escaped black slaves]."

. . . [Union] Gen. Donn Piatt, who canvassed a part of Illinois for Mr. Lincoln in 1860 and spent some time in the company of the President-elect, says: *"He [Lincoln] knew and saw clearly that the free States [that is, the Northern states] had not only no sympathy with the abolition of slavery but held [socialist] fanatics, as abolitionists were called, in utter abhorrence."* And in another place he says: *"Descended from the poor whites of a slave State through many generations, he [Lincoln] inherited the contempt, if not the hatred, held by that class for the negro. . . And he could no more feel a sympathy for that wretched race than he could for the horse he worked or the hog he killed."*[398]

Union Gen. William T. Sherman was only one of many Yankee officials who openly disparaged those of African descent, like President Lincoln, sometimes referring to them as "niggers."

And to all this it is interesting to add the views of John Sherman, the brother of the famous [Union Gen.] William Tecumseh [Sherman]. On April 2, 1862, he said in the Senate: *"We do not like negroes. We do not disguise our dislike. As my friend from Indiana (Mr. Wright) said yesterday: 'The whole people of the Northwestern States are opposed to having many negroes among them and that principle or prejudice has been engraved in the legislation of nearly all of the Northwestern States.'"* And let it not be forgotten that the Northwestern States at that time were inhabited mainly by people who had emigrated, or those whose ancestors had emigrated, from Northern States, most of them perhaps from New England [all emphasis, L.S.]. . . .[399] — COL. B. F. GRADY, CLINTON, N.C.

SLAVEOWNING CONFEDERATE OFFICER OPPOSES SLAVERY

☛ [Confederate] Capt. S. B. Callahan, one of the most noted characters in the Southwest and famous as the last member of the second Confederate Congress, died at the home of his son in Muskogee on February 17, 1911. Captain Callahan was in his seventy-ninth year. He is survived by six children. . . . His last words were: "The way is clear."

His life was replete with dramatic incidents and historic episodes. He was three years old when his father and mother, with a large band of Indians, started from his birthplace at Eufaula, Ala., to the Indian Territory [what would later become the America's Western states]. His father died of privation and exposure on the way to the West.

Though a large holder of negro slaves prior to the Civil War, Captain Callahan was opposed to slavery; yet he was an ardent State rights man, and joined the Confederacy immediately after war was declared. He was a member of the Creek tribal council for a number of years, was chief justice of the Indian court system, was official interpreter for the Creek Nation, and was a delegate many times to Washington to represent the nation in legislative matters. *The Civil War found the Creek Indians largely slave owners, and many of them espoused the cause of the Confederacy* [all emphasis, L.S.].[400]
— CONFEDERATE VETERAN MAGAZINE

MORE EVIDENCE THAT SOUTHERN SLAVE OWNERS PROVIDED HEALTH CARE FOR THEIR BLACK SERVANTS

☛ Some time ago I came across the following entries on the ledger of a deceased [Southern] relative who practiced dentistry during the Confederate war: "1860. Mrs. H.: March 17, to four artificial teeth of gold plate, $20; March 17, to extracting two teeth *for servant (slave) girl, $2; April 19, to extracting one tooth for servant (slave) boy, $1* [my emphasis, L.S.] . . .⁴⁰¹ — DR. B. H. TEAGUE, AIKEN, S.C.

WHITE SOUTHERNER SEEKS INFORMATION ON BLACK SERVANT

☛ A reader of the *Veteran* is interested in tracing the family of a faithful slave, Martha Ann Square, wife of George Square (her master's name), who was taken from Richmond, Va., to Mississippi before the war, leaving behind her five-year-old son and a brother, Hy Thomas Square. She is very anxious to learn something of them, and it may be that some readers of the *Veteran* can give information of them through acquaintance with her master's family in Virginia. This can be reported to the *Veteran* at any time.⁴⁰² — *CONFEDERATE VETERAN* MAGAZINE

William Branch, former black servant, Texas, circa 1937-1938.

BLACK SERVANT SAVES LIFE OF CONFEDERATE SOLDIER

☛ . . . In September, 1861, when [Union] Colonel Mulligan surrendered to [Confederate] General [Sterling] Price, I lived on a farm about six miles south of Lexington [Missouri] and was a private in Bledsoe's Battery. About thirty days after General Mulligan's surrender General Price moved his army to McDonald County, in the southwest corner of the State. I started with the battery, but became ill, and was left near Greenfield at the home of [Confederate] Colonel [John T.] Coffee, who commanded a regiment in [Confederate] General [James E.] Rains's brigade. My brother, Dr. Robert B. Smith, was the surgeon of Colonel Coffee's regiment, and through him I was left in comfortable quarters. *My brother also left his servant, a negro boy about my age, as a nurse for me. Without his excellent service I certainly should have died. He did all that could be done for me, and I believe would have risked his life to save me from the enemy* [my emphasis, L.S.] . . .⁴⁰³ — F. COLEMAN SMITH, COLLIN'S BATTERY, SHELBY'S BRIGADE, C.S.A.

BLACK SOUTHERNER EAGER TO JOIN CONFEDERATE UNIT

☛ . . . An amusing incident occurred in the fight mentioned [a battle in southwestern Missouri, summer 1864]. When we charged the enemy on the hill, the enemy in their haste to get away undertook to have their horses jump across a [creek] branch five or six feet wide; their confusion may be imagined. They claimed to have killed one negro and captured another—maybe killed him also. *I remember having only one negro with us, and he was from Clay County. He wanted to join us, but I would not permit it, but told him he could go South with us and find a job. He was in that charge of our last fight, and was very proud when he captured a rifle and pistol with ammunition* [my emphasis, L.S.]. I know he was not killed. . . .[404] — S. H. FORD, CAPTAIN OF COMPANY F, 2ND REGIMENT MISSOURI CAVALRY, GENERAL SHELBY'S BRIGADE, C.S.A.

WHITE SOUTHERN WOMAN WORKS TO SUPPORT BLACK FAMILY

☛ . . . Near the beginning of the war the ladies of Raymond [Mississippi] gave two concerts for the benefit of the company that went from that town. One of the songs was that sweet old quartet, "Come Where My Love Lies Dreaming," sung by the Misses Calhoun, of Jackson, and their two brothers. There were also tableaux, and in one I was a fairy. The other concert was given in the courthouse, and "The Bonnie Blue Flag" was sung by several young ladies, each representing a Southern State and carrying its flag. After that our entertainments were few, for as the war went on news came of the death on the battlefield of so many of our brave young men, and so many families were in sorrow that no one had the heart to dance and sing. *In 1862 my mother began to teach school, for she knew that if we were not victorious some one would have to make the living for the family; besides, she had to support our negro cook, who had four children* [my emphasis, L.S.]. . .[405] — ESTELLE TRICHELL OLTROGGE, JACKSONVILLE, FLA

THE ALL-IMPORTANT QUESTION A YANKEE WANTS OTHER NORTHERNERS TO ASK THEMSELVES

☛ *Is it not perfectly evident that there was a great rebellion, but that the rebels were the Northerners, and that those who defended the Constitution as it was were the Southerners, for they defended State rights . . . [which is] distinctly entrenched in the Constitution?* [my emphasis, L.S.].[406] — DR. CHARLES E. STOWE, SON OF HARRIET BEECHER STOWE, BEFORE AN ALL BLACK AUDIENCE AT FISK UNIVERSITY, NASHVILLE, TENN.

Copperhead John Wilkes Booth.

LINCOLN'S ASSASSINATION HAD NOTHING TO DO WITH SLAVERY OR EVEN THE WAR

☛ The assassination of Lincoln could never be palliated; but we ought to feel a little differently toward [his murderer John] Wilkes Booth when we learn that he shot Lincoln to avenge the death of a schoolmate whom Lincoln executed after promising Booth to pardon him, and that [therefore] *the killing had no connection with the war* [my emphasis, L.S.].[407] — J. R. PORTER, NEW ORLEANS, LA.

PRESERVATION OF THE ORIGINAL CONSTITUTION WAS MORE IMPORTANT TO THE SOUTH THAN ANYTHING ELSE

☛ The Confederates fought for bigger things than crowns and higher principles than the tenets exploited by [socialist and Union Gen.] John C. Fremont, [radical Left-wing Yankee agitator] John Brown, [history-ignorant Yankee novelist] Mrs. Harriet Beecher Stowe, and the down-East people [that is, Yankees] who sold the negroes to the South, and then came down in 1861 with guns in their hands but without the price paid for them and demanded their return or freedom. . . .[408] — E. H. LIVELY, ABERDEEN, WASH.

"RELIEF" SOUGHT FOR FORMER BLACK CONFEDERATE SOLDIER

☛ N. P. Perrin, of Idabel, Okla., writes of *an old negro* there, *Lewis Crocker by name, who served in the Confederate army*, and who is now in much need, and Mr. Perrin wishes to get in communication with some one who knew him in early life. He belonged to Mrs. Polly Crocker, of Twiggs County, Ga., and he mentions a Mr. Bill Falk and Mr. Henry Land, whom he also knew. *It is hoped that some relief may be secured from his former owners* [all emphasis, L.S.].[409] — *CONFEDERATE VETERAN* MAGAZINE

Miss Lillian C. Reeves, of Camden, Ark., Maid of Honor First Brigade, Arkansas Division.

ALBERT: BLACK CONFEDERATE

☛ . . . A sister-in-law writes of [Confederate Major Joseph W. Anderson]: A nobler, more unselfish man never lived. His father was in Mississippi at the time, but no coffin could be procured, so his body was simply wrapped in a blanket. In November, 1863, Colonel Anderson, *accompanied by a servant, Albert, who had been with Major Anderson from the time of the battle of Bull Run* [my emphasis, L.S.], went to Mississippi and took the body to the grand old home in Botetourt County, Va., and buried it in the Fincastle Cemetery, where a simple stone marks the grave.[410] — *CONFEDERATE VETERAN* MAGAZINE

FAITHFUL BLACK SERVANTS "ALWAYS REMEMBERED"

☛ . . . His was a truly home-loving heart, shown in tenderness for wife, children, and grandchildren. He lived close to nature; he loved his trees and grass and vines. The birds and squirrels on his lawn he always cared for and fed, and *the faithful servant Anna, who had ministered to him and his for many years, was always remembered*. . . . Charles L. Ridley was born in Murfreesboro [Tenn.] in 1847, the youngest of five sons of Chancellor Bromfield Lewis Ridley. The four older boys, Jerome, Lucas, George, and Bromfield, enlisted early in the Confederate army. *The family then moved from Murfreesboro to their country home, Fairmont, near Old Jefferson, where Mrs. Ridley lived with her daughter and young son, Charles, with faithful servants until the stately home was burned by the Federals* [all emphasis, L.S.]. . . .[411] — FROM THE OBITUARY OF CONFEDERATE VETERAN CHARLES LEWIS RIDLEY

THE MYSTERY OF AUNT PATTY & POLYPHEMUS

☛ Away back yonder about the year 1845, when I was a small boy, there was a pleasant-faced, sweet-tempered old black mammy who often sat churning in the shade of the trees near our kitchen, and she always got butter. Churning was her favorite sort of work, for she was too fat to enjoy standing up. *She was a very good person, and was fond of telling stories to the children, white and black.* One which she told made a deep impression in a soft spot (soft then, not now) in my head. It was about a giant much bigger than our old friend Goliath of Gath. He was so big that he could pluck up a good-sized tree by the roots and use it for a walking stick as he waded out into the ocean to recapture his escaped prisoners whom he intended to eat—one every day. She said his name was Polyphemus.

Some years later when at school I got into Virgil to my surprise I read in Latin substantially the same story Aunt Patty the good had told me about terrible Polyphemus. I wondered how Aunt Patty, an unlettered negro, had come to know the story. Had her forbears brought it with them from Africa? or had some smart boy reading Virgil told it to her? If so, what boy? Before I had the opportunity to ask her how she learned it, Aunt Patty died and went to heaven, I believe, for she talked more about heaven than anyone I have ever known in my pilgrimage through this world.

I have retained all these years a good memory picture of Aunt Patty, but a rather shadowy conception of Polyphemus.[412] — A. J. EMERSON

Black female servant at the spinning wheel.

CONFEDERATE VETERAN LOVED BY ALL RACES

☛ On August 9, 1882, he [William L. Jackson] was married to Mrs. Sallie Fleming Winecoff, and in 1884 he joined the Presbyterian Church in Archer, Fla., and remained a faithful member until the call came. He was a noble type of the "old Virginia gentleman," with a cordial, jolly disposition, and he was ever generous toward his fellow men. During an illness of over a year and a half he showed the same courage and unselfishness that characterized his life. He was a devoted husband, and *was universally loved by rich and poor, white and black* [my emphasis, L.S.].[413] — FROM THE OBITUARY OF WILLIAM LITTLETON JACKSON, VETERAN OF COMPANY H, 6^(TH) VIRGINIA CAVALRY, C.S.A.

FORMER BLACK CONFEDERATE "GOES TO JAIL ON HIS HONOR"

☛ Cicero Finch, servant of the Finch family in Jackson County, [Georgia], "espeshully of Mars Ben Finch endurin' de war," is an honest man.

Deputy Sheriff Wiley Roberts took Cicero for a visit to the family whose harness he was accused of appropriating. Cicero had "plenty of chance" to get away, but he waited for the deputy and accompanied him to their destination.

Returning townward, the officer left the old negro to return to the jail alone. He presented himself at the grill door and asked for admittance. "Well, suh, here I is, and you know dem white folks jes natchelly knows I ain't guilty!"

Assembly of United Daughters of the Confederacy in front of Arlington Hotel, Hot Springs, Ark., November 1898.

He was sent back to the prison to await his trial. He was believed to have taken some harness from Mr. Crawford, at whose house he had done some painting.

Cicero stoutly denied guilt, and he said: "I is sixty-six years old, come nex' June. I b'longed to ol' Mars Charlie Finch, on Mulberry River, in Jackson County, eighteen miles from Athens. He give me my name, and I'se had it ever since. I lived wid him ontel he give me to little Mars Ben, and *I went wid him to de war*. You know when Petersburg blowed up? Well, Mars Ben was killed right dere, and *I got wounded in two places*. Dey sent me home to see my folks, and *atter dat I was in de Georgy war* [all emphasis, L.S.] and left here when Atlanta was took. Sence dat time I been workin' at mos' anything.

"Mostly I is a painter, but lemme tell you," the old negro laughed and slapped his leg with his broad-brim hat, "I is jes natchelly one of de finest roasters and hotel cooks in de land. An' lemme tell you somethin' mo': I never was whipped in my life and I never was up fer stealin'. I sho didn't git dem harness, and you knows dem white folks knows it. De ol' nigger is hones'; he is sho, boss."[414] — *CONFEDERATE VETERAN MAGAZINE*

BLACK MAMMY IN NEED SHOWERED WITH LOVE, GIFTS, & MONEY BY WHITE FRIENDS

☛ Tuesday was Aunt Rachel's seventy-ninth birthday, but it promised to mean no gala occasion for the faithful old woman. Until recently she had managed to earn her own living, supplying her simple wants as best she could through money obtained in nursing little children, washing, and general house-work. Now the knuckles of her hands are knotted with rheumatism. It was discovered that the faithful old negro faced her seventy-ninth birthday without coal or provisions in her little cabin. Her case was made public. While the old woman had never accepted charity in her life, she could not refuse the "birthday gifts" which were taken to her, and the gratitude as expressed by her was pathetic [that is, inciting mercy and pity].

Sarah Ashley, former black slave, Texas, 1937.

"I'se jus' bilin' with joy, honey," she said to Mrs. Booth, one of Miss Fannie Battle's right-hand workers in the United Charities of Nashville. All gifts for Aunt Rachel were sent to the United Charities and forwarded by them to her.

When the United Charity worker gave her the gifts, the old honest face lighted up with that "bilin' joy;" but when it came to the money, the old woman said: "Now, honey, you jus' pay de rent fo' a month and pay de dollar I owes on de burial insurance, and den you keep de res' till I jus' has to have it, 'cause shore as I have it myself I might spen' it on somethin' to eat which I might's well git erlong without."

The United Charities will keep the few dollars left after paying the rent and insurance, and will give it to Aunt Rachel as she may need it; but the clothes and the sirup and the pound cake and the roll and the meal and the tea and the bacon and the canned soup and the warm things to wear are in the possession of the old woman as *birthday gifts from white friends.*

The gifts were accompanied by little notes saying, "In memory of an old black mammy," or "For Aunt Rachel, wishing her a happy birthday," or some equally appropriate expression. As the little notes were read to her, the old woman's eyes filled with tears and she said: "Now, ain't dat sweet? De Lord bless whos'ever sent dat" [all emphasis, L.S.].[415] — CONFEDERATE VETERAN MAGAZINE

WHITES DEDICATE STONE TABLET TO THE MEMORY OF BLACK SERVANT JEMIMA RAYBURN

☛ "Aunt" Jemima Rayburn, who was a servant in the family of Maj. William Hume and then in the family of Mr. Leland Hume, serving the two more than forty years, had unusual honor paid her memory in marking her grave some time ago. The sons of the family, Leland, Alfred, Foster, Fred, and John D. Hume, the wife of Mr. Leland Hume, their son, William Hume, Jr., and her sister, Miss Trenholm, and some business associates *went to Murfreesboro in automobiles and dedicated a tablet to her memory in the presence of a large assembly of colored people* [my emphasis, L.S.]. The inscription states:

Erected to the memory of
Mrs. Jemima Rayburn;
Born Sept. 16, 1827; Died Oct. 30, 1908.
Beloved Black Mammy of _____

Names of the Hume sons and other inscriptions follow.
Addresses were made by a colored pastor, by Mr. Leland Hume, who gave a life sketch of the faithful woman, and by Alfred Hume, Vice Chancellor of the University of Mississippi, who was born soon after her service began in the family. It was a fitting event and made the occasion a reunion of the brothers. Mrs. W. C. Branham, of Spring Hill, the only daughter of Major and Mrs. Hume, was not present.[416]
— CONFEDERATE VETERAN MAGAZINE

ALBERT PEETE: LOYAL BLACK CONFEDERATE HONORED

☞ Albert Peete was buried on March 6, 1912, from the Colored Baptist Church of Nashville, Tenn. He was [Confederate] Gen. William B. Bate's cook for forty-five years. He was true and honest.
When the 2nd Tennessee Regiment [C.S.A.] was in Huntsville, Ala., the soldiers gave all their money to General Bate to take care of for them. He took Albert with him one night and buried half of the money, placing the other half under the floor at Martin's store.
Albert ripped up the floor and placed it back. Every cent of the money was returned to the soldiers after the war. The Yankees dug deep all over the yard looking for hidden treasure; and when they came near the crape myrtle tree at the front porch, it was feared they would find the money, but they missed it. Albert was uniformed by the Yankees and pressed into service [note: thousands of Southern blacks were similarly forced into the Union army, usually at gunpoint]; but when [Union] General [Lovell H.] Rousseau was informed that he was "rheumatic and always delicate and unfit for service," Albert was ordered dismissed.[417]
— CONFEDERATE VETERAN MAGAZINE

Albert Peete (Bate).

ALECK KEAN: MUCH ADMIRED BLACK CONFEDERATE

☞ Judge George L. Christian, of Richmond, writes of Aleck Kean, colored, as "faithful unto death":
Early in November, 1911, three of us, ex-members of the second company of Richmond Howitzers [C.S.A.] during the war of the sixties, honored ourselves by attending the funeral services of Aleck Kean, which took place near Green Springs, in Louisa County. *The career of Aleck as an honest, upright, faithful servant and man was so conspicuous and unique that it deserves this public notice.*
When the war broke out, John Henry Vest, a son of the late James M. Vest, of Louisa, entered the Confederate army as a private in the second company of Richmond Howitzers, and *took Aleck along as his body servant and cook*, as was customary in those days. The "Renfrew" mess was

soon formed with Aleck as the cook, and without hesitation I affirm that *he was the most faithful and efficient man in the performance of every duty pertaining to his sphere that I have ever known.* His whole mind and soul seemed bent on trying to get and prepare something for his mess to eat; and if there was anything to be gotten honestly, Aleck always got the share which was coming to his mess, and he always had that share prepared in the shortest time possible and in the most delicious way in which it could have been prepared in camp. *The comfort of having such a man as Aleck around us in those trying times can scarcely be described and certainly cannot be exaggerated.*

Young Mr. Vest (Aleck's young master) died in the fall of 1863, and after that Aleck, *although he had offers to go to others or to return to his home, had become so attached to the members of the "Renfrew" mess that he refused to leave them, and, with his master's consent, remained with that mess up to the very last, when he surrendered with them near Appomattox. He was always loyal, true, brave, honest, and faithful not only to the members of his mess but to every man in the 2nd and 3rd Howitzers, all of whom knew, respected, and admired his fidelity and efficiency.*

When the war ended, he went back to his old home. *His old master, Mr. James M. Vest, gave him a little home* a very short distance from his own dwelling, and it was there within hearing of his own people and always ready and willing to do their bidding that he spent the rest of his life. There was scarcely any one in all that community who was more respected by all the people, white and colored, than Aleck, and certainly no other deserved that respect and confidence more than he did. His funeral was largely attended both by white and colored, all of whom seemed anxious to attest by their presence the high regard in which he was held both as a man and a Christian.

Such a career of fidelity, loyalty, and devotion is worthy of being published to the world and ought to stimulate others, both white and black, to strive to follow his example. Nearly every year since the formation of the Howitzer Association an invitation to its annual banquet has been sent to Aleck, and whenever he was able to do so he attended. Every member of the association knew and respected him, and was glad to extend to him the cordial greeting which he received at these annual gatherings [all emphasis, L.S.].[418] —*CONFEDERATE VETERAN MAGAZINE*

BLACK CONFEDERATE "BLACK HAWK" GOES ON RECORD

☞ I thank you for putting my picture in your magazine. *I am proud of my war record.* I was given when a young man by my old master, Samuel C. Williams, who was a member of the Virginia Secession Convention, to his oldest son, who was then Lieut. James H. Williams, of Chew's Battery [C.S.A.], and I stood by him and his brothers until the close of the war. I was taken prisoner twice, captured once with the watches and money of our boys and others of the Williams mess upon my person, given into my care when the battle began. *I escaped and returned with watches and money all safe* [my emphasis, L.S.].

"Black Hawk."

The picture you published was taken while Dr. [James B.] Avirett was on a visit to Mrs. James H. Williams at Woodstock, Va. I was not Dr. Avirett's camp servant, nor was he ever a member of the Williams mess. As far as I know, Dr. William McGuire, of Winchester, Va., L. B. Morel, of Florida, and myself are the only living members of that mess. Rev. Dr. Avirett was often our guest.

. . . Like the rest of the [Confederate] veterans, I am growing old; but I am with my people in Woodstock, where I was born.[419] — "BLACK HAWK" WOODSTOCK, VA.

HONOR FOR THE OLD-TIME NEGRO

☛ The time is not far distant when a monument will be erected in Montgomery, Ala., or Richmond, Va., as a tribute to the memory of the old-time Southern negro. *The loyal devotion of the men and women who were slaves has had no equal in all history. They took care of the women and children whose natural protectors were with Lee and Jackson, Forrest and Joe Johnston, and were faithful to the trust.*

Women during the great war did not fear to ride alone through large plantations to give directions as to the crops. These women were protected and never outraged. It was the coming of the carpetbagger, with his social equality [that is, at the time, racially divisive communist] *teachings, that caused many negroes to become brutes* [all emphasis, L.S.]. The old-time negro will soon be but a memory, and while a remnant survive an imposing monument should be erected as a tribute to their faithfulness. It should be a monument worth fifty thousand dollars [$1.7 million in today's currency]. This money could be easily raised if the religious and secular papers in the South would take up the matter in the spirit that the cause merits.[420] — JOHN W. PAULETTE, IN THE *MORRISTOWN GAZETTE* (TENN.)

BLACK CONFEDERATE SERVANT PULLS WOUNDED WHITE SOLDIER OFF BATTLEFIELD UNDER "APPALLING FIRE"

☛ This contribution records a deed done during the war by one in the humblest walks of life, as heroic in character as any ever performed by the men who to-day proudly wear the victor's cross of honor. The facts were brought more vividly to mind by an accidental meeting with one of the actors recently. In the lobby of a hotel in Houston I noticed a tall, heavily built man wearing the cross of honor. I spoke to him as a comrade, and learned that he was a member of the staff of [Confederate] Brig. Gen. James H. Clanton, of Alabama. I then recognized him as Baxter Smith, ordnance officer of the command, now a practicing physician of Bay City, Tex.

Well, to the story. On the morning of July 14, 1864, a detachment of the 6th Alabama Cavalry, about one hundred and fifteen men, under the command of General Clanton, encountered a largely superior [Union] force of the Rousseau raiders at Greensport Ferry, on the Coosa River. Colonel Livingstone, with about two hundred and fifty men, was holding back the enemy's main body at Ten Island Ford. It was imperative for us to hold the road until reenforcements could reach us; otherwise the Oxford Iron Works, upon which the Confederate foundries at Selma, Ala., depended, would be destroyed.

The men had been well posted behind trees and rocks on the slope of a thickly wooded hill, and the road extended along the river bluff. The firing on both sides was spirited. The enemy, in spite of superior numbers, could not drive our boys from their position; but they seemed determined to gain possession of the road, and they formed a heavy column with which they could pass our thin line and clear the road before them. General Clanton and two of his staff officers, Capt. R. A. Abercrombie and "Bat" Smith, also Tommy Judkins, were standing in the middle of the road dismounted. A few feet away on the side of the road were five or six young fellows attached to headquarters and eight or ten boys of the 6th Alabama Cavalry, also dismounted. I was behind a large tree, a few feet in advance of the General, and had a good view of everything in front. A heavy column of the enemy on foot was coming around the curve of the road, about two hundred yards distant. Suddenly just behind me I heard a loud, fierce yell, and the two staff officers, followed by the headquarters' boys and the small squad of the 6th Alabama Cavalry, dashed at the enemy, who quickly poured a deadly fire upon them and then halted.

Abercrombie and Tommy Judkins were killed. Bat Smith and the handful of boys close behind him kept on. In a few seconds Smith fell headlong upon his face and then turned over on his back. The effect of the enemy's fire was appalling. Not one of that gallant little band was left standing. The charge was reckless in the extreme, but it illustrated the spirit and high courage of our soldiers. That feat of daring was followed by another of the lowliest and humblest man there present. A tall, strapping, young negro named Griffin approached General Clanton and asked: "General, where is Marse Bat?" The General pointed down the road and said: "There near the enemy's line dead." Griffin at once started down the road. *He was called back, but did not heed. He sped on in the face of that heavy fire, took up the wounded young officer, and carried him in his arms from the field.* He came up the road for a few yards, then stepped into the woods and came out again on the road just where the General was standing. "Is he dead, Griffin?" asked General Clanton. "I don't know, sir," he replied. "Mammy was his nurse, and I am the older. I promised mammy to take care of him and to bring him back to her, and I am going to carry him home."

Simple words, but how much do they convey! *An untutored negro slave carrying out his mother's commands in behalf of her nurseling at the risk of his own life! I have often thought of that day, and the scene is vivid. I can see the deathly pale face of the unconscious and sorely wounded young officer as he was being carried to safety in the arms of his faithful slave* [all emphasis, L.S.].

If some of our Northern neighbors could have witnessed this scene, they might form some conception of the devotion existing in the old days South between master and servant.[421] — SAMUEL COLEMAN, SIXTH ALABAMA CAVALRY [C.S.A.]

Battle of Malvern Hill.

SOUTHERN WHITE WOMAN LOVES "ALL GOD'S PEOPLE"

☛ . . . In all things she was a devout Christian and Bible student and Methodist, *a dear lover of all God's people. Protestant and Catholic. Jew and Gentile, black and white, high and low* [my emphasis, L.S.]. *Her life was strangely long and singularly noble and beautiful.* . . .[422] — FROM THE 1912 OBITUARY OF MRS. ANNE J. HAMILL, CULLMAN, ALA.

Mrs. A. J. Hamill.

BLACK CONFEDERATE ESCAPES YANKEE CAPTURE & RETURNS TO HIS CAMP

☛ Reference to monuments to our servants in the Confederate army in the *Veteran* . . . recalls a work of that grand patriot, William H. Howcott, of New Orleans. With the hearty approval of the citizens of Canton, Miss., from which locality many of us enlisted in Harvey's Scouts, of [Confederate] General [Nathan Bedford] Forrest's army [C.S.A.], he, at his individual expense, bought a lot adjoining the Canton Cemetery and erected a very imposing monument to our faithful negroes. It is splendid and cost about $3,000. Like "Black Hawk" [see articles above] . . . *my "boy" Ben was captured by the Federals, escaped, and returned to our company* [my emphasis, L.S.]. Mr. Howcott belonged to it.[423] — JAMES L. GOODLOE, MEMPHIS, TENN.

BLACK MAMMY STEALS FROM YANKS TO SUPPLY CONFEDERATE FAMILY

☛ . . . [Confederate] General [Samuel Gibbs] French's command was just one mile nearer town [Nashville, Tenn.] on the 15th of December. They fell rapidly back to the Compton Hill, on which [Confederate] General [William Brimage] Bate's command was intrenched. From the windows of our home I watched the camp fires of our boys all night of the 15th of December. They were camped in my father's hills and the hills of my great-uncle, Harry Compton, between the Granny White and Hillsboro Pikes. The next day our line gave way and passed on to the south. There were one hundred and fifty dead and wounded in our home at one time, so I was told. My mother and I were permitted to give water to the Confederates and some bread and milk, for that was all we had for three days *except what an old black mammy stole and begged from the Yankees for us* [my emphasis, L.S.]. . . .[424] — PARK MARSHALL, ESQ., NASHVILLE, TENN.

KINDLY WHITE CONFEDERATE VETERAN EMPLOYS BLACKS

☛ [Confederate] Capt. Robert Alexander Hardie, born at Thornhill, Talladega County, Ala., in 1837, was the fourth son of John and Mary Meade Hardie. He received his education in the Mardisville and Talladega Academies. From an early age he had charge of his mother's farm until the spring of 1862.

He enlisted in the Confederate army. He was elected first lieutenant and later captain of his company in the 31st Regiment of Alabama Infantry. He served to the close of the war. . . . He was a successful farmer as well as merchant, and accumulated much of the choicest land in Perry County. . . . *He was just and kind to the many colored people in his employ* [my emphasis, L.S.]. He had no enemies.⁴²⁵ — JOSEPH HARDIE, LOS ANGELES, CAL.

WHITE & BLACK RELATIONS ON A TYPICAL SOUTHERN PLANTATION

☞ Ring out, memory bells, and carry me back to the golden days of childhood and life on the old plantation, where my mother and father presided over their children in the "great house" and their large family of darkies in the quarters; where "marster" and "mistess" were often relegated to the trundle-bed when all the resources for sleeping were exhausted in order that with true Southern hospitality the best rooms might be given to the honored guests.

Southern servant returning home after selling his garden produce at the local town market. Besides a salary, a home, clothing, food, and medical care, servants were also typically provided with a plot of land to work, and encouraged to peddle their wares for extra income.

I fancy I hear again the soft, sweet melody of the banjo and the pickaninnies danced in front of the cabin door by the light of the moon, or when fair Luna's face was turned away by the lightwood torch burning so brightly on the high scaffold. In some of the cabins I hear the more religious of the old darkies holding prayer meetings and singing hymns, each line of which is given out by some one, making a regular break in the monotone of quavering voices. *I was permitted to go with "mammy" on Sunday afternoons to the church that my father had built for his servants, and where a colored parson literally expounded the gospel*, and his audience responded lustily and shouted with energy as the "Sperit moved them.". . . My father, Judge Edward Thomas Branch, was a native of Virginia, a graduate of the ancient college of William and Mary; . . .

His marriage to Miss Anne Wharton Cleveland, the adopted daughter of Col. and Mrs. William H. Wharton, and the official trusts accepted, fixed his residence in the young republic. In 1842 he returned to Virginia to receive his inheritance of negroes and other property, the death of his mother, who had waited and wept for the absent son, having made such division necessary. This was a journey of two months in transit, with no railroads and with the uncertain navigation of rivers. *Among these negroes was one* [Phoebe Meade] *who had been my father's nurse in his infancy and until he was seven years of age*, when he dismissed her from such duty, as she said "he thought hisself too big a man to be nussed."

She was a high authority on the plantation, having many attentions and privileges not accorded to any other. By the time she came to our home in

Texas she had been the mother of seventeen children, and was married but once. Her [black] husband, Nero Meade, was also a remarkable character. His sense of honor and integrity was as high as that of any man's, and in recognition of this my father had intrusted him with his money on the trip from Virginia to Texas and told him that when the boat landings were made on one side of the Ohio River he was a free man; but he placed this treasure upon him as safer than with himself. It has been the regret of my life that I did not make record of his many expressions in grandiloquent language of his own coinage. Six feet three inches in height, of commanding figure, he seemed fitted to have been the descendant of some African king, and his high-sounding words were most impressive. He poured into my childish ears many accounts of scenes he had witnessed in "Ole Virginny." One of these that I recall was the surrender of [British] "Gineral Bugwine" [John Burgoyne]. The fact that he had never been out of Virginia did not shake my faith in the truth of this statement until my own education saw the discrepancy, and then so firm was my belief in him that I concluded he had perhaps been at Yorktown and had confused the [Charles] Cornwallis surrender with that of Burgoyne at Saratoga. His wife, Phoebe Meade, with whom he lived more than fifty years, by virtue of her distinction and honor in having been my father's nurse, was installed as our "black mammy;" and very dearly was she loved and her authority respected by my brother, my sisters, and myself. She was very religious, of the orthodox kind, and was the only person that I ever heard speak to father on the subject of his faith.

The field servants on the average Southern plantation were typically managed by a trusted black servant overseer, whose relaxed work ethic perfectly harmonized with the already easygoing atmosphere established by the white owners.

My father was an Episcopalian, his mother having reared him in that Church; but his belief was of a sacred kind, "not to be worn upon his sleeve," so to speak. Whenever he was sick, mammy came into his bedroom with this leading question: "Marster, does you pray?" Which question, considering his dignity and reserve, seemed rather audacious; but she was ever ready to declare herself as "not ashamed of Jesus."

When the emancipation proclamation was published, I drove from my own home to my mother's plantation to tell her the news, and then went out to mammy's room to tell her that she was free. She quietly replied: *"What do I want with freedom? The Lord set me free many years ago."*

One of her daughters was my maid, and her husband had been purchased from a neighbor at a cost of $1,600 [$61,000 in today's currency] in gold just one year before he was emancipated to prevent the possible separation of the pair; and when they were freed, my husband gave them a home, where mammy went to live when my mother's financial condition could no longer afford her support. She did not long survive, and mother and I were summoned to see her "cross the river."

When we reached her bedside, she was speechless. I asked her: "Mammy, do you still keep the faith and trust of your lifetime?" A radiance not of earth but of the celestial world came over that dear old black face, transfiguring it, as though she saw the gates of Paradise opening to receive her, and she nodded her head two or three times in reply. So sure was I that she was entering the eternal city that on the impulse I said; "Tell Lena and father that I hope to meet them." *She sleeps in our family burial ground at the feet of the "marster" she loved so well.*

Holidays, like Christmas, were much anticipated on large plantations in the Old South. The usual rules and regulations were loosened, work was suspended, and gifts and merriment were heartily shared among both white and black families.

. . . Christmas on the plantation was a gala time, and the servants thronged into and around the house in the early morning with their chorus of "Christmas gift!" to each one of the family; and none went away empty-handed, for a great baking of cakes and pies, with making of homemade candy, had been kept up by the house servants for a week that all should have an extra share of good things. There were new suits for the men, women, and children to be worn on Christmas day. Big bowls of eggnog were beaten up and served to the older darkies, and all were made happy.

[Black] weddings too were great occasions, and the "infair," or banquet, was the gift of the "marster" under the direction of his wife, and she gave the bridal outfit, in which the veil and orange blossoms had important parts. It was one of the forms observed to ask the consent of "marster" and "mistess," which in nearly all cases was granted, and the ceremony took place on the long veranda of the mansion performed by a colored minister, who made it long and imposing, as the white folks were all present and the darkies were gathered on the lawn to witness the interesting scene. Then the feasting began with much merriment and concluded with a dance, in which the family from the great house were observers for a while.

The darkies prided themselves on the high position of their owners, and fixed their own caste on that basis, boasting that "we are no low-class niggers; we belong to quality folks." In the cabin or in the field their hearts and voices were full of song, and in looking back they seemed to me to have been the happiest people I have ever known, free of all responsibility or care. With plenty to eat and wear, to them there was nothing more to be desired.

My father was a typical gentleman of the old school, cultured and refined, with that high sense of honor which would have scorned to abuse the authority that he possessed as lord of the manor; hence his servants and dependents were always kindly and justly treated, and he taught his children that was an evidence of bad breeding to be otherwise than polite and respectful to the servants and considerate to all who were less fortunately placed in life than themselves.

The negro character takes very naturally to a disregard of personal responsibility, and the freedom of that race has tended to increase this characteristic. Another marked feature of the negro character, either in servitude or as freedmen, is that in physical exertion they have a limit and will not go beyond that gait. So *they were rarely if ever over-worked. Public sentiment in the South was opposed to any cruel treatment of the negroes, and a planter who was not kind to his slaves lost caste and the respect of his neighbors; and even if humanity had not so prompted, it was to the interest of the planter to give the best care to his slaves.* It cannot be denied that there were occasional cases of the abuse of this power, but even under the boasted civilization of the twentieth century men are sometimes brutal to their wives and children.

Those who did not live in the ante-bellum days cannot realize the warm tie of mutual affection which bound together the master's family and these simple, faithful people. This was fully shown during the War of the States, when the wives and mothers of our soldiers in the field were left alone on the great plantations to the protection only of their negroes with no fear of harm from them. My widowed mother was so situated for four long years. "Mammy's" husband, "Uncle Nero," insisted on sleeping on the back veranda in summer and in the mansion in a rear room in winter to serve as a "bodyguard for 'mistress' and her children."

These thoughts are not expressive of a desire to see the institution of slavery again established, for there is only rejoicing in the hearts of the Southern people that it is no more. Aside from the wrong of such servitude, I have the memory of the labor that devolved on my [white] mother [that is, the mistress of the house] in caring for this large family.

White family members were always there to support their black servants in time of need—and vice versa.

She was the greatest slave on the plantation, as upon her fell so largely the burden of care "in sickness and in health." The people of my dear Southland have been misjudged and misunderstood in dealing with that problem of wrong which was inherited at the formation of this government and in which all of the thirteen colonies became participants by signing through their representatives that compact known as the Constitution of the United States, which recognized negroes as property and left the settlement of this question to each one of the States. At that time all of the colonies were slave-holding except Massachusetts, but slave labor was not profitable in the New England States; yet it is a little singular in view of the "irrepressible conflict" and aggressive agitation on this subject, later developed in that section, that the sense of moral wrong was not awakened in these States until most of their slaves had been sold in Southern markets, and only a small proportion were emancipated.

Many planters of the South felt that slavery was wrong, but so difficult and varied were the problems to be solved in abolishing it that concert of action was not easy to secure. In the trend of progress it would have come in time with less of political and financial revolution and without the loss of so many precious lives had the Southern people been allowed to settle this question in each State [all emphasis, L.S.].

Happily these national differences are all adjusted, and under one common government and one flag this republic under wise administration will grow greater and grander from year to year.[426] —
CORNELIA BRANCH STONE, U.D.C., GALVESTON, TEX.

REVERED BLACK CONFEDERATE: GUILDFORD CHRISTMAS

☞ A peculiar mark of respect was paid to a Cumberland County negro by the white people of Fayetteville, N.C. He was Guilford Christmas. His life of devotion in the service of his former master, Col. Wharton J. Green, endeared him to the family of Colonel Green. White people sent flowers and leading white citizens acted as pallbearers. During the war he was body servant to Colonel Green at the front. They understood each other thoroughly; they were reared together. This funeral and the tributes emphasize the kindly feeling that still abides in the South between the whites and those who were slaves [my emphasis, L.S.].⁴²⁷ — *CONFEDERATE VETERAN* MAGAZINE

A VIRGINIA PLANTATION IN THE 1860S

☞ Mechanicsville, Hanover County, Va., where the Seven Days' battle commenced, was a little village of two or three stores and two blacksmith and two carpenter shops, and was five miles north of Richmond and one-half mile north of the Chickahominy River. About one-third of this village was owned by my father. He lived a mile or so east of here, at which place sixteen of us were born.

In Mechanicsville I saw the raising of the first Confederate flag, and I well remember the excitement it created among the boys of the community. My brothers were largely instrumental in raising the flag and talking war, war to everybody. About this time everything was excitement over the war, and the boys used to assemble and see the Confederate soldiers drill as they were mustered in every day.

About this time our family physician, who had gone with the army, came to my father's house to dinner, and many of the neighbors assembled to hear the news. He said the Federals were rapidly approaching Richmond, and he had better send the girls to another part of the State, as he was confident there would be heavy fighting around home. So all were sent away except father, mother, one sister, and myself. I was then eleven years old. I well remember the parting of my sisters and our old slaves when they separated.

About this time I would assemble the many negro children at night, and as their captain I would drill them and have sham battles with stick guns, and we had a big time. All manner of rumors would come to us of the advance of [Union General George B.] McClellan's army, and at last the last Confederate soldier left us. Then my mother called me and placed around my waist a cloth belt, and in it was placed what money my father had at home. This consisted of gold, which we had ceased to use, keeping it sacredly for future needs. Confederate money only was used as exchange among the people, and those who had gold kept it hidden.

Union Gen., George B. McClellan and his wife Ellen Mary Marcy.

After our soldiers left, [one of our servants,] Uncle Tom came running in and said: "Marse William, dey is cum for sure. My God, Marster, de woods is full *of dem Yankees! Well, Marster, I wants to tell you right now: all de young niggers am going to leab you, but you is been a good marster to me, an' you can count on dis nigger stayin' with you till dis war am over."* And how proud we all felt of Uncle Tom! He was one of the most aristocratic of negroes. He seldom worked in the field, just attended to the carriage team and occasionally went to market. He had a consequential air, dressed well, and bossed it over the other darkies, who looked up to him with reverence and respect. I never knew him to open a gate or shut one when a negro boy was in sight. The negroes always rated their standing from the amount of slaves and money their masters possessed. He always occupied the front seat in the gallery at the church; and when the carriage arrived at church, all the small boys stood around and watched him as he drove up. He would open the carriage door, let down the steps, and help my mother and the children out, and with a wave of the hand fold up the steps, close the door, turn his team over to the footman, and go in to church.

Another of our negroes was Uncle Americus. No one knew his age, but he was supposed to be about a hundred years old. Never in my recollection had he performed any work of any kind. He would tell us children about the Revolutionary War, and they were most remarkable stories. I looked up to him in awe and admiration. When the Yankees came, he was in his glory. They would gather around him in crowds. I can see his bald head now shining in the sun, and the way he imposed on their credulity was a "caution." He was a past master in this respect. He would always ask for alms when his story was ended [my emphasis, L.S.].⁴²⁸ . . .
— HENRY CLINTON SYDNOR

New England socialist Wendell Phillips.

WITTY SOUTHERN BLACK SERVANT TAKES ADVANTAGE OF ILL-INFORMED YANKEE SOCIALIST

☛ A long time ago [New England socialist] Wendell Phillips, the [famous] abolitionist, went to Charleston [South Carolina]. He had breakfast served in his room, and was waited upon by a slave. Mr. Phillips took the opportunity to represent to the negro in a pathetic way that he regarded him as a man and brother, and, more than that, that he himself was an abolitionist. Finally Mr. Phillips told the darky to go away, saying that he could not bear to be waited on by a slave. "You must 'scuse me," said the negro. "I is 'bliged to stay here 'cause Ise 'sponsible for de silverware."⁴²⁹
— *CONFEDERATE VETERAN* MAGAZINE

MORE EVIDENCE OF CHRISTIANITY AMONG BLACK SERVANTS
☛ . . . The charge is made in grave histories and in essays and stories by Northern writers and speakers that the slaves were treated like cattle and their religious culture utterly neglected by the Southern people. Yet . . . [it has been proven] that half a million slaves—one-seventh of all—were communicants in churches. The Methodist and Baptist Churches had the largest proportion. But the other denominations had also gathered in a great many. The system of plantation missions of the Methodist Church had brought over a million into that body in the

thirty-five years—1829-1865. The amount expended for work among the slaves by all the Churches in that time was $4,000,000 [$153 million in today's currency].[430] — *CONFEDERATE VETERAN MAGAZINE*

WHAT HISTORY SHOWS

☛ [Anti-South writers show nothing but contempt for white Victorian Southerners but offer] not one word of credit to the [millions] of humble [white Southern] Christians . . . who [reluctantly] inherited slaves and had done so much for them that all through the war crisis in their gratitude as servants and devotion as friends there never occurred an outrage or an insubordination by them. . . .[431] — *CONFEDERATE VETERAN MAGAZINE*

DEVOTED FORMER BLACK SLAVE REMAINS WITH WHITE FAMILY AFTER EMANCIPATION

☛ Comrade John V. McKinney, sitting on the lawn of his residence, McCallie Avenue, Chattanooga, Tenn., is caught by a "snap shot," while near by stands "Ham," Mr. McKinney's cook, housekeeper, and "major domo." Ham is a typical darky of the ante-bellum period. *He was a slave in the Kelso family, of which the lovely Dana Kelso became Mrs. McKinney, and except for a short time has remained with the family throughout his freedom. Ham is devoted to his "people" and takes great interest in them.* He is thoroughly trustworthy, and for the past five years has been Mr. McKinney's housekeeper and purchasing agent. Ham does not know his exact age, but his birthdays are frequent.

Mr. McKinney is the proud father of seven stalwart sons, several of whom have gone out into the world to seek their fortune. When five or six of these sons get home for a reunion, *Ham has a birthday and gets up a big dinner for the boys and pays all expenses of the occasion from his own pocket. He has repeatedly had two birthdays in one year* [all emphasis, L.S.].

Mr. John McKinney and "faithful servant" Ham.

Mr. John V. McKinney was reared at Fayetteville, Tenn., where he enlisted in the Confederate service on April 1, 1861, in Peter Turney's 1st Tennessee Regiment (the Orphan boys). Serving throughout the war in the Army of Northern Virginia, he never missed a roll call until wounded at Seven Pines in May, 1862. He returned to his command in July following, and was in all the lights and campaigns of Stonewall Jackson's corps till Gettysburg. He surrendered with a small remnant of the regiment at the rock fence on Cemetery Heights on the third day of the great battle. He was kept in prison at Fort Delaware until March 2, 1865, when he was paroled for exchange; but he was never exchanged and did not take the oath of allegiance. That was not necessary, for he has performed his full duty as a citizen.[432] — *CONFEDERATE VETERAN MAGAZINE*

BLACK CONFEDERATE GOES TO YANKEE PRISON RATHER THAN TAKE U.S. OATH OF ALLEGIANCE

☛ . . . A negro prisoner named Dial who was a servant in an Alabama regiment preferred to suffer with and for those he loved rather than be released on the terms offered, and he was there when I left. That the Southern people are unceasingly kind to those old slaves who were true during the dark days of the Civil War verifies all that the South claimed of their relation [my emphasis, L.S.] . . .[433]
—W. E. DOYLE, MEXIA, TEX.

NO CREDIT

☛ . . . [Enemies of factual history give] the South no credit for lifting the African savage to a higher plane of civilization; no credit for the fact that her slaves were the best cared for and happiest class of laborers in the world [my emphasis, L.S.]. . . .[434] — MRS. OWEN WALKER, HISTORIAN TENNESSEE DIVISION, U.D.C.

MORE PROOF THAT THE WAR WAS NOT OVER SLAVERY, THIS TIME FROM ABRAHAM LINCOLN

☛ Do the people of the South really entertain fears that a Republican [then the Liberal/Socialistic Party] administration would, directly or indirectly, interfere with the slaves or with them about their slaves? If they do, I wish to assure you as once a friend and still, I hope, not an enemy, that there is no cause for such fear. The South would be in no more danger in this respect than it was in the days of [George] Washington. . . .[435] — FROM A LETTER BY ABRAHAM LINCOLN TO FUTURE CONFEDERATE VICE PRESIDENT ALEXANDER H. STEPHENS, DATED DECEMBER 22, 1860

Confederate Gen. Ambrose Powell Hill.

CRADLE TO GRAVE CARE FOR SOUTHERN BLACK SERVANTS

☛ . . . Many of you think our slaves were treated harshly. I only wish you could go to the South with me and see the devotion which some of those one-time slaves have for the families who once owned them. Many of them are still with the children of their old masters and consider it a high honor to be allowed to remain. It was not real slavery; it was more like a patriarchal government [that is, a domestic system operated by a kind fatherly male]. The slaves looked to their masters and mistresses for everything. If they were ill, they were cared for; if they were hungry, they were fed. They were treated humanely [my emphasis, L.S.]. But the young negro of to-day is not like the old negro of yesterday. . . .[436] — MRS. ALEXANDER B. WHITE, PRESIDENT GENERAL, U.D.C. IN NEW ENGLAND

AFTER FREEDOM BLACK SERVANT FAMILY MEMBERS SPEND THEIR ENTIRE LIVES WITH CONFEDERATE VETERAN

☛ George Leonidas Wrenn was born in Lancaster County, S.C., January 6, 1838; and died at his summer home at Monteagle, Tenn., August 27, 1912. . . . When the McGehee Rifles of one hundred men were organized in 1861, they became Company A, 20th Mississippi Regiment, and were ordered to Iuka.

. . . [An hour after being captured by the Yanks] . . . he was placed in a wagon and guarded to Grand Gulf. On his way up the Mississippi River, as he was nearing his old home, he saw a negro that belonged to his aunt in a dugout filled with watermelons. He had carried the melons to sell to the Federal soldiers, but he was so glad to see his young master that he wanted to give him all of the melons. Through this servant he was able to send a message to his aunt that he was again a prisoner and was being carried North, he knew not where. He was taken to the old State prison at Alton, Ill., where he remained a month.

Confederate veteran George L. Wrenn.

His love, kindness, and justice to every one was very great, especially to his servants. Many of the negroes remained with him on the plantation from the close of the war until his death. The Federals carried away all of his aunt's slaves; but the negro who wished to give him the melons worked his way back from St. Louis and brought his family to serve again the mistress they loved so well, and they were the only help the family had in the house and field until the close of the war. After the death of his aunt, the [black] family lived with Comrade Wrenn until their death [all emphasis, L.S.].[437] — CONFEDERATE VETERAN MAGAZINE

WHY THE SOUTH & NORTH FOUGHT

☛ The present is the era not only of honors to the dead but of justice to the motives and patriotism of both Union and Confederate soldiers. *The [honest] historian no longer repeats the falsehood that the men who lie here before us and their comrades who sleep on a thousand battle fields died that slavery might live, or that the soldiers who rest in those graves over there enlisted to set the negroes free. That was not the issue upon which the war between the North and the South was fought. Four-fifths of the Confederate soldiers were non-slaveholders, and the soldiers in blue did not enlist to emancipate the slave. They fought for the Union, the Confederates for independence. All were freemen, fighting for the perpetuity of free institutions* [my emphasis, L. S.]. *The survivors of the two armies and civilians as well, North and South, now vie with each other in honoring both the Federal and Confederate dead.*

. . .[438] — FROM A SPEECH BY HILARY A. HERBERT AT LAYING OF CORNER STONE AT ARLINGTON CEMETERY

WHITE FAMILY MEMBER GIVES ENTIRE INHERITANCE SHARE TO BLACK SERVANT

☛ Old Aunt Amanda, a negro mammy, lay dying in a hospital in New Orleans. She had been a slave in one of the sugar parishes of Louisiana. After the death of her mistress, she cared for the children. The [white] family scattered, the two daughters making their home in a small city of the same State, while the brother went to Chicago. News of the mortal illness of the old negro mammy brought one of the sisters from her many responsibilities in the care of a large family and several boarders half a day's journey into New Orleans to visit the old nurse. The other daughter, unable to leave, sent her friend, a Christian minister, to offer prayer and to minister the sacrament to the dying woman. The son, whose residence is in Chicago, received the telegram in Pittsburgh while on a business trip, and immediately journeyed all the way to New Orleans to be at her bedside.

Some years ago on the death of the [white] father of these three persons, who had been the owner of the old woman, several thousand dollars came as an inheritance to each member of the family. The son relinquished his share in favor of the old woman that she might be cared for in her declining years [all emphasis, L.S.].[439] — REV. G. L. TUCKER, IN THE LIVING CHURCH

Union prison at Rock Island, Illinois, where, in violation of the Geneva Conventions, Confederate prisoners were routinely tortured by white and black Yankee soldiers.

LINCOLN PERMITS (OR ORDERS) NORTHERNIZED BLACKS TO TORTURE CONFEDERATE PRISONERS

☛ . . . I was severely wounded at Cynthiana on [Confederate] Gen. John [Hunt] Morgan's first campaign into Kentucky, was taken to Covington to a [Yankee] hospital, and remained there for some thirty days, when I was transferred to the [Union] jail in Cincinnati. I tried to send a letter home secretly, but it was intercepted, and I was vilified by a blear-eyed, drunken officer. I was sent away on some cattle cars, being in one of two car loads of "Johnnies." None of us knew our destination. My wounds were still unhealed. We were landed in Rock Island about the last day of October [1863]. This island is in the Mississippi River opposite Rock Island City and Davenport, Ia. I was assigned to Barracks 84, where I found several friends and acquaintances. A large number of Morgan's men were sent to this far-away prison to deter any attempt to escape, for it was alleged as almost impossible to keep them in any ordinary prison walls. I had experienced tough times in the other prisons, but nothing had equaled my sufferings on Rock Island. Our treatment beggars description, and my comrade, B. M. Hord, told only a small part of the terrible and barbarous brutality of the [Yankee] officers and soldiers stationed here to the unfortunate and helpless [Confederate] prisoners confined in this prison.

. . . two most brutal and cowardly men were placed in charge—viz., [Union] Col. A. J. Johnson and [Union] Lieutenant Colonel Carrier. It would be difficult to say which was the more inhuman and brutal. They seemed to vie with each other in inventing some new method of torture for their helpless victims. They belonged to a peculiar class. *They were in command of a [Yankee] negro regiment, and the negroes under them seemed eager and pleased to carry out their brutal orders.*

Confederate monument, Louisville, Kentucky.

The boxes of edibles were often held so long they would spoil. If we complained, we were informed that we should not receive anything more, and then they would appropriate it to themselves or feed it to the hogs or dogs or give it to the negroes about headquarters. Many of the comrades were in rags or had very thin clothing, and the bleak wintry winds almost froze the blood and forced many to remain within the barracks. Coal would often run short, when we would almost freeze to death. Often blankets were lacking, and two or three men would bunk together and "spoon" it to keep from freezing.

About this time there was instituted the worst barbarism and villainy ever heard of. These men, Johnson and Carrier, ordered all the prisoners to be vaccinated for the ostensible purpose of preventing smallpox in this prison, but the real reason was soon demonstrated. Poisonous virus of a loathsome disease was used, and this soon manifested itself among those who had submitted to this diabolical outrage. Many of these helpless victims died with a complication of diseases superinduced by the vaccination, many lost arms and legs and eyes, and those who recovered were maimed for life. I asked permission to attend these unfortunates, but was angrily refused. From this time forward this officer persecuted me almost continuously for trivial offenses. He had me tied up by the thumbs three different times within a month. A four-inch block was placed under my feet, then stout cords were tied around my thumbs, and a strong negro placed above me on the parapet, a heavy spike driven in the wall, and this negro would catch hold of these cords tied to my thumbs and stretch me up, drawing them tight, and the blocks were then kicked from under my feet. I was left thus helpless, a victim of a cowardly, brutal nature that always seemed absolutely callous and devoid of all human sympathy. I look back upon this period and shudder with horror at the remembrance of these inhumanities. Many of my comrades were treated in the same way during my stay in this hell hole of torment [all emphasis, L.S.] . . .[440]

— DR. THOMAS F. BERRY, PAULS VALLEY, OKLA.

HOW SOME YANKEE INDOCTRINATED BLACKS TREATED WHITE SOUTHERNERS

☛ In the latter part of 1861 Horace B. Toombs and John E. Rossen joined the First Arkansas Infantry Regiment. Toombs was in Company H and Rossen was in Company K. The two men lived in St. Charles, Ark. They were friends and partners in business. Each had a wife and child. Rossen's wife was Virginia Rogers. Toombs married Miss Fannie Puckett, of Memphis, Tenn. She, after her husband enlisted, went to Memphis to live with her father, Maj. Richard Puckett, during the crisis. While there she often ministered to the sick and wounded soldiers. Soon after the battle of Shiloh Mr. Rossen became ill near Corinth, Miss., and died near there.

In the fall of 1864 Mrs. Toombs went to St. Charles to attend to some business. While there she was the guest of her friend, Mrs. Rossen. *The town was garrisoned by negro soldiers of the 53rd United States Colored Infantry, commanded by Col. Orlando C. Risden, who ordered all citizens to leave* [my emphasis, L.S.]. Mrs. Toombs was waiting for a boat to return to Memphis. Mrs. Rossen was preparing to go to the home of her stepfather, Mr. John R. Walton, who lived five miles in the country.

On October 23rd Mr. Walton went in for them, but Mrs. Rossen was not quite ready to leave her home, wishing to get a piece of cloth out of the loom, so she told him to return next day. When ready to go, he turned and said: "I don't like to leave them there." They told him not to be uneasy.

That night before 12 o'clock they were awakened by loud knocking upon the door. Mrs. Toombs got up, and was

John Barker, former black servant, Abilene, Texas, 1937.

shot through a window. The bullet entered her heart, and she fell in a kneeling posture across a table. The negro nurse girl, the eyewitness, sought safety under the bed. Mrs. Rossen fled from the house and ran to the negro cabin, where she got in the bed with her old servant. But the negro fiend pursued her and dragged her by the hair into the yard, where he beat her brains out. Then he entered the house and looted it. The clothes he stole led to his identification. The old negro man, Armistead, went for Mr. Walton, who reached the sad scene just as the officers did, at break of day.

The two children, Laura Toombs and Joe Rossen, were found asleep upon the skirt of Mrs. Toombs's gown. When they had cried, the negro threatened to shoot them. Though so young, little Laura remembered the tragic incident as long as she lived, six years. Joe Rossen lived to manhood, married, and practiced law. He died some years ago in Abilene, Tex. The negro [Yankee] soldier was arrested, tried, and executed.441 — MRS. MARGARET MARTIN GALLOWAY, FAYETTEVILLE, ARK.

MORE PROOF THAT MANY WHITE YANKEE SOLDIERS REFUSED TO LEAD BLACK U.S. TROOPS
☛ On August 16, 1862, in the battle of Deep River Run, Va., Company F of the 85th Pennsylvania [U.S.A.] assaulted and drove the Confederates from their intrenchments, and [Yankee soldier] Ed Leonard, of said company, had fired at the retreating [Confederate] color bearer, who was unknown to him. When his gun was empty, he ordered the ensign to halt, which he refused to do. He threw his gun at him, thinking he would knock him down with it; but he was just far enough away for the gun to turn once, and the bayonet went through the body of the color bearer, killing him. Leonard picked up the flagstaff, tore the [Southern] flag from it, and concealed it about his person, intending to send it home; but it was discovered and he was required to turn it in to headquarters. *For this act of bravery Leonard was commissioned a captain. When he was assigned to his* [U.S.] *command, he found it was a negro company; he returned the commission and went back to his company as a private* [my emphasis, L.S.]⁴⁴² — W. T. ROGERS, KNOXVILLE, TENN.

Stonewall Jackson at age twenty-four.

A SIDE OF GEN. STONEWALL JACKSON LEFT OUT OF YANKEE HISTORIES
☛ . . . The health of his negro servants and their general welfare were constantly in his mind. . . .⁴⁴³ — REV. S. PARKES CADMAN IN *METHODIST QUARTERLY REVIEW*

U.S. GEN. ULYSSES S. GRANT ENCOURAGES BLACK INSURRECTIONS IN LETTER TO GEN. WILLIAM T. SHERMAN
☛ On reflection I think better of your proposition. It will be much better to go South than to be forced to come North. You will no doubt clean the country where you go of railroad tracks and supplies. *I would also move every wagon, horse, mule, and hoof of stock, as well as the negroes. As far as arms can be supplied . . . I would put them in the hands of the negro men. Give them such organization as you can. They will be of some use* [my emphasis, L.S.].⁴⁴⁴ — LETTER DATED OCTOBER 12, 1864, FROM THE *MACON TELEGRAPH*

WHITE MASTER DIES, BLACK SERVANTS LOSE THEIR "BEST FRIEND"
☛ At Hebard Mills, Waycross, Ga., on June 4, 1912, Capt. William H. Atwood passed from this life. On June 1 he had gone there from his home, near Darien, to visit his two sons. He seemed in the best of health, but after a brief illness he was taken away from us. His children have lost a most devoted father, McIntosh County one of her noblest sons, and the command of [Confederate Gen.] "Fighting Joe" Wheeler its last commissioned officer. He was brought again to dear old McIntosh County, which to him was always home, and laid beside the devoted and

beloved wife whom he had sorely missed for nearly three years. *All were grieved at his going, and a pathetic feature of this occasion was the sorrow of the few faithful old family servants who felt that in giving up "Marse Henry" they had indeed lost their best friend, as he was just, true, and kind* [my emphasis, L.S.].⁴⁴⁵ — FROM THE OBITUARY OF CONFEDERATE CAPT. WILLIAM H. ATWOOD

FROM THE OBITUARY OF CONFEDERATE CAPT. R. Y. JOHNSON
☛ . . . Captain Johnson was very popular. He was never married, but lived with his sister at the old home. *The house was burned about two years ago; but he refused to move from the place, and lived in one of the outbuildings in the yard, ministered to by faithful servants, his sister having died* [my emphasis, L.S.].⁴⁴⁶ — REV. JAMES H. MCNEILLY, D.D., CONFEDERATE VETERAN, NASHVILLE, TENN.

VIRGINIA: FIRST STATE TO PUSH FOR ABOLITION
☛ Thomas Jefferson Randolph's resolutions on the abolition of slavery [were] introduced for extended debate in the Virginia Assembly in 1832.⁴⁴⁷ — MATTHEW PAGE ANDREWS

The two daughters of Confederate President Jefferson Davis. Left, Margaret "Maggie" Howell Davis; right, Varina "Winnie" Anne Davis.

CHAPTER SIX
1913-1916

VICTORIAN BLACK HUMOR
☛ A [Liberal] Boston couple visited near Augusta, Ga., and during their stay took a great fancy to an old colored woman. They invited her to pay them a visit, which she accepted with the understanding that they were to pay her expenses. She was given a good room and had her meals at the same table with her host and hostess. When at a meal the hostess said: "You were a slave, weren't you?" The darky replied in the affirmative. "I suppose your master never invited you to eat at his table?" queried the Boston woman. "No, honey, dat he didn't. My master was a gentleman. He ain't never let no nigger set at the table 'longside of him."[448] — *POPULAR MAGAZINE*

THE MOST FICTITIOUS & DAMAGING BOOK EVER WRITTEN
☛ In the course of an address delivered last night at the Camden High School, F. Hopkinson Smith, writer, painter, and engineer, said that [Harriet Beecher Stowe's infamous novel] *Uncle Tom's Cabin* had done more harm in the world than any other book ever written. Mr. Smith continued with this assertion that . . . *the colored population of the South were happier, better cared for, and more content in the days of slavery.*

Mr. Smith's criticism of *Uncle Tom's Cabin* was based on his belief that *the book gave to the world an entirely erroneous conception of the negro's life and condition before the war.* He said that *the chief incidents in Mrs. Stowe's work were such as never could have happened in the South that he knew.* He attributed much of the bitter resentment that prevailed in the South many years after the war to a general ill feeling between the two parts of the nation which had its basis largely in the misinformation conveyed broadcast by Mrs. Stowe's work.

Mrs. Stowe, Mr. Smith said, was to be blamed only for making such a use of incidents that came to her knowledge at second hand. *Uncle Tom's Cabin as a whole was a highly colored caricature that did not at all reflect life in the South at that day.*

[Appended note from *Confederate Veteran*:] (It is understood, and is doubtless true, that Mrs. Stowe later in life deplored the errors in her book. Her son [Charles E. Stowe], a minister, made an address in

Confederate Gen. Albert Pike.

Nashville on the hundredth anniversary of her birth in which he declared that *the men of the South were for the Constitution of the government and that the Northerners ignored it* [all emphasis, L.S.]. His extraordinary address to the students of Fisk University (negro) created a sensation and was most gratifying to the white people of the South).[449] — FROM THE *PHILADELPHIA BULLETIN* OF DECEMBER 4, 1912

TRUE SOUTHERN HISTORY WITH MISS MILDRED LEWIS RUTHERFORD

☛ It is difficult to conceive of a more interesting entertainment than that in which [Southern historian] Miss Mildred Rutherford gave her unique and charming lecture, "The South of Yesterday." Mr. Lawton Evans very happily introduced Miss Rutherford, paying a beautiful tribute to this cultured Southern woman, who is impressing the young people with the truths of Southern history. A more attractive picture can hardly be imagined than that presented by Miss Rutherford's appearance.

She began her remarks by giving a splendid and faithful description of "Old Marse," the lordly planter of the Old South, "Old Miss," and the young members of the family. The old plantation, as she pictured it, was seen in the mind's eye of every member of the audience—the "big house," its spacious grounds, the long avenue of magnolias, or possibly oaks, to the rear of the house, along which were the quarters of the contented slaves, whose pride in belonging to "Old Marse" was as intense as the affection cherished for "Old Miss" and "de chillun." She referred to the log-rollings, the corn-shuckings, and particularly the hog-killings, a time to which the little ones, white and black, looked forward with happiness unutterable. And then the Christmases! Such Christmases! One could see the children crawl out of bed and watch the door for the woolly heads that would peep in and joyously exclaim: "Christmas gif! Christmas gif!" Miss Rutherford's lectures are not characterized by flights of rhetoric. Such would be superfluous. She prefers to speak of her lecture as a talk, which makes it all the more entertaining and delightful. Every member of the large and enthusiastic audience went away with impressions and memories that will long be cherished.[450] — *AUGUSTA CHRONICLE*

Mildred Lewis Rutherford, Historian General, U.D.C.

BLACK SERVANT CONSIDERED "FRIEND" BY MRS. ROBERT E. LEE

☛ [Southern black servant] "Aunt Mary [Washington (Logan)]," wife of George Washington, colored, is a woman of unusual character. *She was the constant attendant and nurse of* [antislavery activist Mary Randolph Custis Lee] *the wife of* Gen. Robert E. Lee *during the last two years of Mrs. Lee's life*. She [Mary the servant] has a cataract on both eyes, and is totally blind in one eye and almost so in the other.

The late Dr. Barton, of Lexington, was General Lee's family physician, and for years Mary's mother was Dr. Barton's cook; and Mary, a likely young negress, was first housemaid in Dr. Barton's home, and afterwards the Doctor selected her as the nurse for his distinguished patient.

[Servant] Mary has some prized treasures, presented to her by Mrs. Lee, which she cherishes very dearly. Chief among them is a neat English Testament published by the University Press at Cambridge, Mass. Upon the flyleaf of this little Testament was written by Mrs. Lee: *"Mary Logan, from her friend, Mary Custis Lee, Alexandria, 24th May, 1873."* Mrs. Lee died on November 5 following.

Mary Washington Logan.

Mary tells how she liked to stand by Mrs. Lee and turn the leaves of the Bible for that lady, who, on account of her afflicted arms and hands, could not do so. This was a daily custom with Mrs. Lee and she read aloud for Mary's benefit.

[Servant] Mary was taken to Charlottesville sometime ago to be treated for her cataract by Dr. Hedges. And on December 6, 1912, Drs. Hedges and Compton wrote to me: "We now feel that a cataract extraction would be practically useless. If the cataract should ever develop in the right eye, we shall be glad to operate on it for her. She has been a model patient."

[The enclosed] . . . picture of [servant] Mary is sixty-two years old. She has lived in a rented house for the last twenty-eight years. When overtaken with this affliction, about one year ago, Mary and George, who is now in his eightieth year, did washing and ironing; but they are now entirely dependent. George was a noted blacksmith during the war, making horseshoe nails and shoeing the Confederate cavalry and artillery horses. Both of them were born slaves [all emphasis, L.S.].[451] — JOHN A. MCNEEL, LEXINGTON, VA.

THE OLD BLACK MAMMY

☛ The outside world has never had and never will possess a proper conception of the peculiar relations that existed between "marster" and "mistess" and those who called them such in the old slave days. *The tender kindliness that lay in the hearts of master and slave, mistress and maid, mammy and child, and that threw its grace and glamour over old-time Southern life*, is a lost chord whose melody will never ring again in earth or sea or sky. Looking back to those old days—*to Mary, my old-time nurse, whose gentle care so blessed my tender years*; Mary beside whose coffined form I stood within the chancel of the little church where she had been so long a worshiper and tried to pay an earnest tribute to *her long and blameless life*; and *to all the faithful hearts and hands that made "heaven lie about us in our infancy"*—a tribute comes from my old-time heart [all emphasis, L.S.]. . . .[452]
— WALTER A. CLARK

LIFE ON THE SOUTHERN PLANTATION DURING THE WAR BETWEEN THE STATES

☛ ... The "big house," with its great halls, big rooms, and imposing colonnades, usually dated back to colonial times, as did its furniture of mahogany or walnut, the big "tester" beds, the straight-back chairs and sofas. In the "front yard" were many flowering shrubs, crape myrtle, cape jasmine and magnolia, or maybe an elaborately planned flower garden, the work of an English landscape gardener. The house, surrounded by magnificent oaks, elms, hickories, was fenced off from the fields by brown worm fences or Cherokee rose hedges or the English eglantine. On one side was the orchard, and beyond were the barns and stables. The "back yard," ample and well planned, held the kitchen, the smokehouse (as the meat house was called), the chicken houses, and mammy's house. Farther off were the other buildings necessary for the diversified life of each little village, for such practically was every plantation. The blacksmith shop, the gin and loom houses, and the washhouse were all clustered together; and yet farther away were the "quarters," the homes of the negroes, cabins usually of one room and a shed, each with its small garden plot and orchard in the rear.

A plantation ball.

Somewhat apart were the meetinghouse and the home of the overseer. Over such a community of sometimes hundreds of people was the mistress called to preside, now that husband and sons were at the front.

That strange condition—a strong will and a frail body—how far and how long did it carry many a tenderly reared Southern women in the cruel days of 1861 to 1865. *The mainstays of the mistress were the "aristocrats" among the slaves, who were divided into two large classes, the house servants and the field hands. First of all was her "mammy," who had doubtless nursed her and her children, a most efficient and loyal ally at all times, often serving three generations; then in order of importance came her maid, butler, and carriage driver. Few overseers were to be had during the war, they too having shouldered arms. So her head man was an old [black] uncle, respected alike by both black and white, to whom was intrusted the carrying out of the plans for the field hands. These servants, ready with counsel and work, always faithfully shared with their "mistis" the care of the plantation.*

On the mistress, of course, fell the burden and the heat of the day. She was overseer, doctor, nurse, counselor, seamstress, teacher, housekeeper, protector, mother, priest. Never an hour of the day but her dependents put upon her some demand, real or fancied. She visited their cabins, baptized their children, gathered them on Sunday afternoons for biblical instruction, comforted their sick, and read the ritual of the Church for their dead. All day she was turning here and

Field servants at work picking cotton.

there, pinching, piercing, saving, racking her brain for devices to make both ends meet in the struggle to feed and clothe her children and servants as the coils of the [Yankees' illegal and inhumane] blockade drew ever closer and more relentlessly about her. At night her thoughts and prayers were given to the soldier boys in gray whose chief support and inspiration she was throughout that fierce and awful struggle. Well it was for her that day nor night brought surcease of demand; she was given no time to brood over the black news from the front that steadily grew day by day.

. . . As a rule . . . *the life of the slaves was disturbed amazingly little by the war. At any time they could have torn in twain the thin fabric between them and freedom. Old men, women, and children of the dominant race by thousands, from the Potomac to the Rio Grande, were wholly at their mercy, and the whites knew it. All that the slaves needed to gain their freedom was to rise and assert it, and they knew it. The one thing the distant soldier had to base hope on for his family at the mercy of his slaves was his belief in the character of the negro as he had hitherto known it—a character affectionate, loyal to attachments, usually uncommonly strong in the case of slaves and owners. The bond oftener than not was an intimate one, and upon the almost reverential attitude of the negroes to their masters, strengthened by generations of friendly contact, the people of the South based their faint hope of safety from a slave uprising, that black dread never far from the breasts of the whites. But the negroes worked in the fields as cheerfully as they had always done, or in their cabins, with that calm patience which is a universal characteristic of the race awaiting their inevitable emancipation* [all emphasis, L.S.]. . . .[453] — FRANCES CALDWELL HIGGINS, MONTEVALLO, ALA.

GROUP OF BLACKS ATTEND FUNERAL OF THEIR FRIEND CONFEDERATE GENERAL G. W. C. LEE

☛ Gen. George Washington Custis Lee, oldest son of Gen. Robert E. Lee, died on February 18, 1913, at Ravensworth, in Burke, Fairfax County, Va., the home of his sister, Mrs. W. H. F. Lee, the widow of Gen. W. H. F. Lee.

. . . He was buried at Lexington by the side of his father and mother in the memorial chapel of the university and under [Edward V.] Valentine's wonderful recumbent statue of his father. The casket was borne to its resting place by pallbearers chosen from the student body of Washington and Lee and from the cadets of the Virginia Military Institute; while the officers and faculty of the

Confederate General George Washington Custis Lee, Pres. Jefferson Davis' aide-de-camp.

two institutions, together with a representation of Lee-Jackson Camp, U.C.V., of which General Lee was a member, constituted a guard of honor. The body was carried from the Lee Memorial Church, where the services were held, to the chapel where it was to be buried through long lines of students and cadets. *Following the family and pallbearers as they entered the church came a small body of colored men who had served General Lee during his residence at Lexington and who were numbered among his friends* [my emphasis, L.S.] . . .⁴⁵⁴ — FROM THE OBITUARY OF CONFEDERATE GEN. GEORGE W. C. LEE

MORE SUPPORT FOR PENSIONING BLACK CONFEDERATES

☛ The South loved and revered the old darkies who formerly were servants in the homes and on the plantations of the white people. They will ever occupy a sacred place in the memory of the people of the Old South and their sons. If people ever deserved to be so revered, it is the old darkies.

The people of the South should do something material for the benefit of a particular class of old slaves. The servants who faithfully followed their young masters to the front during the War of the States and served as loyally as if they had been enlisted white men, doing their particular duties well and never tiring, should be allowed to draw pensions paid by the white people of the Southern States.

Black servant artisan, specializing in iron and woodwork. Such highly skilled African craftsman—well paid and in high demand—greatly contributed to the architectural beauty of the Old South.

Behold the picture: Black, ignorant, yet faithful, *the servant of the sixties, at the call of his master, was quick to leave the old plantation and go to the front to bear the burdens of the master, forage for him, and nurse him while sick or wounded, and in death lifted the body of his beloved master, bore it from the battlefield, and took it back to the old plantation and family burying ground. The negro slave delighted in serving his white folks.*

Consider the irony of the situation. The darky knew that the first consequence of the war in case of victory for the enemy would be his immediate "freedom." He knew it because his master told him so. But *no soldier in gray ever fought with greater vengeance than was felt in the heart of the black man with him. Administering to his every want in sickness and in health, seeking food for his hungry body, and bearing him home in death*—in every way the servant was loyal and faithful to his master.

He cannot live much longer, and *we should pension him.* There are not so many old negroes who saw this kind of service in the war that the expense would be heavy. [Editor's note: Today we know that some 1 million blacks served in the Confederate military in one capacity or another; all are now legally considered Confederate soldiers. L.S.] *We are sure that not a normal human bring in all the South would begrudge the old darkies who served their masters at the front a pension commensurate with their great services and the capacity of the State to pay.*

There has been organized in Birmingham [Alabama] an Ex-Slaves' Association with a total membership of 365 old darkies. The organization will be extended finally over the entire South. An ex-slaves' home is one of the objectives of the Birmingham organization. Plans are already under way for this institution, which will be unique in many respects. The plan of the former slaves is to return to ante-bellum simplicity in the manner of living. The home is to be equipped with the old-time loom, spinning wheel, and carders. Pots and ovens with the ash cake will take the place of modern cooking utensils and baker's bread. The idea is to be inaugurated in an old-time mammies' dinner to be given at Birmingham some time this summer. The dinner will be cooked in the old way by old time mammies. Only negroes of both sexes born before 1860 are eligible for membership in the Ex-Slaves' Association. *This move should enlist the hearty support of all our white people* [all emphasis, L.S.].⁴⁵⁵ — *MONTGOMERY ADVERTISER* (ALA.)

Confederate Gen. Jubal Anderson Early.

NEW ENGLAND ACADEMICIAN COMMENTS ON ABOLITIONIST FERVOR AMONG LEFT-WING YANKEE BUSYBODIES
☛ . . . But neither can there be doubt that the antislavery leaders of New England [radical Leftists; that is, Yankee socialists and communists] were of different origin from the Southerners whom they denounced, and that they knew only *by report the things which they abhorred*.
. . . Yet in the fact that the impulses of the New England reformers to set the world right finally *concentrated themselves on the affairs of other people and not on their own*, there proves to be a trait which *reveals how little the temper of New England has ever strayed from the temper of the mother country. For no peculiarity has been more characteristic of the native English than a passion to reform other people than themselves* [all emphasis, L.S.]. . .⁴⁵⁶ — BARRETT WENDELL, PROFESSOR OF ENGLISH, HARVARD UNIVERSITY, CAMBRIDGE, MASS.

WHY THE WAR COULD NOT HAVE BEEN OVER SLAVERY
☛ The Northern people boast, and have published it in their histories, that our great struggle for Southern independence was a slaveholders' rebellion. Never was a more arrant falsehood spread upon the pages of history. I will prove that by the authentic utterances and documents of their own people.
First, President Abraham Lincoln, in delivering his inaugural address on March 4, 1861, distinctly declared as follows (and for fear you might think I am misquoting him, I have written it down and will not trust to memory, though I shall never forget these words) in regard to slavery: "I have no purpose, directly or indirectly, to interfere with the institution of slavery in the States where it exists. I believe I have no lawful right to do so, and I have no inclination to do so." This was the official utterance of Mr. Lincoln.

When Congress met in extra session after the battle of Manassas, in July, 1861, the following resolution was passed by unanimous vote of both branches of Congress:

"Resolved, That this war is not waged upon our part with any purpose of overthrowing or interfering with the rights or established institutions of these States, but to defend and maintain the supremacy of the Constitution and to preserve the Union."

That was the solemn declaration and resolution of the United States Congress at the beginning of the war—that its only purpose in prosecuting the war was for the supremacy of the Constitution and to preserve the Union. So here we have the solemn and deliberate declarations of both the Executive and Legislative Departments of the United States government that the war was not for the purpose of emancipating the slaves.

In August, 1861, [Union] General [John C.] Fremont, a major general in the army, with headquarters at Hilton Head, S.C., issued a proclamation declaring free the slaves of all persons engaged in the rebellion. As soon as Mr. Lincoln heard of that proclamation he at once removed Fremont and declared Fremont's proclamation null and void.

Again, on May 9, 1862, [Union] Gen. David Hunter, of the Federal army, with headquarters at Hilton Head, S.C., issued a proclamation declaring free all the slaves in the States of North Carolina, South Carolina, and Georgia. As soon as Mr. Lincoln heard of that proclamation he issued his proclamation (May 19, 1862) in which he declared Hunter's proclamation null and void, and that no one had authority under the government of the United States to declare any slaves free. Does that look like Lincoln was waging the war in order to liberate the slaves?

What else? Lincoln declared in his second message to Congress, in December, 1862, that "the people of the South are no more responsible for the introduction of slavery into this country than are the people of the North." And he might have said, "Not as much so," because Yankee New England slave traders brought those savages from Africa to the South.

Were you men fighting to keep the negro in slavery? Not one in five of you ever owned or expected to own a negro. Our great leader, the peerless Lee, was not fighting to keep the negroes in slavery. On December 27, 1857, Colonel Lee (then a colonel in the Federal army) wrote to his son, who was afterwards a general in the Confederate army: *"There are few, I believe, in this enlightened age who are not willing to acknowledge that the institution of slavery is a moral and political evil; greater to the white man than to the colored race."*

In the midst of the war General Lee set free the slaves that had been given his wife according to the will of her father. Does that look like he was fighting to keep the negro in slavery?

Union Gen. John C. Fremont.

The Constitution of the United States, when it was first made, permitted the introduction of slavery into the United States and expressly declared that Congress should not have the power to prohibit the importation of slaves into this country before the year 1808. Mark you now, *there was the Constitution of the United States declaring that Congress should not prohibit the importation of slaves into this country before the year 1808; and the Constitution of the Confederate States—which is said to have been a slaveholders' rebellion— expressly declared and prohibited Congress from allowing slaves to be imported into the South! These are the facts.*

Why, even President Lincoln, in his famous Emancipation Proclamation issued January 1, 1863, did not attempt or pretend to set free all the slaves in the South, but only those in certain States and parts of States. That proclamation did not affect Maryland, Kentucky, Tennessee, and certain counties in Virginia and certain parishes in Louisiana. It expressly stated that it was issued as a "military necessity" and "as a fit and necessary war measure for suppressing the rebellion." So you see that *Mr. Lincoln did not attempt to free the slaves because of any love for them or because he thought he had a right to do so, but only as a "war measure" and a "military necessity." The slaves of the South were legally set free by the votes of the Southern States ratifying the Thirteenth Amendment to the Constitution, which amendment would not have been considered necessary if Lincoln had already lawfully emancipated them* [all emphasis, L.S.].[437] — HON. H. A. LONDON, PITTSBORO, N.C.

Miss Mary Watts Wood, Maid of Honor to Miss Varina Howell Davis Hayes.

WHITE SOUTHERNER SUPPORTS BUILDING OF MONUMENT TO BLACK SERVANTS

☛ [Concerning] . . . the suggestion of a monument being erected in memory of the old-time Southern negroes. I hope very much that such a monument will be erected. *I believe there would be a liberal* [that is, a widespread enthusiastic] *response throughout the entire South to such an appeal. No people could be more faithful and more deserving of appreciation. I have the deepest veneration for their memory. Of all the monuments erected in the South, none would appeal to my heart more feelingly. Such a monument would also show to the world the devotion which existed in the South between master and servant* [all emphasis, L.S.].[458] — MRS. EDWARD CARTER, WARRENTON, VA.

BLACK CONFEDERATE REMAINS WITH WHITE MASTER UNTIL HIS DEATH

☛ Capt. R. D. Smith was the friend of everybody. He was the oldest son of Rev. Franklin Gillette and Sara Anthony Smith. He died at Columbia, Tenn., in the house in which he was born and in which he had lived all his life.

. . . Captain Smith was elected Division Commander of the Confederate Veterans of Tennessee some years ago without his

Up until the last Confederate soldier passed away (in the 1950s), Confederate veterans' parades like this one were a common sight in cities across the U.S.A.

solicitation and during his absence from the State. He was ever a devoted Confederate, and on several occasions delivered addresses in the North, where he always defended his native Southland.

When he left his home in defense of the Southern cause, his father gave him a negro boy named John Smith, who was about the same age of the young soldier. John was as true as life itself, and they went through the entire conflict together, returned home together, and were ever afterwards together; for when the summons came, John was at his bedside [my emphasis, L.S.]. The day was the fiftieth anniversary of the battle of Perryville.[459] — FROM THE OBITUARY OF CONFEDERATE CAPT. ROBERT DAVIS SMITH, OF COLUMBIA, TENN.

CONFEDERATE KENTUCKY & THE CONSTITUTION

☛ . . . In the fact that Kentucky for sixty years played such a conspicuous part in the great debates which ushered in the War of the States lies in no small measure the explanation of Confederate Kentucky. *Not to perpetuate human slavery did our fathers leave home and fireside to march under the blood-red cross of the Southland, but to maintain those eternal rights of local self-government* [my emphasis, L.S.] which ever since Runnymede their forefathers had been gradually wresting from the favored few who had gathered all authority unto themselves. . . .[460] — REV. FRANK M. THOMAS, D.D., LOUISVILLE, KY.

OLD DARKEY LEFT BEHIND

☛ Ol' Marse, ol' Mis' done gone away;
He went to de wah, en I heerd 'em say
He wuz at Malvern Hill. Dunno 'bout hit,
But somebody got hurt ef Marse Tom fit.

All de darkies leab de ol' place
'Cept me. I hatter take keer ob Mis' Grace,
'Caze I promised Marse Tom when he lef' home
I'd stay an' wu'k on de farm 'twell he come.

   Po' ol' Mis'!
Her step git slow an' her hair tu'n gray,
En she call me in de big house en say:
"Ned, tain't no use ter wait. I'll hab ter go,
Fur he ain't nebber comin' back home no mo'."

She's buried up on de orchard hill.
When de briers is down, you kin see her grabe still.
Mockin' birds gimme a tune as dey pass,
When Ise wu'kin' aroun' mowin' de grass.

I ax 'em: "Kin you tell me dis? Whar's ol' Marse? Did he ebber find ol' Mis'? De ol' man's lonesome an' doan' want ter stay, Fer ol' Marse en ol' Mis' bofe gone away."⁴⁶¹ — ANNE BACHMAN HYDE, CHATTANOOGA, TENN.

A YANKEE WHO UNDERSTANDS WHY OUR CONFEDERATE ANCESTORS FOUGHT

☞ . . . it must be remembered that the matter of slavery was not the question which was uppermost in the public mind at the beginning of the war. Lee never would have drawn his sword to perpetuate slavery. He did not believe in slavery. But the war complicated and confused matters, and *the only direct and clear issue that Lee and Jackson and their like saw and felt was that of State loyalty, which to them was a plain question of patriotism, of love for the fatherland* [my emphasis, L.S.]. . . .⁴⁶² — REV. G. MONROE ROYCE, NEW WINDSOR, NY.

YANKEE DEBUNKS A LEFT-WING MYTH ABOUT NEW ENGLAND

☞ . . . I was born in Boston [Massachusetts] and have lived here all of my sixty-six years of life . . . While the popular view of Southern people from time immemorial has been that here [New England] is the seat of hostility, past and present, to everything Southern, and that its citizens by a vast majority were of the antislavery party before the war, I assure you this is a mistaken view. *The abolitionists [that is, Yankee socialists and communists] of antebellum days were a small knot of noisy agitators with whom only a very few people were in sympathy.* [Socialist] Wendell Phillips was derisively alluded to as "Windmill Phillips," and [socialist William Lloyd] Garrison was once mobbed in the streets of this city. It was one of these two men who used the expression regarding the Constitution: "A covenant with death and an agreement with hell." This sentiment was universally condemned here [in Boston], though [it seems to be perceived in the South] . . . as the view of Northern people as a whole.

Confederate Gen. Fitzhugh Lee, a nephew of Gen. Robert E. Lee.

The men of the North volunteered for the war to defend the Union. Had they believed the war to be a crusade against slavery, there never would have been a Northern army. The teachings of the two sections have always been different. In the South reverence and loyalty to one's State has been the source of patriotism; in the North it was one's country, the nation before the State. I am making no argument as to which of these theories constituted the higher type of patriotism; I am only striving to set right the attitude of our people [here in New England].

That Boston recognized the war ended when peace was declared cannot be better shown than in the words of the late [Confederate] Gen. Fitzhugh Lee when he was here in 1875 on the centenary of the battle of Bunker Hill: "I always like to come to Boston, for here I am not expected to apologize for my part in the late war." The ovation which that man received in the streets of Boston would have been a revelation to some of your people [in the South]. . . .[463] — H. S. RUGGLES, BOSTON, MASS.

BLACK CONFEDERATES IN KENTUCKY CAVALRY
☛ [The 1st Kentucky Confederate Cavalry] . . . was composed of the flower of the youth of Kentucky. This was one of the first military organizations sworn into the Confederate service, Kentucky being at that time neutral. It was a beautiful sight when this gallant band of Confederates were marching or on parade. Many of the officers were mounted on Kentucky thoroughbred horses owned by their riders, and many had negro servants mounted on extra horses [my emphasis, L.S.]. . . .[464] — THE MILITARY ANNALS OF TENNESSEE, AS CITED BY CONFEDERATE MAJ. SAMUEL H. BUCK, NEW ORLEANS, LA.

NEGRO MINSTRELSY FOR A QUARTER OF A CENTURY
☛ The Al G. Field Minstrels is the oldest traveling theatrical organization and the oldest minstrel show in the world. It has toured continuously, save during summer vacations, since the date of its organization, July 4, 1886, and has not lost a season since its opening, it has never changed name, ownership, or management; and it is understood that Mr. Field has made all arrangements that the company may be perpetuated after he chooses to discontinue at its head.[465] — ANNOUNCEMENT/ADVERTISEMENT IN CONFEDERATE VETERAN MAGAZINE

EMBERS OF FUTURE WAR: SLAVERY & YANKEE TRICKERY
☛ . . . One day, away back in the past centuries, a Yankee skipper was sailing his splendid brig-rigged craft up the African coast, attracted by a good harbor on the shores of which there appeared a settlement. He landed, finding a great gathering of natives. He began bartering trinkets, with which he was supplied, for peltry and wares of crude and envious design. His vessel was a curio to the natives. [After procuring several hundred enslaved Africans from the black owners living at the settlement, the Yankee skipper's] . . . anchor was weighed, and he sailed away to Boston [Massachusetts]. Arriving there, he sold these black people into slavery to his brother Yankees. He sailed back to Africa and brought many other loads of these same black people and sold them all into slavery.

One of many Yankee slave ships that worked the Atlantic Slave Trade for over two centuries. Simultaneously, the South was giving birth to the American abolition movement.

Later on these shrewd Yankees divined that in the years to come a proclamation would be made by the President of the United States releasing from bondage all these black people, and they proceeded to sell their blacks to their Southern brethren. When the money from these sales was safely invested, they made declaration that it was wrong to hold black people in bondage.

This doctrine of wrong was preached from many pulpits, and its echoes extended to the legislative halls at Washington; and, with this beginning of difference, many grievances, imaginary or real, were added, and the representatives of the North and the representatives of the South quarreled, and they quarreled so bitterly that the people of the North and the people of the South became aligned against each other. . . .[466] — COL. ROBERT MCCULLOCH

LIFE OF WHITE CONFEDERATE SOLDIER SAVED BY BLACK CONFEDERATE

☛ . . . Robert S. Wilson was born in Lafayette County, Ark., in 1844. When the War of the States came on, young Wilson was a Texan and joined Company B, 14th Texas Regiment. In the battle of Mansfield, La., he was shot in the right cheek, the ball passing downward, tearing off a part of the left jaw and coming out through his neck. *His life was saved by his faithful negro servant Ike, who got to him and by keeping the blood cleansed from his throat prevented strangulation* [my emphasis, L.S.] . . .[467] — J. O. BRADFIELD, COMPANY E, 1ST TEXAS REGIMENT, HOOD'S BRIGADE, ARMY OF NORTHERN VIRGINIA

Confederate Gen. John Bell Hood.

SOUTHERN BLACK SERVANTS HELP PROTECT & FEED THEIR WHITE FAMILY DURING YANKEE GENOCIDE

☛ . . . The railroads were badly damaged, so it took a long time to reach a place a short distance away. I noticed that a great change had taken place during my confinement of four months. Everything seemed so desolate. When I reached Okolona, Miss., I learned that the enemy had visited our section, taking everything. *My own family, having been left without subsistence, had been taken to a place of hiding by some faithful old darkies. I secured a horse and an old darky to pilot me, and started for that section of the country where I had been told they had gone. The following day I met one of our servants, who was overjoyed to see me* and told me that mother was about two miles away. We turned into an old blind road with bushes in the center and followed it a mile, reaching a scrub pine field. In the center of this field stood a double log cabin, the refuge of my family. Not withstanding the surroundings, our meeting was a happy one. I found that the Yankees had taken from my mother everything, and *those faithful darkies had done odd jobs to get meat and bread for the family* [all emphasis, L.S.]. . . .[468] — SAMUEL HANKINS, CONFEDERATE VETERAN, SOLDIERS' HOME, GULFPORT, MISS.

BLACK SERVANTS MAKE CLOTHES FOR CONFEDERATE SOLDIERS DURING THE WAR

☛ Mrs. Sarah Cunningham was the only child of John Fox, a pioneer of Monroe County, Ala. Her birth occurred on the 2nd of March, 1823, and her ninetieth birthday was celebrated at the home of her son, John Cunningham, of Evergreen, Ala., on Sunday, March 2 [1913]. . . . Mrs.

Cunningham is in splendid health and *cherishes the memories of the [eighteen] sixties, when she superintended the servants who were busily engaged in spinning and weaving clothes for the boys who wore the gray* [my emphasis, L.S.]. Her only children are Miss Willie Cunningham and John Cunningham, both of Evergreen.[469] — *MONTGOMERY ADVERTISER*

WHITE CONFEDERATES CARE FOR NEGLECTED FELLOW BLACK CONFEDERATES

☛ . . . [A massive Civil War reunion was held in 1913 at which Union and Confederate soldiers encamped together in friendship at Gettysburg, under the auspices of the state of Pennsylvania and the G.A.R.] . . . One long street in the camp was devoted to negro soldiers. But the [U.S.] Commission made arrangements only for Union negroes, forgetting that some [actually many thousands] darkies served their masters in the Confederate army. *A few of these came and found no place. They were given straw beds in the big tent, and were found there by a group of Tennessee Confederates. When the Southerners found out who the negroes were they took them into their own camp, set aside a tent for them, and in every way displayed their gratitude to the old slaves* [my emphasis, L.S.].[470] — "PRESS CLIPPING"

FREED BLACKS DURING RECONSTRUCTION

☛ . . . I was a boy under [Confederate Gen. Robert E.] Lee. For a year I belonged to the crack fighters of Mahone's Division in the Army of Northern Virginia [C.S.A.]. When our cannon were silenced and the Stars and Bars were furled at Appomattox, parole in pocket, as a lad of fifteen, I returned to the ruined homes and devastated fields of my people, put reverently aside my gray cap and jacket, and began to make ready for the burden that each vanquished Confederate soldier must bear. Around me were ruined cities and impoverished communities and a brave people who, in the darkest hours that ever fell upon them, had no word of repining nor cry of reproach for the cruel fate that had blasted their hopes and left them in utter poverty and distress. *The millions of bewildered blacks, who for generations had toiled contentedly in the fields of corn and cotton, now demoralized by a freedom for which they were wholly unfit, had as their leaders and corrupters the swarming birds of prey* [Yankee socialists and communists], *whose carrion scent inevitably led them where they could riot amid the helpless victims of a great war* [my emphasis, L.S.]. Not a little of the heavy burden of the returned Confederate was imposed by these conscienceless plunderers of the South, who brought a bitterness to it beyond even the defeat of its armies and the despoiling of its

Confederate States navy men aboard the Confederate cruiser C.S.S. *Alabama*.

homes in the shame and vileness of their presence among us in time of our trial and sorrow. Let others forget and condone their scoundrelism and seek to palliate their evil with mawkish sentiment if they will, for my own part I shall have now or hereafter no words of apology or forgiveness for those [carpetbaggers] who robbed and tortured a defenseless and vanquished people and with alien helpers and native "scalawags" left a mark of destruction and pollution upon the South that a hundred years cannot efface. . . .[471] — DR. H. M. HAMILL, CHAPLAIN GENERAL, U.C.V.

MORE PROOF OF THE BLACK CONFEDERATE
☛ In a register of the "Confederate dead buried in Indiana" [there are two black men listed]: Solomon Littleton, (negro slave), 3rd Mississippi [and] . . . Henry Mayo (negro slave), Co. G, 56th Virginia.[472] — *CONFEDERATE VETERAN MAGAZINE*

BLACK CONFEDERATE SAVES HIS MASTER'S LIFE, THEN LATER BEQUEATHS MONEY TO HIS FAMILY
☛ In the battle of Shiloh my father, William Guy Patteson, of Grenada, Miss., was a boy lieutenant commanding a company in the 25th Mississippi Regiment, afterwards known as the 1st Battalion of Mississippi Sharpshooters. He was desperately wounded there in two places, one ball crippling his hand and another passing entirely through his body. *Back of the firing line his negro body servant, Martin, a boy of about twenty, awaited anxiously the issue of the battle. After the firing ceased he found his young master and protected and cared for him in his helpless condition. Through the long, torturing ride in a rough wagon back to Corinth this boy remained at his master's side and never relaxed his vigilance until my grandfather came to his relief.*

Most 21st-Century Americans may be unaware of the reality of the black Confederate soldier, but he was a well-known figure in the past. The original caption under this old illustration reads: "Rebel negro pickets as seen through a field-glass."

After the war this [black] boy [Martin], ignorant and unlearned, began farming on his own account, and in time he built up a substantial competence for himself and his wife. He had no children. *In his comfortable farmhouse he reserved a room exclusively for his white friends when business should take them into his section of the country. This room was frequently occupied by my father, whose affection for his old servant ended only with his life.*

Surviving his master by two years, Martin also died a few weeks ago. His wife had gone before him, and he had no direct heirs. After his death it was found that his careful business methods had caused him to make a will in due legal form, bequeathing his farm and stock to some nieces of his wife who had been reared by him, thus providing handsomely for them. In addition to this, *all the money he had on deposit drawing interest—no inconsiderable sum—he bequeathed to Misses Emma Percy and Madge Patteson, daughters of the master who had reared and trained him and whose life he had probably saved at Shiloh* [all emphasis, L.S.].[473] — G. E. PATTESON, MEMPHIS, TENN.

BLACK CONFEDERATE SAVES HIS WHITE MASTER FROM STARVATION & CAPTURE BY THE YANKS

☞ Augustus ["Gus"] A. Bracey was born in Clark County, Miss., February 23, 1841, and while yet a child was taken by his parents to Hinds County and reared on their large plantation.

. . . [When he] . . . left for the war *his father sent with him one of the old slaves, a great giant of a negro, who often saved the boy from capture and starvation, at one time literally carrying him seven miles in his arms to save him from capture, as he had broken down and could not keep up with the army.* Just before the battle of Chancellorsville, having a premonition that he would be killed, he started the negro home with a letter to his mother. In this battle he was struck in the breast with a piece of spent shell, which knocked him down, but he recovered and went back into the fight. His cousin, [Confederate] Lieut. Sedley Lynch Bracey, fighting by his side, saw him fall, but could not stop to give him aid. Lieutenant Bracey was himself wounded soon after and from the hospital was sent home, where he reported that Gus had been killed. No more was heard from him, and the mother mourned for her dead boy. He fought on with his command until the dark day of Appomattox, and after getting his parole he went out through North Carolina, overtook [Confederate] President [Jefferson] Davis, and, with eighteen other young Mississippi boys, tried to help him out of the country. These boys escaped when President Davis was captured, and Gus Bracey made his weary way through the desolate country that Sherman had left and finally reached home. His mother was overcome with joy at the return of her long-lamented son, and *the old slave who had followed him throughout the war pulled him off of his horse and took him into the house in his arms* [all emphasis, L.S.].[474] — CONFEDERATE VETERAN MAGAZINE

Whites were not the only racial group that owned slaves in the Old South: At least 25 percent of all free Southern blacks were slave owners. The wealthy African American pictured here was one of the 75 percent of free blacks in Charleston, South Carolina, who owned slaves.

AGED BLACK SERVANT ATTENDS FUNERAL OF HIS FORMER WHITE MASTER

☞ Among the attendants at the funeral of George R. Creel, a member of one of the pioneer families of Parkersburg, W. Va., who died at the age of eighty-one, was "Uncle Ned" Peyton, who owns a small farm on the Ohio side. He was a former slave of the Creel family, and he said he was there to attend the funeral of his *young master*. The records of the family show that Peyton was taken from Virginia by the pioneer of the Creel family in the year 1808, and at the time be rode a horse across the mountains. The family consider him about one hundred and seventeen years of age, but Peyton claims he is one hundred and twenty-one years of age. *It has been his custom to make a visit to the Creel family once a year, generally making the trip afoot* [all emphasis, L.S.].⁴⁷⁵ — *CONFEDERATE VETERAN MAGAZINE*

"AFFECTIONATE LOYALTY" BETWEEN MASTER & SERVANT DESERVES TRIBUTE IN MARBLE

☛ Those of us who were in the South during the war and who cherish tender memories of the old times (and all of us do) are prone to *wonder why the love of truth and justice of the Southern people has not long since consigned the memory of the faithful slaves, who tilled the soil, ground the meal,*

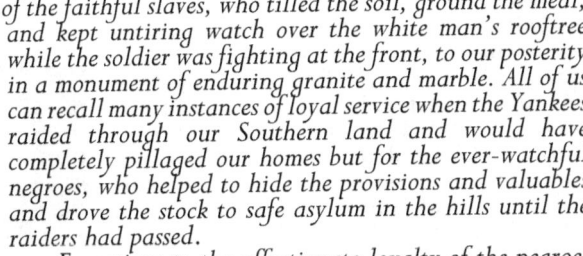

and kept untiring watch over the white man's rooftree while the soldier was fighting at the front, to our posterity in a monument of enduring granite and marble. All of us can recall many instances of loyal service when the Yankees raided through our Southern land and would have completely pillaged our homes but for the ever-watchful negroes, who helped to hide the provisions and valuables and drove the stock to safe asylum in the hills until the raiders had passed.

Exceptions to the affectionate loyalty of the negroes were practically unknown. The "uncles" and dear old "mammies," who helped to clothe and feed the women and children (and soldiers too) of the Southern homes while our men were at the front, were held in as affectionate esteem by the helpless ones at home as if they had been of the same race and bound by the ties of blood. And truly the negroes nobly responded to the need for help and the confidence universally bestowed.

Now seems to be a monumental era in our land and a fitting time to raise a monument to *the faithful slaves who blessed and fortified our homes during that time of despair and gloom with their loyal labor and protection* [all emphasis, L.S.]. Who could take this noble work of grateful appreciation in hand and carry it to a successful completion like our Daughters of the Confederacy? And to whom should such a work appeal as one of gratitude and graceful retribution as to that body of reverent and loyal Southern mothers and daughters? And should it not be done before all the old darkies of the South are dead and gone?⁴⁷⁶ — HUGH G. BARCLAY, MOBILE, ALA.

THE SLAVE'S KIND HAND

☛ Proud Southland, risen from a grievous wrong.
Whose valor earned the wonder of the world
And wove a fadeless wreath of poesy and song
To crown the tattered flag defeat had furled—

O, why has slumbered long our gratitude,
That not a granite shaft in all our land
Tells to the world how bondslaves, brave and good,
Took tender care of all our helpless band?

In all the world there's not a case to stand
Beside this wondrous war song of the ages,
When fettered slave upheld the master's hand
That forged his chains. 'Twill shine in history's pages.

Awake, ye scions of our dear Southland,
And rear a shaft of marble, broad and high,
To tell our children how the slave's kind hand
Brought bread and safety in that time gone by.[477] — HUGH G. BARCLAY, MOBILE, ALA.

CONFEDERATE WHITES WANT "PERMANENT MEMORIAL" FOR FAITHFUL SLAVES

☛ The Omer R. Weaver Camp, of Little Rock, Ark., has started a movement to erect a memorial in the capital city of the State *in recognition of the faithful service of the slaves who guarded the families and property of their masters who were at the front fighting for the Confederacy.* A resolution on the subject was introduced by Jonathan Kellogg, Adjutant General of the State Division, and adopted by the Camp, and the matter will be brought before the State Reunion, which meets in Little Rock November 3-5 [1914]. The U.D.C. Convention at Jacksonville last May *adopted resolutions recommending that each State take proper steps toward the erection of a granite shaft or other permanent memorial that will commemorate the loyalty of the slaves of the South during the war of the* [eighteen] *sixties* [all emphasis, L.S.].[478] — *CONFEDERATE VETERAN MAGAZINE*

James Green, former black servant, San Antonio, Texas, 1937.

U.D.C. CONVENTION VOTES FOR SLAVE MEMORIAL

☛ [At the 21st Annual U.D.C. Convention, held at Savannah, Georgia, November 10-14, 1914,] Mrs. Ernest Walworth, of Memphis, paid a tribute to faithful slaves of the South and urged the placing of a bronze tablet under a memorial window in the [Confederate] Battle Abbey at Richmond in honor of the slaves. The resolution was adopted.[479] — *CONFEDERATE VETERAN* MAGAZINE

THE WORLD'S ONLY MONUMENT TO SLAVES IS IN THE AMERICAN SOUTH

☛ A patron of the *Veteran* writes that he is sure [that the public] . . . will be gratified to know there is at least "one granite shaft in all our land" [that has been thus far erected to the memory of the "faithful slave"].

. . . The little town of Fort Mill, in York County, S.C., is known all over our country, and even across the Atlantic, for its monuments erected to the Confederate women of the South; a monument to the

Confederate soldier, a monument to the Catawba Indian, "always the friend of the white man" (a remnant of this tribe still is in this county under the care of the State), *and a monument to the faithful slaves of the Confederacy, the only one in the world* [my emphasis, L.S.].[480] — *CONFEDERATE VETERAN MAGAZINE*

BLACK MAN ATTENDS FUNERAL OF FOUNDER & EDITOR OF *CONFEDERATE VETERAN* MAGAZINE

☞ Sumner A. Cunningham, soldier and journalist [born July 21, 1843], so widely known as editor of the *Confederate Veteran*, died at Nashville, Tenn., on December 20, 1913 [at the age of 70], after a brief illness.

. . . Many friends from different sections of the State and county gathered [at Nashville's First Presbyterian Church] . . . to pay a last tribute [before his body was taken by train the next day to the "old home town" of Shelbyville, Tenn.]. *Among the last to look upon his mortal remains was an old white-haired negro who had worked for Mr. Cunningham seven years when he lived in Shelbyville* [my emphasis, L.S.]. After a short address by General Young, the simple services at the grave were concluded by his reading the burial ritual, with responses by members of Cheatham Bivouac and Frierson Camp, of Shelbyville. Then the plaintive notes of the bugle sounded "taps," and the soldier, citizen, friend was left sleeping on the hillside [at Willow Mount Cemetery, Shelbyville].[481] — *CONFEDERATE VETERAN* MAGAZINE

BLACK CONFEDERATES WALK MILES TO ATTEND FUNERAL OF THEIR WHITE FRIEND

Confederate General George Edward Pickett.

☞ Col. W. O. Moore, a well-known Confederate and member of the present Virginia House of Delegates, died recently at his home, in Wytheville. . . . He entered the service at the commencement of the war and served in what was afterwards [Montgomery D.] Corse's Brigade, in [George E.] Pickett's Division, until July 1, 1863, when he organized a cavalry company which was assigned to the 22nd Virginia Regiment, commanded by Colonel Bowen, afterwards by Col. John Radford.

. . . After the war Colonel Moore became a farmer and cattle breeder, which occupation he followed successfully for the rest of his life. The circumstances surrounding his death were unusually pathetic [sorrowful]. His youngest daughter, Elizabeth Waller, was to have been married on October 2 to Harry G. Nichol, of Detroit, Mich.; but the illness of Colonel Moore caused a change in plans. So instead of the brilliant church wedding a sad group gathered in the home to witness the marriage ceremony. The bride wore her wedding gown and veil, its beauty being the one bright touch to a somber setting. After this, with shadowed faces, they waited for the end.

Thus, surrounded by his children, Colonel Moore fell asleep. The gray coffin was draped with a faded silk flag which his company had carried throughout the war and which had been presented to them by the ladies of Tazewell. Marching in the sad procession which followed him to the grave were veterans of the William Terry and Ivanhoe Camps U.C.V., carrying Confederate flags. *Negroes and mountaineers walked miles, some with babies in their arms, to see the last of their friend. His old darky, Louis, who was with him all through the fighting days, was faithful to the end* [my emphasis, L.S.].[482] — MRS. MAY WALTON KENT

CONFEDERATE VETERAN SAVES LIFE OF DROWNING BLACK MAN

☛ Among the brave men who answered the South's call to arms was David Rhea, who was sworn into the Confederate service May 16, 1861, in John C. Brown's company, 3rd Tennessee Regiment. When the company was first organized at Pulaski, David Rhea was second lieutenant. Soon afterwards the company was reorganized at Lynnville, Tenn., and here Mr. Rhea was elected first lieutenant.

. . . After the surrender Captain Rhea, like all other brave officers and soldiers of the Confederacy, went to work to recover his fallen fortunes. He was an excellent farmer and splendid citizen, and on account of his many fine traits of character and genial disposition was universally loved and respected. His death, which occurred in the spring of 1881, was very tragic. He was on his way home from Pulaski, with a negro in the buggy with him, when, attempting to cross a swollen creek, he, with his buggy, horse, and all, was swept off into the raging torrent below. *Captain Rhea gallantly swam to the shore with the negro and returned for his horse, which was still struggling in the waters*

Capt. James David Rhea.

[my emphasis, L.S.]. In some way (no one knows how) Captain Rhea, one of the best swimmers in the country, lost his life. His remains were recovered and buried by his bereaved relatives and friends. The members of his company met the funeral procession a mile from town and marched with it to the cemetery, where they buried him with military honors. . . .[483] — *CONFEDERATE VETERAN MAGAZINE*

SLAVERY HAD NOTHING TO DO WITH THE SECESSION OF THE SOUTH

☛ . . . Let me say in the beginning that *human slavery was not the cause of the four years of war between the sovereign states of this republic. Let me say that I deny with all the emphasis of my soul that the people of the South were actuated throughout that dreadful conflict by no higher motive than that of preserving the institution of African slavery. The war was produced by a difference in construction of the organic law of the land.* The [Conservative] *Southern States insisted in 1861, as they had insisted ever since the formation of the government, that the Federal Union was a government with no power other than such as had been delegated to it by the States through the instrumentality of the Constitution* [see Amendments 9 and 10]. *The* [Liberal] *Northern States contended that the Federal government was supreme, while the* [Conservative] *Southern States contended for the sovereignty of the respective States, and this clash of opposing opinion continued until the Southern States sought peaceably to withdraw from* the Federal Union. We believed we had the right to peaceably withdraw from a compact into which we had voluntarily entered. We were willing to remain in the Union so long as the original agreement was respected, so long as the sovereignty of the States was preserved, so long as our rights under the Constitution were safe; but when the Federal government passed into the [radical Left-wing] hands of those who openly trample upon the compact of the Union, denied the sovereignty of the States, and declared the Constitution to be a "compact with the devil and a league with hell," we attempted, as we had the right to do, to peaceably withdraw from the Union of "free and independent" States [my emphasis, L.S.]. . . .[484] — CONGRESSMAN CLARK, FROM AN ADDRESS BEFORE THE U.C.V.

BLACK MAMMY HELPS SAVE REGIMENT OF CONFEDERATE SOLDIERS

Mammy Prater, former servant, at 115 years of age, circa 1920.

☛ Mrs. Betty Keyes Chambers [white] was born in Decatur, Ala., March 20, 1834; and was called from our midst February 21, 1914. . . . [At the beginning of the War she] . . . was living at Carrollton, Miss. Her home there became a refuge for the sick and wounded soldiery. She cared for all who came, whether they wore the blue or the gray. She went farther than this, daring to go and to do what others feared to do. To know she was needed meant to her but to go. Many did she save through her strategy. At one time when the Union army was about her home she knew the Confederate army would soon be coming that way, so she sent her trusted old negro "mammy" out to gather information concerning both forces. When "mammy" returned she found her mistress's home filled with Union officers. [The mammy] . . . feigned sudden illness that her mistress might kneel close enough to hear alone her report in time to save the Confederate soldiers. *This is only one of many deeds that might be told and only meagerly tells of a life so beautifully lived* [my emphasis, L.S.].[485] — KATHRYN CARTER BLANKENBURY

NO CONFEDERATE SOLDIER EVER FOUGHT TO PRESERVE SLAVERY

☛ The Virginia Grand Camp, Confederate Veterans, held a three days' session at Newport News October 20-22 [1914], during which many important matters were considered. . . .The Committee on History submitted a strong plea for action that would result in spreading true knowledge of the causes of the War between the States.

A resolution that stirred the veterans and caused many expressions of feeling was that offered by Captain Lamb, of Richmond, which condemned certain utterances of General [W. Calvin] Wells [Commander of the First Brigade of the United Confederate Veterans of the State of Mississippi] in a speech at the general Reunion at Jacksonville, Fla., in which he took the ground that the South fought for the maintenance of slavery, while the North fought for the abolition of slavery. A number of speeches were made, and some of the veterans were quite warm [that is, angry] in their expressions. *The question by Captain Lamb, "Did any soldier here ever see a Confederate soldier fighting for African slavery?" brought forth a vehement "No" from the body....* [Confederate veterans attending the Alabama Division Reunion around the same time had a similar response to Gen. Well's outrageous statement, saying:] *"We do not believe that the slavery question brought about the war. It was State's rights. It is false even to imagine that the men of the South swapped their homes and patriotism for gain"* [all emphasis, L.S.]....[486] — CONFEDERATE VETERAN MAGAZINE

BLACK CONFEDERATE REFUSES TO ABANDON HIS MASTER AFTER LEE'S SURRENDER & EMANCIPATION

☞ [After Lee's surrender April 9, 1865, of] . . . course all was uncertainty, and none could tell just what the future had in store for us. We knew we were prisoners of war, but were totally in the dark as to what the terms of the surrender were. My first thought was to look after the welfare of my faithful servant George and while there was yet time to give him a chance to make his way home. I called him up and explained the situation to him, telling him that I would probably be sent to some Northern prison, that he was free, and that the best thing he could do was to get home the best way he could. I gave him one of my five-dollar gold pieces, which had been sewed for two years in the collar of my jacket, and told him to take my horse "Trumps" and sell him if necessary and use the money to get home.

The poor fellow looked at me for a moment in silence as if hardly understanding and then blubbered out: *"Mars Thomas, I can't do it. Ise gwine to stay with you. Ef you can stand a Yankee prison, I kin too."* I remonstrated with him and told him that he would not be allowed to go with me, and that he had better lose no time in doing as I said, but all to no avail. He took my hand and with the big tears running down his face said: *"No, Mars Thomas, I dassent face Mammy without you. When I left home with you to jine the army, the last words Mammy said was: 'Now, George, you have the care of that chile, and don't you ever show your face to me without you brings him back with you, dead or alive.' Mars Thomas, Ise got to mind Mammy and stay with you." And stay he did, and was faithful to "de fambly,"* and served us for many years [all emphasis, L.S.]. Poor fellow! He was his own worst enemy, but there never was a more loyal and affectionate nature than his. Peace to his ashes! . . .[487] — THOMAS P. DEVEREUX

Dorothea Sothora Odenheimer, of Jessups, Maryland. A member of the Daughters of the Confederacy, the talented teenage writer was well-known as an "ardent admirer of General Lee."

CONSERVATIVE VIRGINIAN ROBERT E. LEE SPEAKS FOR ALL SOUTHERNERS

☞ Robert E. Lee, then a soldier of the United States army, in a letter to his wife written in 1856, says: "In this enlightened age there are few, I believe, but will acknowledge that slavery as an institution is a moral and political evil in any country. It is useless to expatiate on its disadvantages." He says further: "*The blacks are immeasurably better off here than in Africa, morally, socially, and physically.* The painful discipline they are undergoing is necessary for their instruction as a race and, I hope, will prepare and lead them to better things. How long their subjection may be necessary is known and ordered by a wise and merciful Providence. While *we see the course of the final abolition of slavery is onward, and we give it the aid of our prayers and all justifiable means in our power*, we must leave the progress as well as the results in His hands who sees the end and who chooses to work by slow things and with whom a thousand years are but as a single day. Although the [nosey] abolitionist [that is, the socialist or communist] must know this and must see that *he has neither the right nor the power of operating* except by moral means and suasion, if he means well to the slave he must not create angry feelings in the master; that, although he may not approve the mode by which it pleases Providence to accomplish its purposes, the result will ever be the same; that *the reasons he gives for interference in what he has no concern holds good for every kind of interference with our neighbors when we disapprove their conduct*" [all emphasis, L.S.]. . . .[488] — MISS MARGARET L. VON DER AU, ATHENS, GA.

"The Old Rebel," the nickname General Lee gave himself.

MORE PROOF THAT BLACK SERVANTS WERE CONSIDERED MEMBERS OF THEIR WHITE OWNERS' FAMILIES

☞ The next morning at sunrise [one of our horses] "Old Bill," all that was left of the carriage team from the necessities of the war, was seen standing at the front gate, demanding admission by repeated whinnies. He was too old for the hardships of the march, and yet with him and two mules borrowed from General Guerry, with twenty bushels of corn, the crop was saved; but we had no meat in the larder for the rest of the year, 1865. I can never forget the scene on the morning of April 24, 1865 [several weeks after Lee's surrender], when *my father called his big family, white and black,* around him and explained the situation; *told the thirty or forty negroes that they were no longer slaves, that they were at liberty to leave at once if they wanted to, that he had no money, and that the mules, with most of the provisions, had been taken; that it was impossible for him to pay them wages that year, but that, if they wished to stay with him and help to make the crop, he would clothe, house, and feed them as well as he could. Only two left—one boy, Walker, and George, the carriage driver. The latter left his four children behind, and they were wards of our family until self-supporting. All of them followed my brothers and sisters to the West several years later. Two are dead, and two are still living in our midst* [all emphasis, L.S.]. . . .[489] — DR. W. W. GRANT, DENVER, COLO.

THE TRUTH BEHIND LINCOLN'S ILLEGAL EMANCIPATION PROCLAMATION

☞ *The boasted emancipation proclamation was a legal nullity* and, therefore, had no more legal effect on slavery than if it had been issued by [Yankee socialist William] Lloyd Garrison or the ghost of [Yankee socialist] John Brown. *In fact, it was partial, in that it was to have no application in certain parts of the country where slavery existed—that is, it emancipated the negroes within the Confederate lines and retained in slavery those within the Union lines.* It continued slavery in the following parishes of Louisiana: St. Bernard, Plaquemines, Jefferson, St. John, St. Charles, St. James, Ascension, Assumption, Terre Bonne, La Fourche, St. Marie, St. Martin, and New Orleans, including the city of New Orleans; in the forty-eight counties designated as West Virginia and the counties of Berkeley, Accomac, Northampton, Elizabeth City, York, Princess Anne, and Norfolk, including the cities of Norfolk and Portsmouth, in Virginia. *This proclamation also continued slavery in Maryland, Kentucky, Tennessee, and Missouri, as these States were then "in good faith" represented in the United States Congress.* That wonderful State paper [the Emancipation Proclamation] adds: "Which excepted parts are for the present left precisely as if this proclamation were not issued."

Seemingly, the great emancipator [Liberal U.S. President Abraham Lincoln] was emancipating in such States and parts of States only where the proclamation would likely bring about insurrection resulting in the murder of the white women and children of the South, for he says: "And the executive government of the United States, including the military and naval authority thereof, will recognize and maintain the freedom of such persons (the negroes), and *will do no act or acts to repress such persons or any of them in any efforts they may make for their actual freedom.*" That the United States authorities were not to "repress" the negroes in any efforts they might make for their freedom leads naturally to the conclusion that such authorities hoped that a general uprising of the slaves might result; but the negroes, be it said to their credit, did not rise in insurrection, remaining faithful to their people to the end.

That the emancipation proclamation was a nullity is verified by the fact that the slaves were emancipated by the action of conventions of the

Misleading Victorian engraving of Lincoln signing the Emancipation Proclamation, with a bust of George Washington in the background and a Bible on the table. First, Washington was a political Conservative who had almost nothing in common with Liberal Lincoln; second, Lincoln was a publicly professed "infidel," an agnostic who attacked Christianity, ridiculed Jesus, and denounced biblical miracles. As for the Emancipation Proclamation, there were at least three versions, the best known being the third and final one, issued on Jan. 1, 1863. The second, or "preliminary" version, however, issued on Sept. 22, 1862, contained Lincoln's request for Congressional funding to "continue" to ship American blacks back "to their own native land," as he phrased it earlier in 1854. His liberal colleagues convinced him to remove this particular clause from the third and final version for fear of offending socialists and communists (known deceitfully in Northern history books as "abolitionists"), among whom were, as we have seen, some of his greatest supporters.

several slave States in 1865, and the action of such States was approved and recognized by military satraps acting in a sense as governors and later by the powers at Washington.

[Confederate] General [Robert E.] Lee manumitted all his slaves prior to the first day of January, 1863.

[Union] General [Ulysses S.] Grant was a slave owner and ignored *the emancipation proclamation farce* [all emphasis, L.S.] and retained his slaves in servitude till the end of the war—perhaps till they were legally freed by action of the State Convention of Missouri. . . .[490] — W. E. DOYLE, TEAGUE, TEX.

WHY BLACKS SHOULD CELEBRATE DAVIS' BIRTHDAY NOT LINCOLN'S

☞ . . . [Abraham] *Lincoln believed and urged the colonization* [that is, deportation] *of the negro* [to foreign lands]. [Jefferson] *Davis believed in the gradual emancipation of the negro. He thought the South was the logical home of the black man and that the Southern people better understood him and were most ready to make excuses for his shortcomings. He believed that in the South the negro could always find sympathy, protection, religious instruction, work, and a home.*

It has always seemed to me that when birthdays are being celebrated in the South the negroes had far better celebrate Davis's birthday than Lincoln's. He was their truest friend. Besides, it was [Missouri Senator John Brooks] *Henderson's thirteenth amendment after Lincoln's death that freed them. Lincoln's Emancipation Proclamation did not free all the negroes and was made only to punish the seceding States. The negroes have been kept in ignorance along these lines, and their false worship of Lincoln is pathetic* [all emphasis, L.S.]. . . .[491] — MISS MILDRED LEWIS RUTHERFORD, ATHENS, GA.

Southerner John Brooks Henderson, creator of what would become the Thirteenth Amendment, which officially ended American slavery in December 1865.

HENRY HARRISON: MORE EVIDENCE OF ENLISTED BLACK CONFEDERATES

☞ Mrs. George Macauley, 335 East Forsyth Street, Jacksonville, Fla., asks that survivors of the 24th Mississippi Regiment [C.S.A.] who remember Henry Harrison (colored), *a cook in the* [Confederate] *company under Captain Howard and Colonel Dowd, will give her such information in affidavit form, as she is trying to get a State pension for him. "Uncle" Henry is now one hundred and five years old. He enlisted in Florida, and while driving a provision wagon near Nashville, Tenn., he had the bones of his right wrist shattered by a stray bullet* [my emphasis, L.S.].[492] — CONFEDERATE VETERAN MAGAZINE

OBSERVATIONS OF A NEW YORKER WHILE VISITING A SOUTHERN PLANTATION

☞ . . . *On the grass under the spreading oaks in fine weather the tea table is always laid before sunset, and then until bedtime we stroll, play* whist, sing, or play croquet. It is a charming life, and one quits thinking and takes to dreaming.

This lady [the white mistress of the house] is not rich, merely independent; but by thrifty housewifery and a good dairy and garden she contrives to dispense the most liberal [generous] hospitality. Her slaves appear in a manner free, yet they are so obedient and polite, and the farm is so well worked. With all her gayety and fondness for the young, she is very pious, and *in her apartment every night she has family prayers with her household slaves and often calls upon them to sing or to pray.* When a minister comes, which is very often, prayers night and morning for the assembled household are said, and chairs are always provided for the servants.

The slaves are married by a clergyman of their own color, and a sumptuous supper is prepared. On holidays the negroes have dinner equal to an Ohio barbecue. For a week or ten days at Christmas there is a protracted festival for the blacks. They are such a happy, careless, unreflecting, good-natured race, who, if left to themselves, would assuredly degenerate into drones or brutes. Subjected to wholesome restraints and stimulus, they have become the very best and most contented laborers. They are greatly attached to "old massa" and "old missus," but their devotion to "young massa" and "young missus" amounts to enthusiasm. They have great family pride and are the most arrant aristocrats in the world. In short, these "niggers," as we [Yankees] call them, are the happiest people I have ever seen. So far from being fed on "salted cotton seed," as we were told in Ohio, they are oily, sleek, bountifully fed, well clothed, well taken care of, and one hears them at all times whistling and singing cheerily at their work.

Compared with the ague-smitten and suffering settlers that you and I have seen in Ohio or the sickly and starved operatives we read of in factories and in mines, these Southern slaves are indeed to be envied. *They are treated with great humanity and kindness* [all emphasis, L.S.].[493] — U.S. MAJOR GENERAL JOHN ANTHONY QUITMAN, MEXICAN WAR VETERAN, FROM A LETTER TO HIS FATHER IN 1822

THE CONFEDERATE NEGRO

☞ *The Confederate negro is the proudest being on earth.* A few weeks ago I was standing at the counter of the water office, Municipal Building, in Washington [D.C.], when in came a negro who, standing near by, began his business with one of the clerks. He was rather shabbily dressed, but evidently one of the "old stock," as black as ink and as ugly as Satan, eyes beaming with intelligence and a great depth of human sympathy, a countenance one loves to rest one's gaze upon, and with a bearing of modest and courteous dignity. His business over, I said to him: "How long have you been in Washington?" "Since 1870, suh."

After the War, black Confederate veterans were extremely proud of their C.S. military service and would boast about it to anyone who would listen.

"Where did you come from?" I could see his chest swelling, and I knew the answer before it was spoken. "From Ferginny, suh." "Were your people in the war?" "Yes, suh," with a smile of enthusiasm and a bow that bespoke reverence for the memories of the olden days. "They tell me you people 'fit' [fought] some." I could almost see the lightning dart from his eyes as he straightened himself up. "'Fit?' Why, dey outfit [outfought] de world [of Yankees], suh; never did whip us, suh. If dey hadn't starved us out, we'd been fightin' yit." As he passed me going out of the office he said: *"I was wid 'em foh years, suh. I cahd my young master off de field once when I din't think he'd live till I got him to de doctor; but he's living yit."* I did not tell him I was a Confederate soldier [veteran], and he didn't seem to care. He knew what he was, and that was enough.

I have never seen a Confederate negro that was not full of pride in his record. I believe this sentiment is an evidence of his patriotism as well as a testimony of his love and loyalty to his white folks. During the last year of the war I was on duty as assistant surgeon at Howard's Grove Hospital, Richmond. There were about seventy-five young negro men and about the same number of young women employed as laborers in the three divisions of the hospital. In our division there was a bright young fellow whose avowals of patriotism were so frequent and intense that we suspected his sincerity. When the proposition came to enlist the slaves, we accidentally heard that a meeting was to be held at night outside the hospital grounds to consider the matter and that this young fellow would make a speech. Taking care that no white person attended, two or three of us sneaked up in the darkness to where we could hear without being seen. He was speaking, and for a half hour we listened to a most eloquent and earnest plea for every man to enlist in our glorious [Southern] cause and help to drive the ruthless invader from the sacred soil of Virginia [all emphasis, L.S.].[494] — JOSEPH A. MUDD, HYATTSVILLE, MD.

Southern house servants George and Susan Page.

THE OLD BOATMAN
☛ I changed my name when I got free
To "Mister," like de res';
But now dat I am going home,
I likes de ol' name bes'.

Sweet voices callin' "Uncle Rome"
Seem ringin' in my ears;
An', swearin' sorter sociable,
Ol' master's voice I hears.

De way he used to call his boat
Across de river: "Rome,

You damn ol' nigger, come and bring
Dat boat an' row me home!"

He's passed heaven's river now, an' soon
He'll call across its foam:
"You, Rome, you damn ol' nigger,
Loose your boat an' come on home!"⁴⁹⁵ — MARIA HOWARD WEEDEN

THE OLD-TIME SLAVE

☛ God bless the forlorn and ragged remnants of a race now passing away! God bless the old black hand that rocked our infant cradles, smoothed the pillows of our infant sleep, and fanned the fever from our cheeks! God bless the old tongue that immortalized the nursery rhyme, the old eyes that guided our truant feet, and the old heart that laughed at our childish freaks [that is, capricious acts]!⁴⁹⁶ — PETER FRANCISCO SMITH

Miss Margaret Hoyt, Nashville, Tenn., Maid of Honor Forrest's Cavalry.

WHAT MAKES A REAL CHRISTMAS, ACCORDING TO AN OLD BLACK SERVANT

☛ "'Twuz Chris'mus den, sho' nough,'" he added, the fires of memory smoldering; and then, as they blazed into a sudden flame, he asserted positively: "Dese here free-issue niggers don' know what Chris'mus is. Hog meat and pop crackers don' meek Chris'mus. Hit tecks ole times to meek a sho'-'nough, tyahin'-down Chris'mus. Lord, Ise seen 'em!"⁴⁹⁷ — THOMAS NELSON PAGE

SOUTHERN BLACKS HELP BURY CONFEDERATE DEAD

☛ . . . Beginning with the dark days of the War between the States, Southern women, by a common impulse, associated themselves together for the purpose of caring for wounded soldiers, for securing hospital supplies, *and in many instances, assisted by faithful slaves, in burying the dead* [my emphasis, L.S.]. . . . ⁴⁹⁸ — MRS. ANNE BACHMAN HYDE, OF CHATTANOOGA, TENN.

BLACK SERVANTS CONSIDERED "CHILDREN" OF THEIR WHITE FAMILY

☛ On July 4, 1914, [Confederate] Col. Edwards Jeremiah Gurley passed over the river to "rest under the shade of the trees." . . . *A touching feature of the funeral was the presence of some of his old slaves, who brought a handsome floral tribute and mingled their tears with those of the family. They had never forgotten his kindness when they were nominally his slaves, but practically his children, for he treated them as such. Their being free made no difference, for when they needed assistance they never appealed to their old master in vain* [my emphasis, L.S.].⁴⁹⁹ — J. C. SMITH, WACO, TEX.

BLACK SOUTHERN DOCTOR REJECTS YANKEE MYTH, PAYS TRIBUTE TO WHITE SOUTHERNERS

☞ [An arrogant message to white Southerners from a Northern periodical:] "Our friends down South, being sure that the negroes are inferior, deny them advantages and provide inferior schools for negro children in order that they will continue to be inferior and thus prove the correctness of the contention of the scientists and sentimentalists that the negro is inferior. After all, there is nothing quite so satisfying as the feeling that you have got things fixed so that you will always have an inferior race in your midst." — LIFE MAGAZINE, NEW YORK CITY

[Confederate Veteran responds:] The best answer to this [kind of nonsense] is from the negro himself, who realizes that *the South has done for him what the North neglected to do when he had his freedom thrust upon him*. An address by a negro leader in the South on Emancipation Day sets forth some very pertinent reasons why the negro has preferred living as an inferior in the South rather than to seek the "exalted" station which the North was so eager to give him. This address, by one Dr. Wilkins, [a black doctor] at Little Rock, Ark., has been going the rounds of the country. Among other things, he said:

"I say here now, once for all, if we are to celebrate this occasion (Emancipation Day) we cannot in any conscience forget those who, in anguish and pain, still held out to us a hand without which we must have perished from the earth, our freedom a travesty, and Lincoln's proclamation would have had no place except as an epitaph of what might have been.

"Let us, then, celebrate this day in memory of their helpful friendship and in gratitude that we had the good sense to prove our worthiness of their benefactions by not resorting to torch or anarchy, and with a blush of shame that anywhere in our beloved Southland any negro's pretended friends supposed that Lincoln's proclamation ever contemplated the immediate elevation of the ex-slave to place and power that meant not only the humiliation of the negro's best friends but the destruction of that mutual reliance which was the most important element in the remaking of this Southland.

This image of a mounted member of the original Ku Klux Klan in full regalia was meant to be terrifying—but not for the reasons we have been taught by Left-wing historians. What I call the "Reconstruction KKK" only lasted from 1865 to 1869, and, outside its name and some of its eerie apparel, has no connection whatsoever to the modern KKK founded in 1915. The original intent of the non-racist Reconstruction KKK was to drive Left-wing do-gooders and communized South-haters, *whatever their race*, out of Dixie. A Conservative organization founded by Southern Democrats (then the Right-wing Party), it was devoted, like the Confederate government itself, to the preservation of the principals of the original Constitution. When white racist imposters eventually began to infiltrate the group with the intention of using it to persecute African Americans specifically, the Reconstruction KKK was shut down, for by 1869 it had achieved its goals. But not before an all-black chapter of the organization had formed in Nashville, Tennessee.

. . . *"[As a former black servant] I remember well, as if it were but yesterday, when old mistress [white] came into the kitchen and told my* mother, 'Aunt Jane, you are free, as free as I am. And you can go.' She wore a large gray shawl, and as she turned to go I saw tears on her pale cheeks. My mother caught hold of her shawl and, with streaming eyes, said: 'Miss Jennie, where shall I go? What shall I do? I have nine children, and I know no one but you. Why must I leave you?' We were all crying now. "O no, Aunt Jane,' she said; 'you need go nowhere. You can stay right here if you wish, and as long as I have a crust of bread you and your children shall eat. I will pay you what wages I can. And so long as I live and you stay, if you suffer I will suffer too.'

"We stayed, and she did suffer, much more than we. This scene was at that moment being enacted in thousands of homes all over this broad land. Those words were as the star of Bethlehem on that dark night to every negro then on the plantations of the South as he stood dumfounded at seeing old mistress in tears.

"And when old master came to his dilapidated home from the war, he said 'Amen' to every word that old mistress had said. And all was well until the carpetbagger [Yankee liberals, socialists, and communists] came and, with his damnable practices, preaching, and promises, hatched the hell into which the South was plunged from '65 to '76 and out of which the negro came reft of the friendship and help of those whom he knew and who knew him, those whom he loved and who loved him. And the scamp [Left-wing Yankee] fled with his ill-gotten gains to safer quarters and left us to shift the best we could and meet the storm of an outraged manhood. To-day I wish you to celebrate the release of our friends from a worse slavery, a more galling yoke, than we ever wore. And let us celebrate by returning to our first and best love, and let us join hearts and hands with them and sing with all the soul:

Mary Ellen Johnson, former servant, Dallas, Texas, circa 1937-1938.

'I never will leave nor forsake thee.
Where you live, I will live; your God shall be my God;
And where you die, there will I be buried.'

"If this celebration shall mean this to us, then erelong we shall have occasion to shout, 'Free at last.' This is the only kind of blow that we may strike which will mean liberty and freedom. In this way, and this way only, will the negro in America be free. Let us first free the white man from the impressions we made on him under vicious leadership of false friends, and then we may hope for him to free us from the bonds which our own hands have welded about our feet. And not until that day arrives can we have an emancipation celebration that will mean anything.

"Let us regain the love which we forfeited for the few political husks on which we fed, and that love will make us free. At present I think we are foolish for celebrating an event which has meant nothing to us but humiliation, persecution, alienation, degradation, obloquy, scorn, and contempt. We are celebrating an

event that has never taken place, and you know it as well as I. But some things did take place on that memorable first day of January [1863]. *The ruined Southern white man gave us homes and food. He fed us when hungry, clothed us when naked, administered unto us when sick, and visited us when in prison. And our Lord says for one to do that is to do it for him. Let us not forget it, but celebrate it. Remember, all ye who think that Lincoln's proclamation set you free, that if it is so our Southern white friends were our saviors"* [all emphasis, L.S.].[500]
CONFEDERATE VETERAN MAGAZINE

ESTABLISHING THE TRUE CAUSE OF THE WAR FOR SOUTHERN INDEPENDENCE

☛ At the annual reunion of the Missouri Division, U.C.V., held at Higginsville on September 17, 1914, the following resolutions were adopted:

Whereas [Liberal U.S. President Abraham] Lincoln in his inaugural address clearly stated: "I have no purpose, directly or indirectly, to interfere with the institution of slavery in the States where it exists. I believe *I have no right to do so, and I have no inclination to do so*"; and

Whereas the Congress of the United States in extra session in July, 1861, passed the following resolution: "Resolved, That *this war is not waged upon our part with any purpose of overthrowing or interfering with the rights of established institutions of these States,* but to defend and maintain the supremacy of the Constitution and to preserve the Union"; and

Whereas [Conservative C.S.] President [Jefferson] Davis made the emphatic declaration that *"the cause of war on the part of the South was to establish the Confederate government, to preserve the sovereignty of the States, to the end that the Southern people might have local self-government, so that they could enjoy life, liberty, and the pursuit of happiness in their own way"*; and

Confederate President Jefferson Davis in 1866.

Whereas we believe that President Lincoln was sincere in his statement that he had no purpose to interfere with the institution of slavery and that *his proclamation on slavery, issued later, was a "war measure"* for suppressing the conflict and preserving the Union; and

Whereas we heartily believe in the correctness of the statement of Jefferson Davis that *"slavery was but an incident"* and not the cause of the Civil War; and

Whereas we sincerely believe that *the resolutions passed by the Congress of the United States wherein the declaration was made that the war was not waged by the Northern people for the purpose of freeing the negro, but solely for the preservation of the Union,* was all in good faith; and

Whereas it is an established and a *historical fact that not more than one man in ten who served in the Confederate army was the owner of slaves, and it is therefore unreasonable to presume than any nonslaveholder would risk his entire earthly possessions and his life in battle for the purpose of perpetuating the ownership of slaves of any other person*; therefore be it

Resolved, That we explicitly declare that part of the oration of General [W. Calvin] Wells [Commander of the First Brigade of the United Confederate Veterans of the State of Mississippi] asserting that the Confederate soldier fought for no cause but to perpetuate slavery to be wholly untrue, misleading, and a misrepresentation of the Confederate soldier and the great body of Southern people. . . .[501] — GEORGE P. GROSS, MAJOR GENERAL MISSOURI DIVISION, U.C.V.

MORE PROOF THAT THE WAR DID NOT START OVER SLAVERY

☛ *Did [Abraham] Lincoln intend to free the slaves when war was declared? Certainly he did not.* In his speech at Peoria, Ill., he said: "Free them and keep them here as underlings? That would not better their condition. Free them and make them socially and politically our equals? My own feelings will not admit this, and I know the mass of whites, North and South, will not agree to this. We cannot make them our equals. *Free them and send them to Liberia [Africa] would be my first impulse*, but I know that if they were landed there to-day they would perish in ten days. If all earthly power were given to me, I do not know what to do with slavery as it exists in the South to-day. A system of gradual emancipation seems best, and *we must not too quickly judge our brethren of the South for seeming tardiness in this matter*" [all emphasis, L.S.].[502] — MISS MILDRED LEWIS RUTHERFORD, ATHENS, GA.

THE CONFEDERACY VOTES TO ENLIST BLACK MALES FOR SERVICE IN THE C.S. MILITARY

☛ On account of the South's being practically drained of fighting men by the middle of the year 1864, the question of using the male slaves to reenforce the army was agitated. I shall give few opinions on the subject taken from various sources.

As early as September 9 a gentleman from Augusta, Ga., signing himself a "Native Georgian," wrote to the department thus: "The idea may have been presented to you of employing the negroes as soldiers. They can certainly fight as well for us as against us. Let the negro fight negro, and he will show much more courage than when opposed to whites. Promise freedom when the war is over and colonize them either in Mexico or Central America."

On December 21 the Hon. Judah P. Benjamin, [Confederate] Secretary of State, expressed himself as follows: "It appears to me enough to say that the negro will certainly fight against us if not used for our defense. There is no other means of swelling our armies than that of arming the slaves

Jewish Confederate statesman Judah Philip Benjamin, who occupied a number of important positions in the Davis administration, was just one of many white Southerners who campaigned to enlist blacks in the C.S. military.

and using them as an auxiliary force. I further admit that if they fight for our freedom they are entitled to their own."

... Samuel Clayton, Esq., of Cuthbert, Ga., wrote on January 10, 1865: "All of our male population between sixteen and sixty is in the army. We cannot get men from any other source; they must come from our slaves. Some say that negroes will not fight, but they fought us at Ocean Pond, Honey Hill, and other places. The government takes all of our men and exposes them to death. Why can't they take our property? He who values his property more than independence is a poor, sordid wretch."

[Confederate] General [Robert E.] Lee, who clearly saw the inevitable unless his forces were strengthened, wrote on January 11 [1865]:

"I should prefer to rely on our white population; but in view of the preparation of our enemy it is our duty to provide for a continuous war, which, I fear, we cannot accomplish with our present resources. It is the avowed intention of the enemy to convert the able-bodied negro into soldiers and emancipate all. His progress will thus add to his numbers and at the same time destroy slavery in a most pernicious manner to the welfare of our people. Whatever may be the effect of our employing negro troops, it cannot be as mischievous as this. *If it ends in subverting slavery, it will be accomplished by ourselves, and we can devise the means of alleviating the evil consequences to both races.* I think, therefore, that we must decide whether slavery shall be extinguished by our enemies and the slaves used against us or use them ourselves at the risk of the effects which may be produced upon

our soldiers' social institutions. *My own opinion is that we should employ them without delay. I believe that with proper regulations they can be made efficient soldiers.* They possess the physical qualifications in an eminent degree. Long habits of obedience and subordination, coupled with the moral influence which in our country the white man possesses over the black, furnish an excellent foundation for that discipline which is the best guarantee of military efficiency. *We can give them an interest by allowing immediate freedom to all who enlist and freedom at the end of the war to their families.* We should not expect slaves to fight for prospective freedom when they can secure it at once by going to the enemy, in whose service they will incur no greater risk than in ours. In conclusion, I can only say that whatever is to be done must be attended to at once."

[Confederate] President Davis on February 21 [1865] expressed himself as follows: "It is now becoming daily more evident to all reflecting persons that we are reduced to choosing whether the negroes shall fight for or against us and that all the arguments as to the positive advantage or disadvantage of employing them are beside the question, which is simply one of relative advantage between having their fighting element in our ranks or those of the enemy."

The question was argued and thrashed over in [the Confederate] Congress and *on March 23, 1865, the following order was issued from the adjutant and inspector general's office in Richmond:*

> "The Congress of the Confederate States of America do enact that, in order to provide additional forces to repel invasion, maintain the rightful possessions of the Confederate States, secure their independence, and preserve there institutions, the President be and he is hereby authorized to ask for and accept from the owners of slaves the services of such numbers of able-bodied negro men as he may deem expedient for and during the war to perform military service in whatever capacity he may direct.... That while employed in the service the said troops shall receive the same ration, clothing, and compensation as allowed other troops in the same branch of the service.... No slave will be accepted unless with his own consent and the approbation of his master by a written instrument conferring as far as he may the rights of a freedman.... The enlistment will be for the war" [all emphasis, L.S.].

Confederate Gen. Daniel Harris Reynolds.

On March 28 the following order was issued to various parties: "You are hereby authorized to raise a _____ of negro troops under the provision of [the Confederate] Congress, and you are allowed sixty days' absence and will be detached from your command for that purpose."[503] — JOHN C. STILES, BRUNSWICK, GA.

"FAITHFUL SLAVES" MAKE CLOTHING FOR CONFEDERATE SOLDIERS

☞ Mrs. Frances Burton Smoot Plecker died at her home, in Staunton, Va., on January 11, 1915. She was born September 22, 1833, on her father's plantation, in Madison County, Va. She was the daughter of Daniel Jenifer Smoot and Harriet Medley, a granddaughter of Ambrose Medley and Frankey Burton and a great-granddaughter of Maj. May Burton, a soldier of the Revolution.... She was the widow of Jacob H. Plecker, of Augusta County, who served in Company F, 62nd Virginia Regiment. *While her husband was away fighting she and her faithful slaves spun and dyed the yarn, wove the cloth, and made the clothing for him and his fellow* [Confederate] *soldiers* [my emphasis, L.S.].[504] — CONFEDERATE VETERAN MAGAZINE

WAS THE WAR BETWEEN THE STATES FOUGHT TO HOLD OUR SLAVES?

☛ Ah, how often have we of the South had this cast into our teeth and often by some of our own Southern people! Yes, it is full time that this wrong should be righted.

Had the vote been taken in 1860, there would have been more votes against the abolition of slavery in the North than in the South. There were 318,000 slaveholders or sons of slaveholders in the Northern army, men who enlisted from the border States—Missouri, Kentucky, Tennessee, Maryland—besides those from Illinois, Pennsylvania, New Jersey, and Delaware. There were only 100,000 slaveholders in the Southern army. Only five men out of every one hundred owned slaves in the South [or about 5 percent].

There were many men among the leaders of the Northern army who owned slaves themselves or were sons of slaveholders or had married women who owned slaves. Among these may be mentioned Gen. Winfield Scott, Commodore [David Glasgow] Farragut, Gen. George H. Thomas, General Grant. President Lincoln's wife came from a slave-holding family, and Stephen Douglas's wife was a very large slaveholder, while many of the leaders on the Southern side did not own slaves. General Lee had freed his. Gen. Stonewall Jackson never had owned one until [a black] husband and wife begged him to buy them to prevent separation. Gen. Albert Sidney Johnston never owned a slave, and Gen. William M. Browne, a member of President Davis' staff, never owned a slave. No, the war was not fought in hold slaves; but a few selfish Southern people may have thought so.

Stonewall Jackson.

General Grant said: "If I thought this war was to abolish slavery, I would resign my commission and offer my sword to the other side." The North had no thought of fighting abolish slavery; then why should the South be troubled on that score? President Lincoln sent word to [Union] General [Benjamin F.] Butler that the war was not to be fought with any idea of freeing the slaves. President Lincoln was only concerned about the extension of slavery in the new territory and frankly confessed to [Yankee socialist] Horace Greeley that if the Union could be preserved with slavery he would not interfere with it. It was the preservation of the Union that he so ardently desired. He had no love for the negro in his heart. [Union Gen.] Donn Piatt, who stumped the State of Illinois for him in his presidential campaign in 1860, said in one of his speeches that Lincoln had no love for the negro. "Descended from the poor whites of the South, he hated the negro, and the negro hated him; and he was no more concerned for that wretched race than he was concerned for the horse he worked or the hog he killed" [all emphasis, L.S.].[505]
— MISS MILDRED LEWIS RUTHERFORD, ATHENS, GA.

THE REAL MOTIVES BEHIND SOUTHERN DEFENSE & NORTHERN AGGRESSION

☛ ... In view of the awful tragedy [of the War between the states, the impartial student of history] ... might well weep bitter but unavailing tears that when *the moral sense of the Southern States, never at perfect ease over the institution of slavery, was struggling with the complicated and difficult problem of how best to wipe the stain from her escutcheon—best for the innocent and simple-hearted race that Old England and New England had foisted upon them*—the insulting words and incendiary conduct of the North made of every true son of the South a champion and defender of that which, deep down in his heart, he longed to be rid of.

I utterly deny that the South seceded from the Union and poured out the priceless treasure of her heroic blood to maintain the institution of African slavery. Such sacrifice, such matchless courage, such sublime fortitude, such unfaltering trust in her God sprang not from a source so ignominious. "Do men gather grapes of thorns or figs from thistles?"

I know that [Liberal] Mr. [Abraham] Lincoln in his inaugural address declared: "One section of our country believes slavery is right and ought to he extended, while the other believes slavery is wrong and ought not to be extended. This is the only substantial dispute." But I also know that the inaugural address of [Conservative] Mr. [Jefferson] Davis at Montgomery did not once mention slavery and that the second inaugural at Richmond breathed a spirit and wore a form utterly incompatible with the base motives that Northern abolitionists found it profitable to impute to the people whose cause he represented. Suffer me to quote its concluding sentences: "My hope is reverently fixed on Him whose favor is ever vouchsafed to the cause which is just. With humble gratitude and adoration, acknowledging the providence which has so often visibly protected the Confederacy during its brief but eventful career, to thee, O God, I trustingly commit myself and prayerfully invoke thy blessing on my country and its cause." "The people," says the historian Dodd, "dispersed silently and in meditation, as though they had attended divine services."

Dr. Henry Wilson Battle.

I also know that President Davis, after three years of terrific fighting, declared to representatives of President Lincoln: *"We are not fighting for slavery; we are fighting for independence. Say to Mr. Lincoln for me that I shall at any time be pleased to receive proposals for peace on the basis of our independence. It will he useless to approach me with any other."*

I repeat with all the emphasis I can impart to my words that the South did not secede from the Union to maintain the institution of African slavery. I spurn the calumny. It was what was back of and around that issue. *The question of slavery had become so enmeshed through sectional hate with insult and wrong—wrong both in private and public legislation—that a proud and sensitive people were driven to seek relief from intolerable conditions in what they believed to be the right of peaceable withdrawal from the compact into which they had voluntarily entered.* The most fundamental and sacred purposes of that compact having been ruthlessly disregarded, the South believed it to be her unquestionable right peaceably to withdraw. That such peaceable withdrawal was her intention, I shall show; but before I leave the subject of slavery it is in my heart to say that *the truly noble, unselfish, yes, chivalrous, conduct of Southern slaves during the war, when our men were at the front and our women and children almost wholly under their protection, is a complete and triumphant refutation of the slander which branded that domestic relationship at the South as "the sum of all villainies." That cruelties were perpetrated, I doubt not; but they were exceptional, and the guilty parties belonged to a class which is the curse of every section, essentially base in birth, breeding, and instincts. The Southern gentleman and the Southern gentlewoman were never cruel. With the fine feelings engendered by trustful dependence, they gave to their slaves a watchful care and tender solicitude unique and beautiful. "Old Mistress" and "Old Marster" were words spoken lovingly in those days. Had it been otherwise, think you the millions of negroes in Southern homes and on Southern plantations would not have risen in their might and thrown off their fetters by deeds that would have sent fathers and husbands and brothers and lovers rushing back from the front to protect their dear ones at home? One week of such horrors would have sufficed to work the disbandment of the Southern army and the collapse of the Southern cause. Surely the negroes knew it. But no!* [Yankee socialist] *Theodore Parker might say, "I would like, above all things, to see an insurrection of slaves";* [Yankee socialist William Lloyd] *Garrison might exclaim, "Success to every slave insurrection in the South!" But Southern negroes of the war period were incapable of such atrocities. Not one deed of horror stained their splendid record of devotion during those years. Had some lecherous scoundrel, emboldened by seemingly defenseless conditions, dared to assault the snow-white citadel of one Southern woman's virtue, he would have been torn limb from limb by infuriated defenders who formed a dark but impenetrable cordon about the honor of the Southern home. That not one such attack was made writes "lie" on the imputation of universal, or even frequent, cruelty in letters so large and distinct that a wayfaring man, though a fool, may read* [all emphasis, L.S.]. . . .[506] — HENRY WILSON BATTLE, D.D., OF CHARLOTTESVILLE, VA.

Confederate Generals Clement A. Evans and Joseph Wheeler, on the occasion of "Reception of Gen. Wheeler" in Atlanta, Georgia.

HOUSE SERVANTS WERE IN CHARGE OF THE PLANTATION MANSION

☛ When I was a young girl I frequently had held up to me as the great and shining exemplar of domesticity the Southern woman of ante-bellum days. She paraded rhythmically across a broad green lawn or reclined on a lovely couch, carrying flowers and wearing soft, flowing white things with beautiful long trains. Sometimes, instead of the flowers, she carried a dainty bit of sewing. *Her kitchen was left to the device of a great company of slaves, who ran the house pretty much to suit themselves* [my emphasis, L.S.]. . . .[507] — SARAH PRICE THOMAS, CHARLOTTE, N.C.

Miraculously, this rare photo of a uniformed black Confederate soldier (taken circa 1862) has survived 160 years of vicious Yankee censorship. It shows Confederate Sergeant A. M. Chandler (left) with a family servant, Silas Chandler (right), both of Co. F, 44th Mississippi Infantry Regiment. Countless thousands of such photos of black Confederates must have been taken. Thanks to the illegal and immoral but routine Yankee practice of destroying military and family records—by burning Southern courthouses, churches, hospitals, and universities, and bombing Southern cemeteries—nearly all such images have disappeared. The photographic evidence may largely be gone, but the eyewitness testimonies of thousands of Victorian Southerners, white and black, remain, as this very book chronicles.

MORE YANKEE SLAVERY MYTHS DEBUNKED

☛ . . . Did the slaveholder in the South take an interest in the religious condition of the negro? He certainly did. *More negroes were brought to a knowledge of God and their Saviour under the institution of slavery in the South than under any other missionary enterprise in the same length of time. Really, more were Christianized in the two hundred and forty-six years of slavery than in the more than one thousand years before.*

In 1861 there were, by actual statistics, in the seceding States 220,000 negro Baptists, 200,000 negro Methodists, 31,000 negro Presbyterians, 7,000 negro Episcopalians, and 30,000 negroes belonging to unclassified Christian Churches.

The negro race should give thanks daily that they and their children are not to-day where their ancestors were before they came into bondage.

Was the negro happy under the institution of slavery? They were the happiest set of people on the face of the globe, free from care or thought of food, clothes, home, or religious privileges. The slaveholder felt a personal responsibility in caring for his slaves physically, mentally, morally, and spiritually. By the way, we never called them slaves; they were our people, our negroes, part of our very homes. I do not remember a case of consumption (I should now say tuberculosis) among the negroes in the South. I can recall but one crazy negro in those days. Hospitals and asylums cannot now be built fast enough to accommodate them.

I am not here to defend slavery. I would not have it back if I could. But I do say I rejoice that my father was a slaveholder and my grandfathers and great-grandfathers were slaveholders and had a part in the greatest missionary and educational endeavors that the world has ever known. There never have been such cooks, such nurses or mammies, such housemaids, such seamstresses, such spinners, such weavers, such washerwomen. There never have been such carpenters, blacksmiths, butlers, drivers, field hands, such men of all work, as could be found on the old plantations. Aunt Nanny's cabin was a veritable kindergarten where the young negroes were trained to sew, to spin, to card, to weave, to wash and iron, and to nurse; where the boys were taught to shell peas, to shuck corn, to churn, to chop wood, to pick up chips, to feed pigs, to feed chickens, to hunt turkey, duck, guinea, goose, and hen eggs, to make fires, and to sweep the yards.

Confederate monument, Charleston, West Virginia.

Did the negroes hate their owners and resent bondage? I need only to call to mind what happened when [Yankee socialist] John Brown tried to make them rise and murder their masters and their masters' children. I need only to call to mind what happened when their masters went to battle, leaving in absolute trust "Ole Mis" and the children to their protection. I need only to call to mind what happened after they were free that made [Yankee socialist] Thad Stevens's "Exodus Order" necessary in order to tear them from their old owners. I need only to call to mind the many mammies who stayed to nurse "Ole Marster's" children to the third and fourth generations.

Compare the race morally with what it was then. "Ole Marster" never allowed his negroes to have liquor unless he gave it to them. Crimes now so common were never known then. While the negro under the present system of education may know more Latin and Greek, it does not better fit him for his life work. It is true the negro did not go to school under slavery, but *he was allowed to be taught if he so desired.* I have in mind a young aunt who taught three negro women every night because they wanted to read their Bibles. I have in mind my mother on the plantation every Sunday afternoon teaching to the negro children the same verses of Scripture, the same Sunday school lesson, the same hymns that she taught her own children.

As in family life a child must be punished if disobedient, so in plantation life a negro had to be punished if disobedient. Even admitting that some overseers were cruel, will the most exaggerated cases of cruelty compare with the burning of the witches at Salem, or the awful conditions of the captured Africans on the [Yankee] slave ships or the fearful conditions in the sweat shops of Chicago and New York to-day? The slave was the property of the slaveholder, and a selfish reason would have protected him if there had been no higher motive. No, the slaveholder was no criminal, and slavery under the old regime was no crime. In all the history of the world no peasantry was ever better cared for, more contented, or happier [all emphasis, L.S.].

These wrongs must be righted and the Southern slaveholder defended as soon as possible.⁵⁰⁸ — MISS MILDRED LEWIS RUTHERFORD, ATHENS, GA.

LEE, GRANT, & SLAVERY

☛ . . . It is thought by many that in the War between the States the Federal forces fought to free the slaves and the Confederate forces fought to retain them in bondage. If this be true, then the personnel of the two armies presented a strange spectacle.

[Confederate] General Lee, the great leader of the Confederate army, freed his slaves before the war began; while [Union] General Grant, the great Federal commander, continued his in bondage until after the war closed. It was estimated that *there were fifty thousand soldiers from the slaveholding border States in the Federal army, and we know that there were many more than that in the Confederate army who never owned a slave* [my emphasis, L.S.]. . . .⁵⁰⁹ — FANNIE E. SELPH, HISTORIAN KATE LITTON HICKMAN CHAPTER, U.D.C., NASHVILLE, TENN.

BLACK CONFEDERATE VOLUNTARILY GOES TO PRISON WITH HIS WHITE OWNER

☛ At the age of seventy-nine years, Capt. J. B. Wilson died in Orlando, Fla., on February 2, 1915. He was born in Morgantown, Ky., January 5, 1839, and enlisted as a Confederate soldier in Capt. Thomas H. Hine's company from Bowling Green, Ky., John H. Morgan's regiment, with which he served through the battle of Shiloh. . . . He was captured and sent to New Orleans, from there to New York, thence to Johnson's Island, Ohio, and was released in 1865. *During every battle his old negro servant, "Uncle John," was always near him, and when he was taken prisoner the old negro stayed in prison and cared for him the entire time* [my emphasis, L.S.].⁵¹⁰ — CONFEDERATE VETERAN MAGAZINE

Confederate Gen. John Hunt Morgan.

HAD THE SOUTH SUCCEEDED . . .

☛ The Federals [Yankees] had all the world to recruit from, evidenced by pension rolls. All enlisted under the deceptive cry of "Union." The South took up arms to repel invasion and for her constitutional rights, the rights of the people *of the States. Had we succeeded, the negro would have been given emancipation gradually, which would have resulted to the greatest benefit of that race* [my emphasis, L.S.],[511] — T. E. MOORE, LEXINGTON, KY.

BLACK CONFEDERATE SOLDIERS DEFEND A WAGON TRAIN

☛ On Tuesday or Wednesday following the evacuation of Richmond, on returning from carrying an order from [Confederate] Gen. [Seth Maxwell] Barton, *I saw a wagon train guarded by Confederate negro soldiers* [my emphasis, L.S.], a novel sight to me. When within about one hundred yards of and in the rear of the wagon train, I observed some Union cavalry a short distance away on elevated ground forming to charge and the negro soldiers forming to meet the attack, which was met successfully, the Union cavalry retreating. . . .[512] — R. M. DOSWELL, NORFOLK, VA.

LOYAL BLACK CONFEDERATE HONORED BY ALL

☛ [The accompanying] . . . picture of Uncle Mack Dabney was taken in October, 1913, and he was seventy-one years old in December following. Uncle Mack saw service with the 3rd Tennessee Regiment, Col. C. H. Walker, under [Confederate] Gen. John C. Brown, during the entire four years of the war. Colonel Walker was killed at Jonesboro. History says this one of the best of the Tennessee regiments.

The hardest contested battles which Uncle Mack remembers were Vicksburg and Chickamauga. *From the latter battlefield he carried Mr. Bob Marsh, who was mortally wounded.* Mr. Marsh was from Uncle Mack's home town of Cornersville, Marshall County, Tenn. He also recalls Missionary Ridge and was in the bloody battle of Franklin with the cavalry under Capt. Andrew P. Gordon, now living at Cornersville. *This faithful servant and negro soldier was surrendered at Gainesville, Ga., May 10, 1865.*

"Uncle" Mack Dabney.

The following letter from Capt. Gordon gives authenticity to Uncle Mack's service as a Confederate soldier: "Old Uncle Mack Dabney was born and reared three miles south of this place (Cornersville). His old master, the late J. O. Dabney, one of Giles County's best citizens, *sent five noble boys to the Confederate army and also Uncle Mack to cook and wait upon them, which he did well and faithfully to the end. He was with us in all the marches from Fort Donelson to Atlanta and on to Gainesville, Ala., where we all surrendered.* He came home with us and went to work to try to make an honest living for himself and family, and in all these long fifty years just passed I have never heard one single thing against Uncle Mack Dabney. *He is true and faithful to his family and the old soldier* [all emphasis, L.S.]. He is now, and has been for years, sexton at the Methodist church. All the young masters that he went out with have passed away, except one, Sam D. Dabney, who lives here."[513] — CONFEDERATE VETERAN MAGAZINE

CAUSES OF THE WAR FOR SOUTHERN INDEPENDENCE

☛ The different attitudes of the two sections [South and North]—the point of view from which they regarded the impending, the inevitable conflict, the different temperaments—were due, perhaps, somewhat to climatic influences. The [Conservative] South was warm-hearted, generous, quick to resent wrong, either real or fancied, yet capable of a devotion and self-abnegation unparalleled in history in the defense of the right as she saw it. The [Liberal] North, colder, more calculating, pursued with a relentless persistence any object upon which it had concentrated its energies, illustrated by the historic utterance of [Union] General [Ulysses S.] Grant's: "We will fight it out on this line if it takes all summer."

In seeming contradiction to this characteristic there was a strong element in the North capable of the wildest, the most extreme [Left-wing] fanaticism. Witness the unreasoning attitude of this class toward slavery. The South will always most steadfastly and conscientiously maintain that the responsibility for this great evil cannot justly be laid to her door.

When the Constitution was adopted and the Union formed, slavery existed practically in all the States, and its disappearance in the Northern and its firmer establishment in the Southern States were due to climatic and industrial conditions and not to the existence of any great moral idea.

U.S. Vice President Adlai Ewing Stevenson.

The causes of the war will be found somewhat in the Constitution itself, in *the conflicting constructions that it invited*, in the then established institution of slavery, which it recognized and endeavored to protect.

If asked what was the real cause of the war, the ignorant and unthinking would perhaps say, "The negro"; but that there would have been no slavery if the protests of the South (notably South Carolina and Georgia) could have availed when it was first introduced, history abundantly proves ; and now that it is gone by violence and bloodshed, in no section would its restoration be more strongly and universally resisted.

[Confederate Gen.] General [Robert E.] Lee, than whom no loftier spirit or more conscientious Christian gentleman ever lived, uttered these immortal words: "*We had, I was satisfied, sacred principles and rights to defend, for which we were in duty bound to do our best if we perished in the endeavor.*" Vice President Adlai Stevenson said: "In the dread tribunal of last resort valor struggled against valor; here brave men fought and died for their rights as God gave them to see their rights."

It was claimed by the advocates of secession that the United States was not a single nation, but a collection or confederation of sovereign States, united only for mutual convenience and protection against a foreign foe under a treaty known . . . [first, as "the Articles of Confederation," and second, as] the "Constitution of the United States."[514] *If, then, this Constitution was a treaty between sovereign States, it was plain that any one of the parties to it might, in the exercise of sovereign power, withdraw from the treaty if, in the estimation of the majority of its citizens, the terms of the treaty had been violated* [all emphasis, L.S.].[515] — MRS. LOUISE WINSTON MAXWELL, PADUCAH CHAPTER, U.D.C.

WHY THE EMANCIPATION PROCLAMATION FAILED

☛ Lord John Russell, British Secretary of State for Foreign Affairs, sneered at [Lincoln's illegal Emancipation Proclamation] . . . and sent the following dispatch to the British Minister at Washington: *"It is a measure of a questionable kind, an act of vengeance on the slave owner. It proposes emancipation only where the United States authority cannot make emancipation a reality, but nowhere that the decree can be carried out."*

It was a failure. The Southern States were not under the government of the United States. They had legally withdrawn, and Lincoln had no jurisdiction over them. And even if they had not withdrawn, it was a usurpation of power and was unconstitutional for him to interfere with slavery in the States. Congress so construed it and did not act on it. It would not have stood the test of the court. He did not intend it for the purpose of emancipation. It was a strategic war measure to create conditions in the homes that would affect the Confederate army. Had such conditions been brought about, it would have cast the foulest blot on American history and would have shocked the civilized world. But it failed because the slaves refused, with the exception of a few of the low type, to leave their Southern homes. They stayed with the unprotected women and children and protected them and continued the cultivation of the plantations, by which they, as well as the army, were fed.

British Prime Minister Lord John Russell.

Just here the law of compensation manifested itself. Contrary to the accusations of the radical abolitionists [that is, socialists and communists] of the East, *the Southern master had given to the benighted African civilization and Christianity, had furnished him a home provided with comforts as well as necessities; he was given that tender solicitude bestowed on a child by its parents and was tenderly nursed in sickness and comforted in sorrow. There were special pews for him in the churches. He had his feast days and holidays. In fact, he was made a member of the master's household, and these blessings were his without the care of having to provide them. He slept soundly at night, knowing that everything was being looked after by "marster." His place was allotted to him, and he knew his place and kept it with reverence and affection.*

The tie between master and servant was not only beautiful, but it was strong. A more beautiful character does not figure in any romance or legend than the "black mammy" in the Southern home. What tender memories live in the hearts of those who were so fortunate as to have a "black mammy"! She is intimately associated with the tender grace of that day. Heaven bless her memory!

Yes, we gave them much, and they also gave us much in return. I think often of it. They remained with us after they were freed and gave us protection in another way that we hardly know how to value. They are with us as laborers still; and when the low class of foreigners come to our shores, they do not settle in the South, because they cannot compete with negro labor and do not want to be associated in the same ranks [all emphasis, L.S.]. . . .[516] — FANNIE E. SELPH, HISTORIAN KATE LITTON HICKMAN CHAPTER, U.D.C., NASHVILLE, TENN.

OLD JERRY: FAITHFUL BLACK CONFEDERATE & SERVANT

☞ How memory brings up the faithful service of this old slave! Old Jerry was not old in years, but all of Company C knew him as Old Jerry, belonging to a private in that company. Jerry's make-up might have been the cause of his being dubbed "Old," as he was of very large body and short legs, his feet turning out when he walked and his head being almost nude of wool. Jerry was very black, but he claimed that he was of "ginger cake color, but sorter scorched." Jerry was a merry, laughing, obliging servant, and his laugh was musical and contagious. No member of Company C ever called on Jerry for a favor that did not get a promise; but often he could not fulfill his promises, as they were too many and varied. Jerry had been reared on a large farm in H_____ County and, on account of the formation of his legs and feet, was taught the blacksmith's trade, as his kind master did not think he could stand the plow. The old master was dead, and the indulgent mistress of Jerry and mother of the soldier insisted that Jerry should be the bodyservant of C., as *the mistress had so much confidence in Jerry's fealty to his young master and the Southern cause.*

Although it left the plantation without a blacksmith, *Jerry and his young master entered the army of the Confederacy very early in the beginning of the war.* Every member of Company C had confidence in Jerry, and they often gave him large sums of Confederate money to forage the surrounding country when in camp. Never did Old Jerry fail to get their money's worth, nor did he ever embezzle any funds. Jerry was very polite, especially to "white ladies," as he called all white women. As all ladies were glad to help the soldiers and Jerry's description of their suffering was so vivid, little money had to be used to fill haversacks or canteens. Terry always put the members of Company C as the heroes of his stories and his young master as the principal actor in deeds of chivalry. Although his master was very young and never a neat dresser and far from being a lady's man, Jerry always made him out to the young ladies as a regular gallant and to the old ladies as a "boy." *Jerry was a regular war correspondent as to the news from the front when on his foraging trips, and he never carried any news of defeat; but all was victory for the Confederacy with him* [all emphasis, L.S.].

On one occasion, in the memorable Georgia campaign of 1864, Jerry was given money from all the company and told to go beyond the range of the Buttermilk Cavalry in the rear and buy anything to eat he could find. His master's pass was all he needed; but Jerry had his pass countersigned by the captain, as, to his mind, that gave his pass a military look and seemed more soldierlike. As the mountainous country of North Georgia was sparsely settled and the land on the rocky and sandy hills not very fertile, Jerry had to go a long distance to find a "cove" where provisions were more plentiful and the soldiers had not already foraged. In this cove were several large

Felix Haywood, former black servant, San Antonio, Texas, 1937.

plantations, and few soldiers had been in that isolated cove.

Jerry was in his "elements," as he called it, and the news of the front was eagerly sought by the women, only a few old men being left there, and Jerry could tell things as an eyewitness. Jerry found one house where the lady had charge of her husband's farm, he being an officer in the Virginia Army. Jerry had the lady and two sweet girls about sixteen and eighteen years old to listen to his tales of heroism of Company C and his young master. His young master was described as a model dresser, cleanly even in the ditches of the front, and very brave, often leading the company in its many charges and always with success. The mistress of the plantation loaded Jerry down with everything eatable that he wanted—a nice sugar-cured ham, several chickens, six or eight dozen biscuits baked especially for him, a jug of pure molasses, and, best of all, a haversack full of shelled peanuts. Jerry had made his young master out a very rich planter, the number of slaves on the plantation running up into hundreds and the plantation he owned reaching from Big Black to Pearl River.

After spending the night in the negro quarters, early the next morning Jerry came to the big house to bid the lad good-bye. While talking to them he spied two large covered army wagons up the road leading to the house, and, to his consternation, in the first wagon was this "Adonis" [his young master] he had just been describing to the girls. Ragged, dirty, and pinched by hunger and exposure to the summer sun, naturally dark, he was as black as an Indian. Jerry hurriedly left the ladies to meet the wagon. He stopped it and began thus: "Marse C., what in the name ob God is you doin' drivin' that ole wagin fur? Ah is surprised that you got down to be a common wagin driver." C. explained that it was his time to do fatigue duty, and the wagon driver was sick, and he had been detailed to come here after a load of corn for the officers' horses.

Miss Doris Gautreaux, of Galveston, Texas, Sponsor for Camp Magruder at Richmond Reunion.

Jerry thought for a moment and then said: "Now, boss, Ah's been with you all thu dis wah, and Ah want you to do me a big favor. Doan' tell the folks at the house yoh name and doan' tell 'em even what company you b'long to. Ah sho' has got a good lot of things to eat, and Ah had to stritch the blanket a little about who Ah belonged to. Yoh is lookin' worse dan Ah eber seed you—no coat an' dat old torn shirt an' dat pine straw hat doan' mek yoh look like yohself. Ah will take the wagin back to load it too and tell the ladies that Ah knowed the wagin driver, an' he promised to let me ride back to camp fur loadin' the wagin fur him. Yoh do as Ah says, and Ah sho'ly will be mighty glad."

As C. was not fond of work, he readily agreed to the trade and sat down to raw ham, biscuits, and molasses, and finished off with peanuts. When the wagons were loaded and Jerry came back with the wagon, C. got in and began: "Jerry, you must have told those ladies a lot of lies to bring such a big supply of grub, and, besides, you were afraid to let me go up there and tell the whole truth."

Jerry replied: "Ah wa'n't so skeered ob what yoh saved as Ah was ob what yoh looked. Ah tole dem pretty white ladies yoh wore good clothes, an' yoh sho'ly 'ain't got on good clothes to-day. Ah tole dem yoh eben kep' clean in de ditches, an' Ah am sho' not a man in dat piney wood Company K is as dirty as yoh is. Ah sho'ly am goin' to stop at de fust creek an' wash yoh clean one time an' wash dem clothes too if dey will hol' together."

When Jerry got back to the wagon train and C. had taken his place in the trenches again and the rations had been eaten by the company, the story leaked out of Jerry's description of his boss and his boss's actual looks. Jerry on reaching home after the war told this story to his old mistress and said: "Miss Tilda, Ah neber seed de boss look so ragged endurin' de whole wah as he looked dat mawnin'."

Miss Tilda said: "Well, Jerry, if he looked any worse than when he reached home, he surely was quite different from your description of him to the good lady and her daughters."[517] — ANNIE LAURIE SHARKEY, ST. LOUIS, MO.

ME & MAMMY

☞ Me and Mammy know a child
About my age and size
Who, Mammy says, won't go to heaven
'Cause she's so grown and wise.

She answers "Yes" and "No" just so
When folks speak to her
And laughs at Mammy and at me
When I say "Ma'am" and "Sir."

And Mammy says the reason why
This child's in such a plight
Is 'cause she's had no Mammy dear
To raise her sweet and right,

To stand between her and the world,
With all its old sad noise,
And give her baby heart a chance
To keep its baby joys.

Then Mammy draws me close to her
And says: "The Lord be praised,
Here's what I calls a decent chile,
Cause hit's been Mammy-raised!"[518] — MARIA HOWARD WEEDEN

Mammy Easter Partee and one of her "babies."

IN MEMORY OF A FAITHFUL SERVANT

☞ After the War between the States, Easter Partee, a young negro girl, remained loyal to her "Old Master" and "Old Miss" and during the rest of her life maintained this loyalty and devotion to the white people, whom she always claimed as her friends. She married and became Easter Brownlee. *When widowed and having no children of her own, her big motherly heart embraced the little white babies placed in her care with all the love that only a real Southern "mammy" could give them.* She was nurse in the Houston families of Aberdeen, Miss., before going to Memphis, Tenn., where she entered the family of Mr. Sam Pepper and nursed his four children until the oldest child married; then mammy went with her to care for the "grandbabies." *She was an interested and constant reader of the* Confederate Veteran [magazine], *her name being on its subscription list, and eagerly each month she looked forward to its coming in her mail. "In God we trust" was a favorite motto with her and the real keynote to her life, for she lived in true Christian spirit, giving unselfishly of her time and money to those less fortunate and never too busy to help those who called upon her for aid. On May 2, 1916, this noble woman died at the home of Mrs. Hugh B. Speed, in Chicago, who had been her first charge of the Pepper children, and she brought mammy back to Memphis that she might rest in that Southland which had always been so dear to her heart.*

It is lives like mammy's which make this world a better place [all emphasis, L.S.], *and the sun is setting on these lives in a rosy hue, leaving a sweet memory to cheer those who grieve their loss.*[519] — CONFEDERATE VETERAN MAGAZINE

BLACK SERVANT BELONGED TO NUMEROUS CONFEDERATE GROUPS

☞ In tribute to one of that fast-passing generation of faithful slaves of the South, Mrs. F. C. Fox, of Amarillo, Tex., writes sympathetically of "Uncle" Ned Buchanan, of Harrison County, Tex., who died some months ago, after a long illness. Uncle Ned was purchased by his master, Col. Rene Fitzpatrick, at Talbotton, Ga., in August, 1834, when only one year old, from [a Yankee slave owner named] Young H. Greer, of Baltimore, Md., and the record of this sale is still in the family. After the war Uncle Ned became a prosperous farmer in Texas, owning his own farm, and *was highly respected for his honesty and integrity. He was a member of several Confederate associations and proudly wore the badges of the W. P. Lane Camp, No. 621, U.C.V., Ross's, Ector's, and Granbury's Association, and Company A, 3rd Texas.* Mrs. Fox writes further: "*The old ante-bellum negroes have nearly all crossed the river, and when I meet one of the Old South I feel inclined to lift my hat. No people were more loyal to the South during the war than the negro slaves* [all emphasis, L.S.]. *As a rule, they were all right; but the present generation presents a problem yet to be settled. Uncle Ned was of the old generation and a credit to himself.*"[520] — CONFEDERATE VETERAN MAGAZINE

"Uncle" Ned Buchanan.

HAPPY DAYS ON THE OLD PLANTATIONS

☞ [My family] . . . *had a large plantation with many slaves* . . . [Recently my memory] *takes me back to the good old days of my boyhood, and I can testify to [the reality of] . . . the happy days among the negroes on the old plantations, for I was there. And they certainly were faithful to us while we were in the army* [my emphasis, L.S.].[521] — CLEMENT SAUSSY, SAVANNAH, GA.

SOUTHERN BLACK SERVANTS HAD A HIGHER STANDARD OF LIVING THAN COMMON FREE WHITE LABORERS

☞ ... [The] charge that the wealth of the South was the fruit of the unpaid labor of the negroes was one of the oft-repeated indictments of our system of slavery. Yet a New England author of ability [Prof. Barrett Wendell], a professor in a great university, who quotes this utterance with approval, has the candor to say in another part of his book: *"A very considerable portion of free laborers have never been able to earn more money or to acquire more property than is demanded by the actual and pressing needs of daily existence common to all mankind—the need of food, clothes, and lodging. Now, there can be no question that in return for their services the Southern slaves generally had these needs supplied. They were fed, they were clothed, they were lodged. What is more, they were lodged, fed, and clothed, to all appearances, rather better than they could have lodged, fed, and clothed themselves on any wages which they could have earned."*

I believe that a fair examination would show that no working class the world over was better paid for unskilled labor. Several years ago, while on a visit in Belfast, Ireland, I was entertained by a noted abolitionist. He asked me to tell him what the negroes had to eat and to wear. When I told him, he seemed astonished and said: "No common laborers in this country are so well provided for." I had occasion also on my travels in Europe to see something of the mode of living and the general lack of comfort among the peasantry, especially in Southern Europe, and it was my conviction that the slaves of the South never lived so poorly. A negro would have starved on the wages of these laborers in Italy [all emphasis, L.S.].⁵²² — REV. JAMES H. MCNEILLY, D.D., CONFEDERATE VETERAN, NASHVILLE, TENN.

OLD SOUTH RELIGIOUS BLACKS CONTRASTED WITH NEW SOUTH ATHEISTIC BLACKS

☞ ... In the thirty or forty years just before the war the negroes had the ministrations of able white ministers on the great plantations and in the families of their masters. The Southern Churches of all denominations recognized their responsibility for the spiritual instruction and training of the slaves, and as a consequence *the system of plantation missions of the Methodist Church from 1829 to 1865 led probably a million slaves to Christ as a Saviour*. Other Churches were diligent in the same work, the Baptist Church and the Methodist Church at the close of the war having each about a quarter of a million communicants. The amount expended by the white people of the South in this period for negro evangelization was about four millions of dollars [$130 million in today's currency]. The present generation of the South seem ignorant of what was done by their fathers for the bringing of the slaves to Christianity. It is probable that the real spiritual condition of the half a million slave communicants was superior to that of the three millions of freedmen Church members of to-day, with the wild [African] orgies and superstitious [Pagan] rites of so many of them.

There is no doubt in the mind of the [white] Southerner who knew the old order that in the elements that go to make high and true character the present generation of negroes, with their pertness, conceit, idleness, shirking of responsibility, lack of trustworthiness, is *distinctly inferior to the old-time slave, with his affection for his "white folks," his pride in the family of which he was a part, his faithfulness to a trust, his loyalty and devotion to the interests of the family, his instinctive sense of propriety, and his fine manners. The "mammies" and "daddies," the "uncles" and "aunties" of those days deserved all the confidence and affection given them by every member of the household* [all emphasis, L.S.].

As a general rule, *the slavery of the South was a life of patriarchal simplicity, with contentment and peace, free from the sharp competitions of trade and the struggle for a living.* I seriously doubt if any advantage of freedom as now exercised, with its anxiety for food and raiment and shelter, can compensate for the loss of the old-time relationship. Now it is jealousy and suspicion, breaking out in frequent conflicts with assassinations and lynchings.[523] — REV. JAMES H. MCNEILLY, D.D., CONFEDERATE VETERAN, NASHVILLE, TENN.

MORE REASONS BEHIND SOUTHERN SECESSION

☛ . . . This was the point [in 1860] to which the [Right-wing] Southern people had come. They had submitted to aggressions of the central government, to flagrant denial of their constitutional rights by the [Left-wing] Northern States, to abuse, misrepresentation, and denunciation by a large number of the Northern people. They had seen a sectional [Liberal] party [then the Republican Party] organized on the platform of opposition to their social and domestic life and system of labor and pledged to deny them equal rights in the territories gained largely by their valor and statesmanship. *They saw that party grow in power until it controlled the Northern States and under forms of law gained control of the central government by the election of a sectional President.* They [the Southern people] felt that submission had reached the limit, and the only remedy was to withdraw from a Union which had become a menace to their dearest rights.

That they did not misunderstand the purpose of the party in power is evident from the honors paid to the memory of [Yankee socialist, murderer, and abolitionist] John Brown, who was hanged for invading the State of Virginia and striving to arouse the slaves to insurrection. There was mourning, with draped churches, in many Northern communities the day he was hanged. His execution was compared to Christ's crucifixion. During the war the Union soldiers chanted his dirge as they marched through the South, pillaging and burning as they marched. After the war the bodies of his associates were disinterred and buried with the honors of war by United States soldiers by order of Mr. [Elihu] Root, Secretary of War in Mr. [William] McKinley's Cabinet. John Brown's home was made by the State of New York a shrine of patriotism, and President McKinley was present at the dedication. The State of Kansas dedicated a park to his memory at Osawatomie, the scene of some of his abolition outrages. Ex-President Theodore Roosevelt was

Your children will want to know the truth about the War for Southern Independence. Teach it to them.

the orator of the occasion and glorified the murderer and assassin as a hero entitled to the nation's gratitude.

Under all the circumstances to ask the Southern people to rejoice in the dishonor done to their States is to ask them to stultify themselves and to acknowledge that the fathers of the republic were lacking in wisdom and patriotism in reserving sovereignty to the States. It is asking us to confess that the abolitionists [that is, socialists and communists] were right in refusing to be bound by the Constitution and in denying the equality of the Southern States.[524] — REV. JAMES H. MCNEILLY, D.D., CONFEDERATE VETERAN, NASHVILLE, TENN.

OLD SLAVE COUPLE FEEDS & AIDS CONFEDERATE SOLDIERS

☞ . . . On reaching the bank of the river where stood a log cabin, the only building left of an old Southern home, occupied by an aged couple of slaves, the old darky warned us of the frequent visits of the Yankees from their fleet in small boats. The old woman cooked us some bacon and corn bread from their meager supply, for which we compensated them liberally with some silver coin. While we were hastily discussing plain but well-relished viands, the old man, stationed outside on picket, hurriedly reported the smoke of a steamer above the bend. . . .[525] — C. Y. FORD, CONFEDERATE VETERAN, ODESSA, MO.

Confederate Gen. William Joseph Hardee.

OBSERVATIONS OF A CONFEDERATE SOLDIER PASSING THROUGH CHARLESTON, WEST VIRGINIA

☞ . . . In going toward Harper's Ferry we passed through the pretty little village of Charlestown at an early hour on the 26th of August, 1864. It was a lovely country, and *I thought that if old John Brown ever had a conscience it must have jolted him when he surreptitiously entered that beautiful and healthful land, where even the negro slaves lived like white people and were just as happy* [my emphasis, L.S.]. . . .[526] — JOHN COXE, GROVELAND, CAL.

A YANKEE DEFENDS THE SOUTH

☞ . . . Another impression [I] received [while visiting the Confederate White House in 1916] was that slavery was but an incidental cause of the great fraternal strife. In this retrospect of half a century *one cannot believe that two mighty sections of one blood and language could have hurled themselves in deadly combat at each other over an issue like that of African slavery.* For slavery was doomed both for humane and economic reasons, and, as well, the cosmic law that transforms childhood and dependence into the estate of maturity and self-reliance was acting powerfully to free the bondman. *If slavery was an immediate irritant leading to the War between the States, it was so for the reason that one section attempted prematurely to hasten a process that human and economic and cosmic forces were fast consummating,* and this prematureness that resulted in so much loss of life and treasure led to the crime of an invasion that had no warrant in right and law and to repel which the South and her leaders drew the sword. [Edmund] Randolph once declared: "We have a wolf [referring to slavery] by the ears; we fear to hold it, but dare not let it go." Certainly the deplorable experiences of Reconstruction gave ample justification to the fears and the judgment of the ante-bellum South.

No, the real cause of the war lay far deeper than slavery. As one hastened through this impressive repository of a cause which arises in perennial resurrection (two hours only were available for the visit where two weeks would be insufficient) one most profoundly realized that the differences created by the issues of *Imperialism* [that is, radical Liberalism and/or socialism] and *Republicanism* [that is, Americanism or Conservatism], a controversy at least inherited from ancient Greece and Rome, were fundamentally the *casus belli* in 1861-65. So far as our nationality is concerned, these causes trace back to the Federalist [then the Left-wing Party] and Democratic-Republican [then the Right-wing Party] parties [of the Colonial period].

. . . Here, then, and not in slavery per se, were the roots of the struggle at arms in 1861-65. One could but reflect upon these things as one stood amongst the Confederate memorials in Richmond. And, too, the irony of the situation was brought to mind when one reflected that the Southern people held in bondage four millions of blacks, while at the same time they drew the sword in defense of constitutional Federalism, Republican [Conservative] self-government, and Jeffersonian ideals of human liberty. Yet the explanation is very easy. The whites were an old and mature race; the blacks a young and immature race. Of necessity, therefore, the one must dominate the other, as much so as that parents must control the children in the family life. And as children must perform household tasks unrequited save for care, so must an immature race do the same on a larger scale. If Southern plantations were carried on by slave labor, so Northern farms were largely carried on by the unpaid labor of sons and daughters and minor relatives until they reached legal majority. And the Confederate war, waged to maintain the right to regulate the affairs of the immature, was as justifiable as it would have been for a Northern farmer to resist by force of arms any invasion of his family intended prematurely to free his sons and daughters before they all attained legal majority. The Southern people, guaranteed under the Constitution which they so willingly helped to form the right of regulation of their own local affairs, refused to tolerate invasion of either territory or legal rights. Hence the war then of bullets, now and for years to come of ballots [all emphasis, L.S.]. . . .⁵²⁷ —
A. W. LITTLEFIELD, D.D., NEEDHAM, MASS.

Gen. Robert E. Lee between battles.

THE HYPOCRISY OF YANKEE LIBERALS
☞ . . . we call to mind some of the vagaries of the New England conscience in the past—how the Puritans sought "gainful pillage" in exploiting the Indians and sold hundreds of them, women and children,

captured in 1676, into slavery in the West Indies, yet to-day boast with pious gratulation that no slave ever breathed the air of Massachusetts—that conscience which fled from England to enjoy liberty and freedom from persecution; yet it whipped, hanged, and banished Quakers and persecuted Baptists in behalf of sound doctrine. It burned witches for the glory of God and the safety of the people. *It engaged for over a century in importing slaves from Africa, with all the horrors of the middle passage; and when slave labor became unprofitable in the North on account of the climate, their slaves were sold to the South. Then when there was danger of the South's maintaining her equality in the Union, the New England conscience became outraged over the sin of slavery and strove to limit the rights of the Southern States in the territories won by their valor and statesmanship and so secure the preponderance of the Northern States in the Union* [my emphasis, L.S.].... [528] — REV. JAMES H. MCNEILLY, D.D., CONFEDERATE VETERAN, NASHVILLE, TENN.

SOME DIFFERENCES BETWEEN WHITE & BLACK RELATIONS IN THE OLD SOUTH AS COMPARED TO THE NEW SOUTH

☛ ... Now [in the New South, that is, the South as of the early 20th Century] in the case of the negro the law of the land has supplanted the old relations; and the fact that he stands as an equal before the law seems to release the white man from the higher law of *noblesse oblige*, which was largely recognized by the slaveholder in the former days. Then [in the Old South] cruelty to helpless and dependent negroes was counted dishonorable and cowardly, and public opinion condemned it. Moreover, the higher law that exacted kindness to the weak was reenforced by the sentiments of affection subsisting between master and servant.

Miss Marguerite H. G. Stringer, Sponsor for Florida Division, U.D.C., Louisville Reunion.

Now the tendency of the present generation of [communized] negroes is to look upon the Southern white man as an enemy and to assert their rights aggressively, if not insolently, being too often put up to it by [radical Left-wing] politicians or [socialist] pseudo-philanthropists. *One must recognize the danger when race prejudice is aggravated by contempt on one side and hatred on the other* [my emphasis, L.S.].[529] — REV. JAMES H. MCNEILLY, D.D., CONFEDERATE VETERAN, NASHVILLE, TENN.

SOUTHERN BLACK SERVANT TREATS VISITING YANKEE LIKE AN OUTSIDER

☛ About seven years before the great American conflict [Yankee Liberal] Charles Sumner was visiting at a private home near Gallatin, Tenn. Here there was a shrewd old [black] house servant, a great favorite with his master's family. He was known as "Old Virginia Jeff," and after Senator Sumner's departure Jeff told the following story of a

Black servants who desired an education were schooled by their white owners. Just as often, servants taught each other to read and write—usually for the purpose of studying the Bible.

conversation between the Senator and himself. Senator Sumner: "Jeff, I hear you call all the white folks down here 'Marse'—'Marse Henry,' 'Marse John,' or what not. Isn't that true?'" Jeff: "Yas, suh." Senator Sumner: "And you always call me 'Mister Sumner.' Now, Jeff, here's a quarter. During the rest of my visit call me Marse Charles, you hear?" The old-time negroes intuitively knew who belonged to them and who didn't [my emphasis, L.S.]. Senator Sumner was accorded different treatment and felt like an outsider. Hence his bribe to Jeff.[530] — CONFEDERATE MAJOR JOHN C. WRENSHALL, ENGINEERING STAFF OF GEN. BRAXTON BRAGG

BLACK CONFEDERATE HUMOR
☛ An old negro who was body servant and cook for an Arkansas officer was ambling along with the stragglers in the rear of the Confederate army on the retreat from Helena [Alabama] when a staff officer overtook him. "Sam," asked the officer, "can you tell me where I can find headquarters?" "Naw, suh," replied the negro. "I don't know where dem headquarters is. I ain't seed nothin' 't all ter-day but hindquarters."[531] — CONFEDERATE VETERAN MAGAZINE

SOUTHERN BLACK SERVANTS RESIST YANKEE BULLYING
☛ . . . Our servants they [the Yankee soldiers] "kindly" made free, and told them they must follow them (the officers). [Our black servant] Margret was boasting the other day of her answer, "I don't want to be any free-er than I is now—I'll stay with my mistress." . . . The conduct of all our servants is beyond praise. . . . During the [skirmish around our house] . . . a fleeing [Union] officer stopped to throw a musket in [black servant] Charles Barker's hands, and bade him fight for his liberty. Charles drew himself up, saying, "I am only a slave, but I am a Secesh nigger, and won't fight in such a damned crew!" . . .[532] — SARAH MORGAN DAWSON (20 YEARS OLD), NEW ORLEANS, LA.

The End

Sumner A. Cunningham, founder of *Confederate Veteran* magazine.

U.S. President Theodore Roosevelt, nephew of Confederate soldiers.

> **The Vice President's Chamber**
> **WASHINGTON, D.C.**
>
> Oyster Bay, N. Y., May 31st, 1901
>
> S. A. Cunningham, Esq.,
>
> Nashville, Tenn.
>
> My dear Mr. Cunningham:—
>
> I thank you very much for sending me the copies of the Confederate Veteran. My Uncle, Captain Bulloch always struck me as the nearest approach to Colonel Newcome of any man I ever met in actual life.
>
> With great regard,
>
> Sincerely yours,
>
> Theodore Roosevelt

Theodore Roosevelt sent the personal letter above to Sumner Archibald Cunningham, a former Confederate soldier and the beloved founder, editor, and publisher of *Confederate Veteran* magazine, in the Spring of 1901, while he was serving as vice president under U.S. President William McKinley. (Note that McKinley was our country's first modern Conservative Republican: between 1854 and 1896 the Republicans were the Liberal, or Left-wing, Party, the Democrats were the Conservative, or Right-wing, Party.) In the missive Roosevelt makes reference to Captain James Dunwoody Bulloch, one of his two uncles, both who served in the Confederate military. The Vice President compares Captain Bulloch to "Colonel Newsome," a fictional character created by English novelist William Makepeace Thackeray in 1854, a figure who came to be a personification of morality and righteousness. Vice President Roosevelt, later President Roosevelt, was only one of a number of early American chief executives who encouraged friendly relations with the South, and especially with Confederate veterans. Due to the Left's demonization of the South and the complete whitewash of Southern history, the practice has fallen out of favor, with some U.S. presidents now even publically excoriating the Confederacy and her symbols.

APPENDIX A
Forrest's Independent Order of Pole Bearers' Speech

NO VICTORIAN SOUTHERNER HAS BEEN more maligned, or more spitefully branded with the "white supremacist" label, than Confederate Gen. Nathan Bedford Forrest. Is this fair, accurate, or even historical? Of course not, and the documented facts prove it. One example is the following speech, which I have included here to provide added perspective to the central topic of this book: ethnic studies and the Old South. Forrest delivered it at Memphis, Tennessee, in 1875, before the Independent Order of Pole Bearers, a sociopolitical group of black Southerners and the forerunner of the now Left-wing NAACP. As reported by the Memphis *Daily Avalanche*, July 6, 1875, as Forrest approached the podium, an African American woman named Miss Lou Lewis, stepped forward and handed him a bouquet of flowers "as a token, of reconciliation, an offering of peace and good will." Smiling, Forrest bowed to the crowd and said:

Forrest late in life.

> Miss Lewis, ladies and gentlemen—I accept these flowers as a token of reconciliation between the white and colored races of the South. I accept them more particularly, since they come from a lady, for if there is any one on God's great earth who loves the ladies, it is myself. This is a proud day for me. Having occupied the position I have for thirteen years, and being misunderstood by the colored race, I take this occasion to say that I am your friend. I am here as the representative of the Southern people—one that has been more maligned than any other. I assure you that everyman who was in the Confederate army is your friend. We were born on the same soil, breathe the same air, live in the same land, and why should we not be brothers and sisters. When the war broke out I believed it to be my duty to fight for my country, and I did so. I came here with the jeers and sneers of a few white people, who did not think it right. I think it is right, and will do all I can to bring about harmony, peace and unity. I want to elevate every man, and to see you take your places in your shops, stores and offices. I don't propose to say anything about politics, but I want you to do as I do—go to the polls and select the best men to vote for. I feel that you are free men, I am a free man, and we can do as we please. I came here as a friend, and whenever I can serve any of you I will do so. We have one Union, one flag, one country, therefore let us stand together. Although we differ in color, we should not differ in sentiment. Many things have been said in regard to myself, and many reports circulated, which may perhaps be believed by some of you, but there are many around me who can contradict them. I have been many times in the heat of battle—oftener, perhaps, than any within the sound of my voice. Men have come to me to ask for quarter, both black and white, and I have shielded them. Do your duty as citizens, and if any are oppressed, I will be your friend. I thank you for the flowers, and assure you that I am with you in heart and hand.[533] — NATHAN BEDFORD FORREST, JULY 4, 1875

Louis Napoleon Nelson, one of the 1 million black Confederates who served in the C.S. army and navy—in Private Nelson's case, in Company M, 7th Cavalry Tennessee. Perhaps the first and only officially commissioned black chaplain in the C.S. military, Louis fought under famed Confederate hero General Nathan Bedford Forrest at the Battles of Brice's Cross Roads, Shiloh, and Fort Pillow. His other conflicts include the Battles of Lookout Mountain and Vicksburg. After the War Louis attended 39 Confederate veterans' reunions, and at his funeral his coffin was draped in a Confederate Battle Flag. His grandson, Nelson W. Winbush, a Korean War vet and a lifetime member of the Sons of Confederate Veterans, wrote the foreword to my book, *Everything You Were Taught About the Civil War is Wrong, Ask a Southerner!* Photo © courtesy Nelson W. Winbush.

APPENDIX B
Abraham Lincoln's Real Views on Race & Slavery

THE LEFT HAS NOT ONLY deceived the world concerning the War for Southern Independence, it has also fabricated a completely new mythological Abraham Lincoln, transforming him from a tyrannical white racist, separatist, and supremacist, into a saintly egalitarian figure, one that would have been completely unrecognizable to his contemporaries. The degree of censorship, gaslighting, misrepresentation, and outright lying involved in this sordid ruse can best be seen and understood by comparing the Left's absurdly unrealistic portrait of Lincoln with his actual words, a tiny sampling which I have included below. Compare these statements with those made throughout this book by Victorian Southerners and Confederate soldiers.

★ "Negro equality! Fudge!! How long, in the Government of a God great enough to make and maintain this universe, shall there continue [to be] knaves to vend and fools to gulp, so low a piece of demagoguism as this?"[534] — ABRAHAM LINCOLN, SEPT. 1859

★ "[I have never intended to] . . . set the niggers and white people to marry together."[535] — ABRAHAM LINCOLN, AUG. 21, 1858

Despite the fact that Southern whites and blacks had lived together harmoniously for centuries, white separatist Liberal Abraham Lincoln believed that the two races could not and should not mingle—either socially or genetically. Hence his lifelong membership in the American Colonization Society, whose primary mission was to deport and settle ("colonize") blacks in foreign lands.

★ ". . . this is the true complexion of all I have ever said in regard to the institution of slavery and the black race. This is the whole of it, and anything that argues me into this idea of perfect, social, and political equality with the negro, is but a specious and fantastic arrangement of words, by which a man can prove a horse chestnut to be a chestnut horse."[536] — ABRAHAM LINCOLN, AUG. 21, 1858

★ "In the first place, what is necessary to make the institution national? Not war. There is no danger that the people of Kentucky will shoulder their muskets, and, with a young nigger stuck on every bayonet, march into Illinois and force them upon us. There is no danger of our going over there and making war upon them."[537] — ABRAHAM LINCOLN, AUG. 21, 1858

★ "I had no thought in the world that I was doing anything to bring about a political and social equality of the black and white races."[538] — ABRAHAM LINCOLN, AUG. 21, 1858

★ "[Conservative] Judge [Stephen A.] Douglas is especially horrified at the thought of the mixing of blood by the white and black races. Agreed for once—a thousand times agreed. There are white men enough to marry all the white women, and black men enough to marry all the black women; and so let them be married."[539] — ABRAHAM LINCOLN, JUNE 26, 1857

★ "We were often—more than once at least—in the course of Judge Douglas's speech last night reminded that this government was made for white men—that he believed it was made for white men. Well, that is putting it into a shape in which no one wants to deny it; but the judge then goes into his passion for drawing inferences that are not warranted. I protest, now and forever, against that counterfeit logic which presumes that because I do not want a negro woman for a slave, I do necessarily want her for a wife. My understanding is that I need not have her for either; but, as God made us separate, we can leave one another alone, and do one another much good thereby. There are white men enough to marry all the white women, and enough black men to marry all the black women, and in God's name let them be so married. The judge regales us with the terrible enormities that take place by the mixture of races: that the inferior race bears the superior down. Why, judge, if we do not let them get together in the Territories, they won't mix there. [An audience member: "Three cheers for Lincoln!" The cheers were given with a hearty good will.] I should say at least that that is a self-evident truth."[540] — ABRAHAM LINCOLN, JULY 10, 1858

★ "In the course of his reply, Senator Douglas remarked, in substance, that he had always considered this government was made for the white people and not for the negroes. Why, in point of mere fact, I think so too."[541] — ABRAHAM LINCOLN, OCT. 16, 1854

★ "I will say then that I am not, nor ever have been, in favor of bringing about in any way the social and political equality of the white and black races—that I am not, nor ever have been, in favor of making voters or jurors of negroes, nor of qualifying them to hold office, nor to intermarry with white people. . . . and I will say in addition to this that there is a physical difference between the white and black races which I believe will forever forbid the two races living together on terms of social and political equality. And inasmuch as they cannot so live, while they do remain together there must be the position of superior and inferior, and I as much as any other man am in favor of having the superior position assigned to the white race."[542] — ABRAHAM LINCOLN, SEPT. 18, 1858

★ "I give him [Judge Douglas] the most solemn pledge that I will to the very last stand by the law of this State [Illinois], which forbids the marrying of white people with negroes."[543] — ABRAHAM LINCOLN, SEPT. 18, 1858

★ "If there was a necessary conflict [race war] between the white man and the negro, I should be for the white man . . ."[544] — ABRAHAM LINCOLN, Sept. 16, 1859

★ "The proposition that there is a struggle between the white man and the negro contains a falsehood. There is no struggle. If there was, I should be for the white man."[545] — ABRAHAM LINCOLN, FEB. 27, 1860

★ [Lincoln quoting Z. B. Mayo] 'Our opinion is that it would be best for all concerned to have the colored population in a State by themselves.' ("In this I agree with him"—[Lincoln's note].)[546] — ABRAHAM LINCOLN, SEPT. 15, 1858

★ "There is a natural disgust in the minds of nearly all white people, to the idea of an indiscriminate amalgamation [that is, race mixing or interracial marriage] of the white and black races;[547] — ABRAHAM LINCOLN, JUNE 26, 1857

★ "A separation of the races is the only perfect preventive of amalgamation; but as an immediate separation is impossible, the next best thing is to keep them apart where they are not already together."[548] — ABRAHAM LINCOLN, JUNE 26, 1857

★ "If all earthly power were given me, I should not know what to do, as to the existing institution. My first impulse would be to free all the slaves, and send them to Liberia [Africa],—to their own native land."[549] — ABRAHAM LINCOLN, AUGUST 21, 1858

★ "Now, irrespective of the moral aspect of this question as to whether there is a right or wrong in enslaving a negro, I am still in favor of our new Territories [that is, the as of yet unformed and unnamed Western states] being in such a condition that white men may find a home—may find some spot where they can better their condition—where they can settle upon new soil, and better their condition in life. I am in favor of this not merely (I must say it here as I have elsewhere) for our own people who are born amongst us, but as an outlet for free white people everywhere, the world over. . ."[550] — ABRAHAM LINCOLN, OCT. 15, 1858

★ ". . . it is my purpose, upon the next meeting of Congress to again recommend . . . that the effort to colonize [deport] persons of African descent, with their consent, upon this continent, or elsewhere, with the previously obtained consent of the Governments existing there, will be continued."[551] — ABRAHAM LINCOLN, SEPT. 22, 1862

★ "What I would most desire would be the separation of the white and black races."[552] — ABRAHAM LINCOLN, JULY 17, 1858

NOTES

1. Seabrook, *Abraham Lincoln Was a Liberal, Jefferson Davis Was a Conservative*, p. 55.
2. Schlüter, p. 23.
3. Woods, p. 47.
4. On Lincoln's socialistic, Marxist, and communist thoughts, ideas, and tendencies, see my books: 1) *Lincoln's War: The Real Cause, The Real Winner, the Real Loser*; 2) *Abraham Lincoln Was a Liberal, Jefferson Davis Was a Conservative: The Missing Key to Understanding the American Civil War*; 3) *Abraham Lincoln: The Southern View*. Also see McCarty, passim; Browder, passim; Benson and Kennedy, passim.
5. See J. W. Jones, TDMV, pp. 144, 200-201, 273.
6. See Seabrook, *The Alexander H. Stephens Reader*, passim. See also, Pollard, LC, p. 178; J. H. Franklin, pp. 101, 111, 130, 149; Nicolay and Hay, ALCW, Vol. 1, p. 627.
7. Seabrook, *A Short History of the Confederate States of America* (J. Davis), p. 59.
8. Seabrook, *A Short History of the Confederate States of America* (J. Davis), pp. 55-56.
9. BISG (the "Book Industry Study Group"), for example—a Left-wing organization which describes itself as "the leading book trade association for standardized best practices, research and information, and events"—gives its BISAC ("Book Industry Standards and Communications") listing for works on the War for Southern Independence under the heading "Civil War Period, 1850-1877." Nearly all books published in the U.S.A. today are under the categorizational control of this progressive group located in New York City.
10. See e.g., Seabrook, *The Quotable Jefferson Davis*, pp. 30, 38, 76.
11. See e.g., J. Davis, *The Rise and Fall of the Confederate Government*, Vol. 1, pp. 55, 422; Vol. 2, pp. 4, 161, 454, 610. Besides using the term "Civil War" himself, President Davis cites numerous other individuals who use it as well.
12. See e.g., *Confederate Veteran*, Vol. 20, March 1912, p. 122.
13. Minutes of the Eighth Annual Meeting, July 1898, p. 87.
14. The Left labels *all* topics that it does not like or does not agree with "controversial"—so that people will question them. In reality, being branded "controversial" by the politically correct thought police usually indicates that the topic is *not* at all controversial and probably factual.
15. For a scientific discussion concerning my rejection of the traditional concept of "race," see e.g., my book *Everything You Were Taught About African-Americans and the Civil War is Wrong, Ask a Southerner!*, pp. 13-16.
16. Acts 17:26 (KJV). The Bible touches on the topic of racial unity in numerous other scriptures as well. For example: Galatians 3:28; Acts 10:34-35; John 13:34; Colossians 3:11; Romans 2:9-11; Genesis 1:27; Mark 12:31; 1 Corinthians 12:13; Deuteronomy 10:17; James 2:1-26.
17. For more on the nihilistic, atheistic, anti-life, anti-tradition, anti-American, anti-Constitution, anti-capitalism, anti-South agenda of the Victorian Republican Party (then the Liberal Party) and the modern Democrat Party (now the Liberal Party), otherwise known as "The Communist/Socialist Rules for Revolution," see Hasselberg, pp. 2350-2351; Lenin, passim; Marx and Engels, passim; B. Dodd, passim. Also see my book *What the Confederate Flag Means to Me: Americans Speak Out in Defense of Southern Honor, Heritage, and History*. Spring Hill, TN: Sea Raven Press, 2021.
18. *Confederate Veteran*, Vol. 9, July 1901, p. 318.
19. *Confederate Veteran*, Vol. 20, April 1912, p. 169.
20. *Confederate Veteran*, Vol. 23, December 1915, p. 545.
21. Haley, p. 231.
22. For more on these and hundreds of related topics, see my in-depth book *Everything You Were taught About American Slavery is wrong, Ask a Southerner!*
23. See, e.g., the insightful BBC News article: "My Nigerian Great-Grandfather Sold Slaves," by Nigerian journalist and novelist Adaobi Tricia Nwaubani. Ms. Nwaubani considers her African ancestor, Nwaubani Ogogo Oriaku, a "businessman," not a slave-trader. Website: www.bbc.com/news/world-africa-53444752
24. Source: Anti-Slavery International. Website: www.antislavery.org
25. For a detailed examination of this subject, see my book *Abraham Lincoln Was a Liberal, Jefferson Davis Was a Conservative: The Missing Key to Understanding the American Civil War*.
26. Bell, pp. 402-403.

27. Cited in Messer-Kruse, p. 103. (Note: These particular communist French instigators were known as the Communards. For a communist perspective of the Communards, see Lenin, *The State and the Revolution*, pp. 38-41, 121.)
28. Cited in Messer-Kruse, p. 106.
29. De Bow, Vol. 24, January-June 1858, p. 497. (Note: This excerpt is from Hunter's speech entitled: "Mr. Hunter on the English Negro Apprentice Trade.")
30. Rowland, Vol. 4, p. 183. Also see Fowler, p. 203.
31. Cited in Ansell-Pearson, p. 45.
32. Fitzhugh, p. 154.
33. Fitzhugh, pp. 368-369.
34. Also see my book *The Great Yankee Coverup: What the North Doesn't Want You to Know About Lincoln's War!*
35. See Bell, pp. 402-403.
36. Source: Global Slavery Index. Website: www.globalslaveryindex.org
37. See e.g., Carson, p. 484.
38. See, e.g., my book *Everything You Were Taught About American Slavery is Wrong, Ask a Southerner!*, pp. 255, 605, 635, 681-686.
39. *Confederate Veteran*, Vol. 10, July 1902, p. 310.
40. The many benefits of both xenophobia (shunning strangers) and racial xenophobia (racism) are obvious. Among many other things they help keep the xenophobic group safe from possible crime, disease, and physical violence. See the following note.
41. For more on this and related topics, see Holloway, passim. Also see Wilson, passim; and Ardrey, passim.
42. Due to its prehistoric biological underpinnings, racial xenophobia, or racial supremacy, if you will, has proven indestructible and continues to thrive on every continent and among every ethnic group.
43. Seabrook, *The Unquotable Lincoln*, p. 118.
44. See, e.g., Chesnut, p. 224.
45. See, e.g., Hofstadter, passim.
46. *Confederate Veteran*, Vol. 20, March 1912, p. 103.
47. *Confederate Veteran*, Vol. 20, March 1912, p. 103.
48. *Confederate Veteran*, Vol. 21, December 1913, p. 577.
49. *Confederate Veteran*, Vol. 19, August 1911, p. 390.
50. *Confederate Veteran*, Vol. 11, July 1903, p. 305.
51. *Confederate Veteran*, Vol. 19, February 1911, p. 56.
52. *Confederate Veteran*, Vol. 16, April 1908, p. 185.
53. *Confederate Veteran*, Vol. 17, August 1909, p. 404.
54. *Confederate Veteran*, Vol. 23, February 1915, p. 88.
55. *Confederate Veteran*, Vol. 21, May 1913, p. 217.
56. *Confederate Veteran*, Vol. 15, January 1907, p. 13.
57. *Confederate Veteran*, Vol. 21, December 1913, p. 598.
58. See e.g., *Confederate Veteran*, Vol. 20, June 1912, p. 282.
59. *Confederate Veteran*, Vol. 8, February 1900, p. 75.
60. *Confederate Veteran*, Vol. 17, April 1909, p. 184.
61. *Confederate Veteran*, Vol. 20, March 1912, p. 126.
62. *Confederate Veteran*, Vol. 8, February 1900, p. 67.
63. *Confederate Veteran*, Vol. 18, February 1910, p. 69.
64. Haley, p. 213.
65. *Confederate Veteran*, Vol. 1, March 1893, pp. 73-74.
66. Note that the Republicans (originally left-wing) and the Democrats (originally right-wing) would not switch platforms and become the parties we know today until the presidential election of 1896. For an in-depth discussion on this topic, see my book *Abraham Lincoln Was a Liberal, Jefferson Davis Was a Conservative: The Missing Key to Understanding the American Civil War*.
67. *Confederate Veteran*, Vol. 1, March 1893, p. 80.
68. *Confederate Veteran*, Vol. 1, March 1893, pp. 81-82.
69. *Confederate Veteran*, Vol. 1, March 1893, p. 82. (Note: The title of this excerpt is mine. L.S.)
70. *Confederate Veteran*, Vol. 1, December 1893, p. 365.
71. *Confederate Veteran*, Vol. 1, January 1893, p. 18.

72. *Confederate Veteran*, Vol. 1, February 1893, p. 42. (Note: The title of this excerpt is mine. L.S.)
73. *Confederate Veteran*, Vol. 1, April 1893, p. 104. (Note: The title of this excerpt is mine. L.S.)
74. *Confederate Veteran*, Vol. 1, November 1893, p. 321. (Note: The title of this excerpt is mine. L.S.)
75. *Confederate Veteran*, Vol. 1, May 1893, p. 139. (Note: The title of this excerpt is mine. L.S.)
76. *Confederate Veteran*, Vol. 1, May 1893, p. 147.
77. *Confederate Veteran*, Vol. 1, May 1893, p. 151.
78. *Confederate Veteran*, Vol. 1, June 1893, p. 171. For a detailed look at domestic African slavery, see my book *Everything You Were Taught About American Slavery is Wrong, Ask a Southerner!*
79. *Confederate Veteran*, Vol. 1, May 1893, p. 136.
80. For a detailed study of the Articles, see my book *The Articles of Confederation Explained*.
81. *Confederate Veteran*, Vol. 1, July 1893, pp. 200-205. (Note: The title of this excerpt is mine. L.S.)
82. *Confederate Veteran*, Vol. 1, August 1893, p. 238. (Note: The title of this excerpt is mine. L.S.)
83. *Confederate Veteran*, Vol. 1, November 1893, p. 323. (Note: The title of this excerpt is mine. L.S.)
84. *Confederate Veteran*, Vol. 1, September 1893, pp. 270-271. (Note: The title of this excerpt is mine. L.S.)
85. *Confederate Veteran*, Vol. 2, January 1894, p. 12. (Note: The title of this excerpt is mine. L.S.)
86. *Confederate Veteran*, Vol. 2, February 1894, p. 37. (Note: The title of this excerpt is mine. L.S.)
87. *Confederate Veteran*, Vol. 2, May 1894, p. 152. (Note: The title of this excerpt is mine. L.S.)
88. *Confederate Veteran*, Vol. 2, May 1894, p. 162. (Note: The title of this excerpt is mine. L.S.)
89. *Confederate Veteran*, Vol. 2, July 1894, p. 217. (Note: The title of this excerpt is mine. L.S.)
90. *Confederate Veteran*, Vol. 2, November 1894, p. 336. (Note: The title of this excerpt is mine. L.S.)
91. *Confederate Veteran*, Vol. 2, May 1894, pp. 146-147. (Note: The title of this excerpt is mine. L.S.)
92. *Confederate Veteran*, Vol. 2, August 1894, p. 233. (Note: The title of this excerpt is mine. L.S.)
93. *Confederate Veteran*, Vol. 3, December 1895, p. 366. (Note: The title of this excerpt is mine. L.S.)
94. Haley, pp. 527-528. (Note: The title of this excerpt is mine. L.S.)
95. Haley, p. 6. (Note: The title of this excerpt is mine. L.S.)
96. *Confederate Veteran*, Vol. 3, January 1895, p. 14. (Note: The title of this excerpt is mine. L.S.)
97. *Confederate Veteran*, Vol. 3, October 1895, p. 293.
98. *Confederate Veteran*, Vol. 3, December 1895, p. 367. (Note: The title of this excerpt is mine. L.S.)
99. *Confederate Veteran*, Vol. 3, June 1895, p. 165. (Note: The title of this excerpt is mine. L.S.)
100. Haley, p. 6.
101. *Confederate Veteran*, Vol. 4, November 1896, p. 385. (Note: The title of this excerpt is mine. L.S.)
102. *Confederate Veteran*, Vol. 4, September 1896, p. 286. (Note: The title of this excerpt is mine. L.S.)
103. *Confederate Veteran*, Vol. 4, October 1896, p. 341. (Note: The title of this excerpt is mine. L.S.)
104. *Confederate Veteran*, Vol. 4, January 1896, p. 11. (Note: The title of this excerpt is mine. L.S.)
105. *Confederate Veteran*, Vol. 4, April 1896, pp. 129-130. (Note: The title of this excerpt is mine. L.S.)
106. *Confederate Veteran*, Vol. 4, June 1896, p. 174. (Note: The title of this excerpt is mine. L.S.)
107. *Confederate Veteran*, Vol. 4, June 1896, p. 178. (Note: The title of this excerpt is mine. L.S.)
108. *Confederate Veteran*, Vol. 4, June 1896, p. 193. (Note: The title of this excerpt is mine. L.S.)
109. *Confederate Veteran*, Vol. 4, July 1896, pp. 223-224. (Note: The title of this excerpt is mine. L.S.)
110. *Confederate Veteran*, Vol. 4, September 1896, p. 303. (Note: The title of this excerpt is mine. L.S.)
111. *Confederate Veteran*, Vol. 4, February 1896, p. 43. (Note: The title of this excerpt is mine. L.S.)
112. *Confederate Veteran*, Vol. 4, November 1896, p. 385. (Note: The title of this excerpt is mine. L.S.)
113. *Confederate Veteran*, Vol. 4, May 1896, p. 153. (Note: The title of this excerpt is mine. L.S.)
114. *Confederate Veteran*, Vol. 4, March 1896, p. 74. (Note: The title of this excerpt is mine. L.S.)
115. *Confederate Veteran*, Vol. 5, January 1897, p. 21. (Note: The title of this excerpt is mine. L.S.) For more on these topics, see my 1,000 page book, *Everything You Were Taught About American Slavery is Wrong, Ask a Southerner!*
116. *Confederate Veteran*, Vol. 5, January 1897, pp. 21-22. (Note: The title of this excerpt is mine. L.S.)
117. *Confederate Veteran*, Vol. 5, March 1897, p. 119. (Note: The title of this excerpt is mine. L.S.)
118. *Confederate Veteran*, Vol. 5, March 1897, p. 203. (Note: The title of this excerpt is mine. L.S.)
119. *Confederate Veteran*, Vol. 5, June 1897, p. 263. (Note: The title of this excerpt is mine. L.S.)
120. *Confederate Veteran*, Vol. 5, June 1897, p. 263. (Note: The title of this excerpt is mine. L.S.) Grady was not a friend of the Old South, and in fact, as a white supremacist and the popularizer of the anti-South term "New South," he had far more in common with America's most infamous Left-wing, South-hating member

of the anti-black American Colonization Society, U.S. President Lincoln, than his fellow Southerners. I quote Grady here on emancipation, however, as one who voiced an opinion held by some other Southerners at the time.

121. *Confederate Veteran*, Vol. 5, July 1897, p. 384. (Note: The title of this excerpt is mine. L.S.)
122. *Confederate Veteran*, Vol. 5, September 1897, p. 463. (Note: The title of this excerpt is mine. L.S.)
123. *Confederate Veteran*, Vol. 5, November 1897, pp. 556-567. (Note: The title of this excerpt is mine. L.S.)
124. *Confederate Veteran*, Vol. 5, August 1897, p. 438. (Note: The title of this excerpt is mine. L.S.)
125. Robinson, pp. 12-16. (Note: The title of this excerpt is mine. L.S.)
126. *Confederate Veteran*, Vol. 5, October 1897, pp. 507-508, 509. (Note: The title of this excerpt is mine. L.S.)
127. *Confederate Veteran*, Vol. 6, March 1898, pp. 101-102. (Note: The title of this excerpt is mine. L.S.) Grady seemed to have no understanding whatsoever of why the South took up arms, and wrongly criticized the Confederacy and her leaders with every opportunity. Nonetheless, many of his views about Southern blacks were shared by other white Southerners, thus I have included this edited quote by him.
128. *Confederate Veteran*, Vol. 6, April 1898, p. 170. (Note: The title of this excerpt is mine. L.S.)
129. *Confederate Veteran*, Vol. 6, April 1898, p. 174. (Note: The title of this excerpt is mine. L.S.)
130. *Confederate Veteran*, Vol. 6, September 1898, p. 411. (Note: The title of this excerpt is mine. L.S.)
131. *Confederate Veteran*, Vol. 6, September 1898, p. 439. (Note: The title of this excerpt is mine. L.S.)
132. For a factual examination of the original Confederate KKK (a non-racist conservative organization that is not connected to the modern group of the same name), see my book *Nathan Bedford Forrest and the Ku Klux Klan: Yankee Myth, Confederate Fact*.
133. *Confederate Veteran*, Vol. 6, November 1898, p. 520. (Note: The title of this excerpt is mine. L.S.)
134. *Confederate Veteran*, Vol. 6, December 1898, p. 550. (Note: The title of this excerpt is mine. L.S.)
135. Wyeth, pp. 20-21. (Note: The title of this excerpt is mine. L.S.)
136. *Confederate Veteran*, Vol. 7, May 1899, p. 231. (Note: The title of this excerpt is mine. L.S.)
137. *Confederate Veteran*, Vol. 7, November 1899, pp. 501, 506. (Note: The title of this excerpt is mine. L.S.)
138. *Confederate Veteran*, Vol. 7, March 1899, p. 112. (Note: The title of this excerpt is mine. L.S.)
139. *Confederate Veteran*, Vol. 7, May 1899, p. 196. (Note: The title of this excerpt is mine. L.S.)
140. Powers, pp. 79-90. (Note: The title of this excerpt is mine. L.S.)
141. *Confederate Veteran*, Vol. 7, May 1899, p. 212.
142. Clayton, pp. 21-24.
143. As every reader of my literary works knows, Lincoln was *not* pro-abolition when he first became president. I discuss this topic in detail in my book *Abraham Lincoln: The Southern View*.
144. *Confederate Veteran*, Vol. 7, May 1899, p. 228. (Note: The title of this excerpt is mine. L.S.)
145. *Confederate Veteran*, Vol. 7, June 1899, p. 300. (Note: The title of this excerpt is mine. L.S.)
146. *Confederate Veteran*, Vol. 7, September 1899, p. 408. (Note: The title of this excerpt is mine. L.S.)
147. *Confederate Veteran*, Vol. 7, January 1899, p. 25. (Note: The title of this excerpt is mine. L.S.) For more on Confederate pensions, see *Confederate Veteran*, Vol. 6, January 1898, pp. 17, 38; Vol. 6, September 1898, pp. 412, 473.
148. *Confederate Veteran*, Vol. 7, July 1899, p. 304. (Note: The title of this excerpt is mine. L.S.)
149. *Confederate Veteran*, Vol. 7, October 1899, p. 449. (Note: The title of this excerpt is mine. L.S.)
150. *Confederate Veteran*, Vol. 7, December 1899, p. 561. (Note: The title of this excerpt is mine. L.S.)
151. For more on this specific topic, see my book *Everything You Were Taught About American Slavery is Wrong, Ask a Southerner!*
152. Powers, pp. 41-44. (Note: The title of this excerpt is mine. L.S.)
153. *Confederate Veteran*, Vol. 7, January 1899, p. 37. (Note: The title of this excerpt is mine. L.S.)
154. *Confederate Veteran*, Vol. 7, August 1899, p. 358. (Note: The title of this excerpt is mine. L.S.)
155. *Confederate Veteran*, Vol. 7, May 1899, pp. 209, 210, 211. (Note: The title of this excerpt is mine. L.S.)
156. *Confederate Veteran*, Vol. 8, August 1900, p. 343. (Note: The title of this excerpt is mine. L.S.)
157. *Confederate Veteran*, Vol. 8, September 1900, p. 399. (Note: The title of this excerpt is mine. L.S.)
158. *Confederate Veteran*, Vol. 8, September 1900, pp. 399-400. (Note: The title of this excerpt is mine. L.S.)
159. *Confederate Veteran*, Vol. 8, November 1900, p. 489. (Note: The title of this excerpt is mine. L.S.)
160. *Confederate Veteran*, Vol. 8, May 1900, p. 233.
161. *Confederate Veteran*, Vol. 8, June 1900, pp. 274-275. (Note: The title of this excerpt is mine. L.S.)
162. *Confederate Veteran*, Vol. 8, July 1900, p. 320. (Note: The title of this excerpt is mine. L.S.)

163. *Confederate Veteran*, Vol. 8, August 1900, p. 346. (Note: The title of this excerpt is mine. L.S.)
164. *Confederate Veteran*, Vol. 8, September 1900, p. 401. (Note: The title of this excerpt is mine. L.S.)
165. *Confederate Veteran*, Vol. 8, October 1900, p. 451. (Note: The title of this excerpt is mine. L.S.) Because they were subject to military law, *all* blacks who served in any capacity in the Confederate army or navy, and were paid, were legally defined by the U.S. government, and still are, as legitimate Confederate soldiers. For more on this topic, see my book *Everything You Were Taught About the Civil War is Wrong, Ask a Southerner!*
166. *Confederate Veteran*, Vol. 8, November 1900, p. 480. (Note: The title of this excerpt is mine. L.S.)
167. *Confederate Veteran*, Vol. 8, November 1900, p. 498. (Note: The title of this excerpt is mine. L.S.)
168. *Confederate Veteran*, Vol. 8, October 1900, p. 429. (Note: The title of this excerpt is mine. L.S.)
169. *Confederate Veteran*, Vol. 8, December 1900, p. 516. (Note: The title of this excerpt is mine. L.S.)
170. *Confederate Veteran*, Vol. 9, January 1901, p. 33. (Note: The title of this excerpt is mine. L.S.)
171. *Confederate Veteran*, Vol. 9, May 1901, p. 231. (Note: The title of this excerpt is mine. L.S.)
172. *Confederate Veteran*, Vol. 9, November 1901, p. 496. (Note: The title of this excerpt is mine. L.S.)
173. *Confederate Veteran*, Vol. 9, January 1901, p. 55.
174. *Confederate Veteran*, Vol. 9, January 1901, p. 55. (Note: The title of this excerpt is mine. L.S.)
175. *Confederate Veteran*, Vol. 9, April 1901, p. 173. (Note: The title of this excerpt is mine. L.S.)
176. *Confederate Veteran*, Vol. 9, January 1901, p. 36. (Note: The title of this excerpt is mine. L.S.)
177. *Confederate Veteran*, Vol. 9, January 1901, p. 36. (Note: The title of this excerpt is mine. L.S.)
178. *Confederate Veteran*, Vol. 9, January 1901, p. 36.
179. *Confederate Veteran*, Vol. 9, May 1901, pp. 218-219. (Note: The title of this excerpt is mine. L.S.)
180. *Confederate Veteran*, Vol. 9, June 1901, pp. 262-263. (Note: The title of this excerpt is mine. L.S.)
181. *Confederate Veteran*, Vol. 9, June 1901, pp. 276-277. (Note: The title of this excerpt is mine. L.S.)
182. *Confederate Veteran*, Vol. 9, October 1901, p. 467. (Note: The title of this excerpt is mine. L.S.)
183. *Confederate Veteran*, Vol. 9, November 1901, p. 506. (Note: The title of this excerpt is mine. L.S.)
184. *Confederate Veteran*, Vol. 9, December 1901, p. 536. (Note: The title of this excerpt is mine. L.S.)
185. *Confederate Veteran*, Vol. 9, January 1901, p. 11. (Note: The title of this excerpt is mine. L.S.) This sketch is of the female owner, or "old mistis," of the noted black Southern servant Uncle Ned Hawkins, profiled earlier.
186. *Confederate Veteran*, Vol. 9, March 1901, p. 107. (Note: The title of this excerpt is mine. L.S.)
187. *Confederate Veteran*, Vol. 9, December 1901, p. 553. (Note: The title of this excerpt is mine. L.S.)
188. *Confederate Veteran*, Vol. 9, December 1901, p. 561. (Note: The title of this excerpt is mine. L.S.)
189. *Confederate Veteran*, Vol. 9, December 1901, p. 567.
190. *Confederate Veteran*, Vol. 10, April 1902, p. 181. (Note: The title of this excerpt is mine. L.S.)
191. *Confederate Veteran*, Vol. 10, December 1902, p. 557. (Note: The title of this excerpt is mine. L.S.)
192. *Confederate Veteran*, Vol. 10, February 1902, p. 66. (Note: The title of this excerpt is mine. L.S.)
193. *Confederate Veteran*, Vol. 10, August 1902, p. 355. (Note: The title of this excerpt is mine. L.S.)
194. *Confederate Veteran*, Vol. 10, January 1902, p. 13. (Note: The title of this excerpt is mine. L.S.)
195. *Confederate Veteran*, Vol. 10, July 1902, pp. 309-310. (Note: The title of this excerpt is mine. L.S.)
196. *Confederate Veteran*, Vol. 10, August 1902, p. 374. (Note: The title of this excerpt is mine. L.S.)
197. *Confederate Veteran*, Vol. 10, December 1902, p. 550. (Note: The title of this excerpt is mine. L.S.)
198. *Confederate Veteran*, Vol. 10, June 1902, p. 273. (Note: The title of this excerpt is mine. L.S.)
199. *Confederate Veteran*, Vol. 10, July 1902, p. 327. (Note: The title of this excerpt is mine. L.S.)
200. *Confederate Veteran*, Vol. 10, August 1902, p. 345. (Note: The title of this excerpt is mine. L.S.)
201. *Confederate Veteran*, Vol. 10, November 1902, p. 492. (Note: The title of this excerpt is mine. L.S.)
202. *Confederate Veteran*, Vol. 11, January 1903, p. 35. (Note: The title of this excerpt is mine. L.S.)
203. *Confederate Veteran*, Vol. 11, January 1903, p. 39. (Note: The title of this excerpt is mine. L.S.)
204. *Confederate Veteran*, Vol. 11, March 1903, pp. 108-109. (Note: The title of this excerpt is mine. L.S.) This March 1903 article is a reprint from the March 1893 issue of *Confederate Veteran*, which is why it appears here.
205. *Confederate Veteran*, Vol. 11, March 1903, pp. 109-110. (Note: The title of this excerpt is mine. L.S.)
206. *Confederate Veteran*, Vol. 11, April 1903, p. 172. (Note: The title of this excerpt is mine. L.S.)
207. *Confederate Veteran*, Vol. 11, April 1903, p. 172. (Note: The title of this excerpt is mine. L.S.)
208. *Confederate Veteran*, Vol. 11, May 1903, p. 210. (Note: The title of this excerpt is mine. L.S.)
209. *Confederate Veteran*, Vol. 11, May 1903, p. 214. (Note: The title of this excerpt is mine. L.S.)

210. *Confederate Veteran*, Vol. 11, May 1903, p. 214. (Note: The title of this excerpt is mine. L.S.)
211. *Confederate Veteran*, Vol. 11, May 1903, p. 233. (Note: The title of this excerpt is mine. L.S.)
212. *Confederate Veteran*, Vol. 11, September 1903, p. 407. (Note: The title of this excerpt is mine. L.S.)
213. *Confederate Veteran*, Vol. 11, November 1903, p. 494. (Note: The title of this excerpt is mine. L.S.)
214. *Confederate Veteran*, Vol. 11, February 1903, p. 60. (Note: The title of this excerpt is mine. L.S.) Though this little story was first published in the 1860s, it was reprinted in the February 1903 issue of *CV*, which is why it appears here.
215. *Confederate Veteran*, Vol. 11, June 1903, p. 278. (Note: The title of this excerpt is mine. L.S.)
216. *Confederate Veteran*, Vol. 11, June 1903, pp. 283-284, 285. (Note: The title of this excerpt is mine. L.S.)
217. *Confederate Veteran*, Vol. 11, September 1903, p. 422. (Note: The title of this excerpt is mine. L.S.)
218. *Confederate Veteran*, Vol. 11, October 1903, p. 470. (Note: The title of this excerpt is mine. L.S.)
219. *Confederate Veteran*, Vol. 11, December 1903, pp. 559-560. (Note: The title of this excerpt is mine. L.S.)
220. *Confederate Veteran*, Vol. 11, March 1903, p. 99. (Note: The title of this excerpt is mine. L.S.)
221. *Confederate Veteran*, Vol. 11, May 1903, pp. 202-203. (Note: The title of this excerpt is mine. L.S.) For more Confederate humor, see my book *Support Your Local Confederate*.
222. Stiles, pp. 136-137. (Note: The title of this excerpt is mine. L.S.)
223. *Confederate Veteran*, Vol. 11, May 1903, p. 215. (Note: The title of this excerpt is mine. L.S.)
224. *Confederate Veteran*, Vol. 11, May 1903, p. 228. (Note: The title of this excerpt is mine. L.S.)
225. *Confederate Veteran*, Vol. 11, August 1903, p. 341. (Note: The title of this excerpt is mine. L.S.)
226. *Confederate Veteran*, Vol. 11, September 1903, p. 405. (Note: The title of this excerpt is mine. L.S.)
227. *Confederate Veteran*, Vol. 11, October 1903, p. 447. (Note: The title of this excerpt is mine. L.S.)
228. *Confederate Veteran*, Vol. 11, November 1903, p. 498. (Note: The title of this excerpt is mine. L.S.)
229. *Confederate Veteran*, Vol. 11, December 1903, p. 557. (Note: The title of this excerpt is mine. L.S.)
230. *Confederate Veteran*, Vol. 11, September 1903, pp. 397, 398. (Note: The title of this excerpt is mine. L.S.)
231. *Confederate Veteran*, Vol. 11, December 1903, p. 562. (Note: The title of this excerpt is mine. L.S.)
232. *Confederate Veteran*, Vol. 12, February 1904, p. 68.
233. *Confederate Veteran*, Vol. 12, February 1904, pp. 77-78. (Note: The title of this excerpt is mine. L.S.)
234. *Confederate Veteran*, Vol. 12, February 1904, p. 87. (Note: The title of this excerpt is mine. L.S.)
235. *Confederate Veteran*, Vol. 12, May 1904, p. 214. (Note: The title of this excerpt is mine. L.S.)
236. *Confederate Veteran*, Vol. 12, May 1904, p. 225.
237. *Confederate Veteran*, Vol. 12, May 1904, p. 231.
238. *Confederate Veteran*, Vol. 12, August 1904, p. 404. (Note: The title of this excerpt is mine. L.S.)
239. *Confederate Veteran*, Vol. 12, September 1904, p. 453.
240. *Confederate Veteran*, Vol. 12, March 1904, pp. 122-123. (Note: The title of this excerpt is mine. L.S.)
241. *Confederate Veteran*, Vol. 12, September 1904, p. 443. (Note: The title of this excerpt is mine. L.S.)
242. *Confederate Veteran*, Vol. 12, September 1904, p. 446. (Note: The title of this excerpt is mine. L.S.)
243. For a collection of authentic Southern ghost stories, see my book *Carnton Plantation Ghost Stories*.
244. Thomas, pp. 607-615. (Note: The title of this excerpt is mine. L.S.)
245. *Confederate Veteran*, Vol. 12, January 1904, p. 23. (Note: The title of this excerpt is mine. L.S.)
246. *Confederate Veteran*, Vol. 12, May 1904, p. 234. (Note: The title of this excerpt is mine. L.S.)
247. *Confederate Veteran*, Vol. 12, August 1904, p. 405. (Note: The title of this excerpt is mine. L.S.) The original text was written in late 19th-Century negro dialect, and is thus almost indecipherable. For readability's sake, I have taken the liberty of correcting its many typos.
248. *Confederate Veteran*, Vol. 12, January 1904, p. 30. (Note: The title of this excerpt is mine. L.S.)
249. *Confederate Veteran*, Vol. February 13, 1905, p. 89. (Note: The title of this excerpt is mine. L.S.)
250. *Confederate Veteran*, Vol. February 13, 1905, p. 89. (Note: The title of this excerpt is mine. L.S.)
251. *Confederate Veteran*, Vol. 13, March 1905, pp. 123-124. (Note: The title of this excerpt is mine. L.S.)
252. As a former resident-historian of Franklin, Tennessee, I have written extensively on the McGavock family, Carnton Plantation, and the Battle of Franklin II. See my books listed on pages 2-3 of this work.
253. *Confederate Veteran*, Vol. 13, April 1905, pp. 177-178, 179. (Note: The title of this excerpt is mine. L.S.)
254. *Confederate Veteran*, Vol. 13, July 1905, p. 326. (Note: The title of this excerpt is mine. L.S.)

255. *Confederate Veteran*, Vol. 13, August 1905, p. 369. (Note: The title of this excerpt is mine. L.S.)
256. For more on these topics, see my book *Everything You Were Taught About American Slavery is Wrong, Ask a Southerner!*
257. *Confederate Veteran*, Vol. 13, September 1905, p. 398. (Note: The title of this excerpt is mine. L.S.)
258. *Confederate Veteran*, Vol. 13, September 1905, p. 422. (Note: The title of this excerpt is mine. L.S.)
259. *Confederate Veteran*, Vol. 13, September 1905, pp. 422-423. (Note: The title of this excerpt is mine. L.S.)
260. For more on this topic, see my book *Abraham Lincoln: The Southern View*.
261. *Confederate Veteran*, Vol. 13, September 1905, p. 423. (Note: The title of this excerpt is mine. L.S.)
262. *Confederate Veteran*, Vol. 13, March 1905, p. 111. (Note: The title of this excerpt is mine. L.S.)
263. *Confederate Veteran*, Vol. 13, March 1905, pp. 119-120. (Note: The title of this excerpt is mine. L.S.)
264. *Confederate Veteran*, Vol. 13, May 1905, p. 210. (Note: The title of this excerpt is mine. L.S.)
265. *Confederate Veteran*, Vol. 13, May 1905, p. 225. (Note: The title of this excerpt is mine. L.S.)
266. *Confederate Veteran*, Vol. 13, July 1905, p. 325. (Note: The title of this excerpt is mine. L.S.)
267. *Confederate Veteran*, Vol. 13, September 1905, p. 418. (Note: The title of this excerpt is mine. L.S.)
268. *Confederate Veteran*, Vol. 13, September 1905, p. 425. (Note: The title of this excerpt is mine. L.S.)
269. *Confederate Veteran*, Vol. 13, November 1905, p. 499. (Note: The title of this excerpt is mine. L.S.) My 4th great grandmother was a Rucker from Virginia, making me half third cousins with Col. Edmund W. Rucker.
270. For an in-depth examination of the history of the Confederacy's four national flags, as well as her Battle Flag, see my book *Confederate Flag Facts*.
271. *Confederate Veteran*, Vol. 13, November 1905, pp. 509-510. (Note: The title of this excerpt is mine. L.S.) While this entry may seem out of place, I have included it to further demonstrate the fact that the C.S.A., a government established by white Southerners, was indeed a Conservative body, one founded, in turn, by the Democratic Party (then the Conservative Party), which Democrat Jefferson Davis correctly called "the Conservative power of the country." It was these very Victorians, white Southern Conservatives, who were widely described as "the best friends the black man will ever have."
272. *Confederate Veteran*, Vol. 13, November 1905, p. 510. (Note: The title of this excerpt is mine. L.S.) This entry shows, as nothing else can, that Left-wing, Victorian enemies of the South were utilizing communist methods to attempt to divide and conquer both the South and the U.S.A. even prior to the War for Southern Independence. And in fact, these are the same ploys being used by the Left to this very day. Along with the fabrication of a fake "race war" and a fake "socioeconomic war," modern anti-South communism also includes radical Leftist inventions like "white privilege," "white misogyny," "white supremacy," "white xenophobia," "white karenism," and "white microaggression." New phoney terms are being invented daily.
273. *Confederate Veteran*, Vol. 13, December 1905, p. 577. (Note: The title of this excerpt is mine. L.S.)
274. *Confederate Veteran*, Vol. 13, February 1905, p. 61. (Note: The title of this excerpt is mine. L.S.) I include this entry to show that, along with white and black "slave" owners and white and black "slaves" in the Old South, there were Native American "slaves" as well, nearly all who remained loyal to their owners and the Southern Cause throughout the duration of Lincoln's War. (There were also countless Indian slave owners, many who possessed both black and white slaves in early America. I have detailed these facts in my book *Everything You Were Taught About American Slavery is Wrong, Ask a Southerner!*)
275. *Confederate Veteran*, Vol. 13, February 1905, p. 76. (Note: The title of this excerpt is mine. L.S.)
276. *Confederate Veteran*, Vol. 13, February 1905, p. 82. (Note: The title of this excerpt is mine. L.S.)
277. *Confederate Veteran*, Vol. 14, February 1906, pp. 71, 72.
278. *Confederate Veteran*, Vol. 14, March 1906, p. 101. (Note: The title of this excerpt is mine. L.S.)
279. *Confederate Veteran*, Vol. 14, March 1906, p. 105. (Note: The title of this excerpt is mine. L.S.)
280. *Confederate Veteran*, Vol. 14, April 1906, pp. 162, 163. (Note: The title of this excerpt is mine. L.S.)
281. *Confederate Veteran*, Vol. 14, April 1906, p. 171. (Note: The title of this excerpt is mine. L.S.)
282. *Confederate Veteran*, Vol. 14, April 1906, p. 172. (Note: The title of this excerpt is mine. L.S.) Despite the historical record (including Vice President Stephens' diary), which attests to the reality that Jim Limber was part of the Davis family, to this day history-ignorant—or purely malicious—Left-wing writers continue to deny the mulatto boy's existence. Why? Because "lil' Jimmy" does not fit the fictitious communist narrative that progressives have fabricated about the South, Lincoln's War, slavery, and the Confederacy; and which continues to be taught in our public schools.
283. *Confederate Veteran*, Vol. 14, June 1906, p. 278. (Note: The title of this excerpt is mine. L.S.)

284. *Confederate Veteran*, Vol. 14, June 1906, pp. 279-280. (Note: The title of this excerpt is mine. L.S.)
285. *Confederate Veteran*, Vol. 14, July 1906, p. 295. (Note: The title of this excerpt is mine. L.S.)
286. *Confederate Veteran*, Vol. 14, September 1906, p. 408.
287. *Confederate Veteran*, Vol. 14, November 1906, p. 516. (Note: The title of this excerpt is mine. L.S.)
288. *Confederate Veteran*, Vol. 14, December 1906, p. 546. (Note: The title of this excerpt is mine. L.S.)
289. *Confederate Veteran*, Vol. 14, December 1906, pp. 547-548. (Note: The title of this excerpt is mine. L.S.) The detested "U.S. Oath of Allegiance" appeared in different forms at various times and places, but in general it read as follows: "I, _____, do solemnly swear or affirm in the presence of Almighty God that I will henceforth faithfully support and defend the Constitution of the United States and the Union thereunder, and that I will, in like manner, abide by and faithfully support all laws and proclamations which have been made during the existing rebellion with reference to the emancipation of slaves, so help me God."
290. *Confederate Veteran*, Vol. 14, December 1906, p. 555. (Note: The title of this excerpt is mine. L.S.)
291. *Confederate Veteran*, Vol. 14, July 1906, pp. 297-298. (Note: The title of this excerpt is mine. L.S.)
292. *Confederate Veteran*, Vol. 14, October 1906, p. 467.
293. *Confederate Veteran*, Vol. 14, August 1906, pp. 350-351. (Note: The title of this excerpt is mine. L.S.)
294. *Confederate Veteran*, Vol. 14, October 1906, p. 447. (Note: The title of this excerpt is mine. L.S.)
295. *Confederate Veteran*, Vol. 14, November 1906, p. 485. (Note: The title of this excerpt is mine. L.S.)
296. *Confederate Veteran*, Vol. 14, February 1906, p. 69. (Note: The title of this excerpt is mine. L.S.)
297. *Confederate Veteran*, Vol. 14, March 1906, p. 112. (Note: The title of this excerpt is mine. L.S.)
298. *Confederate Veteran*, Vol. 14, July 1906, p. 317. (Note: The title of this excerpt is mine. L.S.)
299. *Confederate Veteran*, Vol. 15, January 1907, p. 8. (Note: The title of this excerpt is mine. L.S.)
300. *Confederate Veteran*, Vol. 15, February 1907, p. 85. (Note: The title of this excerpt is mine. L.S.)
301. *Confederate Veteran*, Vol. 15, April 1907, p. 174. (Note: The title of this excerpt is mine. L.S.)
302. *Confederate Veteran*, Vol. 15, April 1907, p. 186. (Note: The title of this excerpt is mine. L.S.)
303. *Confederate Veteran*, Vol. 15, May 1907, p. 210. (Note: The title of this excerpt is mine. L.S.)
304. For an in-depth study of the C.S. Constitution, see my book *The Constitution of the Confederate States of America Explained*.
305. *Confederate Veteran*, Vol. 15, July 1907, pp. 297-298. (Note: The title of this excerpt is mine. L.S.)
306. See ORA, Series 4, Volume 2, p. 1193.
307. *Confederate Veteran*, Vol. 15, July 1907, pp. 316-317. (Note: The title of this excerpt is mine. L.S.)
308. *Confederate Veteran*, Vol. 15, August 1907, p. 367. (Note: The title of this excerpt is mine. L.S.)
309. *Confederate Veteran*, Vol. 15, August 1907, p. 369. (Note: The title of this excerpt is mine. L.S.)
310. For an important in-depth discussion of what I call the "Reconstruction KKK" (as separate and distinct from the modern KKK), see my book *Nathan Bedford Forrest and the Ku Klux Klan: Yankee Myth, Confederate Fact*.
311. *Confederate Veteran*, Vol. 15, November 1907, p. 496. (Note: The title of this excerpt is mine. L.S.)
312. *Confederate Veteran*, Vol. 15, December 1907, p. 548. (Note: The title of this excerpt is mine. L.S.)
313. *Confederate Veteran*, Vol. 15, May 1907, p. 239. (Note: The title of this excerpt is mine. L.S.)
314. *Confederate Veteran*, Vol. 15, August 1907, p. 347. (Note: The title of this excerpt is mine. L.S.)
315. *Confederate Veteran*, Vol. 15, October 1907, p. 448. (Note: The title of this excerpt is mine. L.S.)
316. *Confederate Veteran*, Vol. 15, November 1907, p. 487. (Note: The title of this excerpt is mine. L.S.)
317. *Confederate Veteran*, Vol. 15, January 1907, p. 9. (Note: The title of this excerpt is mine. L.S.)
318. *Confederate Veteran*, Vol. 16, March 1908, p. 124. (Note: The title of this excerpt is mine. L.S.)
319. *Confederate Veteran*, Vol. 16, April 1908, p. 201. (Note: The title of this excerpt is mine. L.S.)
320. *Confederate Veteran*, Vol. 16, May 1908, p. 203. (Note: The title of this excerpt is mine. L.S.)
321. *Confederate Veteran*, Vol. 16, June 1908, p. 294. (Note: The title of this excerpt is mine. L.S.)
322. *Confederate Veteran*, Vol. 16, July 1908, p. 323. (Note: The title of this excerpt is mine. L.S.)
323. *Confederate Veteran*, Vol. 16, September 1908, p. 476.
324. *Confederate Veteran*, Vol. 16, October 1908, p. 506. (Note: The title of this excerpt is mine. L.S.)
325. See ORA and ORN in my bibliography.
326. *Confederate Veteran*, Vol. 16, March 1908, p. 111. (Note: The title of this excerpt is mine. L.S.)
327. *Confederate Veteran*, Vol. 16, March 1908, p. 126. (Note: The title of this excerpt is mine. L.S.)
328. For more on this topic, see my book *Abraham Lincoln Was a Liberal, Jefferson Davis Was a Conservative*.

329. It was from out of this horrific situation that what I call the "Reconstruction Ku Klux Klan"—a non-racist, politically conservative, pro-Constitution group that has no connection to today's KKK—was formed in December 1865. For more on this topic, see my book *Nathan Bedford Forrest and the Ku Klux Klan: Yankee Myth, Confederate Fact.*
330. *Confederate Veteran*, Vol. 16, April 1908, pp. 185-186. (Note: The title of this excerpt is mine. L.S.)
331. *Confederate Veteran*, Vol. 16, January 1908, p. 20. (Note: The title of this excerpt is mine. L.S.)
332. *Confederate Veteran*, Vol. 16, July 1908, p. 364. (Note: The title of this excerpt is mine. L.S.)
333. *Confederate Veteran*, Vol. 16, August 1908, pp. 385-386. (Note: The title of this excerpt is mine. L.S.)
334. *Confederate Veteran*, Vol. 16, August 1908, p. 403. (Note: The title of this excerpt is mine. L.S.)
335. *Confederate Veteran*, Vol. 16, September 1908, p. 439. (Note: The title of this excerpt is mine. L.S.)
336. *Confederate Veteran*, Vol. 13, March 1905, p. 119. (Note: The title of this excerpt is mine. L.S.)
337. *Confederate Veteran*, Vol. 17, February 1909, p. 66. (Note: The title of this excerpt is mine. L.S.)
338. *Confederate Veteran*, Vol. 17, February 1909, p. 86. (Note: The title of this excerpt is mine. L.S.)
339. *Confederate Veteran*, Vol. 17, March 1909, pp. 119-120, 121. (Note: The title of this excerpt is mine. L.S.)
340. *Confederate Veteran*, Vol. 17, July 1909, pp. 360, 361. (Note: The title of this excerpt is mine. L.S.)
341. *Confederate Veteran*, Vol. 17, July 1909, p. 361. (Note: The title of this excerpt is mine. L.S.)
342. For detailed discussions of the McGavocks, Carnton Plantation, and the Battle of Franklin II, see my numerous books on these subjects.
343. Rev. McNeilly incorrectly identifies the general as "W. H. Harding." He is referring to W. G. Harding, that is, General William Giles Harding. For those interested in Southern genealogy, I am a descendant of the Harding family of Belle Meade Plantation and a close cousin of General Harding.
344. *Confederate Veteran*, Vol. 17, August 1909, pp. 404-407. (Note: The title of this excerpt is mine. L.S.)
345. *Confederate Veteran*, Vol. 17, August 1909, p. 409. (Note: The title of this excerpt is mine. L.S.)
346. *Confederate Veteran*, Vol. 17, September 1909, p. 476. (Note: The title of this excerpt is mine. L.S.)
347. *Confederate Veteran*, Vol. 17, October 1909, p. 496. (Note: The title of this excerpt is mine. L.S.)
348. *Confederate Veteran*, Vol. 17, February 1909, p. 67. (Note: The title of this excerpt is mine. L.S.)
349. *Confederate Veteran*, Vol. 17, September 1909, p. 466. (Note: The title of this excerpt is mine. L.S.)
350. *Confederate Veteran*, Vol. 17, October 1909, p. 483. (Note: The title of this excerpt is mine. L.S.)
351. *Confederate Veteran*, Vol. 17, October 1909, p. 494. (Note: The title of this excerpt is mine. L.S.)
352. *Confederate Veteran*, Vol. 17, December 1909, pp. 606, 607. (Note: The title of this excerpt is mine. L.S.)
353. *Confederate Veteran*, Vol. 17, February 1909, pp. 61, 62. (Note: The title of this excerpt is mine. L.S.)
354. *Confederate Veteran*, Vol. 17, February 1909, p. 74. (Note: The title of this excerpt is mine. L.S.)
355. *Confederate Veteran*, Vol. 17, March 1909, p. 141. (Note: The title of this excerpt is mine. L.S.)
356. *Confederate Veteran*, Vol. 17, April 1909, pp. 153-154. (Note: The title of this excerpt is mine. L.S.) For more on this topic, see my book *Abraham Lincoln: The Southern View.*
357. *Confederate Veteran*, Vol. 17, May 1909, pp. 203-204. (Note: The title of this excerpt is mine. L.S.)
358. *Confederate Veteran*, Vol. 17, August 1909, p. 386. (Note: The title of this excerpt is mine. L.S.)
359. *Confederate Veteran*, Vol. 17, August 1909, p. 411. (Note: The title of this excerpt is mine. L.S.)
360. *Confederate Veteran*, Vol. 17, June 1909, p. 267. (Note: The title of this excerpt is mine. L.S.)
361. *Confederate Veteran*, Vol. 17, July 1909, pp. 343-344. (Note: The title of this excerpt is mine. L.S.)
362. *Confederate Veteran*, Vol. 18, February 1910, pp. 69-70. (Note: The title of this excerpt is mine. L.S.)
363. *Confederate Veteran*, Vol. 18, May 1910, p. 225. (Note: The title of this excerpt is mine. L.S.)
364. *Confederate Veteran*, Vol. 18, September 1910, p. 423. (Note: The title of this excerpt is mine. L.S.)
365. *Confederate Veteran*, Vol. 18, November 1910, p. 534. (Note: The title of this excerpt is mine. L.S.)
366. *Confederate Veteran*, Vol. 18, November 1910, p. 534. (Note: The title of this excerpt is mine. L.S.)
367. *Confederate Veteran*, Vol. 18, February 1910, p. 56. (Note: The title of this excerpt is mine. L.S.)
368. *Confederate Veteran*, Vol. 18, May 1910, pp. 211-212. (Note: The title of this excerpt is mine. L.S.)
369. *Confederate Veteran*, Vol. 18, May 1910, p. 216. (Note: The title of this excerpt is mine. L.S.)
370. *Confederate Veteran*, Vol. 18, May 1910, p. 227. (Note: The title of this excerpt is mine. L.S.)
371. *Confederate Veteran*, Vol. 18, August 1910, p. 356. (Note: The title of this excerpt is mine. L.S.)
372. *Confederate Veteran*, Vol. 18, August 1910, p. 381. (Note: The title of this excerpt is mine. L.S.)
373. Like the War itself, these figures continue to be avidly debated by both sides.

374. *Confederate Veteran*, Vol. 18, December 1910, p. 558. (Note: The title of this excerpt is mine. L.S.)
375. *Confederate Veteran*, Vol. 18, December 1910, pp. 564-565. (Note: The title of this excerpt is mine. L.S.)
376. *Confederate Veteran*, Vol. 18, May 1910, p. 208. (Note: The title of this excerpt is mine. L.S.)
377. *Confederate Veteran*, Vol. 18, February 1910, p. 72. (Note: The title of this excerpt is mine. L.S.)
378. *Confederate Veteran*, Vol. 18, June 1910, p. 287. (Note: The title of this excerpt is mine. L.S.)
379. *Confederate Veteran*, Vol. 18, June 1910, p. 294. (Note: The title of this excerpt is mine. L.S.)
380. *Confederate Veteran*, Vol. 18, August 1910, p. 388. (Note: The title of this excerpt is mine. L.S.)
381. *Confederate Veteran*, Vol. 18, September 1910, p. 405. (Note: The title of this excerpt is mine. L.S.)
382. *Confederate Veteran*, Vol. 18, November 1910, p. 501. (Note: The title of this excerpt is mine. L.S.)
383. *Confederate Veteran*, Vol. 18, November 1910, p. 513. (Note: The title of this excerpt is mine. L.S.)
384. *Confederate Veteran*, Vol. 18, November 1910, p. 518. (Note: The title of this excerpt is mine. L.S.)
385. *Confederate Veteran*, Vol. 18, December 1910, p. 577. (Note: The title of this excerpt is mine. L.S.)
386. *Confederate Veteran*, Vol. 18, January 1910, p. 28. (Note: The title of this excerpt is mine. L.S.)
387. *Confederate Veteran*, Vol. 18, February 1910, p. 86. (Note: The title of this excerpt is mine. L.S.)
388. *Confederate Veteran*, Vol. 18, March 1910, p. 132. (Note: The title of this excerpt is mine. L.S.)
389. *Confederate Veteran*, Vol. 18, October 1910, p. 466. (Note: The title of this excerpt is mine. L.S.)
390. *Confederate Veteran*, Vol. 19, January 1911, p. 42. (Note: The title of this excerpt is mine. L.S.)
391. For more on Lincoln and his role as a leader and member of the American Colonization Society, see my book *Abraham Lincoln: The Southern View*.
392. *Confederate Veteran*, Vol. 19, July 1911, pp. 326-327. (Note: The title of this excerpt is mine. L.S.)
393. *Confederate Veteran*, Vol. 19, December 1911, pp. 578-579. (Note: The title of this excerpt is mine. L.S.) For an in-depth look at these and related topics, see my book *Everything You Were Taught About American Slavery is Wrong, Ask a Southerner!*
394. *Confederate Veteran*, Vol. 19, April 1911, p. 156. (Note: The title of this excerpt is mine. L.S.)
395. *Confederate Veteran*, Vol. 19, May 1911, pp. 229-230.
396. *Confederate Veteran*, Vol. 19, October 1911, p. 480. (Note: The title of this excerpt is mine. L.S.)
397. *Confederate Veteran*, Vol. 19, November 1911, p. 522. (Note: The title of this excerpt is mine. L.S.)
398. For more on Lincoln's real views of blacks, see my book *Abraham Lincoln: The Southern View*.
399. *Confederate Veteran*, Vol. 19, December 1911, pp. 576-578. (Note: The title of this excerpt is mine. L.S.) For an in-depth look at these and related topics, see my book *Everything You Were Taught About American Slavery is Wrong, Ask a Southerner!*
400. *Confederate Veteran*, Vol. 19, December 1911, p. 586. (Note: The title of this excerpt is mine. L.S.)
401. *Confederate Veteran*, Vol. 19, February 1911, p. 57. (Note: The title of this excerpt is mine. L.S.)
402. *Confederate Veteran*, Vol. 19, August 1911, p. 407. (Note: The title of this excerpt is mine. L.S.)
403. *Confederate Veteran*, Vol. 19, January 1911, p. 11. (Note: The title of this excerpt is mine. L.S.)
404. *Confederate Veteran*, Vol. 19, July 1911, p. 335. (Note: The title of this excerpt is mine. L.S.)
405. *Confederate Veteran*, Vol. 19, August 1911, p. 370. (Note: The title of this excerpt is mine. L.S.)
406. *Confederate Veteran*, Vol. 19, August 1911, p. 402. (Note: The title of this excerpt is mine. L.S.)
407. *Confederate Veteran*, Vol. 19, August 1911, p. 402. (Note: The title of this excerpt is mine. L.S.)
408. *Confederate Veteran*, Vol. 19, August 1911, p. 406. (Note: The title of this excerpt is mine. L.S.)
409. *Confederate Veteran*, Vol. 19, October 1911, p. 506. (Note: The title of this excerpt is mine. L.S.)
410. *Confederate Veteran*, Vol. 19, March 1911, p. 116. (Note: The title of this excerpt is mine. L.S.)
411. *Confederate Veteran*, Vol. 19, May 1911, p. 238. (Note: The title of this excerpt is mine. L.S.)
412. *Confederate Veteran*, Vol. 20, February 1912, p. 58. (Note: The title of this excerpt is mine. L.S.)
413. *Confederate Veteran*, Vol. 20, March 1912, p. 131. (Note: The title of this excerpt is mine. L.S.)
414. *Confederate Veteran*, Vol. 20, April 1912, p. 173. (Note: The title of this excerpt is mine. L.S.)
415. *Confederate Veteran*, Vol. 20, April 1912, p. 173. (Note: The title of this excerpt is mine. L.S.)
416. *Confederate Veteran*, Vol. 20, June 1912, p. 293. (Note: The title of this excerpt is mine. L.S.)
417. *Confederate Veteran*, Vol. 20, June 1912, p. 293. (Note: The title of this excerpt is mine. L.S.)
418. *Confederate Veteran*, Vol. 20, June 1912, p. 293. (Note: The title of this excerpt is mine. L.S.)
419. *Confederate Veteran*, Vol. 20, September 1912, p. 410. (Note: The title of this excerpt is mine. L.S.)
420. *Confederate Veteran*, Vol. 20, September 1912, p. 410.
421. *Confederate Veteran*, Vol. 20, September 1912, p. 410. (Note: The title of this excerpt is mine. L.S.)

422. *Confederate Veteran*, Vol. 20, October 1912, p. 486. (Note: The title of this excerpt is mine. L.S.)
423. *Confederate Veteran*, Vol. 20, November 1912, p. 515. (Note: The title of this excerpt is mine. L.S.)
424. *Confederate Veteran*, Vol. 20, November 1912, p. 523. (Note: The title of this excerpt is mine. L.S.)
425. *Confederate Veteran*, Vol. 20, December 1912, pp. 527, 528. (Note: The title of this excerpt is mine. L.S.)
426. *Confederate Veteran*, Vol. 20, December 1912, pp. 567-568. (Note: The title of this excerpt is mine. L.S.)
427. *Confederate Veteran*, Vol. 20, January 1912, p. 43. (Note: The title of this excerpt is mine. L.S.)
428. *Confederate Veteran*, Vol. 20, March 1912, p. 105. (Note: The title of this excerpt is mine. L.S.)
429. *Confederate Veteran*, Vol. 20, March 1912, p. 123. (Note: The title of this excerpt is mine. L.S.)
430. *Confederate Veteran*, Vol. 20, March 1912, p. 135. (Note: The title of this excerpt is mine. L.S.)
431. *Confederate Veteran*, Vol. 20, May 1912, p. 200. (Note: The title of this excerpt is mine. L.S.)
432. *Confederate Veteran*, Vol. 20, May 1912, p. 202. (Note: The title of this excerpt is mine. L.S.)
433. *Confederate Veteran*, Vol. 20, May 1912, p. 222. (Note: The title of this excerpt is mine. L.S.)
434. *Confederate Veteran*, Vol. 20, May 1912, p. 250. (Note: The title of this excerpt is mine. L.S.)
435. *Confederate Veteran*, Vol. 20, July 1912, p. 342. (Note: The title of this excerpt is mine. L.S.) See also Johnston and Browne, p. 371.
436. *Confederate Veteran*, Vol. 20, November 1912, p. 501. (Note: The title of this excerpt is mine. L.S.)
437. *Confederate Veteran*, Vol. 20, November 1912, pp. 533, 534. (Note: The title of this excerpt is mine. L.S.)
438. *Confederate Veteran*, Vol. 20, December 1912, p. 549. (Note: The title of this excerpt is mine. L.S.)
439. *Confederate Veteran*, Vol. 20, December 1912, p. 582. (Note: The title of this excerpt is mine. L.S.)
440. *Confederate Veteran*, Vol. 20, February 1912, p. 65. (Note: The title of this excerpt is mine. L.S.)
441. *Confederate Veteran*, Vol. 20, April 1912, p. 160. (Note: The title of this excerpt is mine. L.S.)
442. *Confederate Veteran*, Vol. 20, May 1912, p. 213. (Note: The title of this excerpt is mine. L.S.)
443. *Confederate Veteran*, Vol. 20, May 1912, p. 219. (Note: The title of this excerpt is mine. L.S.)
444. *Confederate Veteran*, Vol. 20, September 1912, p. 466. (Note: The title of this excerpt is mine. L.S.)
445. *Confederate Veteran*, Vol. 20, November 1912, p. 534. (Note: The title of this excerpt is mine. L.S.)
446. *Confederate Veteran*, Vol. 20, December 1912, p. 579. (Note: The title of this excerpt is mine. L.S.)
447. Andrews, p. 22. Virginia was indeed the first state to officially call for the destruction of slavery. However, Virginians were seeking the overthrow of the "peculiar institution" far earlier than 1832. In 1655, for instance, a Virginia farmer became the first white person in North American to voluntarily emancipate his slaves. See my book, *Everything You Were Taught About American Slavery is Wrong, Ask a Southerner!*, p. 50.
448. *Confederate Veteran*, Vol. 21, January 1913, p. 8. (Note: The title of this excerpt is mine. L.S.)
449. *Confederate Veteran*, Vol. 21, January 1913, p. 16. (Note: The title of this excerpt is mine. L.S.)
450. *Confederate Veteran*, Vol. 21, February 1913, p. 60. (Note: The title of this excerpt is mine. L.S.)
451. *Confederate Veteran*, Vol. 21, March 1913, p. 129. (Note: The title of this excerpt is mine. L.S.)
452. *Confederate Veteran*, Vol. 21, March 1913, p. 129.
453. *Confederate Veteran*, Vol. 21, April 1913, pp. 161, 166.
454. *Confederate Veteran*, Vol. 21, April 1913, p. 178. (Note: The title of this excerpt is mine. L.S.)
455. *Confederate Veteran*, Vol. 21, October 1913, p. 481. (Note: The title of this excerpt is mine. L.S.)
456. *Confederate Veteran*, Vol. 21, November 1913, p. 532. (Note: The title of this excerpt is mine. L.S.)
457. *Confederate Veteran*, Vol. 21, November 1913, p. 545. (Note: The title of this excerpt is mine. L.S.) For more background on these and related topics, see my books *Abraham Lincoln: The Southern View*, *Everything You Were Taught About American Slavery is Wrong, Ask a Southerner!*, and *Everything You Were Taught About African Americans and the Civil War is Wrong, Ask a Southerner!*
458. *Confederate Veteran*, Vol. 21, February 1913, p. 71. (Note: The title of this excerpt is mine. L.S.)
459. *Confederate Veteran*, Vol. 21, February 1913, p. 80. (Note: The title of this excerpt is mine. L.S.)
460. *Confederate Veteran*, Vol. 21, March 1913, p. 127. (Note: The title of this excerpt is mine. L.S.)
461. *Confederate Veteran*, Vol. 21, May 1913, p. 215.
462. *Confederate Veteran*, Vol. 21, June 1913, p. 292. (Note: The title of this excerpt is mine. L.S.)
463. *Confederate Veteran*, Vol. 21, August 1913, p. 405. (Note: The title of this excerpt is mine. L.S.)
464. *Confederate Veteran*, Vol. 21, September 1913, p. 449. (Note: The title of this excerpt is mine. L.S.)
465. *Confederate Veteran*, Vol. 21, October 1913, p. 469. (Note: The title of this excerpt is mine. L.S.)
466. *Confederate Veteran*, Vol. 21, October 1913, p. 473. (Note: The title of this excerpt is mine. L.S.)

467. *Confederate Veteran*, Vol. 21, October 1913, p. 498. (Note: The title of this excerpt is mine. L.S.)
468. *Confederate Veteran*, Vol. 21, May 1913, p. 227. (Note: The title of this excerpt is mine. L.S.)
469. *Confederate Veteran*, Vol. 21, May 1913, p. 237. (Note: The title of this excerpt is mine. L.S.)
470. *Confederate Veteran*, Vol. 21, September 1913, p. 431. (Note: The title of this excerpt is mine. L.S.)
471. *Confederate Veteran*, Vol. 21, August 1913, p. 365. (Note: The title of this excerpt is mine. L.S.)
472. *Confederate Veteran*, Vol. 22, February 1914, pp. 77, 78. (Note: The title of this excerpt is mine. L.S.) This entry includes this introduction: "The following is a list of inscriptions on bronze tablets on the monument for Confederate soldiers and sailors who, while prisoners of war, died at Camp Morton, Indianapolis, Ind., and were there buried, in Green Lawn Cemetery. Where the branch of service is not given, it is usually infantry."
473. *Confederate Veteran*, Vol. 22, August 1914, p. 378. (Note: The title of this excerpt is mine. L.S.)
474. *Confederate Veteran*, Vol. 22, September 1914, p. 422. (Note: The title of this excerpt is mine. L.S.)
475. *Confederate Veteran*, Vol. 22, September 1914, p. 425. (Note: The title of this excerpt is mine. L.S.)
476. *Confederate Veteran*, Vol. 22, October 1914, p. 474. (Note: The title of this excerpt is mine. L.S.)
477. *Confederate Veteran*, Vol. 22, October 1914, p. 474. (Note: The title of this excerpt is mine. L.S.)
478. *Confederate Veteran*, Vol. 22, October 1914, p. 474. (Note: The title of this excerpt is mine. L.S.)
479. *Confederate Veteran*, Vol. 22, December 1914, p. 542. (Note: The title of this excerpt is mine. L.S.)
480. *Confederate Veteran*, Vol. 22, December 1914, p. 548. (Note: The title of this excerpt is mine. L.S.)
481. *Confederate Veteran*, Vol. 22, January 1914, pp. 6, 8. (Note: The title of this excerpt is mine. L.S.)
482. *Confederate Veteran*, Vol. 22, January 1914, p. 37. (Note: The title of this excerpt is mine. L.S.)
483. *Confederate Veteran*, Vol. 22, February 1914, p. 71. (Note: The title of this excerpt is mine. L.S.)
484. *Confederate Veteran*, Vol. 22, June 1914, p. 253. (Note: The title of this excerpt is mine. L.S.) For a full discussion of the South and the American right of secession, see my book *All We Ask is to be Let Alone: The Southern Secession Fact Book*.
485. *Confederate Veteran*, Vol. 22, July 1914, p. 328. (Note: The title of this excerpt is mine. L.S.)
486. *Confederate Veteran*, Vol. 22, December 1914, p. 534. (Note: The title of this excerpt is mine. L.S.)
487. *Confederate Veteran*, Vol. 22, June 1914, p. 259. (Note: The title of this excerpt is mine. L.S.)
488. *Confederate Veteran*, Vol. 23, February 1915, p. 65. (Note: The title of this excerpt is mine. L.S.)
489. *Confederate Veteran*, Vol. 23, April 1915, p. 165. (Note: The title of this excerpt is mine. L.S.)
490. *Confederate Veteran*, Vol. 23, April 1915, p. 172. (Note: The title of this excerpt is mine. L.S.)
491. *Confederate Veteran*, Vol. 23, May 1915, p. 229. (Note: The title of this excerpt is mine. L.S.)
492. *Confederate Veteran*, Vol. 23, August 1915, p. 380. (Note: The title of this excerpt is mine. L.S.)
493. *Confederate Veteran*, Vol. 23, September 1915, pp. 397-398. (Note: The title of this excerpt is mine. L.S.)
494. *Confederate Veteran*, Vol. 23, September 1915, p. 411.
495. *Confederate Veteran*, Vol. 23, December 1915, p. 545.
496. *Confederate Veteran*, Vol. 23, December 1915, p. 545.
497. *Confederate Veteran*, Vol. 23, December 1915, p. 545. (Note: The title of this excerpt is mine. L.S.)
498. *Confederate Veteran*, Vol. 23, January 1915, p. 13. (Note: The title of this excerpt is mine. L.S.)
499. *Confederate Veteran*, Vol. 23, January 1915, p. 43. (Note: The title of this excerpt is mine. L.S.)
500. *Confederate Veteran*, Vol. 23, March 1915, p. 105. (Note: The title of this excerpt is mine. L.S.)
501. *Confederate Veteran*, Vol. 23, March 1915, p. 112. (Note: The title of this excerpt is mine. L.S.)
502. *Confederate Veteran*, Vol. 23, May 1915, p. 229. (Note: The title of this excerpt is mine. L.S.)
503. *Confederate Veteran*, Vol. 23, June 1915, pp. 246-247. (Note: The title of this excerpt is mine. L.S.)
504. *Confederate Veteran*, Vol. 23, June 1915, p. 273. (Note: The title of this excerpt is mine. L.S.)
505. *Confederate Veteran*, Vol. 23, June 1915, p. 283.
506. *Confederate Veteran*, Vol. 23, July 1915, pp. 295-296. (Note: The title of this excerpt is mine. L.S.)
507. *Confederate Veteran*, Vol. 23, August 1915, p. 351. (Note: The title of this excerpt is mine. L.S.)
508. *Confederate Veteran*, Vol. 23, October 1915, p. 444. (Note: The title of this excerpt is mine. L.S.)
509. *Confederate Veteran*, Vol. 23, December 1915, p. 545. (Note: The title of this excerpt is mine. L.S.)
510. *Confederate Veteran*, Vol. 23, June 1915, p. 273. (Note: The title of this excerpt is mine. L.S.)
511. *Confederate Veteran*, Vol. 23, August 1915, p. 342. (Note: The title of this excerpt is mine. L.S.)
512. *Confederate Veteran*, Vol. 23, September 1915, p. 404. (Note: The title of this excerpt is mine. L.S.)
513. *Confederate Veteran*, Vol. 23, September 1915, p. 425. (Note: The title of this excerpt is mine. L.S.)

514. For a discussion on these two Constitutions, as well as their complete texts, see my book *America's Three Constitutions: Complete Texts of the Articles of Confederation, Constitution of the United States of America, and Constitution of the Confederate States of America.*
515. *Confederate Veteran*, Vol. 23, December 1915, p. 553. (Note: The title of this excerpt is mine. L.S.)
516. *Confederate Veteran*, Vol. 23, December 1915, p. 545. (Note: The title of this excerpt is mine. L.S.)
517. *Confederate Veteran*, Vol. 24, June 1916, p. 265. (Note: The title of this excerpt is mine. L.S.)
518. *Confederate Veteran*, Vol. 24, June 1916, p. 256.
519. *Confederate Veteran*, Vol. 24, October 1916, p. 476.
520. *Confederate Veteran*, Vol. 24, January 1916, p. 42. (Note: The title of this excerpt is mine. L.S.)
521. *Confederate Veteran*, Vol. 24, January 1916, p. 45. (Note: The title of this excerpt is mine. L.S.)
522. *Confederate Veteran*, Vol. 24, February 1916, p. 68. (Note: The title of this excerpt is mine. L.S.)
523. *Confederate Veteran*, Vol. 24, March 1916, p. 113. (Note: The title of this excerpt is mine. L.S.)
524. *Confederate Veteran*, Vol. 24, March 1916, pp. 114-115. (Note: The title of this excerpt is mine. L.S.)
525. *Confederate Veteran*, Vol. 24, April 1916, p. 167. (Note: The title of this excerpt is mine. L.S.)
526. *Confederate Veteran*, Vol. 24, September 1916, p. 407. (Note: The title of this excerpt is mine. L.S.)
527. *Confederate Veteran*, Vol. 24, October 1916, p. 438. (Note: The title of this excerpt is mine. L.S.)
528. *Confederate Veteran*, Vol. 24, November 1916, pp. 486-487. (Note: The title of this excerpt is mine. L.S.)
529. *Confederate Veteran*, Vol. 24, March 1916, p. 112. (Note: The title of this excerpt is mine. L.S.)
530. *Confederate Veteran*, Vol. 24, March 1916, p. 121. (Note: The title of this excerpt is mine. L.S.)
531. *Confederate Veteran*, Vol. 24, July 1916, p. 335. (Note: The title of this excerpt is mine. L.S.)
532. Dawson, pp. 211-212. Note: Though written in 1862, this entry, an excerpt from Sarah M. Dawson's delightful book *A Confederate Girl's Diary*, was published in 1913.
533. Seabrook, *A Rebel Born* (2015 ed.), pp. 459-460.
534. Seabrook, *The Unquotable Abraham Lincoln* (2018 ed.), p. 78.
535. Seabrook, *The Unquotable Abraham Lincoln* (2018 ed.), p. 78.
536. Seabrook, *The Unquotable Abraham Lincoln* (2018 ed.), p. 78.
537. Seabrook, *The Unquotable Abraham Lincoln* (2018 ed.), pp. 78-79.
538. Seabrook, *The Unquotable Abraham Lincoln* (2018 ed.), p. 79.
539. Seabrook, *The Unquotable Abraham Lincoln* (2018 ed.), p. 84.
540. Seabrook, *The Unquotable Abraham Lincoln* (2018 ed.), p. 79.
541. Seabrook, *The Unquotable Abraham Lincoln* (2018 ed.), pp. 79-80.
542. Seabrook, *The Unquotable Abraham Lincoln* (2018 ed.), p. 81.
543. Seabrook, *The Unquotable Abraham Lincoln* (2018 ed.), p. 82.
544. Seabrook, *The Unquotable Abraham Lincoln* (2018 ed.), p. 82.
545. Seabrook, *The Unquotable Abraham Lincoln* (2018 ed.), pp. 82-83.
546. Seabrook, *The Unquotable Abraham Lincoln* (2018 ed.), p. 83.
547. Seabrook, *The Unquotable Abraham Lincoln* (2018 ed.), p. 83.
548. Seabrook, *The Unquotable Abraham Lincoln* (2018 ed.), pp. 84-85.
549. Seabrook, *The Unquotable Abraham Lincoln* (2018 ed.), p. 99.
550. Seabrook, *The Unquotable Abraham Lincoln* (2018 ed.), pp. 67-68.
551. Seabrook, *Abraham Lincoln: The Southern View* (2021 ed.), p. 135.
552. Seabrook, *The Unquotable Abraham Lincoln* (2018 ed.), p. 93.

FOOD FOR THOUGHT
Fruitful Quotes from Confederate Veteran
SELECTED, TITLED, & EDITED BY LOCHLAINN SEABROOK

RESISTANCE TO TYRANNY IS OBEDIENCE TO GOD
❦ Mrs. W. L. Davis, Secretary of the Ladies' [Confederate] Memorial Association of Albany, Georgia: "I believe with Bishop Pierce . . . that 'Our Northern enemies . . . mistook sedition for liberty, cant for piety; that, as loud-mouthed champions of the freedom of the black man, they trampled in the dust the most sacred rights of their people; that, with peace on their tongues they brought on a gigantic war; that, swollen with vanity, they despised the lessons of the past, and, confident in the pride and power of numbers, they began tearing down their own government, with the hope of destroying us and that every step of their progress was marked with aggression, perfidy, and blood;' and I say now, as reverently as he declared in 1861, that resistance to such a people was obedience to God." — *CONFEDERATE VETERAN*, 1902

THE SOUTHERN CAUSE WAS CONSERVATISM
❦ "A past for which we offer no apology, make no excuse, claiming the vindication of the righteousness of our cause at the hands of our Maker. Deo vindice." — *CONFEDERATE VETERAN*, 1904

ATTENTION SOUTH-HATERS
❦ Ulysses S. Grant on his deathbed: "I feel that we are approaching an era of great good feeling between Federal and Confederate soldiers. I shall not be here to witness it in its perfection, but I feel within me that it is to be so. Let us have peace." — *CONFEDERATE VETERAN*, 1905

TRUTH
❦ Truth, crushed to earth, shall rise again,
The eternal years of God are hers;
But error, wounded, writes with pain,
And dies among his worshipers. — *CONFEDERATE VETERAN*, 1905

OUR CONFEDERATE SIRES
❦ Above their wreath-strewn graves we kneel:
They kept the faith and fought the fight:
Through flying lead and crimson steel
They plunged for freedom and the right.
May we, their grateful children, learn
Their strength who lie beneath this sod,
Who went through fire and death to earn
At last the accolade of God! — *CONFEDERATE VETERAN*, 1925

Confederate cemetery, Covington, Georgia.

BIBLIOGRAPHY
And Suggested Reading

NOTE: Some of the books I have listed here are by dogmatic, ill-informed, and/or malevolent anti-South writers, and thus lack educational merit. Nevertheless, I have included them for their value in presenting opposing views—something typically missing from Left-wing histories.

Alexander, Edward Porter. *Military Memoirs of a Confederate*. New York: Charles Scribner's Sons, 1907.
Anderson, Mabel Washbourne. *Life of General Stand Watie: The Only Indian Brigadier General of the Confederate Army and the Last General to Surrender*. Pryor, OK: self-published, 1915.
Andrews, Matthew Page. *The Dixie Book of Days*. Philadelphia, PA: J. B. Lippincott Co., 1912.
Ansell-Pearson, Keith. *Nietzsche Contra Rousseau: A Study of Nietzsche's Moral and Political Thought*. Cambridge, UK: Cambridge University Press, 1991.
Ardrey, Robert. *African Genesis: A Personal Investigation in the Animal Origins and Nature of Man*. New York: Atheneum Books, 1961.
———. *The Territorial Imperative: A Personal Inquiry Into the Animal Origins of Property and Nations*. New York: Atheneum Books, 1966.
Armstrong, J. M. *The Biographical Encyclopedia of Kentucky of the Dead and Living Men of the Nineteenth Century*. Cincinnati, OH: J. M. Armstrong and Co., 1878.
Armstrong, Zella. *Notable Southern Families*. Chattanooga, TN: Lookout Publishing Co., 1922.
Ashe, Samuel A'Court. *History of North Carolina*. 2 vols. Greensboro, NC: Charles L. Van Noppen, 1908.
Avary, Myrta Lockett. *A Virginia Girl in the Civil War, 1861-1865: Being a Record of the Actual Experiences of the Wife of a Confederate Officer*. New York: D. Appleton and Co., 1903.
———. *Dixie After the War: An Exposition of Social Conditions Existing in the South, During the Twelve Years Succeeding the Fall of Richmond*. New York: Doubleday, Page and Co., 1906.
Bailey, Thomas Pearce. *Race Orthodoxy in the South: And Other Aspects of the Negro Question*. New York: Neale Publishing Co., 1914.
Bell, John W. *Memoirs of Governor William Smith, of Virginia: His Political, Military, and Personal History*. New York: self-published, 1891.
Benson, Al, Jr., and Walter Donald Kennedy. *Lincoln's Marxists*. Gretna, LA: Pelican, 2011.
Bernstein, Edward. *Evolutionary Socialism: A Criticism and Affirmation*. New York: B. W. Huebsch, 1911.
Bond, P. S. (ed.). *Military Science and Tactics: A Text and Reference for the Reserve Officers' Training Corps*. Washington, D.C.: P. S. Bond Publishing Co., 1938.
Bourrienne, Louis A. F. de. *Memoirs of Napoleon Bonaparte*. New York: Charles Scribner's Sons, 1895.
Boyd, James P. *Parties, Problems, and Leaders of 1896: An Impartial Presentation of Living National Questions*. Chicago, IL: Publishers' Union, 1896.
Brock, Robert Alonzo (ed.). *Southern Historical Society Papers*. 52 vols. Richmond, VA: Southern Historical Society, 1876-1943.
Browder, Earl. *Lincoln and the Communists*. New York, NY: Workers Library Publishers, Inc., 1936.
Bryan, William Jennings. *The First Battle: A Story of the Campaign of 1896*. Chicago, IL: W. B. Conkey Co., 1896.
Buhle, Mari Jo. *Women and American Socialism, 1780-1920*. Urbana, IL: University of Illinois Press, 1981.
Buhle, Paul. *Marxism in the United States: Remapping the History of the American Left*. London, UK: Verso Press, 1987.
Burns, James MacGregor. *The Vineyard of Liberty*. New York, NY: Alfred A. Knopf, 1982.
Carpenter, Stephen D. *Logic of History - Five Hundred Political Texts: Being Concentrated Extracts of Abolitionism; Also Results of Slavery Agitation and Emancipation; Together With Sundry Chapters on Despotism, Usurpations and Frauds*. Madison, WI: self-published, 1864.

Carson, Clayborne (ed.). *The Papers of Martin Luther King, Jr.* (Vol. 7: *To Save The Soul of America*, January 1961-August 1962). Oakland, CA: University of California Press, 2014.
Cave, Robert Catlett. *The Men in Gray.* Nashville, TN: Confederate Veteran, 1911.
Chapman, Katharine Hopkins. *Love's Way in Dixie.* New York: Neale Publishing Co., 1905.
Chesnut, Mary Boykin. *A Diary From Dixie.* London, UK: William Heinemann, 1905.
Christian, George Llewellyn. *Abraham Lincoln: An Address Delivered Before R. E. Lee Camp, No. 1 Confederate Veterans at Richmond, VA, October 29, 1909.* Richmond, VA: L. H. Jenkins, 1909.
———. *A Capitol Disaster: A Chapter of Reconstruction in Virginia.* Richmond, VA: self-published, 1915.
———. *Confederate Memories and Experiences.* Richmond, VA: self-published, 1915.
Clayton, Victorian V. *White and Black Under the Old Regime.* Milwaukee, WI: The Young Churchman Co., 1899.
Confederate Veteran (Sumner Archibald Cunningham, ed.). 40 vols (original forty year run). Nashville, TN: Confederate Veteran, 1893-1932.
Cunliffe, Marcus. *Chattel Slavery and Wage Slavery: The Anglo-American Context, 1830-1869.* Athens, GA: University of Georgia Press, 1979.
Cunningham, Joe Anderson. *The Blue and the Gray: And Other Poems and Songs.* Nashville, TN: self-published, 1903.
Dabney, Robert Lewis. *Life and Campaigns of Lieut.-Gen. Thomas J. Jackson (Stonewall Jackson).* New York: Blelock and Co., 1866.
Davis, Jefferson. *The Rise and Fall of the Confederate Government.* 2 vols. New York, NY: D. Appleton and Co., 1881.
Dawson, Sarah Morgan. *A Confederate Girl's Diary.* Boston, MA: Houghton Mifflin Co., 1913.
Dean, Henry Clay. *Crimes of the Civil War, and Curse of the Funding System.* Baltimore, MD: self-published, 1869.
De Bow, James Dunwoody Brownson (ed.). *De Bow's Review and Industrial Resources, Statistics, Etc.* New Orleans, LA: De Bow Publishing, 1846-1884.
Destler, Chester McArthur. *American Radicalism, 1865-1901: Essays and Documents.* New London, CT: Connecticut College Press, 1946.
Dodd, Bella. *School of Darkness.* New York, NY: P. J. Kennedy and Sons, 1954.
Draper, John William. *History of the American Civil War.* 3 vols. New York: Harper and Brothers, 1867.
Du Bois, W. E. B. *Black Reconstruction in America.* New York: Harcourt, Brace, and Co., 1935.
Early, Jubal Anderson. *A Memoir of the Last Year of the War for Independence, in the Confederate States of America.* Lynchburg, VA: Charles W. Button, 1867.
Edmonds, George. *Facts and Falsehoods Concerning the War on the South, 1861-1865.* Memphis, TN: self-published, 1904.
Elson, Henry William. *History of the United States of America.* 5 vols. New York: Macmillan Co., 1904.
Evans, Clement Anselm (ed.). *Confederate Military History.* 12 vols. Atlanta, GA: Confederate Publishing Co., 1899.
Everett, Marshall. *Famous Americans: Their Portraits, Biographies, and Thrilling Experiences.* Chicago, IL: The Educational Co., 1901.
Ewing, E. W. R. *Northern Rebellion, Southern Secession.* Philadelphia, PA: The John C. Winston Co., 1904.
Field, Henry Martyn. *Bright Skies and Dark Shadows.* New York: Charles Scribner's Sons, 1890.
Fitzhugh, George. *Cannibals All! Or, Slaves Without Masters.* Richmond, VA: A. Morris, 1857.
Foner, Eric. *Free Soil, Free Labor, Free Men: The Ideology of the Republican Party Before the Civil War.* New York: Oxford University Press, 1970.
Fowler, William Chauncey. *The Sectional Controversy; or, Passages in the Political History of the United States, Including the Causes of the War Between the Sections.* New York: Charles Scribner, 1862.
Franklin, John Hope. *Reconstruction After the Civil War.* Chicago, IL: University of Chicago Press, 1961.
Gardiner, C. *Acts of the Republican Party as Seen by History.* Washington, D.C.: self-published, 1906.
Glasgow, Ellen. *The Battle-Ground.* New York: Doubleday, Page & Co., 1902.

Goodell, William. *Slavery and Anti-Slavery: A History of the Great Struggle in Both Hemispheres, With a View of the Slavery Question in the United States.* New York: William Harned, 1852.
——. *The American Slave Code in Theory and Practice: Its Distinctive Features Shown by its Statutes, Judicial Decisions, and Illustrative Facts.* New York: American and Foreign Anti-Slavery Society, 1853.
Haley, James T. (ed.). *Afro-American Encyclopedia; or the Thoughts, Doings, and Sayings of the Race.* Nashville, TN: Haley and Florida, 1895.
Hamill, H. M. *The Old South.* Nashville, TN: Smith and Lamar, 1904.
Harris, Joel Chandler. *Uncle Remus and His Friends: Old Plantation Stories, Songs and Ballads With Sketches of Negro Character.* 1892. New York: McKinlay, Stone and Mackenzie, 1920 ed.
Harrison, Royden. *Before the Socialists: Studies in Labour and Politics, 1861-1881.* London, UK: Routledge and Kegan Paul, 1965.
Hasselberg, P. D. (ed.). *Parliamentary Debates: First Session, Fortieth Parliament, 1982, House of Representatives* (Vol. 445). Wellington, New Zealand: Government Printer, 1982.
Herreshoff, David. *American Disciples of Marx: From the Age of Jackson to the Progressive Era.* Detroit, MI: Wayne State University Press, 1967.
Hillquit, Morris. *History of Socialism in the United States.* New York: Funk and Wagnalls Co., 1903.
Hobson, Anne. *In Old Alabama: Being the Chronicles of Miss Mouse, the Little Black Merchant.* New York: Doubleday Page & Co., 1903.
Hodgkin, James B. *Southland Stories.* Manassas, VA: The Journal Press, 1903.
Hofstadter, Richard. *The Progressive Historians: Turner, Beard, Parrington.* London, UK: Jonathan Cape, 1968.
Holloway, Ralph L. *Primate Aggression, Territoriality, and Xenophobia: A Comparative Perspective.* New York: Academic Press, 1974.
Holmes, Oliver Wendell. *Dorothy Q: Together With A Ballad of the Boston Tea Party and Grandmother's Story of Bunker Hill Battle.* 1874. Boston, MA: Houghton, Mifflin and Co., 1892 ed.
Jefferson, Thomas. *Autobiography of Thomas Jefferson, 1743-1790.* (Paul L. Ford, ed.). New York: G. P. Putnam's Sons, 1914.
Johnson, Robert Underwood, and Clarence Clough Buel (eds.). *Battles and Leaders of the Civil War.* 4 vols. New York, NY: The Century Co., 1884-1888.
Johnston, Mary. *The Long Roll.* Boston, MA: Houghton Mifflin Co., 1911.
Johnston, Richard Malcolm, and William Hand Browne. *Life of Alexander H. Stephens.* 1878. Philadelphia, PA: J. B. Lippincott and Co., 1883 ed.
Johnstone, Huger William. *Truth of War Conspiracy, 1861.* Idylwild, GA: H. W. Johnstone, 1921.
Jones, John William. *The Davis Memorial Volume; Or Our Dead President, Jefferson Davis and the World's Tribute to His Memory.* Richmond, VA: B. F. Johnson, 1889.
Keller, Martha Caroline. *Love and Rebellion: A Story of the Civil War and Reconstruction.* New York: J. S. Ogilvie, 1891.
Korngold, Ralph. *Two Friends of Man: The Story of William Lloyd Garrison and Wendell Phillips and Their Relationship with Abraham Lincoln.* Boston, MA: Little, Brown and Co., 1950.
Kraditor, Aileen. *The Radical Persuasion, 1890-1917: Aspects of the Intellectual History and the Historiography of Three American Radical Organizations.* Baton Rouge, LA: Louisiana State University Press, 1981.
Lee, Richard Henry. *Memoir of the Life of Richard Henry Lee, and His Correspondence.* 2 vols. Philadelphia, PA: H. C. Carey and I. Lea, 1825.
Lenin, Vladimir Ilyich. *The State and Revolution: Marxist Teaching on the State and the Task of the Proletariat in the Revolution.* London: UK: The British Socialist Party, 1919.
——. *"Left Wing" Communism: An Infantile Disorder.* Detroit, MI: The Marxian Educational Society, 1921.
Lens, Sidney. *Radicalism in America.* New York: Thomas Crowell, 1969.
Levine, Bruce. *The Spirit of 1848: German Immigrants, Labor Conflict, and the Coming of the Civil War.* Urbana, IL: University of Illinois Press, 1992.
Livermore, Thomas L. *Numbers and Losses in the Civil War in America, 1861-65.* 1900. Carlisle, PA: John Kallmann, 1996 ed.
Lunt, George. *Radicalism in Religion, Philosophy, and Social Life.* Boston, MA: Little, Brown, and Co., 1858.
Lynd, Staughton. *Intellectual Origins of American Radicalism.* New York: Pantheon Books,

1968.

Magliocca, Gerard N. *The Tragedy of William Jennings Bryan: Constitutional Law and the Politics of Backlash*. New Haven, CT: Yale University Press, 2011.

Mandel, Bernard. *Labor Free and Slave: Workingmen and the Anti-Slavery Movement in the United States*. New York: Associated Authors, 1955.

Marx, Karl, and Frederick Engels. *Manifesto of the Communist Party*. Chicago, IL: Charles H. Kerr and Co., 1906.

McCarty, Burke (ed.). *Little Sermons in Socialism by Abraham Lincoln*. Chicago, IL: The Chicago Daily Socialist, 1910.

McGuire, Hunter, and George Llewellyn Christian. *The Confederate Cause and the War Between the States*. Richmond, VA: L. H. Jenkins, 1907.

McMurray, William J. *History of the Twentieth Tennessee Regiment Volunteer Infantry, C.S.A.* Nashville, TN: The Publication Committee, 1904.

McNeilly, James Hugh. *Religion and Slavery: A Vindication of the Southern Churches*. Nashville, TN: M. E. Church, South, 1911.

McPherson, James M. *Abraham Lincoln and the Second American Revolution*. New York, NY: Oxford University Press, 1991.

Meriwether, Elizabeth Avery (pseudonym, "George Edmonds"). *Facts and Falsehoods Concerning the War on the South, 1861-1865*. Memphis, TN: A. R. Taylor and Co., 1904.

Messer-Kruse, Timothy. *The Yankee International: Marxism and the American Reform Tradition, 1848-1876*. Chapel Hill, NC: University of North Carolina Press, 1998.

Miller, Francis Trevelyan, and Robert S. Lanier (eds.). *The Photographic History of the Civil War*. 10 vols. New York, NY: The Review of Reviews Co., 1911.

Miller, Kelly. *Race Adjustment: Essays on the Negro in America*. New York: Neale Publishing Co., 1908.

Mins, L. E. (ed.). *Founding of the First International: A Documentary Record*. New York: International Publishers, 1937.

Minutes of the Eighth Annual Meeting and Reunion of the United Confederate Veterans, Atlanta, GA, July 20-23, 1898. New Orleans, LA: United Confederate Veterans, 1907.

Minutes of the Ninth Annual Meeting and Reunion of the United Confederate Veterans, Charleston, SC, May 10-13, 1899. New Orleans, LA: United Confederate Veterans, 1907.

Minutes of the Twelfth Annual Meeting and Reunion of the United Confederate Veterans, Dallas, TX, April 22-25, 1902. New Orleans, LA: United Confederate Veterans, 1907.

Montgomery, David. *Beyond Equality: Labor and the Radical Republicans, 1862-1872*. New York: Alfred A. Knopf, 1967.

Moore, John Trotwood. *Songs and Stories From Tennessee*. Philadelphia, PA: Henry T. Coates & Co., 1903.

———. *Uncle Wash: His Stories*. Philadelphia, PA: John C. Winston Co., 1910.

Moore, Stanley W. *The Critique of Capitalist Democracy: An Introduction to the Theory of the State in Marx, Engels, and Lenin*. New York: Paine-Whitman Publishers, 1957.

Murphy, Jeannette Robinson. *Southern Thoughts for Northern Thinkers*. New York: Bandanna Publishing Co., 1904.

Murrell, Mrs. D. G. *The White Castle of Louisiana*. Louisville, KY: J. P. Morton & Co., 1903.

Muzzey, David Saville. *The United States of America: Vol. 1, To the Civil War*. Boston, MA: Ginn and Co., 1922.

———. *The American Adventure: Vol. 2, From the Civil War*. 1924. New York, NY: Harper and Brothers, 1927 ed.

Nichols, George Ward. *The Story of the Great March: From the Diary of a Staff Officer*. New York: Harper & Brothers, 1865.

Nicolay, John G., and John Hay (eds.). *Abraham Lincoln: A History*. 10 vols. New York, NY: The Century Co., 1890.

———. *Complete Works of Abraham Lincoln*. 12 vols. 1894. New York, NY: Francis D. Tandy Co., 1905 ed.

———. *Abraham Lincoln: Complete Works*. 12 vols. 1894. New York, NY: The Century Co., 1907 ed.

Obermann, Karl. *Joseph Wedemeyer: Pioneer of American Socialism*. New York: International Publishers, 1947.

ORA (full title: *The War of the Rebellion: A Compilation of the Official Records of the Union and Confederate Armies*). 128 vols. Washington, DC: Government Printing Office, 1880.

ORN (full title: *Official Records of the Union and Confederate Navies in the War of the*

Rebellion). 30 vols. Washington, DC: Government Printing Office, 1894.
Page, Arthur W. (ed.). *The World's Work: A History of Our Time.* (Vol. 31, November 1915 to April 1916.) Garden City, NY: Doubleday, Page & Co., 1916.
Page, Thomas Nelson. *In Ole Virginia.* 1887. New York: Charles Scribner's Sons, 1896 ed.
Parker, Theodore. *Speeches, Addresses, and Occasional Sermons.* 2 vols. Boston, MA: William Crosby and H. P. Nichols, 1852.
Parrington, Vernon Louis. *Main Currents in American Thought: An Interpretation of American Literature From the Beginning to 1920.* New York: Harcourt, Brace & Co., 1927.
Peek, Comer Leonard. *Lorna Carswell: A Story of the South.* New York: Broadway Publishing Co., 1903.
Perry, Lewis. *Radical Abolitionism: Anarchy and the Government of God in Antislavery Thought.* Ithaca, NY: Cornell University Press, 1973.
Pollard, Edward Alfred. *The Lost Cause.* New York, NY: E. B. Treat and Co., 1867.
Powers, William Dudley. *Uncle Isaac or the Old Days in the South: A Remembrance of the South.* Richmond, VA: B. F. Johnson Publishing Co., 1899.
Prince, Leon C. *A Bird's-Eye View of American History.* New York: Charles Scribner's Sons, 1907.
Quint, Howard H. *The Forging of American Socialism: Origins of the Modern Movement.* Indianapolis, IN: Bobbs-Merrill Co., 1953.
Rice, Allen Thorndike (ed.). *Reminiscences of Abraham Lincoln by Distinguished Men of His Time.* New York: North American Publishing Co., 1886.
Richardson, John Anderson. *Richardson's Defense of the South.* Atlanta, GA: A. B. Caldwell, 1914.
Robinson, Nina Hill. *Aunt Dice: The Story of a Faithful Slave.* Nashville, TN: M. E. Church, South, 1897.
Rochefoucauld-Liancourt, Duc de La. *Voyage dans les Etats-Unis.* Paris, France: Du Pont, 1798.
Rogers, William P. *The Three Secession Movements in the United States: Samuel J. Tilden, the Democratic Candidate for Presidency; the Advisor, Aider and Abettor of the Great Secession Movement of 1860; and One of the Authors of the Infamous Resolution of 1864; His Claims as a Statesman and Reformer Considered.* Boston, MA: John Wilson and Son, 1876.
Rove, Karl. *The Triumph of William McKinley: Why the Election of 1896 Still Matters.* New York, NY: Simon and Schuster, 2015.
Rowland, Dunbar (ed.). *Jefferson Davis, Constitutionalist: His Letters, Papers, and Speeches.* Jackson, MS: Mississippi Department of Archives and History, 1923.
Russell, Bertrand. *German Social Democracy: Six Lectures.* London, UK: Longmans, Green, and Co., 1896.
Rutherford, Mildred Lewis. *Truths of History: A Fair, Unbiased, Impartial, Unprejudiced and Conscientious Study of History.* Athens, GA: n.p., 1920.
Salter, Frank R. *Karl Marx and Modern Socialism.* London, UK: Macmillan and Co., 1921.
Schlüter, Herman. *Lincoln, Labor and Slavery: A Chapter From the Social History of America.* New York: Socialist Literature Co., 1913.
Sea, Sophie Fox. *"That Old-Time Child, Roberta: Her Home-Life on the Farm.* Louisville, KY: John P. Morton and Co., 1892.
Seabrook, Lochlainn. *Carnton Plantation Ghost Stories: True Tales of the Unexplained from Tennessee's Most Haunted Civil War House!* 2005. Franklin, TN, 2016 ed.
———. *Nathan Bedford Forrest: Southern Hero, American Patriot.* 2007. Franklin, TN, 2010 ed.
———. *Abraham Lincoln: The Southern View.* 2007. Franklin, TN: Sea Raven Press, 2013 ed.
———. *The McGavocks of Carnton Plantation: A Southern History - Celebrating One of Dixie's Most Noble Confederate Families and Their Tennessee Home.* 2008. Franklin, TN, 2011 ed.
———. *A Rebel Born: A Defense of Nathan Bedford Forrest.* 2010. Franklin, TN: Sea Raven Press, 2011 ed.
———. *Everything You Were Taught About the Civil War is Wrong, Ask a Southerner!* 2010. Franklin, TN: Sea Raven Press, revised 2019 ed.
———. *The Quotable Jefferson Davis: Selections From the Writings and Speeches of the Confederacy's First President.* Franklin, TN: Sea Raven Press, 2011.
———. *The Quotable Robert E. Lee: Selections From the Writings and Speeches of the South's Most Beloved Civil War General.* Franklin, TN: Sea Raven Press, 2011 Sesquicentennial Civil War Edition.
———. *Lincolnology: The Real Abraham Lincoln Revealed In His Own Words.* Franklin, TN: Sea Raven Press, 2011.

———. *The Unquotable Abraham Lincoln: The President's Quotes They Don't Want You To Know!* Franklin, TN: Sea Raven Press, 2011.

———. *Honest Jeff and Dishonest Abe: A Southern Children's Guide to the Civil War.* Franklin, TN: Sea Raven Press, 2012.

———. *Encyclopedia of the Battle of Franklin - A Comprehensive Guide to the Conflict that Changed the Civil War.* Franklin, TN: Sea Raven Press, 2012.

———. *The Quotable Nathan Bedford Forrest: Selections From the Writings and Speeches of the Confederacy's Most Brilliant Cavalryman.* Spring Hill, TN: Sea Raven Press, 2012.

———. *Forrest! 99 Reasons to Love Nathan Bedford Forrest.* Spring Hill, TN: Sea Raven Press, 2012.

———. *Give 'Em Hell Boys! The Complete Military Correspondence of Nathan Bedford Forrest.* Spring Hill, TN: Sea Raven Press, 2012.

———. *The Constitution of the Confederate States of America Explained: A Clause-by-Clause Study of the South's Magna Carta.* Spring Hill, TN: Sea Raven Press, 2012 Sesquicentennial Civil War Edition.

———. *The Great Impersonator: 99 Reasons to Dislike Abraham Lincoln.* Spring Hill, TN: Sea Raven Press, 2012.

———. *The Old Rebel: Robert E. Lee As He Was Seen By His Contemporaries.* Spring Hill, TN: Sea Raven Press, 2012 Sesquicentennial Civil War Edition.

———. *The Quotable Stonewall Jackson: Selections From the Writings and Speeches of the South's Most Famous General.* Spring Hill, TN: Sea Raven Press, 2012 Sesquicentennial Civil War Edition.

———. *Saddle, Sword, and Gun: A Biography of Nathan Bedford Forrest for Teens.* Spring Hill, TN: Sea Raven Press, 2013.

———. *The Alexander H. Stephens Reader: Excerpts From the Works of a Confederate Founding Father.* Spring Hill, TN: Sea Raven Press, 2013.

———. *The Quotable Alexander H. Stephens: Selections From the Writings and Speeches of the Confederacy's First Vice President.* Spring Hill, TN: Sea Raven Press, 2013 Sesquicentennial Civil War Edition.

———. *Give This Book to a Yankee! A Southern Guide to the Civil War for Northerners.* Spring Hill, TN: Sea Raven Press, 2014.

———. *The Articles of Confederation Explained: A Clause-by-Clause Study of America's First Constitution.* Spring Hill, TN: Sea Raven Press, 2014.

———. *Confederate Blood and Treasure: An Interview With Lochlainn Seabrook.* Spring Hill, TN: Sea Raven Press, 2015.

———. *Nathan Bedford Forrest and the Battle of Fort Pillow: Yankee Myth, Confederate Fact.* Spring Hill, TN: Sea Raven Press, 2015.

———. *Everything You Were Taught About American Slavery War is Wrong, Ask a Southerner!* Spring Hill, TN: Sea Raven Press, 2015.

———. *Confederacy 101: Amazing Facts You Never Knew About America's Oldest Political Tradition.* Spring Hill, TN: Sea Raven Press, 2015.

———. *The Great Yankee Coverup: What the North Doesn't Want You to Know About Lincoln's War!* Spring Hill, TN: Sea Raven Press, 2015.

———. *Slavery 101: Amazing Facts You Never Knew About America's "Peculiar Institution."* Spring Hill, TN: Sea Raven Press, 2015.

———. *Confederate Flag Facts: What Every American Should Know About Dixie's Southern Cross.* Spring Hill, TN: Sea Raven Press, 2016.

———. *Nathan Bedford Forrest and the Ku Klux Klan: Yankee Myth, Confederate Fact.* Spring Hill, TN: Sea Raven Press, 2016.

———. *Seabrook's Bible Dictionary of Traditional and Mystical Christian Doctrines.* Spring Hill, TN: Sea Raven Press, 2016.

———. *Everything You Were Taught About African-Americans and the Civil War is Wrong, Ask a Southerner!* Spring Hill, TN: Sea Raven Press, 2016.

———. *Nathan Bedford Forrest and African-Americans: Yankee Myth, Confederate Fact.* Spring Hill, TN: Sea Raven Press, 2016.

———. *Women in Gray: A Tribute to the Ladies Who Supported the Southern Confederacy.* Spring Hill, TN: Sea Raven Press, 2016.

———. *Lincoln's War: The Real Cause, the Real Winner, the Real Loser.* Spring Hill, TN: Sea Raven Press, 2016.

———. *The Unholy Crusade: Lincoln's Legacy of Destruction in the American South.* Spring Hill, TN: Sea Raven Press, 2017.

———. *Abraham Lincoln Was a Liberal, Jefferson Davis Was a Conservative: The Missing Key to Understanding the American Civil War.* Spring Hill, TN: Sea Raven Press, 2017.

———. *All We Ask is to be Let Alone: The Southern Secession Fact Book.* Spring Hill, TN: Sea

———. Raven Press, 2017.
———. *The Ultimate Civil War Quiz Book: How Much Do You Really Know About America's Most Misunderstood Conflict?* Spring Hill, TN: Sea Raven Press, 2017.
———. *Rise Up and Call Them Blessed: Victorian Tributes to the Confederate Soldier, 1861-1901.* Spring Hill, TN: Sea Raven Press, 2017.
———. *Victorian Confederate Poetry: The Southern Cause in Verse, 1861-1901.* Spring Hill, TN: Sea Raven Press, 2018.
———. *Confederate Monuments: Why Every American Should Honor Confederate Soldiers and Their Memorials.* Spring Hill, TN: Sea Raven Press, 2018.
———. *The God of War: Nathan Bedford Forrest as He Was Seen by His Contemporaries.* Spring Hill, TN: Sea Raven Press, 2018.
———. *The Battle of Spring Hill: Recollections of Confederate and Union Soldiers.* Spring Hill, TN: Sea Raven Press, 2018.
———. *I Rode With Forrest! Confederate Soldiers Who Served With the World's Greatest Cavalry Leader.* Spring Hill, TN: Sea Raven Press, 2018.
———. *The Battle of Nashville: Recollections of Confederate and Union Soldiers.* Spring Hill, TN: Sea Raven Press, 2018.
———. *The Battle of Franklin: Recollections of Confederate and Union Soldiers.* Spring Hill, TN: Sea Raven Press, 2018.
———. *A Rebel Born: The Screenplay* (for the film). Written 2011. Franklin, TN: Sea Raven Press, 2020.
———. (ed.) *A Short History of the Confederate States of America* (Jefferson Davis, Belford Company, NY, 1890). A Sea Raven Press Reprint. Spring Hill, TN: Sea Raven Press, 2020.
———. (ed.) *Prison Life of Jefferson Davis: Embracing Details and Incidents in his Captivity, With Conversations on Topics of Public Interest* (John J. Craven, Sampson, Low, Son, and Marston, London, UK, 1866). A Sea Raven Press Reprint. Spring Hill, TN: Sea Raven Press, 2020.
———. *What the Confederate Flag Means to Me: Americans Speak Out in Defense of Southern Honor, Heritage, and History.* Spring Hill, TN: Sea Raven Press, 2021.
———. *Heroes of the Southern Confederacy: The Illustrated Book of Confederate Officials, Soldiers, and Civilians.* Spring Hill, TN: Sea Raven Press, 2021.
———. *Support Your Local Confederate: Wit and Humor in the Southern Confederacy.* Spring Hill, TN: Sea Raven Press, 2021.
———. *America's Three Constitutions: Complete Texts of the Articles of Confederation, Constitution of the United States of America, and Constitution of the Confederate States of America.* Spring Hill, TN: Sea Raven Press, 2021.
———. *Vintage Southern Cookbook: 2,000 Delicious Dishes From Dixie.* Spring Hill, TN: Sea Raven Press, 2021.
Shannon, Alexander Harvey. *Racial Integrity and Other Features of the Negro Problem.* Nashville, TN: self-published, 1907.
Smedes, Susan Dabney. *Memorials of a Southern Planter.* Baltimore, MD: Cushings and Bailey, 1887.
Spargo, John. *Karl Marx: His Life and Work.* New York: B. W. Huebsch, 1910.
Steel, Samuel Augustus. *The South Was Right.* Columbia, SC: R. L. Bryan Co., 1914.
Stephens, Alexander Hamilton. *Speech of Mr. Stephens, of Georgia, on the War and Taxation.* Washington, D.C.: J & G. Gideon, 1848.
———. *A Constitutional View of the Late War Between the States; Its Causes, Character, Conduct and Results.* 2 vols. Philadelphia, PA: National Publishing, Co., 1870.
———. *Recollections of Alexander H. Stephens: His Diary Kept When a Prisoner at Fort Warren, Boston Harbour, 1865.* New York, NY: Doubleday, Page and Co., 1910.
Stiles, Robert. *Four Years Under Marse Robert.* New York: Neale Publishing Co., 1903.
Takaki, Ronald T. *Race and Culture in Nineteenth-Century America.* New York: Alfred A. Knopf, 1979.
The National Cyclopedia of American Biography. New York: James T. White and Co., 1897.
Thomas, Henry W. *History of the Doles-Cook Brigade, Army of Northern Virginia.* Atlanta, GA: Franklin Printing & Publishing Co., 1903.
Thompson, Holland. *The New South: A Chronicle of Social and Industrial Evolution.* New Haven, CT: Yale University Press, 1920.
Towne, William T. *With Hooks of Steel: A Tale of Old-Time Virginia.* New York: Neale Publishing Co., 1913.
Trachtenberg, Alexander (ed.). *Karl Marx and Frederick Engels: Letters to Americans, 1848-1895.* New York: International Publishers, 1953.

Tyler, Charles W. *The Scout: A Tale of the Civil War.* Nashville, TN: M. E. Church, South, 1912.
Tyler, Lyon Gardiner (ed.). *Encyclopedia of Virginia Biography.* New York: Lewis Historical Publishing Co., 1915.
VanMeter, B. F., Sr. *A Dead Issue and the Live One.* Lexington, KY: self-published, 1914.
Veysey, Laurence (ed.). *The Perfectionists: Radical Social Thought in the North, 1815-1860.* New York: John Wiley and Sons, 1973.
Warner, Ezra J. *Generals in Gray: Lives of the Confederate Commanders.* 1959. Baton Rouge, LA: Louisiana State University Press, 1989 ed.
———. *Generals in Blue: Lives of the Union Commanders.* 1964. Baton Rouge, LA: Louisiana State University Press, 2006 ed.
Washington, Booker T. *Up From Slavery: An Autobiography.* New York: Doubleday, Page and Co., 1907.
———. *My Larger Education: Being Chapters From my Experience.* Garden City, NY: Doubleday, Page and Co., 1911.
Weeden, Howard. *Shadows on the Wall.* New York: M. Stolz and Co., 1898.
Weyl, Nathaniel. *Karl Marx: Racist.* New Rochelle, NY: Arlington House, 1979.
Wilson, Edward O. *Sociobiology: The New Synthesis.* Cambridge, MA: Belknap Press, 1975.
———. *On Human Nature.* Cambridge, MA: Harvard University Press, 1978.
Wittke, Carl. *Refugees of Revolution: The German Forty-Eighters in America.* Westport, CT: Greenwood Press, 1952.
Woods, Thomas E., Jr. *The Politically Incorrect Guide to American History.* Washington, D.C.: Regnery, 2004.
Wright, Frances. *England, the Civilizer: Her History Developed in its Principles.* London, UK: self-published, 1848.

BEFORE A SOUTHERN AUDIENCE

"In order to understand the Southern people, especially with respect to issues of the war and what grew out of it, in order to understand their present position, one must know that your hearts and emotions are broad enough to entertain entire loyalty to the issues of the past, which you fought so nobly to sustain, and entire loyalty to our present government, for which you would be willing to lay down your lives if occasion required it."

President William H. Taft
Speech at Columbus, Mississippi, circa early 1900s

INDEX

Abercrombie, Mary, 129
Abercrombie, R. A., 304
Abraham (Bible), 87, 245
Abram, Uncle (black servant), 113
Adair, George W., 104
Adams, John, 293
Adams, Mary E. A., 145
Adams, Will, 139
Agnew, Samuel A., 128
Akin, A. N., 125
Akin, Mrs. M. F., 160
Akin, Warren, 159, 160
Albert (black servant), 297
Alexander, Elam, 162
Alexander, Gross, 221
Alexander, Hannibal, 134, 135
Alexander, Lewis, 135
Alexander, Parker, 134
Alexander, Sidney, 134, 135
Alfred (black servant), 90
Allen, James L., 204
Allison, Belle K., 212
Amanda (black servant), 314
Americus (black servant), 311
Amison, William, 83
Amos (black servant), 95
Amy (black servant), 141
Anderson, Joseph W., 297
Anderson, Margaret, 278
Andrew, John A., 293
Andrew, Matthew P., 319
Andrews, Stephen P., 23, 24
Anna (black servant), 297
Ardis, Fed, 133, 134
Ardis, Isaac, 133, 134
Armstrong, Mary, 88
Arnold, Benedict, 161
Arnot, William, 251
Arp, Bill, 159
Asa (black servant), 89
Ashby, Turner, 62, 126, 191
Ashley, Sarah, 300
Aston, Mrs. C. G., 175
Atkins, Chet, 412
Atwood, William H., 318
Au, Margaret L. von der, 343
Avirett, James B., 191, 303
Bailey, Mrs. H. P., 138
Baird, E. T., 250, 251
Bakunin, Mikhail, 22
Baldwin, John B., 60
Bancroft, George, 40
Banks, E. A., 173
Banks, Willis, 173
Barclay, Hugh G., 337
Barker, Charles, 373
Barker, John, 91, 317
Barnett, J. J., 146
Bartlett, William F., 47
Barton, Dr., 323
Barton, Seth M., 361

Bate, Jim, 74
Bate, William B., 74, 75, 242, 301, 305
Battery, Jim, 193
Battle, Fannie, 300
Battle, Frank, 223
Battle, Henry W., 356, 357
Battle, Joel A., 278
Beauregard, Pierre G. T., 195, 283
Beavers, Robert, 159, 160
Beecher, Henry W., 200, 226
Ben (black servant), 139, 305
Bendy, Edgar, 53
Bendy, Minerva, 53
Benjamin, Judah P., 352
Benning, Anna C., 146
Benning, Henry L., 198
Benton, Thomas H., 244
Berry, Thomas F., 316
Bibb, Joseph B., 165, 166
Bibb, Sophia, 151
Birchett, T. G., 167
Birdsong, J. C., 223
Birney, James G., 113, 114
Bishop, John K., 95
Bivins, Josephine, 75
Black Daddy (black servant), 147
Black Hawk (black servant), 191, 302
Black, Jeremiah S., 221
Blackburn, J. S. C., 264
Blackford, L. M., 91
Blaine, George, 184
Blaine, Nick, 184, 185
Blair, Francis P., Sr., 159, 161
Blankenbury, Kathryn C., 341
Bledsoe, Joel T., 206
Blount, Nancy H., 183
Blount, W. A., 183
Bob (black servant), 245
Bolling, Edith, 412
Bolling, W. T., 213
Bonaparte, Napoleon, 59, 230
Boone, Nathan S., 120
Boone, Pat, 412
Booth, John W., 296
Bormer, Betty, 42
Bourne, Edward, 267
Bowen, Col., 339
Boynton, George, 210, 211
Boynton, Lieut., 211
Bracey, Augustus A., 336
Bracey, Sedley L., 336
Bradfield, J. O., 333
Bradford, H. S., 192
Bradford, Hiram S., 192
Bradford, Taul, 225
Bradshaw, Matt, 112
Brady, Wes, 84
Bragg, Braxton, 89, 125, 147, 373
Bragg, Braxton (black servant), 125
Branch, Edward T., 306

Branch, Lawrence, O., 183
Branch, Nancy H., 183
Branch, William, 295
Branham, Mrs. W. C., 301
Breckenridge, John C., 223
Breckinridge, John C., 100
Brewster, B. B., 283
Bronte, Charlotte, 204
Brooks, John M., 222
Brothers, O. C., 207
Broun, William le Roy, 183
Brown, H. A., 125
Brown, John, 48, 68, 101, 102, 126, 127, 146, 200, 221, 275, 287, 293, 297, 344, 359, 369, 370
Brown, John C., 340, 361
Brown, Robert, 114
Brown, Tom, 111
Brown, Zek, 157
Browne, William M., 355
Browning, Elizabeth B., 204
Brownlee, Easter P., 291, 366
Brownlow, William G., 200
Bryan, John R., 258
Bryan, Joseph, 258
Buchanan, John A., 258
Buchanan, Ned, 367
Buchanan, Patrick J., 412
Buck, Samuel H., 332
Buckner, Mrs. Simon B., 259
Buckner, Simon B., 83, 90, 258, 259
Buford, Elizabeth B., 90
Buford, Mrs. Pattie, 131
Bull, John, 276
Bulloch, James D., 374
Burge, J. G., 78
Burgoyne, John, 307
Burnett, Mary, 216
Burnett, Mrs. Theodore L., 216
Burnett, Theodore L., 216
Burns, Anthony, 288
Burns, Jennie G., 216
Burress, L. R., 290
Burrows, F. M., 47
Burton, Frankey, 354
Burton, May, 354
Butler, Benjamin F., 146, 198, 261, 355
Butler, Col., 69
Butler, Ellen, 111
Butler, Thomas, 123
Byrd, Sylvia, 283
Cabell, William L., 210
Cabiness, S. D., 20
Cadman, S. Parkes, 318
Caesar, 46
Calacut, Staward, 85
Caldwell, John H., 225
Calhoun, Bettie L., 203
Calhoun, John C., 68, 69, 217, 244, 289
Calhoun, W. Lowndes, 199
Callahan, S. B., 294
Cameron, W. E., 138

Camp, Benjamin, 178
Camp, W. C., 283
Campbell, W. A., 135
Candler, Allen D., 199, 254
Carnegie, Andrew, 262
Carnes, William W., 72
Carrier, Lieut. Col., 316
Carson, Martha, 412
Carter, H. W., 279
Carter, Mrs. Edward, 329
Cash, Johnny, 412
Catiline, 46
Cave, R. C., 66
Cesar (black servant), 120
Chadwick, William D., 20, 293
Chalaron, J. A., 114
Chalmers, Anne, 141
Chalmers, Col., 141
Chalmers, James R., 133
Chalmers, S. J., 206
Chambers, Betty K., 341
Chambliss, Nathaniel R., 89
Chancellor, Dr., 209
Chandler, A. M., 358
Chandler, Silas, 358
Chap, Uncle (black servant), 131
Chappel, Alonzo, 281
Charles (black servant), 281
Charles, R. K., 128
Chase, Salmon P., 20, 25, 102, 114, 293
Cheatham, Benjamin F., 85, 212
Cheney, H. J., 282
Chloe, Aunt (black servant), 116, 117
Choate, J. Wesley, 166
Christian, George, 64
Christian, George L., 221, 301
Christian, Julia J., 96
Christian, Thomas J. J., 96
Christian, William E., 96
Christmas, Guildford, 310
Claiborne, Maria E., 202
Clanton, James H., 303, 304
Clark, Congressman, 341
Clark, George R., 257
Clark, Walter A., 323
Clay, Clement C., 113
Clay, Henry, 200, 217, 244, 284
Clayton, Samuel, 353
Clayton, Victoria V., 113
Cleburne, Patrick R., 282
Cleveland, Anne W., 306
Cleveland, Grover, 46, 69, 75, 202
Clingan, Ella, 252
Cobb, Howell, 48, 272
Cobb, Rufus, 225
Cobb, Thomas R. R., 48
Coffee, John T., 295
Coleman (black servant), 77, 91
Coleman, Preston B., 146, 147
Coleman, Samuel, 304
Colley, Thomas W., 254
Combs, Bertram T., 412
Compton, Dr., 323

Compton, Felix, 132
Compton, Harry, 305
Cone, Martha, 151
Cook, H. H., 136
Cook, Philip, 180
Cooper, Douglas H., 137
Cooper, Milan, 284
Cora (black servant), 264
Corbett, A. W., 284
Cornwallis, Charles, 307
Corse, Montgomery D., 339
Councill, W. H., 149, 178
Cowan, George L., 17, 189
Cox, Elijah, 277
Coxe, John, 370
Craig, Tully, 282
Crandall, Prudence, 286
Crawford, Cindy, 412
Crawford, W. P., 153
Creel, George R., 336
Crenshaw, Lewis D., 145
Crocker, Lewis, 297
Crocker, Polly, 297
Cromwell, Oliver, 159, 244
Cruise, Tom, 412
Culp, L. N., 121
Cumming, C. C., 83, 210
Cunningham, Frank, 138
Cunningham, John, 333
Cunningham, Miss Willie, 334
Cunningham, Paul D., 131
Cunningham, Sarah, 333
Cunningham, Sumner A., 83, 149, 256, 339, 374
Cupid (black servant), 126
Curry, Manly B., 54
Cushing, Caleb, 22
Cussons, John, 29
Cyrus, Billy Ray, 412
Cyrus, Miley, 412
Dabney, J. O., 361
Dabney, Mack, 361
Dabney, Sam D., 361
Daffan, John W., 216
Daffan, Lawrence A., 216
Daffan, Mary J., 216
Dana, Charles A., 26, 261
Dancy, Lucy, 264
Dangerfield, Mrs., 126
Davis, Jefferson, 11-13, 29, 41, 43, 49, 50, 69, 81, 114, 122, 135, 138, 150, 163, 192, 196, 205, 210, 213-215, 224, 231, 247, 255, 256, 263, 264, 272, 273, 284, 291, 319, 325, 336, 345, 351, 354-356, 412
Davis, Jefferson H., 210
Davis, Jefferson, Jr., 205
Davis, Margaret H. "Maggie", 205, 224, 247, 319
Davis, Martha, 126, 127
Davis, Mrs. W. L., 392
Davis, Sam, 77, 91, 92
Davis, Varina A. "Winnie", 41, 205, 319
Davis, Varina H., 49, 50, 114, 205, 213, 214, 224
Dawson, Capt., 180
Dawson, Sarah M., 373
Deane, Samuel H., 178
DeLauney, Francis V., 203
Delia (black servant), 134
Demosthenes, 289
Denison, Ruth E., 282
Derry, Joseph T., 175
Devereux, Thomas P., 342
Dial (black servant), 313
Dibrell, George G., 72
Dice (black servant), 95, 97
Dick (black servant), 181, 195
Dickinson, Jacob M., 172, 256
Dix, John A., 293
Dodge, Granville, 77, 92
Donelson, Sam, 122
Donnell, Robert, 120
Doswell, R. M., 361
Douglas (black servant), 126
Douglas, Alfred H., 92
Douglas, C. M., 70
Douglas, Stephen A., 275, 355, 377, 378
Dowd, Col., 345
Downing, Emanuel, 86
Downing, L. L., 207
Doyle, Mahala, 287
Doyle, W. E., 313, 345
Dozier, Tennie P., 227
Draper, W. W., 225
Dromgoole, Miss, 188
Duncan, Nellie, 136
Duvall, Robert, 412
Early, Jubal A., 327
Edgar, Dr., 247
Edwards, A. N., 131, 134
Edwards, Anderson, 46
Edwards, Harry S., 148
Edwards, Minerva, 46
Elmore, Capt., 69
Elmore, Stephen, 33
Elson, Henry W., 30
Emerson, A. J., 298
Emmaline (black servant), 229
Emory, William H., 260
Endicott, John, 86
English, Tom, 92
Enslen, Julia V., 163
Ephriam (black servant), 47
Epperson, Lulu B., 112, 113
Eugenia (black servant), 264
Evans, Clement A., 80, 91, 236, 254, 356
Evans, H. G., 125
Evans, Lawton, 322
Evans, Mark L., 201, 202
Everett, Edward, 85
Ewing, Frank, 256
Fairbairn, Patrick, 250
Fairfax, William H., 235

Falk, Bill, 297
Falkner, J. M., 148
Fanny (black servant), 132, 133
Faris, A. A., 188
Farragut, David G., 355
Faulkner, Charles J., 56
Faulkner, E. C., 133
Fay, Rose, 203
Field, Al G., 332
Finch, Ben, 298
Finch, Charlie, 299
Finch, Cicero, 298
Fisher, Col., 153
Fitzgerald, O. P., 217
Fitzhugh, George, 23
Fitzpatrick, Rene, 367
Flora (black servant), 113
Fly, George W. L., 159
Folsom, Sim, 137
Fontaine, Mrs. G. de, 81
Foot, Samuel A., 66
Foote, Shelby, 412
Ford, C. Y., 370
Ford, S. H., 296
Forney, William H., 225
Forrest, Nathan B., 12, 13, 17, 78, 81, 103, 118, 120, 121, 123, 135, 146, 148, 155, 175, 201, 212, 220, 223, 237, 250, 290, 303, 305, 348, 375, 376
Fox, Amos, 199, 254
Fox, John, 333
Fox, John, Jr., 204
Fox, Mrs. F. C., 367
Franklin, Benjamin, 293
Franklin, Mrs. Herbert M., 93
Franks, Richard, 46
Frederick the Great, 81
Fremont, John C., 297, 328
French, Mary, 129
French, Samuel G., 129, 170, 305
Freytag-Loringhoven, Baron von, 164
Friend, Ed, 119
Furlow, Tim M., 180
Furlow, William L., 180
Gailor, Thomas F., 154
Gaines, J. N., 142, 239
Galloway, Charles B., 227
Galloway, Margaret M., 317
Gano, Richard M., 210
Gardner, Franklin K., 118
Garibaldi, Giuseppe, 236
Garrison, William L., 23, 24, 255, 286, 331, 344, 357
Gass, Jim, 166
Gass, W. T., 166
Gautreaux, Doris, 365
Gayheart, Rebecca, 412
George (black servant), 82, 342, 343
George III, King, 12, 257, 293
Gill, Dr., 264
Gillette, Franklin, 329
Glover, Thomas C., 178
God, 14, 24, 33, 46, 47, 55, 61-64, 66, 95, 97, 110, 113, 120, 139, 140, 142, 149, 155, 157, 161, 162, 168-171, 175, 184, 196, 201, 210, 221, 223, 235, 239, 243, 246, 252, 284, 288, 293, 305, 310, 348, 350, 356, 358, 362, 367, 372
Goethels, G. W., 256
Goliath (Bible), 298
Goodell, William, 23, 24
Goodlett, Caroline D. M., 215
Goodloe, James L., 305
Goodman, Andrew, 147
Goodrich, John T., 230
Goodsell, Bishop, 187
Goolrick, Frances B., 280, 282
Gordon, Andrew P., 361
Gordon, George W., 222
Gordon, James P., 266, 278
Gordon, John B., 13, 66, 91, 211, 260
Gorgas, Josiah, 89
Goulding, Frank, 274
Grady, B. F., 286, 294
Grady, Henry W., 45, 90, 99, 100
Graham, A. T., 206
Graham, Hugh, 225
Graham, Louise, 225
Granbery, Tom, 163
Granger, Gordon, 228
Grant, Frederick D., 256
Grant, Ulysses S., 67, 164, 229, 231, 256, 269, 318, 345, 355, 360, 362, 392
Grant, W. W., 343
Graves, Robert, 412
Greeley, Horace, 23, 26, 28, 355
Green, A. L. P., 43
Green, James, 338
Green, Mrs. M. T., 150
Green, Nathanael, 213
Green, Wharton J., 310
Green, William, 70
Green, William M., 43, 44
Greene, Nancy L., 142
Greer, Young H., 367
Gregg, Maxey, 69, 129, 130
Grier, Fereba, 241
Griffin (black servant), 304
Griffith, Andy, 412
Griffith, B. W., 208
Gross, George P., 352
Grundy, Felix, 189
Gurley, Edwards J., 348
Haley, James T., 71, 74
Hall, Washington, 202
Halleck, Henry W., 230
Ham (black servant), 312
Hamby, Gen., 276
Hamby, W., 235
Hamer, F. A., 241
Hamer, Rev., 241
Hamill, Anne J., 305
Hamill, H. M., 335

Hamilton, Betsy, 65
Hammer, Mary A., 121
Hampton, Wade, 104, 161, 168
Hancock, F. W., 220
Hankins, Samuel, 333
Hanna, Marcus A., 149, 150
Hannibal (black servant), 72
Hardee, William J., 370
Hardeman, Etta, 47
Hardie, John, 305
Hardie, Joseph, 306
Hardie, Robert A., 305
Harding, William G., 245, 248, 412
Harris, Joel C., 203
Harris, Judge, 164
Harris, S. F., 266
Harrison, Henry, 345
Harrison, Mildred R., 225
Harry (black servant), 225, 264
Hart, Ben, 151
Hart, Col., 201
Hartman, J. C., 273
Harts, W, W,, 256
Harvie, Lewis, 110
Hatcher, Dave, 102, 103
Hatcher, James, 102
Havner, M. B., 217
Hawes, Harry B., 192
Hawkins, Ned, 124, 125
Hawthorne, Nathaniel, 246
Hayes, Jefferson A., 210
Hayes, Joel A., Jr., 224
Hayes, Margaret A., 224
Hayes, Margaret H. D., 247
Hayes, Mrs. Jefferson A., 213
Hayes, Varina H. D., 329
Haywood, Felix, 364
Haywood, Sherwood, 183
Hedges, Dr., 323
Heiskell, C. W., 226
Helper, Hinton R., 275
Hemmingway, Emma G., 30
Henderson, G. F. R., 105, 106
Henderson, John B., 345
Hendley, H. L., 125
Hendricks, James H., 260
Henry (black servant), 72
Henry VIII, King, 218
Henry, John C., 114
Henry, Patrick, 58, 63, 217, 279
Henry, Will, 151
Herbert, Hilary A., 314
Herod, 66
Hewett, R. M., 195
Hewitt, Tod, 225
Heywood, John D., 246
Hickman, John P., 222
Hickman, Kate L., 360
Higgins, Frances C., 325
Hilary, Charles, 126
Hilburn, F. A., 199, 254
Hill, Ambrose P., 62, 138, 143, 313
Hill, H. W., 115
Hill, Isaac, 286

Hill, James W., 124
Hill, Lucy L., 138
Hill, Mr., 240
Hillis, N. Dwight, 290
Hindman, Thomas C., 147
Hine, Thomas H., 360
Hines, Claiborne, 172
Hinton, E. H., 221
Hodge, J. M., 125
Hoge, Moses, 250, 251
Holder, Col., 82
Holderby, Dr., 199
Holland, J. Sid, 199, 254
Hollis, Rufus, 92
Hood, John B., 132, 235, 248, 272, 333
Hopkins, Judge, 113
Hord, B. M., 316
Horsley, William G., 280
Hoss, E. E., 91
Houssaye, Edna S. de la, 198
Houston, George S., 234
Houston, Locke, 291
Houston, Robert E., 143, 291
Howard, Capt., 345
Howcott, William H., 305
Howell, Katherine, 63
Hoyt, Margaret, 348
Hume, Alfred, 300, 301
Hume, Foster, 300
Hume, Fred, 300
Hume, H. H., 270
Hume, John D., 300
Hume, Leland, 300, 301
Hume, Mrs. William, 228
Hume, William, 300
Humphreys, B. G., 155
Hunter, David, 229, 230, 328
Hunter, Robert M. T., 22
Hurley, Metamora K., 269, 270
Hursey, Mose, 208
Hutson, William M., 78
Hyde, Anne B., 331, 348
Ike (black servant), 333
Isaac (black servant), 110, 186
Isaiah (Bible), 59
Isham (black servant), 181
Jack (black servant), 95, 120, 264, 279
Jackson, Alfred, 184
Jackson, Andrew, 69, 201, 245, 289
Jackson, James A., 133
Jackson, Julia, 96
Jackson, Mary A., 106, 206
Jackson, Thomas J. "Stonewall", 43, 46, 52, 62, 69, 96, 105, 106, 138, 139, 165, 178, 180, 191, 193, 195, 206, 207, 214, 233, 260, 264, 303, 312, 318, 331, 355
Jackson, William H., 155
Jackson, William L., 298
Janney, John, 60
Jarrett, C. F., 236, 237

Jayroe, A. B., 167
Jeff (black servant), 168, 372
Jefferson, Thomas, 30, 44, 58, 59, 63, 145, 192, 200, 213, 279, 293, 371
Jenkins, R. H., 181
Jenkins, W. F., 181
Jerry (black servant), 103, 364, 365
Jesus, 97, 106, 261, 288, 307, 358
Jim (black servant), 101, 239, 240, 253
John (black servant), 191, 195, 360
Johnson, A. J., 316
Johnson, Ben, 123
Johnson, Bradley T., 99
Johnson, Mary E., 349
Johnson, R. Y., 319
Johnson, William, 123, 124
Johnston, A. D., 223
Johnston, Albert S., 114, 196, 355
Johnston, George D., 284
Johnston, Joseph E., 13, 107, 138, 158, 193, 212, 277, 303
Jones, Agnes C., 208
Jones, Horace W., 171
Jones, J. William, 47, 139, 161, 214
Jones, James, 264
Jones, James H., 225
Jones, Jim, 224
Jones, Jimmie, 291
Jones, Lewis, 101
Jones, Mary K., 86
Joplin, James W., 265
Judd, Ashley, 412
Judd, Naomi, 412
Judd, Wynonna, 412
Jude (black servant), 141
Judkins, Tommy, 304
Judy (black servant), 158
Kalmbach, C. L., 124
Kautz, August V., 18
Kean, Aleck, 301, 302
Keene, John R., 114
Keller, Dr. J. M., 130
Keller, Helen, 185
Keller, Irvin, 130, 147
Keller, James M., 147
Keller, Mrs. J. M., 130
Keller, Murray, 130, 147
Keller, Sadie P., 147
Kelley, David C., 155, 223
Kelley, Judge, 113
Kellogg, Jonathan, 338
Kelso, Dana, 312
Kent, Mrs. May W., 340
Keough, Riley, 412
Key, William H., 131
King, Bill, 278
King, Jack, 278
King, Martin L., 26
Knox, Watson, 150
Koch, Louis L. J., 168, 169
Lafayette, Marquis de, 203
Lairy (black servant), 163

Lake, John, 164
Lamb, Capt., 341
Land, Henry, 297
Landon, Melville D., 103
Lane, W. P., 367
Lankford, A. H., 30
Lankford, George W., 280
Latham, Mrs. T. J., 177
Lawrence, Fannie V. C., 226
Leadbetter, Danville, 117
Ledyard, Emily S., 266
Lee, Ab, 181
Lee, Baker P., 125
Lee, Fitzhugh, 331
Lee, George W. C., 325, 326
Lee, Henry, 58
Lee, Henry, III, 161
Lee, Mary R. C., 322
Lee, Richard H., 58, 62, 279
Lee, Robert E., 32, 46, 62, 91, 105, 106, 127, 129, 138, 148, 159, 161, 165, 180, 183, 193, 195, 196, 203, 209, 212, 213, 217, 219, 223, 227, 228, 230, 231, 256, 260, 267-270, 281, 289, 303, 322, 325, 326, 328, 331, 334, 342, 343, 345, 353, 355, 360, 362, 371
Lee, Robert E., III, 217, 219
Lee, Stephen D., 214, 272
Leight, Watkins, 255
Lenin, Vladmir, 22
Leonard, Ed, 318
Letcher, John, 60
Lewis, Miss Lou, 375
Lieurner, C. T., 117
Light Horse Harry, 161
Lillard, Julia, 124
Lillard, Lizzie, 124
Limber, Jim, 205, 206
Lincoln, Abraham, 11-13, 15, 19-22, 25, 26, 29, 31, 32, 41, 43, 44, 58, 60, 61, 70, 76, 77, 102, 105, 114, 132, 141, 146, 159, 161, 168, 192, 194, 196, 198, 218, 230, 232, 236, 255, 257, 260, 261, 263, 264, 268, 269, 273, 275, 279, 284, 293, 294, 296, 313, 327-329, 344, 345, 349, 351, 352, 355, 356, 363, 377, 378
Little, D. D., 284
Littlefield, A. W., 371
Littleton, Mary B., 205, 237
Littleton, Solomon, 335
Lively, E. H., 230, 297
Livingston, Robert R., 293
Livingstone, Col., 303
Locke, Victor M., 137
Logan, Mary W., 322, 323
London, H. A., 329
Long, Crawford W., 274
Long, Littleton, 115
Longfellow, Henry W., 204, 246

Longstreet, James, 13, 274
Longstreet, James, Sr., 274
Louis (black servant), 340
Lovejoy, Elijah P., 286
Loveless, Patty, 412
Lowell, James R., 32, 33, 204
Luna, Frances H., 263
Lunt, George, 218, 220, 237
Lyle, John N., 102
Macauley, Mrs. George, 345
Madison, James, 58, 101, 279
Manson, H. W., 65
Marcy, Ellen M., 310
Margret (black servant), 373
Marion, Francis, 213, 225
Marlow, Mary, 203
Marsh, Bob, 361
Marshall, Arthur, 64
Marshall, Park, 305
Marshall, Stephen B., 181
Martin (black servant), 335
Martin, Eva, 176
Marvin, Lee, 412
Marx, Karl, 22, 28, 261
Masey, Annie G., 17
Mason, George, 58, 217
Mason, R. B., 171
Mathews, Harvey, 189
Maury, Dabney H., 118
Maury, Matthew F., 138
Maxwell, Harriet V., 172
Maxwell, Louise W., 362
Maxwell, Mary, 172
May, Jerry W., 148, 193, 194
May, Reuben, 152, 153
May, W. H., 153
Mayo, Henry, 335
Mayo, Z. B., 378
McAllister, Anderson, 141
McClain, Elizabeth E., 45
McClatchy, W. P., 78
McClellan, George B., 272, 273, 310
McClellan, Gus, 64
McClish, J. W., 192
McCosh, James, 251
McCulloch, Ben, 137
McCulloch, Grace, 73
McCulloch, Robert, 333
McDaniel, Col., 201
McDavid, Mrs. P. A., 214
McDonald, George, 157
McDowell, James, 56
McDowell, John H., 222
McGavock, Caroline E. "Carrie", 189
McGavock, John W., 189, 244, 245
McGhee, Perry, 121
McGowan, Anna M., 141
McGraw, Tim, 412
McGuire, Hunter, 107
McGuire, William, 303
McKim, Randolph H., 196, 237
McKinley, William, 369, 374
McKinney, C. C., 230
McKinney, John V., 312
McKnight, Lieut., 283
McLean, Sallie J., 124
McLeary, Sam, 163
McLendon, J. R., 152
McNeel, John A., 323
McNeilly, James H., 190, 252, 256, 319, 368, 370, 372
McReynolds, Dr., 89
McReynolds, Mrs., 89
Meade, George G., 129
Meade, Mary, 305
Meade, Nero, 307
Meade, Phoebe, 306, 307
Medley, Ambrose, 354
Medley, Harriet, 354
Meriwether, Mrs. Minor, 67
Mernaugh, James, 132
Merritt, Wesley, 229, 230
Miller, Polk, 71, 107, 138
Mills, B., 202
Mitchell, Frank H., 173
Mitchell, Mimi, 187
Mitchell, William H., 173
Mobley, Aline, 19
Mobley, E. B., 153
Moffett, George H., 210
Moody, Andrew, 127
Moody, Tildy, 127
Moore, George H., 85, 87
Moore, James B., 198
Moore, Kate W., 190
Moore, Olivia, 283
Moore, T. E., 361
Moore, Thomas V., 250
Moore, W. O., 339
Morel, L. B., 303
Morgan, John H., 142, 315, 360
Morris (black servant), 182
Morris, J. C., 88
Morrison, Joseph G., 206
Morton, Bob, 135
Morton, Hugh T., Jr., 181
Morton, Jeremiah R., 239
Morton, John W., 135, 136
Morton, Marmaduke B., 258
Mosby, John S., 412
Moses (Bible), 44, 61
Moses, Patsy, 61
Moton, Robert R., 8
Mudd, Joseph A., 347
Mudd, Major, 193
Mulligan, Col., 295
Nanny (black servant), 359
Napier, J. C., 256
Ned (black servant), 116, 127, 282
Nelson (black servant), 150
Nelson, Hugh M., 60
Nelson, J. O., 128
Nelson, Louis N., 376
Nelson, Thomas, Jr., 58
Nero, 66
Nero (black servant), 309
New South, 50
Nichol, Harry G., 339

Nicholson, A. O. P., 195
Nickerson, Edmonda A., 165
Nietzsche, Friedrich W., 23
Nwaubani, Adaobi T., 19
Obenchain, William A., 145
Ochenden, Mrs. J. M. P., 166
Odenheimer, Dorothea S., 342
Olds, Mrs. Fred A., 174
Oliver, Mr., 228, 229
Oltrogge, Estelle T., 296
Onesimus (Bible), 288
Oriaku, Nwaubani O., 19
Osbourne, R. S., 254
Otey, Mercer, 123, 141
Ousley, Clarence, 171
Overley, Milford, 239
Overstreet, Horace, 120
Overton, Harriet V. M., 172
Overton, John, 172, 248
Owens, Aaron, 132
Owens, Bob, 92
O'Neal, Edward A., 283
Page, Frank, 223
Page, George, 346
Page, Susan, 346
Page, Thomas N., 52, 64, 107, 203, 348
Palmer, Ella, 278
Parker, Theodore, 357
Partee, Easter, 366
Parton, Dolly, 412
Patillo, Marie E., 162
Patterson, Ed, 135, 136
Patterson, T. L., 48
Patteson, G. E., 336
Patteson, Madge, 336
Patteson, William G., 335
Patty (black servant), 298
Paul, Saint, 66, 288
Paulette, John W., 303
Paxton, Dr., 158
Peak, C. S., 201
Peak, Jacob, 201
Peete, Albert, 301
Pemberton, John C., 100, 167
Pendleton, Mrs. E. C., 159
Pepper, Sam, 367
Pepper, Samuel A., 291
Percy, Emma, 336
Perkins Charles, 192
Perkins, Jerry, 192
Perrin, N. P., 297
Pete (black servant), 180
Pettus, Edmund W., 165
Peyton, Ned, 336, 337
Philemon (Bible), 288
Phillips, R. L., 137
Phillips, Sallie, 130
Phillips, Wendell, 21, 286, 311, 331
Piatt, Donn, 294, 355
Pickett, George E., 138, 213, 339
Pickett, William D., 212
Pierce, Bishop, 392
Pierce, Franklin, 246

Pike, Albert, 321
Pillow, Gideon, 118
Pinckney, Charles C., 279
Pink (black servant), 264
Plane, Helen J., 128
Plecker, Frances B. S., 354
Plecker, Jacob H., 354
Plummer, Ann, 150
Polk, George W., 142
Polk, James K., 59
Polk, James K. (black), 236
Polk, Leonidas, 122, 125
Polk, William M., 122
Pope, Benjamin, 74
Pope, John, 140
Porter, J. R., 296
Porter, James D., 226
Pouncey, Frederick, 151, 152
Powell, James W., 234
Power, S. F., 283
Powers, William D., 119
Prater, Mammy, 341
Presley, Elvis, 412
Presley, Lisa M., 412
Preston, Julia J. C., 96
Preston, William B., 60
Price, Sterling, 137, 212, 295
Proctor, John, 77, 78
Proudhon, Pierre-Joseph, 23
Puckett, A. J., 101
Puckett, Fannie, 317
Puckett, Richard, 317
Purvis, George E., 90
Quiggle, J. W., 236
Quitman, John A., 346
Rachel (black servant), 101, 300
Radford, John, 339
Rains, James E., 295
Rambo, Regina E., 146
Randolph, Edmund, 58, 370
Randolph, George W., 60
Randolph, John, 226
Randolph, Thomas J., 319
Ransom, T. D., 138
Rastall, John E., 115
Ravenel, Samuel W., 277
Ray, Billy, 233
Rayburn, Jemima, 300, 301
Raynor, J. B., 154
Reagan, John H., 69, 163
Reed, Julia B., 117
Reed, Robert, 115, 116
Reese, George, 215
Reeves, Lillian C., 297
Reid, A. S., 181
Remus, Uncle, 18, 107
Reynolds, Daniel H., 354
Rhea, David, 340
Rice, C. S. O., 167
Richard I, King, 81
Richards, Samuel L., 124
Ridley, Bromfield L., 73, 297
Ridley, Bromfield, Jr., 297
Ridley, Charles L., 72, 297

Ridley, George, 297
Ridley, George C., 72
Ridley, J. L., 72
Ridley, J. S., 72
Ridley, Jerome, 297
Ridley, Lucas, 297
Risden, Orlando C., 317
Rives, William C., 60
Roberts, N. B., 163
Roberts, Press, 267
Roberts, Wiley, 299
Robertson, Mrs. A. G., 130
Robinson, Nina H., 97
Rochefoucauld-Liancourt, Duc de La, 293
Rock, R. S., 139
Rockefeller, Mr., 149
Roddy, Thomas, 225
Rogan, Charles B., 75
Rogan, Theophilus, 225
Rogers, Virginia, 317
Rogers, W. T., 318
Roosevelt, Theodore, 154, 213, 369, 374
Root, Elihu, 369
Roper, Mrs. Preston L., 138
Rosa (white servant), 186
Rose, William, 69, 70, 129
Ross, Lawrence S., 179
Rossen, Joe, 317
Rossen, John E., 317
Rousseau, Jean-Jacques, 23
Rousseau, Lovell H., 301
Royce, G. Monroe, 331
Rucker, Amos, 198, 199, 254
Rucker, Edmund W., 198, 412
Rucker, Sandy, 254
Ruggles, H. S., 332
Russell, Irwin, 107
Russell, John, 363
Rutherford, Mildred L., 221, 322, 345, 352, 355, 360
Rutherford, Mrs. James, 48
Sallie (black servant), 81, 280
Sam (black servant), 92, 95, 162, 230
Sam, Uncle (black servant), 113
Sanchez, Eugenia, 253
Sanchez, Lola, 253
Sanchez, Mauritia, 252, 253
Sanchez, Panchita, 253
Sandiford, Ralph B., 215
Sandy (black servant), 164
Saunders, Olivia, 258
Saussy, Clement, 367
Saxton, Rufus, 205
Schofield, John M., 224
Schuler, Squire, 92
Schurz, Carl, 21
Scott, Burgess H., 89
Scott, Col., 111
Scott, Dred, 288
Scott, George C., 412
Scott, Harriet, 288
Scott, Miss Charlie, 50
Scott, Mrs. C. C., 52
Scott, Robert E., 60
Scott, Sarah, 111
Scott, Winfield, 59, 355
Sea, Sophie F., 202
Seabrook, Lochlainn, 17-35, 392, 412, 413
Seales, D. C., 223
Sebring, Mrs. W. H., 79
Seddon, James A., 60
Selph, Fannie E., 17, 360, 363
Semple, H. C., 233, 234
Senter, DeWitt C., 89
Seward, William H., 268, 269
Sewell, Samuel, 87
Sharkey, Annie L., 366
Sharp, Thomas, 102
Shelburn (black servant), 259
Shelby, John O., 280
Shelby, Joseph O., 295, 296
Sheliha, V., 117
Shenandoah Valley, 146
Shepard, Mrs. M. P., 262
Shepperd, Lieut., 100
Sherer, J. A. B., 159
Sheridan, Philip H., 146, 229, 230, 260, 261
Sherman, John, 294
Sherman, Roger, 293
Sherman, William T., 77, 116, 130, 261, 294, 318, 336
Shields, Jefferson, 138
Shreve, Robert S., 175
Silas (black servant), 96, 116
Simpson, Samuel R., 215
Sitting Bull, 76
Skaggs, Ricky, 412
Slatter, W. J., 197
Smartt, Myra, 233
Smith, Alleen, 220
Smith, Bat, 304
Smith, Baxter, 303
Smith, Charles H., 159
Smith, Edmund K., 201
Smith, F. Coleman, 295
Smith, F. Hopkinson, 203, 321
Smith, Gerrit, 23, 24
Smith, J. C., 348
Smith, J. D., 207
Smith, Jessica R., 199, 200
Smith, John, 330
Smith, Orren R., 199, 200
Smith, Peter F., 348
Smith, Robert A., 252
Smith, Robert B., 295
Smith, Robert D., 330
Smith, Sara A., 329
Smith, Thomas B., 278
Smith, W. A., 125
Smith, William T., 264, 279
Smoot, Daniel J., 354
Snedecor, Dr., 284
Snow, Peter, 142
Snuffer, Owen, 157

Socrates, 263
Solari, Mary M., 189, 190
Sooky, Aunt (black servant), 112
Sophia (black servant), 103
Sparks, Jesse W., 75, 76
Speed, Mrs. Alan P., 292
Speed, Mrs. Hugh B., 367
Square, George, 295
Square, Hy T., 295
Square, Martha A., 295
Stacker, Clay, 222
Stephens, Alexander H., 11, 13, 97, 115-117, 198, 205, 206, 313, 412
Stevens, Thaddeus, 275, 359
Stevenson, Adlai, 362
Stewart, Alexander P., 72, 73, 164
Stewart, William H., 47, 62, 138, 229
Stiles, John C., 354
Stiles, Robert, 163
Stiles, William H., Jr., 162
Stinson, R. D., 154
Stockton, Maude B., 187
Stone, Cornelia B., 309
Stoughton, Israel, 85
Stowe, Charles E., 284, 285, 296, 321, 322
Stowe, Harriet B., 23, 143, 144, 226, 246, 275, 296, 297, 321
Strange, W. H., 193
Stratford, Hampton, 153
Stratton, Matt, 282
Streater, Wallace, 264
Stringer, Marguerite H. G., 372
Stuart, Alexander H. H., 60
Stuart, James E. B. "Jeb", 62, 110, 196
Stubbs, William, 11
Summers, George Y., 60
Sumner, Charles, 227, 372
Susan (black servant), 64
Susan, Mammy, 64
Sutton, Schuyler, 33
Suvorov, Aleksandr V., 66
Swedenborg, Emanuel, 185
Sydnor, Henry C., 311
Taft, William H., 17, 262, 400
Talleyrand, Charles-Maurice de, 218, 261
Tappan, Arthur, 286
Tappan, Lewis, 286
Taylor, Bob, 241
Taylor, Mrs., 47
Taylor, Richard, 13, 118
Taylor, Zachary, 289
Teague, B. H., 103, 295
Tell, William, 37
Terry, William, 340
Thackeray, William M., 374
Tholey, Augustus A., 232
Thomas, B. S., 125
Thomas, Bryan M., 198
Thomas, Frank M., 330

Thomas, G. E., 163
Thomas, George H., 160, 161, 355
Thomas, Henry W., 175, 182, 183
Thomas, Sarah P., 358
Thompson, Charles, 215
Thompson, George, 286
Thompson, John, 247-249
Thompson, Joseph H., 247
Thompson, Mary, 247-249
Thoreau, Henry D., 287
Thornwell, James H., 121
Tilton, Theodore, 21
Tinsley, Howard, 180
Tip (black servant), 64, 65, 159
Todd, Harry, 74
Todd, Luzerne, 115
Tom (black servant), 80, 141, 311
Toombs, Augustus G., 253
Toombs, Horace B., 317
Toombs, Laura, 317
Toombs, Robert A., 253
Townsend, Samuel C., 20
Traylor, Albert W., 145
Trenholm, Miss, 300
Trotsky, Leon, 22
Trousdale, William H., 125
Tucker, Elizabeth C., 258
Tucker, G. L., 315
Tucker, John R., 63
Turner, Nat, 258
Turney, Peter, 312
Turpin, W. H., 180
Tyler, John, 59, 60
Tyler, Robert C., 197
Ussery, W. T., 125
Valentine, Edward V., 46, 325
Vauban, Marquis de, 90
Vaulx, Joseph, 226
Vest, James M., 301, 302
Vest, John H., 301, 302
Viny (black servant), 239, 240
Virgil, 298
Walker (black servant), 343
Walker, Andrew, 283
Walker, Annie K., 225
Walker, C. H., 361
Walker, Mrs. Owen, 313
Walker, W. H. T., 254
Wallace, George (black servant), 180
Wallace, James, 114
Wallace, L. W., 270
Waller, Elizabeth, 339
Waller, William, 278
Walton, John R., 317
Walworth, Mrs. Ernest, 338
Ward, John S., 77
Ward, R. S., 276
Ward, W. C., 127
Washington, Booker T., 8, 71, 131, 150, 203
Washington, Elizabeth W., 217
Washington, George, 12, 37, 58, 59, 101, 105, 161, 213, 260, 262, 279, 289, 313, 344

Washington, George (black servant), 322, 323
Waterman, George S., 100, 117, 118
Watie, Stand, 137
Watson, Joseph, 274
Weaver, Omer R., 338
Webb, T.S., 77
Webster, Daniel, 101, 244, 289
Weed, Mrs. Edwin G., 43
Weeden, Maria H., 113, 203-205, 237, 348, 366
Weir, Sally R., 229
Wells, W. Calvin, 341, 352
Wendell, Barrett, 327, 368
West, A. J., 199, 254
West, Decca L., 34
West, Eliza, 150
Wharton, William H., 306
Wheeler, Joseph, 118, 223, 318, 356
White, Aaron C., 184
White, B. F., 123, 124
White, Benjamin F., 118
White, J. W., 78
White, John M., 121
White, Mrs. Alexander B., 313
White, P. J., 260
White, Samuel, 291
White, Samuel E., 121, 122
Whitney, Eli, 274
Whitthorne, W. J., 125
Whittier, John G., 204, 286
Wightman, Mrs. M. D., 187
Wiley (black servant), 183
Wilkes, Mary A., 197
Wilkins, Dr., 349
Will (black servant), 178
Williams, James H., 191, 302
Williams, Mrs. James H., 303
Williams, Samuel C., 302
Williamson, J. T., 125
Williamson, James, 206
Williamson, Person, 206
Williamson, William A., 206

Willich, August von, 261
Willingham, J. W., 72
Willis (black servant), 47, 89
Wilson, J. B., 360
Wilson, J. R., 195
Wilson, James H., 283
Wilson, Mrs. James H., 148
Wilson, Robert S., 333
Wilson, Woodrow, 412
Winbush, Nelson W., 376
Winchester, James R., 264
Winder, Caroline E., 189
Winder, Florence T., 202
Winder, John H., 213
Winecoff, Sallie F., 298
Winnie (black servant), 168
Winship, Mr., 180
Winthrop, John, 85, 86
Witherspoon, Reese, 412
Womack, Lee A., 412
Wood, Henry E., 219
Wood, Mary W., 329
Worthington, Lillie F., 264
Worthington, T. F., 264
Worthington, W. W., 264
Wrenn, George L., 314
Wrenshall, John C., 373
Wright, Fanny, 24
Wyeth, John A., 81, 104, 125
Wyley, C. M., 194
Wynn, William, 194
Yancey, WIlliam L., 267
Yarbrough, Billie, 184
Young, Bennett H., 15
Young, Edward E., 43, 46
Young, Gen., 339
Young, George, 202, 203
Young, Litt, 106
Zeke (black servant), 150
Zollicoffer, Anna M., 148
Zollicoffer, Felix K., 148

MEET THE AUTHOR

NEO-VICTORIAN SCHOLAR LOCHLAINN SEABROOK, a descendant of the families of Alexander Hamilton Stephens, John Singleton Mosby, Edmund Winchester Rucker, and William Giles Harding, is a 7th generation Kentuckian and one of the most prolific and widely read writers in the world today. Known by literary critics as the "new Shelby Foote" and the "American Robert Graves," and by his fans as the "Voice of the Traditional South," he is a recipient of the United Daughters of the Confederacy's prestigious Jefferson Davis Historical Gold Medal. As a lifelong writer he has authored and edited books ranging in topics from history, politics, science, religion, astronomy, military, and biography, to nature, music, humor, gastronomy, alternative health, genealogy, and the paranormal; books that his readers describe as "game changers," "transformative," and "life altering."

One of the world's most popular living historians, he is a 17th generation Southerner of Appalachian heritage who descends from dozens of patriotic Revolutionary War soldiers and Confederate soldiers from Kentucky, Tennessee, North Carolina, and Virginia. Also a history, wildlife, and nature preservationist, he began life as a child prodigy, later transforming into an archetypal Renaissance Man. Besides being an accomplished and well respected author-historian and Bible authority, he is also a Kentucky Colonel, eagle scout, screenwriter, nature, wildlife, and landscape photographer, artist, graphic designer, songwriter (3,000 songs), film composer, multi-instrument musician, vocalist, session player, music producer, genealogist, former history museum docent, and a former ranch hand, zookeeper, and wrangler.

Currently Seabrook is the author and editor of 82 adult and children's books (a total of 12,700,900 words) that have earned him accolades from around the globe. His works, which have sold on every continent except Antarctica, have introduced hundreds of thousands to vital facts that have been left out of our mainstream books. He has been endorsed internationally by leading experts, museum curators, award-winning historians, bestselling authors, celebrities, filmmakers, noted scientists, well regarded educators, TV show hosts and producers, renowned military artists, esteemed heritage organizations, and distinguished academicians of all races, creeds, and colors.

Of northern, western, and central European ancestry, he is the 6th great-grandson of the Earl of Oxford and a descendant of European royalty through his Kentucky father and West Virginia mother. His modern day cousins include: Johnny Cash, Elvis Presley, Lisa Marie Presley, Billy Ray and Miley Cyrus, Patty Loveless, Tim McGraw, Lee Ann Womack, Dolly Parton, Pat Boone, Naomi, Wynonna, and Ashley Judd, Ricky Skaggs, the Sunshine Sisters, Martha Carson, Chet Atkins, Patrick J. Buchanan, Cindy Crawford, Bertram Thomas Combs (Kentucky's 50th governor), Edith Bolling (second wife of President Woodrow Wilson), Andy Griffith, Riley Keough, George C. Scott, Robert Duvall, Reese Witherspoon, Lee Marvin, Rebecca Gayheart, and Tom Cruise.

A constitutionalist, an avid outdoorsman, and a gun rights advocate, Seabrook is the author of the international blockbuster, *Everything You Were Taught About the Civil War is Wrong, Ask a Southerner!* He lives with his wife and family in beautiful historic Middle Tennessee, the heart of the Old South.

For more information on author Mr. Seabrook visit
LOCHLAINNSEABROOK.COM

LOCHLAINN SEABROOK ∞ 413

If you enjoyed this book you will be interested in Colonel Seabrook's popular related titles:

☞ ABRAHAM LINCOLN WAS A LIBERAL, JEFFERSON DAVIS WAS A CONSERVATIVE
☞ EVERYTHING YOU WERE TAUGHT ABOUT THE CIVIL WAR IS WRONG, ASK A SOUTHERNER!
☞ EVERYTHING YOU WERE TAUGHT ABOUT AFRICAN AMERICANS AND THE CIVIL WAR IS WRONG, ASK A SOUTHERNER!
☞ EVERYTHING YOU WERE TAUGHT ABOUT AMERICAN SLAVERY IS WRONG, ASK A SOUTHERNER!
☞ CONFEDERATE FLAG FACTS: WHAT EVERY AMERICAN SHOULD KNOW ABOUT DIXIE'S SOUTHERN CROSS
☞ LINCOLN'S WAR: THE REAL CAUSE, THE REAL WINNER, THE REAL LOSER

Available from Sea Raven Press and wherever fine books are sold

ALL OF OUR BOOK COVERS ARE AVAILABLE AS 11" X 17" COLOR POSTERS, SUITABLE FOR FRAMING

SeaRavenPress.com

www.ingramcontent.com/pod-product-compliance
Lightning Source LLC
Chambersburg PA
CBHW021139160426
43194CB00007B/630